Islamic Wealth and the SDGs

Mohd Ma'Sum Billah
Editor

Islamic Wealth and the SDGs

Global Strategies for Socio-economic Impact

Editor
Mohd Ma'Sum Billah
Professor of Finance
Insurance, Fintech and Investment
Islamic Economics Institute
King Abdulaziz University
Jeddah, Saudi Arabia

ISBN 978-3-030-65312-5   ISBN 978-3-030-65313-2 (eBook)
https://doi.org/10.1007/978-3-030-65313-2

© The Editor(s) (if applicable) and The Author(s), under exclusive license to Springer Nature Switzerland AG 2021
This work is subject to copyright. All rights are solely and exclusively licensed by the Publisher, whether the whole or part of the material is concerned, specifically the rights of translation, reprinting, reuse of illustrations, recitation, broadcasting, reproduction on microfilms or in any other physical way, and transmission or information storage and retrieval, electronic adaptation, computer software, or by similar or dissimilar methodology now known or hereafter developed.
The use of general descriptive names, registered names, trademarks, service marks, etc. in this publication does not imply, even in the absence of a specific statement, that such names are exempt from the relevant protective laws and regulations and therefore free for general use.
The publisher, the authors and the editors are safe to assume that the advice and information in this book are believed to be true and accurate at the date of publication. Neither the publisher nor the authors or the editors give a warranty, expressed or implied, with respect to the material contained herein or for any errors or omissions that may have been made. The publisher remains neutral with regard to jurisdictional claims in published maps and institutional affiliations.

This Palgrave Macmillan imprint is published by the registered company Springer Nature Switzerland AG
The registered company address is: Gewerbestrasse 11, 6330 Cham, Switzerland

This book is dedicated to the remembrance of my most beloved parents Allamah Mufti Nur Mohammad (r) *and* Ustazah Akhtarun Nisa' (r) *who have nourished me with their love and wisdom. May* Allah (swt) *shower them with His Love and Mercy and grant them* Jannat al-Ferdaus. *I would also like to dedicate this book to my lovely wife Dr Khamsiah Binti Nawawi (Head, OSHE-Hospital UKM) and our heart-touching kids Dr Ahmad Mu'izz Billah (HCTM), Ahmad Mu'azz Billah (OP-RMC Cadet), Ahmad Muniff Billah (OP-RMC Cadet) and Akhtarun Naba' Billah (ANSARA MRSM) for their continuous supports and sacrifices.*

May all be blessed with Muwaddau Wa Rahmah, Qurratu A'yun *and* Mardhaati Allah (swt) *in the life and the next.*

This book is also dedicated to the Ummah *and the whole of humanity.*

—*Mohd Ma'Sum Billah, Ph.D.*
Islamic Economics Institute
King Abdulaziz University
Saudi Arabia

Preface

The *Islamic Wealth* is a holistic paradigm to care about all creatures as to one's well-being by cooperative helping hands. *Islamic Wealth* is not a mere commercial component in satisfying one's material happiness but it also care about needies in their day-to-day needs, which is a holistic medium of contributing toward a sustainable balanced economy and development for the benefit of individual, family, society, nation, as well as globe as to one's needs with food, clothing, health care, education, shelter, environment, spiritual enrichment, personality development and other needs and comforts, which are with much wider scope and objectives than the coverage and goals of the SDGs. There is a huge *Islamic Wealth* available across the world, which may reach trillions in dollars. They can be in the form of property, asset, wealth, currency, reserved, gold, diamond, mining and so on with value impact. Such *Islamic Wealth* may significantly contribute to the wakeup of the global economy should they are carefully identified by professional research, structured and managed with socio-economic impact within the *Maqasid al-Shari'ah*. But due to poor constructive and effective research, ineffective structuring and unskilled management, the *Islamic Wealth* is yet to contribute to a socio-economic impact as ought to be. Thus, an attempt is made in this book to share different impact-oriented solutions to *Islamic Wealth* in its holistic sustainable capacity as a socio-economic vehicle with impact in today's reality in meeting the goals of SDGs and added values. The book however contributes toh *Islamic Wealth and the SDGs:*

vii

viii   PREFACE

Global Strategies for Socio-economic Impact by addressing some core and specialized issues, which are into **Five Parts** with **Thirty Two** specialized chapters besides an introduction and an index.

Part I provides a Chemistry of Islamic Wealth for SDGs, which consists of ten chapters addressing different core issues of *Islamic Wealth*. Chapter 1 contirbutes on How compatible are SDGs with Divine Principles? A Critical Literature Review (CLR). Chapter 2 provides a paradigm of The Worldview of Islamic Ethical Wealth and its implications for SDGs: The Case of Waqf. Chapter 3 focuses on How Islamic Ethical Wealth May Strategically and Technically Support SDGs Plan? Chapter 4 analyzes on *Shari'ah* Ethical Wealth and SDGs: A *Maqasid* Perspective. Chapter 5 analyzes on the Compatibility of SDGs With Development Goals Based on Divine Principles. Chapter 6 presents a paradigm of an integrated Islamic Social and Commercial Finance to Achieve SDGs. Chapter 7 goes on analyzing the Urban Sustainability and the Role of Islamic Wealth in Mega-OIC Cities: Implications for SDGs. Chapter 8 analyzes on the Structural Mechanisms for Islamic Ethical Wealth for SDGs. Chapter 9 analyzes on *Baitul Maal wat Tamwil* as Integrated Islamic Microfinance Institution to Support SDGs. Chapter 10 focuses on How Islamic Social Finance Contributes to the Sustainable Development Goals: an impactful Story of Al-Khidmat Foundation, Pakistan.

Part II focuses on how Islamic Ethical Wealth May Strategically and Technically Support SDGs' Schemes? which consists of eight chapters. Chapter 11 provides on Why Does Business *Zakat* Contribute Insignificantly to Achieving 'SDG-1: Ending Poverty' in Nigeria? Evidence from Recordkeeping Practices. Chapter 12 discovers the Role of Islamic Ethical Wealth in Strategically and Technically Supporting 'No Poverty'-SDGs 1. Chapter 13 advocates on How Islamic Ethical Wealth May Strategically and Technically Support 'Zero Hunger' Scheme? Chapter 14 presents on How Islamic Ethical Wealth May Strategically and Technically Support 'Zero Hunger' Scheme? Chapter 15 discusses on the Structures of Healthcare Waqf in Indonesia to Support SDGs. Chapter 16 provides on How Islamic Ethical Wealth Manages the risks that threaten 'Good Health and Wellbeing' Mission? Chapter 17 analyzes on the Role of *Waqf* in the Youth of Empowerment to attain the Quality Education in Kano for sustainable development goals. Chapter 18 provides on how Islamic Ethical Wealth May Strategically and Technically Support 'Reduced Inequality' Mission?

Part III contributes on How is the Strategic Mechanism of '*Zakat*' to Support SDGs? The part consists of four different applied issues and experiences of *Islamic Wealth* in four chapters. Chapter 19 discusses on *Zakat* on Wealth and Asset: Lessons for SDGs. Chapter 20 analyzes on the Bridging *Zakat* Impacts toward *Maqasid Shari'ah* and sustainable development goals (SDGs), Influence of Corporatization and Experiences on COVID-19. Chapter 21 contributes on How far Corporate *Zakat* May Contribute to Sustainable Development Goals? Chapter 22 analyzes on Global Zakat Cooperation Chain to SDGs: How Shall Mechanisms and Master Plan be?

Part IV contributes on How Potential of '*Awqaf*' in Supporting SDGs? The part consists of seven different applied issues and experiences of *Awqaf* in seven chapters. Chapter 23 provides a comprehensive analysis of the concern of 'Not Yet Fully Understood Divine Status of *Waqf* and its Social Welfare Role.' Chapter 24 analyzes on the Global Ethical Wealth Based on *Maqasid al-Shari'ah*: The Case of *Waqf*. Chapter 25 discusses on the Forms of *Waqf* Funds and SDGs. Chapter 26 analyzes on the Contributions of *Waqf* Investments in Achieving SDGs. Chapter 27 contributes on presents Corporate *Waqf* for Healthcare in Malaysia for B40 and M40. Chapter 28 analyzes on How Corporate *Awqaf* Can Support SDGs? *Chapter twenty-nine* provides an analysis on the Cash *Awqaf:* How It May Contribute to SDGs?

Part V focuses on How *Sukuk* Structure May Support SDGs? The part consists of three different applied issues and experiences of *Sukuk* in three chapters. Chapter 30 discusses on *Sukuk al-Waqf* Structure for Financing BOT-Based Development Programs. Chapter 31 discusses on *Sukuk* and SDGs-9 'Industry, Innovation and Infrastructure' in Sub-Saharan Africa: Achievements, Challenges and Opportunities. Chapter 32 discusses on How Green Sukuk Structure Contributes to SDGs?

Needless to submit that, the idea of *Islamic Wealth led SDGs* and its emergence are capturing the attention and appreciation of all levels of mankind across the contemporary world, yet no significant or comprehensive research with applied solution on *Islamic Wealth* led SDGs to be used as a reliable reference for continuing academic or industrial research in meeting the demand of practical market niche and develop further with technical know-how, except mostly with jurisprudential thoughts available in the library and/or as occasional research or in the social media. Thus, this title (*Islamic Wealth and the SDGs*) is expected to be among the pioneers with organized and comprehensive applied solutions to *Islamic*

Wealth Led SDGs led by holistic approach of *Islamic Wealth,* which may be a guide to academia, researchers, UNDP-led organizations, SDGs-related organizations, practitioners, decision makers, programmers, professionals, promoters and students for their technical know-how, future research and development of furtherance niche products, and SDGs solutions. It is not impossible for the book to contain any shortcomings. We are thus grateful to all readers should any shortcomings be notified to us for a further improvement.

Jeddah, Saudi Arabia   Mohd Ma'Sum Billah, Ph.D.

Acknowledgments

There is no strength and power except in *Allah (swt)*, To Him comes the praise, the Savant, the Wise, the Omniscient, the most beautiful names belong to Him. May the blessing of Allah (swt) and peace be upon *Muhammad (saw)* and all the Prophets (*aws*) from the first to the last.

I am humbly privileged to acknowledge King Abdulaziz University, Kingdom of Saudi Arabia and its prestigious wing Islamic Economics Institute for supporting us with every facility in research, academic, human capital and professional development activities outreaching the global *Ummah*. It is also a great honor for me to humbly acknowledge His Excellency Professor Dr Abdulrahman Obaid Al-Youbi, the President of King Abdulaziz University, Professor Dr Amin Yousef Mohammad

Noaman, the Vice President of King Abdulaziz University and Dr Abdullah Qurban Turkistani, the Dean of the Islamic Economics Institute (IEI), King Abdulaziz University (KAU), Dr Mohammad A. Naseef (Vice Dean, IEI-KAU), Dr Maha Alandejani (Vice Dean, IEI, KAU), Dr Faisal Mahmoud Atbani (Head, Department of Insurance, IEI-KAU), Dr Adnan M. A. Al-Khiary (Head, Department of Finance, IEI-KAU) and Dr Albara Abdullah Abulaban (Head Department of Economics) for their continuous supports and encouragements towards dynamic professional development, excellent academic contributions and specialized advance scientific research activities. Heartiest acknowledgement is also extended to my respected fellow-colleagues from the Islamic Economics Institute, King Abdulaziz University including Dr Majed Mohammad Rafea Aljuhani (Director, Administrative Division) and my talented colleague Mr Mohammed Alabdulraheem, Lecturer in FinTech and Islamic finance. I would like to express my full-hearted thanks with appreciation to Y. Bhg. Tan Sri Ahmad Zaki Ansore Bin Mohd Yusof (Former Director General, Implementation Coordination Unit, Prime Minister's Department, Malaysia), Y. Bhg. Prof Datuk Dr Daud bin Mohamad (Former Deputy Director General & Head, Department of Nuclear Science and Applications, International Atomic Energy Agency, Vienna, Austria), Y. Bhg. Prof Datin Dr Siti Rahayah Binti Ariffin (Former Dean of Education, UKM), Major Sharif Mahmud Hasan (Rtd), Mr Nazrul Islam Azad (Chairman, Starktree Group), Dr Adil Abdelaziz Hamid (International Business Consultant, UK), Mr Azzuddin Zud Ismail (Malaysian Politician), Mr Muhammad Zahidul Islam (Executive Director, International Institute of Media and e-Journalism (IIMEJ), Germany) for supporting this research with strategic ideas aligning with noble objectives of the UNDP underlined with SDGs towards global socio-economic wellbeing and also Mohamed Kabir Hossain Bin Ruhul Amin. Further acknowledgement is extended to organizations, public and private sectors including the UN, UNDP, CIBAFI, ICD of IDB, universities, industries and professional firms whose direct and indirect supports with knowledge, experiences and resources are full-heartedly recorded.

Mohd Ma'Sum Billah, Ph.D.
Islamic Economics Institute
King Abdulaziz University
Jeddah, Saudi Arabia

INTRODUCTION

The prime idea of sustainable development goals (SDGs) was initiated at the United Nations Conference on Sustainable Development in Rio de Janeiro in 2012. The idea of SDGs replaced the millennium development goals (MDGs), which commenced its global implementation in 2000. There are 17 core objectives promulgated in the SDGs, namely No Poverty, Zero Hunger, Good Health and Well-being, Quality Education, Gender Equality, Clean Water and Sanitation, Affordable and Clean Energy, Decent Work and Economic Growth, Industry, Innovation and Infrastructure, Reduced Inequality, Sustainable Cities and Communities, Responsible Consumption and Production, Climate Action, Life Below Water, Life on Land, Peace and Justice, Strong Institutions and Partnerships to achieve the Goal. With a closer look, SDGs are noble and for the holistic humanity and humanitarian causes with mutual care and concern. Among the core objectives of *Shari'ah* (*Maqasid al-Shari'ah*) are to care and concern with possible helping hand among mankind in no exception to other creatures as enshrined in the holy *Qur'an* 2:5 '...*cooperate amongst you in righteousness and piety*...' The efforts and scope of SDGs are thus, within the noble teaching of Islam and hence, the underlying objectives SDGs may well be structured within the spirit of *Maqasid al-Shari'ah* in caring for the well-being of humanity in no question of one's religion, race, color, gender, status, nationality or background, but with universal holistic value.

The initiative of SDGs is undoubtedly timely to contribute to world peace as to socio-economic stability with fair distribution and humanitarian care and concern. If anyone is individually, domestically, socially, professionally and economically sound and secured, the world may declare its peace with no destruction or tension; hence, the efforts with SDGs are the driving force with significant way forward by contributing to the world peace. There is huge ethical wealth available across the world within the definition of *Shari'ah*, which may reach trillions of dollars. Those ethical wealths may be defined and duly structured with *Zakat* (alms), *Awqaf* (endowment), *Al-Waqf al-Muwaqqat* (temporary endowment), *Manihah* (granting usufruct), *Tabarru'at* (donation), *Sadaqah* (philanthropies), *Hibah* (gift), *Hadiah* (token), *Musahamah* (contribution), *Sukuk* (bond) and so on. Unfortunately, that wealth is not seriously searched, identified, structured or managed with true socio-economic impact. If that wealths is well managed, the socio-economic catastrophe may be significantly reduced while the global socio-economic status quo may uplift with significant results.

SDGs' effort is to achieve seventeen goals for mankind with socio-economic impact; thus, in maximizing, the target of SDGs by 2030 may require US 5–7 trillion per annum. This figure represents only 7–10% of global GDP and 25–40% of annual global investment. However, only US 1.4 trillion are invested annually, from both the public and the private sector, in developing countries. The annual investment gap in major SDG sectors in developing countries alone has been estimated at around US 2.5 trillion per annum. Today, in the private sector participation, there may be a funding shortfall of US 1.6 trillion to be covered by the public sector including the official development assistance (ODA).[1] Looking at the current business phenomena, the public sector may not be able to finance the implementation of the 2030 plan. Therefore, a step-change in private investment in SDG sectors is required. The global community has the financial resources to address the needs of the 2030 plan. Today, the most important sources of capital are largely absent from the funding of the 2030 plan, and only a fraction of the worldwide invested assets of banks, multinational enterprises, pension funds, insurers, as well

---

[1] See, Financing for SDGs Breaking the Bottlenecks of Investment from Policy to Impact June 11, 2018, UNHQ Concept Note, p. 1.

as philanthropies and foundations is in SDG sectors and even less in developing countries. Furthermore, the share of private investment in climate change adaptation remains around 20% in both developing and developed countries. Private flows amount to less than 20% of total financial flows to the least developed countries. In the group of lower-middle-income countries, that share is around 30%.[2] Therefore, it may be submitted that if the global Islamic ethical wealth is carefully and smartly identified and wisely structured, it may significantly contribute to the SDGs with socio-economic impact. The proposed title is timely to address the global Islamic ethical wealth and their potentials along with technical know-how in supporting SDGs with socio-economic impact within the principles of *Maqasid al-Shari'ah*.

---

[2] See, Financing for SDGs Breaking the Bottlenecks of Investment from Policy to Impact June 11, 2018, UNHQ Concept Note, p. 2.

CONTENTS

Part I Chemistry of Islamic Ethical Wealth for SDGs

1   How Compatible Are SDGs with Divine Principles?
A Critical Literature Review (CLR)   3
T. O. Yusuf and L. Raimi

2   The Worldview of Islamic Ethical Wealth and Its
Implications for SDGs: The Case of Waqf   29
Ayman Bakr, Mohamed Cherif El Amri,
and Mustafa Omar Mohammed

3   How Islamic Ethical Wealth May Strategically
and Technically Support SDGs Plan?   53
Irfan Syauqi Beik and Laily Dwi Arsyianti

4   Shari'ah, Ethical Wealth and SDGs: A Maqasid
Perspective   69
Mohammad Abdullah

5   Analysis of the Compatibility of SDGs
with Development Goals Based on Divine
Principles   87
Mustafa Helvacıoğlu, Mustafa Omar Mohammed,
and Mohamed Cherif El Amri

xvii

xviii CONTENTS

6   Integrated Islamic Social and Commercial Finance
    to Achieve SDGs   105
    Ascarya and Ugi Suharto

7   Urban Sustainability and the Role of Islamic Wealth
    in Mega-OIC Cities: Implications for SDGs   129
    Salim Refas, Mohamed Cherif El Amri,
    and Mustafa Omar Mohammed

8   Structural Mechanisms for Islamic Ethical Wealth
    for SDGs   155
    Shariq Nisar and Umar Farooq

9   Baitul Maal wat Tamwil as Integrated Islamic
    Microfinance Institution to Support SDGs   175
    Ascarya

10 How Islamic Social Finance Contribute
    to the Sustainable Development Goals: An Impactful
    Story of Al-Khidmat Foundation Pakistan   197
    Suhail Ahmad

Part II   How Islamic Ethical Wealth May Strategically
          and Technically Support SDGs' Schemes?

11 Why Does Business Zakat Contribute Insignificantly
    to Achieving "SDG-1: Ending Poverty" in Nigeria?
    Evidence from Recordkeeping Practices   219
    Umar Habibu Umar, Mustapha Abubakar,
    and Ibrahim Ibrahim Sharifai

12 The Role of Islamic Ethical Wealth in Strategically
    and Technically Supporting 'No Poverty'-SDGs 1   241
    Mustafa Omar Mohammed, Mohamed Cherif El Amri,
    and Ayman Bakr

13 How Islamic Ethical Wealth May Strategically
    and Technically Support 'Zero Hunger' Scheme?   257
    Irfan Syauqi Beik, Randi Swandaru,
    and Priyesta Rizkiningsih

14 Islamic Ethical Wealth and Its Strategic Solutions
    to 'Zero Hunger' Scheme   273
    Aishath Muneeza and Zakariya Mustapha

CONTENTS   xix

15 Structures of Healthcare Waqf in Indonesia
    to Support SDGs   305
    Ascarya and Hendri Tanjung

16 How Islamic Ethical Wealth Manages the Risks That
    Threaten 'Good Health and Wellbeing' Mission?   325
    T. O. Yusuf and I. A. Oreagba

17 The Role of Waqf in the Youth Empowerment
    to Attain the Quality Education in Kano
    for Sustainable Development Goals   345
    Gwadabe Nura Abubakar and Asmak Ab Rahman

18 How Islamic Ethical Wealth May Strategically
    and Technically Support "Reduced Inequality"
    Mission?   359
    Irfan Syauqi Beik, Mohd Hasbi Zaenal,
    and Abdul Aziz Yahya Saoqi

Part III   How is the Strategic Mechanism of 'Zakat' to
           Support SDGs?

19 Zakat on Wealth and Asset: Lessons for SDGs   375
    Mustafa Omar Mohammed, Mohamed Cherif El Amri,
    and Ramadhani Mashaka Shabani

20 Bridging Zakat Impacts Toward Maqasid Shariah
    and Sustainable Development Goals (SDGs),
    Influence of Corporatization and Experiences
    on COVID-19   393
    Muhammad Iqmal Hisham Kamaruddin
    and Mustafa Mohd Hanefah

21 How Far Corporate Zakat May Contribute
    to Sustainable Development Goals?   421
    Suhail Ahmad and S. Ghiasul Haq

22 Global Zakat Cooperation Chain to SDGs: How Shall
    Mechanisms and Master Plan Be?   439
    Fauzia Mubarik

xx CONTENTS

Part IV How Potential of 'Awqaf' in Supporting SDGs?

23 Not Yet Fully Understood Divine Status of Waqf and Its Social Welfare Role   453
Syed Khalid Rashid

24 Analysis of Global Ethical Wealth Based on Maqasid al-Shari'ah: The Case of Waqf   469
Suheyib Eldersevi, Mustafa Omar Mohammed, and Mohamed Cherif El Amri

25 Forms of Waqf Funds and SDGs   485
Hichem Hamza

26 Contributions of Waqf Investments in Achieving SDGs   501
Barae Dukhan, Mustafa Omar Mohammed, and Mohamed Cherif El Amri

27 Corporate Waqf for Healthcare in Malaysia for B40 and M40   521
Khairul Fikry Jamaluddin and Rusni Hassan

28 How Corporate Awqaf Can Support SDGs?   539
Rusni Hassan and Fatimah Mohamad Noor

29 Cash Awqaf: How It May Contribute to SDGs?   559
Rusni Hassan, Jawwad Ali, and Fatimah Mohamad Noor

Part V How Sukuk Structure May Support SDGs?

30 Analysis of *Sukuk* Al-*Waqf* Structure for Financing BOT-Based Development Programs   581
Mustafa Omar Mohammed, Mohamed Cherif El Amri, and Ramadhani Mashaka Shabani

31 Sukuk and SDG-9 "Industry, Innovation and Infrastructure" in Sub-Saharan Africa: Achievements, Challenges and Opportunities   599
Abubakar Jamilu Baita and Hassan Hassan Suleiman

32 How Green *Sukuk* Structure Contributes to SDGs?   621
Mohamed Cherif El Amri, Mustafa Omar Mohammed, and Mohamed Hamoud Abdi

Index   639

ABOUT THE AUTHOR/EDITOR

Mohd Ma'Sum Billah, DBA, Ph.D., M.B.A., MCL, MMB, LLB (Hons.) is Professor of finance, insurance, fintech and investment, Islamic Economics Institute, King Abdulaziz University, Kingdom of Saudi Arabia. Billah is also affiliated with University of South Australia as Adjunct-Professor. He is currently the Member of the Audit Board of ACIG (appointed by the Saudi Monetary Authority / Central Bank of Saudi Arabia), Saudi Arabia. Billah had been serving and contributing both academic and corporate industries and international organizations for more than 25 years with management, teaching, research, solution proving and sharing of strategic and technical know-how towards the advancement of Islamic finance, fintech, business, investment, capital market and insurance (*Takaful*) besides *Halal* standard. Billah has published 36 books and chapters in books besides more than 200 articles in internationally reputable journals and social media. Most of his books were published by world top publishers, namely Thompson Reuters, Sweet & Max Well, Palgrave Macmillan, Springer, Routledge, Edward Elgar and others. Most of his books and articles are used as among the lead references (solutions to reality) by universities, industries, professional firms, governments, policymakers, regulators, NGOs, academia, researchers and students of higher learning in different parts of the contemporary world. He had been presenting in more than 300 conferences, seminars, executive workshops, professional development and industrial trainings in different parts of the

xxi

world. In addition, he had also been affiliated with corporate, academic and financial industries including central banks, international corporate organizations, governments and NGOs in his capacity as a member in boards, director, advisor, strategic decision maker, transformer and reformer with strategic solutions and technical know-how. Among the areas of his interest and contributions are: Islamic finance, insurance (*takaful*), crowd-funding, investment, *Zakat, waqf*, capital market (*Sukuk*), social finance, SDGs, petroleum finance, trade, fintech, e-Commerce, Crypto-asset, cryptocurrency, industrialization, privatization, national entrepreneuring models, standards, policies strategies and technical know-how.

Notes on Contributors

Mohamed Hamoud Abdi, B.Sc. is currently enrolled in two Master's programs: M.B.A. and Islamic economics and finance at Istanbul Sabahattin Zaim University. After completing his high school in 2013, he moved to Turkey to pursue his higher education. He then obtained Bachelor's degree in business administration from Selçuk University in Konya before enrolling for the present postgraduate education.

Mohammad Abdullah, Ph.D. is an expert in the theory and practices of Islamic sciences, Islamic jurisprudence and Islamic finance. He is a well-trained and highly experienced Shariah Scholar, providing Shariah consultancy and advisory services to various Islamic financial institutions in Europe, South America and the UAE. He is a reputed researcher and has produced several research papers and book chapters on the comparative study of *Waqf* and English trust, *Shariah* governance, Islamic finance and development studies. He holds a bachelor's degree in Shariah Sciences from Darul Uloom Nadwatul Ulama, Lucknow, India, and Masters in Islamic Banking, Finance and Management from the Markfield Institute of Higher Education, UK. He received his Ph.D. at the University of Gloucestershire (UK) and he is a Certified Shariah Advisor and Auditor (CSSA) by the AAOIFI. He is a frequent presenter of research papers and he has presented a number of research papers on different aspects of Islamic banking and finance in different American, European and Asian countries including Germany, Norway, Italy, Ireland, Scotland, UK,

Trinidad & Tobago, Indonesia, Malaysia, India and UAE. He is currently based in Dubai.

Gwadabe Nura Abubakar, M.A. is from Kano State of Nigeria. She obtained a Bachelor's degree in Islamic Studies from University of Maiduguri, 2007, Master of Fiqh from Al-Madinah International University, Malaysia, 2014, and currently a Ph.D. candidate in the Department of Shariah and Economy, University of Malaya, Malaysia, effective from 2018 to date. He is a Lecturer in the Department of Islamic Studies, Faculty of Humanities, Yusuf Maitama Sule University, Kano State, Nigeria. He has published a quite number of articles related to Islamic economics and finance in many peer-reviewed journals.

Mustapha Abubakar, Ph.D. is a Senior Lecturer in the Department of Banking and Finance at Ahmadu Bello University Business School, Zaria, Nigeria. Prior to joining the academic community, he worked as a banking officer in Union Bank of Nigeria for nearly three years from 1996 to 1999. He obtained a Diploma in Accounting, B.Sc. Business Administration, M.B.A., M.Sc. Business Administration and Ph.D. all from Ahmadu Bello University, Zaria, Nigeria in 1989, 1993, 1995, 2010 and 2017, respectively. He has participated in many academic conferences as a paper presenter in conventional and Islamic finance, banking and economics areas in Nigeria, Malaysia, Saudi Arabia and Bangladesh. He has also published papers in academic journals and books in Nigeria and abroad, and as a member of editorial advisory board, had reviewed several academic papers for seminars, theses, journal articles and books in areas of Islamic banking, economics and finance. This is in addition to other numerous supervisions works of undergraduate and postgraduate students he undertook.

Suhail Ahmad, M.B.A. is currently a Ph.D. Research Scholar in the Department of Business Administration at the Sarhad University of Science and Information Technology Peshawar, Pakistan. After getting his graduation, i.e., (BBA HONS) in Finance with *Distinction* and awarded (*Certificate of Merit*) from Government Postgraduate College of Management Sciences Thana Malakand, University of Malakand, Chakdara, Pakistan, he moved to his M.B.A./M.S. in Finance with research thesis of (*Issues & Problems of Islamic Banking in Pakistan with special reference to poverty alleviation*) from University of Malakand, Chakdara, Pakistan. His area of interest is Islamic finance and poverty alleviation through Islamic finance and microfinance. He has the will to alleviate poverty in the economy, not only in Pakistan but also in the globe. He published research papers in the field of finance, Islamic finance, microfinance, poverty alleviation, etc. He just recently published a paper titled '*Developing and proposing a Model for Zakat Management System: A case of the Malakand District of KP, Pakistan with special reference to Poverty Alleviation in the district*' in International Journal of Zakat (Volume 04 No. 01, 2019) an Indonesian-based journal and won the **Best Paper Award** of a cash prize.

Jawwad Ali, M.A. is a Shari'ah researcher involved in Shari'ah-cum-legal research on various aspects of waqf in Malaysia as well as India. He received his undergraduate education at traditional schools of India with specialization in Islamic law and jurisprudence. He has published papers on comparative study of governance of waqf institutions in India and Malaysia besides carrying research on issues and challenges in the management of waqf institutions in India. He presented papers in conferences such as the Colonial Interventions and the Modern States (ICHGA) (2018), International Conference on Contemporary Issues and Maqasid al-Shariah at Sultan Abdul Halim Mu'adzam Shah International Islamic University, Malaysia (2018), and Religion, Culture and Governance the Contemporary World at (ICRCG2018) IIUM. He was part of research projects such as Tawidh and Gharamah in the context of Majlis Agamah Selangor (MAIS), Cash Waqf and its Implementation in the Modern Islamic Finance: A Comparative Study. Also, he contributes in book chapters such as Commentaries of Forty Hadiths on Riba, and Collection of Forty Hadiths on Sale Contract with English Translation and Commentarial Notes. He was a proud recipient of the award for second position in second and third years of bachelor study and the award for third position in PG diploma in Fiqh and Fatawa. He received specialized training in delivering Fatwa. He has Master's of Islamic Revealed Knowledge and Human Sciences (Fiqh & Usul al Fiqh) from IIUM (Malaysia) Currently, he is pursuing Ph.D. (Law) at IIUM (Malaysia).

Laily Dwi Arsyianti, Ph.D. is an Assistant Professor at IPB University. She holds an *amanah* as Deputy Head of the Department of Islamic Economics, Faculty of Economics and Management. She graduated from the same university for Bachelor's in economics (Hons.) and from International Islamic University of Malaysia for her Master of Science in Finance and Ph.D. in Islamic Banking and Finance. Her area of interest includes Islamic wealth management, Islamic social finance and behavioral finance. She published 32 papers in *SCOPUS Indexed* journals and national accredited journals. She also has presented selected papers in various reputable conferences, especially those that are organized by IRTI-IDB and Bank Indonesia.

Ascarya, Ph.D. is a Magister of Economics and Waqf, University of Darussalam Gontor, Indonesia. He serves as editorial team member of several international scientific journals (SCOPUS indexed) and editorial board member of other international scientific journals. He is also a reviewer of several international (SCOPUS Indexed) and national scientific journals. He is an expert in the field of Islamic economics, monetary, banking, Islamic microfinance and Islamic social finance (especially zakat and waqf), as well as a lecturer in several universities. In addition, he is a trainer in the Analytic Network Process (ANP) and Data Envelopment Analysis (DEA) research methods. He holds Ph.D. in Islamic Economics and Finance from IEF-Trisakti University, Indonesia. He has also received Ph.D. candidate in International Development, M.B.A. in Finance and M.Sc. in Management Information System from University of Pittsburgh, USA. He has produced 26 international journals and books, 70 international papers, 22 national journals, 23 national papers, 41 working papers, 3 occasional papers, 22 books, 4 proceedings, 12 periodical publications and 6 research notes. He has presented in 70 international conferences and 90 national conferences. He has received four International Best Paper Awards in 2013, 2014, 2015 and 2016. He has also received BAZNAS Award 2018 as 'Tokoh Pendukung Kebangkitan Zakat.'

Abubakar Jamilu Baita, M.Sc. obtained B.Sc. and M.Sc. Economics at Bayero University, Kano, and presently, he is undergoing a Ph.D. program in the Department of Economics, Usmanu Danfodiyo University, Sokoto. His ongoing Ph.D. thesis focuses on the determinants of sukuk market development in OIC member countries. Currently, he is a Lecturer in the Department of Economics and a Part-Time Lecturer for IJMB Programme in the Institute of Continuing Education (ICE), Yusuf Maitama Sule University, Kano—Nigeria. He is one of the recipients (serving as a core researcher) of the Islamic Research and Training Institute (IRTI)'s research grant for the year 2017. His areas of research interest include sukuk market development, Islamic economics and fiscal policy.

Ayman Bakr, M.B.A. is presently a Ph.D. student in the Department of Islamic Economics and Finance at Istanbul Sabahattin Zaim University. He holds two bachelor's degrees, one in electrical electronics engineering from Bilkent University and the other in mathematics from Southern New Hampshire University from which he earned two outstanding academic achievements rewards. Ayman earned his Master's degree in business administration with distinction from Strathclyde University. He has several industrial experiences; more than ten years are in an international financial institution. He wrote several research papers and his interests are e-waste, circular economy, econometrics of FX rates and trade, waqf and waqf worldview.

Irfan Syauqi Beik, Ph.D. is an Associate Professor in the Department of Islamic Economics, Bogor Agricultural University (IPB), Indonesia, and holds the position of the Director of the Centre of Islamic Business and Economic Studies (CIBEST) at IPB. Besides as an academician, he has been appointed as the Director of the Centre of Strategic Studies at the National *Zakat* Board of the Republic of Indonesia (BAZNAS) since August 2016. He is also a member of the National Shari'ah Board of the Indonesian Council of Ulama (DSN-MUI) and the Deputy Chairman of the Indonesian Association of Islamic Economist (IAEI). He is member of Shari'ah supervisory council in several Islamic financial institutions. In addition, he has published books and scientific articles in both national and international journals and has contributed regularly in various national newspapers in Indonesia.

Barae Dukhan, M.Sc. is an expert in the field of organizational excellence and improvement. His field of expertise also includes Islamic banking. He has worked as independent consultant in leading excellence assessment teams for several awards including the Global Islamic Business Award. He holds a M.Sc. Quality Management from the University of Wollongong in Dubai. Currently, he is a Ph.D. candidate in the Department of Islamic Economics and Finance, Istanbul Sabahattin Zaim University.

Mohamed Cherif El Amri, Ph.D. is working as an Assistant Professor in the Faculty of Business and Management Sciences and specialized in Islamic Economics and Finance at Sabahattin Zaim University. He completed his bachelor's degree in Islamic Studies from IbnTofail University in Morocco. He had his Masters in Islamic Jurisprudence and its principles, while his Ph.D. in Islamic Banking and Finance from International Islamic University Malaysia. He worked as an intern at several Islamic financial institutions, such as the Islamic Capital Market Business Group, Securities Commission, Kuala Lumpur, Malaysia, and Maybank Islamic. He worked as a Researcher at the Institute of Islamic Banking and Finance, Malaysia. He was an Associate Consultant at Amanie Advisors, Kuala Lumpur, Malaysia. He is a member of the Scientific Committee of the International Review of Entrepreneurial Finance Journal and Journal of Islamic Economics and Finance. He has multiple research publications and presentations in the field of Islamic finance and economics.

Suheyib Eldersevi, M.Sc. is presently an Associate Shari'ah Auditor at Raqaba for Shari'ah Audit and Islamic Financial Advisory. He holds a M.Sc. Islamic Banking and Finance from IIUM Institute of Islamic Banking and Finance. Currently, he is a Ph.D. candidate in the Department of Islamic Economics and Finance, Istanbul Sabahattin Zaim University.

Umar Farooq, M.Sc. is currently an Assistant Professor at Rizvi Institute of Management Studies and Research, Mumbai, where he teaches subjects in the domain of finance. He is also associated as a trainer with Institute of Chartered Accountants of India. In the past, he has worked with Centre for Monitoring Indian Economy as an Industry Analyst. He also undertook consulting assignments with Deutsches Asienforschungszentrum (DAfz) and Dun & Bradstreet (D&B), India. At DAfz, he developed an economic model for Malaysian Palm Oil Council (MPOC) to help them understand the potential economic losses it will suffer due to adverse Transnational NGO campaigns. At D & B, he prepared sectoral reports to appraise its clientele of the prevalent economic risks in various industries of the Indian economy. Academically, Umar Farooq holds a master's in management Studies from the University of Mumbai, specializing in finance. He is pursuing his doctoral studies from Jamnalal Bajaj Institute of Management Studies, Mumbai. He also received complete scholarship from University of Luxembourg for a Certificate Course in Law and Regulation of Inclusive Finance. Umar Farooq has published and presented research papers in conferences, contributed chapters to books and has reviewed books.

S. Ghiasul Haq, Ph.D. is currently a Professor and the Dean of Faculty of Management Sciences, Sarhad University of Science and Information

Technology, Peshawar, Khyber Pakhtunkhwa, Pakistan. He holds Ph.D. in Economics from Glasgow University, UK. He is one of the top supervisors and supervised many doctorate scholars in the university in the field of economics and management sciences. He has a vast experience in the field of economics and management sciences. He published different research papers in the field of economics, and Islamic economy and Islamic finance. He also worked on SMEs financing in Khyber Pakhtunkhwa, Pakistan.

Hichem Hamza, Ph.D. holds Ph.D. in Economics from the University of Economics and Management in Clermont-Ferrand, France. He started his career at Tunis higher School of Business in 2003. Since 2016, he is an Associate Professor and Researcher at the Islamic Economics Institute—King Abdulaziz University. His research interests include Islamic finance and banking, monetary and financial economics, Awqaf (Endowments) and non-profit organization. He has published, among others, in *Research in International Business and Finance*, *Studies in Economics and Finance*; *International Journal of Islamic and Middle Eastern Finance and Management*; *Journal of Islamic Accounting and Business Research*, *Borsa Istanbul Review*.

Mustafa Mohd Hanefah, Ph.D. is a Professor of Accounting, Shariah Auditing and Zakat, Faculty of Economics and Muamalat, Universiti Sains Islam Malaysia (USIM). He was a former Deputy Vice-Chancellor (Research and Innovation), USIM, the Dean of Research and Innovation and Faculty of Economics and Muamalat. He also was a Visiting Professor at the Economic Research Centre, Nagoya University (2011) and Aoyama Business School, Aoyama Gakuin University (2016), Japan. Dato' Dr. Mustafa obtained his bachelor's degree in accounting (Hons.) from Universiti Kebangsaan Malaysia (UKM). Later, he obtained his master's degree in accountancy from the University of Wollongong, Australia, and his Ph.D. in Islamic Accounting from Memphis University, USA. He has published many papers in international journals and books in the areas of Islamic financial reporting and accounting, shariah auditing, taxation, zakat and waqf. He also serves as a member of the editorial boards in a number of international journals.

Rusni Hassan, Ph.D. is a Professor at the IIUM Institute of Islamic Banking and Finance, IIUM. She graduated with LLB (Honours), LLB (Shariah) (First Class), Master of Comparative Laws (MCL) and Ph.D. in Law. She is actively involved in various Islamic Financial Institutions as the

Shariah Committee locally and internationally. She has spoken extensively in conferences, workshops and trainings on various Islamic Finance issues. A prolific writer and researcher in Islamic finance, she has published books on Islamic banking and Takaful, Islamic banking under Malaysian law, Islamic banking cases and commentaries, corporate governance of Islamic financial institutions, remedies for default in Islamic banking and termination of contractual obligations in Islamic finance. She has published more than 100 articles in local and international journals. She received a few awards for her contribution to Islamic finance such as Top 10 Women in Islamic Finance (2013); Most Talented Women Professional in Islamic Banking (2014); Women of Distinction in Islamic Finance and Law (2016); Distinguished Woman in Management (2017); 100 Influential Women in Islamic Finance (2017); Top 50 Most Influential Women in Islamic Finance (2018); and Top 10 Most Influential Women in Islamic Business and finance 2019.

Mustafa Helvacıoğlu, M.Sc. was born in Konya, Turkey, in 1981. He is presently pursuing his Ph.D. program in Islamic Economics and Finance at Istanbul Sabahattin Zaim University. He completed his higher education in civil engineering at Istanbul Technical University. He had earlier received M.Sc. degree in Transport & Sustainable Development at the University of London, Imperial College, in 2007. He served for 13 years in engineering and managerial positions in various private companies, and during his tenure, he was assigned several construction projects in Turkey and abroad. He has been working as the Quality and Internal Audit Manager of Seha Construction Co. since March 2016.

Khairul Fikry Jamaluddin, LLB (Hons.) is currently undergoing his pupillage in one of the prestigious law firms in Malaysia—Azmi & Associates under the tutelage of Encik Ahmad Lutfi Abdull Mutalip, the managing partner of the firm. He graduated from the International Islamic University Malaysia (IIUM) with a LLB (Hons.) in 2017 and LLB_S (Hons.) (Shariah) in 2018. Further, he will be graduating with Master in Islamic Banking and Finance in 2020, Master of Islamic Banking & Finance (MIBF). He has consistently received awards as the holder of Dean's List Awards for several semesters during his Master's study. Other than that, during the period of his study in IIUM, he did not limit his scope to just participating in academic-oriented activities since he had actively participated in events organized by IIUM among others being a Program Manager of National Client Consultation Competition (2015), IIUM Lex Sports Carnival (AIKOLFEST 2015) and Ahmad Ibrahim Client Consultation Competition (2016). In addition, he has also undergone a special training organized by Securities Industry Development Corporation (SIDC) under Securities Commission (SC) in 2019. Throughout the period of his training, he was exposed to fundamental knowledge of Islamic capital market (ICM) and Islamic banking and finance.

Muhammad Iqmal Hisham Kamaruddin, Ph.D. is a USIM Graduate Fellow from Universiti Sains Islam Malaysia (USIM). He received his Bachelor's degree of Accountancy with Honours (2014) and Master of Economics and Muamalat Administration (2016) from University Sains Islam Malaysia (USIM). Further, he received his Ph.D. in Islamic Accounting from Universiti Kebangsaan Malaysia (UKM) in 2020. He was a recipient of the Royal Education Award for his Bachelor's degree and the Accounting Best Student Award 2014 from the Malaysian Institute of Accountants (MIA). He also received Faculty Book Award (Master by Research) for his Master's degree. His area of several expertise is in the field of Islamic social accounting, shariah audit, Islamic non-profit organizations and halal management. He has also presented and published several articles and chapters in books in various national and international conferences, journals and book publications.

Fatimah Mohamad Noor, M.A. is a Ph.D. student in the Institute of Islamic Banking and Finance, International Islamic University of Malaysia (IIiBF/IIUM). Her research revolves mostly around the areas of mualamat, waqf and governance. Her doctoral research investigates the practice of good governance in the context of corporate waqf institutions as an attempt to find the best practice for the ongoing issues of governance in waqf institutions across the globe. She holds M.A (2017) and B.A. (2014) in Islamic Revealed Knowledge majoring in Fiqh and Usul from the same university. For her master thesis, she explored the issue related to the purification methodology of Shariah-compliant stocks, whereby Maqasid al-Shari'ah was used as a framework of analysis. Her thesis topic is 'Purification Methodology of Shariah-Compliant Stocks: A Maqasidic approach.' She also had presented her master topic at several conferences and published a chapter book. Until today, she is actively developing an array of publications in journal articles and chapter books that focus more on waqf and its governance issues, and any other muamalat issues. She co-authored an article journal that was published in (2019) and a chapter book in (2020). In addition to that, she also has spanned her research skills by getting involved in a research project funded by a Malaysian state government institution in (2019) as a research assistant. She remains dedicated as a research assistant to further develop her skills in academic research in order to bridge the gap between theory and practices. Currently, she involves in a new research project related to cash waqf and its implementation in modern Islamic finance.

Mustafa Omar Mohammed, Ph.D. is presently the Director of the Institute of Islamic Economics and an Associate Professor in the Department of Economics, International Islamic University Malaysia [IIUM] where he has been teaching for more than 15 years now. He has published more than 50 refereed journal articles and presented more than 70 papers, mostly at international conferences. He is actively involved in funded and commissioned research projects. His present research areas of interest are in *Waqf*, *Zakat*, Islamic microfinance and *Maqasid al-Shari'ah*. He has supervised more than 45 dissertations at Ph.D. and Master Levels. He is also a journal editorial member and reviewer panel to 11 academic entities. He has received several quality awards for teaching and research. He was part of a committee responsible for setting up the Institute of Islamic Banking and Finance and recently, the Department of Islamic Finance at IIUM. He also has long experience in translations, Arabic and English. He undertook projects for several organizations, including MIFC, IBFIM, AIBIM, IFSB—affiliates of the Central Bank of Malaysia. He offers consultancy and has conducted several trainings on Islamic economics, banking and finance in several countries including Kazakhstan, Singapore, Sri Lanka, Bangladesh, Philippines, Indonesia, South Africa and Uganda. He holds a Bachelor's and master's degrees in economics from IIUM and Ph.D. in Finance from Universiti Sains Malaysia.

Fauzia Mubarik, Ph.D. is serving as Assistant Professor in the Faculty of Management Sciences, National University of Modern Languages (NUML), Islamabad Campus. She attained the degree of Doctor of Philosophy in Management Sciences (Finance) in 2017 and has the achievement of attaining honors in the Ph.D. degree. Since 2017, she is serving as the Finance Cluster Incharge in the Faculty of Management Sciences. She is the member of the National Curriculum Review Committee (NCRC), HEC. She has published numerous research papers in the HEC recognized journals and few editorials in *The Frontier Post*

Newspaper and has the honor to attend and present the research papers at the local conferences. She also has in her credibility various trainings/workshops conducted and attended under the Faculty Development Programs.

Aishath Muneeza, Ph.D. is an Associate Professor at INCEIF. She is the first female Deputy Minister of Ministry of Islamic Affairs and is the Deputy Minister of Ministry of Finance & Treasury of Republic of Maldives. She is also the chairwoman of Maldives Center for Islamic Finance. She is considered as the founder of Islamic finance in Maldives. Her contribution to Islamic finance includes structuring of the corporate sukuks and sovereign private sukuk of the country including the Islamic treasury instruments. She also drafted the Islamic Capital Market framework of the country and is the only registered Shari'ah adviser for Islamic capital market in the country since 2013. She played a key role in setting up of the Tabung Haji of Maldives, Maldives Hajj Corporation, and was the first chairperson of it. She sits in various *Shari'ah* advisory bodies nationally and internationally and is chairman for many of these *Shari'ah* advisory bodies including the apex Shari'ah Advisory Council for capital market in Maldives. She has assisted more than eleven institutions to offer Islamic financial products/services. She won various national and international awards for her contribution made towards the development of Islamic finance industry. She is also a role model and a mentor for females who aspire to build their careers in Islamic finance industry and is the Vice President of Women on Boards, an NGO advocating women representation on boards of companies. She is an invited speaker in Islamic finance conferences and events held in different parts of the world. She was listed in 2017 as number seven among the 50 Influential Women in Business and Finance by ISFIRE which is an official publication of Islamic Bankers Association based in London, and she is among the most influential 500 in Islamic Economy. She is a member of the Association of Shari'ah Advisors in Islamic Finance Malaysia (ASAS), Malaysia. She holds a doctorate in law from International Islamic University of Malaysia.

Zakariya Mustapha, LLM practices law in Nigeria where he is an advocate and solicitor of Nigeria's Supreme Court since 2008. In 2010, he joined Faculty of Law Bayero University, Kano, Nigeria, as a lecturer where he taught conventional and Islamic banking and finance law, alongside other Islamic law courses until 2017. He specializes in legal and *Shari'ah* issues in Islamic banking and finance and offers legal and Islamic financial advisory services about legal framework, dispute resolution and Shari'ah-compliant product development in Islamic banking and finance. He has published numerous articles, and he has presented research papers at national and international conferences. He holds a LLB, LLM and BL with membership of Nigerian Bar Association and Nigerian Institute of Management (Chartered). He is currently pursuing his Ph.D. in Islamic Finance Law in the Faculty of Law, University of Malaya, Kuala Lumpur.

Shariq Nisar, Ph.D. is a Professor at Rizvi Institute of Management Studies and Research, Mumbai, and received his Ph.D. in Economics from Aligarh Muslim University, India. In the past, he worked at Harvard Law School as a Senior Visiting Fellow. Before moving to academics, he spent over a decade and a half in the Indian finance industry developing financial products and services aimed at improving financial inclusion. He made seminal contributions to India's financial sector by launching India's first Shariah index at Bombay Stock Exchange, first mutual fund scheme and first venture capital scheme. He played a key role in the design and launch of Shariah Index at Chittagong Stock Exchange, Bangladesh. He was invited to make a presentation before the Select Committee of Indian Parliament during the discussion on Insurance Amendment Bill 2015. He established India's first Center for Alternative Finance at ITM Business School, Mumbai. He has authored three books and 60 research papers and articles. He received Skoch Digital Inclusion Award for inclusion of minorities in India's financial system and Honorary Award from Islamic Finance Forum of South Asia (IFFSA), Colombo, for his contribution to Indian finance industry. He is on the board of various companies and member Academic Steering Committee of ICMIF, UK.

I. A. Oreagba, Ph.D. is a Consultant Pharmacist and Clinical Pharmacologist with a master's and Doctorate degree in Pharmacology. He also has a Postgraduate Certificate in Pharmaco-epidemiology and Pharmacovigilance from the London School of Hygiene and Tropical Medicine London, UK. He is a Fellow of the West African Postgraduate College of Pharmacists. He is also a seasoned resource person and examiner of the college. He is currently a Professor and Head of the Department of Pharmacology, Therapeutics and Toxicology, College of Medicine, University of Lagos Idi-Araba. He is an immediate past Editor-in-Chief of the *West African Journal of Pharmacy*, one time Editor-in-Chief of the *Nigerian Journal of Pharmacy*, currently an Editor in the *West African Journal of Pharmacology and Drug Research* and an Editorial Consultant for the

Nigerian Quarterly Journal of Hospital Medicine, Journal of Basic Medical Sciences and the *Journal of Basic and Social Pharmacy Research*. He is also a reviewer to many local and international journals. He has published over 70 original scientific papers in the field of pharmacology, pharmacy practice, public health, rational drug use, drug abuse, pharmacovigilance, pharmacoepidemiology, chemotherapy and toxicology in local and international journals. He is currently the Executive Director of a welfare-oriented NGO named 'Human Concern Foundation International' and Chairman of a Quality Assurance Organization known as Halal Certification Authority. He is also the current Vice President of the Islamic Medical Association of Nigeria and the National Secretary of the Muslim Pharmacists Association of Nigeria.

Asmak Ab Rahman, Ph.D. is currently an Associate Professor and Head, Department of Shariah and Economy, Academy of Islamic Studies, University of Malaya. She obtained her Ph.D. in Islamic Economics, Masters in Shariah, Bachelors of Shariah from University of Malaya. She is expert in the areas of Takaful, Islamic banking, economics of waqf, peace economy among other Islamic finances. She published many articles in the peer-reviewed journals, books and chapters in book.

L. Raimi, Ph.D. is an Assistant Professor of Entrepreneurship, American University of Nigeria, Yola, Adamawa State. He also doubles as the Chair of Entrepreneurship, the Coordinator of Graduate Program at the School of Business & Entrepreneurship and the Assistant Director of the AUN Centre for Entrepreneurship. Previously, he was a Principal Lecturer/Coordinator of Training/Coordinator Part-Time Programme at the Centre for Entrepreneurship Development (CED), Yaba College of Technology Nigeria. He is an Entrepreneurship Educator trained at the Entrepreneurship Development Institute (EDI), Ahmedabad, India, under the World Bank-Step B Project. He had similarly undergone a special training in Enterprise Education for Employability in Africa facilitated by the Oxford Brookes University and Pan African University, Nigeria, under the British Council's sponsorship. He is an alumnus of Cumberland Lodge, Windsor, UK, having participated in the 2014 Residential Mentoring. He recently attended the Experiential Classroom XX organized for Entrepreneurship Educators at the University of Tampa, Tampa, Florida, USA. Dr. Raimi has a strong passion for development-oriented issues in the fields of entrepreneurship, development, HRM and CSR. He has delivered papers at conferences/seminars in Turkey,

Malaysia, Ghana, UK, France, Morocco, Togo, India, Belfast, Leicester and USA. A number of his peer-reviewed articles and book chapters are published by Springer, Sage, Emerald, Elgar, Palgrave Macmillan, Inderscience, Routledge and IGI. His publications are listed in Scopus, Orchid, Publons, Researchgate and Google Scholar with encouraging citations and a growing number of downloads.

Syed Khalid Rashid, Ph.D. served as a Professor of Law, Ahmad Ibrahim Kulliyah of Laws, International Islamic University, Malaysia, for 25 years (1990–2015). He has 50 years of research and teaching experiences mainly in waqf laws and management in four different universities in Malaysia, India and Nigeria. His Ph.D. thesis on 'Waqf laws and administration in India,' was awarded in 1971, the first doctorate in Islamic law by Aligarh Muslim University in India in its century-long history. For 10 years, he served as a Professor of Law and Dean at Usmanu Danfodiyo University, Sokota, Nigeria (1980–1990). For a total of 12 years, he was Associate Professor of Law at Aligarh Muslim University and Kurukshetra University, India. His publication includes 13 books and 88 papers, out of which 8 books and 27 papers are on waqf laws and management. He won the Best Researcher Award in Law at IIUM during 2004. Islamic Development Bank, Jeddah, Saudi Arabia, invited him as a Visiting Scholar (Waqf) in 2011 and JAWHAR (Prime Minister's Department, Federal Government of Malaysia) appointed him as the chief consultant (Waqf) during 2010–2011. He was the Founding Director, International Centre for Waqf Research, IIUM, during 2014–2015. In 2019, he was awarded by the Deputy Prime Minister of Malaysia, the 'Lifetime Achievement Award' conferred by the Global Waqf Conference 2019 held in Kuala Lumpur, organized by the International Madinah University, for excellence in waqf researches.

Salim Refas, M.Sc. is a Ph.D. student in Islamic Economics and Finance at Istanbul Zaim University. He has a diversified 13-year international experience in the infrastructure, transport and development industries. Salim Refas contributed, managed or led some research initiatives in the transport sector, such as the World Bank economic sector work on container dwell times in sub-Saharan African ports published in World Bank publications in January 2012 (ISBN: 9780821395004). As division manager for the transport division at Islamic Development Bank, he participated in 2017 the launch of the Sustainable Mobility for All initiative (SuM4ALL).

Priyesta Rizkiningsih, M.Sc. is a Senior Researcher in Center of Strategic Studies, the National Board of *Zakat* the Republic of Indonesia (Puskas BAZNAS). Previously, she worked as a Research Assistant at the Central Bank of Indonesia. She earned her Master's degree in Islamic Finance and Management from Durham University, UK, with a full scholarship from Indonesia Endowment Fund for Education. Her research interests are Islamic social finance as well as governance and social reporting.

Abdul Aziz Yahya Saoqi, M.Sc. was born in Tasikmalaya, Indonesia, on 10 February 1989. He accomplished a Bachelor's degree in Islamic economics from Tazkia University in Indonesia with cum laude predicate. Moreover, in 2015, he received a scholarship from Maybank Islamic Berhad to continue a Master's degree in Islamic finance at International Islamic University Malaysia and accomplished the study in 2017. From the year 2018 until 2019, he served as a Research Fellow at Central Bank of Indonesia in Islamic Economics and Finance Department. From 2019 until the present, he has a career in BAZNAS Center of Strategic Studies (Puskas BAZNAS) of the Republic of Indonesia and holds a position as Senior Researcher in the organization. Amid his career, he involved in several national strategic projects in the Islamic social finance area. In Central Bank, he involved in designing Shariah and Internal Audit Standards for Zakat Institution and other projects related to the Islamic social finance issues. Nevertheless, in BAZNAS Center of Strategic Studies, he leads significant and impactful projects and surveys such us National Zakat Literacy Index and Shariah-Compliance Index for Zakat Institutions across the Nation and other related projects. Besides, he also actively became a speaker in the webinars that discussed the issue of Islamic social finance.

Ramadhani Mashaka Shabani, B.Sc. is a Master student in the Faculty of Business and Management Sciences, Islamic Economics and Finance Department, at Istanbul Sabahattin Zaim University. He obtained his Bachelor's degree in Customs and Tax Management from the Institute of Tax Administration in Tanzania. He worked as an Assistant Tax Officer for 1 year in the Tanzania Revenue Authority.

Ibrahim Ibrahim Sharifai, B.A. was born and brought up in Kano city, Kano State, Nigeria. He obtained a Bachelor of Arts (B.A.) degree in Islamic Studies from Ahmadu Bello University, Zaria, Nigeria. He has been working with the Kano State Zakat Commission for more than two decades. He is currently the Director, Planning, Research and Statistics of the Commission.

Ugi Suharto, Ph.D. is currently Lecturing at the University of Buraimi, Sultanate of Oman. He was among the early students of Islamic Economics at the International Islamic University Malaysia (IIUM). His Bachelor's degree (1990) and Master's degree (1993) are from the Kulliyah of Economics and Management Sciences (KENMS). He obtained his Ph.D. in year 2000 from the International Institute of Islamic Thought and Civilization (ISTAC, IIUM) with a dissertation turned into a book entitled 'Kitab al-Amwal: Abu Ubayd's Concept of Public Finance' published by ISTAC in 2005. He has been serving in full-time tenure in various universities in different countries including Malaysia, Bahrain, UK and now in Oman. He used to be a visiting lecturer for postgraduate program in public university in Indonesia as well. His highest academic rank is Associate Professor and he used to hold the position of Vice President for Academic Affairs in the University College of Bahrain (UCB). His research interests include Islamic economics, Islamic banking and finance, history and methodology of *hadith, fiqh mu'amalat* and Islamic thought and civilization.

Hassan Hassan Suleiman, Ph.D. holds a Ph.D. in Economics from Abertay University, Dundee, UK. He also holds a Master of Science and a Bachelor's degree in Economics from Bayero University, Kano, Nigeria. At present, he is an Economist and Strategist with the Nigerian Securities and Exchange Commission. Previous to that, he was Technical Assistant to the Director General of the Securities and Exchange Commission. Before joining the Commission, he taught Economics at Bayero University, Kano, for over 12 years. He has also held visiting positions at Al Qalam University, Katsina, and Bauchi State University in Nigeria. He has acted as a consultant to Women for Health Programme (W4H). He is a member of the Editorial Board of the *Nigerian Journal of Securities Market* and also an Associate Editor of the *Yobe State Journal of Economics*. His recent research interest is on emerging capital markets and Islamic finance.

Randi Swandaru, M.Sc. is Head Division of Zakat Utilization at the National Board of Zakat, the Republic of Indonesia (BAZNAS). He is responsible to utilize zakat fund for economic empowerment programs ιe aims of poverty alleviation. He leads four economic empowerment programs, namely BAZNAS Zakat Community Development, BAZNAS Microfinance, BAZNAS Institute of Mustahik Breeder Empowerment and BAZNAS Institute of Mustahik Economic Empowerment. He graduated with Master Program of Islamic Finance and Management at Durham University in 2017 as the best academic performance student. He also achieved several awards such as Young Southeast Asian Leaders Initiative (2020), Obama Foundation Leaders Asia Pacific (2019), Future Leaders Connect British Council (2018) and 3rd place in Indonesia Financial Authority Financial Inclusion Competition.

Hendri Tanjung, Ph.D. holds Doctor Philosophy in economics from the International Institute of Islamic Economics, International Islamic University, Islamabad, Pakistan, in 2012. He is author of 33 books; reviewer and editor of 14 journals; 66 publications in newspapers and magazines; 40 publications of research papers; 1958 citations, h-index 11, Google Scholar version. He is Vice-Director of the Postgraduate School, University of Ibn Khaldun, Bogor, Indonesia; Chairman of International Council of Islamic Finance Educators (ICIFE) Indonesia Chapter; Commissioner of Waqf Board Indonesia.

Umar Habibu Umar is a pioneer staff of Yusuf Maitama Sule (Formerly Northwest) University Kano, Kano, Nigeria, founded in 2012 and began operation in 2013. He is a Lecturer in the Department of Accounting. Currently, he is the acting Head of the Department of Accounting in the university. His area of research interest is Islamic accounting, banking and finance. He has also developed a special interest in research that links accounting to Islamic inheritance. Consequently, he published many papers in reputable journals and edited books in this research area. Besides, he is a member of the Institute of Chartered Accountants of Nigeria (ICAN).

T. O. Yusuf, Ph.D. is in his early fifties was born in Mushin, Lagos State. He bagged his Bachelor's and Master's degrees in Insurance and Management from the University of Lagos. As a Lecturer in the Department of Actuarial Science and Insurance, University of Lagos, he traveled to England in 2004 to obtain his second Master's degree in Islamic Management, Banking and Finance (with Distinction) from the Loughborough University and a Ph.D. in Insurance in Nottingham University Business School in 2009. He is currently an Associate Professor in the Faculty of

Management Sciences, University of Lagos. As an academic, he has traveled to several countries, including the USA, UK, Malaysia, Japan and Kenya to deliver lectures and participate in learned conferences, seminars and workshops. He has published up to fifty articles in referred and peer-reviewed journals both locally and internationally in Islamic finance and risk management. He is an Associate Member and Chartered Insurer of Chartered Insurance Institute of London. Currently, he is the Chairman of the Lagos State Muslim Pilgrims' Welfare Board and the Founder and Fellow of the Institute of Islamic Finance Professionals (IIFP) in Nigeria. As an Islamic scholar, he is one of the Imams of the University of Lagos Muslim Community and former Staff adviser for the Muslim Students' Society of Nigeria, University of Lagos Branch. He is an oratory speaker who regularly gives lectures on varied Islamic subjects in public, radio and television. His hobbies are traveling and keeping tab on current affairs. He has also authored Islamic books such as *Winning Souls for Allah*, *Conquering Shaytan, Mosque: Basics and Management.*

Muhammad Hasbi Zaenal, Ph.D. is a Deputy Director in Center of Strategic Studies, the National Board of Zakat the Republic of Indonesia (Puskas BAZNAS), and Research Fellow in Islamic Economic Studies and Thoughts Centre (IESTC). He graduated from Al-Azhar University (Bachelor's degree) and Universiti Kebangsaan Malaysia (Master and Ph.D.). His previous experiences include as Researcher at Research Center for Islamic Economics and Finance, School of Economics, Universiti Kebangsaan Malaysia, from 2011 to 2014, and Research Assistant at Islamic Research and Training Institute, Islamic Development Bank, from 2013 to 2017.

LIST OF FIGURES

Fig. 3.1	Sustainable Development Goals (*Source* United Nations [2020])	54
Fig. 3.2	Foundational alignment for human development (*Source* Beik [2020])	56
Fig. 3.3	Conceptual framework of Zakat (*Source* Beik [2020])	59
Fig. 3.4	Zakat Programs of BAZNAS and SDGs Priority (*Source* BAZNAS Center of Strategic Studies [2017])	60
Fig. 3.5	Zakat Foundational Goals and SDGs (*Source* Noor and Pickup [2017])	63
Fig. 3.6	Pillars of Zakat Programs (*Source* BAZNAS Center of Strategic Studies [2017])	64
Fig. 5.1	The Venn-diagram Model applied of SDG Goals (*Note* The dimensions of SD are mostly shown with simple illustrations, such as Venn-diagram model, Russian-doll model, 3-pillar model or wedding cake model, to reflect the jointly balanced pillars of SD. Here, the preferred illustration for the SDGs are Venn-diagram model)	97
Fig. 7.1	Population growth 2000–2020 of largest OIC cities (> 3Mn inhabitants in 2020) (*Source* United Nations Stats)	133
Fig. 9.1	Integrated Islamic Microfinance IIMFI-1 model	178
Fig. 9.2	Integrated Islamic Microfinance IIMFI-2 model	180
Fig. 9.3	Integrated Islamic Microfinance IIMFI-3 model	182
Fig. 9.4	Integrated Islamic Microfinance IIMFI-4 model	183
Fig. 9.5	Integrated Islamic Microfinance IIMFI-5 model	185
Fig. 9.6	Integrated Islamic Microfinance IIMFI-6 model	187

xli

xlii LIST OF FIGURES

Fig. 9.7	Graduation model	191
Fig. 9.8	Social Waqf project to build public facility	192
Fig. 9.9	Productive Waqf project to build commercial business	193
Fig. 10.1	Different health care facilities provides by Al-Khidmat foundation across the country	207
Fig. 10.2	Beneficiaries through health services by Al-Khidmat foundation across the country	208
Fig. 10.3	Details of clean water initiative	210
Fig. 10.4	Details of community service by Al-Khidmat foundation across Pakistan	212
Fig. 10.5	Details of community service by Al-Khidmat foundation across Pakistan (Provincial Disaster Management Authority, Khyber Pakhtunkhwa)	213
Fig. 13.1	GHI trend score for Indonesia (*Source* Global Hunger Index [2019])	263
Fig. 13.2	Islamic social finance model (*Source* Bank Indonesia [2019])	264
Fig. 13.3	The role of Zakat, Infaq, and Waqf in national economic development (*Source* Bank Indonesia [2019])	265
Fig. 13.4	Food bank activities (*Source* BAZNAS [2020])	266
Fig. 13.5	Food bank program output (*Source* BAZNAS [2020])	266
Fig. 13.6	*Rumah Sehat* BAZNAS activities—monitoring children development (*Source* BAZNAS [2020])	267
Fig. 13.7	Sustainable agriculture and farmers empowerment program (*Source* BAZNAS [2020])	269
Fig. 13.8	Productivity of organic farmers (*Source* BAZNAS [2020])	269
Fig. 14.1	A Muzara'ah agriculture financing scheme (*Source* Shafiai and Moi [2015])	284
Fig. 14.2	Proposed Islamic food banking model (*Source* Author's Own)	294
Fig. 15.1	General structure of social healthcare waqf (a) and (b)	307
Fig. 15.2	General structure of productive healthcare waqf	308
Fig. 15.3	General structure of integrated social-productive healthcare waqf-1 (a) and (b)	310
Fig. 15.4	General structure of integrated social-productive healthcare waqf-2 (a) and (b)	312
Fig. 15.5	Layanan Kesehatan Cuma-Cuma—Dompet Dhuafa (LKC-DD) Clinic	313
Fig. 15.6	Structure of Rumah Sehat Terpadu—Dompet Dhuafa (RST-DD) Hospital Social Healthcare Waqf, Early Model	315

Fig. 15.7	Structure of Sultan Agung Islamic Hospital (SA-IH) productive healthcare waqf	316
Fig. 15.8	Structure of RBC Maternity Hospital social-productive healthcare waqf	317
Fig. 15.9	Structure of RST-DD integrated social-productive healthcare waqf	318
Fig. 15.10	Structure of Achmad Wardi Eye Hospital integrated social-productive healthcare waqf	319
Fig. 16.1	Islamic ethical wealth and holistic health and wellbeing model (*Source* Authors)	331
Fig. 18.1	The latest global Gini index (*Source* World Bank [2018])	360
Fig. 18.2	The factors of inequality (*Source* World Bank [2015])	361
Fig. 18.3	World wealth map 2019 (*Source* Credit Suisse Research Institute [2019])	362
Fig. 18.4	The Islamic wealth management process (*Source* Shafii et al. [2013])	363
Fig. 18.5	The instruments of wealth distribution in Islam (*Source* Author's Document)	366
Fig. 18.6	Division of Waqf asset (*Source* Author's Document)	369
Fig. 18.7	The model of corporatization of Waqf asset (*Source* Author's Document)	370
Fig. 19.1	Zakat collection and distribution in Indonesia in 2018 (*Source* BAZNAS [2020])	376
Fig. 19.2	Zakat-SDGs framework based on their dimensions	385
Fig. 20.1	*Zakat* impacts on *Maqasid Shariah* elements in Malaysian ZIs	408
Fig. 20.2	*Zakat* impacts on SDGs goals in Malaysian ZIs	411
Fig. 20.3	*Zakat* impacts on *Maqasid Shariah* and SDGs by Malaysian ZIs	412
Fig. 22.1	Outlay of the global Islamic financial technology industry	443
Fig. 22.2	Islamic financial technology landscape	447
Fig. 28.1	Model of corporate Waqf WANCorp (*Source* Hanefah et al. 2011)	548
Fig. 28.2	Corporate Waqf Model Perbadanan Wakaf Selangor (PWS) and Bank Muamalat Malaysia Berhad (BMMB) (*Source* Ibrahim et al. 2016)	549
Fig. 28.3	Funding Scheme of the Bencoolen Street Waqf Project (*Source* Shinsuke 2016)	551
Fig. 28.4	Profit Distribution Scheme of the Bencoolen Waqf Project (*Source* Shinsuke 2016)	552
Fig. 29.1	Modus operandi of direct cash waqf (*Source* Ismail and Mohsin 2014)	568

xliv LIST OF FIGURES

Fig. 29.2	Modus operandi of indirect cash waqf (*Source* Ismail Abdel Mohsin 2014)	568
Fig. 29.3	CWFI framework for low-risk investment (*Source* Ismail Abdel Mohsin 2013)	571
Fig. 29.4	CWFI framework for high-risk investment (*Source* Ismail Abdel Mohsin 2013)	572
Fig. 29.5	Figure cash waqf investment model of IEF (*Source* Firdaus et al. 2017)	574
Fig. 30.1	Cash *Waqf* linked *Sukuk* structure (*Source* Authors' illustration)	591
Fig. 31.1	Sustainable Development Goal 9 (SDG-9) Index in 2019 (*Source* Bertelsmann Stiftung and SDSN [2019])	603
Fig. 31.2	Competitive Industrial Performance (CIP) Index (*Source* UNIDO [2019])	605
Fig. 31.3	Innovation index in 2019 (*Source* World Economic Forum [2019])	606
Fig. 31.4	Infrastructure index in 2019 (*Source* World Economic Forum [2019])	607
Fig. 31.5	Outstanding sukuk issues in 2018 (*Source* Islamic Financial Service Board [IFSB] [2019])	611
Fig. 32.1	Generic structure for Green *sukuk* (*Source* Adapted from [Mat Rahim and Mohamad 2018])	625
Fig. 32.2	The structure of the Orasis Green *sukuk* Project (*Source* Adapted from Dorsman et al. [2016])	627

LIST OF TABLES

Table 1.1	The 17 Sustainable Development Goals (SDGs)	11
Table 2.1	Reasons for digressing from waqf worldview	40
Table 2.2	Framework of the Islamic worldview of waqf	43
Table 2.3	Framework of the Islamic worldview of the Islamic ethical wealth	44
Table 3.1	Sustainable Development Goals and Maqasid al-Sharia	57
Table 5.1	Seventeen goals of SDGs and their explanation	91
Table 6.1	ISF and ICF Instruments to Achieve SDGs	121
Table 7.1	Largest 20 cities in the world from 1950 to 2030 (forecast), OIC cities highlighted	130
Table 7.2	Typical policy and public intervention instruments to address sustainability issues in mega cities	136
Table 9.1	Examples of BMT applying IIMFI-1 model	179
Table 9.2	Examples of BMT applying IIMFI-2 model	181
Table 9.3	Examples of BMT applying IIMFI-3 model	183
Table 9.4	Examples of BMT applying IIMFI-4 model	184
Table 9.5	Examples of BMT applying IIMFI-5 model	186
Table 9.6	Examples of BMT applying IIMFI-6 model	188
Table 9.7	Balance sheet of BMT before managing Zakat and Cash Waqf	189
Table 9.8	Balance sheet of BMT after managing Zakat and Cash Waqf	190
Table 10.1	Orphan care program details	205

xlv

xlvi LIST OF TABLES

Table 10.2	Region wise beneficiaries across Pakistan through orphan care program (Annual Report 2018 of Al Khidmat Foundation, Pakistan)	206
Table 10.3	Details of educational facilities	209
Table 10.4	Details of service wise beneficiaries	210
Table 11.1	Profile of the interviewees	228
Table 11.2	Categorical Themes and Interview Questions	228
Table 12.1	Gaps in the literature	249
Table 12.2	Seven targets of SDG-1 (United Nations 2020)	250
Table 14.1	Actions for strengthening food banking by Global Food Banking Network	292
Table 16.1	Proposed Islamic ethical wealth deployment for holistic health and wellbeing	334
Table 20.1	Relationship between *Zakat* impacts, *Maqasid Shariah*, and SDGs	403
Table 20.2	ZIs in Malaysia	405
Table 20.3	*Maqasid Shariah* elements and SDGs goals	407
Table 20.4	Comparison between corporate and non-corporate ZIs in Malaysia based on *Zakat* impacts	412
Table 20.5	Malaysian ZIs' Zakat allocation funds for COVID-19	415
Table 21.1	Four years campaign and details of Shaukat Khanum Cancer Hospital	431
Table 25.1	Forms and impacts of Waqf funds	490
Table 26.1	UNCTAD SDGs investment areas	505
Table 26.2	Guido Schmidt-Traub SDGs investment areas	507
Table 26.3	UNCTAD vs Schmidt-Traub SDG investment areas	509
Table 26.4	Waqf-SDGs Investment Areas	515
Table 28.1	The five protections and the role of waqf	543
Table 31.1	Global sovereign sukuk issuances in sub-Saharan Africa (Jan. 2001–Dec. 2018)	612
Table 31.2	Global sovereign sukuk issuances by countries in SSA (Jan. 2001–Dec. 2018)	612
Table 32.1	PNB Merdeka Ventures Sdn Bhd *sukuk* Highlight	631
Table 32.2	Asset-based and Asset-backed *sukuk* compared	632

PART I

Chemistry of Islamic Ethical Wealth for SDGs

CHAPTER 1

How Compatible Are Sdgs with Divine Principles? A Critical Literature Review (CLR)

T. O. Yusuf and L. Raimi

INTRODUCTION

Islam is described by Allah as the most standard creed (Din-ul-Qayyimah) because its divine principles are eternally consistent for achieving global peace, human progress, economic growth, and sustainable development. The divine principles of Islam have been categorized by Maududi (1967) into three parts, namely: At-Tawheed, Ar-Risalah, and Al-Khilafah. At-Tawheed focuses on discussion of Allah as the Creator, the Sovereign Law Giver, and the Management of affairs of heavens and earth are vested in Him. Ar-Risalah explains the concept of Prophethood including the medium through which the Sovereign Laws are transmitted to us, from the Prophets. Al-Khilafah on the other hand explicates the concept of Vicegerency and/or the management of the affairs of the world by man, after exit of the Prophets of Allah (Peace be upon them all).

T. O. Yusuf (✉)
University of Lagos, Lagos, Nigeria

L. Raimi
American University of Nigeria, Yola, Nigeria

© The Author(s), under exclusive license to Springer Nature Switzerland AG 2021
M. M. Billah (eds.), *Islamic Wealth and the SDGs*,
https://doi.org/10.1007/978-3-030-65313-2_1

3

The divine principles of Islam unlike man-made principles transcend theorization, but pragmatically impact on the lived experiences of Muslims in the areas of laws, social norms, economics, and property rights (Sait and Lim 2006). Leveraging the divine principles of Islam, Prophet Muhammad (Peace be upon him) reinvented and rebuilt the state of Madinah al-Munawwarah (Madinah the City of Light) into an inclusive society where Muslims, Christians, and Jews lived together under the constitution of Madinah. After the Prophet (Peace be upon him), early Muslims established their presence in different parts of the world including Iberia peninsula (Andalusia) under the leadership Tariq Bin Ziyad on the strengths of the divine principles of Islam (Kennedy 2014).

It is falsely believed that modernism started in Europe as renaissance, reformation, and spread like wild-fire to other parts of the globe including Muslim world. History however asserts that different civilizations including Islam contributed to modernism in different degrees. Modernism in the Muslim world started during the era of the Prophet but became amplified during the era of Abbasid, Umayyad, Fatimid, Andalus, Ottoman empires, India, and Africa, where early Muslims achieved landmark achievements in liberal arts, sciences, and technology (Sibāʿī and Khan 1996). Muslims' confrontation with modernism generated different responses, which shaped the contemporary thoughts of Muslims (AbdurRaheem 2013). The two key responses are: Proactive Response (PR) and Total Rejection Response (TRR). The proactive response is the view that modernism is consistent with Islam, and that Allah raised Prophet Muhammad (SAW) to spread Islam and modernize the era of Jahiliyyah with the divine principles. To proponents of proactive response, modernity is a renewal with the past, a return to the original ethos of Islam of Makkah and Madinah taken cognizance of new realities. However, the total rejection response is the opinions that modernity portends grave danger for the Muslims because it came with adulterations and thoughts that are alien to Islam. The total rejection response extends to the perception of modernity as nothing more than secularism and banishment of religious values from personal and communal aspects of Muslims' daily lives, hence should be fought consistently (AbdurRaheem 2013).

One of the contentious modern agenda is the sustainable development goals (SDGs), which was adopted by the United Nations on September 2015, as a new development blueprint that builds on the success of the Millennium Development Goals (MDGs). It was officially launched on January 1, 2016, with the recommendation to member countries to take ownership of the SDGs and establish national frameworks for the achievement of the 17 Goals (United Nations 2018). The seventeen (17) SDGs include: (i) Eradication of poverty, (ii) ending hunger and malnutrition, (iii) ensuring health facilities and promoting well-being of the people, (iv) providing quality education to all and promoting life-long learning opportunities for all, (v) promoting gender equality and working for empowerment of women, (vi) ensuring pure drinking water and sanitation, (vii) ensuring reliable, affordable modern electricity for all, (viii) ensuring economic growth by creating job opportunities for unemployed people, (ix) promoting industry, innovation, and infrastructure, (x) reducing income inequality, (xi) creating safe, resilience and sustainable cities and communities, (xii) ensuring sustainable consumption and production of goods, (xiii) ensuring environmental sustainability, (xiv) protecting life below water, (xv) protecting life above land, (xvi) promoting peace, justice, and strong institutions, and (xvii) developing global partnership for sustainable development (Mukhtar et al. 2018).

The SDGs are targets to be implemented and tracked by the United Nations member countries for the next fifteen years (2015–2030) at the regional, national, and international levels (Raimi et al. 2019). The failure of several international development blueprints is linked to the absence of the ethical climate (Fapohunda 2012). An ethical climate takes cognizance of working environment, ethical consequences of organizational issues, policies, procedures, and practices (Mulki et al. 2008; Moore 2012) and extends to the execution of ethical standards to reward ethical activities and sanction unethical conduct (Schwepker 2001; Martin and Cullen 2006). Poor compliance and absence of ethical environment for the implementation of SDGs justify the need for exploring the compatibility of the SDGs with the divine principles of Islam.

Based on the foregoing, this chapter critically discusses SDGs compatibility with divine principles of Islam. This study seeks to answer the research question (RQ): Are SDGs compatible with the divine principles of Islam? The research question is suitable for an exploratory study because there is no intent to test hypotheses or propositions, rather it attempts to enrich existing body of knowledge on connection between SDGs and Islamic law. There are seven (7) sections in this chapter contribution. Section "Introduction" provides an introductory background on the nature of divine principles of Islam from historical records. Section "Methods and Analysis" discusses the adopted methods and analysis. Section "Theoretical Framework" provides the theoretical foundation for the study. Section "Doctrine of Maqāṣid al-Sharīʿah (Objectives of Divine-Revelations)" critically discusses the doctrine of Maqāṣid al-Sharīʿah (Objectives of divine-revelations). Section "Development of Modern Day Global Bodies and SDGs" narratively explores the development of modern day global bodies and SDGs. Section "Discussing Each of the SDGs in the Light of Qur'an and Sunnah" discusses each of the SDGs in light of Qur'an and Sunnah. Section "Conclusion and Implications for Policy and Practice" concludes with implications for policy and practice.

Methods and Analysis

This paper adopts a qualitative research method because of its exploratory nature. Archival technique was employed in sourcing the required information from diverse materials, which include Qur'an, Hadith, online resources and scholarly articles on the subject matter. The required pieces of information sourced from Qur'an, Hadith, online resources and scholarly articles were subjected to critical literature review (CLR). A critical literature review (CLR) is the systematic and objective analysis and evaluation of scholarly articles on a specific subject matter for the purpose of developing new insights, richer findings, and enriching understanding about the subject of inquiry (Saunders and Rojon 2011; Saunders et al. 2012).

Theoretical Framework

Two theories provide the needed theoretical foundations for this discourse, these are: Maududian affirmative Islamic revivalism theory and theory of Islamic Revivalism. The Maududian affirmative Islamic revivalism theory asserts that Muslims with more knowledge, understanding, and exposure to the provisions of the Qur'an and Sunnah, they are strongly motivated to revive their religion. Islamic revivalism based on this theory is a reaction to certain issues found undesirable, unethical, and repulsive in the society. The issues that made Islamic revivalism imperative in the contemporary times include: (a) negative onslaught of modernity and secularism, (b) unfulfilled aspirations of the citizens, and (c) increasing level of impoverishment and income inequality (Ali 2012; Raimi 2015).

Comparatively, the theory of Islamic Revivalism presupposes that face with challenges and disappointment brought by modernism, Muslims have different perception and rethinking about religion, they have changed their liberal notion of seeing Islam as a private affair with God limited to the mosques, rather Islam is viewed as the viable solution to poverty and other depravation facing the Muslims (Carvalho 2009). In the contemporary times, the Muslims have made a transition from elitist lifestyles to Islamic lifestyles rooted in religious orthodoxy (fundamentals of Islam). Islamic revivalism is strongly evident in the daily lives of Muslims ranging from increasing participation of young and old in religious activities and preference for ethical values, lifestyles, and traditions (Raimi et al. 2014). Both theories underscored the fact that Islamic revivalism is rooted in awareness and consciousness about Islam, and the benefits of exploring the provisions of the Qur'an and Sunnah for spiritual, social, economic, and political solutions.

Doctrine of Maqāṣid al-Sharīʿah (Objectives of Divine-Revelations)

Islamic scholars in the field of Islamic Economics, Islamic law, Islamic philosophical thoughts, Islamic political economy, Islamic Finance, and Islamic Management have consistently used the doctrines of Maqāṣid al-Sharīʿah to explain the compatibility of Islam with the positive aspect contemporary discourse in the fields of economics, ethics, and management (Darus et al. 2013; Duderija 2014; Ibrahim et al. 2019). In the comparative literature, there are diverse reformist thoughts on Maqāṣid al-Sharīʿah for the purpose of promoting different reformist agenda in the Muslim societies (Duderija 2014). What is Maqasid al-Shariah?

Functionally, the term Maqasid al Shariah translated as the objectives of divine-revelations or the objectives of the Shariah is an approach used by Islamic Jurists in analyzing and assessing bioethical issues with a view to determining their compatibility and relevance to the principles of Islamic law. Analysis of issues based on Maqasid al-Shariah is based essentially on three aspects, namely: intention, method, and output/final goal, while the assessment of issues based on Maqasid al-Shariah is based on human interest hierarchy, inclusivity, and degree of certainty (Ibrahim et al. 2019).

However, Duderija (2014) defines the Maqāṣid al-Sharīʿah as a system of values that practically contributes to a desired and sound application of Islamic law (explicitly derived or inferred from the Qur'ān and the Sunna). It is based on the idea that Islamic law is naturally purposive and is ordained by Allah to serve particular purposes especially promoting people's benefit and safeguarding the welfare of people and protecting humans from harm. Maqāṣid al-Sharī'ah also include other concepts in the pre-modern Islamic tradition such as the idea of public interests (al masaliḥ al-ammah), unrestricted interests (al-masaliḥ al-mursala), juridicial preference (istiḥsān), presumption of continuity (istiḥsāb), and avoidance of mischief (mafsadah).

From another perspective, Ismail and Arshad (2009) stated that Islamic Economics is based on five divine principles because of consideration for the welfare of the society. These principles are: (a) principle of right and wrong, (b) principle of uses, (c) principle of moderation, (d) principle of economic freedom, and (e) principle of justice. The principle of right and wrong emphasizes that Islamic economic system principally make distinction between what is permitted being lawful (Halal) and what is forbidden being unlawful (Haram). The principle of uses makes it an obligation that within the bounds of lawful (Halal) and unlawful (Haram) prescribed by Allah, humans have been allowed to make full use of God's gifts bestowed on him. The principle of moderation states that Islam unequivocally discourages its followers to cross the limits set by Allah with emphasis on moderation and avoidance of extremism. The principle of economic freedom accords every individual freedom tied to accountability in the world, and that good actions will be rewarded and bad actions punished in the hereafter. The principle of justice emphasizes that Islamic principle of justice operates in production, distribution, consumption, exchange and other aspects of economic life (Ismail and Arshad 2009).

Maqāṣid al-Sharī'ah as a Fiqh concept has been classified into five broad categories by Imam Shatibi in their different discourses. These categories are: safeguarding the well-being by preserving the religion (Hifzul Deen), safeguarding the well-being by preserving the souls (Hifzul Nafs), safeguarding the well-being by preserving the intellect (Hifzul 'Aqeel), safeguarding the well-being by preserving the offspring/posterity (Hifzul Nasl), and safeguarding the well-being by preserving the wealth/money (Hifzul Mal). Inability to preserve these five principles considered as a Maslahah (interest) leads to social problems (Auda 2008; Ibrahim et al. 2019). Although the five traditional Maqasid are popular and well-rooted in the literature, Duderija (2014) explained that the scope has been broadened and enriched by a number of scholars. Rashid Rida (d. 1935) added to the five traditional Maqasid, the concept of reform and women's rights; Muhammad Al Ghazali (d. 1996) introduced the concept of justice and freedom; Yusuf al-Qaradawi included human dignity and rights into the themes of Maqāṣid al-Sharīʿah; and Ibn Ashhur included concepts of equality, freedom, and orderliness. For this chapter, the five thematic areas of Maqāṣid al-Sharīʿa as categorized by Imam Shatibi have been adopted, and they will be used for explaining the compatibility of Islamic laws with the SDGs.

DEVELOPMENT OF MODERN DAY GLOBAL BODIES AND SDGS

To sustainably drive socioeconomic and political development after World War II, the United Nations made the issues of peace, human rights and global cooperation important tools for achieving equitable, inclusive and sustainable development. The UN Charter that was launched in 1945 accorded people across the globe economic, social, and cultural rights (MacNaughton and Frey 2018). Unfortunately, the 1945 Charter proved to be a mere pronouncement with very low compliance among member nations of the UN. In 1948, the Universal Declaration of Human Rights Charter was launched by the United Nations for adoption by the international community. The new Charter guarantees protection of the person and provides classical freedom and rights such as freedom of expression, as well as economic, social, and cultural rights. The rights apply to all people irrespectively of their race, gender, and nationality, as all people are born free and equal (Association of Human Rights (2011). The Declaration elicits cooperation of governments as critical segments of the society for enforcement.

In January 1999, the United Nations came up with a nine-point Global Compact as a blueprint for promoting the shared values and international principles regarding issues of human rights, labor, and the environment (UN Global Compact 2014).

According to Raimi et al. (2010), the millennium development goals (MDGs) that was adopted in 2000 as another worthwhile agenda that sought to eradicate extreme poverty and hunger (MDG 1), achieve universal primary education (MDG 2), promote gender equality and empower women (MDG 3), reduce child mortality (MDG 4), improve maternal health (MDG 5), combat, HIV/AIDS, malaria, and other diseases (MDGs 6), ensure environmental sustainability (MDG 7), and develop a global partnership for development (MDG 8). By the terminal date of 2015, the targets of Mdgs were not realized in several countries across the world.

The United Nations adopted the sustainable development goals (Sdgs) in September 2015, as a new development blueprint that builds on the success of Mdgs across the globe. It was officially launched on January 1, 2016, with the recommendation to member countries to take ownership of the Sdgs and establish national frameworks for the achievement of the 17 Goals (United Nations 2018). The Sdgs is an all-inclusive sustainable development blueprint to be implemented and tracked for the next fifteen years by the international community at the national and international levels (Raimi et al. 2019). Historically, the Sdgs are seventeen (17) interconnected social, economic, and environmental goals to be achieved by 2030. These goals as shown in Table 1.1 are necessary to reinvent a better and more sustainable future for all in the face of daunting global challenges facing the developed and developing countries (United Nations 2018).

DISCUSSING EACH OF THE SDGS IN LIGHT OF QUR'AN AND SUNNAH

There are five thematic objectives of Islamic law as earlier discussed under the Maqasid al-Shariah in previous section. These five Maqasid include (i) preservation of religion, (ii) preservation of life, (iii) preservation of intellect, (iv) preservation of progeny, and (v) preservation of wealth (Kamali 2008; Ismail and Arshad 2009). Comparatively, the 17 targets of Sdgs when critically examined align with the five thematic objectives of Islamic law. This section discusses the compatibility of each of the Sdgs in light of Qur'an and Sunnah.

SDG 1: No Poverty. Islam views poverty as a harsh social-economic condition that denied people basic needs of life, quality living, and self-esteem. The pangs of excruciating poverty are experienced more in the Muslim Majority Nations by the vulnerable groups like widows, sick people, aged, orphaned children, landless and ethnic minorities (Raimi et al. 2013). No poverty target of SDG 1 comes under Preservation of wealth. Consequently, Allah instituted the Zakat, Sadaqah, and Waqf as tools for redressing poverty condition in the Muslim societies. To achieve the no poverty target of SDG 1, there is need to ensure that funds accumulated from Zakat be disbursed to the eight beneficiaries mentioned by

1 HOW COMPATIBLE ARE SDGS ... 11

Table 1.1 The 17 Sustainable Development Goals (SDGs)

SN	Goal description	Practical policies for goal actualization
Goal 1	No poverty	Economic growth must be inclusive to provide sustainable jobs and promote equality
Goal 2	Zero hunger	The food and agriculture sector offers key solutions for development and is central for hunger and poverty eradication
Goal 3	Good health and well-being	Ensuring healthy lives and promoting the well-being for all at all ages is essential to sustainable development
Goal 4	Quality education	Obtaining a quality education is the foundation to improving people's lives and sustainable development
Goal 5	Gender equality	Gender equality is not only a fundamental human right, but a necessary foundation for a peaceful, prosperous, and sustainable world
Goal 6	Clean water and sanitation	Clean, accessible water for all is an essential part of the world we want to live in
Goal 7	Affordable and clean energy	Energy is central to nearly every major challenge and opportunity
Goal 8	Decent work and economic growth	Sustainable economic growth will require societies to create the conditions that allow people to have quality jobs
Goal 9	Industry, innovation, and infrastructure	Build resilient infrastructure, promote sustainable industrialization, and foster innovation
Goal 10	Reduced inequality	Reduce inequalities, policies should be universal in principle, paying attention to the needs of disadvantaged and marginalized populations
Goal 11	Sustainable cities and communities	Ensure access to safe and affordable housing

(continued)

12   T. O. YUSUF AND L. RAIMI

Table 1.1   (continued)

SN	Goal description	Practical policies for goal actualization
Goal 12	Responsible production and consumption	Responsible production and consumption
Goal 13	Climate action	Climate change is a global challenge that affects everyone, everywhere
Goal 14	Life below water	Careful management of this essential global resource is a key feature of a sustainable future
Goal 15	Life on land	Sustainably manage forests, combat desertification, halt and reverse land degradation, halt biodiversity loss
Goal 16	Peace, justice and strong institutions	Access to justice for all, and building effective, accountable institutions at all levels
Goal 17	Partnerships for the goals	Revitalize the global partnership for sustainable development

Source United Nations (2018)

Allah in the Qur'an. However, Sadaqah and Waqf can be utilized for flexible and innovative utilization and disbursement. By and large, all funds earmarked for CSR, Waqf, and Zakat are trust that must be properly kept and utilized for poverty reduction (Raimi et al. 2013). Allah warns those who do not show empathy to the poverty-stricken people thus:

Verily, he used not to believe in Allah, the Greatest. And urged not the feeding of the poor. So, no friend has he here this Day, Nor any food except filth from Ghislin. (Q69:33–36)

The Zakah are only for the Fuqaraa´ (poor), and the Masaakeen (the needy) and those employed to collect (the funds); and for to attract the hearts of those who have been inclined (towards Islam); and to free the captives; and for those in debt; and for Allah's Cause, and for the wayfarer (a traveler who is cut off from everything); a duty imposed by Allah. And Allah is All-Knower, All-Wise. (Q9:60)

The Zakah are only for the Fuqaraa´ (poor), and the Masaakeen (the needy) and those employed to collect (the funds); and for to attract the hearts of those who have been inclined (towards Islam); and to free the captives; and for those in debt; and for Allah's Cause, and for the wayfarer (a traveler who is cut off from everything); a duty imposed by Allah. And Allah is All-Knower, All-Wise. (Q9:60)

SDG 2: Zero Hunger. The pivotal role of Islamic governance is to mitigate hunger and poverty in the society. Within the Islamic state of Madinah, Prophet Muhammad (Peace be upon him) managed poverty sustainably leveraging the age long Baitul Mal. The word Baitul Mal itself refers to the treasury of the Muslims established for safeguarding the common wealth of the State (Ummah). It is a replica of the modern day Central Bank. Fiscal matters such as Zakat computation, collection, and distribution for poverty reduction are handled by officials working in the Baitul Mal. Baitul Mal housed the Gold (Dinar), Silver (Dirham), Grains, Crops, and other valuables collected from sources like Zakat (Obligatory charity), Sadaqat (Voluntary charity), Jizyah (Capitation tax), Rikaz (Discovered minerals). Allah says:

> So, let them worship the Lord of this House. Who has fed them against hunger, and has made them safe from fear. (Q106:3–4)
> Nothing is worse than a person who fills his stomach. It should be enough for the son of Adam to have a few bites to satisfy his hunger. If he wishes more, it should be: One-third for his food, one-third for his liquids, and one-third for his breath. (Tirmidhi and Ibn Majah).

> Nothing is worse than a person who fills his stomach. It should be enough for the son of Adam to have a few bites to satisfy his hunger. If he wishes more, it should be: One-third for his food, one-third for his liquids, and one-third for his breath. (Tirmidhi and Ibn Majah)

SDG 3: Good Health and Well-being. Islam places very high importance on healthy living and human well-being, as this falls under preserving the souls (Hifzul Nafs). The Muslim governments and authorities in the Muslim communities are expected to find cure for diseases and ailments through provision of physician, drugs, vaccines, and other remedies. Prophet Muhammad (Peace be upon him) explicated the importance of good health and well-being, when he said,

> A strong believer is better and dearer to Allah than a weak one and both are good. Adhere to that which is beneficial for you. Keep asking Allah for help and do not refrain from it. If you are afflicted in any way, do not say:

If I had taken this or that step, it would have resulted into such and such but say only: Allah so determined and did as He willed. This word opens gates of evil thoughts. (Sahih Muslim 6954)

SDG 4: Quality Education. Quality education refers to varieties of knowledge disseminated to humans as information, technical skills, and understanding of natural laws. Education is needed for worship and self-awareness, to dispel conjecture and false belief, and survival on earth and beyond. A quality education is therefore one of the fundamental rights of the citizens and the primary duty of the government. Quality education based on the thematic objectives of Islamic law falls under protection of life, intellect, and progeny (Kadi 2006; Mukhtar et al. 2018). Part of the reasons for raising the Prophets of *Allah* is to educate humanity and reduce high-level ignorance about Allah and the universe. *Allah* says:

He it is Who sent among the unlettered ones a Messenger from among themselves, reciting to them His Ayat, purifying them, and teaching them the Book and the Hikmah. And verily, they had been before in manifest error. (Q62:1–3)

Read! In the Name of your Lord Who created. He has created man from a clot. Read! And your Lord is the Most Generous. Who has taught by the pen. He has taught man that which he knew not. (Q 96:1–5)

We made (David's) kingdom strong and gave him wisdom and sound judgement in speech and decision. (Sad 38:20)

In the hadith, the Noble Prophet Muhammad (Peace be upon him) said:

If anyone travels on a road in search of knowledge, Allah will cause him to travel on one of the roads to Paradise. Angels will lower their wings in their great pleasure with one who seeks knowledge, inhabitants of the heavens and the Earth and fish in deep waters will ask forgiveness for the learned man. The superiority of learned man over devout is like that of the moon on the night when it is full over rest of stars. The learned are heirs of Prophets and Prophets leave neither dinar nor dirham (currencies) leaving only knowledge and he who takes it takes an abundant portion. (Sunan Abu Dawud 3641)

O people, knowledge only comes by learning and understanding only comes by seeking understanding. For whomever Allah intends good, he gives him understanding of the religion. Verily, only those with knowledge fear Allah among his servants. (35:28). (al-Mu'jam al-Kabīr 929)

SDG 5: Gender Equality. Gender equality is a fundamental right in Islam, hence the males and females have been accorded same spiritual rights and privileges when they both abide by the divine instructions. As far as Islamic law is concerned, all people, men and women are equal in terms of spirituality, morality, and value, but have natural differences. The universal truth of Islam with regard to gender equality is that there is a complementary relationship between male and female. Allah says:

➤ Verily, the Muslim men and Muslim women, the believing men and believing women, the obedient men and the obedient women, the truthful men and truthful women, the patient men and patient women, the humble men and humble women, the charitable men and charitable women who give Sadaqat, the fasting men and fasting women, the men who guard their chastity and women who guard their chastity, and the men who remember Allah often and the women who remember Allah, Allah has prepared for them forgiveness and a great reward. (Q33:35)

Believers men and women, are helpers/protectors of one another, they enjoin good (all that Islam orders one to do) and forbid (people) from bad (all that Islam has forbidden); they perform prayers and give compulsory charity/zakah and obey Allah and His Messenger. Allah will have His Mercy on them. Surely Allah is Almighty, All-Wise. Allah has promised believers (men and women) gardens under which rivers flow to dwell therein forever and beautiful mansions in gardens of 'Adn (Eden Paradise) but the greatest bliss is the Good Pleasure of Allah. That is the supreme success (Q9:71–72)

For men there is reward for what they have earned, (and likewise) for women there is reward for what they have earned and ask Allah of His bounty. Surely, Allah is ever all knower of everything (Q4:32)

The Prophet (Peace be upon him) affirmed this reality, saying:

Verily, women are the counterparts of men. (Musnad Ahmad 25663)

SDG 6: Clean Water and Sanitation. Water and sanitation are central to Islam, hence the four schools of thought (madhhab) made water purity and related topics such as water classifications, ablution/bathing central matters in the Islamic jurisprudence such as al-Mughni of the Hanbali madhhab; Kifayah al-Akhyar fi Halli Ghayah al-Ikhtisar of the Shafi'i madhhab; al-Mudawwanah al-Kubra of the Maliki madhhab; and Badai' al-Sanai' fi Tartib al-Sharai' of the Hanafi madhhab (Mokhtar et al. 2015). Therefore, access to clean water and sanitation by the citizens is part of the obligations of government, business organizations, philanthropists, and relief organizations where governments are incapable of fully discharging the obligations. Practically, clean water and sanitation (purity of the environment) are necessary for protection of life. Allah says:

> He will send rain to you abundantly. And give you increase in wealth and children, and bestow on you gardens and bestow on you (humans) rivers. (Q71:10–12)

> Do not ever stand there (in prayer). In fact, the mosque that was founded on Taqwa (piety) from the first day has greater right that you stand in it. In it are people who like to observe purity; and Allah loves those observing purity. (Q9:108)

Prophet Muhammad (Peace be upon him) said:

> Cleanliness is half of faith and Al-Hamdu Lillah (Praise be to Allah) fills the scale and Subhan Allah (Glory be to Allah) and Al-Hamdu Lillah (Praise be to Allah) fill up-what is between the heavens and the earth and prayer is light and charity is proof (of one's faith) and endurance is brightness and Holy Qur'an is proof on your behalf or against you. All men go out early in the morning and sell themselves thereby setting themselves free or destroying themselves. (Sahih Muslim 223)

SDG 7: Affordable and clean energy. Responsible government is obligated to provide clean, adequate, regular, and affordable energy for the citizens. In the traditional societies, oil, wood, coal, wind, solar, geothermal, and hydropower are common energy sources. In the contemporary times, energy sources such as electricity, nuclear, and fossil fuel have become common. Irrespective of the energy sources, the most important consideration is that, energy should be affordable and clean. The Qur'an encourages humans to ensure proper use and conservation of all forms of energy as one of the creations of Allah.

And We certainly gave David from Us bounty. [We said], "O mountains, repeat [Our] praises with him, and the birds [as well]." And We made pliable for him iron, [Commanding him], "Make full coats of mail and calculate [precisely] the links, and work [all of you] righteousness. Indeed I, of what you do, am Seeing. (Q34: 10–11)

Trees play a critical role in quality livelihood of the people and sustainability of the planet, flora and fauna. Therefore, tree planting and other green policies are measures designed to ensure access to clean energy. Prophet Muhammad (Peace be upon him) said:

If a Muslim plants a tree or sows seeds, and then a bird, or a person or an animal eats from it, it is regarded as a charitable gift (Sadaqah) for him. (Ṣaḥīḥ al-Bukhārī 2195)

SDG 8: Decent Work and Economic Growth. Government in Muslim countries and employers of labor are obligated by Islamic law to provide decent work to fellow citizens for purpose of accelerating economic growth. Prophet Muhammad (Peace be upon him) was a merchant before his prophetic mission. After his prophethood, he provided guidance to the Muslims on business ethics and workplace conditions/standards. Therefore, Islam has its own guiding principles on decent work and economic growth based on the Qur'an and the Sunnah. Since, the phenomenon of indecent work poses serious existential threats to people and the economy, it falls under preserving the souls (Hifzul Nafs), preserving the intellect (Hifzul 'Aql), and preserving the wealth/money (Hifzul Mal). Allah enjoins:

But seek, with that which Allah has bestowed on you, the home of the Hereafter, and forget not your portion of lawful enjoyment in this world; and be generous as Allah has been generous to you, and seek not mischief in the land. Verily, Allah likes not the mischief-makers. (Q28:77)

SDG 9: Industries, Innovation, and Infrastructure. The tremendous impact that these three modern concepts portend for the modern societies cannot be over-emphasized. Flourishing industries supported by cutting-edge innovations powered through science and technologies generate massive employment and comfortability for the people. Functional infrastructures also guarantee ease of doing businesses in the modern time—all meant to achieve the good wish of Allah for mankind and so as to ease the task of vicegrency:

Allah intends for you ease and does not intend for you hardship. (Q2:185)

SDG 10: Reduced Inequality. As far as Islamic law is concerned, all people are equal before the law, and there is no basis for discrimination (Spierings et al. 2009). Islam's agenda to reduce inequality extends to recognizing, accommodating, understanding and accepting personality differences of people based on their race, ethnicity, gender, age, class, physical ability, religion, and other social orientations, although absolute equality does not exist anywhere in the world, the equality which is required and enforceable is equality before law, hence the needs of excluded and marginalized people should be given attention and consideration by the authorities. Furthermore, Mukhtar et al. (2018) cautioned that Islam and its divine principles do not recognize, accommodate and protect sexual rights of Lesbian, Gay, Bisexual and Transgender persons (LGBT) because there is no space for unnatural lust and perverted practices, rather Islamic law prescribed strong punishment for Lesbian and Gays in order to serve as deterrent for future perverts.

O mankind! We have created you from male and female and made you into nations and tribes that you may know one another. Verily, the most honorable of you with Allah is that (believer) who is pious. Verily, Allah is All-Knowing, All-Aware. (Q49:13)

In addition, economic power and opportunities are the major factor for unbridled inequality hence it is curtailed by the institution of Zakat:

...so that it may not circulate only between the rich among you... (Q59:7)

SDG 11: Sustainable cities and communities. Theologically, Islam makes it an obligation on governments, individuals, and groups to protect their cities and communities from war, perils and all forms of aggression for the benefit of the present and future generations. Historically, cities and communities are only destroyed by Allah, after series of warning. Allah reminds:

Nay! I swear by this city. And you are free in this city. (Q90:1–2)

And how many a town have We destroyed, which was thankless for its means of livelihood! And those are their dwellings, which have not been inhabited after them except a little. And verily, We have been the heirs. And never will your Lord destroy the towns until He sends to their mother town a Messenger reciting to them Our verses. And never would We destroy the towns unless the people thereof are wrongdoers. (Q28:58–59)

With regard to the sanctity of the City of Makkah, the Prophet (Peace be upon him) said:

Verily, Allah made this city sacred on the Day that He created the heavens and the earth. Therefore, it is sacred by the sanctity of Allah until the Day of Judgement. Its trees should not be uprooted, and its bushes and grasses should not be removed. And it was only made lawful for me (to fight in) for one hour of a day. Today its sanctity has been restored just as it was sacred yesterday. So, let the one who is present inform those who are absent. (Bukhari and Muslim)

SDG 12: Responsible Production and Consumption. In the globalized world, the production and consumption activities of humans pose serious existential threat to the ecosystems. Unfriendly environmental activities such as blockage of drainages by solid wastes, oil spillages into rivers, pollutions of agricultural land, chemical diffusion in the communities and emissions of carbon monoxides into the atmosphere are manifestations of irresponsible production and consumption. Therefore, Islam views responsible production and consumption as central issues that must be given considerations by humans while exploiting earth resources. Allah says:

O you mankind! Eat of what is on earth, Lawful and good; and do not follow the footsteps of the devil, for he is to you an avowed enemy. (Q2:168)

O believers, wine and gambling, idols and divining arrows are abominations from the work of Satan. Avoid them, in order that you prosper. (Qur'an 5:90)

Evil has appeared in the land (Al-Barr) and the sea (Al-Bahr) because of what the hands of men have earned, that He may make them taste a part of that which they have done, in order that they may return. Travel in the land and see what was the end of those before (you)! Most of them were idolators. (Q30:41–42)

In a sound narration, the need for responsible use of water was emphasized to drive home the culture of responsible consumption by the Prophet (Peace be upon him).

> "Abdullah ibn Amr ibn Al-'Aas (May Allah be pleased with him) reported that the Prophet (Peace be upon him) passed by Sa'd ibn Abi Waqas (May Allah be pleased with him) while he was performing wudu' (ritual water purification in preparation for prayers). The Prophet asked Sa'd, "Why is this water wastage?" Sa'd replied "Is there wastage in water purification also?" The Prophet said, "Yes, even if you are at a flowing river." (Ahmad)

SDG 13: Climate Action. The repercussions of irresponsible production and consumption caused by effects of solid waste contamination and carbon/gas emission from industrial plants on people, plant and planet affect everyone, everywhere. Climate change is therefore a serious environmental challenge facing humanity across the globe with different degrees of intensity. The policymakers across countries are working tirelessly at mitigating the adverse effects of climate change. Affirmative actions formulated at national and international level to combat climate change include eco-vigilance, conservation of the flora and fauna, zero-tolerance for gas flaring, adoption of environmental friendly manufacturing techniques, and carbon emission reporting/disclosures. Islam recommends both preventive and curative approaches to climate action (UN Global Compact 2014; Ortar 2015). Allah narrates the wonders of creation, and cautions against environmental abuse that could lead to climate change. Allah says:

> Have We not made the earth as a bed. And the mountains as pegs. And We have created you in pairs. And We have made your sleep as a thing for rest. And We have made the night as a covering. And We have made the day for livelihood. And We have built above you seven strong. And We have made (therein) a shining lamp. And We have sent down from the clouds (Mu'sirat) water in abundance (Thajjaj). That We may produce therewith grains and vegetations. And gardens that are gathered. (Q78:6–16)

> Do not make mischief on the earth after it has been set in order. Supplicate to Him in fear and hope. Surely the mercy of Allah is close to those who are good in deeds. He is the One who sends the winds carrying good news before His blessings, until when they lift up the heavy clouds; We

drive them to a dead land. Then we pour down water. Then We bring forth with it all sorts of fruits... (Q7:56–57)

The adverse effects of climate change are connected to human actions, disobedience, and excesses. Allah reminds:

> And Allah gives the example of a township, it was secure and peaceful: its provision coming to it in abundance from every place, but it (its people) denied the favors of Allah. So Allah made it taste extreme hunger (famine) and fear, because of what they did. There has come to them a Messenger from among themselves, but they denied him, so the torment seized them while they were wrongdoers. (Q16:112–113)

SDG 14: Life Below Water. Islam views life below water as equally important as life on land, hence Allah always caution on excesses on the use of land and its diverse resources that extend to life below water. Below the water, there are living creatures such as plants, fishes, and other aquatic animals. They all need to be protected from harms and environmentally degrading activities of humans on the land. Allah recounts His blessings on humans thus:

> And He it is Who subjected the sea to you, that you may eat from the fresh tender meat, and that you bring forth out of it ornaments to wear. And you see the ships plowing through it, that you may seek from His bounty and that you may perhaps be grateful. And He has driven firm standing mountains into the earth, lest it should shake with you; and rivers and roads, that you may guide yourselves. And (by the) landmarks; and by the stars, they guide themselves. Is then He Who creates the same as one who creates not? Will you not then reflect). And if you would try to count the favors of Allah, you would never be able to count them. Truly, Allah is Forgiving, Most Merciful. (Q16:14–18)

Prophet Muhammad (Peace be upon him) has serious concerns for the environment and its sustainability, hence he draws connection between green practices and the rewards of the Hereafter.

> Mu'adh (May Allah be pleased with him) reported that the Prophet (Peace be upon him) warned, *"Beware of the three acts that cause you to be cursed: relieving yourselves in shaded places (that people utilize), in a walkway or in a watering place."* (Ranked sound, hasan, by Al-Albani)

SDG 15: Life on Land. Land and its resources are the gifts that Allah entrusted on humans on earth as vicegerents. Life on landfalls with the thematic objective of preservation of life in Islamic law. As the vicegerents of Allah on earth, it is compulsory to manage sustainably the land, forests, animals, vegetation, and work collaboratively to halt all forms of abuse of land and its resources for sustainable development. Allah says:

> Evil has appeared in Al-Barr(land) and Al-Bahr (sea) because of what the hands of men have earned, that He may make them taste a part of that which they have done, in order that they may return. (Q30:41)

> Those who, if We give them power in the land, establish the Salah, enforce the Zakah, and they enjoin the good and forbid the evil. And with Allah rests the end of all matters. (Q22:41)

In Islamic law, there are rewards from Allah for maintaining life on land as required by SDG 15. Prophet Muhammad (Peace be upon him) said,

> While a man was walking he felt thirsty and went down a well and drank water from it. On coming out of it, he saw a dog panting and eating mud because of excessive thirst. The man said, this (dog) is suffering from the same problem as that of mine. So, he (went down the well) filled his shoe with water, caught hold of it with his teeth and climbed up and watered the dog. Allah thanked him for his (good) deed and forgave him. The people asked, "O Allah's Messenger (Peace be upon him), Is there a reward for us in serving animals?" He replied, "Yes, there is a reward for serving any animate. (Sahih Al-Bukhari 2363)

SDG 16: Peace, Justice, and Strong Institutions. Access to justice in the society supported by accountable institutions is a divine principle cherished by Islam. The issues of peace, justice, and strong institutions all come under preservation of religion and preservation of life. Islam brings peace to human communities judging by its etymology. Peace refers to a state of tranquility and calmness that individuals, groups, and nations experience by submitting to the Will of Allah (Islam), the Owner and Creator of all things. Peace has link with Islam in many respects. It is not by coincidence that one of the names of Allah is As-Salaam (Source of peace). Allah and His Prophet (Peace be upon him) enjoin peace and justice. Relevant verses of the Qur'an that supports SDG 16 are quoted below.

1 HOW COMPATIBLE ARE SDGS ... 23

Allah says; Verily, Allah commands that you should render back the trusts to those, to whom they are due; and that when you judge between men, you judge with justice. Verily, how excellent is the teaching which He (Allah) gives you! Truly, Allah is Ever All-Hearer, All-Seer. (Q4:58)

O you who believe! Stand out firmly for Allah and be just witnesses and let not enmity and hatred of others make you avoid justice. Be just: that is nearer to piety and fear Allah. Verily, Allah is Well Acquainted with what you do (Q5:8)

Prophet Muhammad (Peace be upon him) ordered Muslims to uphold peace and justice. He said:

Do not commit injustice, because injustice is darkness in the Day of Judgment. (Muslim)

Ibn Al-Jawzi said: *"Injustice necessitates two sins: usurping others' rights and defying Allah with disobedience. The sin of doing injustice is more evil than other sins because it is usually committed against the weak, who are powerless to fend for themselves. The cause of injustice is the darkness of the heart; a man whose heart is lit with guidance would not commit injustice."*

Ibn Taymiyyah said: *"People unanimously agree that the consequences of injustice are dire and that the outcomes of justice are good." He also said that, "Allah The Exalted grants victory to a just state even if it is a non-Islamic state, and lets an unjust state be defeated, even if it is an Islamic state."*

Beyond maintaining justice, Islam makes it an obligation on those in authority at different levels of governance to establish institutions for public welfare. Almighty Allah counsels,

Those who, if We give them power in the land, establish the Salah, enforce the Zakah, and they enjoin the good and forbid the evil. And with Allah rests the end of (all) matters. (Q22:41)

SDG 17: Partnerships for the Goals. Islam as a community-driven religion emphasizes the need for partnership for task accomplishment and implementation of developmental efforts. Partnership for development is inevitable in the contemporary times for promoting the ideals of SDGs because international players are tired of engaging in unprofitable efforts and unnecessary rivalries that are time-wasting and very expensive to sustain. Partnership is a working practice whereby individuals, groups, organizations, and countries work together for a common purpose thereby achieving short, medium, and long-term benefits. The noble Prophet Muhammad (Peace be upon him) practically demonstrated the importance of partnership in the building of the state of Madinah.

> Help one another in furthering virtue and Allāh-consciousness, and do not help one another in furthering evil and aggression. (Q5:2)
> Allah says of Dhul-Qarnayn: "That in which my Lord had established me is better. So help me with strength, I will erect between you and them a barrier. Give me Zubar of iron;" then, when he had filled up the gap between the two mountain-cliffs, he said: "Blow;" then when he had made them (red as) fire, he said: "Bring me Qitran to pour over them. (Q18:95–96)

According to Elias (2016), the precedent for cooperation and partnership with Non-Muslims is the alliance called Hilf al-Fudul. Hilf al-Fudul is a pre-Islamic pact of justice launched to support an oppressed person and restoration of his rights and privileges. The Prophet spoke highly of this pact and made clear that he would support any similar pact with non-Muslims after the advent of Islam. He said:

Certainly, I had witnessed a pact of justice in the house of Abdullah ibn Jud'an which, if I were called to it now in the time of Islam, I would respond. Make such alliances in order to return rights to their people, that no oppressor should have power over the oppressed (al-Dalā'il fī Gharīb al-Hadīth 243)

Conclusion and Implications for Policy and Practice

The chapter sets out to discuss the compatibility of SDGs with divine principles of Islam using a critical literature review (CLR). After the review, it was found that the seventeen (17) SDGs are compatible with the five (5) thematic objectives of Islamic law, namely: (i) preservation of religion, (ii) preservation of life, (iii) preservation of intellect, (iv) preservation of progeny, and (v) preservation of wealth. Therefore, the ideals of SDGs should be adopted, implemented, and monitored by all member countries of the United Nations for the betterment of this world and the hereafter as well. Two practical/managerial implications emerged. Firstly, discussing the compatibility of Sdgs; drawing evidences from the Qur'an and Hadith has provided theological foundation for SDGs as Shari'ah-compliant ideals. Secondly, the evidence-based justification would strengthen adoption and compliance with the SDGs by Muslim nations and policymakers because the sustainable development ideals of the United Nations have been situated within the realm of Maqasid al-Shariah (Objectives of Islamic law). This supports the theory of Islamic Revivalism and Maududian Affirmative Islamic Revivalism. The suggestion for the future is for researchers to carry out an empirical investigation on the compatibility of SDGs with the divine principles of Islam.

References

AbdurRaheem, L. (2013). *Muslim Face to Face with Modernism*. Special Annual Lecture. Available: https://web.facebook.com/TheMuslimCongress/posts/islam-face-to-face-with-modernity-imam-luqman-abdurraheem-amir-tmcpos ted-mon-100/602503116473308/?_rdc=1&_rdr. Accessed May 27, 2020.

Ali, J. A. (2012). *Islamic Revivalism Encounters the Modern World: A Study of the Tabligh Jama'at*. New Delhi: Sterling Publishers.

Association of Human Rights. (2011). *The Universal Declaration of Human Rights (UDHR)—1948*. Available: https://www.humanrights.ch/en/standa rds/udhr/. Accessed April 17, 2020.

Auda, J. (2008). *Maqasid al-Shariah: An Introductory Guide*. Herndon: International Institute of Islamic Thought (IIIT).

Carvalho, J.-P. (2009). *A Theory of the Islamic Revival*. Available http://tuvalu.santafe.edu/~bowles/TheoryIslamicRevival.pdf. Accessed June 4, 2020.

Darus, F., Yusoff, H., Naim, A., Milianna, D., Mohamed Zain, M., Amran, A., et al. (2013). Islamic Corporate Social Responsibility (i-CSR) Framework from the Perspective of Maqasid al-Syariah and Maslahah. *Issues in Social & Environmental Accounting, 7*(2), 102–112.

Duderija, A. (2014). Contemporary Muslim Reformist Thought and Maqāṣid cum Maṣlaḥa Approaches to Islamic Law: An Introduction. In *Maqāṣid al-Sharī'a and Contemporary Reformist Muslim Thought* (pp. 1–11). New York: Palgrave Macmillan.

Elias, A. (2016). *Cooperation with All Humanity for Justice in Hilf al-Fudul. Faith in Allah Article*. Available https://abuaminaelias.com/justice-for-all-humanity-hilf-al-fudul/. Accessed June 4, 2020.

Fapohunda, T. M. (2012). Towards Improved Access to Full Employment and Decent Work for Women in Nigeria. *International Journal of Humanities and Social Science*, *2*(8), 104–112.

Ibrahim, A. H., Rahman, N. N. A., Saifuddeen, S. M., & Baharuddin, M. (2019). Maqasid al-Shariah Based Islamic Bioethics: A Comprehensive Approach. *Journal of Bioethical Inquiry*, *16*(3), 333–345.

Ismail, A. G., & Arshad, N. C. (2009). Islamic Economic System: From Principles to Microeconomics and Macroeconomics Fields. In *International Conference on Islamic Economics, Banking and Finance* (pp. 1–16).

Kadi, W. (2006). Education in Islam—Myths and Truths. *Comparative Education Review*, *50*(3), 311–324.

Kamali, M. H. (2008). *Maqasid al-Shariah Made Simple*. London and Washington, DC: International Institute of Islamic Thought (IIIT).

Kennedy, H. (2014). *Muslim Spain and Portugal: A political history of al-Andalus*. London: Routledge.

MacNaughton, G., & Frey, D. (2018). Challenging Neoliberalism: ILO, Human Rights, and Public Health Frameworks on Decent Work. *Health and Human Rights*, *20*(2), 43–55.

Martin, K. D., & Cullen, J. B. (2006). Continuities and Extensions of Ethical Climate Theory: A Meta-Analytic Review. *Journal of Business Ethics*, *69*(2), 175–194.

Maududi, A. A. (1967). *Islamic Way of Life*. Al-Bat'ha. Available http://www. islamindepth.com/books/Islamic%20Way%20Of%20Life.PDF. Accessed May, 24, 2020.

Mokhtar, M. I., Abdullah, R., & Baharuddin, A. (2015). An Islamic Perspective on Water Quality: A Case of Malaysia. *Water Policy*, *17*(3), 454–471.

Moore, H. L. (2012). *Ethical Climate, Organizational Commitment, and Job Satisfaction of Full-Time Faculty Members.*

Mukhtar, S., Zainol, Z. A., & Jusoh, S. (2018). Islamic Law and Sustainable Development Goals. *Tazkia Islamic Finance and Business Review*, *12*(1), 81–99.

Mulki, J. P., Jaramillo, J. F., & Locander, W. B. (2008). Effect of Ethical Climate on Turnover Intention: Linking Attitudinal-and Stress Theory. *Journal of Business Ethics*, *78*(4), 559–574.

Ortar, L. (2015, December). *Climate Change and CSR: Can Voluntarism Pay? UNFCCC (COP 21) meeting in Paris.*

Raimi, L. (2015). Waqf and Zakah as Social Safety nets for Poverty Reduction in Nigeria. *WIEF-UiTM Occasional Papers* (2nd ed), 89–103. https:// www.researchgate.net/profile/Lukman_Raimi2/publication/288825661_ WAQF_AND_ZAKAH_AS_SOCIAL_SAFETY_NETS_FOR_POVERTY_R EDUCTION_IN_NIGERIA/links/5684370408ae197583937ca1.pdf#pag e=89.

Raimi, L., Adelopo, A. O., &Yusuf, H. (2019). Corporate Social Responsibility and Sustainable Management of Solid Wastes and Effluents in Lagos Megacity Nigeria. *Social Responsibility Journal*, 1–21. https://doi.org/10.1108/SRJ-09-2018-0239.

Raimi, L., Bello, M. A., & Mobolaji, H. I. (2010). Faith-Based and Business System Models: A Policy Response to the Millennium Development Goals (MDGS) in Nigeria. *Humanomics, 26*(2), 124–138. Emerald Publishing UK.

Raimi, L., Patel, A., & Adelopo, I. (2014). Corporate Social Responsibility, Waqf System and Zakat System as Faith-Based Model for Poverty Reduction. *World Journal of Entrepreneurship, Management and Sustainable Development, 10*(3), 228–242.

Raimi, L., Patel, A., Adelopo, I., & Ajewole, T. (2013). Tackling Poverty Crisis in the Muslim Majority Nations (MMNs): The Faith-Based Model (FBM) as an Alternative Policy Option. *Advanced Journal of Business Management and Entrepreneurship, 1*(1), 1–12.

Sait, S., & Lim, H. (2006). *Land, Law and Islam: Property and Human Rights in the Muslim World* (Vol. 1). London and New York: Zed Books.

Saunders, M, Lewis, P., & Thornhill, A. (2012). Research Methods for Business Students (Eds). Edinburgh Gate, Harlow, UK: Pearson Education Limited.

Saunders, M. N., & Rojon, C. (2011). On the Attributes of a Critical Literature Review. *Coaching: An International Journal of Theory, Research and Practice, 4*(2), 156–162.

Schwepker, C. H., Jr. (2001). Ethical Climates Relationship to Job Satisfaction, Organizational Commitment, and Turnover Intention in the Salesforce. *Journal of Business Research, 54*(1), 39–52.

Sibāʿī, M., & Khan, S. A. (1996). *Some Glittering Aspects of the Islamic Civilization*. International Islamic Book Center.

Spierings, N., Smits, J., & Verloo, M. (2009). On the Compatibility of Islam and Gender Equality. *Social Indicators Research, 90*(3), 503–522.

UN Global Compact. (2014). *Corporate Sustainability in The World Economy. UN Global Compact Office*. United Nations, New York. Available http://www.unglobalcompact.org/docs/news_events/8.1/GC_brochure_FINAL.pdf. Accessed 12 April, 2020.

United Nations. (2018). *About the Sustainable Development Goals*. Available at www.un.org/sustainabledevelopment/sustainable-development-goals/. Accessed 23 April 2020.

United Nations Development Programme. (2020). *Goal 8: Decent Work and Economic Growth*. Available https://www.undp.org/content/undp/en/home/sustainable-development-goals/goal-8-decent-work-and-economic-growth.html. Accessed April, 24, 2020.

CHAPTER 2

The Worldview of Islamic Ethical Wealth and Its Implications for SDGs: The Case of Waqf

Ayman Bakr, Mohamed Cherif El Amri, and Mustafa Omar Mohammed

INTRODUCTION

There are many issues facing the Islamic ethical wealth. Currently, zakāh management suffers from a lot of inefficiencies and bureaucracies and is not compatible with today's challenges. Perhaps that is what led Kidwai and Zidani (2020) to call for a review of zakāh management. In comparison, waqf was subjected to various deteriorations from time-to-time commensurate with the requirements of each period in history. A lot has been said about the reasons for the deterioration of the waqf system since the fall of the Ottoman Caliphate. Bagby (2012, p. 24) and Kahf (1998,

---

A. Bakr · M. C. El Amri (✉)
Department of Islamic Economics and Finance, Istanbul Sabahattin
Zaim University, Istanbul, Turkey

M. O. Mohammed
Department of Economics, International Islamic University Malaysia [IIUM],
Gombak, Malaysia

© The Author(s), under exclusive license to Springer Nature
Switzerland AG 2021
M. M. Billah (eds.), *Islamic Wealth and the SDGs*,
https://doi.org/10.1007/978-3-030-65313-2_2

29

p. 5), for example, talked about underfunding as the reason for this deterioration. Others like Abdullah Nadwi (2014, pp. 6, 8) and Rashid (2012, p. 135) discussed the issue from the perspective of mismanagement, misconduct, and corruption. Other reasons involve colonial abandonment and appropriation of waqf (Abdur-Rashid 2020, p. 26), aggression and lack of governmental support (Abdullah Nadwi 2014, pp. 5–6; Dogarawa 2010, p. 22), and legislative issues (Kahf 1998, p. 6; Nawa 2015).

Today, the issues are not less serious than the above-mentioned ones, albeit of a different kind. With more and more writings about Islamic ethical wealth, aberrations continue to crop in several works on Islamic ethical wealth. Such aberrations have created diversions and detachment from the true identity of the Islamic ethical wealth system. It is evident that this is happening partly due to lack of proper understanding of its worldview and partly due to the laxity of Shari'ah constraints on the topic. Yet, the literature has remained silent on the issue of aberrations. Therefore, this chapter fills in this research gap by investigating the extent of Islamic ethical wealth worldview.

Review of Related Works on Worldview of Islamic Ethical Wealth

Islamic ethical wealth follows from the great ethical values established by Islam. The purpose is multi-folded. First, it creates a state of strong social ties among the people. Second, it helps eliminate hardships and poverty. Third, it establishes ways for Muslims to come closer to Allah. These outcomes are common to all the institutions and tools provided by the Islamic ethical wealth. But, since waqf stands out from the other institutions and tools in terms of its perpetual nature, it makes sense to visit the case of waqf in reviewing the related works on the worldview while bearing in mind that to some extent the same consequences follow for the other institutions.

There are volumes of literary works on waqf, for example (Bonine 1987; Çizakça 1995; Ariff 1996; Dogarawa 2010; Orbay 2012; Rashid 2012; Bulut & Korkut 2019). The focus of most of these studies is not linked directly to the worldview of waqf. The authors might have assumed that such worldview is implied and is a common knowledge to the reader. Yet spelling them out clearly makes great difference in putting arguments and issues into contexts and perspectives. On the other hand, few studies have discussed dimensions and worldviews related to waqf. However, in some of the studies the discussion on the issues and dimensions is general, disjointed, and has not been contextualized within the scope of waqf worldview or at least a worldview framework. While some of the other studies have based waqf worldview on other worldviews such as Islamic worldview and Tawḥīdī worldview.

For example, in a study Abdur-Rashid (2020) mentioned interesting dimensions of waqf worldview, namely 'ṣadaqah jāriyah' (ongoing charity), perpetuity, and ownership. However, these dimensions were not articulated and contextualized into waqf worldview let alone the framework of the worldview. Abdur-Rashid (2020) explored the chronological transformations a philanthropic institution such as waqf had undergone. He explained that the desire for having an ongoing charity that extended beyond the donor's life contributed to the creation of waqf as a separate and uniquely developed Islamic institution. More precisely, he maintained that Muslim scholars have interpreted 'ṣadaqah jāriyah' (ongoing charity) as a reference to Islamic waqf (Abdur-Rashid 2020, p. 8). He explained the formative phase of waqf, and in the process, he discussed the elements of waqf and its parameters such as perpetuity. He described the various scholars' thoughts on perpetuity and ownership. Whereas he could identify critical dimensions of waqf worldview, his work was not able to develop them further. This constitutes an important gap in this group of literature.

Meanwhile, there are works that have used Islamic worldview in general to explain the motives for waqf. For example, Shaikh et al. (2017) mentioned Islamic worldview as a motive for charitable giving in Islam. This worldview underpins the importance of waqf in the Islamic redistribution framework to demonstrate the possibility of using waqf for financing and development. This Islamic worldview would in turn leads to the creation of a waqf institution. Other studies have used the Tawḥīdī worldview to explain waqf. The study of Mahamood and Rahman (2015) is one such example. They approach the waqf from a Tawḥīdī worldview to explain the motives for financing universities through waqf, though the study was not able to relate to all the dimensions of a waqf worldview.

In the same vein, Choudhury e al. (2019) studied waqf in Malaysia from the worldview of Tawḥīdī unity of knowledge. They attempted to isolate waqf from the ethically exogenous socio-economic treatment under "Sharī'ah compliance". They concluded that if there is a future for waqf as a truly Islamic institution with Tawḥīdī worldview, then it must return to the classical understanding of the underpinning principles of sustainability and perpetuity (Choudhury et al. 2019, p. 791). This study is exceptional in that it has demonstrated a clear and strong sense for a worldview of waqf. The gap left in the study is, again, to articulate the worldview through the lens of dimensions related to the worldview of waqf.

In summary, the study has identified the following gaps in literature. Firstly, the vast literatures are general and descriptive. They have not linked their discussions directly to the worldview. Secondly, few literatures have either discussed the dimensions of a worldview or have used other worldviews to explain an Islamic ethical wealth. Those that discussed the dimensions were unable to articulate them and contextualize them to develop framework of a worldview. Similarly, those that have adopted other worldviews to explain an Islamic ethical wealth missed out on the dimensions of the worldview. The present study aspires to fill in these three major research gaps.

The Socio-Economic Role of Islamic Ethical Wealth and the History of Waqf

The Islamic ethical wealth constantly provided support for the various facets of life throughout history. Its fundamental role in alleviating poverty, developing the non-profit non-governmental organizations, and contributing to the socio-economic welfare of the society has been acknowledged by many researchers. For example, many researchers discussed the socio-economic implications of waqf (Dogarawa 2010, p. 1; Haneef et al. 2015, p. 250; Kahf 1998, p. 9; 1999, p. 39). Similarly, many researchers delineated the socio-economic effect of zakāh and its role in alleviating poverty (Joan et al. 2019; Kidwai and Zidani 2020; Syed et al. 2020). Therefore, the Islamic ethical wealth possesses enormous potential to easily close the gap created by the other two sectors, the public and private sectors, in any economy. Mentioning waqf as the first example is of no surprise. This is because it possessed the space for huge and constant development and modifications while surviving over a span of more than a millennium. Thus, it is of utmost injustice to overlook its significance and how it had evolved. Therefore, it is inevitable that we mention a brief history of how waqf developed over time.

The Qubā' mosque in al-Madīnah formed the first waqf in Islam followed by the Prophet's mosque. These were waqfs for 'ibādah (worshiping), i.e., for religious purposes. However, scholars disagreed on what was the first philanthropic waqf in Islam. According to Kahf (2003, pp. 3–4), the well of Rūmah bought by 'Uthmān Ibn 'Affān, the companion of the prophet (ﷺ), was the first one. Whether it really was or not, does not affect the great implications it had on the welfare of the Muslims as everyone started to have access to free drinking water since then. In 4 Hijri (ﷺ) himself had declared that the seven orchards given to him by Mukhairīq become a remainder charitable waqf (AlMunajjid 1979; Kahf 2003, p. 4). It is also narrated that 'Ā'ishah, the wife of the prophet (ﷺ), said, "The prophet (ﷺ) made seven of his orchards in al-Madīnah ṣadaqah (charity) on the children of 'Abd al-Muṭṭalib and the children of Hāshim" (Bayhaqī's sunan al-kubrā: 11896). The latter marked a third type of waqf: the family waqf, though it is still philanthropical. Nonetheless, regardless of the type of waqf, the sīrah (biography of the prophet, pbuh, and his companions), is rich of similar examples where the companions of the prophet (ﷺ) have devoted their properties for waqf. Al-Shafi'ī has reported that he enumerated eighty of the Ansār companions who dedicated their properties for that purpose (AlMunajjid 1979).

Later during the Umayyad period, waqf was so prolific that they established an organization for supervising them, while the appointing of trustees (mutawallīs) was tasked to judges (AlMunajjid 1979). The latter held the former accountable of their work. Judges also monitored the distributional channels of the returns. The 'Abbasids added to their predecessors the position of ṣadr al-waqf (minister-like of waqf) who was responsible for managing waqf and recruiting assistants (AlMunajjid 1979). This continued on and during the Ottoman period waqf evolved tremendously. During their reign, the Ottomans developed complex managerial structures (AlMunajjid 1979) to further improve organizing waqf affairs, the outcome of which manifested itself with its widespread (Bulut and Korkut 2019, p. 8). Soon every facet of life was enjoying the benefits of waqf: feeding and caring for animals was reported like the waqf for cats and unwanted animals, both in Damascus (Kahf 2003, p. 10); Bulut and Korkut (2019, p. 8) listed that educational and religious institutions and infrastructural services, like sidewalks and bridges, were funded; hospitals and libraries were built; students, poor, needy, and orphans were supported; graveyards and cemetery ceremonies were financed (Dogarawa 2010, p. 8).

It must be clear, though, that the word 'waqf' was not used until around the middle of the third century in Islam (Abdur-Rashid 2020,

p. 9). Therefore, you will not be able to find that word in Qurān or Sunnah. Nonetheless, other words in Sunnah were used to refer to the act of endowment. The prophet (ﷺ) said to 'Omar, "Sequester the principal [of the orchard] and devote its proceedings" (Narrated by al-Nasā'ī: 3603, and Ibn Mājah: 2397). So, what was common at their time was the word 'habs' (seizure or sequestering) or any derivative of that word. Thus, 'habs al-asl' or 'habs al-'ayn' would mean to seize the principal from being sold, gifted, or inherited. Also, the word 'sadaqah' and any form of its derivates were also used for that purpose. However, by the early period of the 'Abbāsid dynasty, a terminological problem started to emerge (Abdur-Rashid 2020, p. 13); different jurists employed different words to refer to waqf which could have caused great confusion. Notwithstanding, the jurists of all sects, except for Malikīs, eventually united by adopting the word 'waqf' going forward.

ISLAMIC WORLDVIEW AND ITS SIGNIFICANCE TO THE COMPONENTS AND DIMENSIONS OF ISLAMIC ETHICAL WEALTH

In order to get a sound understanding of the Islamic worldview of the Islamic ethical wealth, it is critical that we refer to its original sources and the understandings of the former companions and scholars. The sources from Qur'ān and Sunnah will help us to identify the components and dimensions of the Islamic ethical wealth from an Islamic worldview. However, before delving further, it is worth noting that the various institutions and tools of the Islamic ethical wealth share almost the same components and dimensions except that the waqf exceeds them with a few more due to its nature. Therefore, studying the specific case of waqf first allows us to capture all the components and dimensions related to the Islamic ethical wealth and then it would be possible to generalize for the remaining institutions.

Two remarkable stories that help trace the worldview of waqf institution are worth mentioning here. The first was the narration of Anas ibn Mālik who reported that Abū Talhah came to the prophet (ﷺ) when the following verse was revealed:

[But as for you, O believers,] never shall you attain to true piety unless you spend on others out of what you cherish yourselves; and whatever you spend - verily, Allah has full knowledge thereof. (*Qur'an* 3:92)

He came to him and said, "*O messenger of Allah, Allah says in His book (and recites Qur'ān [3:92]), and the dearest of my property is Bairuḥā' so I have given it as ṣadaqah (charity) for Allah's sake, and I anticipate its reward with Him; so spend it, O Messenger of Allah, as Allah guides you*". Messenger of Allah (saw) said, "*Well-done! That is a profitable property, that is a profitable property. I have heard what you have said, but I think you should spend it on your nearest relatives*". So Abū Talḥah (May Allah be pleased with him) distributed it among his nearest relatives and cousins. (Narrated by al-Bukhārī and Muslim—Riyāḍ al-Ṣaliḥīn: 297).

It is worth noting that Bairuḥā' was a large grove owned by Abū Talḥah where the prophet (saw) used to visit and drink from its sweet water. It is also worth noting that, although many refer to this specific ḥadīth as evidence for waqf, this case didn't actually form a waqf since Abū Talḥah transferred full ownership of the grove to his relatives.

The other story happened during the 7th year of Hijrah when the Muslims came from Khaybar with booties. 'Omar Ibn Khaṭṭāb went to the prophet (saw) seeking his advice about what he should do with the orchard of palm trees called Thamgh. The prophet (saw) said, "Donate its corpus [land and trees], [so that the corpus] will neither be sold, nor given as a present, nor inherited, but the fruits are to be spent in charity" (Narrated by al-Bukhārī: 2764). 'Omar made the donation of this waqf for Allah's Cause, the emancipation of slaves (fi al-Riqāb) and the needy, guests and wayfarer (Ibn al-Sabīl), kinsmen (Dhī al-Qurbā), and who administers the waqf. It is clear from the above that the benefits of waqf are not restricted to the poor and needy only, rather it can be declared to any beneficiary, or it can be confined to certain beneficiaries; there is no limit on the category of the beneficiary. We also deduce the importance of appointing a trustee (Nāẓir or Mutawallī) to overlook the waqf and the significance of having a clear and explicit declaration of the waqf asset and its beneficiaries.

While the above two stories outlined the components of waqf from an Islamic worldview, we have a plethora of evidence in Qurān and Sunnah that delineate the dimensions of waqf. Perhaps the ḥadīth narrated by imām Muslim is one of the clearest. The prophet (saw) said, "If a human-being dies, his work comes to an end, except for three things: except for ongoing charity, or knowledge benefitted from, or a pious child who prays for him" (Narrated by Muslim: 1631). The ongoing charity, or ṣadaqah jāriyah, suggests a sustainable benefit to the community and thus an ongoing reward in the Hereafter, in other words, one that is intended for perpetuity. In fact, scholars regard the ongoing charity, ṣadaqah jāriyah, the one that actually alludes to waqf.

Apart from the above social effect of waqf (perpetuity of the benefits), we have already provided in the previous section many examples that demonstrated the philanthropical dimension of waqf and briefly discussed its tremendous contributions toward the socio-economic welfare of the people. Beyond this are two things. Firstly, is the goal of achieving true piety. In Qur'ān [3:92], attainment of true piety is tied to expending from one's properties that which he cherishes the most. Such a goal was the driver for the companions of the Prophet (saw) to make waqf such as the story of Abū Talḥah and 'Omar above. Secondly, is the act of altruism that is derived from waqf practice. The act gives the donors the sense of satisfaction that stems from the belief that such acts would not go unrewarded. However, the reward sought is not a worldly one but rather one that is saved for the Hereafter as stated in the following verse of the Quran.

> The example of those who give their wealth in the way of Allah is like a grain of corn that sprouts seven ears, in every ear a hundred grains. Allah multiplies to whom He will, Allah is the Embracer, the Knower. [*Qurān* 2:261]

The Quranic verse above has far-reaching implications for waqf worldview. For example, the act of solidarity will not only ensure sustainability for the poor and needy but reinforce and strengthen social ties as well. The affluent and poor are brought together under the umbrella of mutual care. Economically, waqf acts as an institution that helps in the distribution and circulation of wealth thereby eliminating any possibility of its concentration in the hands of just a few. And so, does the remaining institutions and tools of the Islamic ethical wealth.

To tie up everything together, we attempt to put the Islamic worldview of Islamic ethical wealth into context. It needs to fulfill the religious, social, and economical aspects for which it was initiated for. For waqf, perpetuity is furthermore added. In other words, before attempting the practice of an Islamic ethical wealth, the religious dimension is only attainable when the donor purely seeks Allah's blessings and satisfaction. Thus, there should be no element of hypocrisy nor there should be any violation to Sharī'ah laws. The social dimension is achieved by the solidarity created for the community and by ensuring that the beneficiaries are receiving their complete rights without any loss or reduction. For waqf, the social solidarity should be sustainable. Attaching 'sustainable' to 'solidarity' was purposefully intended here in order to ensure that the perpetual dimension of waqf is realized and in order to set it apart from normal charity. Finally, the economical aspect of the Islamic ethical wealth is realized by the continuous circulation of wealth in the society.

The Worldview of Waqf as Distinct from Other Types of Islamic Ethical Wealth

Waqf worldview has often been marred by the question of how this institution differs from charity or the other types of the Islamic ethical wealth, which also help to distribute and circulate wealth, create solidarity in the community, provide a means for sustainability among the poor and needy, and indeed promote a sense of caring and solidarity. It is obvious that waqf is an act of charity. But what sets it apart from other Islamic ethical wealth charities is the dimension of perpetuity and the continuous recurrence of the benefits. When one declares a property as a waqf property, it is understood that the charity here is perpetual and should accrue benefits to the beneficiaries forever. For example, the benefits of mosques for worshiping Allah are perpetual. The perpetuity worldview also has implications for other dimensions of waqf. It is embodied in the Shari'ah rulings the waqf's nature, characteristics, and purpose. Other kinds of charities do not require similar rulings. They can be included in the current general Shari'ah laws. Perpetuity of waqf also has implications for its management, which requires record keeping, governance structure, maintenance, and investment of the waqf assets for sustainability. This is in addition to waqf manager/trustee who needs to be appointed to carry out these tasks and to liaison with the governmental entity and other relevant waqf stakeholders.

In addition to perpetuity and its implications, there are other features that differentiate waqf from other types of the Islamic ethical wealth. One of these features is ownership. With waqf, does the ownership transfer? If indeed it does, to whom does it transfer to? If it doesn't, can the benefactor revoke the waqf? All these questions make waqf a highly delicate subject and an intricate institution. For other Islamic ethical wealth charities, the donation simply changes hands from the benefactor to the beneficiary and the worldly act ends here; nothing else needs to be made. Therefore, the status of ownership provides yet another distinguishing feature. A consequence of the issue of ownership is that no individual, party, or entity has the right to claim or destroy waqf property. While these questions are jurisprudential in nature, it is necessary to understand that, from a worldview perspective, ownership of the usufruct should remain in the hands of the beneficiaries.

The flawless description of the components and dimensions in the previous section derived from the Islamic worldview of the Islamic ethical wealth and the clear distinction between waqf and other charities makes it very significant for several reasons. Donors of Islamic ethical wealth, establishers of Islamic ethical wealth entities, cooperatives, and organizations, Islamic ethical wealth trustees, Islamic ethical wealth investors, and Islamic ethical wealth researchers can all measure themselves against those dimensions. Performing against these dimensions guarantees setting the proper set of activities and tasks within the guidelines of Shar'īah. This way it will help guide the objectives, develop the required activities, measure them, guide the direction on how to use māl, and guide the overall behavior and caring.

Developing the Islamic Ethical Wealth Worldview Framework

Stagnation in the Islamic ethical wealth knowledge and mechanisms, especially zakāh and waqf, is not desired because, obviously, drastic changes had occurred in people's way of life since the introduction of the Islamic ethical wealth over a millennium ago. The development and evolution in waqf and zakāh management, for instance, are thus strongly recommended and deemed inevitable. But it is imperative that they should not be on the expense of digressing from the intended objectives for which they were established for by Islam, that is, an Islamic worldview. In essence, a worldview is a well-defined philosophical conception of the intended's world, clearly defining its components and outlining its dimensions. Fundamentally, a worldview will provide clear objectives, as well as serve to ensure all work or innovations in the intended field/thing do not digress from the original philosophical conceptions and objectives. The authors believe that this is where Islamic worldview of Islamic ethical wealth turns out to be handy, providing an answer to the problem in the aforementioned paragraph. The Islamic worldview of Islamic ethical wealth will set the path straight and help keep sight on the actual objectives. But before delving any further, the authors again take the example of waqf in order to calibrate the understanding of the components of Islamic ethical wealth and discuss their practices.

Waqf consists of five components: the donor/benefactor, the donation (or waqf asset), the beneficiary/s, the explicit statement, and the trustee. For the other Islamic ethical wealth tools and institutions, there are three main components (donor/benefactor, donation, and beneficiary/s). This is so, because the explicit statement is not necessary for the other types of Islamic ethical wealth; there is no requirement for detailing the donation and to whom it should go and how should it be managed because the donation is not continuous/perpetual. However, the components of the other types of Islamic ethical wealth can become four if an agency, or government, carries out the responsibilities of distributing it; in which case the fourth component will be the trustee. The donor needs to be a free, sane, and mature person who has passed puberty. As for the waqf asset, 'ulema' originally stipulated that it should be of an unconsumable type. The reason for that condition is to ensure that the asset provided benefits perpetually. However, today we have the form of cash waqf where cash is consumable, nonetheless because it is fungible and can be grown via legal transactions, equivalent cash plus profits can compensate for perpetuality. Therefore, a waqf asset should be an existing, legal, and specific object that is capable of creating benefits in perpetuity; it can either be of a type that you can sequester its corpus and make its usufruct perpetual (e.g., agricultural land), or it can be of a type that can be invested and grown continuously (e.g., cash waqf). These conditions are not required for the donations of the other types of Islamic ethical wealth. In contrast, the beneficiary of a waqf is not restricted to the category of the poor and needy as in most of the other types of Islamic ethical wealth. For zakāh, the beneficiary/s are restricted to the eight categories outlined in Qur'ān [9:60], whereas the beneficiaries of a waqf are unrestricted, unless restricted by the donor, and can also be families, warriors in the way of Allah, and even animals. The purpose of the explicit statement is to explicitly and clearly declare the waqf, with the pure intention, and delineate what constitutes the waqf asset and who are the beneficiaries, in addition to appointing the trustee. The trustee, on the other hand, should be an experienced, truthful, and trustworthy person/entity who/that is capable of managing, preserving, and growing the waqf for its best interest.

While the trustee's role in a zakāh agency is confined to daily managerial tasks and distribution works, the trustee's role of a waqf involves one extra responsibility. Being perpetual necessitates the development of the waqf asset. Therefore, the management of a waqf property involves two aspects: administrative and developmental. With the former, waqf practices involve optimally preserving the properties in hand and ensuring that the revenues of the beneficiaries are maximized (Kahf 2003, p. 5). To realize such a potential, the trustee needs to nurture an environment of competition among the staff for the management of waqf. The latter, i.e., the developmental aspect, implies considerations for financing. There are many financing modes trustees can seek to finance the waqf property they are appointed for. Traditional forms of finance available include financing by introducing new waqf properties, replacing a waqf property by another with a higher usufruct, and borrowing on the waqf with repayment from the net revenues. Kahf (1999, p. 40) outlines new forms of financing based on Islamic financial institutions. In these modes, the trustees can utilize financial instruments such as murābaḥah to the purchase orderer, istiṣnāʿ, parallel istiṣnāʿ, leasing, and Muḍārabah by the trustee. Yet, another, not less important, way of financing is restoring the concept of investment waqf and encouraging Muslims to create these types of waqf properties (Kahf 1998, p. 9). Such waqf involves the investment of waqf assets and using the generated income to develop and grow the existing waqf. Henceforth, we attempt to develop a worldview-based waqf definition that aids in setting the path straight and helps keeping sight on the actual objectives of an Islamic ethical wealth. Later, from the worldview-based waqf definition we can develop a framework for Islamic ethical wealth worldview.

Captured by our quick survey of the literature of waqf, Table 2.1 summarizes the reasons for digressions from waqf worldview since its first

Table 2.1 Reasons for digressing from waqf worldview

No.	Reasons for digressions
1	Confusing waqf with charity
2	Unjustified bias and intervention to make a deed fall under waqf's definition
3	Confusing waqf with investment leading to the distribution of profits on establishers and shareholders
4	Confusing waqf partner investors with waqf beneficiaries
5	Violating Sharīʿah laws

occurrence until this date. The first two reasons are directly related to the lack of understanding of the definition of waqf. The third and fourth reasons again follow, albeit not directly, from the lack of a proper and accurate definition of waqf. The definition of waqf in literature ranged from a mere one-word translation (e.g., endowment) to a description of waqf as a perpetual philanthropical charity that can alleviate poverty. There is no single comprehensive, accurate, and universal definition for waqf that captures its worldview dimensions. Hence, why we have four of the five reasons for digression is related to definition issues. The remaining reason can be alluded to the misunderstanding, even ignorance, of the Islamic commercial laws.

A clear and accurate definition then becomes urging. But before we attempt to put forth such a definition a few things have to be clarified. The first reason in Table 2.1 dictates to have a clear distinction between waqf and other types of Islamic ethical wealth (non-waqf) in the definition. For that we have to note that waqf is a more intricate venture which involves continuous management and development to ensure perpetuity, whereas the other types of Islamic ethical wealth cannot fulfill such a description. Thus, the word 'institution' can be used for this purpose alongside some keywords that demonstrate perpetuality like 'sustainable' and 'develop'. Nonmaterial-based charities like volunteer services with time, effort, and expertise cannot be sustainable because they end with the end of each project/job/task and end by the volunteer's death, unless these are materialized like in a book that is turned into waqf. In order to eliminate the second reason causing digression, the donation has to be of a type that generates continuous benefits or can be developed or increased. A phrase like 'can be sustainable' can suffice for such a purpose.

From the outset of the definition, ṣadaqah (charity) has to be stressed in order to avoid reason 3. Reason 4 can be easily overcome by observing that no return should be requested from the beneficiaries of the waqf. Although difficult to incorporate in a definition, mentioning Sharī'ah laws within the definition can help remind of the importance of compliance and consultation with scholars. Lastly, but not least, the definition should include the key players in waqf: donor/benefactor (wāqif), trustee (mutawallī), and beneficiaries. The reason is twofolds. First, it can help provide a further distinction between waqf and non-waqf Islamic ethical wealth. Second, when developing the concept of waqf, these key players form an essential framework that helps to avoid deviating from waqf worldview. By now, we are ready to present the following worldview-based waqf definition:

> Waqf is a ṣadaqah (charity) institution whereby the wāqif's (donor) donations are such that they do not violate Sharī'ah laws and can be sustainable by the mutawallī (trustee) who will trustfully develop them and ensure that they are distributed among the intended beneficiaries with no return from them whatsoever.

The above definition helps to capture the dimensions of the worldview of waqf where the religious aspect, social solidarity, and economic objective can be indirectly deduced. Donors of waqf and establishers of waqf entities can observe the Islamic worldview dimensions of waqf using the worldview-based definition of waqf above. That will help them to guide setting their objectives and measure their activities.

We can further develop this definition into a framework, the effect of which can further reduce the possibility of departing from the actual worldview of waqf. This is followed by a generalization to develop an Islamic ethical wealth worldview framework. Table 2.2 depicts the waqf worldview framework at the heart of which sits Sharī'ah compliance. The framework looks at both the components of waqf and the dimensions of a waqf worldview. Similarly, we can modify Table 2.2 to generalize the framework into a one that incorporates the components and dimensions of an Islamic ethical wealth worldview in general. This is illustrated in Table 2.3.

In essence when forming or practicing an Islamic ethical wealth, the individual or entity creating or performing it will need to ensure that the components are in place while observing that the dimensions are met. The framework can be used to measure certain Islamic ethical wealth that are in existence. Hereafter, since waqf has more components and details than the rest of the institutions or tools of Islamic ethical wealth and without loss of generality, we will utilize a couple of the current waqf practices and measure them against the worldview framework. Doing so will help to easily identify issues with a future endeavor to correct them or even avoid them.

Table 2.2 Framework of the Islamic worldview of waqf

Shari'ah compliance

Waqf worldview dimensions

Religious
- No hypocrisy (Riyaʾ)
- Paradise is the return

Economic
- Wealth circulation
- Continuity of usufruct

Social
- Solidarity in the community
- Beneficiary & his rights
- Benefactor & his obligations
- Trustee & his responsibility

Waqf worldview components

Wāqif	**Waqf asset**	**Beneficiary**	**Explicit statement**	**Mutawalli**
• Free	• Material-based	• Declared by wāqif	• Detail waqf asset	• Experienced
• Sane	• Existing	• Observes philanthropy	• Detail the beneficiaries	• Truthful
• Mature	• Legal	• No return is expected whatsoever		• Trustworthy
• Puberty	• Specific			
	• Continuous or capable of growing			

Table 2.3 Framework of the Islamic worldview of the Islamic ethical wealth

Shari'ah compliance

Islamic ethical wealth worldview dimensions

Islamic ethical wealth worldview components

	Donor	**Donation**	**Beneficiary**	**Explicit statement**[a] **(Only waqf)**	**Trustee**[a] **(In case of agency)**
Religious • No hypocrisy (Riya') • Paradise is the return **Economic** • Wealth circulation **Social** • Solidarity in the community • Beneficiary rights • Benefactor obligations • Trustee responsibilities	• Free • Sane • Mature • Puberty	• Existing • Legal • Specific	• Observes philanthropy • No return is expected whatsoever	• Detail waqf asset • Detail the beneficiaries	• Experienced • Truthful • Trustworthy

[a]Not applicable

ANALYSIS OF SELECTED ISSUES BASED ON WAQF WORLDVIEW FRAMEWORK

By observing the timeline of waqf since the period of the prophet (ﷺ) until today, we find that the first crucial deviation from the worldview of waqf was the introduction of cash waqf during its initial stages. These cash waqfs operated on interest-based lending (Abdur-Rashid 2020, p. 24). Çizakça (2004, p. 2) reported that a borrower of cash waqf during the Ottoman period would provide a big collateral, usually his house. Although the borrower would remain in his own house, however he will be paying its rents during the borrowing period until full repayment of the debt. The way it was described shows that the rents were a condition for borrowing. This cannot be viewed except as a clear usury because any debt that leads to a benefit is usury (Ribā). Needless to say, that there are many narratives during the time of the prophet (ﷺ) demonstrating the same. Projecting this case on the worldview framework discussed in the previous section reveals that it doesn't fulfill the condition of being confined to Sharī'ah laws.

Today, a lot of innovations happened on waqfs and cash waqfs which also have their own problems. Perhaps the most inexplicable and eccentric of these problems is the idea of creating waqf through nonmaterial contributions, e.g., Iman and Mohammad (2017). In essence callers of these models introduce time waqf, knowledge waqf, expertise waqf, and skills waqf! Knowledge can become waqf if for example one dedicates a material-based item like a book to be waqf for the general public to benefit from. However, the waqf concepts they intend here are nonmaterial-based and, thus, are really very confusing; it is very difficult, if not impossible, to see how they fall under the general understanding of waqf. Proponents of such ideas explain that people can provide volunteering services as a charity by offering their time, knowledge, expertise, or skills for a project free of charge. It must be reminded that, although a charity by itself, waqf is set apart from any other kind of charity with the characteristics that we have delineated before. What becomes very clear here is that these people are, indeed, confusing waqf with other types of Islamic ethical wealth (non-waqf charity).

In contrast, Iman and Mohammad (2017) attempted to segregate the nonmaterial-based contributions from normal charity by giving these volunteer services monetary value; the reason being is to add the perpetual dimension to them. Unfortunately, the tweaking provided is an unjustified bias that is not substantiated by any evidence. Otherwise, we can attach a monetary value to any ṣadaqah made and claim that it is waqf. By analogy, then, everything in life can be considered a waqf! How is this monetary value determined is yet another ambiguous case and therefore the proposal is further weakened.

Projecting time waqf and volunteer services on the framework, it is found that it doesn't satisfy the concept of the waqf asset which necessitates that the waqf should be material-based and continuous or capable of growing. To be continuous the asset should be of the type that has a corpus which can be sequestered and a usufruct which continuously gives non-terminating benefits. Or it could be of a type where it can be invested and continuously grown. Moreover, such act can't be a waqf because it doesn't satisfy the component of possibly appointing a trustee. Therefore, such a volunteer act is a general charity.

Another group that digressed from the real worldview of waqf introduced waqf bank, integrated cash waqf, cash waqf cooperatives, and corporate waqfs (e.g., Haneef et al. 2015; Mohd Thas Thaker 2018). Unfortunately, with these models the system becomes purely that of investment where, on the worldview framework, the social and religious dimensions are missing. The philanthropical dimension is restricted to the act of lending cash to microenterprises and requestors of microfinance and any profits earned from such investments are only distributed to shareholders and establishers of waqf. Besides these issues, the economic dimension is violated by the misconduct in corporate waqfs, for example, where low profits go to developmental projects while the huge chunk of waqf goes into the pockets of the shareholders. Following is a presentation of what went wrong in the evolution of cash waqf.

Integrated waqfs (IW) and integrated cash waqfs (ICW) defy the purpose of waqf from a couple of points of view. First, while the principal is preserved, in fact increased through various modes, there is no sign of use of 'usufruct' or any foreseen benefit. In other words, the increase over the principal, alongside the principal itself, is repumped for financing purposes with the expectation of a return on investment! The very legitimate and essential question here is who is the beneficiary of this investment then? The perception that the requestors of funds for purchase purposes, business financing, or carrying out their projects, whatever the purpose is, the perception that they are the beneficiaries is untenable. The simplest reason is that such practice is one where these fund requestors are expected to return the funds fully with a markup—hence violating the worldview framework condition which states that no return is expected from beneficiaries whatsoever. Second, indisputably, those in charge of managing the cash waqf are entitled for a share of the waqf in return for their efforts. However, the concept of distributing the profits of the investments among the establishers of IW and ICW is a great violation to what the waqf was established for on the first hand. The least that can be said about this situation is that there is a major misinterpretation and misconception of the matter. In this case, the donors of the cash waqf would have not attained their purpose of seeing their money go into the hands of those who deserved it. Saying that the whole system is flawed is unequivocal. Rather, the microenterprises and receivers of microfinances should be viewed as investment partners with waqf. The return on investment should then be distributed among the beneficiaries as determined by the fund contributors of the waqf. Distribution among establishers of waqf should only be on the basis of covering costs and paying for efforts and work done. As a matter of fact, establishers and trustees of waqf funds are, indeed, considered a special case of beneficiaries.

Some argue that the philanthropical dimension is indeed fulfilled by allowing the microenterprises to enjoy the 'usufruct' of the cash a period of time, after which the money will be returned, similar to having people benefit from the usufruct of a rented machinery. It is easy to say that this argument is flawed too. First, in the case of cash the microenterprises are expending the money and not returning the same original chapter money that was given to them. Second, even if for the sake of argument, we do not take the first point into consideration, conspicuously the amount returned is more than the principal given; in other words, the case of cash cannot be likened to the case of rented machinery. Third, in the case of cash, constraints are relaxed in terms of who deserves to receive the financing and any microenterprise can apply regardless of their need or whether the donors wanted it or not. In summary, this kind of 'waqf' doesn't fulfill the economic and social dimensions for the simple fact that the return on investment is only repumped for financing purposes and not for any foreseen beneficiary. The entrepreneurs and small businesses benefitting from the finance provided by the integrated cash waqfs can't be the beneficiaries since they are expected to give some return. They are only venture partners who will help the waqf asset to grow.

Implications for SDGs

In 2015, all United Nations member states adopted the sustainable development goals (SDGs) to end poverty in the world and ensure that everyone enjoys peace and prosperity by 2030 (UNDP 2020). This came by as an answer to the already failing Millennium Development Goals (MDGs) which extended from 2000 to 2015 (Khan 2019). Only four years later from its launch, the SDGs program was declared by the UN Deputy Secretary-General (2019) as not being on track for the target date of 2030. The UN Deputy Secretary-General (2019) further announced that the financing gap is US$2.5 trillion per year! The Islamic ethical wealth possesses huge potential to fill the gaps needed for the SDGs. After all, and as mentioned previously, waqf is estimated to be worth billions of dollars (Rashid 2012, p. 105) while the potential size of the annual zakāh pool has been estimated between US$200 billion and US$1 trillion (Rehman and Pickup 2018). However, such potential is undermined by the various obstacles, issues, and challenges that face the Islamic ethical wealth. Most of these issues are caused by the aberrations and digression from its worldview. The worldview framework developed in this chapter will help to eliminate these challenges and release the full potential of the Islamic ethical wealth institutions and therefore have the utmost positive effect on the SDGs program.

From the perspective of its dimensions, the worldview framework has several contributions to offer. For instance, the social dimension necessitates social solidarity within the society. So, by maintaining the rights of the beneficiaries while the benefactors fulfill their obligations and the trustees trustfully and efficiently observe their responsibilities, the Islamic ethical wealth can help to "promote... inclusive societies" and "access to justice for all" (United Nations 2020) which are the requirements for attaining sustainable development goal 16: 'peace, justice, and strong institutions'. In contrast, the sustainable development goal 10, which is 'reduced inequality', can be supported by the economic dimension demonstrated by the wealth circulation of the Islamic ethical wealth. Goal 10 stipulates reducing "inequality within and among countries" (United Nations 2020) and that is exactly what wealth circulation of the Islamic ethical wealth can achieve. The effect is multiplied as both the social solidarity and wealth circulation of the worldview framework contribute to Goals 1 to 4: 'no poverty', 'zero hunger', 'good health and well-being', and 'quality education', to which waqf support has been proven over several centuries.

Yet, the effect of the religious dimension of the worldview of the Islamic ethical wealth is far more reaching than the other dimensions. This is so because the religious dimension is the driver for the other dimensions. The altruism dictated by the expectation of return, not in this world, but in the Hereafter ensures the continuity of wealth circulation and social solidarity. As such, the worldview of Islamic ethical wealth has more to offer than the 17 goals sought by the United Nations. While the target goals are the same, the SDGs do not aspire to solve the root cause of the actual issues. One of these root causes is the current flawed economic system. On the other hand, the worldview framework of the Islamic ethical wealth exactly tackles the root cause of the issue by stipulating wealth circulation, the concept which the current economic system fails to recognize and in fact plays a big role in increasing the inequality gap within the societies of a country and between countries.

CONCLUSION

Islamic ethical wealth possesses an enormous potential for solving today's SDG challenges and issues as it is worth billions to trillions of dollars. It has been proven throughout history that the Islamic ethical wealth has contributed heavily to the welfare of the society as it affected every facet of life: alleviating poverty, helping the poor and needy, providing education, building the infrastructure, supporting scholars, financing orphanages, providing care for the elderly, widows, and single women, caring for animals, and providing health services and health supplies, just to mention a few. Thus, it is quintessential to have it revitalized, while innovating new models of it is not less important. Unfortunately, a quick screening in the history of waqf development and evolution and other institutions of the Islamic ethical wealth revealed that people eventually started to digress from its original understanding— the understanding that once the companions of the prophet (ﷺ) possessed and contentedly applied. While stagnation in Islamic ethical wealth development is not desired, it should not happen on the expense of diluting its intended purpose and sloughing off its true identity.

The authors believe that the main reason for this diversion is losing sight of the Islamic worldview of the Islamic ethical wealth. The significance of having a worldview is manifested in guiding people's objectives and providing them with a means to measure their activities. In this study, we aimed to contribute in laying down a simple, yet very effective, Islamic worldview-based definition of waqf, a specific worldview-based framework of waqf, and a general worldview-based framework of Islamic ethical wealth. The developed frameworks combine worldview dimensions [religious, economic, and social] and components [donor, donation, beneficiary, explicit statement (only for waqf), and trustee (for waqf or if an agency exist for the other institutions/tools)] in a way that helps to preserve the declared Islamic ethical wealth from digressing from its original worldview. It is hoped that the definition and framework discussed in this chapter will be a reference going forward for Islamic ethical wealth-related economics.

References

Abdullah Nadwi, M. (2014). Fate of Awqaf in India: A Critical Appraisal. *SSRN*, 1–8. https://doi.org/10.2139/ssrn.2384283.

Abdur-Rashid, K. (2020). *Financing Kindness as a Society: The Rise & Fall of Islamic Philanthropic Institutions (Waqfs)* (pp. 1–27). Yaqeen Institute for Islamic Research.

AlMunajjid, S. (1979). *al-Waqf ihya' Sunnah*. Retrieved January 25, 2020, from https://almunajjid.com/lectures/lessons/202.

Ariff, M. (1996). The Islamic Voluntary Sector in Southeast Asia. *Islamic Economics, 8*, 73–77.

Bagby, I. (2012). *The American Mosque 2011: Activities, Administration and Vitality of the American Mosque.*

Bonine, M. E. (1987). Islam and Commerce: Waqf and the Bazaar of Yazd, Iran (Islam und Handel: Waqf und der Bazar von Yazd, Iran). *Erdkunde, 41*(3), 182–196. Retrieved from https://www.jstor.org/stable/25645162.

Bulut, M., & Korkut, C. E. M. (2019). Ottoman Cash Waqfs: An Alternative Financial System. *Insight Turkey, 21*(3), 91–112. https://doi.org/10.25253/99.2018EV.07.

Choudhury, M. A., Pratiwi, A., & Hoque, M. N. (2019). Waqf, Perpetual Charity, in a General System Theory of Tawhidi Metascience. *Thunderbird International Business Review, 61*(5), 777–792. https://doi.org/10.1002/tie.22039.

Çizakça, M. (1995). Cash Waqfs of Bursa, 1555–1823. *Journal of the Economic and Social History of the Orient, 38*(3), 313–354. Retrieved from https://www.jstor.org/stable/3632481.

Çizakça, M. (2004). *Incorporated Cash Waqfs and Mudaraba, Islamic Non-bank Financial Instruments from the Past to the Future*. MPRA Munich Personal RePEc Archive.

Dogarawa, A. B. (2010). Poverty Alleviaton Through Zakah and Waqf Institutions: A Case for the Muslim Ummah in Ghana. *SSRN*, 1–27. https://doi.org/10.2139/ssrn.1622122.

Haneef, M. A., Pramanik, A. H., Mohammed, M. O., Bin Amin, M. F., & Muhammad, A. D. (2015). Integration of waqf-Islamic microfinance model for poverty reduction: The case of Bangladesh. *International Journal of Islamic and Middle Eastern Finance and Management, 8*(2), 246–270. https://doi.org/10.1108/IMEFM-03-2014-0029.

Iman, A. H. M., & Mohammad, M. T. S. H. (2017). Waqf as a Framework for Entrepreneurship. *Humanomics, 33*(4), 419–440. https://doi.org/10.1108/H-01-2017-0015.

Joan, K., Pambudi, B. C., & Adjie, D. P. (2019). Blending Islamic Microfinance and Productive Zakat to Support SDGs in Fisheries Sector. *International Journal of Islamic Economics, 1*(2), 136–150. https://doi.org/10.32332/ijie.v1i02.1805.

Kahf, M. (1998). *Awqaf of the Muslim Community in the Western Countries: a Preliminary Thoughts on Reconciling the Shari'Ah Principles with the Laws of the Land* (pp. 1–25). Retrieved from http://monzer.kahf.com/%5Cn http://monzer.kahf.com/papers/english/AWQAF_OF_THE_MUSLIM_COMMUNITY_IN_WESTERN_COUNTRIES.pdf.

Kahf, M. (1999). Financing the Development of Awqaf Property. *American Journal of Islamic Social Sciences, 16*(4), 39–68.

Kahf, M. (2003). The Role of Waqf in Improving the Ummah Welfare. *The International Seminar on Waqf as a Private Legal Body*, 2–24. https://doi.org/10.1108/IMEFM-08-2013-0094.

Khan, T. (2019). Reforming Islamic Finance for Achieving Sustainable Development Goals. *Journal of King Abdulaziz University, Islamic Economics, 32*(1), 3–21. https://doi.org/10.4197/Islec.32-1.1.

Kidwai, A., & Zidani, M. E. M. (2020). A New Approach to Zakat Management for Unprecedented Times. *International Journal of Zakat, 5*(1), 45–54. https://doi.org/10.37706/ijaz.v5i1.207.

Mahamood, S. M., & Rahman, A. A. (2015). Financing Universities Through Waqf, Pious Endowment: Is It Possible? *Humanomics, 32*(4), 430–453.

Mohd Thas Thaker, M. A. B. (2018). A Qualitative Inquiry into Cash Waqf Model as a Source of Financing for Micro Enterprises. *ISRA International Journal of Islamic Finance, 10*(1), 19–35. https://doi.org/10.1108/IJIF-07-2017-0013.

Nawa, F. (2015). *Internal Struggles at US Mosques Seep into Secular Courts.* Retrieved January 25, 2020, from Reveal website: https://www.revealnews. org/article/internal-struggles-at-us-mosques-seep-into-secular-courts/.

Orbay, K. (2012). Financial Development of the Waqfs in Konya and the Agricultural Economy in the Central Anatolia (Late Sixteenth-Early Seventeenth Centuries). *Journal of the Economic and Social History of the Orient, 55*(1), 74–116. https://doi.org/10.1163/156852012X628509.

Rashid, S. K. (2012). Measures for the Better Management of Awqaf. *IIUM Law Journal, 20*(1), 103–138.

Rehman, A. A., & Pickup, F. (2018). *Zakat for the SDGs.* Retrieved September 5, 2020, from United Nations Development Programme (UNDP) website: https://www.undp.org/content/undp/en/home/blog/2018/zakat-for-the-sdgs.html.

Shaikh, S. A., Ismail, A. G., & Mohd Shafiai, M. H. (2017). Application of Waqf for Social and Development Finance. *ISRA International Journal of Islamic Finance, 9*(1), 5–14. https://doi.org/10.1108/IJIF-07-2017-002.

Syed, M. K, Mustafa, R. R., & Thalassinos, Y. E. (2020). An Artificial Intelligence and NLP Based Islamic FinTech Model Combining Zakat and Qardh-Al-Hasan for Countering the Adverse Impact of COVID 19 on SMEs and Individuals. *International Journal of Economics and Business Administration, VIII*(2), 351–364. https://doi.org/10.35808/ijeba/466.

UN Deputy Secretary-General. (2019). *Citing $2.5 Trillion Annual Financing Gap during SDG Business Forum Event, Deputy Secretary-General Says Poverty Falling Too Slowly.* Retrieved September 5, 2020, from United Nations Meetings Coverage and Press Releases website: https://www.un.org/press/en/2019/dsgsm1340.doc.htm.

UNDP. (2020). *Sustainable Development Goals.* Retrieved August 27, 2020, from https://www.undp.org/content/undp/en/home/sustainable-development-goals.html.

United Nations. (2020). *The 17 Goals.* Retrieved September 22, 2020, from United Nations website: https://sdgs.un.org/goals.

CHAPTER 3

How Islamic Ethical Wealth May Strategically and Technically Support SDGs Plan?

Irfan Syauqi Beik and Laily Dwi Arsyianti

INTRODUCTION

Millennium Development Goals (MDGs) have been replaced by Sustainable Development Goals (SDGs) as stated in the Resolution adopted by the General Assembly on September 25, 2015, when MDGs have reached its goals. Unlike MDGs, SDGs bring more localities: local realities, local values, and local aspirations which could be have been available and relevant to the population segments (Khan 2019). SDGs have been set by United Nations (UN) to call all nations to end poverty, protect the earth and improve human living environments. This concept is basically a concept that Islam has been taught to its believer as mentioned in QS al-Qashash: 77:

> So seek the abode of the Hereafter through what God has given you, and do not forget your part in this world. Do good to others as God has done

---

I. S. Beik (✉) · L. D. Arsyianti
Department of Islamic Economics, Bogor Agricultural University (IPB University), Bogor, Indonesia
e-mail: irfan_beik@apps.ipb.ac.id

© The Author(s), under exclusive license to Springer Nature
Switzerland AG 2021
M. M. Billah (eds.), *Islamic Wealth and the SDGs,*
https://doi.org/10.1007/978-3-030-65313-2_3

53

good to you, and do not try to spread corruption (exploitation) in the land. Surely God does not like corrupters.

There are 17 SDGs that should be achieved within 15 years until 2030 (United Nations 2015). Those goals consist of no poverty; zero hunger; good health and well-being; quality education; clean water and sanitation; affordable and clean energy; decent work and economic growth; industry, innovation, and infrastructure; reduced inequalities; sustainable cities and communities; responsible consumption and production; climate action; life below water; life on land; peace, justice, and strong institutions; and partnerships for the goals. The logos of each goal are presented in Fig. 3.1.

It has been five years since the Sustainable Development Goals have been launched in 2015. The spirit of SDGs is basically accordance with Islamic teachings that human should do good and not try to undermine the earth and spoil the nature. Thus, every aspect in human life should be concurrent with this ethical teaching, including in managing wealth. The goal of 'no poverty' is actually only one among those goals that supposedly can be achieved through Islamic ethical wealth way, specifically through Islamic social finance instrument, zakat.

Zakat is a financial instrument in Islam that have multiple impacts toward, at least, three aspects, namely economic, social, and spiritual aspects. It is a type of charity, but obligatory for Muslims. Ahmed et al. (2015) highlighted the role of nonprofit institution engagement for

Fig. 3.1 Sustainable Development Goals (*Source* United Nations [2020])

significant mobilization of resources to achieve SDGs. Zakat has itsown officer explicitly mentioned in the Quran. This paper attempts to elaborate the concept of zakat: How zakat can actually be the tool in Islam that covers all SDGs agenda?

Conceptual Framework of Zakat on Sustainable Development Goals (SDGs)

Ethical wealth management in Islam is correlated with *maqasid* sharia. *Maqasid* Sharia in Islam comprises five points that are being upheld in every aspect in human life. These five points, fundamentally, preserving human's potential of intellectual, spiritual, physical, and social relations. The original concept of Islamic wealth management that explains ethical wealth management is wealth purification. Wealth purification is a concept that acquiring human to get and use money in accordance with sharia, that is by the permissible way (halal). It starts from creating job or earning income until generating or distributing wealth. It is indeed not merely purifying the earned money that is unknowingly.

Zakat, as one of financial as well as social instruments, is aimed to acquire these maqasid al-sharia. Align with the 17 SDGs, zakat is proclaimed to protect religion including human religiosity and spirituality (hifzul dien), to protect human life and physicality (hifzul nafs), to protect human intellectuality (hifzul aql), to protect lineage for future generation (hifzul nasb), and to protect human wealth (hifzul maal) (Fig. 3.2).

Protecting religion and human spirituality (hifzul dien) is the essential aspect as the *dien* is guiding human being to be more discreet in performing *ibadah*, including to do daily activities. Human's heart is highly correlated with human spirituality. How human can be in tranquility, to be more calm and deliberately solve problems, as well as to be grateful on what human have been given are among the purposes of protecting *dien*. No poverty; good health and well-being; decent work and economic growth; responsible consumption and production; peace, justice, and strong institutions; as well as partnership for goals are among SDGs that related with this *maqasid* that can be realized by performing ethical wealth management, particularly in paying zakat. Zakat brings its payers to be more selective in creating wealth that musts comply with sharia: no riba, no uncertainty, no gambling, no harmful and deceit activities, not dealing with any non-permissible products and services. Zakat also guides its payer to be more active in generating wealth that wealth

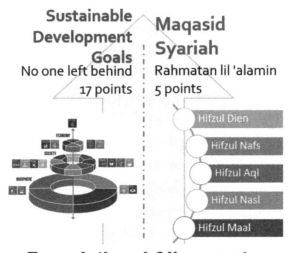

Fig. 3.2 Foundational alignment for human development (*Source* Beik [2020])

musts provide benefit for others as well, and considering the life of future generation.

Protecting human soul and physicality (hifzul nafs) is essential in keeping human to stay healthy and uphold the dignity. Activities that strengthen productivity and innovation are some efforts to achieve the goals of no poverty; zero hunger; good health and well-being; decent works and economic growth; industry, innovation, and infrastructure; reduce inequalities; sustainable cities and communities; responsible consumption and production; peace, justice, and strong institutions; as well as partnerships for the goals. Works covering ecological economics, social responsibility, and governance concerns are considered ethical indeed support the circular economy paradigm (Khan 2019). Thus, *maqasid* sharia in ethical wealth creation and distribution concurrent with SDGs. This includes paying and distributing zakat in responsible way.

Protecting human intellectuality and mind (hifzul aql) and its alignment with SDGs of no poverty; zero hunger; quality education; decent works and economic growth; industry, innovation, and infrastructure; as well as partnerships for the goals facilitate access to healthy nourishment which make children and those who seeking knowledge be productive in the future (Julia and Kassim 2020). This may also be applied for protecting lineage for future generation (hifzul nasb). Knowledge and its derivatives such as innovation, critical thinking, and adaptive attitudes help to implement productive life, move enthusiastically, happy mind and balanced emotion. Rasulullah *sallallahu alaihi wasallam* had once giving an axe from a part of income earned from an auction of a poor's possession who asked Rasulullah to overcome his poverty. Rather than giving the person a full amount of money from the auction, Rasulullah gave him a tool that could make him earn his own living. This example fulfills the maqasid of being creative and productive to protect human mind and intellectuality. Utilizing zakat for productive program is one of ways concurrent with *maqasid* sharia and its SDGs alignment (Table 3.1).

Table 3.1 Sustainable Development Goals and Maqasid al-Sharia

No.	SDGs	Dominant Maqasid	Level of Needs
1	No poverty	Wealth	Daruriyah
2	Zero hunger	Life, wealth	Daruriyah
3	Good health and well-being	Life, wealth	Daruriyah
4	Quality education	Intellectual	Daruriyah
5	Gender equality	Wealth, intellectual, life, lineage	Daruriyah
6	Clean water and sanitation	Life, lineage	Daruriyah
7	Affordable and clean energy	Lineage	Hajiyah
8	Decent work and economic growth	Wealth	Daruriyah
9	Industry, innovation, and infrastructure	Wealth	Hajiyah
10	Reduced inequalities	Wealth	Daruriyah
11	Sustainable cities and communities	Lineage, life, wealth	Hajiyah
12	Responsible consumption and production	Lineage, life	Hajiyah
13	Climate action	Lineage, intellectual	Hajiyah
14	Life below water	Lineage, wealth, intellectual	Hajiyah
15	Life on land	Lineage	Hajiyah
16	Peace, justice and strong institutions	Life, wealth, lineage	Daruriyah
17	Partnership for the goals	Wealth, intellectual	Hajiyah

Source BAZNAS Center of Strategic Studies (2017)

Protecting lineage for future generation (hifzul nasb) is in line with SDGs of gender equality; clean water and sanitation; affordable and clean energy; sustainable cities and communities; responsible consumption and production; climate action; life below water; life on land; peace, justice, and strong institutions. Long list of alignment aspects indicates that this matter is very important, essential, and fruitful if the efforts are tightly discipline (but not too hard), and effectively implemented. Community empowerment-based zakat programs preferably start from families or households that earned low-income, had persistent food insecurity, no sustainable job opportunities, and no arable land to be cultivated as studied by Mahmud et al. (2015). This means that family as a unit of empowerment can then be sustainable and resilient together the head of household and the family member. The successors or the children are expected to have better life in the future.

Protecting wealth (hifzul maal) is very crucial in countries that poverty level is still elevated, especially during this pandemic situation. Mergaliyev et al. (2019) found that in Indonesia, Bangladesh, Pakistan, and Jordan, most Islamic institutions are very keen to safeguard 'life', 'posterity' and 'social entity' and more active in social and development role as oppose to Bahrain, Kuwait, Qatar, and United Kingdom. This indicates that those countries are not only concerning about economic growth, to be specific in Islamic institutions, but also about social connection and development which are considered as assets to protect wealth regardless the current wealth position.

Zakat, in this regard, has inclusively embedded in the financial system because Islamic value comprises not only human relationship with God but also with society and the environment. Figure 3.3 shows an example of zakat role in poverty alleviation. Zakat framework includes the economy, social, and dakwah or advocacy. Economy aspect of zakat aims on growth, how capital can be grown by improving production with the help of market. Social aspect of zakat focuses on access, how everybody gets access and equal opportunity to access education, health facilities, emergency, and disaster response. Meanwhile, dakwah or advocacy aspect of zakat invites participation of every Muslim to contribute in enacting laws, networking, and capacity building. Zakat, even in non-Muslim countries like India, has manifested itself as a successful means to meet financial needs and possesses a robust potential critical role to apply the SDGs of alleviating the poverty (Intezar and Zia 2020).

Fig. 3.3 Conceptual framework of Zakat (*Source* Beik [2020])

Zakat Programs and SDGs Priority

After reviewing on conceptual framework of zakat as part of wealth purification in ethical wealth concept in Islam, in regard of *maqasid* sharia and achieving SDGs, this paper discusses how specific zakat program can achieve SDGs and what is the SDGs priority of each program. Can zakat actually have those kinds of programs?

Zakat program emphasizes on two categories: consumptive and productive program. Consumptive programs are those with relatively aim on short-term goals, while productive programs are relatively aiming on long term empowerment. However, it does not mean both consumptive and productive programs are separated. Both can be integrated, notwithstanding that the consumptive programs support the productive ones. For instance, scholarship to attain degree for students can be integrated with empowerment program that the students are encouraged to live better life through creating and generating wealth for future endeavor. Priority of the programs should consider the Sustainable Development Goals Priority Criteria (Fig. 3.4).

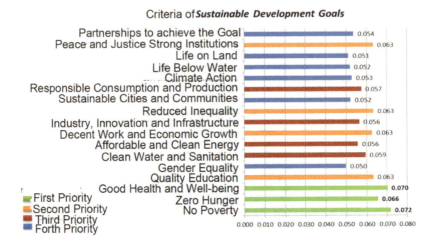

Fig. 3.4 Zakat Programs of BAZNAS and SDGs Priority (*Source* BAZNAS Center of Strategic Studies [2017])

Zakat Community Development (ZCD) is a structured program to have the zakat fund distributed to emancipate a village or a region in multi-sector development such as economy, social, health, education, and *da'wah* by giving capacity building, seed funding, assistance and supervision, market enlargement, and providing and opening access for basic life support. ZCD aims to achieve all 17 aspects in SDGs, thus *maqasid* sharia.

Economic empowerment program focuses on poverty alleviation by providing seed funding, production enhancement, capacity building, and market enlargement. It is structured to have the zakat fund distributed into three main program, namely Zmart (traditional yet modern-modified convenience store), creating *mustahik* entrepreneur, and building food barn to emancipate farmers by introducing sustainable farming. The program mainly aims to achieve SDGs of no poverty; zero hunger; good health and well-being; quality education; gender equality; decent work and economic growth; industry, innovation, and infrastructure; reduced inequalities; and partnerships for the goals. Ismail and Shaikh (2018) found that risk-sharing shifts the emphasis of credit-worthiness to be placed on the value creation and economic viability of investments (including real sector) that create new wealth. Islamic social finance package can cater to the financially excluded households.

Economic empowerment for *Mustahik* Breeder program is dedicated to empower breeder to tackle rural poverty. In this program, *amil* zakat (zakat administer) emancipates the breeder by providing capacity building, opening access to the best seed, livelihood support, organization strengthening, and uplifting their spirituality. In Qurban season the *amil* mainly get the livestock from these breeders to facilitate market in acquiring the best *qurban*, as well as to empower the breeders. This program relatively almost has the same focus on SDGs' aspect for economic empowerment as aforementioned, except for gender equality. Almost none of the breeders are female. The occupation might be more intense and intrigued if female was prioritized for this profession, this can be an opportunity for female as well.

Mustahik Emergency Services program is dedicated to help poor people, vulnerable groups, and especially fast response to any emergency situation. Besides, this team also educates and promotes health and well-being to the society. The program aims to attain no poverty; zero hunger; good health and well-being; clean water and sanitation; reduced inequalities; and partnerships for the goals. This program is integrated with economic empowerment to encourage those who are being marginalized to have more spirit to live, being treated like others, acquire equal opportunities to enter job market or to create jobs, while emergency services provide the basic necessities, such as wheelchair for those who are in need.

Disaster Response is specialized to give first aid and fast response to any disaster in Indonesia and abroad. They do not only respond the disaster by providing rescue and help but also increasing the awareness of the society about the disaster so that they become resilience. The program supports the SDGs of no poverty; zero hunger; good health and well-being; clean water and sanitation; climate actions; and partnerships for the goals. This program also provides post-disaster recovery program to supports the people who affected by traumatic events, by building facilities such as public kitchen, public shelter, clean water, and sanitation infrastructure.

Health services are structured to give free basic health services for the poor. The program does not only provide medication but also promote and educate the poor about good sanitation and healthy food. There are now six Hospitals that were built by the National Board of Zakat of

Republic of Indonesia in Jakarta, Sidoarjo, Yogyakarta, Makassar, Parigi Moutong, and Pangkal Pinang. Good health well-being; clean water and sanitation; and partnerships for the goals are the most priority SDGs to be achieved by this program. These hospitals also provide their own medical staffs including doctors, nurses, and pharmacists.

Education Program has two focuses: Building a Boarding School for the Poor and Providing Scholarship for Students at any level of education. For Building a Boarding School for the Poor program, the program is designed to become an ideal model of zakat disbursement program in education. The National Board of Zakat of Republic of Indonesia has been operating a boarding school for junior high school level in Bogor. This program is expected to create access for the poor to have good quality in education and to shape great leaders in the future. Therefore, the priority SDGs to be achieved through this program are quality education; reduced inequalities; and partnerships for the goals.

Meanwhile, Education Program that provides scholarship for students is available for students at every level of education. This scholarship is dedicated not only to pay the tuition fee but also to run capacity building program such as personal development, writing workshop, leadership camp, and many more. The program also promotes scholarship for young *ulema* to create thousands future *ulema*. Similar with building a boarding school program, scholarship program also aims to achieve quality education; reduced inequalities; and partnerships for the goals.

Microfinance services program with *qard al hasan* mode is funded by zakat and *infaq* (charity) to target, specifically the poor. The program provides capital for them to run their business. The program also offers business development services and market enlargement facilities. Thus, this zakat distribution program aims to achieve SDGs of no poverty; zero hunger; gender equality; decent works and economic growth; reduced inequalities; and partnerships for the goals.

Associated with the concept of empowering the poor through zakat fund distribution, providing business coaching and supervision, Tawhidi String Relations (TSR) is introduced for more structured and planned concept. TSR was introduced by Choudhury in Harahap (2018) and widely published in Choudhury (2019). TSR has manifested the concept of zakat, entrepreneurship and poverty alleviation support to social-wellbeing through pervasive interaction, integration, and evolution process.

Another program from zakat distribution is Education and Training for *Muallaf*. This program provides dakwah and public support in Islamic teaching. The program also supports vulnerable groups and enlightens the society on how beautiful Islam is in daily life. The priority goals of this program are achieving the SDGs of no poverty; quality education; and partnerships for the goals. As *muallaf* is a new comer in Islam that must have strong supportive environment to strengthen their intention to perform, convey and obey the Islamic teaching, education, and training for *muallaf* is highly expected and depended to support them.

Strategic Researches and Studies program is aimed to do strategic research on zakat. The results are taken as consideration to establish relevant policies in particular related with SDGs of no poverty; quality education; and partnerships for the goals. The program basically is also taking the policy-making role in order to alleviate poverty and support public welfare. The specific zakat foundational goals and SDGs are shown in Fig. 3.5.

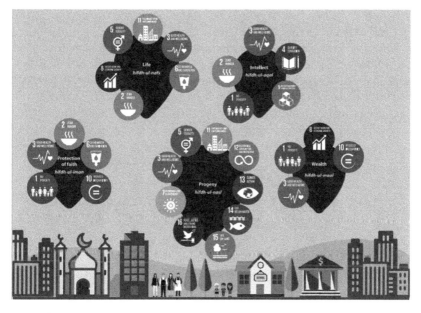

Fig. 3.5 Zakat Foundational Goals and SDGs (*Source* Noor and Pickup [2017])

Pillar of Zakat Programs

As aforementioned, wealth purification as the original concept in Islamic wealth management persuades the wealthy to create and distribute the wealth in an ethical, decent, and modest way, that is the permissible or halal way. Wealth purification is represented by one of Islamic social finance instrument: zakat. The payers are basically setting the base of society empowerment which eventually aim for economic growth and protecting human being in all aspects as presented in *maqasid* sharia that is in line with SDGs.

Even though, up to this date, zakat is well-known and recognized for its role in direct contribution to poor, zakat actually has been contributing a lot through many programs. It is not only the one-time direct contribution, but far beyond consumptive support, as mentioned under the subtitle of 'Zakat Programs and SDGs Priority.' Many programs have been settled to transform *mustahik* into *muzakki*, up until when *mustahik* not eligible to receive zakat, rather they have to pay and become *muzakki*.

Figure 3.6 shows the pillars of zakat programs that the National Board of Zakat of Republic of Indonesia hold on to in every plan they have and will made. There are basically five pillars: economy, education, social-humanity, health, and *da'wah*. Economy is the first pillar since no poverty, zero hunger, and good health and well-being are also the SDGs priority in zakat programs. As mentioned by Khan (2015) that there are six elements

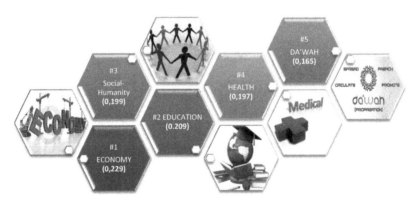

Fig. 3.6 Pillars of Zakat Programs
(*Source* BAZNAS Center of Strategic Studies [2017])

of SDGs including dignity, prosperity, justice, partnership, palnet, and people which are included in the priority criteria of zakat programs. Notwithstanding, zakat is one of pillars in Islam that has to be fulfilled by its believer and directly related with economy aspect in human life. So, it is the best fit that economy should be put at the first pillar in zakat program. For the payer, zakat is considered as an obligation, while for the receiver, zakat can uplift their life by fulfilling basic needs and, beyond that, empowering them to be more resilience in the future and later transformed to become the payer.

In terms of second pillar: Education, Indonesia is among those countries that showed progression in the international assessment performance although Indonesia was also among those countries whose education policy faced the major issues and numerous challenge to deliver quality education. Equitable quality education indicators comprise high intake, high completion rate, full learning experience, through teacher quality, school readiness, school management and leadership, physical facilities in school. One of Indonesia's problem was the teachers being away from schools, although Indonesia showed positive improvement. The result might lead to the low rate of resilience student, which is defined as students that fall under poor category from low-middle income countries but have high international assessment performance (COMCEC 2018). Therefore, zakat program for education is expected to contribute into better performance of Indonesia, not only among OIC countries but also in the world.

Social-humanity pillar is dedicated to protect human life and well-being, to protect progeny and future generation, as well as SDGs related goals, such as reduced inequalities. The related program is expected to provide the opening of equal opportunities in accessing provided facilities for every citizen.

The pillar of health is also essential to protect life and furthermore to protect progeny and future generation as health is the fundamental in doing every well-done work. Healthy body and healthy mind both are the key to happy life, thus fulfilling every single SDGs that in line with *maqasid* sharia.

Da'wah is crucial to protect *dien*, the first *maqasid* sharia. The programs are specified for the new comer in Islam and to people living in the inland like far away in the deep forest or mountain or living in the borderlines of Indonesia. Da'wah is basically transferring knowledge, supervising *ibadah* activities, and spreading Islamic values.

Conclusion

Ethical wealth management is a process managing wealth by upholding the concept of decent, modest, and environment oriented activities. All the concepts are embedded in *maqasid* sharia, which then translated by United Nation by SDGs. SDGs are more local and embrace the local values in comparison with MDGs. This ethical wealth management has already been thought in Islam, where wealth purification through zakat is the original concept introduced in Islam.

Zakat programs have brought activities to achieve SDGs as mentioned in this study. Every program has been described on how their approach in achieving SDGs, along with five pillars in zakat programs that have been upheld up to this very date. Economy, education, social-humanity, health, and *da'wah* are among those that prioritized since those are considered the top issues in developing country like Indonesia.

References

Al Quran App for Windows 8.

Ahmed, H., Mohieldin, M., Verbeek, J., & Aboulmagd, F. (2015). *On the Sustainable Development Goals and the Role of Islamic Finance.* The World Bank.

BAZNAS Center of Strategic Studies. (2017). *Sebuah Kajian Zakat on SDGs: Peran Zakat Dalam Sustainable Development Goals Untuk Pencapaian Maqashid Syariah* (A Study on Zakat on SDGs: The Role of Zakat in Sustainable Development Goals to Achieve Maqasid Al Shariah). Jakarta, Indonesia: BAZNAS Center of Strategic Studies.

Beik, I. S. (2020). *Implementation of Zakat on SDGs.* Islamic Economics Winter Course 2020 Presentation Module, Department of Islamic Economics, IPB University (Bogor Agricultural University), Indonesia.

Choudhury, M. A. (2019). Establishing Tawhidi String Relation as the Epistemic Foundation of Tawhidi Methodological Worldview. In *The Tawhidi Methodological Worldview* (pp. 15–25). Singapore: Springer. https://doi.org/10.1007/978-981-13-6585-0_2.

COMCEC. (2018). *Education Quality in the OIC Member Countries.* Ankara, Turkey: COMCEC Coordination Office. Retrieved from http://ebook.com cec.org/Kutuphane/Icerik/Yayinlar/Analitik_Calismalar/Yoksullugun_Azalti lmasi/Toplanti11-rev/files/assets/common/downloads/publication.pdf.

Harahap, L. R. (2018). Zakat Fund as the Starting Point of Entrepreneurship in Order to Alleviate Poverty (SDGs Issue). *Global Review of Islamic Economics and Business, 6*(1), 063–074.

Intezar, M. T., & Zia, S. B. (2020). *Zakat, SDGs, and Poverty Alleviation of Muslims in India. In Impact of Zakat on Sustainable Economic Development* (pp. 1–20). IGI Global. Retrieved from https://www.igi-global.com/chapter/zakat-sdgs-and-poverty-alleviation-of-muslims-in-india/259755.

Ismail, A. G., & Shaikh, S. A. (2018). *Role of Islamic Economics and Finance in Sustainable Development Goals.* Islamic Economic Studies and Thoughts Centre (IESTC), 1(1).

Julia, T., & Kassim, S. (2020). *Green Banking.* Banking and Finance. IntechOpen.

Khan, T. (2015). Access to Finance and Human Development—Essays on zakah, awqaf and Microfinance: An Introduction to the Issues and Papers. In H. A. El-Karanshawy, et al. (Eds.), *Access to Finance and Human Development—Essays on zakah, awqaf and Microfinance.* Bloomsbury Qatar Foundation: Doha, Qatar.

Khan, T. (2019). Reforming Islamic Finance for Achieving Sustainable Development Goals. *Journal of King Abdulaziz University: Islamic Economics, 32*(1), 3–21.

Mahmud, K. T., Hassan, M. K., Sohag, K., & Alam, M. F. (2015). Impact of zakat in Alleviating Rural Poverty: A Case Study of Masjid Council for Community Advancement (MACCA) in Bangladesh. In H. A. El-Karanshawy, et al. (Eds.), *Access to Finance and Human Development—Essays on zakah, awqaf and Microfinance.* Bloomsbury Qatar Foundation: Doha, Qatar.

Mergaliyev, A., Asutay, M., Avdukic, A., & Karbhari, Y. (2019). Higher Ethical Objective (Maqasid al-Shari'ah) Augmented Framework for Islamic Banks: Assessing Ethical Performance and Exploring Its Determinants. *Journal of Business Ethics, 2019,* 1–38.

Noor, Z., & Pickup, F. (2017). *The Role of Zakat in Supporting the Sustainable Development Goals.* BAZNAS and UNDP Brief Series.

United Nations. (2015). *Transforming Our World: The 2030 Agenda for Sustainable Development.* General Assembly: Resolution adopted by the General Assembly on 25 September 2015.

United Nations. (2020, May). *Sustainable Development Goals: Guidelines for the Use of the SDG Logo Including the Colour Wheel, and 17 Icons.* United Nations Department of Global Communications. Retrieved from https://www.un.org/sustainabledevelopment/wp-content/uploads/2019/01/SDG_Guidelines_AUG_2019_Final.pdf.

CHAPTER 4

Shari'ah, Ethical Wealth and SDGs: A Maqasid Perspective

Mohammad Abdullah

INTRODUCTION

The global consensus on the significance and vitality of Sustainable Development Goals (SDGs) heralded a new dawn in the arena of international development. Though agreed on a moral rather than legal ground, the adoption of SDGs by the international community as a framework and measurement of development in their respective countries exhibits their determination for an inclusive development (Ahmad et al. 2015). The SDGs if achieved within its timeframe will be not only a game-changer for the world community in present, but a harbinger of a much better world for the future generations as well (Sachs 2012). In its scope and objectives, the SDGs capture a comprehensive roadmap for the betterment of the planet earth and its dwellers (Steiner 2018). Though the SDGs cover a broad range of developmental issues, many goals revolve around different dimensions of existing lacuna in the mechanism of either

---

M. Abdullah (✉)
Markfield Institute of Higher Education, Markfield, UK

© The Author(s), under exclusive license to Springer Nature Switzerland AG 2021
M. M. Billah (eds.), *Islamic Wealth and the SDGs*,
https://doi.org/10.1007/978-3-030-65313-2_4

69

distribution of resources or the method of their consumption and deployment (Abdullah 2018). The issue of wealth in this discussion finds some constructive critique.

There are many interconnections between wealth and Sustainable Development Goals (SDGs). The linkages of SDGs and wealth are of both types, i.e. explicit and implicit (ESCAP 2019). Broadly, some of the key objectives of SDGs are achievable simply by correcting the course of how the phenomenon of wealth is conceptualised and treated by individuals as well as by the community (Abdullah 2018). For example, if the objectives of wealth and the related responsibilities are properly understood and acted upon, the problem of its insufficient circulation as well as its improper utilisation can be remedied to a great extent (ESCAP 2019). As a result, this exercise may directly help achieve, particularly, the SDG 10 as well as SDG 12. While the SDG 10 is aimed at reducing inequalities within and among the countries, the SDG 12 is meant to ensure responsible production and consumption pattern (Kate and Nicholas 2019).

Wealth has multiple forms of relationships and diverse functions towards the accomplishment of SDGs. Primarily, a massive amount of wealth is needed to functionalise the SDGs as a global programme and initiative. Secondly, wealth is immensely critical to reduce extreme poverty which is the SDG 1, or to accomplish zero hunger which is SDG 2 (World Bank 2018). Without wealth, there is hardly any scope of either ensuring a healthy life or providing quality education which constitutes the SDG 3 and SDG 4, respectively. Similarly, the provision of clean water and clean energy which appears as SDG 6 and SDG 7, respectively, is dependent on the existence of wealth and its appropriate employment (Abdullah 2018). Thus, be it in the form of deployment from national exchequers of different countries, from pockets of civil societies, from NGOs or from international aid agencies, the role of wealth is critical in the discussion of SDGs and their realisation. Without wealth and its strategic utilisation, there is no scope of SDGs' realisation (World Bank 2020).

There are assertions that wealth and its accumulation are imperative at individual as well as at national levels to enhance the quality of life and to participate in the developmental progress of the twenty-first century (Abdullah 2020). With the wealth comes the scope of growth, innovation, advancement and progression. However, generally the argument on the critical role of wealth in bringing development and improving the overall standard of life appears to neglect any constructive discussion on the ethics and values of wealth (Ariff 2017). Though there is hardly any scope for negating the indispensable function of wealth in securing a dignified and respectable quality of life, there is little doubt that creation and amassment of wealth in an unethical manner cause and fetch more socio-economic evils in the society than the virtues (Gadhoum 2017). In this background, it is essential to dissect the means, mechanism and manners of ethical versus unethical wealth creation, its accumulation and consumption.

This study aims at examining the nexus and inter-linkages between ethical wealth and Sustainable Development Goals from a *Maqasid al-Shariah* (the higher objectives of *Shariah*) perspective. The study attempts to conceptualise the concept, characteristics and premises of ethical wealth from a *Shariah* perspective followed by delineating its creation and consumption process and pattern. The study endeavours to locate the underlying relationship between ethical wealth and SDGs within the established parameters and paradigm of the higher objectives of *Shariah*. The objective of the study is to underline the role and relevance of ethical wealth in materialising the SDGs. The focus of the study is limited to discuss, in particular, the existing connections and overlapping between SDGs and *Shariah*-based ethical wealth. It is argued in this study that the concept of ethical wealth has an underlying bond with the all SDGs in general, and with some SDGs in particular. Ethical wealth is particularly relevant with the SDGs containing the goals of ending poverty, ensuring zero hunger, reducing inequality and emphasising on responsible production and consumption, respectively.

The study is based on a library-oriented research approach and it adopts a qualitative research paradigm to report the conclusion. An extensive review of available literature on SDGs and other developmental initiatives has been conducted to develop a comprehensive understating of the topic. For *Shariah* dimensions, the primary and secondary sources of *Shariah* in different languages have been referred to. The conclusion on *Maqasid al-Shariah* aspects has been drawn based on the textual analysis technique.

The study is divided into five key sections. Section "Introduction" provides the introduction of the study. The concept and features of ethical wealth and its relationship with SDGs are examined in section "Ethical Wealth and Sustainable Development Goals" of the study. Section "Wealth and *Maqasid al-Shariah*" focuses on analysing the *Shariah* approach and parameters of ethical wealth and its treatment in the alignment of *Maqasid al-Shariah*. The interconnections between ethical wealth, SDGs and *Maqasid al-Shariah* are delved into section "SDGs, Ethical Wealth and *Maqasid al-Shariah*". The conclusion and recommendations of the study are provided in section "Conclusion".

Ethical Wealth and Sustainable Development Goals

In the arena of development, the subject of wealth receives repeated reference. The discussion on the role of wealth in development can be of multifaceted (Ariff 2017). From the argument that wealth is panacea to all socio-economic problems, to the contention that wealth is root of all ills and evils in the society, there exists a wide range of opinion in the literature (Retno 2015). The opinion on wealth and its status varies based on the approach one adopts towards it. The status of wealth from a religious perspective is different from the status it is afforded in the opinion of economists. The divergence of opinion on wealth may also extend from a liberal capitalistic approach to a moralist or value-based pro-poor approach. Thus, the treatment of wealth may differ in line with the applied approaches and perspectives towards it. Notwithstanding the differences of opinion on wealth, there is no denial of the fact that wealth is critical towards the betterment of human life on this planet (Khattak 2018).

There is no concrete definition of wealth in the literature. It is defined variously. As per the neoclassical economic theory, wealth can be defined as a valuable asset which produces revenues (Clark 2015). The general perception of wealth is that it refers to money or a valuable which is exchangeable in the market. Broadly, wealth can be defined as any valuable asset which can be stored, exchanged for another valuable and can be used for economic activity (Gadhoum 2017). Based on the ownership structure, the nature of wealth can differ as individually owned or jointly owned. The possession and ownership of wealth may originate from a plethora of sources. Wealth can be gained by production, inheritance, gift and through other acceptable modes of transfer and acquisition (Kamali 2017).

The concept and characteristics of ethical or unethical wealth are not easily found in the contemporary literature. Wealth in the literature is generally treated as an abstract concept without any particular reference to its qualification into ethical or unethical (Moran 1901). Whether wealth can be classified into ethical and unethical on the basis of the source and modes of its acquisition or by methods of its creation is scarcely discussed in the literature (Clark 2015). The modes of consumption and deployment of wealth aside, the first yardstick to judge the ethicality of wealth is to examine its origin. From this angle, the legality and illegality of the originating source of wealth is the primary focus. Hence, in this context, whether wealth has been acquired through legal or illegal sources can be the initial defining criteria for ethical wealth.

Compared to legality vis-à-vis illegality approach, another approach to ascertain the ethicality of wealth is based on morality and sustainability criteria. For this, there is an argument on determining the nature of wealth as ethical or unethical on the basis of whether it has been obtained by being considerate to the sustainability of environment or not (Hudson 2005). In contrast, the modes and paradigm of investment have also been considered as one of the defining criteria of ethical vis-à-vis unethical wealth. To this end, if the wealth is invested in a socially and environmentally sustainable manner, it is fit to qualify for the term 'ethical' (Clark 2015; Hudson 2005). From the perspective of this approach, avoidance of investment in sin industries is a condition to maintain the ethicality of wealth (Keitsch 2018). Another approach towards defining wealth into ethical or unethical lays emphasis on examining the manner of its consumption. As per this approach, if wealth is consumed in an environmentally sustainable manner, it is qualified as ethical wealth. In an otherwise scenario, the wealth is unethical (Kamali 2017). There is a possibility of another approach to characterise wealth as ethical or unethical. This characterisation can be done on the basis of the magnitude and amount of wealth that an individual can own and possess. According to this approach, for instance, if an individual owns beyond a certain threshold, the residual wealth becomes unethical (Salim et al. 2016). Finally, there is scope of determining ethicality or un-ethicality of wealth on the basis of how the owner of such wealth behaves. For example, if the owner of wealth is duly fulfilling all his/her financial responsibilities towards his/her dependent and is actively participating in charitable and social activities, the underlying wealth is ethical. In an otherwise case, the subject of wealth becomes unethical (Ariff and Mohamad 2017).

There are some overtures on the contour of good and bad wealth in the literature (Clark 2015). However, such discussion on the qualification of wealth is rather limited in its nature. Apparently, the study by Clark (2015) categorises wealth into good and bad based on the consequentialist approach of moral theory. As the normative theory of consequentialism considers the end result of an action or conduct to decide its merit, so is the approach of Clark (2015) in treating the wealth. The qualification of good or bad wealth, according to him, is determinable by looking into the means and mechanism of its creation and the method and pattern of its consumption. Clark argues:

> Good wealth consists of assets that are created, distributed and used in a manner that respects human dignity and promotes the common good, thus leads to increases in well-being. Bad wealth consists in assets that are accumulated in an unjust manner (using force or fraud), is distributed in a manner that benefits only elites and excludes the poor and marginalized, and is used to create invidious distinctions and not for the common good. (Clark 2015, p. 2)

Despite all the varied methods and approaches of classifying wealth into good and bad or ethical and unethical, there is no unanimity of opinion on any such classification. The concept of wealth as defined and understood within the prism of a religious framework may not necessarily fit with the definitions given by the moralists or economists. The religious approach may stipulate further conditions and parameters to determine the nature and qualification of wealth. Thus, even if an agreement is reached on the definition of ethical and unethical wealth in a secular frame, there is no guarantee that the same will be acceptable from a religious perspective. In other words, it is not necessary that the above-discussed criteria of wealth are accommodated within the religious framework of ethical wealth. However, perhaps, all approaches unite in recognising the paramount significance of wealth for an individual, a household and a society. Presumably, there is a perception among the different stakeholders of the society that certain pattern of wealth consumption may have a constructive or destructive implications for individual as well as for the community. Thus, wealth has the potential of either making or breaking a household as well as a society.

In the discussion of development, lack of equity and fairness in distribution of wealth appears to be one of the many reasons of widespread deprivation and sub-standard quality of life for many (Kate and Nicholas 2019). In the context of SDGs, wealth has a distinctive role to play. Without existence of wealth and its proper deployment, neither the goal of poverty alleviation nor the objective of zero hunger can be achieved. Similarly, be it the goal of reducing inequalities within and outside nations, or the goal of ensuring sustainable consumption and production pattern, the concept of wealth and its functions requires due conceptualisation. Wealth is crucial to provide affordable housing and for arrangement of drinkable water. Without wealth, there is little scope for the system and mechanism of education as well as for the continuity of healthcare infrastructure and apparatus. Notwithstanding these, if the concept and function of wealth are not conceptualised and practised appropriately, it may end up backfiring, causing numerous evils and deprivation in the society (Abdullah 2018).

The subsequent section of the study analyses the ethics of wealth and its role in the society from a *Maqasid al-Shariah* perspective.

Wealth and *Maqasid al-Shariah*

Preservation of wealth (*hifz al-maal*) includes among the five unanimously agreed upon major objectives of *Shariah* (*Maqasid al-Shariah*). The other four key objectives of *Shariah* comprise protection of religion, life, intellect and progeny (Abdullah 2020). There is an implicit assumption that these objectives are subtly interconnected. Within the *Shariah* paradigm, wealth constitutes a gift of God (*fadl al-Allah*) and thus be strived for (Ibrahim et al. 2014). In Quranic term, wealth has been counted among the essentials of human life (Kamali 2017). Without wealth and its proper utilisation, the divine plan on earth cannot be implemented (Abdul-Rasul 1980). From a *Shariah* perspective, the role that human being has been assigned on this planet can hardly be played without acquisition of wealth and its due deployment. Wealth is a means to achieve a dignified life and to enjoy the blessings of God (Al-Shaybani 2015).

The Islamic jurisprudence makes the primary categorisation of wealth (*maal*) into *Mutaqawwam* (an asset which is considered as wealth in *Shariah*) and *Ghair Mutaqawwam* (an asset which is not considered as wealth in *Shariah*) (Bashir 2002). This primary categorisation of wealth in *Shariah* excludes such objects and items from the definition of wealth which are intrinsically prohibited in *Shariah*. The example of such objects includes pork and liquor, among others (AAOIFI 2015). This initial categorisation is indicative of the *Shariah* stand that all that has a value and is exchangeable in the market is not necessarily deemed as wealth in the sight of *Shariah*. Thus, at the initial stage, *Shariah* filters out the assets and valuables which qualify for the merit of being termed as wealth from the ones which do not stand to this test.

To be defined as ethical wealth, a valuable has to meet some other layers of *Shariah*-filtering criteria as well. In this context, the second layer of *Shariah*-filtering process sieves out unethical assets and objects based on their source and origination. A wealth acquired illegitimately either by force, exploitation, without consent of the relevant party or through an unfair means is excluded at this stage from the qualification of ethical wealth (Kamali 2017). This is applicable for the wealth which is not prohibited intrinsically, but is impermissible due to being originated from a Shariah-prohibited means. Thus, a wealth acquired by theft, deceit, fraud, embezzlement or through bribery falls under this category. Since *Shariah* deems acquisition of wealth through such illicit means among the major sins, it is natural that such wealth can never be treated as ethical.

Another filtering process which *Shariah* applies to examine the merit of wealth is to confirm whether the wealth has been acquired through *Shariah*-compliant agreements and contracts or not. At this stage, wealth obtained through, for example, interest or gambling-based contracts automatically falls disqualified from the race of ethical wealth (MIFC 2016). In this example, though such contracts may have been reached through mutual agreement of the relevant parties, the breach of fundamental *Shariah* principles on prohibition of interest and gambling makes it impermissible in the sight of *Shariah*. Thus, due to being labelled as *Shariah* non-compliant, the question of passing the ethicality criteria does not arise for such wealth.

The next level of filtering criteria for an ethical wealth, from a *Shariah* perspective, is composed of two-dimensional requirements. Whether an underlying wealth has been accumulated without resorting to misery, greed or through hoarding tactics is the first indicated dimension of this level of filtering. The second dimension of this process is to examine whether the underlying wealth is utilised moderately or extravagantly (Al-Ghazali 2004). In case, wealth is used as a means to indulge in an extravagant lifestyle or to inflate the sense of self-pride or to hone arrogance, the ethicality of such wealth comes into question. The *Shariah* stipulations and qualifying criteria of ethical wealth are not over at this stage. Rather, *Shariah* requires to confirm whether the requisites of *Shariah* are properly met in the process of preserving and investing the wealth or not (Al-Shaybani 2015).

Shariah neither condones hoarding of wealth in the name of preservation, nor does it promote taking an unduly heightened risk in investing. Rather, a moderate and middle attitude towards saving and investment decision is desired (Ibrahim et al. 2014). Thus, neither the wealth which is lying idle due to extra risk-averse approach nor does the one which is put carelessly to unwarranted risk commands *Shariah* appreciation. In terms of investment, the *Shariah* paradigm prohibits investment in certain *Shariah* non-compliant avenues. The *Shariah* impermissible avenues include investment in sin industries, interest-based institutions, in gambling or social and environmentally harmful industries. The qualification of an underlying wealth as ethical in view of *Shariah* is dependent on satisfying these and other similar *Shariah* criteria of investment (MIFC 2016).

In relation to wealth, *Shariah* stipulates certain duties, responsibilities and obligations which need to be fulfilled in a *Shariah*-prescribed manner. To this end, the *Shariah* prescriptions are multidimensional. Broadly, these may be divided into individual, religious, social and environmental obligations (Abdullah 2020). The primary obligation arising out of wealth is that it is moderately spent on self and on the dependents of the owner. In addition, among the primary *Shariah*-prescribed obligations of wealth is that it is spent appropriately on achieving a balanced and dignified life of oneself and the dependent family members (Singer 2008). Satisfying the essential needs, which require usage of wealth for their fulfilment, is included in this requirement. Other than this, the religious obligations of wealth are of two forms. These include dispensing wealth as a part of *Shariah*-prescribed charities such as *Zakat* and *Sadaqah al-Fitr* and establishing the worship which requires consumption of wealth such as performing pilgrimage to Mecca (Sabra 2000).

To sum it up, the term "ethical wealth" within the prism of *Shariah* can be conferred to such wealth which fulfils the *Shariah*-prescribed qualifying criteria. Apparently, these criteria are set by *Shariah* in the spirit of its higher objectives which could be summarised as bringing ease and removing hardship and harm (Abdullah 2018). The essence of *Shariah* paradigm of wealth is, seemingly, encapsulated in its broader theme of respecting the individual property rights and dignity, while blocking the scope of harm to the society by its misuse. Finally, ethical wealth in *Shariah* can be defined as the wealth which is sourced through a *Shariah*-permissible method, consumed in a *Shariah*-prescribed manner, dispensed in a *Shariah*-desired way, preserved and invested in a Shariah-compliant avenue and is used as a means to securing a gracious, dignified and better life in this world and Hereafter.

SDGs, Ethical Wealth and *Maqasid al-Shariah*

Since the turn of the twenty-first century, the theme and cause of sustainable development and environmental-friendly practices have attracted a remarkable amount of interest from the academia, industry and other national and international stakeholders. Sustainability warrants permanence, continuity and recurrence of a given activity or business, which is ensured by adoption of responsible pattern of production, consumption and resource deployment. In economic terms, sustainability amounts to stability which is obtainable by underlining the merits of responsible economic behaviour and shunning the irresponsible forms and patterns of production and consumption. To induce the urgency of sustainable behaviour among the masses, calibrated efforts of public, private and civil society are vital. In this process, formulation of appropriate policies and promotion of responsible decision-making are the key (Abdullah 2018).

The framework of Sustainable Development Goals (SDGs) encapsulates a comprehensive and inclusive set of social, economic and climate-based goals to be achieved by the global community. The international acceptance of the SDGs indicates the emergence of global sensitivity and consciousness towards restoring and maintaining a more equitable socio-economic order. For this, the need for countering the menace of poverty, hunger, illiteracy, ill-health and inequality has been unanimously agreed among the different stakeholders. In addition, the significance of conserving a habitable environment, protecting ecological system, developing institutions to promote peace and justice along with taking care of the life on land and the life under the sea has successfully captured the attention of the international development community. Similarly, the essentials of socio-economic well-being such as provision of clean water, clean energy, decent work and sustainable infrastructure development have emerged to draw the notice of the pertinent stakeholders (Ahmad et al. 2015).

In achieving the SDGs, the critical role that ethical wealth can play is scarcely delineated in the literature. In line with the above-discussed *Shariah* criteria, the notion and significance of ethical wealth need to be conceptualised in literature and promoted in practice. Through the promotion of *Shariah* merit and attributes of ethical wealth coupled with its translation into practice, the wealth-related objective of *Shariah* can be achieved, which ultimately hit and match several SDGs (Abdullah 2018; Kamali 2017). For example, the process and pattern of creating, consuming and deploying *Shariah*-based ethical wealth necessitate honouring individual's property rights, fulfilling socio-economic obligations and considering environmental and ecological implications. These criteria, as a result, automatically help resolve several dimensions of SDGs.

The production, utilisation and deployment of ethical wealth are critical to lay the foundation of a just, equitable and responsible society as well as a progressive and imitable socio-economic order. Creation and circulation of ethical wealth are key to beget an active, robust and prosperous economy and infrastructure. In a nutshell, deployment of wealth in a responsible, transparent, accountable and goal-oriented manner is a prerequisite for a smooth functioning and burgeoning society. In contrast, misuse of wealth or its usage without planning may harm the wider society more than benefitting it. To curtail the scope of any such misuse and its spillover, it is imperative to instil in the different stakeholders the *Shariah*-based guiding principles on ethical usage of wealth. In this context, the primary focus of *Shariah* guidelines is on infusing the spirit of responsibility and accountability in relation to creation and utilisation of wealth (Abdullah 2020).

Since the framework of SDGs does not, in general, contradict with the higher objectives of *Shariah*, there is a greater scope of collaboration between the stakeholders of *Shariah* and SDGs. Drawing a unified pitch of coordination, the two stakeholders need to put their calibrated efforts to achieve the SDGs in a timely manner. In general, most of the SDGs are amenable to *Shariah* objectives. *Shariah* provides an axiomatic socio-ethical paradigm, which exhorts its stakeholders to maintain the path of moderation in production, consumption, investment, distribution and other activities. Establishing fairness and equity coupled with transparency, particularly, in monetary dealings is among the key objectives of *Shariah* (Abdullah 2018). Similarly, instilling the sense of responsibility and pitching for creation of a considerate society towards human, nature and other creatures are some of its vital values and ethos (Abdullah 2020).

The objective of maximising positive impact and reducing the effects of negative, harmful and detrimental activities is included in the list of *Shariah*-based principles. The impacts of efforts towards materialising SDGs can be magnified by raising awareness about *Shariah* objectives in general and promoting the *Shariah*-based notion of ethical wealth in particular (Abdullah 2018). It is pertinent to note that there is an existing gap between the theory and practice of ethical wealth as prescribed by *Shariah*, which needs to be effectively bridged. In this way, the dual objectives of introducing the true position of *Shariah* with reference to wealth and its unique proposition of ethical wealth can be accomplished. Consequently, on the practical ground, the approach and paradigm of *Shariah* towards wealth and its ideal treatment can become clearer for all.

The inter-linkage among the ethical wealth, SDGs and *Maqasid al-Shariah* is brightly visible in different *Shariah*-based benevolent institutions. The institutions of Islamic obligatory and voluntary charities, for instance, constitute the prominent examples of this phenomenon (Yalawae and Tahir 2008). Among the different forms and shapes of Islamic charitable institutions include *Zakat*, *Sadaqah al-Fitr*, *Waqf*, *Qard Hasan*, etc., to name a few. These institutions are predominantly focused on fighting poverty, hunger, malnutrition and other socio-economic deprivations. In addition, some of these institutions are meant to supply many basic necessities and essentialities of life (Kamali 2017). The institution of *Waqf*, for example, is envisaged to ensure provision of all necessary services that are needed in functioning of a society. *Waqf* aims to voluntarily bridge any existing gap in the sufficient supply of public goods. The role of *Waqf* in providing food, drinkable water, free education and respectable employment is widely acknowledged throughout the history of the institution. Similarly, the role of *Waqf* has been significant in infrastructure development as well as in supporting the institutions of peace and justice among the societies (Lev 2005).

In comparison to the function of *Waqf*, the role of *Qard Hasan* (interest-free benevolent loan) and other *Shariah*-prescribed charities is critical in supporting communities and societies on a voluntary basis (Abdullah 2015). The benevolent character of *Qard Hasan*, for example, facilitates financial help to the deserving entities without encumbering the recipient with the burden of interest. Finally, being obligatory upon the wealthy and privileged annually, the institutions of *Zakat* and *Sadah al-Fitr* ensure the mandatory redistribution of wealth among the underprivileged and deserving entities on an annual basis. Importantly, since *Shariah* recognises a charity as acceptable only if this is exercised from the wealth which qualifies the *Shariah*-described criteria of ethical wealth, the need to understand and acknowledge the relevance of ethical wealth becomes self-explanatory.

Along with institutionalising charities, the emphasis of *Shariah* on engaging in equity-based financing and avoiding gambling-like highly ambiguous transactions blocks the way of hoarding wealth as well as making unjust enrichment at the cost of another. The objective of these *Shariah* injunctions is to ensure circulation of wealth in the economy and reduction of inequalities. In addition, the *Shariah* prohibition of interest is aimed at safeguarding the society from its ill effects. The mechanism of interest runs counter to the *Shariah*-prescribed concept of benevolence. Interest causes selfishness, and it induces risk-averse behaviour by enabling the capitalist to make money on money by shifting the underlying risk of money to the borrower. The concept and mechanism of interest are arguably one of the many factors of growing inequalities among the societies. In comparison, *Shariah* reprimands shifting risks and urges to share it along with being fair and just. *Shariah* advises to be easy in contracts and compassionate in dealings: waiving-off the non-payable debt due to hardship of debtor, providing flexibility in contractual terms, delaying the repayment and being benevolent when and as required.

To sum it up, the *Shariah* objectives of ensuring justice in society, providing equal opportunities to all, treating the underprivileged with compassion, helping others and being considerate to the environment are evidently encapsulated in many SDGs. And, to actualise the shared objectives of *Shariah* and SDGs' framework, the role of ethical wealth is far more critical than being generally perceived. Finally, by underlining the shared aspirations, values and objectives of SDGs and *Shariah*, an integrated pitch of collaboration between the two can be drawn. Lastly, due to its critically essential role, overlooking the significance of ethical wealth in this collaboration can hardly be afforded.

CONCLUSION

The framework of Sustainable Development Goals (SDGs) provides a comprehensive development programme in the form of globally agreed seventeen key goals to be targeted and accomplished by the international community by 2030. In the process of materialising these goals, the significance of wealth and its role can be hardly overstated. It is argued that the concept of wealth in itself does not possess any specific relevance for SDGs, unless it is transformed into ethical wealth. However, there is a noted dearth of discussion in the literature on the concept of ethical wealth and its features. This study attempted to conceptualise the framework of ethical wealth from a *Shariah* perspective and aimed to underscore the relationship between ethical wealth and SDGs. For the analysis of the existing nexus between ethical wealth and SDGs, the *Maqasid al-Shariah* paradigm and its approach towards wealth were delineated.

This study found that for qualifying for the *Shariah*-prescribed concept of ethicality, a wealth has to meet several criteria. The *Shariah* approach on wealth and its treatment is based on its fundamental values and principles. The *Shariah* values manifest in the form of inculcating to respect the property rights of individuals and counter-parties, rights and obligations of poor and other deserving entities along with considering the environment and ecological system. Similarly, the values of *Shariah* require shunning any unjust enrichment or using exploitative means to acquire wealth. In addition, indulgence in unethical activities for wealth generation or its consumption is unequivocally condemned in *Shariah* for contradicting its values. The principles of *Shariah* lay down specific rules regarding the permissible means, methods and mechanism of wealth generation, its consumption, deployment investment and redistribution. Once the *Shariah* values and principles are abided in the process, the resultant wealth is treated as being ethical in *Shariah*.

This study argued that there are many possible inter-linkages between the SDGs and *Shariah*-based concept of ethical wealth. Many SDGs are vividly linked with ethical wealth while some other are implicitly dependent on it. From poverty alleviation to hunger mitigation, the role of ethical wealth is critically important. Similarly, in achieving the goal of quality education for all, provision of clean water, clean energy, decent work, as well as in reducing the inequalities and ensuring sustainable pattern of production and consumption, the significant role of ethical wealth remains in limelight. Thus, in the context of SDGs and their materialisation, the potential impacts and implications of ethical wealth towards SDGs can hardly be overlooked.

Finally, this study found that in a broad term, the SDGs are generally consistent with the *Maqasid al-Shariah* (the higher objectives of *Shariah*). In summary, achieving ease, peace, dignity and sustainability in life and in the environment constitutes the essence of *Maqasid al-Shariah*. The framework of SDGs, apparently, focuses on accomplishing similar goals though in somewhat a different form. Hence, there is an existing underlying bond connecting the essence of *Shariah* with the objectives of

SDGs. In a nutshell, the spirit and essence of both, i.e. SDGs and *Maqasid al-Shariah*, unify in urging that the prospects of a liveable and vibrant future shall not be compromised due to greed of maximising the enjoyment and the benefit of resources in the present. Future, in this context, is limited to this world only for the stakeholders of SDGs. In comparison, from the prism of *Maqasid al-Shariah*, connotations of future extend to Hereafter as well.

REFERENCES

AAOIFI. (2015). *Shariah Standards for Islamic Financial Institutions*. Bahrain: Accounting and Auditing Organisation for Islamic Financial Institution.

Abdullah, M. (2015). Analysing the Moral Aspect of Qard: A Shariah Perspective. *International Journal of Islamic and Middle Eastern Finance and Management, 8*(2), 171–184.

Abdullah, M. (2018). Waqf, Sustainable Development Goals (SDGs) and Maqasid al-Shariah. *International Journal of Social Economics, 45*(1), 158–172.

Abdullah, M. (2020). Waqf, Social Responsibility, and Real Economy. In B. Saiti & A. Sarea (Eds.), *Challenges and Impacts of Religious Endowments on Global Economics and Finance* (pp. 23–36). Hershey, PA, USA: IGI Global.

Abdul-Rasul, A. (1980). *Al-Mabadi' al-Iqtisadiyyah Fi Al-Islam*. Cairo: Dar Al-Fikr Al-Arabi.

Ahmad, H. Mohieldin, M. Verbeek, J., & Aboulmagd, F. (2015). *On the Sustainable Development Goals and the Role of Islamic Finance* (Policy Research Working Paper 7266). Washington: World Bank Group.

Al-Ghazali, A. H. (2004). *Ihya Uloom al-Deen (Kitab al-Faqr wa al-Zuhd)* (Vol. 4, pp. 259–330). Cairo: Dar al-Afaq.

Al-Shaybani, M. H. (2015). *al-Kasb*. Abu Dhabi: Tourism and Cultural Authority.

Ariff, M. (2017). Wealth Management, Its Definition, Purpose, Structure. In M. Ariff & S. Mohamad (Eds.), *Islamic Wealth Management: Theory and Practice* (pp. 12–24). Gloucester: Edward Elgar.

Ariff, M., & Mohamad, S. (2017). Wealth as Understood in Economics and Finance. In M. Ariff & S. Mohamad (Eds.), *Islamic Wealth Management: Theory and Practice* (pp. 3–11). Gloucester: Edward Elgar.

Bashir, A. (2002). Property Rights, Institutions and Economic Development: An Islamic Perspective, *Humanomics, 18*(¾), 75–91.

Clark, M. (2015). *Promoting Good Wealth: CST and the Link Between Wealth, Well-Being and Poverty Alleviation* (A Background Paper).

ESCAP. (2019). *A Guide to Inequality and the SDGs*. Bangkok: Social Development Policy Guides.

Gadhoum, M. (2017). Wealth from the *Shariah* Perspective. In M. Ariff & S. Mohamad (Eds.), *Wealth Management: Theory and Practice* (pp. 13–24). Gloucester: Edward Elgar.

Hudson, R. (2005). Ethical Investing: Ethical Investors and Managers. *Business Ethics Quarterly, 15*(4), 641–657.

Ibrahim, A., Eltrash, J., & Farooq, O. (2014). Hoarding Versus Circulation of Wealth From the Perspective of Maqasid Al-Shari'ah. *International Journal of Islamic and Middle Eastern Finance and Management, 7*(1), 6–21.

Kamali, H. (2017). The Shari'ah Purpose of Wealth Preservation in Contracts and Transaction. *Islam and Civilizational Renewal, 8*(2), 153–175.

Kate, D., & Nicholas, L. (2019). *From Disparity to Dignity Tackling Economic Inequality Through the Sustainable Development Goals: Human Rights Policy Brief*. New York: CESR.

Keitsch, M. (2018). Structuring Ethical Interpretations of the Sustainable Development Goals-Concepts, Implications and Progress. *Sustainability, 10*, 829.

Khattak, M. (2018). Protection and Distribution of Wealth, Islamic Commercial and Financial Transactions: A Maqasid Al-*Shariah* Perspective. *European Journal of Islamic Finance* (10), 1–8.

Lev, Y. (2005). *Charity, Endowments and Charitable Institutions in Medieval Islam*. Gainesville, FL, USA: University Press of Florida.

MIFC. (2016). *Islamic Wealth Management: Growing Stronger Globally*. Kuala Lumpur, Malaysia.

Moran, T. (1901). The Ethics of Wealth. *American Journal of Sociology, 6*(6), 823–838.

Retno, W. (2015). *Redistribution Adjusts Efficiency in Economy; Islamic Paradigm* (MPRA Paper No. 67809). Available at https://mpra.ub.uni-muenchen.de/67809/, accessed on 25 December 2019.

Sabra, A. (2000). *Poverty and Charity in Medieval Islam: Mumluk Egypt. 1250–1517*. Cambridge: Cambridge University Press.

Sachs, J. D. (2012). *From Millennium Development Goals to Sustainable Development Goals*. Available at: http://www.thelancet.com/journals/a/article/PII S0140-6736%2812%2960685-0/fulltext, accessed on 20 September 2015.

Salim, R., Hossain, R., & Mawali, N. (2016). Distribution of Wealth and Resources in Islam: Restoring Social Justice, Peace and Prosperity. *International Journal of Economic Research, 13*(2), 571–586.

Singer, A. (2008). *Charity in Islamic Societies*. Cambridge: Cambridge University Press.

Steiner, A. (2018). *The Role of Islamic Finance: Opening Remarks on "Innovative Financing for the SDGs: The Role of Islamic Finance"*. Available at: https://www.undp.org/content/undp/en/home/news-centre/speeches/2018/-the-role-of-islamic-finance.html, accessed on 21 October 2019.

World Bank. (2020). *Poverty and Equity Brief*. Available at: https://databank.worldbank.org/data/download/poverty/33EF03BB-9722-4AE2-ABC7-AA2972D68AFE/Global_POVEQ_IND.pdf, accessed on 20 March 2020.

World Bank. (2018). *Piecing Together the Poverty Puzzle*. Available at: https://openknowledge.worldbank.org/bitstream/handle/10986/30418/211330ov.pdf, accessed on 20 March 2020.

Yalawae, A., & Tahir, I. M. (2008, September, 10–13). *The Role of Islamic Institution in Achieving Equality and Human Development: Waqf or Endowment*. Paper presented at the 5th annual conference of the HDCA, New Delhi, India.

CHAPTER 5

Analysis of the Compatibility of SDGs with Development Goals Based on Divine Principles

Mustafa Helvacıoğlu, Mustafa Omar Mohammed, and Mohamed Cherif El Amri

Introduction

The United Nations mooted the ideas of Sustainable Development Goals [SDGs] in 2015. Yet the concept of sustainable development is not new to the primary and secondary sources of Islam. With the demise of the Ottoman Empire, almost all of the superseding states changed their institutions in parallel to the idea of Westernization, even though the majority of their population were still Muslims. Therefore, the teachings of Islam lost ground and were relegated from institutional levels to individual

---

M. Helvacıoğlu · M. C. El Amri (✉)
Department of Islamic Economics and Finance, Istanbul Sabahattin Zaim University, Istanbul, Turkey

M. O. Mohammed
Department of Economics, International Islamic University Malaysia [IIUM], Gombak, Malaysia
e-mail: mustafa@iium.edu.my

© The Author(s), under exclusive license to Springer Nature Switzerland AG 2021
M. M. Billah (eds.), *Islamic Wealth and the SDGs*,
https://doi.org/10.1007/978-3-030-65313-2_5

87

levels. Thus, institutions in the Islamic world were transformed into a status where they relied largely on ideas and innovations from their corresponding Western institutions, which have long remained in pioneering positions for decades (Helvacıoğlu et al. 2020). Apparently, many ideas from the Western world have been imported by the Muslim world after these ideas were well entrenched in the West. Such is the adoption of sustainable development by the governments of Muslim societies, which has happened lately too (Aburounia and Sexton 2006, p. 763).

Sustainable development is considered as a re-discovery by the Western world, since they were finally able to generate the idea as an outcome of social, economic and environmental drawbacks through the end of the twentieth century. Although sustainable development is a concept introduced by the Western world in the late 1980s, it is not a new concept to Islam, which, in theory and practice, has its roots in the sustainable development principles enshrined in the primary sources of Islam for ages (Aburounia and Sexton 2006, p. 757). The original institutions of Islamic societies have had a strong foundation in the practice of this concept. This arises from the responsibility approach between human-creator, human-human and human-environment relationships guided by the divine principles (Dariah et al. 2016, p. 159). Muslims as a general principle and as a norm care and worry for others, a behaviour that emanates from their religious philosophy that does not discriminate others in all good dealings. Therefore, SDGs, or any other sustainable developments concept, are part of these good dealings in Islam.

Islamic societies are expected to take the opportunity to evaluate and lead sustainable development concept, and thus supporting SDGs. Divine principles will provide the basis regarding any activities related to SDGs. Muslims shall therefore refrain from expecting solutions from Western institutions to prepare for them a what to-do list on SDGs. Instead, they should derive principles, ideals and key features related to these goals from divine principles. Past Islamic civilizations are full of SDG-related examples and guidelines. So, revisiting SDGs in relation to sustainable development based on divine principles shall be an important step towards the right direction. There are few literatures that have discussed the concept of sustainable development and SDGs from Islamic perspectives. These works are largely informative, normative and suggestive.

Review of Related Works

There are few studies that have discussed the relationships between divine principles, development, sustainability and SDGs. These studies are largely descriptive focusing on concepts and philosophies of divine principles, sustainable development and to a lesser degree SDGs. For example, Kahf (2002) argues for the operationalization of divine principles at the institutional levels. He explained that utilizing divine revelation only at the spiritual level without operationalizing it at the institutional level would hamper the realization of actual progress and development and would keep the reforms called for by the divine guidance static behind the curtains. He substantiated his arguments with the verses 13:11 and 8:53 from Qur'an, that "Verily never will God change the condition of a people until they change what is in themselves" and thus God will never change the condition of the people towards progress and development unless they change what is in their own soul.

In the same vein, Martı (2018) opined that divine principles need to be operationalized. As a background, she relates that economic, social and ecological crisis arises from the selfish lifestyle of human being, that is, incompatible with the universal balance and harmony. The core issue is not the physical pollution but the mind's pollution. Unconsciousness and unawareness in moral values transform a human being into a harmful creature against other humans, non-human beings and even the future habitants of the Earth. She thinks that listing the verses of Qur'an about the natural life or the hadith about cleanness, protection of animals, prohibiting the extravagancy is not sufficient commitments from Muslims for sustainability.

Martı (2018)'s view is shared by Sarkawi et al.'s (2016) who examined the issue of sustainability from Islamic perspective. They reviewed the concept of sustainability based on its three dimensions [economic, social and environment]. They concluded that sustainability is part of Islamic perspective, especially in relation to the environment. Meanwhile, Aburounia and Sexton (2006, p. 757) explained that sustainable development is a concept introduced by the Western world in the late 1980s, yet it is not a new concept to Islam. They explained that Islam had long since included the main ideas of Sustainable Development Goals in its primary sources both in principles and in practice.

There is a dearth of literature that discussed SDGs from Islamic perspective. One important recent study about the approach for SDGs in

Islamic perspective is conducted by Dariah, Salleh and Shafiai in 2016. They argue that SDGs cannot fully fulfil the basic needs of humans without including the spiritual components and divine principles as the main determinants for development. They conclude that human ideals can only be manifest through spiritual development from divine revelation and humans with such ideals can play a significant role in social and environmental awareness, and they can develop attitudes and behaviours that will lead to the success of SDGs. In another study, Aliyev and Aslanlı (2015, p. 43) consider SDGs as neither products nor projects with a beginning or ending, but ongoing processes of exploring and binging solutions to economic, social and environmental problems of today and tomorrow. Human problems can be overcome from various sources of solutions. One such source is divine principles, which can provide important inputs to SDGs when they are accepted and included in the evaluation process of SDGs (Aliyev and Aslanlı 2015, p. 43).

Moreover, SDGs are supposed to encompass both material and moral dimension to bring a long-run development to humanity (Ajanovic 2017, p. 6). Meanwhile, Ahmed et al. (2015) describe the finance-related divine principles of Islam as supportive, socially-inclusive, environmentally-friendly and developmental, with the ability to reveal the activities for the achievement of SDGs. However, they also emphasize that the contribution of Islamic institutions to SDGs has been lower than its potential in practical terms (p. 30).

SDGs and Their Philosophies

As stated in section one above, SDGs were mooted by the United Nations in 2015. SDGs succeeded in the Millennium Development Goals (MDGs), which was announced by the United Nations during the last 20 years. The eight goals embodied in MDGs were global development agendas determined in 2000 and were to last until 2015. The seventeen Sustainable Development Goals (SDGs), mooted in 2015 to last until 2030, are updated and expanded versions of MDSs, and thus, SDGs have taken over the unfinished business of MDG. The seventeen goals of SDGs and their explanations are reproduced in Table 5.1 below. This will be followed by a discussion on the philosophy of SDGs.

Sustainable Development Goals are well-acknowledged concepts for humanity to stay focused on their course to progress and development. They embody a philosophy that harmonizes the economic, social and

Table 5.1 Seventeen goals of SDGs and their explanation

No	Goal	Explanation
Goal 1	No Poverty:	End poverty in all its forms, everywhere
Goal 2	Zero Hunger:	End hunger, achieve food security and improved nutrition and promote sustainable agriculture
Goal 3	Good Health and Well-Being:	Ensure healthy lives and promote well-being for all
Goal 4	Quality Education:	Ensure inclusive and equitable quality education and promote lifelong learning opportunities for all at all ages
Goal 5	Gender Equality:	Achieve gender equality and empower all women and girls
Goal 6	Clean Water and Sanitation:	Ensure available and sustainable management of water and sanitation for all
Goal 7	Affordable and Clean Energy:	Ensure access to affordable, reliable, sustainable and modern energy for all
Goal 8	Good Jobs and Economic Growth:	Promote sustained, inclusive and sustainable economic growth, full and productive employment and decent work for all
Goal 9	Industry, Innovation and Infrastructure:	Build resilient infrastructure, promote inclusive and sustainable industrialization and foster innovation
Goal 10	Reduced Inequalities:	Reduce inequality within and among countries
Goal 11	Sustainable Cities and Communities:	Make cities and human settlements inclusive, safe, resilient and sustainable
Goal 12	Responsible Consumption and Production:	Ensure sustainable consumption and production patterns
Goal 13	Climate Action:	Take urgent action to combat climate change and its impacts
Goal 14	Life Below Water:	Conserve and sustainably use the oceans, seas and marine resources for sustainable development

(continued)

Table 5.1 (continued)

No	Goal	Explanation
Goal 15	Life on Land:	Protect, restore and promote sustainable use of terrestrial ecosystems, sustainably manage forests, combat desertification, and halt and reverse land degradation and halt biodiversity loss
Goal 16	Peace, Justice and Strong Institutions:	Promote peaceful and inclusive societies for SD, provide access to justice for all and build effective, accountable and inclusive institutions at all levels
Goal 17	Partnerships for the Goals:	A successful SD agenda requires partnerships between governments, the private sector and civil society

environmental dimensions of sustainable development. SDGs try to bring awareness that human activities shall be undertaken in the context of a holistic approach balancing between economic, social and environmental sustainability issues. None of these three dimensions should be neglected, traded off between each other or preferred over the other. The word sustainability refers to a continuous balance between these dimensions, while the word development refers to continuous progress. Sustainable development requires a yardstick and benchmark to measure its performances as it progresses from past, present and future. Of course, there are several ways of measuring the progress to determine if the balance between the three dimensions is sustained or not. It is worth noting that no matter how high the progress is in one dimension, still sustainable development should be measured as a balanced progress encompassing all the dimensions, regionally and globally.

Any form of development strategies that extend to the future requires targets and methods for measuring their achievement. The Sustainable Development Goals (SDGs) have formulated such targets for themselves. SDGs make human beings think about sustainable development in their own environments and remove obstacles to economic, social and environmental sustainability. SDGs create a bridge of sustainability between the present generations and future generations as the present generations are supposed to generate proper activities of sustainable development without compromising the abilities of future generations. Hence, fundamentally SDGs are both destinations and means that interpret, motivate and activate development towards economic, social and environmental sustainability. SDGs are the measures to address the common problems of humanity and to seek solutions for them. According to KPMC International (2015), SDGs serve as a worldwide memorandum which guides the institutions in their core businesses towards achieving economic, social and environmental sustainability.

Unless SDGs are acknowledged and enhanced at the national and institutional levels, it would be slow to achieve a significant improvement in the expected outcomes. National strategy that includes development plans, policies and regulations is necessary for achieving any of the SDGs (Ahmed, Contribution of Islamic Finance to the 2030 Agenda for Sustainable Development, 2017). Any idea and activity related to sustainable development that finds its place among institutions or nations would be disseminated to the public through policies and regulations. SDGs' ability to transcend time and space on economic, social and environmental dimensions depends on learning from each other. The good practices of an institution or a nation should be made accessible to other institutions and nations on a common platform. Sometimes an economic sustainability problem in an Asian country can be solved by a practice in a European country. And sometimes a local NGO may inspire a multinational company about an issue of long-term environmental concern.

If SDGs claim to have a worldwide philosophy, this means that they shall focus on the common basics of all in the world instead of limited specific issues of some. That brings us to a major assumption that SDGs aim at determining and considering the basics of life. Basic economic, social and environmental measures and their progress are the primary aims of SDGs. However, those basics must be tracked and evaluated globally. A progress in one aspect of life in a region is necessary but not sufficient for a worldwide sustainable life. Special cases and isolated issues of excessive luxuries cannot be considered the aim of SDGs, whose objectives are assumed to accommodate a shared vision and the idea of the basic needs that make the world a better place. Everyone breathing on the Earth has to be aware of the impacts of his own existence on others free from the borders and governments. SDGs help all stakeholders to detect if their social, economic and natural environment is retrogressive or progressive and to overcome any obstacles of meeting their basic human needs. SDGs enable people to formulate interactions, trade-offs and mutual reinforcements between the three dimensions of sustainable development. SDGs create a systematic action plan within the three dimensions. In short, they help people to make their development decisions sustainable. SDGs create a systematic action plan for balancing the three dimensions (Purvis et al. 2018, p. 692) (Fig. 5.1).

COMPATIBILITY OF SDGs WITH SUSTAINABLE DEVELOPMENT BASED ON DIVINE PRINCIPLES

Kahf (2002) thinks that "the real challenge in the Muslim countries today is to develop new behavioural patterns of governance". He emphasizes that SDGs can only be achieved by "culture-friendly, development-motivating, societal institutions and policies" (p. 61). The success of the SDGs is expected to be even greater when the efforts equipped with divine principles and supported by institutional or political structures (Dariah et al. 2016, p. 165).

Divine Principles Relative to Sustainable Development

Islam encourages human beings to utilize earthly resources for production, consumption and distribution of wealth among all people. Such utilization is guided by divine principles from revelation and practices through observations. Islam looks at human being, regardless of their innate qualities and features, as an integrated whole. Human being is guided by the divine message of Allah (swt) in Qur'an and Sunnah, for using and distributing earthly resources to achieve salvation (Kahf 2014, pp. 6–9). According to Martı (2018), Islam establishes a universal ethical code for human beings to guide their attitudes, decisions and behaviours towards other humans, non-human beings and future livings on the Earth.

The following are some of the main principles that are derived from the divine messages of Allah (swt) in Qur'an and Sunnah which have relevance to SDGs. Firstly, the Oneness of Allah (swt). Based on this concept, Allah (swt) is the only supreme and humans are noble creations of Allah (swt). The attitude, decision and behaviours of humans shall be based on and emanate from divine messages by Allah (swt). Secondly, the Obedience to Allah (swt). Any quality and superiority among humans vary with their attitudes, decisions and behaviours towards worshipping

Allah. The more a believer avoids associating partners with Allah (swt) and works in His obedience, the higher is his status in the sight of Allah (swt). Thirdly, the Human Equality. All humans in the past, present and future are equal in the sight of Allah (swt) just like the teeth of a comb. No privileges are granted to anybody over others. Divine principles of Islam promote sustainability for all mankind, irrespective of whether one is a believer or not, and therefore, professing religion is not a limitation for the implementation of divine principles (Sarkawi et al. 2016, pp. 115–116).

Fourthly, the Vicegerency of Allah (swt) on Earth. The universe is created for mankind, and humans are given the advantage of benefitting from all its resources. Working and managing the resources for one's own benefits and for the benefits of others is a divine command upon all humanity. It is not confined to specific race, colour, religion or class. Availing resources is the task of every human being, believers or otherwise. Human beings need to be aware of their empowerment from Allah (swt) and act accordingly. Everything is a trust to human beings by Allah (swt), and they cannot imagine about the universe without the control of Allah (swt) (Martı 2018, s. 7–8). There are some key elements related to the vicegerency duty that need to be reflected upon:

a. Wisdom (Hikmah): It represents a common effort to knowingly and willingly take wisdom from all nationalities and internalize it. The cross-fertilization of inclusive knowledge, encouraged by the divine principles, is a critical element of turning societies into sustainable communities that accept sustainability as a way of life.
b. Justice (Adl): It is the sine qua non foundation of any good governing structure that represents a sustainable willpower based on human rights in broadest terms, emphasized by the divine principles.
c. Public Interest (Maslahah): It represents the public consensus that concludes the good for everyone based on the divine principles. This element forms a middle ground for all local and global communities.
d. Renewal and Innovation (Tecdid): It represents the intellectual capital and efforts derived from the divine revelation and guidance, to be used to solve the existing and emerging problems of humanity. It enables a continuous renewal process of methods for sustainable development (Aliyev and Aslanlı 2015, p. 43).

Fifthly, Accountability in front of Allah (swt). Everything that is done by an individual affects him or her and others that preceded him or her, his or her contemporary, and those that succeed him or her. There will be resurrection and a day of judgement where all individuals are held accountable for their deeds and rewarded accordingly. All actions of life, including the economic, social and environmental activities, are also forms of worship. Helping a poor person, facilitating the marriage of a couple, forestation, among others, are activities that invite the pleasure of Allah (swt). The Qur'an deems progress and development as good action (Kahf, Sustainable Development in Muslim Countries, 2002, p. 61). On the other hand, the distribution of wealth and the use of resources change from time to time between individuals, nations and generations. Human beings are responsible and held accountable for the usage of what they acquired within these given periods.

Compatibility of SDGs with Sustainable Development Based on Al-Maqasid

The previous sections discussed the philosophy and concept of SDGs as well as the divine principles in relation to sustainable development. This section focuses on determining and analysing the compatibility of SDGs with sustainable development concepts based on divine principles. To facilitate to the reader, the section is structured into four subsections to discuss the compatibility of SDGs with sustainable development concepts based on divine principles. These four subsections are: the concept of Maslahah, the concept of needs, the concept of limitations and the concept of objectives.

The Concept of Maslahah

Maslahah or well-being is the pillar of divine principle related to the objective of Shari'ah. Broadly speaking, every activity, including development, must aim at achieving Maslahah and avoid Mafsadah (harm). Maslahah extends to human, society and the environment. In relation to SDGs, Maslahah encompasses all the three dimensions: economic, social and environment. The scholar of Maqasid al-Shari'ah has categorized Maslahah into three:

> Necessities (dharûrriyât); that are essential or indispensable
> Conveniences (hâjiyyât); that are complementary to the necessities

5 ANALYSIS OF THE COMPATIBILITY OF SDGS … 97

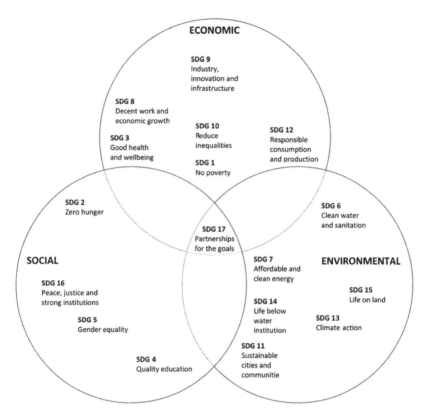

Fig. 5.1 The Venn-diagram Model applied of SDG Goals (*Note* The dimensions of SD are mostly shown with simple illustrations, such as Venn-diagram model, Russian-doll model, 3-pillar model or wedding cake model, to reflect the jointly balanced pillars of SD. Here, the preferred illustration for the SDGs are Venn-diagram model)

> Beautifications (tahsîniyyât); that are comforts and embellishments. (Kahf 2014)

These three categories of Maslahah create the basis of legal decisions, rulings and judgements independently, and they don't require additional reference for judgement. The necessities must be secured by the state, legal system, society and members of society (Orman 2018). On the other hand, conveniences and beautifications require additional references for judgement, and they are conditions for individual preferences (Kahf 2014). This key approach of Islamic tradition opens the main gate for us to approach and evaluate the compatibility of SDGs to sustainable development based on divine principles.

The activities of humans shall care and foster environment and protect human rights based on the divine principles of Maslahah. Therefore, today's activities for meeting the economic, social and environmental needs shall ensure that they do not compromise the necessities (dharuriyyat) of life in social, environmental and economic field in future (Aburounia and Sexton 2006). This view overlaps SDGs' point of origin perfectly. SDGs can be identified in two basic concepts according to the Brundtland Report: "the concept of needs" and "the concept of limitations" (WCED 2019, p. 41). These two concepts are the key terms that relate SDGs to the divine principles. The first one is to seek the compatibility of the intention of SDGs, while the second one is to seek the compatibility of the method of activities for achieving SDGs. An additional concept must be pointed when looking at the compatibility of SDGs based on the divine principles. That's the "concept of objectives" structured onto the other two concepts. This concept is to seek the compatibility of the outcome of activities for achieving SDGs.

The Concept of Needs

SDGs are introduced within the concept of needs as the essentials of the people living in poverty and those essentials must be supplied as a priority (WCED 2019, p. 41). The essentials are common and usually do not change between nations and cultures: an honourable life with sufficient water, food, dress, shelter and health care and the ability to develop to obtain these necessities by an individual within a community without causing harm to anyone.

In parallel to this, the necessities (dharuriyyat) mentioned in the first level of Maslahah are the point of origin to every economic, social and environmental behaviour, activity and transaction of human beings. Therefore, Islamic law addresses these basic needs as a must to be supplied for all human beings. This creates a right on the needy members of the society and the members with abilities are entitled to meet the needs of others in this manner. Today's wealthy can fall into poverty tomorrow and today's needy can be converted to tomorrow's benevolent. People will be questioned about how they behaved in their good and bad circumstances.

The concept of needs (dharuriyyat) helps us to determine the extent of SDGs needs and their priorities in relation to our economic, social and environmental aspects. Any SDG needs must be carefully defined, understood and evaluated based on this concept so that it does not lead to any wrong activity or outcome from the beginning.

The Concept of Limitations
SDGs are introduced within the idea of limitations assuming that the environment's capacity of supplying essentials of today and tomorrow is insufficient due to unfair distribution and excessive consumption. SDGs imply limitations on natural resources imposed by the technological and social structure that considers the ability of the Earth to negate the effects of human activities. That's why technological and social improvement shall be balanced with the ecological changes (WCED 2019, pp. 16, 41).

Divine principles oblige human being to seek the pleasure of Allah (swt) in their every economic behaviour, activity and transaction. According to the Qur'an, the path to the pleasure of God is through adding value to human life and serving other human beings. This philanthropic and altruistic approach embedded in the concept of divine principles is supposed to be the internal limitation in parallel to the external physical limitations addressed by SDGs. Divine principles put a limitation on consumption by calling humans to avoid extravagance and consume modestly (Kahf, Sustainable Development in Muslim Countries, 2002, p. 21). Higher rates of savings create an internal resource for investments and philanthropic activities which attract the pleasure and blessing of Allah (swt). This allows sustainable development to achieve wider welfare both in material and in moral terms. The concept of limitations helps to determine how to achieve SDGs in economic, social and natural environment. Any activity planned for achieving an SDG must be evaluated based on this concept without losing the essence and intention of SDG.

The Concept of Objectives
It is a known fact that sustainable development operationalizes its objectives through SDGs. SDGs serve as a global compass that guides economic, social and environmental life (KPMG International 2015, p. 11). No matter how many goals are determined, their common objective is to build a sustainable human life on the three dimensions: environmental, social and economic at the same time. The fundamental

rights of human beings can only be provided in a social, economic and natural environment that permits a quality life with "dignity and well-being" (WCED 2019, p. 271).

The major teaching of Islam that is revealed by Allah (swt) created humans as the highest of all creatures in the universe, and all other creations are subservient to humans to achieve their main goal of knowing, loving and obeying Allah. Therefore, humans shall make the best use of all the things controlled by them, with the sense of accountability and justice.

Since the divine principles cover all the human-related actions and ideas, they offer more than any other economic, social and natural system offer. It is not a surprise to have some common objectives between the divine principles and other human systems. However, the outcome must not contradict the clear rules of Islamic tenets, which are always for the benefit of human being even though they don't understand it. Establishing justice and respect for human dignity must be positioned as the first and best outcome of SDGs.

There are five commonly accepted objectives under divine principles known as *"Maqasidal-Shari'ah"*. These five basic objectives correspond to basic human needs. Therefore, they are aspects to be considered for the constitution of SDGs. The objectives of SDGs must aspire to preserve and sustain at least one of the elements listed below:

1. Preservation of faith/religion (deen)
2. Preservation of life (nafs)
3. Preservation of mind/intellect (aql)
4. Preservation of lineage/progeny (nasl)
5. Preservation of wealth/property (mâl) (Dariah et al. 2016, p. 161).

The concept of objectives helps us to determine what SDGs could achieve in the economic, social and environment and provides the benchmark for the progress of SDGs. Any activity planned for achieving an SDG must be evaluated based on this concept without leading to any unwanted and unproductive outcome in the end.

Conclusion and the Way Forward

This chapter initially addressed the origins of sustainable development tracing how the Western world discovered it, and the chapter pointed out the reasons for the Islamic world adopting this concept late. Due to world politics and wars, Muslim communities abandoned their institutional structure, which embodies the main concepts of sustainable development. The scattered relations of Muslim communities and the political and economic hegemony of the Western powers resulted in an import of alien concepts to Muslim institutions. SDGs were also imported in stock and barrel.

Therefore, there is a need for developing a methodology of assessing SDGs based on divine principles that shall guide Muslims to understand their objectives and motives. Even though a set of goals for sustainability are defined by a collective international structure, they must be analysed with reference to divine principles for being claimed as universal and useful. Such analysis is not only confined to the definition of SDGs but also extends to their methods and objectives. Similarly, steps taken for achieving SGDs must also be questioned for their compatibility with divine principles.

Following the categorization of current SDGs, based on the supportive concepts between SDG and divine principles, a three-step assessment process is suggested in this paper, for evaluating the determination, implementation and objectives of SDGs. As discussed in the last section of this paper, SDGs relate to divine principles in three main concepts:

1. The Concept of Needs.
2. The Concept of Limitations.
3. The Concept of Objectives.

Therefore, the issues of compatibility of all existing and future SDGs with the divine principles could be evaluated based on these three steps of concepts. Firstly, the intention of an SDG must be evaluated based on the concept of needs. Secondly, the method of achieving an SDG must be evaluated based on the concept of limitations. Lastly, the outcome of achieving the SDG must be evaluated based on the concept of objectives.

Muslim nations have a chance to play a significant role in the achievement of SDGs with reference to their divine principles that bring an inclusive approach to all human-creator, human-human and human-environment relationships. There is a huge area for Muslims to reflect and highlight their abilities on SDGs. This shall trigger a win-win process globally when the Islamic governments, Muslim communities and Muslim businessmen discover their potential to contribute to the achievement of SDGs based on the divine principles and the international communities take the advantage of bringing such dimensions to the attention of SDGs to policymakers.

The common problems of our world cannot be solved without enabling the contributions of all cultures. All the opportunities shall be seriously considered and discussed with their pros and cons, and so divine principles should not be left out given their huge potentials and contributions to development. The divine principles shall be recognized and examined closely through all current and possible future SDG themes. The SDGs will offer a positive impact worldwide as they are defined and applied in connection with the divine principles. Muslim communities shall embrace SDGs based on divine principles into their business and life and track their practical measures to introduce their contributions and improvements on SDGs to the world.

Taking all these suggestions into considerations would have far-reaching outcomes for SDGs. Firstly, global institutions would be encouraged to involve Muslim stakeholders more in their discussion and decision processes. Secondly, it would activate Muslim communities on SDGs and increase their involvement. Thirdly, Muslim stakeholders would be highly motivated to implement the process of SDGs compatible with divine principles. Finally, there will be increasing attention and interest on divine sources of Islam in relation to SDGs. All these are in line with the notion that inclusive partnerships built upon principles and values, a shared vision and shared goals that place people and the planet at the centre are needed at the global, regional, national and local level (KPMG International 2015).

References

Aburounia, H. M., & Sexton, M. (2006). Islam and Sustainable Development. In G. Aouad (Ed.), *The 3rd International Salford Centre for Research and Innovation (SCRI) Research Symposium: In Conjunction with the International Built and Human Environment Research Week* (pp. 757–764). Rotterdam: School of Construction & Property Management, University of Salford.

5 ANALYSIS OF THE COMPATIBILITY OF SDGS ... 103

Ahmed, H. (2017, November 29). *Contribution of Islamic Finance to the 2030 Agenda for Sustainable Development*. 40. Durham, UK: Durham University Business School.

Ahmed, H., Mohieldin, M., Verbeek, J., & Aboulmagd, F. (2015, May). *On the Sustainable Development Goals and the Role of Islamic Finance* (Policy Research Working Paper 7266).

Ajanovic, N. (2017). Islamic Finance and SDGs. In I. D. Bank (Ed.), *High-Level Conference on Financing for Development and the Means of Implementation of the 2030 Agenda for Sustainable Development* (p. 24). Doha.

Aliyev, E., & Aslanlı, K. (2015). İslam Ülkelerinin Sürdürülebilir Kalkınma Performansı; Kavramlar, Teoriler, Ölçümler. *Avrasya Etüdleri, 47*(1), 37–70.

Dariah, A. R., Salleh, M. S., & Shafiai, H. M. (2016). A New Approach for Sustainable Development Goals in Islamic Perspective. *Procedia—Social and Behavioral Sciences, 219*, 159–166.

Helvacıoğlu, M., Bulut, M., El-Amri, M. C., & Mohammed, M. O. (2020, June 14–20). *A Critical Analysis of the Economic Dimensions of SDGs Based on Islamic Economics Perspective* (Conference presentation). Istanbul, Turkey: 12th International Conference on Islamic Economics & Finance. Retrieved from https://www.youtube.com/watch?v=Y7l0QYLpvcw&t=7625s.

Kahf, M. (2002). *Sustainable Development in Muslim Countries*. monzer.kahf.com. Retrieved October 5, 2020, from http://monzer.kahf.com/papers/english/Sustainable_development_Revised_First_Draft.pdf.

Kahf, M. (2014). *Notes on Islamic Economics; Theories and Institutions (Book 1)*. Westminister: Monzer Kahf.

KPMG International. (2015). *SDG Industry Matrix: Financial Services*. United Nations Global Compact.

Martı, H. (2018, February). İslam, Çevre ve Ahlak. Diyanet Aylık Dergi (326), 6–9. October 5, 2020 tarihinde T.C. Diyanet İşleri Başkanlığı Din Hizmetleri Genel Müdürlüğü: https://www2.diyanet.gov.tr/DiniYay%C4%B1nlarGenelMudurlugu/DergiDokumanlar/Aylik/2018/subat_aylik.pdf.

Orman, S. (2018). Al-Ghazâlî on Justice and Social Justice. *Turkish Journal of Islamic Economics, 5*(2), 1–68.

Purvis, B., Mao, Y., & Robinson, D. (2018). Three Pillars of Sustainability: In Search of Conceptual Origins. *Sustainability Science, 14,* 681–695.

Sarkawi, A. A., Abdullah, A., & Dali, N. M. (2016, April). The Concept of Sustainability from the Islamic Perspectives. *International Journal of Business, Economics and Law, 9*(5), 112–116.

WCED. (2019, December 16). *Report of the World Commission on Environment and Development: Our Common Future*. Retrieved from Sustainable Development Goals Knowledge Platform: https://sustainabledevelopment.un.org/content/documents/5987our-common-future.pdf.

CHAPTER 6

Integrated Islamic Social and Commercial Finance to Achieve SDGs

Ascarya and Ugi Suharto

INTRODUCTION

In Islam, the commercial and social activities had never been dichotomized. Early Islamic society, for example, was showing a rich Companion of the Prophet (p.b.u.h.), Uthman ibn Affan, bought a well from a Jew named Ruma for two million dirhams and allowed the society to consume as much water as they needed for free. In another occasion, Uthman also gave up all of his trading merchandises, comprising a thousand camels full with wheat and food, as a charity for the poor section of the society when Madinah suffered a drought during the period of Caliphate of Abu Bakr. Personal economic motives have been blended with the social economic concerns in this example of early Islam.

In the modern time, there is a concept of TBL (Triple Bottom Line) in conventional social finance aiming for the objectives of outreaching,

---

Ascarya (✉)
Institut Agama Islam Tazkia, Bogor, Indonesia

U. Suharto
University of Buraimi, Al Buraimi, Oman

© The Author(s), under exclusive license to Springer Nature Switzerland AG 2021
M. M. Billah (eds.), *Islamic Wealth and the SDGs*,
https://doi.org/10.1007/978-3-030-65313-2_6

105

sustainability, and welfare impacts which seem cannot be achieved by itself (Zeller and Meyer 2002). One of the reasons is that the conventional commercial finance emphasizing solely on commercial motives makes it incompatible with the concept of TBL. Meanwhile, there is a kind of a transformation of social missions to reach the poor section of the society and try to improve the welfare of communities into more profitable sustainable commercial missions (Armendariz et al. 2013) which are still preserving the basis of commercialization.

Islamic social finance, however, can achieve the TBL goals (Ascarya 2016). There is already an Islamic social finance instrument through zakat, for example, which is obligatory upon rich Muslims to pay. In addition, there is also another social instrument called "waqf" which is encouraging rich Muslims to involve in it. These instruments will drive the economy and create commercial and social investment. Furthermore, Islamic commercial finance calls upon the community to be more productive in the real sector. Islamic finance also encourages well-managed business partnership-based and ethically based business activities.

The Islamic Research and Training Institute (IRTI)–Islamic Development Bank (IDB) published two series of reports on Islamic Social Finance in 2014 and 2015, respectively. The fact that the IRTI-IDB has extended its focus from Islamic commercial finance to Islamic social finance shows the importance of this sector. The reports provided information about the developments, future challenges, and prospects for different sectors of Islamic social finance covering both the regions of South and Southeast Asian countries (Indonesia, India, Pakistan, Bangladesh, Malaysia, Singapore, and Brunei Darussalam) and sub-Saharan African countries (Sudan, Nigeria, Kenya, Mauritius, South Africa, and Tanzania).

Social and Commercial Finance in Islam

Islamic Social Finance

The Islamic Research Institute (IRTI) in its 2015 annual report pointed out that the scope of Islamic social finance includes institutions which work with the Islamic tradition of financing humanity using instruments such as charity, sadaqa, and waqf. It also covers aid-based institutions such as qard (interest-free loan) and assurance (kafala), as well as microfinance institutions aimed at reducing poverty. Another instrument, Zakat, can also be included to meet the most important needs of the poor, such as food, clothing, and shelter. The objective of all the instruments is to enable these unfortunate classes to move to a better level so that they can turn into more productive citizens and make more meaningful contributions to economic life.

In order to attain the objectives, this vulnerable group is certainly in need of help and support through the social finance. In order to elevate them from the dependence on donations to the development of enhanced skills through which these people can earn an income, it is necessary to set up social finance in both its personal and institutional forms. The poverty level of these people can also be eradicated via mechanism of social financing. At the most basic level, poverty is characterized as the obstruction of opportunities and the ability to make choices (i.e., the denial of choices and opportunities). This is an area in which Islamic social finance can play its role in terms of creating and providing opportunities for the less fortunate groups of the society. All these possibilities can exactly be provided through Islamic charitable institutions such as zakat, waqf, and microfinance institutions.

In its practical level, we can cite Indonesia as an example. The establishment of the National Zakat Agency (Badan Amil Zakat Nasional, BAZNAS), Indonesia Waqf Board (Badan Wakaf Indonesia, BWI), as well as microfinance institutions such as Baitul Maal wat Tamwil (BMT), Islamic cooperatives, and others that have grown in Indonesia are tangible forms of Islamic social finance institutions that are inseparable in Islamic muamalah. What is instrumental today, on top of the personal donations in the form of zakat, infaq, and waqf, is the support of established institutions and organizations in the field of zakat, waqf, and microfinance as has been exemplified in Indonesia.

Islamic Commercial Finance

Islamic commercial finance is usually defined as the application of Shariah-based financing, especially through the banking system. Historically, the first modern Islamic bank was established in 1975 as Dubai Islamic Bank. This was subsequently followed by other Islamic banks around the world, such as Bahrain Islamic Bank (1979), Bank Islam Malaysia Berhad (1983), Bank Muamalat (1991) in Indonesia, and Bank Nizwa (2013) in Oman. Over the course of four decades, Islamic banks all over the world have been established in more than 60 countries (IMF, Press Release no 17/53).

Islamic commercial finance, represented by Islamic banking institution, relates to profit-motivated financial institutions by complying with the principles of the Shariah as the cornerstone of their theories and operations. The usury (ribawi) system, which is the backbone of conventional banking, is replaced by a system based on fiqh al-muamalat, such as buying and selling, leasing, and profit sharing. Any Islamic banking product or service must pass through a specific verdict (fatwa) of the Muslim jurists ('ulama) to ensure that it must be Shariah compliance. The Shariah Supervisory Board (SSB), whether at the institutional level or at the national level, becomes the essential part of the Islamic banking organizational structure.

Islamic Financial Institutions that are originally run merely for-profit motive and commercial activity in a Shariah-compliant way are gradually integrating their efforts into a socially financial institution themselves. In addition to being influenced by the external development of social contributions from conventional banking in the form of the Corporate Social Responsibility (CSR) concept, Islamic banking is also influenced by the internal Shariah system itself. Just to cite as an example, almost every Islamic bank is allocating its zakat payment from profits earned or from owned assets. Zakat is a good example of social finance in Islamic financial system.

Integration of Islamic Social and Commercial Finance

At the structural level, there is an urgent need to look into a close relationship between the commercial finance and the social finance in the form of a business organization. On top of the concepts such as CSR and TBL outlined above, as used by conventional financial institutions as part of their attempts to link the commercial and social financial activities, the concepts of zakat, infaq, qard, and waqf can certainly be integrated into Islamic commercial and social financial unified institutions as well.

In fact, Islamic muamalah does not condone a dichotomy between the taking of commercial advantage and providing social assistance. This is guided by the Qur'anic verse that states "In their possessions there is a certain right to the one who asks for help and for the one who is deprived of the opportunity" (Al-Ma'arij 70: 24–25; Al-Dzariyat 51: 19). If this injunction can be practiced at the personal and private level, the same can also be exercised at the institutional level. In the modern time of course, the integration between commercial and social finance must be carried out in the form of financial institutions such as Islamic commercial banks and other types of financial institutions.

The purpose of this study, therefore, is to attempt to find suitable models for the meaningful integration of the commercial and social financial systems within a Shariah-compliant financial business organization. Despite its complexities, it is hoped that there will be a continuation of this study so that efforts to obtain the best and appropriate model can be achieved. In accordance with Islamic principle of non-separation between commercial finance and social activities, the writers are confident that in the near future there will emerge strong and well-established Islamic Financial Institutions which can forge an ideal linkage between the commercial and social financial practices that are needed by the world community.

MODELS OF INTEGRATED ISLAMIC SOCIAL AND COMMERCIAL FINANCE

The integration model can be implemented at various levels, namely: (1) Islamic Bank Model at the national level; (2) Islamic Community Bank Model at the community level; and (3) Islamic Microfinance Model at the micro-level. The integration model at the national level can be implemented by Islamic banks, including Islamic commercial banks (BUS), Islamic business units (UUS), and Islamic regional development banks (Islamic BPD), especially those that have been registered as Islamic financial institution–receiver of cash waqf (IFI-RCW), which means they are ready as recipient of the cash waqf collected by the Nazir of cash waqf. In this study, we will focus on the integration model in the national level, which could have several variations. Each integration model will be discussed in detail.

Integrated Islamic Commercial and Social Bank

a. IBANK-1 Model

In this IBANK-1 model, Islamic bank acts as IFI of zakat institution that collects zakat, infaq, and sadaqa (ZIS) funds and as IFI-RCW for waqf institution that collects cash waqf.

Islamic bank as IFI of zakat institution collects deposits of ZIS funds, including zakat and infaq (ab) from the wealthy Muslims as zakat payer (muzakki) or general donor. These ZIS funds would be distributed by zakat institution for consumptive programs (a) and productive programs (b). ZIS funds usually be distributed within one lunar/Islamic calendar. The productive programs, in the form of qardh financing (benevolent loan), are intended to assist the poor (mustahiq) to establish micro-business/enterprise (ME) to get out of poverty. The successful MEs could then expand their businesses by getting micro-small financing from the Islamic bank.

Meanwhile, Islamic bank as IFI-RCW of waqf institution collects deposits of direct cash waqf (y) and indirect cash waqf (xz) from waqf donor (waqif) for designated waqf institution. Then, waqf institution could use the direct cash waqf for its intended use (such as build a mosque or establish productive waqf facility), as well as invest the indirect cash waqf to financial sector with the Islamic bank as waqf investment deposits (x), or invest the cash waqf in the real sector (z). The returns from financial sector (r_1) and real sector (r_2) would be used by waqf institution to finance various social programs ($r = r_1 + r_2$).

In the organizational structure of Islamic bank applying the IBANK-1 model, there is no work unit or staff specifically assigned to manage ZIS, while Islamic bank as obligatory zakat payer would pay its company zakat directly to the selected zakat institutions, including zakat and infaq collected from employees and customers.

Examples of Islamic banks applying the IBANK-1 model include Bank Bukopin Syariah, Bank CIMB Niaga Syariah, BRI Syariah, and Islamic Regional Development Bank (BPD) of Central Java.

b. IBANK-2 Model

IBANK-2 model has similarity with IBANK-1 model, where Islamic bank acts as IFI of zakat institution that collects zakat, infaq, and sadaqa (ZIS) funds and as IFI-RCW for waqf institution that collects cash waqf. In addition, the Islamic bank also forms social unit as zakat collection unit (ZCU) of zakat institution.

Islamic bank in this model forms social unit as ZCU of zakat institution and collects ZIS from the bank itself, the employees, the customers, as well as from general Muslim society. This social unit also carries out the duties of Islamic bank as IFI for zakat institutions and as IFI-RCW of waqf institutions, as described in the previous model. ZIS collected by the social unit will be passed on to the parent zakat institution to be distributed to mustahiq (zakat beneficiaries) in the form of consumptive program (a) and productive program (b). The rest is similar as described in the previous model of IBANK-1.

In cash waqf collection, this social unit carries out the duties of Islamic bank as IFI-RCW of waqf institutions. Cash waqf received will be passed on to respected waqf institutions (yz) or be invested in the Islamic bank (x) as ordered by the waqf institution. The rest is similar as described in the previous model of IBANK-1.

Within the organizational structure of the Islamic bank applying IBANK-2 model, there is already a work unit (social unit) specifically assigned to manage ZIS collected from employees, customers, and general Muslim society. Meanwhile, Islamic bank zakat as zakat payer is channeled directly to the social unit as ZCU, so that it can be recorded as a tax deduction.

An example of a Islamic bank applying the IBANK-2 model is the Islamic Regional Development Bank (BPD) DKI Jakarta, which has been registered as IFI-RCW. Zakat Management Unit with 6 (six) staff collects zakat and infaq and distributes it in the form of consumptive programs and productive programs. Cash waqf received will be forwarded to Indonesian Waqf Board (BWI) as Nazir.

c. **IBANK-3 Model**

IBANK-3 model is a further development of IBANK-2 model, where Islamic bank established Baitul Maal, which could be registered as amil of zakat collecting ZIS. As IFI-RCW of waqf institution, the Islamic bank receives cash waqf collected by waqf institutions.

Baitul Maal of Islamic bank as amil collects ZIS (ab) using (or deposited in) Islamic bank account from Islamic bank itself, Islamic bank employees, Islamic bank customers, and general Muslim society, which subsequently distributes the collected ZIS for consumptive program (a)

and productive program (b). Zakat has to be distributed to eight types of mustahiq, while infaq and sadaqa could be distributed to mustahiq or non-mustahiq. Infaq and sadaqa could also be used for various social programs for general society.

Islamic bank as IFI-RCW of waqf institutions receives cash waqf (xyz) collected by waqf institutions and deposited in Islamic bank accounts, which then will be used as initially intended, such as indirect cash waqf invested in the investment account of the Islamic bank (x), direct cash waqf invested in the real sector (z), and direct cash waqf to build waqf facilities (social waqf or productive waqf).

Within the organizational structure of Islamic bank applying the IBANK-3 model, Baitul Maal as a foundation is established by the Islamic bank on behalf of commissioners and can be registered as regional or national zakat institution. The management of the Baitul Maal is totally separated from the Islamic bank. The Baitul Maal as zakat institution would have collection division and disbursement division.

Examples of Islamic banks with the IBANK-3 model are: (1) Bank Syariah Mandiri (BSM) which established LAZNAS BSM, national zakat institution, as Baitul Maal that manages ZIS, and BSM serves as IFI of several zakat institutions and IFI-RCW of several waqf institutions; and (2) Bank BNI Syariah (BNIS) which established LAZ, regional zakat institution, as Baitul Maal that manages ZIS, and BNIS is the IFI of several zakat institutions and the IFI RCW of several waqf institutions, such as the Indonesian Waqf Board (BWI), Global Waqf, Dompet Dhuafa, Rumah Zakat, and Zakat Al-Azhar.

d. **IBANK-4 Model**

IBANK-4 model is an expansion of IBANK-3 model, where the Baitul Maal established by the Islamic bank is registered not only as amil of zakat collecting ZIS, but is also registered as Nazir of waqf capable of collecting all types of waqf.

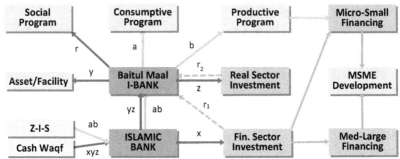

Islamic bank as IFI could establish Baitul Maal which is then registered as zakat institution and waqf institution, while the Islamic bank serves as IFI and IFI-RCW of the Baitul Maal in receiving ZIS funds and cash waqf. The Islamic bank still also serves as IFI and IFI-RCW of other zakat and waqf institutions as described in IBANK-1 model. The Baitul Maal of Islamic bank collects ZIS funds (ab) using Islamic bank accounts, which will be distributed to the mustahiq in the forms of consumptive program (a) to fulfill the basic needs and productive program (b) to provide qardh financing to develop micro-business/enterprise.

The Baitul Maal of Islamic bank also collects cash waqf (xyz), direct and indirect, deposited in Islamic bank's accounts. Direct cash waqf could be intended to build social and/or productive waqf facilities, while indirect cash waqf could be invested in financial sector (x) or in the real sector (z). The returns of productive waqf (r) would be used to finance social waqf facilities and social programs.

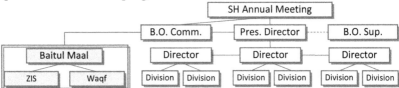

Within the organizational structure of the IBANK-4 model, Baitul Maal, which was established on behalf of the Islamic bank's commissioners, was registered as zakat institution (regional or national level) and waqf institution. ZIS and waqf from employees, customers, and Islamic banks as zakat payer are collected by the Baitul Maal.

Examples of Islamic bank applying the IBANK-4 model are Bank Muamalat Indonesia (BMI), which established Baitul Maal Muamalat (BMM) registered as national zakat institution and waqf institution.

e. IBANK-5 Model

IBANK-5 model is a real integrated Islamic commercial and social finance within Islamic bank, where it has Islamic bank division and Baitul Maal division within the bank, and the Baitul Maal division is registered as zakat institution and is also registered as waqf institution.

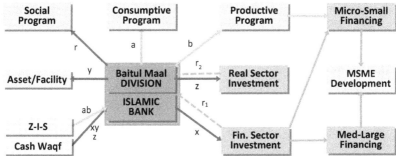

Islamic bank adopting IBANK-5 model is mimicking Baitul Maal wat Tamwil (BMT) described in the previous section, where the Islamic bank establishes Baitul Maal division to carry out Islamic social finance (ISF) as Amil of zakat and Nazir of waqf using ISF instruments, ZIS, and waqf. Meanwhile, the Islamic bank carries out Islamic commercial finance offering Islamic banking services, as well as acts as IFI of zakat institution and IFI-RCW of waqf institution. Baitul Maal division as Amil of zakat collects zakat, infaq, and sadaqa (ZIS) funds (ab) deposited in the Islamic bank accounts, to be distributed to mustahiq through consumptive program (a) and productive program (b). Since the Islamic bank has Baitul Maal division, the productive program could be carried out fully including qardh financing, weekly meeting, skill training, and technical assistance to guide mustahiq to establish micro-business/enterprise.

Baitul Maal division as Nazir of waqf collects all types of waqf, such as land and building. Cash waqf collection (xyz) will be deposited with the Islamic bank, where direct cash waqf would be used as initially intended to build social waqf facilities (y) or to establish productive waqf in the real sector (z). Indirect cash waqf would be invested in productive waqf, either in the real sector (z) or in the financial sector (x). Baitul Maal division will also manage the productive waqf returns (r) and organize various social programs for the general society, such as free health care and free education.

Within the organizational structure of the IBANK-5 model, there will be a division of Baitul Maal led by a director, which formed specifically to manage Islamic social finance, including ZIS and waqf. Example of Islamic bank applying IBANK-5 model does not yet exist, because some laws do not allow Islamic bank to become Amil of zakat or Nazir of waqf. Amendments of Islamic bank Act and related regulations are needed to allow Islamic bank to become Amil of zakat and Nazir of waqf.

f. IBANK-6 Model

IBANK-6 model is a corporate model where in the corporate level zakat institution and waqf institution are established to manage Islamic social finance. The Islamic bank will serve as IFI of the zakat institution and as IFI-RCW of the waqf institution.

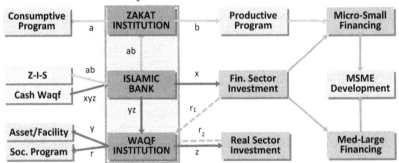

Islamic bank adopting IBANK-6 model operates similar to IBANK-1 as IFI of zakat institutions and IFI-RCW of waqf institutions. However, in corporate level, it has close collaboration with zakat institution and waqf institution established by the corporation, where all Islamic social finance activities in the zakat and waqf institutions could be integrated with Islamic commercial finance activities in the Islamic bank. The zakat programs in the zakat institution and waqf programs in the waqf institution could be carried out professionally and fully in coordination with the Islamic bank's programs. The key performance indicator (KPI) of the

Islamic bank could also be integrated with the KPI of the zakat and waqf institutions.

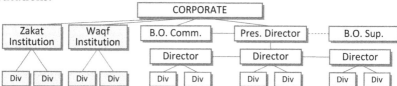

The organizational structure of the IBANK-6 model within the corporation is in the same level with the organizational structure of the zakat and waqf institutions established by the corporation. The zakat institution would have collection division and disbursement division, as well as other divisions needed, such as risk management division and internal control division. Meanwhile, the waqf institution would have at least collection division, investment division and social program division. Example of BUS-6 model does not yet exist, but it does not rule out the possibility of this IBANK-6 model in the future.

Discussion

Islamic banks before managing ZIS-Waf funds generally did not have funding problems where the financing to deposit ratio (FDR) was less than 100%, but during the crisis FDR increased above 100% (averaging around 104% in 2008 and 100% in 2012 and 2013) so they were dependent from other sources (Other Liabilities) to meet their needs. During the 2012–2014 crisis, ROA and ROE declined dramatically (from 2.1 to 0.4% and from 24.1 to 4.2% at the end of 2014), while NPF and BOPO increased dramatically (from 2.2 to 4.3% and from 0.75 to 0.97 at the end 2014). Islamic banks are very vulnerable to financial crisis. In the era of COVID-19 pandemic, Islamic banks are exposed to two problems at the same time in assets side as well as in liabilities side. In assets side, many borrowers could not pay their installments due to decline in their businesses or forced unemployment, so that non-performance financing (NPF) increases sharply. In liabilities side, many depositors withdraw their savings to support their daily life due to income loss/decrease.

Moreover, commercial banks, including Islamic banks, have some structural weaknesses because they apply fractional reserve banking system (FRBS) and leverage system. FRBS, which is applied by commercial banks, and leverage system, which is implemented by investment banks, where these banks can provide credit/financing far greater than the deposits collected thus can create bubbles (and inflation) which is one of the causes of the financial and banking crisis. The problem of FRBS in commercial banks is not only voiced by Islamic economists, such as Othman et al. (2012, p. 12), Trabelsi (2011, p. 17), Mirakhor and Krichene (2009, pp. 14–15), Meera and Larbani (2004, p. 10), and Garcia et al. (2004, p. 1), but also put forward by conventional economists, such as Stiglitz (2010, p. 325) and Claessens et al. (2010, p. 9). Meanwhile, the problem of leverage systems in investment banks was raised by many Islamic economists, such as Ahmed (2010, p. 318), Smolo and Mirakhor (2010, p. 372), Hassan and Kayed (2009, p. 36), Mirakhor and Krichene (2009, p. 26), Siddiqi (2009, p. 3), Ahmed (2009, p. 15), and Chapra (2007, pp. 165 and 166), and also suggested by conventional economists such as Claessens et al. (2010, p. 7).

Furthermore, the pool of funds system creates problems of mismatch and liquidity that prolonged without any real solution, because bank deposits are short-term funds from many small deposits which are channeled to medium/long-term large credit/financing. Claessens et al. (2010, p. 6) stated that maturity mismatch is also one of the causes of the global financial crisis. Before managing ZIS and cash waqf from ISF activities of zakat institution and waqf institution, the balance sheets of Islamic bank look like table.

Assets	Liabilities
Cash	*Wadiah* demand deposit
Bank deposits	*Wadiah/Mudharabah* savings deposit
Receivables (*Murabahah, Qardh*, etc.)	*Mudharabah* investment deposit
Financing (*Mudharabah, Musharakah*, etc.)	Other liabilities
Services (*Fee-based Services*)	
Inventory	Reserves
Fixed assets	Capital

Islamic banks after managing ZIS and cash waqf funds slowly but surely have a source of funds from cash waqf (Long-Term Waqf Investment Deposits) which can replace their dependence from more expensive other sources (Other Liabilities). The more the Islamic banks are trusted by the public, the more the people choose to use Islamic banks, so that the sources of funds from depositors also increase. The nature of cash waqf (especially indirect cash waqf), which continuously increasing with infinite maturity, makes the problem of mismatch and liquidity risk decreases continuously. Vulnerability of Islamic banks to the financial crisis gradually diminishes with the ever-stronger liabilities. When cash waqf is intended to finance certain productive programs (commonly called indirect waqf), this scheme is more of an allocation of funds (not pool of funds) and asset driven (not liability driven), which makes Islamic banks operate more ideally, as stated by IFSB & IRTI-IDB (2010, p. 17), thereby minimizing bubble, mismatch, and liquidity risk.

In addition, the cash waqf can also be placed as capital participation (waqf capital) which, in addition to cheap funds, can also strengthen the capital standing of Islamic banks. This is in line with the statements of Stiglitz (2010, p. 325) and Claessens et al. (2010, p. 8) that one of the causes of the global financial crisis is the low capital of banks (undercapitalized) and the erosion/decline of bank capital. The existence of cash waqf on the capital side will also reduce the cost of funding for customers, because waqf capital is not part of the third-party funds deposited with the Islamic bank. The balance sheets of the Islamic bank after managing ZIS and cash waqf funds would look like table.

Assets	*Liabilities*
Cash	*Wadiah* demand deposit
Bank deposits	**Zakat savings deposit**
Receivables (*Murabahah, Qardh*, etc.)	*Wadiah/Mudharabah* savings deposit
Financing (*Mudharabah, Musharakah*, etc.)	*Mudharabah* Investment deposit
Services (*Fee-based Services*)	**Long-term Waqf investment deposit**
Long-term Investment	**Waqf capital**
Inventory	Reserves
Fixed assets	Capital

Waqf capital in Islamic banks can be obtained, among others, through the mechanism of "Initial Waqif Offering" (IWO) which is similar to an IPO (Initial Public Offering) of shares of companies that will go public, but this IWO is an offer representing a potential general waqif (including Islamic bank owners) on a large scale/target.

Integrated Islamic Commercial and Social Finance to Achieve SDGs

The idea of Sustainable Development Goals started in 2015 was inspired by the success of Millennium Development Goals (which seemed to be uneven across regions and countries, especially the most vulnerable by virtue of their sex, age, disability, ethnicity, or geographic location, to be achieved by 2030. Meanwhile, the goals of Sustainable Development Goals (SDGs) are to achieve a combination of economic development, environmental sustainability, and social inclusion (triple bottom line approach to human well-being), which are in line with the developmental motives of nations, while the multi-dimensional matrix of SDGs comprises more social goals (9 goals) and less economic goals (4 goals) or environmental goals (4 goals), suggesting the important role of social economic and finance. Islamic economic and finance could better address SDGs' goals, especially in improving the well-being of the poor and micro-enterprises, through integrated Islamic commercial and social finance (IICSF).

When Islamic banks apply IICSF model, it will not only make Islamic banks more resilience to financial crisis and more sustainable, but also it will make Islamic banks capable of playing their role in achieving all goals of SDGs, especially social goals using the addition of ISF instruments, including zakat, infaq, sadaqa, and waqf. Goals of SDGs could be achieved by using instruments of ICF (especially funding, financing, services, and takaful), by using instruments of ISF (especially zakat, infaq, and sadaqa), as well as by using the combination of instruments ICF and ISF, which can be seen in Table 6.1.

Table 6.1 shows that the commercial finance instruments, including Islamic commercial finance (ICF) instruments, could not be used to achieve all goals of SDGs, but it could be used to achieve economic goals of SDGs and it could be used as complement to achieve some social and environmental goals of SDGs. Meanwhile, Islamic social finance (ISF) instruments could be used to achieve all goals of SDGs. ISF instruments could be used to achieve all social goals of SDGs, as well as all environmental goals of SDGs. Moreover, ISF instruments, especially productive waqf, could be used to better achieve all economic goals, since waqf does not have shareholders.

6 INTEGRATED ISLAMIC SOCIAL ... 121

Table 6.1 ISF and ICF Instruments to Achieve SDGs

SDGS		Instruments	
Goal	Type	ICF	ISF
1. No poverty	Social		Zakat, infaq, waqf
2. Zero hunger	Social		Zakat, infaq, waqf
3. Good health & wellbeing	Social	Takaful, financing, Services	Zakat, infaq, waqf
4. Quality education	Social	Funding, takaful	Zakat, infaq, waqf
5. Gender equality	Social	Financing, services	Zakat, infaq, waqf
6. Clear water & sanitation	Environmental	Financing	Infaq, waqf
7. Affordable & clean energy	Social		Zakat, infaq, waqf
8. Decent work & Ec. growth	Economy	Financing, services, takaful	Zakat, infaq, waqf
9. Industry innovation & infrastructure	Economy	Financing, services, takaful	Waqf
10. Reduced inequalities	Economy	Financing, services, takaful	Zakat, infaq, waqf
11. Sustainable cities & communities	Social		Zakat, infaq, waqf
12. Responsible consumption & production	Economy	Financing, services, takaful	Waqf
13. Climate action	Environmental	Financing	Infaq, waqf
14. Life below water	Environmental		Infaq, waqf
15. Life on land	Environmental		Infaq, waqf
16. Peace, justice & strong institutions	Social		Infaq, waqf
17. Partnerships for the goals	Social		Infaq, waqf

Note ISF instruments could include zakat, infaq, waqf, sadaqa, hibah, hadiah, etc., but we summarized them into zakat (compulsory), infaq (compulsory/voluntary), and waqf (voluntary)

1. No Poverty

End extreme poverty in all forms. This goal can be achieved using ISF instruments, especially zakat for mustahiq to fulfill the basic needs using consumptive program and infaq to develop micro-business/enterprise (ME) to move out of poverty. Semi-commercial financing using cash waqf could be used for the transition period from social finance qardh financing to commercial finance Islamic micro-financing.

2. Zero Hunger

End hunger, achieve food security and improved nutrition, and promote sustainable agriculture. This is also part of fulfilling basic needs for mustahiq, which could be achieved using ISF instruments, especially zakat using consumptive program. Sustainable agriculture could be achieved by using productive waqf to develop agriculture, agro-business, and agro-industry. Moreover, infaq could be used as a complement of productive waqf projects to cover initial operational costs.

3. Good Health & Well-being

Ensure healthy lives and promote well-being for all at all ages. Health care is part of basic needs for mustahiq using consumptive program of zakat. Wealthy people could use healthcare takaful offered by Islamic bank, when health care could not be provided free by the government. Meanwhile, to improve the well-being of the poor could be achieved in three stages. Stage 1, the poor (mustahiq) will be given zakat through consumptive program to fulfill their basic needs. Stage 2, the poor will be involved in multi-level productive program of qardh financing using infaq to develop micro-businesses/enterprises (MEs). Stage 3. When the financing increases above the level of mustahiq, the poor have graduated from poverty and they will be provided with commercial micro-small financing to expand their businesses and improve their well-being further. For non-mustahiq, well-being improvement could be achieved using ICF instruments, including financing, services, and takaful.

4. Quality Education

Ensure inclusive and equitable quality education and promote lifelong learning opportunities for all. Education is also part of basic needs for mustahiq using consumptive program of zakat. Social waqf supported by productive waqf run by waqf institution could also provide free education for general society. Non-mustahiq could also use infaq scholarship provided by zakat/social institution, when education could not be provided free by the government. Moreover, education saving and education takaful could also be provided commercially by Islamic bank.

5. Gender Equality

Achieve gender equality and empower all women and girls. Although there is no gender inequality in Islam, if it is existed it can be resolved using ISF instruments if the affected subjects are mustahiq. Public services provided by social waqf would provide all public services with equality, such as in education, health care, and employment. Productive waqf could also provide and operate their businesses free of inequality in accordance with Shariah principles.

6. Clear Water & Sanitation

Ensure availability and sustainable management of water and sanitation for all. Clear water and sanitation are also part of basic needs for mustahiq, which could be fulfilled using zakat through consumptive program. The clear water and sanitation as public utility could also be provided using social waqf, combination of social-productive waqf, or productive waqf with commercial financing to provide free or cheap clear water and sanitation for general society.

7. Affordable & Clean Energy

Ensure access to affordable, reliable, sustainable, and modern energy for all. This goal could be achieved using ISF and ICF instruments similar to goal 6, since energy is also part of basic needs and public utility.

8. Decent Work & Economic Growth

Promote sustained, inclusive, and sustainable economic growth, full and productive employment, and decent work for all. This macroeconomic goal of SDGs could be achieved using the combination of ISF and ICF instruments, although this is more economic than social goal, since this is also part of the objective of Islamic economic and finance to achieve full employment and economic growth (Chapra 1985).

9. Industry Innovation & Infrastructure

Build resilient infrastructure, promote inclusive and sustainable industrialization, and foster innovation. Infrastructure is public goods, which should be provided by the government for free. Social waqf and productive waqf could help the government in providing these public goods for free. Industrialization and innovation are more economic goals, which could be achieved using ICF instruments or productive waqf. However, costly research and development could also be provided using combination of social-productive waqf.

10. Reduced Inequalities

Reduce inequality within and among countries. This macroeconomic goal of SDGs could be achieved similar to goal 8, using combination of ICF and ISF instruments, since this goal is also part of Islamic economic and finance objectives of justice and equitable distribution of income and wealth (Chapra 1985).

11. Sustainable Cities & Communities

Make cities and human settlements inclusive, safe, resilient, and sustainable. This goal needs more free or affordable public goods, such as public housing, public transport, and public spaces, which can be build using social waqf or combination of social-productive waqf. For mustahiq, these can be provided using ISF instruments.

12. Responsible Consumption & Production

Ensure sustainable consumption and production patterns. This goal can be reduced to dispose, reduce, and recycle waste in business, consumption, and production, which can be achieved through ICF instruments, such as responsible or green financing and services, and takaful mitigation, and ISF instruments, such as responsible or green social-productive waqf, including responsible or green sukuk link waqf.

13. Climate Action

Take urgent action to combat climate change and its impacts. To achieve this environmental goal by limiting the climate change requires political will and technological measures, including in financing. Meanwhile, to deal with the impacts of climate change, such as earthquakes, tsunamis, floods, and, ISF instruments, especially infaq and waqf, could be used to rebuild the impacted areas and help the people affected.

14. Life Below Water

Conserve and sustainably use the oceans, seas, and marine resources for sustainable development. This environmental goal also needs political will and technological measures not to abuse life below water. The impacts of abuse of ocean, such as clean the ocean, could be dealt with ISF instruments, especially infaq and waqf.

15. Life on Land

Protect, restore, and promote sustainable use of terrestrial ecosystems, sustainably manage forests, combat desertification, and halt and reserve land degradation and halt biodiversity loss. This is another environmental goal that requires political will and technological measures not to abuse life on land and conserve them. The efforts of conservations could be possible using ISF instruments, especially infaq and waqf.

16. Peace, Justice, & Strong Institutions

Promote peaceful and inclusive societies for sustainable development, provide access to justice for all, and build effective, accountable, and inclusive institutions at all levels. Peace and justice are also part of Islamic economic and finance goals to achieve well-being and prosperity in this world and the hereafter (Chapra 1985), and require political will, which can be promoted by applying Islamic values. Specific efforts to promote peace and justice could use ISF instruments, especially infaq and waqf.

17. Partnerships for the Goals

Strengthen the means of implementation and revitalize the global partnership for sustainable development. These global partnerships require political will. Specific efforts to involve in these global partnerships to achieve SDGs could use ISF instruments, especially infaq and waqf.

POLICY IMPLICATIONS

In order for Islamic bank to be able to manage Islamic social finance effectively, the Islamic bank has to be allowed to become Amil of zakat and Nazir of waqf officially, so that the management of Islamic commercial finance (ICF) and Islamic social finance (ISF) could be fully integrated within one management. The key performance indicator (KPI) of the employees managing ICF and ISF could be integrated to optimize the synergy between them. The collection of zakat, infaq, and waqf could be integrated into the front office and customer services of ICF, so that customers entering the Islamic bank could be targeted as potential donor of ISF, either as muzakki to pay zakat, as munfiq to participate in social programs financed by infaq, or as waqif to donate his/her assets to establish waqf facilities.

Meanwhile, the emergence of financial technology (fintech) has posed threat and opportunity for Islamic banking industry, in the commercial side as well as in the social side. Therefore, the future of Islamic bank implementing integrated Islamic commercial and social finance must adopt fintech for its ICF operation, especially in adopting digital banking, payments, and peer-to-peer (P2P) financing. Moreover, the future Islamic bank could also adopt fintech for its ISF operation, especially in adopting peer-to-peer (P2P) social to raise zakat, infaq, and waqf to reach out wider external potential donors.

REFERENCES

Ahmed, H. (2009). Financial Crisis: Risks and Lessons for Islamic Finance. *ISRA International Journal of Islamic Finance, 1*(1), 7–32.

Ahmed, A. (2010). Global Financial Crisis: An Islamic Finance Perspective. *International Journal of Islamic and Middle Eastern Finance and Management, 3*(4), 306–320.

Armendariz, B., D'Espallier, B., Hudon, M., & Szafarz, A. (2013). *Subsidy Uncertainty and Microfinance Mission Drift* (CEB Working Paper, 11).

Ascarya. (2016). Holistic Financial Inclusion Based on Maqashid Shariah Through Baitul Maal Wat Tamwil. *Middle East Insights: Islamic Finance Special, 1,* 1–8.

Chapra, M. U. (1985). *Towards a Just Monetary System: Islamic Economics Series-8.* Markfield, UK: The Islamic Foundation.

Chapra, M. U. (2007). The Case Against Interest: Is It Compelling? *Thunderbird International Business Review, 49*(2), 161–186.

Claessens, S., Dell'Ariccia, G., Igan, D., & Laeven, L. (2010). *Lesson and Policy Implications from the Global Financial Crisis* (IMF Working Paper, WP/10/44).

Garcia, V. F., Cibils, V. F., & Maino, R. (2004). Remedy for Banking Crises: What Chicago and Islam Have in Common. *Islamic Economic Studies, 11*(2), 1–22.

Hassan, M. K., & Kayed, R. N. (2009). The Global Financial Crisis, Risk Management and Social Justice in Islamic Finance. *ISRA International Journal of Islamic Finance, 1*(1), 33–58.

IFSB & IRTI-IDB. (2010). *Islamic Finance and Global Financial Stability*. Kuala Lumpur, Malaysia: Islamic Financial Services Board.

Meera, A. K. M., & Larbani, M. (2004). The Gold Dinar: The Next Component in Islamic Economics, Banking and Finance. *Review of Islamic Economics, 8*(1), 5–34.

Mirakhor, A., & Krichene, N. (2009). Recent Crisis: Lessons for Islamic Finance. *Journal of Islamic Economics, Banking and Finance, 5*(1), 9–57.

Othman, R., Aris, N. A., Azli, R. M., & Arshad, R. (2012). Islamic Banking: The Firewall Against the Global Financial Crisis. *The Journal of Applied Business Research, 28*(1), 9–14.

Siddiqi, M. N. (2009). Current Financial Crisis and Islamic Economics. In Islamic Economic Research Center (Ed.), *Issues in the International Financial Crisis from an Islamic Perspective* (pp. 1–10). Jeddah: Scientific Publishing Center King Abdulaziz University.

Smolo, E., & Mirakhor, A. (2010). The Global Financial Crisis and its Implications for the Islamic Financial Industry. *International Journal of Islamic and Middle Eastern Finance and Management, 3*(4), 372–385.

Stiglitz, J. E. (2010). Lessons from the Global Financial Crisis of 2008. *Seoul Journal of Economics, 23*(3), 321–339.

Trabelsi, M. A. (2011). The Impact of Financial Crisis on the Global Economy: Can the Islamic Financial System Help? *The Journal of Risk Finance, 12*(1), 15–25.

Zeller, M., & Meyer, R. (2002). *The Triangle of Microfinance. Financial Sustainability, Outreach and Impact*. Washington, DC: The International Food Policy and Research Institute.

CHAPTER 7

Urban Sustainability and the Role of Islamic Wealth in Mega-OIC Cities: Implications for SDGs

Salim Refas, Mohamed Cherif El Amri, and Mustafa Omar Mohammed

INTRODUCTION

Urbanization is increasingly dominating the global discourse. Studies show that two-thirds of the global population will live in cities by 2050 (UN 2019). Meanwhile, more than 52% of the 1.8 billion population of the 57 Organization of the Islamic Cooperation (OIC) countries live in urban areas as of 2020. This figure represents an increase of more than 8% compared to the year 2000 (SESRIC 2019). In 2020 (see Table 7.1), five of the world's largest 20 cities are located in OIC member countries

---

S. Refas · M. C. El Amri (✉)
Department of Islamic Economics and Finance, Istanbul Sabahattin Zaim University, Istanbul, Turkey
e-mail: charif1982@gmail.com

M. O. Mohammed
Department of Economics, International Islamic University Malaysia, Gombak, Malaysia

© The Author(s), under exclusive license to Springer Nature Switzerland AG 2021
M. M. Billah (eds.), *Islamic Wealth and the SDGs*,
https://doi.org/10.1007/978-3-030-65313-2_7

129

Table 7.1 Largest 20 cities in the world from 1950 to 2030 (forecast), OIC cities highlighted

1950		1970		1990		2010		2020		2030 (forecast)	
New York	12,338	Tokyo	23,298	Tokyo	32,530	Tokyo	36,834	Tokyo	38,323	Tokyo	37,190
Tokyo	11,275	New York	16,191	Osaka	18,389	Delhi	21,935	Delhi	29,348	Delhi	36,060
London	8361	Osaka	15,272	New York	16,086	Mexico City	20,132	Shanghai	27,137	Shanghai	30,751
Osaka	7005	Mexico City	8831	Mexico City	15,642	Shanghai	19,980	Beijing	24,201	Mumbai	27,797
Paris	6283	Los Angeles	8378	São Paulo	14,776	São Paulo	19,660	Mumbai	22,838	Beijing	27,706
Moscow	5356	Paris	8208	Mumbai	12,436	Osaka	19,492	São Paulo	22,119	**Dhaka**	27,374
Buenos Aires	5098	Buenos Aires	8105	Calcutta	10,890	Mumbai	19,422	Mexico City	21,868	**Karachi**	24,838
Chicago	4999	São Paulo	7620	Los Angeles	10,883	New York	18,365	**Dhaka**	20,989	**Cairo**	24,502
Calcutta	4513	London	7509	Seoul	10,518	**Cairo**	16,899	**Cairo**	20,568	**Lagos**	24,239
Shanghai	4301	Moscow	7106	Buenos Aires	10,513	Beijing	16,190	Osaka	20,523	Mexico City	23,865
Los Angeles	4046	Chicago	7106	**Cairo**	9892	**Dhaka**	14,731	**Karachi**	19,230	São Paulo	23,444
Mexico City	3365	Calcutta	6926	Delhi	9726	Calcutta	14,283	New York	18,793	Kinshasa	19,996
Berlin	3338	Rio de Janeiro	6791	Rio de Janeiro	9697	Buenos Aires	14,246	**Lagos**	16,168	Osaka	19,976
Philadelphia	3128	Nagoya	6603	Paris	9330	**Karachi**	14,081	Buenos Aires	15,894	New York	19,885
Rio de Janeiro	3,026	Shanghai	6036	Moscow	8987	**Istanbul**	12,703	Calcutta	15,726	Calcutta	19,092
Saint Petersburg	2903	Mumbai	5811	Nagoya	8407	Rio de Janeiro	12,374	Chongqing	15,233	Guangzhou	19,092

7 URBAN SUSTAINABILITY AND THE ROLE ... 131

1950		1970		1990		2010		2020		2030 (forecast)	
Mumbai	2857	**Cairo**	**5585**	Jakarta	8175	Los Angeles	12,160	Guangzhou	15,174	Chongqing	17,574
Detroit	2769	Seoul	5312	London	8054	Manila	11,891	**Istanbul**	15,099	Buenos Aires	17,380
Boston	2551	Beijing	4426	Manila	7973	Moscow	11,461	Kinshasa	14,118	Manila	16,956
Cairo	2494	Philadelphia	4396	Shanghai	7823	Chongqing	11,244	Manila	13,942	**Istanbul**	**16,756**

Source United Nations Stats

(Dhaka, Cairo, Karachi, Lagos, and Istanbul). This has increased from one OIC city from 1950 to 1970 (Cairo), two in 1990 (Cairo and Jakarta), and four in 2010 (Dhaka, Cairo, Karachi, and Istanbul). By 2030, four mega-OIC cities will be among the 10 largest cities in the world, up from two cities today. Each one of these cities will host population of more than 24 million inhabitants, 10 times the population of Cairo in 1950.

This booming growth of mega cities in OIC countries or more generally in the world creates a set of urban planning and sustainability challenges unprecedented in human history. According to UN data (UN 2019), 67 cities in the world had populations of more than 5 million inhabitants in 2018, up from 18 in 1970, and this number is expected to grow to 109 by 2030. The cities of more than 5 million inhabitants were housing 1 in every 25 persons living on earth in 1970; they are housing one in every 9 persons today and will be housing one in every 7 by 2030. In the fastest-growing cities, this proportion is expected to increase in the next decade.

Defining Sustainability of Megacities in OIC Countries

Mega-OIC Cities

There is no formal definition of megacity in the economic literature, but the word generally refers to urban areas with a permanent population above 10 million inhabitants. By extension, the cities of the 57 member states of the Organization of Islamic Cooperation (OIC) with population above 3 million inhabitants are still referred to as mega-OIC cities in this chapter due to the fast growth observed.

Demographic Pressure in Mega-OIC Cities

The demographic expansion of OIC cities has not been uniform over the last decades. Figure 7.1 presents the average growth rate between 2000 and 2020 of the 35 largest OIC cities in 2020, all having a population over 3 million inhabitants in 2020. In a sample of 35 cities, 80% of them (28 cities) have an average annual growth rate of over 2% in the period 2000–2020 and the average growth rate of the overall OIC population over that period (SESRIC 2019). These 28 cities have therefore added an impressive 50% total population to their urban area in a period of 20 years.

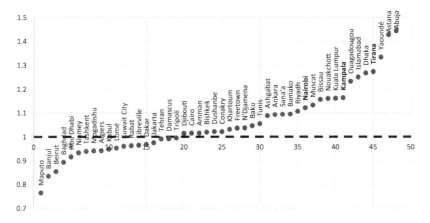

Fig. 7.1 Population growth 2000–2020 of largest OIC cities (> 3Mn inhabitants in 2020) (*Source* United Nations Stats)

Defining Urban Sustainability in Megacities

Adopting a people-centric agenda, and in reference to the UN definition of sustainable development as a development that promotes "prosperity and economic opportunity, greater social well-being, and protection of the environment," this chapter proposes the definition of sustainable urban development in mega-OIC city context as **the most efficient and resilient path to provide housing, employment, and access to basic services for all urban dwellers**. By efficiency and resilience, the definition refers both to the economic and environmental dimensions of the sustainability agenda. Based on universal housing and access issues (i.e., access to employment and basic services) on the other hand, this definition focuses on the socioeconomic dimensions of sustainability onto the basic social requirements of individuals. Derived into operational strategies, this definition focuses on the planning efforts coupled with two dimensions: land-use strategies first, for the efficient and resilient provision of housing, employment, and basic services at all locations required in the city grid, and transportation planning on the other hand, to move urban dwellers and goods between these locations. This echoes the targets 11.1 and 11.2 of the Sustainable Development Goal 11.[1]

---

[1] https://sustainabledevelopment.un.org/sdg11.

The Main Dimensions of Urban Sustainability Issues in Mega-OIC Cities

Access to Adequate Safe and Affordable Housing

According to most recent data on percentage of population living in slum areas in the OIC countries (UN Stats, April 2020), slums and informal settlements are prevalent in mega-OIC cities. Statistics are available in 39 countries, mainly in Arab, South Asia, and sub-Saharan African regions. The data available show that the level of deprivation of urban residents in OIC countries is very acute and of great concern. With more than half of their population leaving in slums and informal settlements, 21 OIC countries out of 39 in the sample have extremely high deprivation rates, which run the risk of being compounded by environmental and social unrest risks. In 7 countries, more than 70% of the population live in slums. Only 10 out of 39 OIC countries for which data are available have a percentage of population living in slums below world average (33.3% of the urban population living in slum areas).

Access to Safe, Affordable, Accessible, and Sustainable Transport Systems

Beyond access to housing and basic services, access to transport is seen as the other main requirement to support inclusive, safe, resilient, and sustainable cities. OIC country performance in terms of access to safe, affordable, accessible, and sustainable transport for all varies markedly. In particular, a great divide is observed between low-income and high or middle-income countries in urban transport infrastructure stocks: despite numerous success stories of metro systems (Kuala Lumpur, Dubai, Istanbul, and Cairo), Bus Rapid Transit systems (Jakarta, Istanbul, Tehran, Tabriz, and Shiraz) or Light Rail systems (Rabat, Casablanca, Algiers, Oran, Tunis, Lusail, Dubai, etc.) in middle-income OIC countries, no mega-OIC city in low-income countries in OIC regions has been able thus far to develop a mass urban transit system (metro, tramway, or BRT system) to serve the growing mobility needs of their massive urban populations. Even in lower-middle-income countries, the provision of public transport options remains scanty and only few exceptions have managed to launch, with the support of international financial institutions, massive public transport projects in recent years. The detailed analysis of this public transport infrastructure gap, and the resulting access gaps to sustainable mobility for urban dwellers, is beyond the scope of this chapter, but it is important to add to that acute infrastructure gaps the compounding effects of efficiency of the transport services, environmental performance of the transport systems, and road safety issues, which are discussed, for example, in Sum4All (2017)

Sustainability Issues in Mega-OIC Cities and Current Policy Interventions

Sections "Access to Adequate Safe and Affordable Housing" and "Access to Safe, Affordable, Accessible and Sustainable Transport Systems" have briefly exposed current concerns related to the poor performance of mega-OIC cities in providing access to housing, employment, and basic services for all urban dwellers. These concerns are further aggravated by two urbanization challenges which are commonly found in developing countries: (i) the demographic pressure, discussed in section "Demographic Pressure in Mega-OIC Cities" with an unprecedented growth in urban population in these cities that will continue over the next decades and (ii) the fast-paced urban sprawl that is observed in these cities with car-centric urban planning that drives city expansion over ever-expanding city boundaries.[2] On the other hand, central or local public administrations do not remain idle against the issues faced and typically use the instruments mentioned in Table 7.2 to control the related social, environmental, or economic issues, within the limitations of their available resources. Not all of these measures are found that lead to positive short-term and long-term impacts however, and this is briefly discussed in the table.

The dominant policy actions in developing countries, including OIC countries, are traditionally found in public investment programs and traditional land-use taxation. The last section of this chapter will discuss the application of these instruments in relation to the topic of this chapter.

---

[2] A detailed description of the urban sprawl phenomenon is beyond the scope of this paper, but classical works on this phenomenon can be found in the literature: Whyte et al. (1958) and Harvey and Clark (1965), etc. It is important also to note that urban sprawl is not a uniform outward growth of urban settlements but rather the extensive suburbs are generally of much lower density than the historic cores (Cox 2020). Therefore, the geographic expansion of cities happens at an even faster pace than the demographic growth in some contexts.

Table 7.2 Typical policy and public intervention instruments to address sustainability issues in mega cities

Typical instruments used in mega-OIC city context	Short-term impact	Long-term impact
Traditional land-value taxation (developed sites)	**Positive** efficient and progressive tax collection, non-distortionary	**Positive (with risks)** Efficient tax to fund public improvements but possible capital flight
White-land taxation	**Positive** progressive tax collection	**Neutral** Perceived as penalty rather than incentive to develop
Affordable housing schemes	**Positive** Addresses housing supply shortfalls and creates employment	Mainly **Negative** low livability, uncontrolled city expansion, aggressive resettlements
Public investment in infrastructure	**Negative** Resettlements, congestion	**Positive** urban sustainability
	Positive Employment, value creation, city attractiveness	**Negative** Sprawl, land predation/speculation, public debt, environment

Source Authors

The Funding Gap

While there is no global consensus on a methodology to precisely assess the funding requirements to meet individual SDG targets, an interesting attempt to quantify these investment needs by compiling numbers from multiple sources can be found for SDG-11 in UN-Habitat (2020). The main data source is the Global Infrastructure Outlook published by the G20 which builds on a top-down econometric approach using panel data to draw inferences on infrastructure investment. The Global Infrastructure Outlook uses two main inputs: (i) the forecasted infrastructure investment in each country derived from recent history, with growth in investment occurring only when there is a substantial change to country's economic and demographic fundamentals; (ii) an investment need forecast which is derived from the performance of their best performing peers (i.e., in the same income bracket), after controlling for differences in the characteristics of each country.

UN-Habitat then crosses the Global Infrastructure Outlook results with data from the McKinsey Global Institute, United Nations Sustainable Development Solutions Network, and UNCTAD to fine-tune the total investment gap forecasts. Results from this UN-Habitat estimation show that the total investment needed to meet all SDGs is estimated at $38 trillion for the decade 2020–2030, a figure which can hardly be commented due to its aggregate nature. However, a very interesting outcome of UN-Habitat (2020), developed using a sample of developing cities and using the data sets presented above, is an estimate of individual investment requirements at the level of a typical city based on the city size and characteristics to meet SDG 11 targets by 2030. The results indicate that for a small city in a developing country, total average annual costs can be expected of around $20–50 million. For a medium-sized developing city, the costs range from around $140 million to more than $500 million. And large developing cities, which is the category of concern in this chapter, can expect an average annual cost from around $600 million to over $5000 million, with average results being in billions of USD per city and year.

The Role of Islamic Ethical Wealth Toward Megacities Development: Review of Best Practices

Against the backdrop of the first section of this chapter, where the present-time sustainability issues of mega cities in OIC countries are discussed, this section will draw some lessons from best practices of ethical wealth in funding mega cities development and addressing sustainable development needs of large cities. The review will start by discussing urban planning considerations of Islamic cities in the history and the role played by ethical wealth in supporting the development of these cities. A brief comparative analysis with other historical setups will then be discussed to compare especially the historical urban development context of mega-OIC countries to other developing countries. The third part of this section will finally propose a taxonomy of the main channels through which Islamic ethical wealth has the potential to positively impact the urban development path of the mega-OIC cities in the post-industrial era and draw lessons from best practices.

Islamic Ethical Wealth in the Development of Cities: A Brief Historical Perspective

From pre-urban times to post-industrial era, cities and urban settlements have been formed by human societies originally inclined to nomadic and agricultural life for specific functions which can generally be characterized around three essential elements: an administrative and military element (the "stronghold"), a religious element ("the temple"), and a commercial element ("the market"). While historians would argue that the religious and law and order imperatives have dictated the early formation of cities, it is evident that in modern days, with few exceptions, the economic functions have become the primary character of mega cities, including in OIC countries: the most common feature of the largest cities in each country remains that they are "economic capitals" and as a result, millions or tens of millions of workers and their families, in some instances, agglomerate in their urban areas extending over thousands of square kilometers in search of employment and the promise of a (relatively) safe comfortable living.

However, cities have a history and have become the lively result of multiple transformations through ages, sometimes in periods of peace, sometimes in periods of war. Even if the study of the genesis of cities, or more particularly of mega-OIC cities is beyond the scope of this chapter, looking at the historical formation and transformation of Islamic cities and comparing it to post-industrial cities may shed light on the available options for solving their sustainability issues. In particular, it is important to discuss how religion and power historically played an important part in shaping Islamic cities, even if the modern manifestation of this role is subdued today. In a fascinating review of waqfs and urban structures in Ottoman Damascus, Van Leeuwen (1999), for example, provides an interesting history of how Muslims transfigured the city of Damascus after its conquest in year 635. The choice of the location of the Mosques and the institution of endowments to fund the religious activities as well as other public services determined the urban landscape of the city up until modern times. In a more generic account of the role of waqfs in shaping cities, Deguilhem (2008) mentions that:

> Waqf increasingly influenced and shaped numerous infrastructural aspects in cities in the Islamic world as well as in the daily lives of individuals living in the cities from the early Islamic centuries up through the medieval period to modern and contemporary times. Along with the expansion of Islam in newly-founded settlements and cities or its advent within already-existing inherited urban centres, the endowments played a major role in determining the physical configuration of cities due to the addition of Islamic edifices and complexes in the urban landscape or the adaptation

of existing ones in the form of mosques, madrasas, dâr al-hadîth, dâr al-qurân, zâwiyas, ribâts, bîmâristâns, soup kitchens, etc., the great majority of which were financed by waqf revenues. This income accrued to the endowments mostly by the rent of commercial buildings which belonged to the endowments such as boutiques, bakeries, artesian workshops, caravanserai, coffeehouses, bathhouses, etc., or plots of agricultural land such as orchards, vegetable gardens, etc. (Page 928)

Even if scholarly attention has been mostly dedicated to major mosques (for Friday prayers) or religious edifices, it is interesting to note that the organization around Islamic edifices is also observed around secondary mosques, as explained, for example, by González Gutiérrez (2015) in the city of Madinat Qurtuba in Muslim Spain. The religious functions and activities of the city become therefore not only a manifestation of the urban life of its Muslim dwellers, but they have remained constant through centuries one of the most determining drivers of the urban development patterns. In parallel, the administrative functions of the cities, especially during Imperial times, required the institution of central buildings for the exercise of the judicial or executive powers of the state, which also played a role in shaping the administrative quarters, but their impact in shaping the overall development of cities may be limited to the central districts where these functions were generally agglomerated.

Comparative Analysis of the Historical Urban Development of Cities in Islamic and Other Developing Countries

The global discourse on the spatial organization of cities and megalopolis in regional or urban development studies has been dominated since the advent of the twentieth century by the study of European, North American, or East Asian contexts. The classical theories of urban sociology developed by Marx, Engels, Durkheim, Simmel, or Weber, for example, all theorize the structure of the cities against the backdrop of social relationships in the European context with specific cultural and social models that are hardly replicable to other parts of the world. Park and Burgess (2019), in their seminal work "the City" published in 1925, propose the paradigm of the "concentric ring theory," and more than thirty years later, Mumford (1961) is credited for his effort to define and describe what a "Megalopolis" is and will become. Among the classical authors of the twentieth century, Max Weber (1966) could be credited, in his seminal book "the City" first published in German and translated in 1958, for the effort extended to study Asian, Jewish, or Muslim cities and comparing them to European contexts. However, this comparison merely serves the purpose of contrasting "Occidental urbanism" with "Oriental urbanism" with the intention of reinforcing the legitimacy of the sociological paradigms that he proposes for the former. Therefore, it is very difficult to find, from among the authoritative authors of classical economic or social studies of the last century, relevant references to depict what urbanization and spatial organization processes characterize the structural transition of major urban centers in Islamic countries from periods of administration under Muslim rule (e.g., during Ottoman times) in pre-industrial era, to post-independence context with mega cities of several million inhabitants as discussed in the first section of this chapter.

In the absence of such knowledge in the literature, this chapter will briefly mention below three stylized facts about mega cities in Islamic countries that characterize their historical urban development patterns and which played a part in their modern time structures.

First and foremost, as described, for example, in Abu-Lughod (1980), the "chief contrast with cities generated under other legal systems" would be that Islamic cities have been structured around "communal settlements" or quarters attributed to supra-individual groups related to "kinship, descent, common origin or function." In other words, the Islamic city was always by definition a multi-polar city, where each quarter, each district, was "administered" by some form of informal local authority and where the relationships between dwellers were dictated by a strong social interaction sometimes preceding the state rules. Until today, it is not uncommon therefore to travel across Islamic cities in the world and still find reminiscences of the Dyers district, the Sharqawa or Maghariba district, or the Jewish district, for example, with a spatial organization that has survived history (although the social organization has not in most instances). The quarters are bounded by what Eickelman (1999) calls "*Qaraba*," which could be translated by kinship, that he defines as "the exchange of visits on feast days and on other occasions, by assistance and participation in the activities connected with births, circumcisions, wedding and funerals, graduation from school or memorization of the Qur'ân. The "heads of household (…) share certain minimal collective responsibilities," and the administration of the quarter responds to unwritten communal rules that are transmitted from generation to generation. Eickelman (1999) therefore concludes that critics of Weber toward

Oriental cities and Muslim cities, in particular, that he blames for lacking the formal organization into urban communes (*Gemeinde*) and therefore being merely cities in an economic sense are at best idealistic, at worst biased and ethnocentric, and therefore should be rejected and denied.

Secondly as described shortly in the previous section of this chapter, the religious buildings played a central role in the spatial organization of towns and urban centers, and until today, codes of urbanism still give a high importance to the Mosque and the educational institutions.

Thirdly, as described, for example, in Van Leeuwen (1999), the waqf institution is presented as a determining factor in the growth and structure of Muslim cities which is absent (or secondary) in the Occidental cities but which has hardly survived to modern times (under colonial rule or in independent countries). Today, waqfs play therefore only a marginal role in shaping cities while they use to be of central importance, in particular, for example, under Ottoman rule.

Other theories attempt to analyze urban development patterns of Islamic cities by contrasting them to European or North American cities, but such studies generally refer to sociological or cultural factors to attempt to explain the relative difference in the fate of urban centers in the Islamic world which used to be the most advanced from an economic development perspective and are today lagging behind. For example, Bosker et al. (2013) try to find in religious practice a relevant instrument to describe the relative dip in economic performance of Islamic cities. In this sense, such studies even if econometrically correct fall into ethnocentric bias when identifying model variables.

This being said that even if comparatively the structure of cities in Islamic countries and in other sociological contexts varies markedly as briefly exposed above, in particular in relation to the religious institutions established in the Islamic cities, it is evident that these differences have been overshadowed by the most determining factor shaping the development of large cities since the second half of the twentieth century: the dominance of cars and motorized vehicles as primary transport mode. A substantial body of knowledge has been developed in regional studies and urban planning studies to analyze the advent of cars and the way this has profoundly changed the structure and shape of cities, especially suburban developments, but it is probably sufficient for the scope of this chapter to mention the main channel by which this revolution happened: the standards of road and street construction. As Southworth and Ben-Joseph (2013) puts it: "Each era of urban expansion has had its own conceptions of the good city, its own processes and standards for city building." And since the domination of the car in urban transport has been a universal phenomenon over the last century in all large cities across the globe, urban planning has developed across all geographies along one main dimension: the road and street network. The colonization of most developing countries by European powers has then led to the rapid diffusion of the dominant models of urban planning in Western Europe to most parts of the world, and accordingly very little marked differences remain between the urban planning of Islamic cities and their Western counterparts today. The next section will question whether this is welcomed or regretted historical fact.

The Positive Impact of Islamic Ethical Wealth on the Urban Development Path of the Mega-OIC Cities in the Post-industrial Era

In summary, the previous two sections have established that: (i) during pre-industrial era, the structure of Islamic cities was in stark contrast to the structure of Western cities, mainly in consideration of the polycentric nature of Islamic cities along communal subdivisions by kinship, origin, function or else, and in consideration of the primary role of waqfs and religious institutions in shaping city development, and (ii) this contrast has gradually disappeared in the course of the industrial and colonial era, and car-centric street and road design standards have subsequently dictated urban planning considerations.

At the same time, it was established in section "The Main Dimensions of Urban Sustainability Issues in Mega-OIC Cities" that mega-OIC cities are not sustainable, and in particular due to unsustainable transport planning and lack of provision of adequate housing. Three categories of policy instruments offer the opportunity to address these issues (tax instruments, non-tax incentive measures, and regulatory instruments), but massive public investment is also required and a recent study has established that for large developing cities, the annual investment effort required to transform the sustainability performance of the mega cities and achieve the SDG targets is in the range of billions of dollars of sustainable public or private investment (UN-Habitat 2020).

This chapter proposes now to discuss the role that Islamic Ethical Wealth can play in this context, both in light of the historical role it played in shaping cities in the pre-industrial era and in light of the financing gaps identified which are far beyond the capacity of the public sector and local governments. Building upon Banister (1998), the implementation issues are addressed at four levels: decisions relating to the use of existing resources; decisions relating to new development; decisions relating to transport; and decisions relating to increasing resource efficiency[3] within urban areas.

The Role of Islamic Ethical Wealth in the Use of Resources in Megacities

Islamic Ethical Wealth plays a dual role with regard to the use of existing resources in mega-OIC cities:

- High net-worth individuals and families are often the largest property owners in the mega-cities, having heavily invested in land or real estate assets throughout recent decades, or having maintained their ownership of family properties and land assets despite incapacity (or absence of will) to develop them into "positive use";
- At the same time, being the largest capital owners and having access to private finance, High net-worth individuals and families have the greatest potential to fund the regeneration of brownfield areas within cities, both on their own land and on the land of third parties.

The scale of the challenge is unprecedented due to the booming real estate prices in the fastest-growing cities. Doubling of land prices in less than a decade is observed in some contexts due to massive demographic pressure and due to supply and offer dynamics, and as a consequence, a large number of owners decide to hold land and property for long periods, even if not turned into productive use, to maximize value instead of developing it for housing or commercial activities. Land vacancy across OIC mega cities has not been studied to the authors' knowledge but some examples offer good insights into the scale of the challenge. In the Kingdom of Saudi Arabia (KSA), for example, and as discussed in Zakaria et al. (2019), the issue is of magnitude, and as a consequence, KSA's Council of Ministers approved a White Land Tax in November 2015. Under the new law, owners of empty plots of urban land designated for

---

[3] Banister (1998) mentions energy efficiency but we chose to extend the thinking on resource efficiency in general i.e. including water and food in particular which pose great challenge in the developing context of mega-OIC cities.

residential or commercial use will have to pay a tax of 2.5% of the value of the land each year.

Yet the tax instrument faces implementation issue, and beyond tax contributions, Islamic Ethical Wealth should lead the way in putting to use the extended land banks instead of speculating on their value appreciation. The waqf structure in particular, and the historical uses of it as discussed in the second section, is particularly adapted to turn these lands into productive assets, and some best practices have been recently implemented. Ali et al. (2016) mention the example of Penang State Islamic Religious Council which successfully enhanced value of waqf real estate developments through the implementation of nine housing project developments using the ijarah concept in Malaysia. The Abraj-Al-Bait project in Makkah al Mukarramah and Awqaf Al-Rajhi developments in the main cities across Saudi Arabia are other examples of multi-billion dollar investment by private waqfs into brownfield real estate developments in city centers. The second mechanism identified, still with the same objective of regenerating city centers into denser and more efficient uses to enhance the sustainability of cities, is to establish public-private partnership to mobilize private funding of Islamic Ethical Wealth for the regeneration of vacant or derelict lands inside city boundaries. Multiple forms of partnerships exist including the setup of joint ownership structures where public land or public property is privatized and collateralized at incentivized rates to leverage on debt funding of the real estate projects for social uses. The governance of such structures is, however, a major challenge.

The Role of Islamic Ethical Wealth Relating to New Developments

Referring here to the historical role waqfs (hence Islamic Ethical Wealth) played in shaping Islamic cities, it is legitimate to ask how Islamic Ethical Wealth should in present-day mega cities be invested into new urban developments. The funding requirements estimated to meet the urban sustainability challenges of mega-OIC cities have been briefly mentioned in section "The Funding Gap" above: for large cities, experts expect an average annual cost from around $600 million to over $5,000 million to meet SDG 11 targets by 2030. A significant proportion of these costs is required to fund new sustainable projects. In particular, social housing projects house the millions of urban dwellers that are deprived from housing and basic social needs. The first role of Islamic Ethical Wealth relating to new developments is therefore a financing role for social and affordable housing schemes. The channels and financing instruments through which this financing should be mobilized differ, however, from country to country.

In the context of less mature markets, Islamic Housing Micro Finance (HMF) schemes or waqfs are called upon to provide temporary solutions until financial markets develop. In fact, issues such as ownership rights, legal and regulatory frameworks, ineffective land registration systems, or high transaction costs are found to significantly impede the capacity to raise finance for social housing in the countries studied (Shirazi et al. 2012). This echoes Renaud (1999) which also concludes that in undeveloped housing systems, the financing of basic urban infrastructure and the adoption of adequate urban planning regulations and policies should be given priority over financing of housing sector.

The second role of Islamic Ethical Wealth this chapter calls for, in relation to new developments, is to support the resilience of urban areas. The historical context of Islamic cities mentioned in sections "Islamic Ethical Wealth in the Development of Cities: A Brief Historical Perspective" and "Comparative Analysis of the Historical Urban Development of Cities in Islamic and Other Developing Countries" has described the importance of communal or sub-communal settlements/quarters, bounded together by central waqf buildings (mosques or educational institutions) and kinship "*Qaraba*" relationships, in the original shaping of cities. This has been lost in time to the benefit of alternative urbanization patterns, especially car-centric developments toward ever-expanding city boundaries. This chapter recommends that Islamic Ethical Wealth is channeled toward the most sustainable urban developments along three dimensions at least: environmental and "sociocultural" resilience, density, and inclusiveness. Through environmental resilience, the objective is to address long-term environmental concerns of cities and avoid the damaging tendency of low-quality buildings for social uses and affordable housing which bring major challenges of refurbishment and regeneration at the end of their useful life. Through "sociocultural resilience," the objective is to revive the "heart and soul" of quarters in the cities, or even develop it with the help of historical and religious ties, to build again the cohesion and solidarity at the level of the quarter which characterized Islamic cities in their glorious past and helped address social issues (unemployment, poverty, etc.) as well as maintain attachment to the land over generations (an efficient way to tackle suburban migrations). At the same time, it is demonstrated that density is one of the most important characteristics of sustainable cities and massifying urban centers are critical to deliver sustainable mobility and address socioeconomic needs of the urban populations. Finally, inclusiveness refers to sharing economic outcomes fairly across society and creating opportunities for all. This inclusiveness is reinforced with kinship and through the establishment of "trust networks" at the local level. Islamic Ethical Wealth has a critical role to play in this, and this will be further developed in the last section of this chapter.

The Role of Islamic Ethical Wealth Relating to Transport

The main urban sustainability challenges relating to transport are to encourage reduction of the motorized travel needs and the use of sustainable transport modes, such as public transport or non-motorized modes of travel. Islamic Ethical Wealth has here a critical role to play. In particular, massive investment in public transport is often beyond the reach of local governments in low-income countries or lower-middle-income countries as discussed in section "The Main Dimensions of Urban Sustainability Issues in Mega-OIC Cities". This situation was faced by Islamic empires in the past, and it is reported, for example, that Ottoman-era Turkey lacked a budget for public infrastructure and to fill the infrastructure gaps, more than 35,000 private foundations, known as *Vakif* in Turkish, funded public work projects and municipal services, from water systems and schools to hospitals, bridges, and roads.

The local governments also face difficulties to implement major innovations in sustainable mobility that have the potential to transform the future of cities. Islamic Ethical can help bridge the gaps. In particular, it can provide financing and grants to local operators, invest in buses or minibuses, provide free transport or transport at subsidized rates, improve viability of public transport (e.g., by investing in metro station naming rights), and provide funding to public transport innovations such as car-sharing systems. In addition, the transfer and sale of private lands owned by high net worth individuals or families to the municipalities for public transport projects should be encouraged or facilitated (with tax or non-tax incentives). Land acquisition is indeed a major obstacle to the development of public transport in megacities, and Islamic Ethical Wealth has a role to play to address this issue.

The Role of Islamic Ethical Wealth in Increasing Resource Efficiency in Megacities

Finally, the role of Islamic Ethical Wealth in increasing resource efficiency, in particular energy efficiency, in mega-OIC cities is comparable to its role relating to sustainable transport: the objective is at the same time to support through funding innovations and public investments (through public-private partnerships, for example) in sustainable energy and at the same time, at a more micro-level support through donations or lending the transition from polluting to environmental friendly resource uses.

Practical Considerations of the Findings for the Realization of the SDG Agenda

The previous sections of this chapter have provided an overview of the scale of the urban sustainability challenges faced by mega-OIC cities and the main dimensions of interventions that are recommended. The scale of the challenge is such, and the timeline before 2030, the target year for achievement of the SDG agenda, is so tight that the window of action is now and the interventions must be of massive scale: billions of dollars in annual investments are required in each megacity to achieve SDG 11 alone, the main SDG related to urban sustainability.

Islamic Ethical Wealth has a multi-dimensional role to play in helping local governments achieve the ambitious targets. The recommendations on the role Islamic Ethical Wealth should play to support the transition to sustainable urban development in mega-OIC cities can be looked at from the perspective of the financing instruments or interventions available, or as this chapter has proposed, from the perspective of the type of interventions and various roles that can be played. The following four roles have been identified, building upon urban planning literature:

- support through brownfield developments and use of vacant land/properties
- support through new developments
- support through the development of sustainable transport
- support through the increased efficiency in the use of resources.

While these interventions, from an analytical perspective, can be easily understood and justified, this chapter further hypothesizes that these interventions are not common approaches in the context of the SDG agenda and are often overlooked. And the question must be asked of why Islamic Ethical Wealth role is most commonly understood, in the context of the sustainable development agenda, as a philanthropic or humanitarian financier of social responsibility projects and not as a key player in the development agenda. Three hypotheses can be made at this stage and should be subject to further research.

First, the question of the governance systems in place for the urban areas can be asked. In the distant past, Islamic cities were ruled in a cohesive manner by a mix of formal and informal leadership systems. The formal leadership system that we could qualify by top-down system generally consisted of an administrative system appointed by the central regime for each governorate, under different varieties according to the ruling systems: governors, emirs, beys, deys, etc., would administer on behalf of the state the major localities of the Islamic Empire, collect the taxes, and depending on the military organization, be directly or indirectly responsible for the security and state affairs. But at the same time, such centrally appointed administrators would have never succeeded in running, sometimes at times of wars, famines or social unrest, major urban areas distant by several days or weeks from the capital of the empire without a strong local support. And this local support that helped especially control the suburban and agricultural areas feeding the cities respected historical traditions of each country and people administered. The "Elders," the chiefs, or even the "heads of households" only (as Eickelman 1999 puts it) shared collective responsibility and self-administer sometimes entire quarters of the urban area without the need for intervention from the local authority. This sub-communal self-administration has almost disappeared in present-day cities. Some remains of these systems can be seen, for example, in Arab cities where the "Omda" (Mayor) of each quarter can still be seen in Cairo or Jeddah, for example, or the Cheikh (Elder) of a tribe or of a given profession can be met. But their role is very limited and is relevant only for the settlement of local disputes or some ceremonies. Building back these informal responsibility systems, and empowering wealthy families to play a more central role in the governance of cities and quarters, seems crucial to deepen their role in the transition to more urban sustainability. In a way, the governance system would need to be reformed therefore to put back in the driving seat the individuals that have most leverage to support the sustainable transition of mega cities.

The second hypothesis relates to the financialization of the real estate and land markets. This chapter has discussed the central role of land-use planning in managing sustainability of mega cities. It must be recognized that urban planners have generally failed in mega-OIC cities over the last decades in creating the conditions for resilient and liveable cities for the present and future generations. And this explains in part the unsatisfactory performance of mega-OIC cities in terms of economic, social, and environmental sustainability. Beyond the car-centric and centrifugal development strategies that have been very detrimental as nobody would challenge today to the future of these cities, one of the main reasons why the urban planners have failed to design and implement sustainable urban master plans has arguably been the poor management of land banks and real estate property markets. This leads to the unfortunate situation today where major cities and urban areas know exactly what to do to transform the city into sustainable cities (in particular through providing sustainable mobility and massifying developments), but lack the means to do so because of the unavailability of land to build the public infrastructure required to deliver the sustainability promise: the land acquisition costs and resettlement costs of massive public transport projects often exceed the investment cost of the infrastructure itself. But urban planners are not the only one to blame. The upper social classes have heavily invested—and sometimes without realizing via pension funds, investment vehicles, or shares of Real Estate Operating Companies (REOC)—into available land and properties in urban areas creating ever-increasing boom-bust cycles in land and property markets and unprecedented city expansions that have completely transformed urban structures for decades to come (modern-day examples would be the cities of Dubai or Istanbul for example). Yet, land, in its legal, historical, or even in its accounting nature, is not expected to change hands frequently. In fact, the mere possibility of allowing buying and selling land and making profit out of this in cities where every single square meter has a crucial importance for the generations to come could be questioned. Even without going to that extreme, the question of the financialization of land and property markets and the direct impact this has on sustainable development prospects of cities must be studied.

Finally, a third perspective remains the question of incentives. Based on the estimates of purchasing power, a present-day estimate of the waqf of Uthman ibn Affan in the city of Madinah at the time of the Prophet (PBUH), a well that he is reported to have purchased for 20,000 dirhams, is in the range of only USD 50–70,000 based on Zarra-Nezhad (2004) in present-day US Dollars. Yet, it is well known that this waqf has created enormous amount of wealth which has been continuously redistributed in part to poor and orphans and reinvested in part since its inception, leading to a situation today where the waqf owns expensive property in the city of Madinah and is endowed with large sums of money.[4] The specific feature of waqfs as productive assets, and the corresponding investment and management challenges that arise to generate the best economic outcomes out of their use, is an important subject from a behavioral economics perspective. Questions must be asked as to the social and moral incentive frameworks that would entail more investment from wealthy individuals into waqf structures supporting sustainable urban development, and on a wider scale, other sustainable development projects, and at the same time, proper attention must be given to the anthropologic and legal challenges that have caused their derelict in recent generations.

CONCLUSION

By 2030, four mega-OIC cities will be among the 10 largest cities in the world, up from two cities today and none in 1990. Each one of these cities will be home for more than 24 million inhabitants, the majority of which living in slums or informal settlements. In just 10 years, between 2020 and 2030, these mega cities are expected to see a population increase, through natural growth or migrations, of 3 to 8 million inhabitants each. Another three mega-OIC cities are increasing their population by more than 2.5 million each during the same period. Relatively smaller large OIC cities, between 1 and 10 million inhabitants, also see rapid growth and expansion trends and overall, by 2050, an expected 68% of the OIC population will live in urban areas, a large proportion of which in the largest urban areas of each country. On many accounts, these trends are not sustainable. This chapter has proposed a new approach to analyze the urban sustainability challenges for mega-OIC cities. Adopting a people-centric agenda, and in reference to the UN definition of sustainable development as a development that promotes

---

[4] Some unverified sources report that this Waqf generates today up to USD 50 Mn in revenue every year (see: https://millichronicle.com/2019/04/did-you-know-the-third-cal iph-uthman-bin-affan-owns-a-hotel-and-a-bank-account-in-madinah/).

"prosperity and economic opportunity, greater social well-being, and protection of the environment," this chapter proposes the definition of sustainable urban development in mega-OIC city context as the most efficient and resilient path to provide housing, employment, and access to basic services for all urban dwellers. The stylized facts presented show that the current performance of mega-OIC cities in meeting urban population needs for access to safe and adequate housing or to sustainable systems is not satisfactory. Due to booming demographics and urban sprawl, this performance is expected to further deteriorate over next decades. To face these unprecedented challenges, public administrations use a variety of instruments which are found to bring limited positive impacts, especially in the long term. The funding gaps estimated also amounting to billions of dollars per city and per year are such that public administration alone cannot face the urban sustainability challenges identified.

In this context, and informed by Islamic history, Islamic Ethical Wealth is found to have a critical role to play to address the challenges. This role can be looked at from a financing perspective only, or as this chapter proposes, from the perspective of all support roles that can be played by Islamic Ethical Wealth and which are classified into four categories: support through brownfield developments and use of vacant land/properties, support through new developments, support through the development of sustainable transport, and support through the increased efficiency in the use of resources. The use of waqfs in shaping future sustainable cities is exemplified. The chapter concludes by analyzing why, while these interventions from an analytical perspective and based on the historical context of Islamic cities can be easily understood and promoted, Islamic Ethical Wealth role in addressing sustainable urban development issues in the context of the SDG agenda is marginalized and overlooked. Three hypotheses are proposed: the question of the governance systems in place in the mega-OIC cities, the question of the financialization of the real estate and land markets, and the question of incentives. Further research is needed along these three dimensions to unlock the great potential of Islamic Ethical Wealth in shaping sustainable and resilient cities for all by 2030 and beyond.

References

Abu-Lughod, J. (1980). *Contemporary Relevance of Islamic Urban Principles (extract)*. Ekistics, 6–10.

Ali, S. N. M., Noor, A. H. M., Johari, N., Fauzi, N. S., Chuweni, N. N., & Ismail, N. R. P. (2016). Hungry for Housing: Waqf Real Estate Development-A Social Welfare Alternative. In *MATEC Web of Conferences* (Vol. 66, p. 00068). EDP Sciences.

Banister, D. (1998). Barriers to the Implementation of Urban Sustainability. *International Journal of Environment and Pollution, 10*(1), 65–83.

Bosker, M., Buringh, E., & Van Zanden, J. L. (2013). From Baghdad to London: Unraveling Urban Development in Europe, the Middle East, and North Africa, 800–1800. *Review of Economics and Statistics, 95*(4), 1418–1437.

Cox, W. (2020). *Demographia World Urban Areas* (11th Annual ed.).

Deguilhem, R. (2008). The Waqf in the City. In *The City in the Islamic World* (2 vols., pp. 929–956). Boston: Brill.

Eickelman, D. F. (1999). The Coming Transformation of the Muslim World. *Middle East Review of International Affair, 3*(3), 78–81.

Gutiérrez, C. G. (2015). Secondary Mosques in Madinat Qurtuba: Islamization and Suburban Development Through Minor Religious Spaces. *Papers from the Institute of Archaeology, 25*(1).

Harvey, R. O., & Clark, W. A. (1965). The Nature and Economics of Urban Sprawl. *Land Economics, 41*(1), 1–9.

Mumford, L. (1961). The Myth of Megalopolis. In L. Mumford (Ed.), *The City in History: Its Origins, Its Transformations, and Its Prospects*. London: Secker and Warburg.

Park, R. E., & Burgess, E. W. (2019). *The City*. Chicago, IL: University of Chicago Press.

Renaud, B. (1999). The Financing of Social Housing in Integrating Financial Markets: A View from Developing Countries. *Urban Studies, 36*(4), 755–773.

SESRIC. (2019). *Urban Development in OIC Countries: Towards Sustainable Urbanization*. Infrastructure Development Studies. The Statistical, Economic and Social Research and Training Centre for Islamic Countries. Ankara.

Shirazi, N. S., Zulkhibri, M., & Ali, S. S. (2012). Challenges of Affordable Housing Finance in IDB Member Countries using Islamic Modes. *Journal of Islamic Business and Management, 219*(1236), 1–10.

Southworth, M., & Ben-Joseph, E. (2013). *Streets and the Shaping of Towns and Cities*. Washington, DC: Island Press.

Sum4All. (2017). *Global Mobility Report 2017*. Sustainable Mobility for All Consortium of Partners. Accessed at http://www.sum4all.org/publications/global-mobility-report-2017.

UN-Habitat. (2020). *The Sustainable Investment Gap and How to Close It: Cities, Infrastructure and SDG Investment Gap*. Nairobi 2020. https://unhabitat.org/the-sustainable-investment-gap-and-how-to-close-it-cities-infrastructureand-sdg-investment-gap.

United Nations. (2019). *The Population and Vital Statistics Report* (Vol. LXXI). Accessed at https://unstats.un.org/unsd/demographic-social/products/vitstats/index.cshtml.

Van Leeuwen, R. (1999). Waqfs and Urban Structures: The Case of Ottoman Damascus (Vol. 11). Boston: Brill.

Weber, M. (1966). *The City*. Glencoe, IL: Free Press.

Whyte, W., Jacobs, J., Bello, F., Freedgood, S., & Seligman, D. (1958). *The Exploding Metropolis*. Garden City, NY: Doubleday.

Zakaria, N., Ali Z., & Awang, M. Z. (2019). *White Land Tax: Evidence in the Kingdom of Saudi Arabia*.

Zarra-Nezhad, Mansour. (2004). A Brief History of Money in Islam and Estimating the Value of Dirham and Dinar. *Review of Islamic Economics, 8*, 51–65.

CHAPTER 8

Structural Mechanisms for Islamic Ethical Wealth for SDGs

Shariq Nisar and Umar Farooq

INTRODUCTION

The 2030 Agenda for Sustainable Development, adopted by all United Nations (UN) Member States in 2015, provides a shared blueprint for peace and prosperity for people and the planet, now and into the future. At its heart are the 17 Sustainable Development Goals (SDGs), which are an urgent call for action by all countries—developed and developing—in a global partnership. They recognize that ending poverty and other deprivations must go hand in hand with strategies that improve health and education, reduce inequality, and spur economic growth—all while tackling climate change and working to preserve our oceans and forests (United Nations 2020).

SDGs are a culmination of decades of work done by countries and the UN dating back to the first global effort in 1992 at the Earth Summit in Rio De Janeiro, Brazil, with over 178 countries adopting Agenda 21. Millennium Development Goals (MDGs) followed this in the year 2000 by adopting eight common goals for 2015, which aimed to eradicate

S. Nisar (✉) · U. Farooq
Rizvi Institute of Management Studies and Research, Mumbai, India

© The Author(s), under exclusive license to Springer Nature Switzerland AG 2021
M. M. Billah (eds.), *Islamic Wealth and the SDGs*,
https://doi.org/10.1007/978-3-030-65313-2_8

155

extreme poverty as the primary goal. The world saw some progress, but the goals of MDG were not achieved completely and this led to the UN member states adopting SDGs. The SDGs are an extension of MDGs. The SDGs are not just broader in their scope but also have well-defined 169 targets, which the member countries should strive to achieve by 2030. Seven of the SDGs comprise of the end goals of development narrowed down to people's well-being, while the remaining are the means to reach the end (Dariah et al. 2016). The SDGs acknowledge the interlinked nature of goals and hence an action (or the lack of it) on one will have an impact on the others too. Between MDGs and SDGs, the core focus remains the eradication of extreme poverty as it is not just humanitarian but the progress and success of others like hunger, health, education and gender equality directly depend on it.

Owing to a varying degree of economic development within and across countries, the UN while understanding the need and importance of these goals refrains from prescribing any specific tools and techniques to member states to achieve them. Rather, it restricts its role in suggesting broader guidelines on how to achieve them and sharing best practices. Releasing the interconnected nature of the goals and also the impact of actions by countries on one another, the 17th goal of SDGs, *Partnerships for the Goals*, encourages forging partnerships to achieve the 16 other goals. These partnerships are to be in the domain of finance, technology, capacity building and systemic issues.

While the aim of the UN is common global good and welfare of everyone and the ecosystem at large, the events of the past decade pose an adverse challenge and run the risk of derailing the efforts and even reversing the progress and gains achieved over the past two decades. The major events are the global economic slowdown post the 2008 financial crisis, the European Debt Crisis, the disintegration of European Union with Britain's exit and the calls for separation in Spain, Ireland and Italy, the European migrant crisis, wars and displacements in South-East Asia and the Middle East and North Africa, the US-China trade war, increasing backlash against globalization and rising nationalism giving rise to politics of extremes (either left or right), trade wars for economic supremacy among a host of other factors make it difficult to achieve these individual and shared goals.

The key factors, in the success of the world in achieving progress in uplifting millions out of poverty and eradication or reducing the incidences of polio or HIV/AIDS, are an easy flow of knowledge, technology and the availability of finance, the fruits of globalization, which drove the global economic growth across the world. Nevertheless, globalization has its share of pitfalls. Much of the gains of global progress and success have been concentrated with a limited set of corporates and individuals. For instance, between 1995 and 2014, the global wealth grew by 66% but inequality was substantial as wealth per capita in high-income Organisation for Economic Cooperation and Development (OECD) member countries was 52 times higher than in low-income countries (Lange et al. 2018). A decline in per capita wealth was recorded after the 2009 financial crisis. This indicates that assets critical for generating future income may be depleted, a fact not often reflected in national GDP growth figures. As of 2019, the top 1% population owned 44% of the global wealth while the bottom 56% accounted for just 1.8% (Shorrocks et al. 2019). This highlights the stark difference in the wealth of individuals within and across countries and subsequently the economic opportunities for growth and development.

The global order is in desperate need of a mechanism, which shall help in enhancing global welfare through better redistribution of resources. There are abundances of resources on this planet for the consumption and welfare of all living beings. Can Islamic finance and economics through its emphasis on risk and reward sharing provide that alternative in a better redistribution of wealth and resources, enhance the quality of human life and yet, preserve the ecology?

Eco-Vision of Islam

Islam is a religion that puts a strong emphasis on wealth creation on the principle of sharing of risk and rewards between capital provider and entrepreneur. It gives strong support to entrepreneurship by making capital ineligible for reward without sharing the risk.

The trade-off in Islam is between not only the risk and return but it is also mandated that people should not try to take each other's wealth in any wrongful manner.[1] Emphasis on the circulation of wealth among masses is another important condition that distinguishes Islam from any

---

[1] And do not consume one another's wealth unjustly or send it [in bribery] to the rulers in order that [they might aid] you [to] consume a portion of the wealth of the people in sin, while you know [it is unlawful] (*Qur'an* 2:188).

other religion. *Qur'an* specifically ordains that wealth should not remain confined among the rich only.[2]

In addition to the above, Islam, driving from its worldview and unlike conventional economics, has a unique way of approaching the question of cost-benefit. It declares people as trustees of the resources[3] spread on the earth[4] and reminds that people should exercise moderation[5] in the exploitation of these resources keeping in view the requirements of the future generation as well. Hence, overexploitation, misuse and wastes are disapproved in no uncertain terms. From an Islamic point of view, cost-benefit can be looked at from the following three angles:

I. Cost-benefit analysis within the current generation: In this approach, permissibility is evaluated keeping in view the quantum of benefits it brings against its cost. *Qur'an* declares *Khamr* and *Maysir* impermissible because the cost of it is far greater than its benefits.[6]

II. Cost-benefit analysis between current and future generation: Protecting the interest of future generation is obligatory upon the current generation. *Shari'ah* scholars who have dealt with the subject of the objectives of the *Shari'ah* (*Maqasid-e-Shari'ah*) are unanimous that protection of progeny is one of the important objectives of *Shari'ah*. Islamic law of inheritance makes it very clear that the interest of future generations cannot be ignored or overlooked.

---

[2] "...... So that it will not be a perpetual distribution among the rich from among you" (*Qur'an* 95:7).

[3] Indeed, We have made that which is on the earth adornment for it that We may test them [as to] which of them is best in deed (*Qur'an* 18:7). And O you who have believed, let not your wealth and your children divert you from remembrance of Allah. And whoever does that—then those are the losers (*Qur'an* 63:9).

[4] "He it is who made the earth smooth for you, therefore go about in the spacious sides thereof, and eat of His sustenance, and to Him is the return after death" (*Qur'an* 67:15).

[5] And [they are] those who, when they spend, do so not excessively or sparingly but are ever, between that, [justly] moderate (*Qur'an* 25:67).

[6] They ask you about wine and gambling. Say, "In them is great sin and [yet, some] benefit for people. But their sin is greater than their benefit." And they ask you what they should spend. Say, "The excess [beyond needs]" (*Qur'an* 2:219).

III. Cost-benefit analysis between the present life and the hereafter: This is another unique contribution of Islamic economics in the sense that it declares life in this world as a test.[7] Islam emphasizes that life in this world is finite as compared to life in the hereafter. It exhorts believers to take their worldly decisions (economic, social, political, etc.) keeping in view this aspect.[8]

Overall, Islamic rules can be put into three categories such as **Compulsory** (*Mandoob*), **Permissible** (*Mubah*) and **Prohibitory** (*Haram*). Compulsory are those actions commission of which is mandated by Islamic law. Those who submit and follow are promised rewards and those who do not are warned of punishment for their negligence in the matter. Most of the rules related to worship (*Ebadaat*) fall in this category. From the economic point of view, only the obligation of *Zakah* falls in this category.

The second category is of those, which are considered permissible from the *Shari'ah* point of view. These are matters that are left to the discretion of people to pick and choose according to their respective utility and convenience. Much of the worldly matters fall in this category (such as trade, business and profession).[9]

The third is the category of those, which are specifically prohibited in *Shari'ah*. This is most important as far as the worldly affairs are concerned. All our economic, political and social matters fall in this category. *Qur'an* highlights all the things that are prohibited and instructs people to stay away from it clearly and in all situations. It even warns people not to go even near the boundary lines of prohibitions.[10] Other than these prohibitions, *Qur'an* gives people the freedom to indulge in their affairs as per mutual consent and free will. Those who flout the prohibition rules are declared wilful offenders and therefore deserving

---

[7] [He] who created death and life to test you [as to] which of you is best in deed (*Qur'an* 67:2).

[8] The Quran reminds believers not to sell life in the hereafter for the life in this world (*Qur'an* 2:86 and 4:74).

[9] "And I have made lawful for you, trade and business, and made unlawful for you dealing and interest" (*Qur'an* 2:275).

[10] These are the limits [set by] Allah, so do not approach them. Thus does Allah make clear His ordinances to the people that they may become righteous (*Qur'an* 2:187).

punishment and those who avoid prohibitions are promised rewards for their commitments to stay within the rules.

A general *Shari'ah* principle in the matters of worship is prohibition,[11] whereas in the matters of worldly affairs things are generally permissible.[12] Relations and rights of people are categorized into two: the rights of the Creator (*Huquq-Allah*) and the rights of the people over each other (*Huquq-al Ebaad*).[13] In terms of priority, rights of people prevail over the rights of Allah, as on the Day of Judgment Allah can forego/waive His rights over the people but not the right of the people over each other. He will leave it to people concerned about whether to extract recompense or forgive.

EVOLUTION OF ECONOMIC TOOLS

There are rules and regulations designed to support the attainment of Islamic economic vision. However, we find it pertinent to highlight that these tools were not created by the Prophet Muhammad ﷺ. There are hardly any tools that we can claim were designed by the Prophet himself. Based on the divine guidance, he declared certain practices (among the people) as prohibited and certain practices (among the people) as permissible. In some cases, he modified certain aspects/conditions to make it fall within the Islamic requirements of permissibility. For example, *riba* was declared prohibited (*haram*), while partnership (*shirkah*) was declared permissible and contracts like *Salam* were modified/tweaked to meet the clarities required to avoid Islamic prohibition of *gharar*. Prophet guided people in the further elaboration of these rules through his practices and instructions (e.g., describing types and nature of *riba*, etc.).

[11] Things are prohibited except those allowed or as required.

[12] Things are allowed except what is prohibited.

[13] And from their properties was [given] the right of the [needy] petitioner and the deprived (*Qur'an* 51:19).

SHARI'AH RULES FOR WEALTH MANAGEMENT
What Is Prohibited/Discouraged?

- *Riba*: Gain without risk and consideration to the business outcome.
- *Gharar*: Strong emphasis on contractual transparency, clarity and integrity.
- *Maysir*: No win at the cost of others even with mutual consent.
- Cheating/Frauds/Short sale/ *Najash/ghaban*.
- All cooperation that brings/cause harm to society.
- Delinquencies and non-payment of debt/dues on time.

Riba is the most important prohibition impacting business and wealth management. *Qur'an* is emphatic and commands believers to stay away from dealing with *riba*[14] as a mark of their commitment to the faith.[15] It also warns that those who do not stop dealing in *riba* are at war with Allah and His Prophet.[16] There is no other prohibition (except *"Shirk"*— joining partners with God), which attracts as severe punishment as *riba*. Prophet cursed all the parties that are involved in *riba* in any manner be they receiver, payer, writer or witness. During his lifetime, Prophet highlighted various types of *riba*. People ever since the Prophet have been very cautious in identifying and avoiding *riba* as much as they can. According to the majority of the Islamic scholars, modern-day bank interest falls in the same category as *riba* and hence believers seek to establish a banking operation that performs all the useful functions of a bank without involving itself in the prohibited *riba*. The most underlying feature of any Islamic prohibition is the injustice it causes to the society,

[14] "Those who eat *Riba* (usury) will not stand (on the Day of Resurrection) except like the standing of a person beaten by Satan leading him to insanity. That is because they say: "Trading is only like *Riba*," whereas Allah has permitted trading and forbidden *Riba*. So whosoever receives an admonition from his Lord and stops eating *Riba* shall not be punished for the past; his case is for Allah (to judge); but whoever returns [to Riba], such are the dwellers of the Fire - they will abide therein" (*Qur'an* 2:275).

[15] Allah destroys interest and gives increase for charities. And Allah does not like every sinning disbeliever (*Qur'an* 2:276).

[16] O you who have believed, fear Allah and give up what remains [due to you] of interest, if you should be believers (*Qur'an* 2:278). And if you do not, then be informed of a war [against you] from Allah and His Messenger. But if you repent, you may have your principal—[thus] you do no wrong, nor are you wronged (*Qur'an* 2:279).

and therefore, Islamic scholars have always attempted to identify injustices in an economic transaction and bring it under the prohibition of *riba*. Prophet also identified various types of economic injustice as *riba*.

Gharar is another important prohibition in Islamic finance, though not with as much severity as *riba*. *Gharar* is a kind of situation wherein parties to a transaction have a potential risk of a dispute arising between them due to lack of clarity on key objects of the transaction. This is also known as the presence of contractual ambiguity or lack of clarity. Price, delivery, quantity and quality are important aspects of a business transaction. If there is a lack of absolute clarity on these matters or certain promises or representations are contingent upon circumstances not within the reasonable control of the contracting parties, then it is known as infested with *gharar*. This *gharar* is further classified as major and minor.[17] In compensatory contracts (like trade), even the presence of minor *gharar* is disallowed whereas, in gratuitous contracts, scholars generally permit the availability of *gharar*. Islam for its emphasis on peace and tranquillity among people wants all aspects having a potential of causing disputes between the parties are minimized, understood and addressed.

In Islam, the return is always linked with effort, risk and responsibility borne by participating stakeholders. Naturally, return that is delinked from above or returns that are earned at the cost of another participating partner is not allowed. Hence, it is not only the gains from betting and gambling (*Maysir* or *Qimar*) but also participation in such activities is disallowed.

Any earning through wrongful manners such as cheating, fraud, misrepresentation, malpractices, hiding of material defect, bribe and a short sale is prohibited. *Qur'an* not only instructs for cooperation in good and virtuous things but also requires believers for non-cooperation in things that cause harm to society. The purity of income is one of the important considerations for acceptance of supplication in Islam. Prophet has said that a body which is nourished from *Haram* sources is good for hellfire only.

Non-payment of debt at maturity, or when the borrower is capable of repayment, is considered as an injustice to the lender and dealt with in the strongest possible words. The Prophet always encouraged people to

---

[17] *Gharar* can also be identified at individual and group levels such as in insurance and *Takaful*.

pay their debt on time and with better measurement. He practised this and encouraged others to do so.

What Is Encouraged/Recommended?

- Seeking beauties of this world and hereafter is virtuous.
- Considering wealth as blessings of Allah.
- Strong emphasis on entrepreneurship.
- Cooperation in good and virtuous things.
- Sharing of risk and rewards.
- Moderation in expenses.
- Avoid wastages/overexploitation.

Wealth like in many other religions is not considered taboo in Islam. Islam recognizes and appreciates the importance of wealth in human lives. Among the most important daily prayers *Qur'an* has taught is one that seeks God to grant the best of things in both the worlds (here and hereafter).[18] At many places in *Qur'an*, wealth is considered as a blessing and believers are encouraged to spread on earth seeking bounties of God. Wealth is also compared with children as a form of blessing from God.

Prophet himself practised entrepreneurship and Islam as a religion gives strong emphasis on entrepreneurship. Honest[19] entrepreneurs, traders and businessmen are compared with those fighting in the cause of God and promised rewards of the company of the Prophet himself in the life hereafter.[20]

Partnership among people is encouraged in no mean term. Prophet taught that when two people join in a partnership God brings Himself as the third partner and remains there until one of the partners becomes dishonest. Most of the businesses that Prophet himself was involved in were based on partnership concept (like *Musharaka* and *Mudaraba*).

---

[18] "Our Lord, give us in this world [that which is] good and in the Hereafter [that which is] good and protect us from the punishment of the Fire" (*Qur'an* 2:201).

[19] And O my people, give full measure and weight in justice and do not deprive the people of their due and do not commit abuse on the earth, spreading corruption (*Qur'an* 11:85).

[20] "The truthful, trustworthy merchant is with the Prophets, the truthful, and the martyrs" (Sunan al-Tirmizi-1209).

Even in agriculture, Prophet encouraged partnership between the landowner and farmer based on sharing of produce.

There are different models of partnership, which parties can choose from depending upon their respective roles and preferences but in no situation, the interest of other stakeholders can be overlooked or jeopardized. Society is considered to be the biggest stakeholder. No business arrangements between parties are allowed which can adversely affect the well-being of the society. Employees are another important stakeholder in Islamic arrangement whose interest and well-being are recognized with high importance.

Many teachings of the Prophet give guidance on how to spend.[21] While miserliness in Islam is considered as a sort of shortcoming and believers are exhorted not to be stingy.[22] It is also recommended that wastage or misuse is not allowed.[23] Prophet said food of one is enough for two and food of two is enough for three. He recommends people not to eat too much and not to overuse water even when they are on the bank of a river.

Wealth Redistribution

- *Zakah*: Helping near and dear one is compulsory and considered as purification of wealth in Islam.
- *Awqaf*: Encouraging rich and wealthy in society to dedicate their financial and other resources for the welfare of identified beneficiaries. Considered this as a perpetual charitable activity in favour of the donor.

---

[21] And spend in the way of Allah and do not throw [yourselves] with your [own] hands into destruction [by refraining]. And do good; indeed, Allah loves the doers of good (*Qur'an* 2:195).

[22] Behold, ye are those invited to spend (of your substance) in the Way of Allah: But among you are some that are niggardly. But any who are niggardly are so at the expense of their own souls. But Allah is free of all wants, and it is ye that are needy. If ye turn back (from the Path), He will substitute in your stead another people; then they would not be like you! (*Qur'an* 47:38).

[23] And do not make your hand [as] chained to your neck or extend it completely and [thereby] become blamed and insolvent. Indeed, your Lord extends provision for whom He wills and restricts [it]. Indeed, He is ever, concerning His servants, Acquainted and Seeing. And do not kill your children for fear of poverty. We provide for them and for you. Indeed, their killing is ever a great sin (*Qur'an* 17:29–31).

- *Hiba*: Giving power/authority to donate up to $1/3^{rd}$ of wealth to anyone without affecting the rights of the inheritors.
- Protecting the interest and rights of descendent and other family members including women by giving them property rights assigned from God.
- Foregoing of debt or giving time to borrowers who face difficulties.

Capability to earn wealth is considered as blessings from God, bestowed upon a chosen few. Hence, believers are expected to express their gratitude towards God[24] by acknowledging this special favour by assuming responsibilities in discharging their roles in the society for promoting good and meeting needs of the society.[25] At many places in *Qur'an*, people are reminded that their wealth is a test for them.[26] They are encouraged to spend on their family members,[27] relatives, neighbours, orphans,[28] friends and society at large.[29] There are verses in *Qur'an* that

[24] And those who thank are promised even better rewards, ""If you give thanks, I will give you more (of My Blessings)" (*Qur'an* 14:7). He will send rain to you in abundance; And give you increase in wealth and children and bestow on you gardens and bestow on you rivers" (*Qur'an* 71:10–12). And "I said (to them): 'ask forgiveness from your Lord; verily He is Oft-Forgiving. He will send rain to you in abundance; And give you increase in wealth and children, and bestow on you gardens and bestow on you rivers" (*Qur'an* 71:10–12).

[25] And Allah has favored some of you over others in provision. But those who were favored would not hand over their provision to those whom their right hands possess so they would be equal to them therein. Then is it the favor of Allah they reject? (*Qur'an* 16:71).

[26] And know that your properties and your children are but a trial and that Allah has with Him a great reward (*Qur'an* 8:28).

[27] And give the relative his right, and [also] the poor and the traveler, and do not spend wastefully. Indeed, the wasteful are brothers of the devils, and ever has Satan been to his Lord ungrateful (*Qur'an* 17:26–27).

[28] Have you seen him who belies the rewards and punishments of the Hereafter? It is he who drives away the orphan and does not urge giving away the food of the poor. (*Qur'an* 107:1–3). "And give to the orphans their properties and do not substitute the defective [of your own] for the good [of theirs]. And do not consume their properties into your own. Indeed, that is ever a great sin" (*Qur'an* 4:2).

[29] Allah has said: "Spend oh son of Adam and I shall spend on you" (*Bukhari*).

exhort people to spend their wealth openly[30] and silently.[31] The Prophet encouraged people to spend their wealth instead of saving it all for one's children.[32] It does not mean that leaving wealth for children is considered bad. Prophet taught one of his companions who had a daughter and requested Prophet to allow him to bequeath all his wealth for the social cause. Prophet did not permit him to bequeath his wealth beyond one-third with a recommendation that it is better to leave your children in a comfortable situation so that they are not required to seek help from others.

Qur'an reminds people that wealth should not circulate only among rich and hence makes the provision of its circulation among the poor through a strong redistributive mechanism such as *Zakah*. *Zakah* is one of the five most important pillars of Islam. Every person who has wealth beyond a measurement is required to pay a percentage (2.5%) towards meeting the needs of poor and needy.[33] This is considered as purification of wealth.[34] During Prophet's time and later period also, this was implemented vociferously and *Zakah* continued to play a very important role in ameliorating the situation of the poor. However, in modern times after the emergence of nation-states, *Zakah* management in many countries have fallen in private hands leading to a lot of mismanagement and leakages.

[30] [O Muhammad], tell My servants who have believed to establish prayer and spend from what We have provided them, secretly and publicly, before a Day comes in which there will be no exchange, nor any friendships (*Qur'an* 14:31).

[31] If you disclose your charitable expenditures, they are good; but if you conceal them and give them to the poor, it is better for you, and He will remove from you some of your misdeeds [thereby] (*Qur'an* 2:271).

[32] They ask you, [O Muhammad], what they should spend. Say, "Whatever you spend of good is [to be] for parents and relatives and orphans and the needy and the traveler. And whatever you do of good - indeed, Allah is Knowing of it" (*Qur'an* 2:215).

[33] There are eight categories of recipients, but all can be identified with the two. Those working in zakat collection and distribution are permitted to draw their salaries or meet their expenses. Qur'an says, "Zakah are only for the poor and for the needy and for those employed to collect [*Zakah*] and for bringing hearts together [for Islam] and for freeing captives [or slaves] and for those in debt and for the cause of Allah and for the [stranded] traveler - an obligation [imposed] by Allah. And Allah is Knowing and Wise" (*Qur'an* 9:60).

[34] Take, [O, Muhammad], from their wealth a charity by which you purify them and cause them increase, and invoke [Allah's blessings] upon them. Indeed, your invocations are reassurance for them (*Qur'an* 9:103).

Waqf is another very important redistribution economic tool used since the very early days of Islam. Making *Waqf* is not compulsory, but highly encouraged in *Qur'an* and teachings of Prophet as a charity with a lot of emphasis and promise of rewards in both the worlds.[35] Many companions of the Prophet dedicated a significant portion of their wealth for public causes such as making provisions for water, food, treating the sick and medicines. Visitors, travellers and state guest were also supported through provisions of *Awqaf*. During Islam's ascendency, wealthy people through the provision of *Waqf* supported the laboratories, libraries, hospitals, motels, etc. In Islam, the value of *Waqf* can be understood from the fact that these are considered as perpetual charities in favour of the donor. We find millions of *Awqaf* across the globe meeting the needs of the society and sharing the burden with their respective governments.

Hiba (gift), *Wasiyah* (will) and *Mirath* are other economic tools in Islam, which play a very important role in directing wealth from rich to others. Hiba is a plain gift given during the lifetime of a person, whereas *Wasiyah* is a will where the donor grants wealth to someone after his/her death. There is a cap prescribed on *Wasiyah* to make sure that rights of the inheritors are not compromised with. It is important to mention that Islam recognizes the right of women in the wealth of their parents, husbands and other relatives just like men. However, the share in the wealth is prescribed according to their respective responsibilities towards their dependents. Another very important feature of Islamic economic rule is the recommendation of forgoing debt owed by others. Those who can afford are encouraged to give relaxation in time to those who are unable to repay their debts.[36] Creditors are encouraged to not only provide relaxation in time and amount but also exhorted to waive the entire loan should they find their borrowers in difficulty. This in Islam is

---

[35] [Charity is] for the poor who have been restricted for the cause of Allah, unable to move about in the land. An ignorant [person] would think them self-sufficient because of their restraint, but you will know them by their [characteristic] sign. They do not ask people persistently [or at all]. And whatever you spend of good—indeed, Allah is Knowing of it (*Qur'an* 2:273).

[36] And if someone is in hardship, then [let there be] postponement until [a time of] ease. But if you give [from your right as] charity, then it is better for you, if you only knew (*Qur'an* 2:280).

considered as *Qard-e-Hasana*, a benevolent loan for which Allah promises multiple rewards.[37]

BASIC HUMAN NEEDS AND *SHARI'AH*

Islamic scholars agree that *Shari'ah* has twofold objectives: saving people from harm and seeking benefits for them. Ibn Qayyim al-Jawziyyah emphasizes the primacy of ethical norms to the structure of Islamic values in these words, "The *Shari'ah* is founded in wisdom and realization of people's welfare in this life and the next. It is all about justice, mercy, and the common good. Thus, any ruling that replaces justice with injustice, mercy with its opposite, common good with mischief, and wisdom with indiscretion does not belong to the *Shari'ah*, even if it is claimed to be so according to some interpretations" (Qayyim 1973). Therefore, all the *Shari'ah* regulations revolve around seeking these two goals. The main idea behind the emergence of Islamic banking and finance was to create strong linkages between the real economy and financial sector on the principle of sharing of risk and reward. Another equally important target was enabling finance for socially, ethically and morally beneficial sectors and activities of the society. Rafe Haneef, CEO of CIMB Islamic succinctly, puts it, "From an Islamic viewpoint everything on this earth and beyond belongs to God Almighty. And whatever human beings own on this earth is held on trust for God. God gives some an abundance of wealth and to others a pittance. The wealth is but a test on the rich. If the rich consume the wealth wisely, invest the wealth in socially responsible activities and give charity to the poor, they as God's trustee will pass the test and be rewarded with a place in heaven. But, if the rich spend the wealth wastefully, engage in usurious lending, and ignore the poor, they will fail the test" (Haneef 2019).

It may not be an overstatement to claim that Islamic finance drew the attention of masses on the concept of ethical finance and investments. However, it was the Global Financial Crisis of 2008–2009, which exposed the faultiness of the financial system before the Western academia and policymakers. People started evaluating the cost of excessive financialization and its benefits to society. Ever since many such ideas have emerged such as "Responsible Investments", "Ethical Investments",

---

[37] Whoever gives a goodly loan to Allah, he will multiply it for them abundantly, Allah is the one who withholds and gives, and to him is your final return (*Qur'an* 2:145).

"Values-Based Intermediation", "Environmental, Social and Corporate Governance (ESG)", "Ethical Finance" and "Impact Investing". Sustainable Development Goals (SDGs) is an extension of the same idea with the concurrence of the members of the United Nations. Countries have unanimously agreed to target 17 specific areas concerning human dignity and welfare.

Al-Shatibi is among the scholars who have dealt with in detail about the objectives of *Shari'ah* concerning five most basic human interests such as (i) religion (*din*); (ii) life (*nafs*); (iii) progeny (*nasl*); (iv) intellect (*aql*); and (v) wealth (*maal*). He categorizes protection of these five into three layers, namely (Nassrey et al. 2018):

(a) The Necessities: This refers to basic universal human needs, provision of which is must by society or state.
(b) Needs/Requirements: This refers to the provision of removal of hardships in attaining the necessities by allowing required exceptions.
(c) Complementariness: This is the final layer of human needs which aims at complementing and beautifying human culture and aesthetics.

In the light of the above discussion on the objectives of *Shari'ah*, we find following SDGs directly addressed through Islamic economics tools.

Mapping SDGs with Islamic Teachings

The verses of the *Qur'an* and life of the Prophet shed light on the importance attached to the well-being of all living beings and the ecology at large and guide us on the road to attaining welfare for all. Below we map the Islamic teachings with the objectives of SDGs (Obaidullah 2019).

SDGs 1–3: Poverty, Hunger and Well-Being

- "And they give food in spite of love for it to the needy, the orphan, and the captive, [Saying], "We feed you only for the countenance of Allah. We wish not from you reward or gratitude" (*Qur'an*, 76:8–9). Poverty in Islam is compared with disbelief. Prophet used to regular pray for safety against poverty. Ending poverty is considered as a collective responsibility of the society.

- Not making provision for feeding poor is considered great sin and believers are required to make sure that there is no one hungry in their locality. Prophet taught that a person is not Muslim if he eats full while his neighbour is hungry. He said: "Give food to the hungry, visit the sick and set free the captives" (*Bukhari*, Vol. 7, No. 552). Moderation in food consumption is encouraged along with the focus on agriculture.
- Cleanliness is compared with faith (*Imaan*). Looking after one's hygiene and cleanliness is important requirements of the five daily prayers. *Qur'an* says, "O you who have believed when you rise to [perform] prayer, wash your faces and your forearms to the elbows and wipe over your heads and wash your feet to the ankles…. Allah does not intend to make difficulty for you, but He intends to purify you and complete His favour upon you that you may be grateful" (*Qur'an* 5:6). At another place, Qur'an declares, "Indeed, Allah loves those who are constantly repentant and loves those who purify themselves" (*Qur'an*, 2:222).
- The Prophet commanded Muslims to seek treatment of every ailment. He said Allah has not made a disease without appointing a remedy for it (*Abu Dawud*, Book 22, No. 3846). A healthy and strong believer is praised over a weak and unhealthy believer.
- Prophet prescribed a maximum time limit for clipping the moustache, cutting the nails, plucking hair under the armpits, shaving the pubes (*Sahih Muslim* 258: Book 2, Hadith 66).
- Consumption of unclean animals is prohibited for safety and hygiene reasons. *Qur'an* commands, "He has only forbidden to you dead animals, blood, the flesh of swine, and that which has been dedicated to other than Allah" (*Qur'an*, 2:173).

SDGs 4–6: Quality Education, Gender Equality, Clean Water and Sanitation

- Education is given paramount importance in Islam. The first verse to be revealed on Prophet Muhammad ﷺ was, "Recite in the name of your Lord who created" (*Qur'an* 96:1). Prophet said, "When a man dies, his acts come to an end, but three, recurring charity, or knowledge (by which people benefit), or a pious son, who prays for him (the deceased)" (*Muslim*, Book 25, No. 20).

- The Prophet commanded:

  - "Seeking knowledge is an obligation upon every Muslim" (*Sunan Ibn Majah*).
  - "He who follows a path in quest of knowledge, Allah will make the path of Jannah easy to him....... The superiority of the learned man over the devout worshipper is like that of the full moon to the rest of the stars. The learned are the heirs of the Prophets" (*Riyad as-Salihin* 1388, Book 12, Hadith 13).
  - "Whoever goes out seeking knowledge, then he is in Allah's cause until he returns" (*Jami at-Tirmidhi* 2647: Book 41, Hadith 3).
  - "Acquire knowledge and impart it to the people" (*Al-Tirmidhi*, 107).
  - "A father gives his child nothing better than a good manner" (*Al-Tirmidhi*, Vol 4, 1952).
  - "He who has a slave-girl and teaches her good manners and improves her education and then manumits and marries her will get a double reward" (*Bukhari* 2547).

- Regarding gender equality, *Qur'an* declares, "And of all things We created two mates; perhaps you will remember" (*Qur'an* 51:49). "And of His signs is that He created for you from yourselves mates that you may find tranquillity in them, and He placed between you affection and mercy. Indeed, in that are signs for a people who give thought" (*Qur'an* 30:21). And "O you who have believed, it is not lawful for you to inherit women by compulsion. And do not make difficulties for them to take [back] part of what you gave them unless they commit a clear immorality. And live with them in kindness. For if you dislike them - perhaps you dislike a thing and Allah makes therein much good" (*Qur'an* 4:19).
- "And do not wish for that by which Allah has made some of you exceed others. For men is a share of what they have earned, and for women is a share of what they have earned. And ask Allah of his bounty. Indeed Allah is ever, of all things, Knowing" (*Qur'an* 4:32).
- Prophet warned, "I forbid usurpation of the right of two weak persons – the orphan and the woman" (*Muslim*).

SDGs 10–13: Reducing Inequality, Sustainable Cities and Communities, Responsible Consumption and Production, Climate Action

- "And from their properties was [given] the right of the [needy] petitioner and the deprived" (*Qur'an* 51:19). "And those within whose wealth is a known right, for the petitioner and the deprived" (*Qur'an* 70:24–25).
- "And be not excessive. Indeed, He does not like those who commit excess" (*Qur'an* 6:141). "....eat and drink, but be not excessive. Indeed, He likes not those who commit excess" (*Qur'an* 7:31). "And give the relative his right, and [also] the poor and the traveller, and do not spend wastefully" (*Qur'an* 17:26).
- "And [they are] those who, when they spend, do so not excessively or sparingly but are ever, between that, [justly] moderate" (*Qur'an* 25:67).
- "Corruption has appeared throughout the land and sea by [reason of] what the hands of people have earned so He may let them taste part of [the consequence of] what they have done that perhaps they will return [to righteousness]" (*Qur'an* 30:41).

SDGs 15–17: Life on Land, Peace, Justice and Strong Institutions, Partnerships for the Goals

- "Do you not see that to Allah prostrates whoever is in the heavens and whoever is on the earth and the sun, the moon, the stars, the mountains, the trees, the moving creatures and many of the people?" (*Qur'an* 22:18)
- "And there is no creature on [or within] the earth or bird that flies with its wings except [that they are] communities like you. We have not neglected in the Register a thing. Then unto their Lord, they will be gathered" (*Qur'an* 6:38).
- "And the heaven He raised and imposed the balance. That you not transgress within the balance. And establish weight in justice and do not make deficient the balance" (*Qur'an* 55:7–9),
- "If the Resurrection were established upon one of you while he has in his hand a sapling, then let him plant it" (*Musnad Aḥmad*, 12491).

- "They who believe and do not mix their belief with injustice - those will have security, and they are [rightly] guided" (*Qur'an* 6:82).
- "And [all] faces will be humbled before the Ever-Living, the Sustainer of existence. And he will have failed who carries injustice" (*Qur'an* 20:111).
- The *Qur'an* equates the unwarranted killing of even a single individual with the killing of the whole of mankind, and the saving of a single life with the saving of the whole of mankind, "...whoever kills a soul unless for a soul or for corruption [done] in the land - it is as if he had slain mankind entirely. And whoever saves one - it is as if he had saved mankind entirely" (*Qur'an* 5:32).
- "Indeed, the best one you can hire is the strong and the trustworthy" (*Qur'an* 28:26).
- "And cooperate in righteousness and piety, but do not cooperate in sin and aggression" (*Qur'an* 5:2).

CONCLUSION

Despite all technological advancements and wealth creation, humanity is still unable to provide minimum assured quality of life to a great majority of people on the globe. A great amount of wealth generated every year goes in the hands of very few people. At the same time, the major cost of technological and industrial advancement is borne by masses who are finding it increasingly difficult to cope up with the challenges thrown by global warming, displacements, war, political upheavals and social strife. In such a scenario, United Nations member countries launched Millennium Development Goal (MDG) which after few years was expanded into Sustainable Development Goals (SDGs). The basic idea behind SDGs is to require member countries to commit human and financial resources for achievements of minimum agreed targets by the year 2030. A large number of countries who are much behind on SDGs parameters are members of the Organization of Islamic Cooperation (OIC). Islamic Banking and Finance is a thriving business in these countries with the potential to reach masses in the coming years. We have explored and discussed the relationship between SDGs and *Shari'ah* objectives. In the light of *Shari'ah* objectives, we have highlighted that 12 objectives of SDGs are matching with basic *Shari'ah* stipulated quality of life. Through this paper, we aim to create better understanding and appreciation of

SDGs in the light of *Shari'ah* and hope that Islamic finance fraternity will play a positive role in assisting their respective governments in achieving SDGs goals.

REFERENCES

Dariah, A., Salleh, M., & Shafiai, H. (2016). A New Approach for Sustainable Development Goals in Islamic Perspective. *Procedia—Social and Behavioural Sciences*, 159–166.

Haneef, R. (2019). Convergence of Islamic and Sustainable Finance. In *SOAS-QFC Public Lecture on Convergence of Islamic and Sustainable Finance* (p. 36). London: Centre for Islamic and Middle Eastern Law, SOAS, University of London and Qatar Financial Centre Authority.

Lange, G.-M., Wodon, Q., & Carey, K. (2018). *The Changing Wealth of Nations 2018: Building a Sustainable Future*. Washington, DC: World Bank.

Nassrey, I., Ahmed, R., & Tatari, M. (2018). *The Objectives of Islamic Law: The Promises and Challenges of Maqasid al-Shari'a*. Lanham, MD: Lexington Books.

Obaidullah, M. (2019, September 21). *The Sustainable Development Goals from a Shariah Perspective—VII*. Retrieved from IBF Net Blogs: https://ibfnet.blog/2019/09/21/the-sustainable-development-goals-from-a-shariah-perspective-vii/.

Qayyim, I. A. (1973). *Ilam al Muwaqqi'in an Rabbi al Alameen* (Vol. 1). Beirut: Dar al Jeel.

Shorrocks, A., Davies, J., & Lluberas, R. (2019). *Global Wealth Report*. Zurich: Credit Suisse.

United Nations. (2020, July 7). *Sustainable Development Goals*. Retrieved from Sustainable Development Goals Knowledge Platform: https://sustainabledeve lopment.un.org/sdgs.

CHAPTER 9

Baitul Maal wat Tamwil as Integrated Islamic Microfinance Institution to Support SDGs

Ascarya

Introduction

The principles of Islamic economic and finance are not only focused on the commercial side, such as the prohibition of riba, gharar, maysir, dharar, dzalim and muharramat, but it is also focused on the social side, such as zakat, infaq, shadaqa and waqf. Zakat is not only an instrument to achieve equitable distribution of income and wealth inclusively, but zakat is also an instrument to control individual wealth to be channeled to productive activities in the real sector. Waqf, along with infaq and shadaqa, is an instrument intended to encourage members of the community to participate in social and commercial activities aiming to improve the welfare of the community. With the integration of Islamic commercial finance and Islamic social finance, economy would run sustainably to achieve equitable distribution of income and wealth with stable and just monetary and financial system. Moreover, Islamic commercial finance is inherently stable (IRTI-IDB 2010), while Islamic social finance could

Ascarya (✉)
Institut Agama Islam TAZKIA, Bogor, Indonesia

© The Author(s), under exclusive license to Springer Nature Switzerland AG 2021
M. M. Billah (eds.), *Islamic Wealth and the SDGs*,
https://doi.org/10.1007/978-3-030-65313-2_9

175

simultaneously achieve triple bottom-line stated by Zeller and Meyer (2002), including outreach to the poor, sustainability and welfare impact.

However, zakat, infaq, sadaqa and waqf, as elements of Islamic social finance, have not been given the same attention to Islamic commercial finance, so that Islamic financial institution (IFI) has mostly focused on commercial finance. Conceptually, IFI, especially Islamic bank (IB), Islamic rural bank (IRB) and Islamic microfinance institution (IMFI), operates differently compared to conventional financial institution (CFI). While CFI applies fractional reserve banking system (FRBS), pooling of funds and liability driven, IFI applies non-FRBS, allocation of funds and asset driven. However, the development of IFI has been mimicking the CFI, so that IFI has also been exposed to risks associated with FRBS, pooling of fund and liability driven, such as bubble, mismatch and liquidity risk. Therefore, IFI has also been affected greatly by financial crisis.

Baitul Maal wat Tamwil

Baitul Maal wat Tamwil or BMT is a typical Indonesian Islamic microfinance institution (IMFI) that was originally established and developed to be able to adapt to regulations and market needs. The first BMT, Teknosa, the Expertise Service Cooperative, was established on July 4, 1984, with an initial capital of Rp34 million and 18 members, which then grew to Rp1.4 billion with 300 members. Because of the high non-performing financing (NPF), BMT Teknosa stopped its operation in 1989. In the following year, the second BMT, Ridho Gusti Cooperative, was established in Bandung. Since then, other BMTs have begun to grow like mushrooms in the rainy season. The latest estimate recorded that there were more than 5000 BMTs spread all over Indonesia. Meanwhile, the largest BMT UGT has reached Rp3.2 trillion total assets, 327 branches spread in 10 provinces, serving more than 420 thousand members, managed by more than 1600 employees.

BMT has two functions or work units, namely: (1) Baitul Maal (Bait = House, al-Maal = Wealth)—whose activities collect Islamic social funds (mandatory or voluntary) such as zakat from muzakki (zakat payer), infaq from munfiq (infaq donor), sadaqa from general Muslim and waqf and cash waqf, from waqif (waqf donor), to financed social waqf, productive waqf, as well as optimizing their distribution according to Shariah principles—and (2) Baitut Tamwil (Bait = House, at-Tamwil = asset development)—carry out activities to develop productive businesses and investments in improving the economic quality of micro- and small entrepreneurs, especially by encouraging various savings and investments, as well as supporting various financings, especially for productive activities (Ascarya 2017).

BMT applies an integrated approach by providing Islamic social financial services to fulfill the basic needs of mustahiq or the poor (to get out of poverty) and to fulfill the needs of the society in general, as well as providing a variety of Islamic commercial financial services on a smaller scale to low-income groups to improve their quality of life. Thus, besides BMT integrating Islamic social and commercial finance, BMT also integrates social inclusion (in Baitul Maal) and financial inclusion (in Baitut Tamwil), which is a real application of holistic financial inclusion (Ascarya 2016). By integrating Islamic social finance in the Baitul Maal and Islamic commercial finance in the Baitut Tamwil, the BMT would be able to achieve triple bottom-line stated by Zeller and Meyer (2002), including outreach to the poor, sustainability and welfare impact.

MODELS OF INTEGRATED ISLAMIC MICROFINANCE

The integration model of Islamic commercial finance (ICF) and Islamic social finance (ISF) at the micro-level can be carried out by Islamic microfinance institutions (IMFI) with legal entity MFI (Microfinance Institutions) under the OJK (Financial Services Authority) regulation or by IMFI with legal entities KSPPS (Islamic Savings and Financing Cooperative) under the regulations of KemKop & UKM (Ministry of Cooperatives and Small and Medium Enterprises). Baitul Maal wat Tamwil or BMT, which carries out social financial activities in Baitul Maal and commercial finance in Baitut Tamwil (Ascarya 2014, p. 54, 2016, pp. 2, 6; Wulandari and Kassim 2016, pp. 217, 230), as Indonesian original IMFI, constitutes the largest part of this integrated IMFI model, especially those with KSPPS legal status.

Integrated Islamic Microfinance

IIMFI-1 Model
In this IIMFI-1 model, the BMT as IMFI appoints person in charge (PIC) or forms a Social Unit to collect zakat, infaq and sadaqa (ZIS)

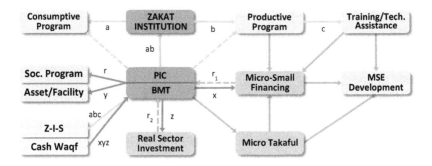

Fig. 9.1 Integrated Islamic Microfinance IIMFI-1 model

funds as Zakat Collection Unit (ZCU) of zakat institution and to collect cash waqf as waqf institution (see Fig. 9.1).

BMT as IMFI with KSPPS legal status with very small total assets (less than Rp1 billion) or small total assets (less than Rp10 billion) designates a person in charge (PIC) or forms a Social Unit (the forerunner of the Baitul Maal Unit) as ZCU of zakat institution and as a Nazir of waqf (including cash waqf). Meanwhile, BMT (specifically the Baitut Tamwil or BT) as IFI who have Wadiah saving deposits are also officially becomes IFI of Receiving Cash Waqf (IFI-RCF).

As Amil of zakat or ZCU, the BMT collects and deposits ZIS funds (abc) in the BMT saving deposits, mainly collected from BMT's stakeholders, especially the BMT members and employees, as well as surrounding communities, and then channeled to the zakat institution. These funds will be distributed by the zakat institution to mustahiq (zakat recipients) through consumptive program (a) to fulfill the basic needs, productive program (b) and training/technical assistance (c). The productive program with training and technical assistance is intended to assist the mustahiq out of poverty by providing qardh financing to start a business and be self-sufficient, as well as developing mustahiq's business further accessing commercial micro-small financing.

As Nazir, the BMT collects cash waqf (xyz) direct and indirect cash waqf), and deposits the cash waqf funds in the BMT saving deposits (for direct cash waqf) and investment deposits or waqf equity (for indirect cash waqf). Direct cash waqf (y) will be used to build social waqf facility or productive waqf asset, including real sector investment (z). Indirect cash waqf will be used productively to extend micro-small financing to

Table 9.1 Examples of BMT applying IIMFI-1 model

BMT	Asset	Branch	BT employee	Member	Location
NU Sumenep	Rp95.24 Bi	29	161	22.17 Th	Sumenep
Amanah Ummah	Rp11.68 Bi	2	22	5.32 Th	Surabaya
Manfaat	Rp2.40 Bi	1	4	0.27 Th	Surabaya

BMT	Zakat	Infaq	ID-Cash aqf	D-Cash aqf	PIC BM
NU Sumenep	–	Rp17.7 Mi	–	–	2 Persons
Amanah Ummah	Rp19.4 Mi	Rp4.5 Mi	Rp5.7 Mi	–	2 Persons
Manfaat	Rp29.0 Mi	Rp24.0 Mi	Rp11.0 Mi	Rp7.0 Mi	1 Person

Note 2017 data from BMT's Annual Reports. BT = Baitut Tamwil; D = Direct; ID = Indirect; BM = Baitul Maal; Bi = Billion; Mi = Million; Th = Thousand

prime member-customer. Micro-takaful is used to mitigate the financing. The returns from micro-small financing (r_1) and real sector investment (r_2) will be used to finance various social programs ($r = r_1 + r_2$).

Examples of BMT applying the IIMFI-1 model (see Table 9.1) are quite numerous, such as BMT: (1) BMT NU in Sumenep; (2) BMT Ummah Amanah in Surabaya; and (3) BMT Manfaat in Surabaya. These IIMFI-1 model BMTs have assets ranged from Rp2.40 to Rp95.24 Billion, with 1–29 branches, 4–161 employees, 0.27–22.17 thousand members, which are spread especially in Java. These IIMFI-1 model BMTs manage Rp17.7–Rp53.0 million in zakat and infaq, manage Rp0 – Rp18 million of cash waqf, and are managed by 1–2 PICs.[1] Even though BMT Sumenep has quite large assets, it does not have Social Unit or Baitul Maal Unit to manage ZIS. It also does not manage waqf (including cash waqf).

IIMFI-2 Model

In this IIMFI-2 model, the BMT as IMFI establishes formal Baitul Maal Unit as ZCU of zakat institution to collect zakat, infaq and sadaqa (ZIS) funds and to collect cash waqf as waqf institution (see Fig. 9.2).

BMT applying IIMFI-2 model is an IMFI that has legal status as KSPPS with medium total assets (Rp10–Rp50 billion). The BMT formed the Baitul Maal Unit as a Zakat Collection Unit (ZCU) or zakat

---

[1] 1 USD = Rp14,125.00 at June 15, 2020, by Bloomberg.

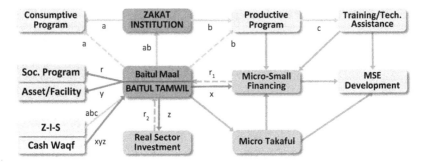

Fig. 9.2 Integrated Islamic Microfinance IIMFI-2 model

management partner (ZMP) of a zakat institution, and as Nazir of waqf (including cash waqf). Meanwhile, BMT (specifically Baitut Tamwil or BT) as IFI who has Wadiah saving deposits also officially becomes IFI and IFI-RCW of the BM Unit as Amil of zakat and Nazir of cash waqf.

The BM Unit will carry out the duties of Amil of zakat and Nazir of waqf similar to PIC or Social Unit of IIMFI-1 model with more resources and capabilities. As ZMP, the BM Unit could manage the ZIS funds (abc) by itself with zakat institution assistance/collaboration to distribute ZIS to mustahiq, by organizing consumptive program (a), productive program (b) and training/technical assistance (c). Infaq could also be used to finance various social programs needed for general Muslim society conducted by the BM Unit itself.

As Nazir of waqf, BM Unit could organize to raise waqf to build larger social waqf facility (y), such as Islamic kindergarten, musholla and mosque, or to develop larger productive waqf business in the real sector (z), such as home-office and mini store. the BM Unit could also receive waqf assets directly from the waqf donor (waqif). As Nazir of indirect cash waqf, the BM Unit will collect cash waqf (x) from stakeholders and invested the funds in the BMT (especially in Baitut Tamwil), as has been described in IIMFI-1 model.

Examples of BMT applying IIMFI-2 model include: (1) BMT Hudatama in Semarang; (2) BMT Mardlotillah in Sumedang; and (3) BMT Mustama in Lembang (see Table 9.2). These IIMFI-2 model BMTs manage assets ranged from Rp5.27 to Rp40.00 billion, with 1–5 branches, 9–45 employees, 1.71–30.23 thousand members, which are

Table 9.2 Examples of BMT applying IIMFI-2 model

BMT	Asset	Branch	BT Employee	Member	Location
Hudatama	Rp40.00 Bi	5	45	7.00 Th	Semarang
Mardlotillah	Rp19.65 Bi	5	9*	30.23 Th	Sumedang
Mustama	Rp5.27 Bi	1	10	1.71 Th	Lembang

BMT	Zakat	Infaq	ID-Cash aqf	D-Cash Waqf	BM Unit
Hudatama	Rp500.0 Mi		Rp300.0 Mi	–	1 unit
Mardlotillah	Rp23.8 Mi	Rp29.7 Mi	Rp10.1 Mi	–	1 staff
Mustama	Rp6.1 Mi	Rp52.9 Mi	Rp1.1 Mi	–	1 unit

Note 2017 data from BMT's Annual Reports. BT = Baitut Tamwil; D = Direct; ID = Indirect; BM = Baitul Maal; Bi = Billion; Mi = Million; Th = Thousand

spread especially in Java. The IIMFI-2 model BMTs manage Rp59.0–Rp500.0 million annually of zakat and infaq and manage Rp1.1–Rp300.0 million of cash waqf, and the BM Units are managed by 1–3 staffs. Hudatama could collect zakat and cash waqf of IDR 0.5 billion or 1.25% of the total assets and could collect Rp0.3 billion or 0.75% of the total assets, so that the ZIS and cash waqf collected annually equivalent to 2.00% of the total assets.

IIMFI-3 Model
In this IIMFI-3 model, the BMT as IMFI divides the BMT into two full divisions, namely Baitul Maal division responsible to manage ZIS and waqf, and Baitut Tamwil division responsible to manage commercial Islamic microfinance, and acts as IFI and IFI-RCF receiving ZIS and cash waqf of Baitul Maal division (see Fig. 9.3).

BMT adopted IIMFI-3 model is an IMFI under KSPPS legal status with quite large total assets (Rp50–Rp100 billion) or large total assets (Rp100–Rp250 billion). Generally, the BMTs with IIMFI-3 model have a Baitul Maal (BM) division and a Baitut Tamwil (BT) division. BM division officially becomes the ZMP (Zakat Management Partner) or a fully independent zakat institution, and also becomes a Nazir of waqf (including cash waqf). Meanwhile, BT division acts as IFI of ZIS and IFI-RCW of cash waqf of BT division.

As a further expansion of IIMFI-2 model, the IIMFI-3 model BM division as zakat institution fully could carry out and develop extensive

Fig. 9.3 Integrated Islamic Microfinance IIMFI-3 model

and better zakat programs, including consumptive program, productive program and training/technical assistance, since they have better resources, better infrastructure, better system and better capabilities. The zakat programs are expected to have graduation system capable of assisting mustahiq out of poverty. ZIS in terms of cash will be deposited in BT division, while ZIS in kind could be managed directly by BM division.

Moreover, as Nazir of waqf or waqf institution fully, the BM division could also carry out and develop larger and better waqf projects, including social waqf project, productive waqf project, integrated social-productive waqf project and various social programs. Fund-raising of indirect cash waqf could also be carried out expansively to strengthen the capital and liabilities of the BMT, therefore improving the sustainability of the BMT. Waqf in terms of cash will be deposited/invested in BT division, while waqf in kind could be managed directly by BM division.

Examples of BMTs with the IIMFI-3 model are quite numerous, such as: (1) BMT Beringharjo in Yogyakarta; (2) BMT L-Risma in Metro, Lampung; (3) BMT Bina Ihsanul Fikri in Yogyakarta; (4) BMT Surya Abadi in Central Lampung, Lampung; and (5) BMT Barrah in Bandung (see Table 9.3). BMT Beringharjo can collect zakat and infaq of Rp3.0 billion or 2.22% of its total assets, as well as Rp209.0 million cash waqf or 0.15% of its total assets.

IIMFI-4 Model
In this IIMFI-4 model, BMT or Baitut Tamwil (BT) as IMFI establishes separate Baitul Maal as Amil of zakat managing ZIS, and as Nazir managing waqf, including cash waqf, while the BMT or BT acts as IFI

Table 9.3 Examples of BMT applying IIMFI-3 model

BMT	Asset	Branch	BT Employee	Member	Location
Beringharjo	Rp135.00 Bi	16	135	9.72 Rb	Yogyakarta
L-Risma	Rp103.00 Bi	21	196	66.48 Th	Lampung
Surya Abadi	Rp101.00 Bi	7	101	20.91 Th	Lampung
Bina I. Fikri	Rp78.60 Bi	11	93	36.35 Th	Yogyakarta
Barrah	Rp37.48 Bi	6	59	16.33 Th	Bandung

BMT	Zakat	Infaq	ID-Cash Waqf	D-Cash Waqf	BM Employee
Beringharjo	Rp3000.1 Mi		Rp132.7 Mi	Rp69.3 Mi	6 Staffs
L-Risma	Rp115.7 Mi	Rp201.2 Mi	Rp345.0 Mi	Rp1500.0 Mi	6 Staffs
Surya Abadi	Rp18.2 Mi	Rp70.2 Mi	Rp11.0 Mi	Rp555.3 Mi	2 Staffs
Bina I. Fikri	Rp233.5 Mi	Rp95.7 Mi	Rp98.3 Mi	Rp148.7 Mi	5 Staffs
Barrah	Rp90.9 Mi	Rp749.5 Mi	Rp80.7 Mi	–	1 Staff

Note 2017 data from BMT's Annual Reports. BT = Baitut Tamwil; D = Direct; ID = Indirect; BM = Baitul Maal; Bi = Billion; Mi = Million; Th = Thousand

and IFI-RCW receiving ZIS funds and cash waqf of the Baitul Maal (see Fig. 9.4).

Fig. 9.4 Integrated Islamic Microfinance IIMFI-4 model

BMT and/or BT as IMFI with KSPPS legal status focus their businesses on providing Islamic microfinance services to their member-customers. Meanwhile, they also want to expand and focus on managing ZIS and waqf, so that the BT establishes new separate Baitul Maal, while the Baitul Maal Unit of the BMT is spin off to become independent Baitul Maal, still under the foundation. The Baitul Maal is officially registered as zakat institution and also as waqf institution capable of carrying out the duties of Amil of zakat and Nazir of waqf.

The BM as zakat institution would launch zakat collection programs targeting muzakki (zakat payer) not only from the BMT circle, but also from wealthy Muslims in general. The BM would also launch several programs to be financed by infaq, not only for productive program and training/technical assistance, but also other social programs, such as providing clean water (artesian wells) in arid villages and providing food for those affected by COVID-19 pandemic by establishing public kitchen.

The BM as waqf institution would have various waqf programs targeting potential donor (waqif) to develop social waqf facilities (such as free health clinics, free Islamic kindergarten, and free Islamic elementary school), productive waqf businesses (such as home-shop, home-office and mini store) and integrated social-productive waqf combining social waqf facility to be financed by productive waqf business. The BM would also still collect indirect cash waqf to be invested in the BMT/BT to strengthen the liabilities and capital of the BMT/BT.

Examples of BMT/BT with the IIMFI-4 model include: (1) BT Tamzis in Wonosobo, Central Java, and (2) BMT ItQan in Bandung, West Java (see Table 9.4). BMT ItQan has collected zakat and cash waqf

Table 9.4 Examples of BMT applying IIMFI-4 model

BMT	Asset	Branch	BT Employee	Member	Location
Tamzis	Rp527.00 Bi	37	487	117.12 Th	Wonosobo
ItQan	Rp39.04 Bi	7	68	17.47 Th	Bandung

BMT	Zakat	Infaq	ID-Cash Waqf	D-Cash Waqf	BM Employee
Tamzis	Rp410.0 Mi	Rp704.0 Mi	Rp119.0 Mi	Rp0.0 Mi	6 Staffs
ItQan	Rp253.0 Mi	Rp1060.0 Mi	Rp252.0 Mi	Rp300.0 Mi	12 Staffs

Note 2017 data from BMT's Annual Reports. BT = Baitut Tamwil; D = Direct; ID = Indirect; BM = Baitul Maal; Bi = Billion; Mi = Million; Th = Thousand amounting to Rp1.31 billion or 3.36% of assets and Rp0.55 billion of cash waqf or 1.41% of assets, so that ZIS and cash waqf collected have reached the equivalent of 4.77% of the total assets. Moreover, BMT ItQan also has established Islamic daycare, Islamic playgroup, Islamic kindergarten and Islamic elementary school, all based on integrated social-productive waqf.

IIMFI-5 Model
In this IIMFI-5 model, Islamic Cooperative as IMFI with KSPPS legal status establishes Social Unit to manage ZIS and waqf (especially cash waqf), while the Islamic Cooperative acts as IFI and IFI-RCW receiving ZIS funds and cash waqf of the Baitul Maal (see Fig. 9.5).

Islamic Cooperative, which is not a BMT, naturally does not have Baitul Maal Unit, and initially only conducts Islamic commercial microfinance activities. To be able to manage ZIS and waqf, Islamic Cooperative could form a Social Unit or Baitul Maal Unit to conduct Islamic social finance activities to collect and manage ZIS funds and waqf, especially cash waqf. This Social Unit can officially become a ZMP of a zakat institution and become a Nazir of cash waqf.

The Social Unit as ZMP collects ZIS funds (abc) from wealthy stakeholders (zakat payer) and deposits the funds in the Islamic Cooperative as savings account. Subsequently, the Social Unit distributes the ZIS through consumptive program, productive program and training/technical assistance for mustahiq as zakat recipients. The Social Unit could do all these programs by itself, or it could also collaborate

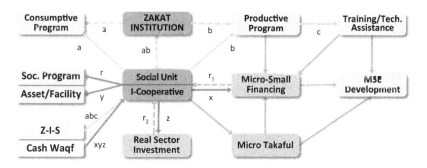

Fig. 9.5 Integrated Islamic Microfinance IIMFI-5 model

186   ASCARYA

Table 9.5 Examples of BMT applying IIMFI-5 model

IMFI	Asset	Branch	BT Employee	Member	Location
Benteng Mikro Indonesia	Rp327.00 Bi	5	492	127.52 Th	Banten

IMFI	Zakat	Infaq	ID-Cash Waqf	D-Cash Waqf	Social Unit
Benteng Mikro Indonesia	Rp308.0 Mi	Rp665.0 Mi	–	–	PIC 1 staff

Note 2017 data from IMFI's Annual Report. BT = Baitut Tamwil; D = Direct; ID = Indirect; BM = Baitul Maal; Bi = Billion; Mi = Million; Th = Thousand

with the parent zakat institution to be more effective, as well as to learn from the experts.

The Social Unit is also at least officially registered as Nazir of indirect cash waqf to be able to collect it especially from the employees, the member-customers and other stakeholders. The indirect cash waqf would be beneficial not only for the general Muslim society, but also for the Islamic Cooperative itself to strengthen its liabilities and capital/equity.

One example of Islamic Cooperative applying IIMFI-5 model is KSPPS Benteng Mikro Indonesia, in Serang, Banten (see Table 9.5).

By the end of 2019, the total assets of BMI have increased to Rp603.46 billion, with 761 employees, and Rp8.93 billion ZIS and cash waqf. By May 2020, during COVID-19 pandemic, BMI has collected Rp10.36 billion indirect cash waqf and awarded as the KSPPS with the highest achievement in collecting cash waqf.

IIMFI-6 Model

In this IIMFI-6 model, BMT, BT or Islamic Cooperative as IMFI with KSPPS legal status collaborates with zakat institution and waqf institution established by the parent organization or foundation to focus on managing ZIS and waqf professionally (see Fig. 9.6).

IMFI with KSPPS legal status which only focuses on conducting Islamic commercial microfinance activities could work together with zakat institution and waqf institution established separately by the parent organization or foundation to conduct Islamic social finance activities to

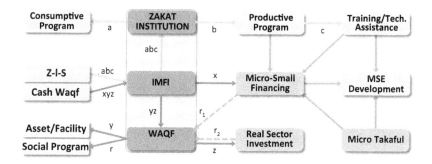

Fig. 9.6 Integrated Islamic Microfinance IIMFI-6 model

collect and manage ZIS funds and waqf (including cash waqf) professionally. Meanwhile, the IMFI which has Wadiah saving accounts could officially become IFI of the zakat institution and IFI-RCW of the waqf institution.

As Amil of zakat, the zakat institution will focus on managing zakat programs professionally, including collection, management, disbursement, empowerment, other social programs and reporting. The ZIS funds collected (abc) will be deposited as savings account in the IMFI and managed with good Amil governance. The zakat distribution to mustahiq will be done through consumptive program (disbursement) to fulfill their basic needs, as well as through productive program (empowerment), combined with training/technical assistance, to help the mustahiq establish and progress micro-businesses/enterprises to graduate and get out of poverty. For mustahiq graduated from empowerment program will be recommended to the IMFI to apply for commercial micro-small financing for further development of their micro-enterprises. The zakat institution will also have various social programs financed by infaq.

Meanwhile, as Nazir of waqf, the waqf institution will focus on managing various waqf projects, including social waqf, productive waqf and integrated social-productive waqf by collecting direct cash waqf (yz) deposited in the IMFI. The waqf institution could also collect indirect cash waqf (x) and invested it in the IMFI, which could be used to extend micro-small financing to its member-customers, mitigated by micro-takaful. The returns from productive waqf in the real sector and in the financial sector will be used to finance various social programs needed by the Muslim community.

188   ASCARYA

Table 9.6   Examples of BMT applying IIMFI-6 model

BMT	Asset	Branch	BMT Employee	Member	Location
UGT Sidogiri	Rp2.50 Tr	280	1494	896.32 Th	Pasuruan
BMT	*Zakat*	*Infaq*	*ID-Cash Waqf*	*D-Cash Waqf*	*LAZ-LKAF Staff*
UGT Sidogiri	Rp9.90 Bi	Rp13.64 Bi	Rp373.2 Mi	–	152 – 4

Note 2017 data from BMT's Annual Report. BT = Baitut Tamwil; D = Direct; ID = Indirect; BM = Baitul Maal; Bi = Billion; Mi = Million; Th = Thousand

Example of IMFI with the IIMFI-6 model can be seen in BMT UGT under the Sidogiri Islamic Boarding School in collaboration with zakat institution LAZ Sidogiri and waqf institution L-Kaf Sidogiri Waqf, both establish by the Sidogiri Islamic Boarding School as well (Table 9.6).

By the end of 2019, the total assets of BMT UGT have reached Rp3.2 trillion, with 327 branches spread in 10 provinces, managed by more than 1600 employees.

Discussion

The BMTs (including BT and Islamic Cooperative) prior to managing ZIS funds and cash waqf generally had structural problems on the funding side so that they had to rely on external sources such as Islamic bank financing to meet up to more than 50% of their funding needs, which caused financing to deposit ratio (FDR) to reach more than 200%. Meanwhile, BMTs' capital was also not as strong as Islamic rural banks (IRBs) to support their financing, because BMTs' capital as a Shariah-based cooperative came from members' contributions which were almost all included in the low-income group. The poorer the BMT members, the smaller the BMT capital and the greater the FDR percentage. With all their shortcomings, IMFIs are considered sustainable and robust in the face of financial crisis (Obaidullah 2008, p. 58), while commercial banks in general often need help from the government.

The BMTs in general also operate as a commercial bank that implements fractional reserve banking system (FRBS) and pooling of fund system which creates bubbles (and inflation), but on a micro-scale. However, BMTs are not systemic because they are independent institutions that are not inter-dependent (Obaidullah 2008, p. 58). However, BMTs, similar to IRBs, have a problem of acute funding dependence from external sources (Ascarya 2014, p. 83; 2016, p. 6; 2017, p. 1) and limited capital (Ascarya 2017, p. 1), even some BMTs need funding assistance from donors (Wulandari and Kassim 2016, pp. 222–224). The more BMTs have a not-for-profit mission, the more they rely on donors. Other problems faced by BMTs are the quality of human resources (Hamzah et al. 2013, p. 215), weak regulation (Seibel 2005, p. ii; Hamzah et al. 2013, p. 215), high operating costs, high financing margins, weak management and weak technology.

In addition, like Islamic banks, the pool of fund system creates problems of mismatch and liquidity (on a microscale) that prolong without any tangible solutions, because the BMTs' third-party funds are short-term funds, collected from members' micro-deposits, which are channeled into short/medium-term microfinancing. BMTs' financings mainly are extended to micro-businesses/enterprises or MEs (Seibel 2005, p. 7; Obaidullah 2008, p. 57; Masyita and Ahmed 2013, p. 42; Ascarya 2014, p. 82; Ascarya), including small businesses/enterprises or SEs for members who want to develop their business (Ascarya 2016, p. 3). Before managing ZIS and cash waqf of the Baitul Maal as zakat institution and waqf institution, the balance sheets of the BMT would look like Table 9.7.

After managing ZIS and cash waqf funds, the BMT slowly but surely gains source of funds from cash waqf, especially indirect cash waqf (placed as Long-Term Waqf Investment Deposits and/or Waqf Capital) which could replace its dependence on expensive Islamic bank financing and burdensome to the BMT (see Table 9.8). A very high FDR of more than 200% would go down from time to time to a healthy level below 100%,

Table 9.7 Balance sheet of BMT before managing Zakat and Cash Waqf

Assets	Liabilities
Cash	*Wadiah/Mudharabah* Savings Deposit
Bank Deposits	*Mudharabah* Investment Deposit
Receivables (*Murabahah*, *Qardh*, etc.)	Islamic Bank Financing
Financing (*Mudharabah*, *Musharakah*, etc.)	
Fixed Assets	Capital

190 ASCARYA

Table 9.8 Balance sheet of BMT after managing Zakat and Cash Waqf

Assets	Liabilities
Cash	*Wadiah/Mudharabah* Savings Deposit
Bank Deposits	**Zakat Savings Deposit**
Receivables (*Murabahah, Qardh*, etc.)	*Mudharabah* Investment Deposit
Financing (*Mudharabah, Musharakah*, etc.)	**Long-Term Waqf Investment**
Long-Term Investment	**Waqf Capital**
Fixed Assets	Capital

even below 80%, which would ultimately reduce the cost of funds and reduce financing margins to its member-customers. When the mandate of managing cash waqf is carried out properly, the BMT would also gain trust from the surrounding community and more and more local people choose to use the BMT, which could increase the deposits and capital further.

Meanwhile, the nature of cash waqf which continues to grow and perpetual makes the problems of mismatch and liquidity would decrease gradually, the liquidity ratio could be maintained at a safe level, while the need for higher liquidity on Eid al-Fitr and the new school year could be better anticipated. When cash waqf is intended to finance certain productive programs, these schemes are more of an allocation of funds (not a pool of funds) and asset driven (not liability driven), which makes the BMT operates more ideally, as stated by IFSB-IRTI (2010, p. 17), thereby minimizing bubble, mismatch and liquidity risk.

In addition, cash waqf could also be placed as capital investment (Waqf Capital), which, in addition to cheap funds, could also strengthen the capital standing of the BMT, so that the capital adequacy ratio (CAR) could be maintained at a high level above the minimum limit without the need for additional capital from members to expand the BMT business. With the strengthening of capital, the BMT would no longer experience prolonged undercapitalized structural problems.

The BMTs would most likely gain the benefits from managing cash waqf because their assets are small, ranging from under Rp1 billion to Rp2.5 billion, with the mode of Rp1 billion to Rp10 billion total assets, so that the accumulation of small amount of cash waqf would mean a lot, since it accounted as a large percentage of the total assets.

Integrated Islamic Microfinance to Support SDGs

Naturally, the BMT applies integrated Islamic commercial finance in the Baitut Tamwil (BT) and Islamic social finance in the Baitul Maal (BT), so that various commercial goals (4 goals) and social goals (9 goals), including environmental goals (4 goals), could be supported in micro-small level. In general, all goals could be supported by Islamic social finance of zakat, infaq and waqf, since social and environmental goals could be supported by all Islamic social finance instruments (including zakat, infaq and waqf), while commercial goals could be supported by waqf, since waqf could also be used for commercial productive waqf.

For example, some of the BMTs apply graduation model to assist mustahiq out of poverty, which consists of several stages of qardh financing using zakat/infaq combined with semi-commercial financing using cash waqf (see Fig. 9.7). Stage 1, the mustahiq are provided with basic needs in consumptive program, including Dharuriyat Asasiyat (food, clothing, shelter and worship) and Hajjiyat Asasiyat (education, health and transportation), to achieve basic needs security. Stage 2, the mustahiq are provided with extensive productive program including training qardh financing, technical assistance and savings. Qardh financing could include several steps, for example, three-step qardh financing using zakat/infaq from Rp1.0 million, Rp2.0 million and Rp3.0 million in group lending, followed by two-step semi-commercial microfinancing using cash waqf from Rp4 million and Rp5.0 million. All of these financing will be combined closely with technical assistance and further training. Stage 3, the mustahiq have graduated from the graduation program and provided with commercial micro-small financing in gradual progression from above Rp5.0 million to Rp50.0 million or more by the Baitut Tamwil.

Fig. 9.7 Graduation model

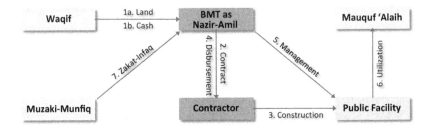

Fig. 9.8 Social Waqf project to build public facility

This graduation model applied by BMT would support SDGs number 1 to 5 in small scale for the stakeholder and surrounding community, namely: (1) no poverty; (2) zero hunger; (3) good health and well-being; (4) quality education; and (5) gender equality.

Meanwhile, the BMT with active Baitul Maal could collect and manage various social waqf projects to build, improve and maintain public facility in the local community (see Fig. 9.8). First, the BMT plans a certain public utility project needed by the community and raises waqf (land and cash) from the stakeholders, community and general Muslims. Subsequently, the public facility will be built by the contractor as planned. Upon the completion, the Baitul Maal of the BMT will manage and maintain the public facility and provide the services to the local community for free. The operational costs incurred will be financed by raising zakat and infaq. Zakat could be used to serve poor people, while infaq could be used to serve general community.

These social waqf projects could be used to provide/support clear water and sanitation (goal 6) as public utility, such as by establishing artesian wells, for every surrounding village that does not have access to clear water and sanitation. Social waqf and integrated social-productive waqf could also be used to provide/support affordable and clean energy (goal 7) as public utility too. Social waqf of BMT could also be used to support the impacts of climate action (goal 13), life below water (goal 14) and life on land (goal 15) for the stakeholders and surrounding community in micro-small level.

Furthermore, the BMT could also collect and manage productive waqf to support commercial goals of SDGs (see Fig. 9.9). First, the BMT plans to establish a certain productive waqf needed by the community

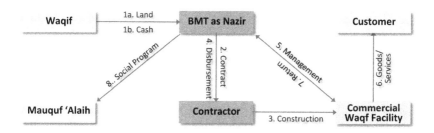

Fig. 9.9 Productive Waqf project to build commercial business

which coincides with commercial goals of SDGs and raises waqf, including land and cash, from general Muslim society, internally and externally. Second, the BMT will hire contractor to build the productive waqf facility according to the plan and schedule. Subsequently, the BMT will assign and/or hire the right persons to manage the commercial business of productive waqf. The returns could be used to expand the business and to finance social programs supporting social goals of SDGs.

The productive waqf, integrated social-productive waqf and Islamic commercial finance could be used to support decent work and economic growth (goal 8), industry innovation and infrastructure (goal 9), reduce inequalities (goal 10) and responsible consumption and production (goal 12) for the stakeholders and surrounding community in micro-small level.

The Way Forward

Financial technology (fintech) has disrupted the financial industry, including Islamic finance and Islamic microfinance. Fintech in Islamic microfinance (Islamic micro-fintech) is inevitable and has been recognized by the IMFI including BMT, BT and Islamic Cooperative, which is in line with what have been said by Pytcowska and Korynsky (2017), while most IMFIs lack in resources to adopt Islamic micro-fintech, but they do not want to lose their competitiveness and their member-customers. Meanwhile, although Islamic micro-fintech companies have their competitive advantage in financial technology, they do not have data to access the micro-small enterprises (MSEs) owned by the BMT (including BT and Islamic Cooperative), since most MSEs are the member-customers of BMT.

Meanwhile, Islamic micro-fintech could benefit BMT greatly in Islamic social finance to collect zakat, infaq and cash waqf from external donors using crowdfunding peer-to-peer (P2P) social, as well as in Islamic commercial finance to collect funding from external investors using crowdfunding peer-to-peer (P2P) financing. According to Yahaya and Ahmad (2018), Islamic micro-fintech P2P social could improve the effectiveness and efficiency of zakat collection and zakat distribution, while micro-fintech could improve lending, as well as spending and earning services of MFI. Islamic micro-fintech is also considered as a tool to survive and thrive, so that the adoption of Islamic micro-fintech by the BMT is a must in the near future to be sustainable.

Moreover, Sancha-Navarro et al. (2018) found that commercial crowdfunding (P2P financing) and social crowdfunding (P2P social) would help to improve the life quality of the poor. When the BMT adopt P2P social, it could reach out to more muzakki (zakat payer) of zakat, more waqif (waqf donor) of waqf and more munfiq (infaq donor) of infaq. Therefore, the activities of Islamic social finance by the Baitul Maal of BMT would be greatly improved to further support the social goals and environmental goals of SDGs. In the meantime, the adoption of P2P financing would be able to reach out external investor to invest in the BMT, which could improve funding and solve the BMT's structural problems of mismatch and liquidity.

References

Ascarya. (2014). Sustainable Conventional and Islamic Microfinance Models for Micro Enterprises. *ISRA International Journal of Islamic Finance, 6*(2), 49–85.

Ascarya. (2016). Holistic Financial Inclusion Based on Maqashid Shariah Through Baitul Maal wat Tamwil. *Middle East Insights: Islamic Finance Special, 1,* 1–8.

Ascarya. (2017). Baitul Maal wat Tamwil (BMT). as an Integrated Islamic Social and Commercial Financial Institution in Indonesia. In ISRA-TR-IRTI (Eds.), *The Islamic Commercial Law Report 2018* (pp.104–107). Kuala Lumpur, Malaysia: ISRA, Thompson Reuters and IRTI.

Hamzah, H., Rusby, Z., & Zulfadli, H. (2013). Analysis Problem of Baitul Maal Wat Tamwil (BMT) Operation in Pekanbaru Indonesia Using Analytical Network Process (ANP) Approach. *International Journal of Academic Research in Business and Social Sciences, 3*(8), 215–228.

IFSB & IRTI-IDB. (2010). *Islamic Finance and Global Financial Stability*. Kuala Lumpur, Malaysia: Islamic Financial Services Board.

Masyita, D., & Ahmed, H. (2013). Why Is Growth of Islamic Microfinance Lower Than Its Conventional Counterparts in Indonesia? *Islamic Economic Studies, 21*(1), 35–62.

Obaidullah, M. (2008). *Introduction to Islamic Microfinance*. New Delhi: IBF Net Limited, India.

Pytcowska, J., & Korynsky, P. (2017). *Digitalizing Microfinance in Europe* (Research Paper). Poland: Microfinance Centre.

Sancha-Navaro, J. M., Sanchis-Pedregosa, C., & Oliver-Alfonso, M. D. (2018). Relationship Between Crowdfunding and Microfinance: A Theoretical Approach. *Finance, Markets and Valuation, 4*(2), 83–99.

Seibel, H. D. (2005). *Islamic Microfinance in Indonesia*. Deutsche Gesellschaft für Technische Zusammenarbeit (GTZ).

Wulandari, P., & Kassim, S. (2016). Issues and Challenges in Financing the Poor: Case of Baitul Maal Wa Tamwil in Indonesia. *International Journal of Bank Marketing, 34*(2), 216–234.

Yahaya, M. H., & Ahmad K. (2018). Financial Inclusion Through Efficient Zakat Distribution for Poverty Alleviation in Malaysia: Using FinTech & Mobile Banking. In *Proceeding of the 5th International Conference on Management and Muamalah 2018 (ICoMM 2018)*.

Zeller, M., & Meyer, R. (2002). *The Triangle of Microfinance: Financial Sustainability, Outreach and Impact*. Washington: The International Food Policy and Research Institute.

CHAPTER 10

How Islamic Social Finance Contribute to the Sustainable Development Goals: An Impactful Story of Al-Khidmat Foundation Pakistan

Suhail Ahmad

INTRODUCTION

Islamic ethics has been applied to the economy since the advent of Islam. The first verse of Islam already refers to the moral principles on which it is necessary to manage one's material activities such as usury (usury), Zakat (solidarity tax) pay to every Muslim), private property, etc. Although its basic principles are far away, the way Islamic funding exists today is a recent development. It is also a solid application of Islamic economic ideology; this ensures fundraising and their injection into the economic circuit. However, Islamic banks and other moral and social institutions should not agree to a simple financial and moral approach, but should move toward an Islamic "land management" approach, that is, effective economic and social participation in the development of

S. Ahmad (✉)
Sarhad University of Science and Information Technology, Peshawar, Pakistan

© The Author(s), under exclusive license to Springer Nature Switzerland AG 2021
M. M. Billah (eds.), *Islamic Wealth and the SDGs*,
https://doi.org/10.1007/978-3-030-65313-2_10

197

Muslim society. The gradual transformation of short-term instruments from Islamic banking and financing toward the Islamic social and moral financial practices, in fact, reflects a major evolution in the concept of Islamic finance.

The initial idea of the Islamic Bank was linked to the global vision of the Islamic economy, aimed at a new alternative economic and social order. However, the prohibition on interest has a moral significance when it comes to the principles of profit and loss sharing and the connection to real assets. In relation to the real economy, it is possible to argue that "Islamic finance was not involved in the causes of the financial crisis, because the risk of mortgage lending is prohibited and the derivative (subprime, securitization) is subject to uncertainty, because the basic asset is a package of credit sold in the market.

Like the Christian moral treasure, the outgoing standards apply to Islamic investment. The list is variable, but the wine, guns, gambling, and pork industries need it. In addition, Islamic finance manages the control of products manufactured under the name of "Compatible with *Shari'ah*." In cases where genocide is judged on the basis of interest, "purification" schemes are arranged in the form of donations to the poor. But it is clear that Islamic finance is immoral about its destiny, it is for its inspiration, which is the law of the fundamentally based Muslim religion based on the Holy Qur'an, is none other than *Shari'ah*. The most well-known prescription is the prohibition of usury, which is usually a higher interest rate, but which results in a prohibition on interest-bearing loans. This prohibition is also found in the Old Testament, as in Aristotle's policy. Interest is not converted into Islamic finance (Daoud 2013).

The lender who lends does not receive a fixed interest in advance and is guaranteed, shares it with his debtor, lends him or her profits he/she receives. It contributes to the loss No more claims or loans, no lenders or lenders, the joint venture involves two actors, a joint venture of two people to carry out a joint venture. Financial transactions have to do with the real economy; they can't create anything on their own. The financial cycle should be a fruitful cycle of goods or services. Then, in Islamic finance, financial speculation is forbidden, as is "excessive uncertainty" in contracts (Daoud 2013).

Even then, it is clear that this relationship with the real must be manifested, and that all these actions must be fairly transparent. Islamic finance is in fact a moral treasure. It is even more stringent that investments are not allowed in certain sectors, such as the gaming industry, tobacco, alcohol, armaments, in companies with more than a few percent of the debt. Even this Islamic social and ethical financial support can be seen as a service to the people, aimed at protecting human, family, social harmony, and even the environment (Jouaber 2011). This respect for the environment with respect for future generations brings Islamic social finance closer to the goals of sustainable development, as well as to corporate social responsibility practices (Forget 2009). Other provisions of the Qur'a help to Islamic and social finance morally like Zakat, which is a religious tax levied on all believers on all their property and which is usually paid by banks is charged, but can be paid directly to the associations or other individuals of the community. But most importantly, giving alms is always linked to prayer. Almsgiving, one of the five religious precepts of Islam seems to be a tax on the poor or a purification tax when interest is charged illegally. It becomes a means of transporting goods to the poorest and beyond, a means of achieving balance and social justice. However, these principles whether always respected or only partially respected are excellent features of moral treasure because it is generally appreciated.

ETHICAL AND SOCIAL FINANCE AND SUSTAINABLE DEVELOPMENT IN ISLAMIC FINANCE

Islamic business principles are rooted in *Shari'ah*, the biblical basis of faith. Its goals are to achieve good and prevent harm, especially in the protection of religion, life, intellect, property, and the new generation. Interpreting Islamic ethics in business and financial matters requires sharing risk, rather than changing risk. Perhaps the most notable principle, which has been shared by other religions, is to avoid "riba," which is translated as interest, which prevents the sale of debts and toxic assets in the current global crisis is considered helpful. The Qur'an warnings about the riverbank are presented in an interesting way, along with donations and charities which show that it contradicts the latter in its moral significance and collective consequences (Moghul 2015).

Some have interpreted the law to emphasize the consequences of creating spiritual and material well-being. As part of the broader religious discourse, Muslim communities are increasingly debating stability, resilience, and interpersonal ethics. Various commentators have recognized Islamic finance as a viable means of tackling development challenges, alleviating extreme poverty, and bringing prosperity to developing and emerging economies. The reason for this is to link Islamic finance to the comprehensive results of the need to divide the real economy's assets and its risk. For many of these, and perhaps for other reasons, the global post-financial crisis shows that Islamic finance is more flexible than its counterparts and, therefore, can promote military financial stability.

Based on routine business experience, modern Islamic finance has integrated a layer of responsible consultants to evaluate the ethical value of products under Islamic principles. Some give private advice, while others do central work. While everyone interprets the law, their commitments are certainly not solid. As the responsible market discusses stakeholder views, it will be helpful for them to learn about Islam's "traded multi-storyter stakeholder approach," which includes not only animals, the natural environment and work communities are strengthened (Moghul 2015).

Sustainable development is now at the center of many reflections (politics, environment, finance). However, the very concept of sustainable development is often misunderstood because it is considered incomplete. The goal is to fight poverty in the service of as many people as possible, with the distribution of maximum wealth and the protection of nature. After all, in each of the economic, social, and environmental aspects, there is an interim demand for inter-ethnic solidarity. There are three main ways; economic growth through investment, reduction of social inequalities (working conditions, wages), and sustainable consumption of natural resources and reduction of pollution. Individuals, institutions, or other government and non-governmental organization, on their own initiative, voluntarily integrate social and environmental concern in their relationships with stakeholders. When examining the relationship between ethical finance and Islamic finance, we will ask ourselves whether the latter covers many topics of sustainable development and social responsibility.

In fact, the purpose of Islamic law, influenced by Islamic law (*Shari'ah*), is to promote the well-being of all individuals so that excess needs can be met at no cost. It also emphasizes the protection of future generations, resources, and the environment; therefore, achieving these goals requires dynamic interaction between social processes and environmental priorities. As a result, Islamic social and ethical finance offers many guidelines that have hitherto been called sustainable development. It also proposes a model of corporate social responsibility based on more sustainable moral and ethical principles that has a broader meaning based on moral and religious action (Ougoujil and Rigar 2019).

The entrepreneur no longer guides through the maximum justice, mutual respect, God, and the concept of responsibility through honesty. The declaration issued by this working group (an interfaith declaration: a code of ethics for international business for Christians, Muslims and Jews), a code of business ethics common to all three religions is good in each is prepared to adopt methods, especially with regard to stakeholders. The purpose of Islamic social and ethical finance is to improve human condition, establish social equality and prevent injustice in trade, social, and moral aspects of the individuals and society. This is the essence of the prohibition of interests and its change through the system of distribution of benefits and risks. These goals are consistent with ethical finance because of the sustainable development of its economic and social pillars in recent years.

The environmental pillar is not absent from Islamic finance either one of the foundations of Islam is that man fulfills a task of managing God's creatures. Therefore, God's creation, which is not limited to nature and the environment, but also encompasses man and society, belongs to God and is entrusted to man. Therefore, it has a duty to manage and protect it. As a result, unnecessary waste and consumption is unacceptable because the link between religion and business ethics was studied by an interfaith grouping of representatives of three more monotheistic religions (Christianity, Islam, and Judaism) at the initiative of the British and Jordanian royal families and under the patronage of Prince Philip. From Duke Edinburgh, Prince Hassan of Jordan and Sir Evelyn de Rothschild (Ougoujil and Rigar 2019).

They relate to financial processes that offer the beginning of interests or activities that are deemed necessary if they are illegal. As a form of social responsible investment and enterprises, the distribution of funds involves returning some of the proceeds to NGOs or humanitarian organizations. Islamic finance practices this in two ways; i.e., in the introducing of financial products, Islamic filtering involves locating the financial title according to Islamic law. Once the stock passes this test, it can be added to the investment portfolio. Let's mention one important factor in filtering. It is a refinement of income. Purity is two aspects of income: on the one hand, purity under Zakat, which is one of the five pillars of Islam. Any Muslim who has more than 85 grams of gold on his doorstep will have to pay 2.5% to any one of the eight categories of deserving people. On the other hand, the purification of dirty income avoids accidental situations, whether or not a company must pay money or interest from one of the sectors prohibited by Islamic law from the outset.

This purification is supervised by the Shariah Board. Finally, Islamic filtering can be improved to reinforce the need for ethical and sustainable development. Whether quantitative or qualitative information is required to make an ethical choice, Islamic filtering also depends on it. In quantitative information, Islamic filtering can be improved by indicating the use of natural resources (water, energy, raw materials) the same is true of merit. It will be about knowing the relationships that societies maintain with organizations environmental protection, professional integration, education, and human rights defense, providers and the population (Ougoujil and Rigar 2019).

Objectives of the Study

The study has the following objectives;

1. To elaborate the statues of Pakistan toward the SDGs,
2. To see and analyze the philanthropic efforts of the Al-khidmat Foundation of Pakistan,
3. To see how the Islamic ethical and social finance model best fit for the attainment of the SDGs of the UN agenda 2030, and
4. To encourage other individuals and philanthropic institutions to follow and adopt the Islamic ethical and social finance model for efficiently achieving the SDGs in its true letter and spirit.

RESEARCH METHODOLOGY

Case Study Research Design

A case usually stays within certain limits. It can be an individual, an organization, a behavior, an event, or another social phenomenon. It is possible that the boundary between the case and the context cannot be easily distinguished. Integrated case study research design enough the embedded case is made up of the unique features of a selected case to investigate the characteristics of each embedded case and searching for embedded cases will ultimately expand the scope of this case (Budiyanto et al. 2019). Case study research is one of the various strategies for conducting social science research activities. This research strategy has the potential to help us discover complex social phenomena. From this the researcher can derive features such as real-life events, such as life cycle, administrative and organizational processes, and changes in neighborhoods, international affairs, and industry development (Teiu and Daniel 2011).

The case study method is the most widely used method in academia for researchers interested in quality studies. Research students choose case studies without understanding the various factors that may affect the results of their research. It takes a lot of time and resources to conduct an investigation any misrepresentation can be made about the purpose and methodology of the investigation as well as the validation of the findings (Rashid et al. 2019).

Thus, this study adopts the case study approach of research design, in which a real case study which is a philanthropic organization which practicing Islamic social finance in its true letter and spirit and resulted a real impact in the society and country toward not only the socioeconomic development of Pakistan but also has a promising results in the achievement of SDGs.

Philanthropic Institution Which Practicing Islamic Social and Moral Finance in Pakistan

Al-Khidmat Foundation Pakistan is a non-profit organization dedicated exclusively to humanitarian services since 1990. Their dedicated services include disaster management, health services, education, orphan care, clean water, timeless debt, and other social services across the country and also abroad in other countries in the time of emergency and any disaster situation when faces across the globe. Al-Khidmat Foundation Pakistan a non-political non-governmental and non-profit organization is committed to serving humanity by contributing to any form of discrimination, humanity, health, education, financial stability. By mobilizing resources for economics, housing, clean water availability, mosques, disaster-related, and other aspects of life and the welfare of its employees, and partnerships with NGOs, other interested government and private organizations (Newsletter 2017). Promoting and participating in useful programs and doing all the necessary work to achieve the above with all these functions, initiatives, and sustainability.

It is a high profile organization dedicated entirely to the cause of humanity. Despite the fact that the Al-Khidmat Foundation was officially registered as a non-governmental organization in 1990, its humanitarian and relief record dates back to the days of Pakistan's independence, initially providing safe houses, backwardness and focused on their treatment and care, which later became the trademark of Al-Khidmat Foundation Pakistan (Wikipedia 2017).

The Foundation is present throughout Pakistan, including all provinces and territories administered by the Government of Pakistan. It has a fast and wide base that is always alert in case of a sudden emergency. Its latest initiative is its orphanage care program, where the foundation conducts two activities, namely "Aghosh Homes" and "Orphan Family Support." Both programs are for orphans under the age of 14 where the foundation provides full support to the child and his family. Al-Khidmat Foundation Orphan Houses is a great place to provide state-of-the-art facilities for children. The program is sponsored by many people and international donors (Al-khidmat Foundation 2018a).

Together with other NGOs, the Al-Khidmat Pakistan Foundation has been involved in relief efforts for the victims of the 2005 earthquake. The service reportedly provided more than 10,000 temporary shelters and houses for those affected by the quake.[1] Trucks carrying relief supplies are heading to the flood-hit areas after the 2010 floods in Pakistan, the Japanese government provided financial assistance to the Al-Khidmat Foundation to help the people of Charsadda (a city of Khyber Pakhtunkhwa) who were affected by the floods. In addition, the Japan Disaster Relief Team conducted operations in Multan, Pakistan and is engaged in medical assistance activities in South Punjab.[2] Therefore, the foundation has the following specific program undertaken for the welfare of the society and socioeconomic development of the country and sharing their part in the SDGs of Pakistan laid down by the UN agenda 2030.

[1] Disaster Management Authority of Pakistan.

[2] www.ndma.org.pk

Table 10.1 Orphan care program details

S. No.	Particular	Numbers/Strength
1	Activities held	1240
2	Clusters	57
3	Study centers	140
4	Beneficiaries	12,011
5	Total expenditure annually	1,009 Million PKR

Source www.alkhidmat.org.pk

ORPHAN CARE PROGRAM (SUSTAINABLE DEVELOPMENT GOALS NUMBER, 1 & 2)

Orphans are the innocent souls who suffer the most on earth due to lack of proper parental support. As the most vulnerable section of society, they need a lot of support to get their lives back on track. Those who come to the aid of these orphans can reduce their risk and reap the best rewards in the future. According to the United Nations, Pakistan has more than 4 million orphans and the majority of the population is under 17 years of age.[3] This important section of the population is suffering from social ills which need immediate attention. Support the Al-Qaeda Orphan Care Program to ensure a bright future for orphans (Al-khidmat Foundation 2018b).

In the Table 10.1, it is quite clear about the orphan care program of the foundation on yearly basis. It indicates that 1240 number of various activities held regarding the orphans across the country, which divided by different cluster of about 57 in the whole country. In addition, there are one hundred forty study and educational centers including, schools, colleges, tuitions centers, and many other training and learning insti tutes for the orphan children across the country. Furthermore, there are number of children who facilitated to this initiative of the foundation and more than twelve thousands of children/orphans across the country benefited in a year and costs more than one thousand million Pakistani Rupees which is estimated more than 6 million US Dollars (Foundation 2019). The orphan care program of Al-Khidmat Foundation is extensively spreading across the whole country and provides a number of facilities to

---

[3] United Nations Report for Pakistan.

206   S. AHMAD

Table 10.2 Region wise beneficiaries across Pakistan through orphan care program (Annual Report 2018 of Al Khidmat Foundation, Pakistan)

S. No.	Name of region	Number of children/orphans	Expenditure
1	Azad Jammu & Kashmir	890	74.77 Million PKR
2	Baluchistan	298	25.03
3	Gilgit-Baltistan	167	14.03
4	Khyber Pakhtunkhwa	3555	298.64
5	Punjab	5297	445
6	Sindh	1804	151.54
Total		**12011**	**1009**

Source www.alkhidmat.org.pk

the needy and helpless children in the country, that's why the role of the foundation is an indispensable for the enhancement of well-being in terms of education, health, and food and shelter and ultimately ramping up their role for achieving the SDGs of the humanity across the globe set by United Nations agenda for 2030 to empower the humanity in terms of each and every aspects of a prosperous life.[4]

Table 10.2 shows the expansion of the orphan care program by Al-Khidmat foundation in different provinces in the whole country and their incurred expenditure through the different facilities provides to the orphan and children in different centers for caring them under the supervision and control of Al-Khidmat foundation Pakistan. The table mentioned that highest number of children and orphan facilitated in Punjab province of the country due to its larger population followed by Khyber Pakhtunkhwa, then Sindh followed by Azad Jammu & Kashmir followed by Baluchistan and the last but not the least is the Gilgit-Baltistan (Foundation 2019).

HEALTH FACILITIES (SUSTAINABLE DEVELOPMENT GOALS NUMBER 3)

Al-Khidmat Pakistan foundation is always striving to serve the poor section of the society. Given the state of poor infrastructure in the health

[4]United Nations Agenda 2030, Sustainable Development Goals.

sector in Pakistan, they have launched a series of projects to improve the situation by providing facilities to the common man, regardless of the socioeconomic situation.

Figure 10.1 is about the health care facilitation by the foundation in the country, the figure highlight that there are forty-four hospitals established along with sixty-six medical care centers and clinics for the sack of health facilitation to the people of the country irrespective of their religion, race, ethnicity, gender, and other sociocultural differences. Despite a widespread network of hospitals and medical centers and clinics they also caring the diagnosis facilities of laboratories and investigation for various treatment purposes they set up more than 115 collection points along with a network of forty-four pharmacy and medical stores in which the medicine provides to the people free or a nominal charges from the patients which hardly cover the utilities of the stores. On the other hand, they also have a wide network of medical camps along with the ambulatory services across the country.

There are more than 7 million patients are covered by their health care facilities in the different regions of the whole country including urban and rural localities irrespective of their geographical location and community spread but the prime purpose is to serve the humanity by providing the health care facilities to the society. In addition, all these health facilities incurred cost about more than two thousands Million of PKR which is almost a huge amount ever any non-governmental organization in the country only for the health facilities of the community (Foundation 2019).

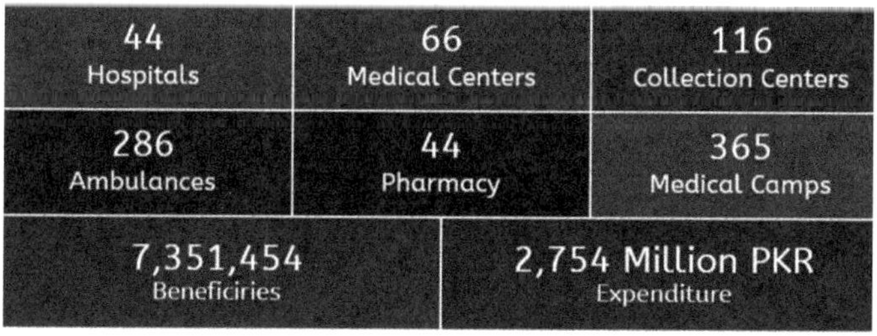

44 Hospitals	66 Medical Centers	116 Collection Centers
286 Ambulances	44 Pharmacy	365 Medical Camps
7,351,454 Beneficiries		2,754 Million PKR Expenditure

Fig. 10.1 Different health care facilities provides by Al-Khidmat foundation across the country

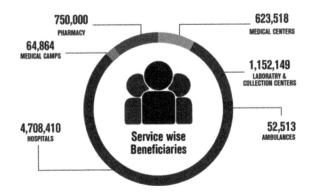

Fig. 10.2 Beneficiaries through health services by Al-Khidmat foundation across the country

Figure 10.2 indicates the different health care services provide in a year across the country to help and support the community which resulted the socioeconomic development of Pakistan. The figure mentions that there are 750 thousands of individuals benefited through the pharmacy and medical store facilities along with a number of 1.15 million of individuals facilitated through laboratories and collection points for the patient's investigations and diagnosis the illness. Similarly, about more than sixty-four thousands visited and acquired the services in medical camps and more than 623 thousand of patients visit the medical centers and clinics established by Al-Khidmat foundation across the country.

The foundation has full-fledged and well equipped ambulatory services for facilitated the patients toward the hospitals and medical centers for the early treatment, about more than fifty-two thousand of patients used the facilities of ambulatory services of the foundation across the country. Despite the various facilitations services to the community in terms of health care and more than 4.7 million individuals treated in the hospitals network in the country.

Education (Sustainable Development Goals Number 4)

Education is the only solution for the prosperity of humanity. Allied service businesses cover all issues and problems of education in Pakistan.

It provides equal opportunities to all talented and deserving students across the country without any discrimination. The proportion of male and female students in the list of beneficiaries of the educational programs is equal, as it has a literacy rate of 100% in Pakistan (Report 2017).

Table 10.3 labeled the educational facilities for caring the needs of the education in the community of the country and playing a social responsible entity of the country. There are 31 centers for child protection, about seventy has the skill development centers where the skillful personnel produce in which different individuals irrespective of their age trained and skilled to work for the community and afford their homes and dependents. Whereas five schools along with two hostels established for educational purposes to the children and youth of the country, on the other hand, there are a numbers of scholarships also provides to the needy and able students for their future education and careers, therefore more than three thousands scholarship availed by the deserving students for facilitated them in their educational activities and future career. About more than twenty-nine thousands students facilitated which incurred cost about 126 Million PKR. Table 10.4 indicated different services attained through educational program of Al-Khidmat foundation, in which we can see child protection services along with skill development centers followed by hostel facilities, followed by schools, scholarships and school supplies including furniture, equipments, stationery, and other miscellaneous items.

Table 10.3 Details of educational facilities

S. No.	Name of facilities	Numbers
1	Child protection centers	31
2	Skill development centers	70
3	Hostels	2
4	Al-Khidmat schools	5
5	Alfalah scholarships	3872
6	Beneficiaries	29795
7	Expenditure	126 Million PKR

Source www.alkhidmat.org.pk

210   S. AHMAD

Table 10.4 Details of service wise beneficiaries

S. No.	Name of facilities	Beneficiaries
1	Child protection centers	5000
2	Skill development centers	1000
3	Youth hostels	100
4	Al-Khidmat schools	17695
5	Alfalah scholarships	3872
6	Schools supplies	6000

Source www.alkhidmat.org.pk

CLEAN WATER (SUSTAINABLE DEVELOPMENT GOALS NUMBER 6)

Pakistan is on track to become a water-storage country, ranking 30th among the world's most water-scarce countries. Clean drinking water is an urgent and important issue in Pakistan which needs to be addressed first. Al-Khidmat foundation is actively working to ensure safe drinking water supply by installing hand pumps in arid areas, digging water wells in remote areas, and installing water filtration plants in cities and providing water to households in rural areas through their water schemes. Al-Khidmat Saaf Pani (clean water) program takes all possible steps to carry out its mission in accordance with the needs of water-scarce areas.

In Fig. 10.3, it stated that the foundation worked for the clean drinking water and tries to provide the clean and drinking water to the poor and the deprived sector of the society. For this purpose, they set up more than six thousand water hand pumps in different localities in the country

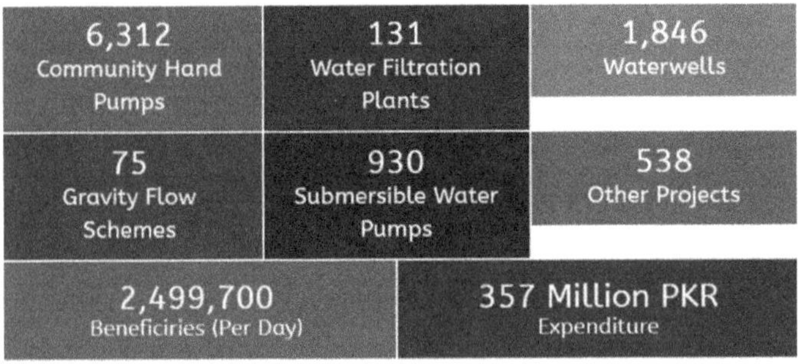

6,312 Community Hand Pumps	131 Water Filtration Plants	1,846 Waterwells
75 Gravity Flow Schemes	930 Submersible Water Pumps	538 Other Projects
2,499,700 Beneficiries (Per Day)		357 Million PKR Expenditure

Fig. 10.3 Details of clean water initiative

along with more than 1800 water wells. Furthermore, they also established about 131 water purification plants and 75 gravity flow schemes (Report 2018).

About more than nine hundred submersible water pumps and also other running project of 538 in the country for the clean and drinking water. These projects cost about 357 Million PKR and more than 2.4 million individuals benefited through these clean and drinking water daily.

COMMUNITY SERVICES (SUSTAINABLE DEVELOPMENT GOALS NUMBER 11)

Pakistan has been facing a number of social problems over the years ranging from poverty to civic ignorance and lack of basic living facilities. People face serious problems in terms of health, education, and economy. The country ranks 145th in the Human Development Index (HDI) and 50% of Pakistan's population lack basic necessities. "The best of you is the one who helps others." Al-Khidmat foundation has a vision of a safe, educated, and healthy community and has been known for solving the social problems of the poor and needy for the past three decades. They are working on a peaceful social mission with a responsible attitude toward good health, education, conscience, and overall development of the country (Report 2018).

Al-Khidmat community services alleviate the suffering caused by poverty, physical disability and imprisonment through its various initiatives. It solves these problems through various humanitarian projects throughout Pakistan.

In the Fig. 10.4 shows a details service of the foundation imparting to the welfare of the community in the country by helping and supporting the needy and poor segment of the society. Taking the services of the community initiative there are more than 12 million peoples across the country benefited and about 539 Million PKR is spent on the welfare of the society. The community services initiative program consist of various humanitarians and welfare causes such as, gifts (about 11,298) in the occasion of Eid (religious festivals of muslin community), (2,335) gifts in Diwali and Christmas for the minorities in the country.

Whereas the winter packages (25,111), prisoner's welfare (3,470), about more than fifty-eight thousand slaughters meats packs distributed in the community, 42,329 Ramadan packages consists of all food items for a family distributed. In addition, 2,967 wheelchairs were handover to the

Fig. 10.4 Details of community service by Al-Khidmat foundation across Pakistan

needy and deserving segment of the society. Despite all these activities the foundation also constructed about thirty-six mosques in the country by their own resources and funding from the rich and the well off community of the society and spent among the deserving an deprived class of the society across the country (Report 2018).

Disaster Management

Disaster is a word that brings thousands of dangerous thoughts to one's mind. It reminds us of the unfortunate time of the deadly 2005 earthquake that struck northern Pakistan, killing thousands and displacing millions. Also in 2010, a catastrophic flood devastated a large part of Pakistan. Occasional terrorism, accidents, and other catastrophic incidents have also played a key role in exacerbating humanitarian problems in Pakistan (Report 2011).

It indicated in the above Fig. 10.5, that foundation worked in disaster whenever face by the country, so in the difficult situation the foundation worked side by side with the government of Pakistan for serving the people and community across the country. There are 3,157 shelter homes established for the needy and affected community in the country, they also provided the food for the affected people in the disaster and 4,565 food packages were distributed in the time of disaster. Response hub also set

Fig. 10.5 Details of community service by Al-Khidmat foundation across Pakistan (Provincial Disaster Management Authority, Khyber Pakhtunkhwa)

up in the different regions in the country along with 85 training centers. Volunteers groups were also set up through which various services and help provided to the door step of the people, thus about more than 6,506 volunteers join the foundation for serving the humanity. In the disaster about 221,066 individuals get benefited and about 236 million PKR is spent in these welfare and support services in the country by foundation.

COVID-19 Outbreak

The foundation working in the current pandemic in the cities, villages, towns, and other community places, whether urban or rural but reached to each and every needy and poor individuals in the country and help them in terms of providing various food packages, medicines, hygienic accessories along with other safety and preventive kits for the deserving and needy individuals and patients.

There is a complete lockdown about two months in the country, and peoples were asked to stay in home and not exposes to the markets, shopping malls, parks, and other places. There is a massive destruction in the economy of the country and the employees were unemployed due to the lockdown and did not bore the expenses by the owners and employer. A sever affected people are the daily wagers, and laborers segment in the community who depends on the daily activities and feed themselves along with their families and kids. A Khidmat foundation as its previous practice, about more than twenty-two thousand of volunteers, join the foundation for the sack of the humanity and their services in the pandemic and lockdown across the country. They are launching fund raising campaign in different cities of the country and requesting the rich and well off segment of the society to donate their Zakah, Sadaqah, Sadaqah-Ul-Fitre, and other charities to combat to the needy and deserving class of the society especially affected due to the current pandemic across the globe. Just in thirty days, more than one Billion PKR collected and directly spent among the community across the whole country by more than five million individuals get benefited in a short time span of a month only (Foundation 2020).

CONCLUSION

Throughout this article, we have seen that the Islamic financial system is based on moral and religious principles that support a particular economic and social prosperity. This so-called financial support of Halal is generating amazing enthusiasm, which is largely explained by the cyclical interest in sustainable development. From a conceptual point of view, Islamic finance and moral finance have been demonstrated to be in compliance with Islamic *Shari'ah* law, which requires believers to record their daily activities, especially economic activities, with respect to the environment and future generations. Therefore, the *Shari'ah* requires believers to behave in a "socially responsible" manner. Social responsibility, the primary center of moral investment, therefore, must play an important role in Islamic finance. This requires a new definition of the responsibilities of each party confirmation of the fundamental role of finance, implementation of appropriate regulatory, ethical and ethical tools that will restore trust and correct some of the existing asymmetries in the system. These changes are key factors that will enable finance to move toward more sustainable development where the human economy and the environment are at the heart of their concerns.

The widespread awareness of political decision makers and civil society should allow the development of ethical finance, which has good prospects for them as they have come to understand that the understanding of financial profit and economic profit was not contradictory, but reform and it was decisive in decision making to continue your activities. In this context, Islamic social and ethical finance will have a prominent place, with an institution of principles that is a matter of jurisprudence in times of questioning of the financial system as a whole. The evolution of demand for financial actors in terms of social and environmental inclusion should be a necessary axis of development for *Shari'ah-compliant* fundraisers.

REFERENCES

Alkhidmat Foundation. (2018a). *Progress of Alkhidmat Foundation*, Peshawar.

Alkhidmat Foundation. (2018b). *Who We Are and What We Do?* Lahore. www.alkhidmat.org.com.

Alkhidmat Foundation. (2019). *Our Services and Project for Community*. Lahore, Pakistan: Alkhidmat Foundation.

Alkhidmat Foundation. (2020). *Serving in the Pandemic*. Lahore, Pakistan: Alkhidmat Foundation.

Budiyanto, C., Prananto, A., & Ter-Chian Tan, F. (2019). Designing Embedded Case Study Research Approach in Educational Research. *International Journal of Pedagogy and Teacher Education, 3*(1), 1–16.

Daoud, K. B. (2013). L'intermédiation financière participative des banques islamiques. *Les Cahiers de La Finance Islamique, no, 5,* 28–40.

Forget, E. (2009). Le développement durable dans la finance éthique et la finance islamique. *Les Cahiers de la finance islamique, no, 1,* 1–4.

Jouaber, K. a. E. (2011). *La finance islamique est-elle une finance durable?* In *P. Grandin et D. Saidane (dir.), La finance durable: une nouvelle finance pour le XXIème siècle?* (pp. 137–152). Paris: Revue Banque Editions.

Moghul, U. (2015). Islamic Finance and Social Responsibility. *Stanford Social Innovation Review,* 1–4.

Newsletter. (2017). *Progress of Al Khidmat Foundation*. Lahore: Al Khidmat Foundation.

Ougoujil, S., & Rigar, S. M. (2019). Ethical Finance and Islamic Finance: Possible Convergence and Potential Development. *World Academy of Science, Engineering and Technology International Journal of Economics and Management Engineering, 12*(7), 958–972.

Rashid, Y., Rashid, A., & Akib Warraich, M. (2019). Case Study Method: A Step-by-Step Guide for Business Researchers. *International Journal of Qualitative Methods, 18,* 1 13.

Report, A. (2011). *Progress of Alkhidmat in Disaster*. Peshawar, Pakistan: Alkhidmat Foundation.

Report, A. (2017). *Progress of Alkhidmat Foundation*. Lahore, Pakistan: Alkhidmat Foundation.

Report, A. (2018). *Inside Story of Alkhidmat Foundation*. Lahore, Pakistan: Alkhidmat Foundation.

Teiu, M. C., & Daniel, J. (2011). A Practical Approach on Making Use of Case Study Research in Economics (*Munich Personal RePEc Archive MPRA Paper No. 37204*), 1–13.

United Nations Report. (2019). *UN Agenda 2030 Sustainable Development Goals*. New York: United Nations.

Wikipedia. (2017). *Introduction of Al Khidmat Foundation Pakistan*. www.wekipedia.org.pk.

www.alkhidmat.org.pk.

www.ndma.org.pk.

www.un.org.

www.undp.org.

PART II

How Islamic Ethical Wealth May Strategically and Technically Support SDGs' Schemes?

CHAPTER 11

Why Does Business Zakat Contribute Insignificantly to Achieving "SDG-1: Ending Poverty" in Nigeria? Evidence from Recordkeeping Practices

Umar Habibu Umar, Mustapha Abubakar, and Ibrahim Ibrahim Sharifai

INTRODUCTION

Globally, poverty is considered to be a social disorder and a recurrent problem from economic, social, and political points of view, especially in developing and third-world countries (Nadzri et al. 2012, p. 62). Poverty

---

U. H. Umar (✉)
Department of Finance, Universiti Brunei Darussalam, Bandar Seri Begawan, Brunei

M. Abubakar
Department of Banking and Finance, Ahmadu Bello University Business School, Zaria, Nigeria

I. I. Sharifai
Kano State Zakah Commission, Kano, Nigeria

© The Author(s), under exclusive license to Springer Nature Switzerland AG 2021
M. M. Billah (eds.), *Islamic Wealth and the SDGs*,
https://doi.org/10.1007/978-3-030-65313-2_11

219

becomes an international subject of concern because of the extreme level it has reached (Muhammad 2010, p. 139). It is a serious problem and a challenge, particularly in developing economies (Shirazi 2014, p. 80). For Nigeria, the Brookings Institution revealed that at least 87 million Nigerians live in extreme poverty and every one minute, six Nigerians become poor (Vanguard 2018). Similarly, the World Data Lab's Poverty Clock around June 2018 disclosed that about 90 million Nigerian, representing almost 50%, lived in extreme poverty (World Economic Forum 2019) and roughly six persons in Nigeria fell into the poverty trap per minute (World Economic Forum 2019). Further, the World Poverty Clock revealed that as of June 5, 2019, out of 197,686,877, (sometimes approximated to 200 million), 91,885,874 of Nigeria's population (representing 46.5%) live in extreme poverty (Sahara Reporters 2019). Unfortunately, it was found that 87% of poor Nigerians are located in the Northern region (PM News 2020). Ironically, this region is generally dominated by Muslims and Kano State in particular, is the most populated state not only in Nigeria but also in sub-Saharan African.

Poverty remains a major macroeconomic problem in Nigeria, particularly in Muslim-dominated states (Mustafa et al. 2020). Hence, the dethroned Emir of Kano and former Governor of the Central Bank of Nigeria, Muhammad Sanusi II, cautioned the people of Northern Nigeria region to change their culture, otherwise, they would continue to remain backward and in extreme poverty (Gusau 2020). On another occasion, on the 60th birthday for Governor of Kaduna State, Nasir Nasir El-Rufai, Sanusi II raised the alarm again to northern Nigerian leaders that the region would destroy itself if the leadership did not change (PM News 2020). Unfortunately, the activities of Boko Haram and the recent appearance of Corona Virus (COVID 19) have contributed significantly to the increase in poverty in Nigeria. COVID 19, in particular, having become a pandemic, is leading to the recession of the global economy.

However, considering the intensity of poverty in the Muslim world, zakat as a social empowerment tool in Islam is considered to be one of the institutions that could play a significant role in poverty eradication if properly deployed. Regrettably, it has been abandoned in Muslim countries, making Muslims vulnerable to poverty (Shirazi 2014, p. 80). There is historical evidence that zakat was used to eliminate poverty in Islamic society. Dogarawa (2009, p. 17) states that during the periods of Umar bin al-Khattab (13–22A.H) and Umar bin Abdul-Azeez (99–101A.H), poverty was totally eradicated whereby it became difficult to find people willing to receive any amount from the zakat collections. Even though zakat was used to effectively and completely eradicate poverty during the rule of Caliph Umar bin Al Khattab and Umar bin Abdul Aziz, this achievement was short lived. In contemporary times, for example, zakat has become ineffective when colonial masters conquered and controlled the Islamic state (Nadzri et al. 2012, p. 61). Many Nigerian studies, such as Mustafa and Maiyaki (2011), Mustafa and Idris (2015), Mustafa et al. (2017, 2018), among others, justified that the potential of zakat were yet to be utilized in such a way as to eradicate poverty in Nigeria. Recently, Mustafa et al. (2017, 2020, p. 44) believed that Kano state has the potential to generate at least ₦25billion per annum as zakat revenues.

Further to this, we note, here on the one hand, that a significant amount of zakat mostly comes from business persons. This signifies that the importance of business zakat in Islamic society is very profound. Previous studies like Umar and Kurawa (2019), Umar and Haron (2020) and Umar et al. (2020) emphasized on the general importance of the business sustainability for the benefit of heirs, non-heirs, and other members of Islamic societies and, in particular, the payment of business zakat. They recommended for the admission of heirs into an inherited business as partners (or shareholders). Moreover, to prevent heirs from voluntary liquidation during inheritance distribution, previous studies like Saleem (n.d.), Umar and Haron (2020), and Umar et al. (2020), etc., called on the founder/owner of any family inheritable business to integrate it with *waqf*. The integration will ensure the going concern of the business to generate income, growth, and development. Therefore, as long as the business remains a going concern, zakat must be paid which could be unitized for poverty eradication among the Muslim ummah.

On the other hand, we recognize that accounting serves as a tool for the computation of zakat, as it plays a key role in ensuring a proper and fair assessment of zakat liability (Adnan and Abu Bakar 2009, p. 33). The development of accounting records was originally for zakat accountability, a delegation of business and government responsibilities as well (Zaid 2000, p. 73). Hence, Muslim businessmen need to develop and implement books of accounts, systems, and recording procedures in line with the Shari'ah with the view to properly calculate business zakat (Zaid 2000, p. 76). Therefore, business zakat could only be fairly and correctly calculated if complete and proper records of business transactions are kept. However, a number of African studies, such as Zotorvie (2017), Pavtar (2017), Nketsiah (2018), Nyathi et al. (2018) and Aladejebi and

Oladimeji (2019), among others, found enterprises maintaining either improper or incomplete records. Although these studies did not evaluate the recordkeeping of zakatable assets, it can be inferred that there is a tendency to underpay enterprise zakat. Thus business zakat contributes insignificantly to eradicating poverty in Africa.

Given the above background, this study aims to assess the record-keeping practices of traders in Kano state in order to establish the extent of the accuracy of the zakat levies being collected with a view to finding the reasons why zakat contributes insignificantly to the achievement of "SDG-1: Ending Poverty" in Kano State, Nigeria. Only the record-keeping practices of traders in the famous traditional markets in the state, such as Kurmi, Sabon Gari, Rimi, Kofar Ruwa, and Singer, among others, were assessed. These traders were targeted because they constitute the highest number of businesspersons in the state. Therefore, they have more potential to contribute to zakat revenue than the other classes of business. Hence, the assessment of the recordkeeping practices of corporations, manufacturing companies, and other companies for the purpose of zakat does not fall within the scope of this study. The remainder of the paper is organized into five sections, which are arranged as follows: literature review, methodology, research findings, discussion of findings and conclusion and recommendations.

LITERATURE REVIEW

A Brief Background to the Case Study

The city of Kano is a regional trade hub for more than 300 million people in northern Nigeria and other countries that share borders with Nigeria, such as the Niger Republic, Chad and Cameroon and other countries located in the Sahel economic zone/North Africa (KSIHB 2013). The history of trade in Kano could be traced back to the seventh century, where various forms of markets exist in the state, such as of the community, the metropolitan, the regional, and the international, which are attended every day by thousands of people not only from other parts of Nigeria but also neighboring countries like Benin, Burkina Faso, Cameroun, Central Africa Republic, Chad, Ghana, Niger, and Togo (Ibrahim 2015, p. 31).

According to the World Bank Report, the population of Kano State in 2016 was 15 million people, representing 8.06% of the estimated

Nigeria's population of 186 million people in 2016 (Mustafa et al. 2018). Kano is an Islamic state with at least 95% of its population as Muslims (Mustafa et al. 2018). The state has an estimated number of 1.6 million Micro Small and Medium Enterprises (MSME) that cut across all economic activities in the state and provide about 60–70% output and employment opportunities (KSIHB 2013). It is densely populated with uncountable successful Muslim entrepreneurs. It accommodates high ability zakat payers like the richest African Business Icon—Alhaj (Dr.) Aliko Dangote (Mustafa et al. 2018). The selection of Kano State as the focus in this study was made in consideration of at least four major reasons. Firstly, it is an Islamic state dominated by Muslims. Secondly, it is a popular commercial state with its slogan of "Center of Commerce" not only in Nigeria but also in the West African region. Thirdly, most of the poor and the needy in Nigeria are found in Northern Nigeria where the state is located. Fourthly, it is the most populated state not only in northern Nigeria but also in West Africa.

Determination of Business Zakat

The payment of business zakat is unanimously agreed by all scholars (Hamzat 2009, p. 14). Adnan and Abu Bakar (2009, p 35) defined business zakat as a compulsory contribution, which is charged on specified assets of the business that meet certain conditions for the benefit of identified persons, who are not under any obligation to pay zakat. It is chargeable on assets and not income (Haniffa et al. 2008, p. 13; AAOIFI 2017, p. 874). It must be paid whether or not the business earned a profit, provided that it has positive working capital that reaches the *nisab* (Awang and Mokhtar 2012, p. 286; AAOIFI 2017, p. 874). Assets of the business that are zakatable include inventories, cash in hand, cash at bank and receivables (Abdul Rahman 2007, p. 92). However, zakat is not paid on operational or income-generating non-current assets (fixed assets), such as premises, plants and equipment, land and buildings, motor vehicles, patent rights, trademarks, computer software, and leased assets (AAOIFI 2017, pp. 874–875). The Department of Islamic Development Malaysia (JAKIM) in its published book, entitled "Panduan Zakat di Malaysia," provided two methods of calculating business zakat: *urfiyyah* (adjusted growth capital) and *syariyyah* (adjusted working capital) (Hamzat 2009, p. 15). These methods are adopted and recommended by the Malaysian Accounting Standards Board (MASB) in its Technical Release *i*-1 (Accounting for Business Zakat).

The formula for computing zakat by using adjusted growth capital model is "equity + long term equity − fixed asset − noncurrent Asset ± adjustments" and to compute the zakat payable by the business, the formula is given as "current assets − current liabilities ± adjustments)." But both methods provide the same outcomes (Abdul Rahman and Awang 2003, p. 37; Awang and Mokhtar 2012, p. 289). Both the adjusted growth capital method and the adjusted working capital method yield the same results, which are extracted from the same statement of financial transactions, but most of the business persons apply the adjusted working capital method (Hamzat 2009, p. 15).

From the above formulae, it could be seen that adjustments must be done before arriving at the zakat base. Under the growth capital model, the equity and other financial resources of the zakat payer are adjusted (where necessary) with the view to take care of *halal and haram* and different opinions on conventional and Islamic values on the recognition of income and expenses (Awang and Mokhtar 2012, p. 287). In the case of the working capital model, total current liabilities should be subtracted from total current assets and adjustments should also be made to ensure that the components are in line with the Shari'ah (Abdul Rahman and Awang 2003, p. 39; Awang and Mokhtar 2012, p. 287). Further, Hamzat (2009, p. 15) shades more light on three adjustments that should be made if the adjusted working capital method is applied: (a) non-allowable items, such as limited ownership and non-productive current assets, should be deducted from the current assets; (b) all donations made to the charitable organizations and all fixed assets purchased in the last quarter of the year using internal funds should be added back to the current assets; (c) only current assets that emerge from operational activities of the business, such as payables (creditors), accrual salaries, accrual rent, are allowed to constitute the current liabilities. Therefore, non-operational liabilities like unpaid dividends and bank overdrafts are not supposed to be deducted from the current assets as current liabilities. Zakat is also chargeable on assets earned through lawful ways. Hence, it is not charged on illegal assets or assets acquired through ways rejected by Islam, such as interest income and stolen items (Mohsin 2015, p. 42).

Similarly, the AAOIFI (2017, p. 870) in its Shari'ah Standard No. (35) states two methods of computing the zakat base: the net assets method and the net investment assets method, which are all expected to give the same result if such a difference is well considered. However, the standard recommends the application of the net assets method. Basically, the application of the method entails that liabilities should be subtracted from zakatable assets, i.e., zakatliability = zakatable assets-current liabilities. It is worth noting that the adjusted working capital and net assets methods are the same, so also are the adjusted growth model and net investment assets method similar.

Having identified and determined the zakatable assets, the next issue is to ascertain their value. It is unanimously agreed that the assets should not be assessed based on their historical costs but current values (a prevailing market price or cash equivalent values) on the date the zakat falls due (Abdul Rahman and Awang 2003, p. 34; Abdul Rahman 2007, p. 97; Haniffa et al. 2008, p. 14; Ather and Ullah 2009, p. 14; Awang and Mokhtar 2012, p. 289). The market value is expected to be applied in order to avoid negative wealth transfer from the rich to the beneficiaries (Awang and Mokhtar 2012, p. 289) or observe justice to the payers and the beneficiaries concurrently (Abdul Rahman 2007, p. 97).

Review of Empirical Studies on Business Recordkeeping Practices in Africa

In recent years, many empirical studies were conducted on the prevalent recordkeeping practices of businesses. Zotorvie (2017) assessed the financial accounting practices of SMEs in the Ho municipality in Ghana using a sample of 225 owner-managers. The study found that the majority of SMEs did not keep proper records of their transactions. Consequently, the enterprises found it difficult to find the actual profit or loss for a particular accounting period as well as their assets and liabilities for the purpose of making strategy and necessary adjustments for their success. Pavtar (2017) evaluated the accounting practices and explored the challenges of SMEs in Makurdi Metropolis in Benue State Nigeria. Through the administration of questionnaires, the study established that the SMEs maintained sales and purchases daybooks only and had challenges that negatively affected their operations. Moreover, the assessment of the recordkeeping practices of SMEs at Vigaeni Ward in the Mtwara-Mikindani Municipality, Tanzania, was one of the major objectives of a study carried out by Ghasia et al. (2017). The data were collected through interviews and observations. The study found that the majority of the SMEs did not practice sound recordkeeping management. Another finding of the study is the lack of understanding of the importance of keeping business records by SMEs owner-managers. Nketsiah (2018) assessed the recordkeeping practices of Small Business Operators in the Sekondi-Takoradi Metropolis, Ghana. The study used a descriptive cross-sectional survey to establish how they maintained their accounting records by selecting a sample of 200 SMEs randomly. The study revealed that 85% of the businesses maintained records of their receivables but maintained the least records for assets.

Based on the above empirical studies, it is understandable that most MSMEs in Africa do not maintain proper records of their transactions. Keeping proper and complete records by businesses is very profound. Hence, there is a group of studies that examined the relationship between proper recordkeeping and financial performance, growth or success of businesses, particularly MSMEs. Adeyemi et al. (2015) investigated the determinants of demand and supply of accounting and auditing for SMEs in Lagos State, Nigeria. Semi-structured questionnaires were used to collect the data from 300 SME owner-managers and 80 accounting firms. A key finding relevant to this study is that accounting and services have significant effects on the success of SMEs. This study recommended that SME owner-managers should be oriented on the role of accounting and auditing services on the success of their business. Solanke et al. (2016) examined the effects of keeping accounting records on the growth of SMEs in the North Central region of Nigeria. Questionnaires were used to generate data from a sample of 307 entrepreneurs. The study found that 62.90% of the SMEs maintained poor accounting records. The study also established a significant positive relationship between maintenance accounting records and the growth of SMEs in North Central Nigeria. Okpala (2017) studied the impact of accounting records on the financial performance of SMEs in Anambra State, Nigeria. The data were collected by administering questionnaires to a sample of 176 SMEs in the state. It found the SMEs maintaining proper records of their financial transactions, which improved their financial performance significantly. Similarly, Aladejebi and Oladimeji (2019) examined the application of accounting information to assess the performance of SMEs in Lagos Metropolis, Nigeria. The data were collected through the administration of 200 questionnaires to 200 SME owners out of which 197 were returned. It was found that the respondents believed keeping proper records enabled them to know their performance as well as consider it as a crucial factor to the success of the business. Unfortunately, the majority of them were found to have no basic knowledge of recordkeeping. Nyathi et al. (2018) carried out a survey to examine the role of accounting information in the success of selected SMEs in Harare, Zimbabwe. The study established that the majority did not utilize accounting information to make decisions for their success. This happened because they maintained incomplete or improper records.

Methodology

This study applied a qualitative approach by conducting a semi-structured interview in order to achieve the objective of the study. The semi-structured interview enables the interviewee to express their views on a particular subject (Nor and Hashim 2015, p. 6). The qualitative approach is believed to be the best way of getting a clear and in-depth understanding of phenomena (Eldabi et al. 2002). This is adapted from various studies like Nor and Hashim (2015), Thaker and Thaker (2015), Abu Bakar and Yusof (2016), Thaker (2018), and Umar et al. (2019). Traders and professional accountants were selected as respondents, who are in a better position to enable the study to ascertain whether or not the traders keep complete and accurate records of their zakatable assets.

Further, this study used a purposive sampling technique in selecting the interviewees. This sampling technique is the most suitable way of pre-selecting respondents based on a particular research question (Thaker 2018, p. 23). Concerning sample size, a sample of seven respondents was used based on data saturation. The small sample size is preferable to a large one in qualitative research because a small sample size enables the researchers to understand the complexity, depth, variation, or context surrounding the phenomena (Gentles et al. 2015, p. 1782). Table 11.1 shows the profile of the interviewees.

Table 11.1 presents seven interviewees. The four interviewees (B1, B3, B4, and B6) are entrepreneurs, who have gone through educational training as accountants with many years of business experience. And B2 and B5 are professional accountants that work in reputable accounting firms in the state. They render professional services to different businesses in the state for many years. The last respondent (B7) was interviewed to explore from him primarily about the potential of the Kano State Zakat and Hubsi Commission to generate adequate income to eradicate poverty in the state. Eight (8) questions were substantially developed based on *syariyyah* (adjusted working capital). This is because it is the most common method used by companies in Malaysia to compute their business zakat (Hamzat 2009, p. 15).

Table 11.2 contains eight categorical themes and their respective interview questions, which were adapted from previous studies (see Thaker and Thaker 2015; Thaker 2018; Umar et al. 2019; Umar 2020).

Table 11.1 Profile of the interviewees

No.	Occupation/place of employment	Code
1	Trader	B1
2	Professional accountant	B2
3	Trader	B3
4	Trader	B4
5	Professional accountant	B5
6	Trader	B6
7	Staff of Kano State Zakatand Hubsi Commission	B7

Table 11.2 Categorical Themes and Interview Questions

No.	Categorical themes	Interview questions
1	Inventories	To what extent do the traders keep proper records of their inventories?
2	Receivables	Do the traders keep complete records of their credit sales?
3	Cash and bank balances	Do the traders keep complete records of their cash receipts and payments?
4	Payables	Do the traders keep complete records of their credit purchases?
5	Valuation of inventories	Could you explain how the traders value their inventories for the purpose of zakat?
6	Zakat base	Do the traders charge zakat on profit or working capital?
7	Employment of bookkeepers/accountants	Do the traders employ permanent staff to work as bookkeepers/accountants?
8	The potential of generating business zakat revenue by Kano State Zakat and Hubsi Commission for the alleviation of poverty in the state	Does the Kano State Zakat and Hubsi Commission have the potential to generate business zakat revenue to alleviate poverty in the state?

Research Findings

In this section, the interview results generated from seven respondents for eight themes were presented. The seventh respondent was able to provide an answer to the last theme only as he does not know the recordkeeping practices of the traders. This is because not only does he not have such knowledge but also he has no power to investigate the recordkeeping practices of zakat payers in the state.

Inventories

Inventories constitute a significant portion of the current assets of the business. The respondents were asked about the recordkeeping practices for inventories by the traders in Kano state. Six respondents said that they did not maintain proper and complete records of their inventories. In particular, B5 said:

> The majority of the traders do not keep proper records of their inventories. Due to poor and inadequate storage systems, it is not uncommon to find two or more traders jointly using one warehouse and each of them could not provide comprehensive and genuine records showing the movements of their inventories.

Based on this finding, it is noted that the traders keep incomplete and proper records of their inventories. Consequently, this would negatively decrease the businesses zakat payable by them.

Receivables

Receivables were previously known as debtors. They emerge when the business sells goods on credit to its customers. Six respondents believed that most of the traders did not keep proper and complete records of their receivables. B1 described the attitude of the traders toward keeping records of their receivables as follows:

> The traders do keep records of their credit sales to customers improperly or in unprofessional ways. Therefore, there is a tendency of forgetting to write some transactions in totality or incorrectly which might lead to a dispute between the traders and their debtors.

The findings in respect of the receivables imply that the traders do not keep proper and adequate records of their receivables which tend to reduce the zakat to pay by the businessmen.

Cash Receipts and Payments

Keeping cash receipts and payments records could easily enable the traders to prepare cash books to ascertain their cash balance for the purpose of zakat. All the respondents viewed that most of the traders maintained incomplete and improper records of their receipts and payments. Quoted verbatim, B6 said:

> At least 60% of the traders do not issue receipts for cash collections unless they are required to provide. Also, more than 90% of them do not safely keep their receipts for future use and as such, they could not provide complete receipts for at the end of the financial year.

Based on the responses on the records for cash receipts and payments, it is understandable that the businessmen do not maintain proper and complete records of cash receipts and payments. In addition, the personal expenses of the traders are mostly settled out of the cash collections. Consequently, business zakat would be underpaid.

Payables

Payables were previously known as creditors. Normally, businesses buy goods on credit from their suppliers. They become due within a period that does not exceed a year. In the opinion of all the respondents, credit sales are normally kept in the books of the suppliers but mostly unprofessionally. Two respondents provide better descriptions of the nature of recordkeeping for payables by traders as follows:

> Most of the credit purchases and other accruals are not recorded rather they (traders) memorize them in their memories which could easily be forgotten which easily lead to disagreement between the business owners and their suppliers or creditors. B1
>
> Credit purchases are mostly recorded in the books of the suppliers in a way that is not in line with the modern principles of recordkeeping for financial transactions. But in most cases, credit purchases from relatives and friends are not recorded because of trust and closeness. B4

Valuation of Inventories

The respondents were asked on the basis of the valuation of inventories for the purpose of zakat. They all opined the majority of the traders did not revalue their inventories at market value. The three most import important excerpts from the responses are as follows:

> The majority of the traders do not give special consideration to their inventories for the purpose of determining the business zakat. It is hard to find traders valuing their inventories for the purpose of zakat, which is usually paid in the month of Ramadan. B2
>
> Most of the traders do not apply any right method that could enable them to value their inventories for the purpose of computation of the businesses zakat, but rather they estimate the value based on their unreasonable personal estimations. B5
>
> At least 60% of the traders do not perform inventory-taking for the purpose of zakat. Not more than 20% of the traders that carry out the inventory –taking revalue the inventories at the market value. B6

Zakat Base

Unlike taxation, which is normally charged on the profits of businesses, zakat is normally chargeable on the working capital of the business when it reaches the *nisab*. The interviewees were asked whether the traders pay business zakat based on profit or working capital. The respondents unanimously believed that most of the traders paid zakat based on the profit they earned or sales or they just paid the amount they liked without reasons. Some wealthy persons do not pay at all. B1 illustrated the basis on which some traders pay business zakat as follows:

> The majority of the traders charge zakat on the amount by which their wealth appreciated. For example, if at the beginning of the year the capital of the business is $10,000,000 and at the end of zakat year the wealth becomes $15,000,000, the trader would charge zakat on the increment, that is, $5,000,000. However, they still have a way of paying the little amount as zakat if the wealth is depreciated.

Employment of Bookkeepers/Accountants

For the businesses to maintain proper and complete records of their financial transactions and prepare a complete set of financial statements, competent bookkeepers/accountants must be employed. The respondents were asked about the employment of bookkeepers/accountants to maintain proper and complete records of their transactions. All the respondents said that most of the traders had no competent employees that are primarily employed to keep proper and complete records.

> At least 90% of the traders do not employ bookkeepers/accountants due to illiteracy about the importance of the bookkeeping. In addition, confidentiality is another reason why the traders do not want anybody to know their net worth. B1
>
> The traders have not yet realized the benefits of employing the bookkeepers/accountants to their businesses as they hardly have employees who are primarily responsible for bookkeeping and accounting for their businesses. Most of their employees are the ones who attend to the customers and collect cash sales. B5

The Potential of Generating Business Zakat Revenue

Formally, all forms of zakat whether business or individual are collected by Kano State Zakat and Hubsi Commission. The respondents were asked to state whether the commission had the potential to generate business zakat that could be utilized to eradicate poverty in the state. Five respondents believed that the commission had the potential to generate business zakat revenue that could adequately finance various poverty alleviation programs and that if judiciously implemented and utilized, poverty could be reduced to the barest minimal in the state. An excerpt from the B7 response, being a staff of the commission with more than a decade working experience in the commission, is as follows:

> One thing that clearly shows the potentials of business zakat revenue to alleviate poverty in the state is that in 1992, before this commission (Kano State Zakat and Hubsi Commission) was established, one of the successful entrepreneurs' business zakat was the sum of N700,000,000 (equivalent to $136,718,750) […]. He found it difficult to decide where, how and to whom to share the fund because there was no Kano State Zakat and Hubsi Commission then. Today, there are uncountable numbers of young millionaires and billionaires' entrepreneurs in this (Kano) state that if they pay the correct amount of zakat that could be the end of the poverty here. Believe me, if this commission gets all the necessary supports from the

government and the trader, it would definitely compete with Kano State Internal Revenue Service (KIRS) in terms of revenue generations [...].

DISCUSSION OF FINDINGS

The findings of the study indicate that most of the traders in Kano maintain incomplete and improper records of basic zakatable assets (inventories, cash, and receivables) and current liabilities to arrive at chargeable assets. These findings are substantially attributed to the fact that most of them do not employ bookkeepers/accountants that could handle and maintain a robust, complete, and proper record of business transactions in a professional way. These findings reveal that the traders in Kano state did not maintain proper and complete records of their financial transactions. These correspond with the earlier African studies, such as Solanke et al. (2016), Zotorvie (2017), Ghasia et al. (2017), Nyathi et al. (2018), and Aladejebi and Oladimeji (2019), among others. It was also found that the traders did not revalue their inventories for the purpose of zakat. Earlier mentioned in Islamic accounting, inventories are measured at their market values for the purpose of zakat with a view to maximizing zakat revenue for the socioeconomic development of the Ummah (Abdul Rahman and Awang 2003, p. 34; Abdul Rahman 2007, p. 97; Awang and Mokhtar 2012, p. 289). In specific, Mustafa et al. (2020) established that lack of proper recordkeeping of zakat revenue by the Kano State Zakat and Hubsi Commission is among the major problems of zakat institution in the state. This contributes significantly to low zakat collections. Moreover, most of the traders were found paying business zakat only when they earn profits. The fact is that business zakat is chargeable on specified assets when they reached the minimum (Haniffa et al. 2008, p. 13; Awang and Mokhtar 2012, p. 289; AAOIFI 2017, p. 874). Therefore, like individuals, it is compulsory to pay business zakat whether or not profit is earned provided that such asset values reached the minimum. Therefore, it is not like in the case of the conventional sense where tax it is usually charged on business profits.

More importantly, it is believed that if the Kano State Zakat and Hubsi Commission would get all the necessary resources and support from the government and traders, it would have generated as much the amount generated by the Kano State Internal Revenue (KIRS). For example, in the first two-quarters of 2019, KIRS generated the sum of N18, 564,546,104 (National Bureau of Statistics 2019). Therefore, the sum

N 37,129,092,208 could be generated for the year ended December 31, 2019. Similarly, if these amounts could be generated as business zakat revenues annually and used judiciously in the state, poverty would fall drastically in a few years. There are many young millionaire and billionaire entrepreneurs in the state. It is also believed that there are key and notable entrepreneurs (who are not up to 10 in number) in the state, who, if they pay the correct amount of business zakat and the amount is given to the right beneficiaries and used it judiciously, the frightening levels of poverty would be eliminated in the state within a few years. This finding corresponds with that of Mustafa et al. (2018), who found 98.65% of the respondents were business persons (men and women) with some of them paying as much as N100 million as zakat in the last 15–20 years. They added that 80% of zakat payers are relatively young people, as their ages fall within the range of 25–55 years. Fortunately, some of them were previous beneficiaries of the zakat. Similarly, Mustafa (2020) found that 707 zakat payers, who represented 78.6% of the respondents, were found to fall into the class of high ability zakat payers between 5,000–₦1 m and above. They believed this is a clear indication of a high level of the potential revenue base of the zakat institution in Kano state.

CONCLUSION AND RECOMMENDATIONS

Zakat is one of the five pillars of Islam which entails the movement of wealth from the rich to the needy. It is widely believed that if it is applied judiciously, poverty could be alleviated in the Muslim world. Despite the fact that many studies re-justified the potential of zakat revenue to alleviate poverty, it still remains the problem of most Muslim-dominated countries. Hence, this study sought to establish the reason why business zakat does not contribute significantly to the achievement of the "SDG-1: Ending Poverty" in Nigeria by assessing the recordkeeping practices of traders in Kano State, Nigeria. The study established that they did not maintain proper and complete records of their zakatable assets and deductible liabilities. Most of them also paid business zakat only when they earn profit not when their zakatable assets reach the *nisab*. Consequently, they underpay business zakat, which does not contribute to poverty alleviation in the state significantly. It was also found that the Kano State Zakat and Hubsi Commission have the potential to earn revenues as much as KIRS.

Based on these findings, three recommendations were pointed out. First, in line with Mustafa et al. (2020), a law should be enacted to convert the Kano State Zakat and Hubsi Commission into a Ministry of Zakat and Hubusi to be headed by a seasoned scholar that has both Islamic and conventional backgrounds, preferably in the area of Islamic Social and Management Sciences. The state government should give all the necessary power and resources to the Ministry to discharge its duties efficiently and effectively. The Ministry is also expected to develop a standard or manual to guide traders on the computation of business zakat in line with the Shari'a. Each business must be mandated to file its annual reports and accounts to the Ministry in the month in which the zakat is due, which is usually Ramadhan. It should be given an enabling law to audit and investigate the recordkeeping practices of traders with a view to ensuring that correct amounts of business zakat are paid. Second, the Kano State Traders Associations, the proposed Ministry of Zakat and Hubsi and accounting professional associations (such as the Institute of Chartered Accountants of Nigeria and the Association of National Accountants of Nigeria) should collaborate to organize periodically training for traders on bookkeeping practices and the preparation of financial statements. Third, the disbursement of zakat revenue to beneficiaries should be monitored and all the necessary measures put in place to ensure that the beneficiaries utilize what they collect in such a way as to ensure that poverty is alleviated to the barest minimum.

REFERENCES

Abdul Rahman, A. (2007). Pre-requisites for Effective Integration of Zakat into Mainstream Islamic Financial System in Malaysia. *Islamic Economic Studies, 14*(1 & 2), 91–107.

Abdul Rahman, R., & Awang, R. (2003). Assessing Business Zakat at Pusat Zakat Selangor: Between Theory and Practice. *Journal of Financial Reporting and Accounting, 1*(1), 33–48.

Abu Bakar, F., & Yusof, M. A. M. (2016). Managing CSR Initiatives from the Islamic Perspective: The Case of Bank Islam Malaysia Berhad (BIMB). *JurnalPengurusan, 46*, 67–76.

Accounting and Auditing Organization for Islamic Financial Institutions (AAOIFI). (2017). *Full Text of Shari'ah Standards for Islamic Financial Institutions Accounting, Auditing and Governance Standards*. Manama: Dar AlMaiman for Publishing & Distribution.

Adeyemi, S. B., Obaha, S., & Udofia, I. E. (2015). Determinants of Demand and Supply of Accounting and Audit Services in SMEs: Evidence from Nigeria. *Accounting and Management Information Systems, 14*(3), 546–574.

Adnan, M. A., & Abu Bakar, N. B. (2009). Accounting Treatment for Corporate Zakat: A Critical Review. *International Journal of Islamic and Middle Eastern Finance and Management, 2*(1), 32–45.

Aladejebi, O., & Oladimeji, J. A. (2019). The Impact of Record Keeping on the Performance of Selected Small and Medium Enterprises in Lagos Metropolis. *Journal of Small Business and Entrepreneurship Development, 7*(1), 28–40. https://doi.org/10.15640/jsbed.v7n1a3.

Ather, S. M., & Ullah, H. (2009). *Islamic Accounting Systems and Practices*. Retrieved from https://www.researchgate.net/publication/263809688. Accessed 13 November, 2017.

Awang, R. N., & Mokhtar, M. Z. (2012). Comparative Analysis of Current Values and Historical Cost in Business Zakat Assessment: Evidence from Malaysia. *International Journal of Business and Social Science, 3*(7), 286–298.

Dogarawa, A. B. (2009, October 3). *Poverty Alleviation Through Zakat and waqf Institutions: A Case for the Muslim ummah in Ghana*. Paper Presented at the First National Muslim Summit, Organized by Al-Furqan Foundation, Tamale, Ghana, Held at Radach Memorial Centre, Lamashegu, Tamale, Ghana.

Eldabi, T., Irani, Z., Paul, R. J., & Love, P. T. D. (2002). Quantitative and Qualitative Decision-making Methods in Simulation Modelling. *Management Decisions, 40*(1), 64–73.

Gentles, S. J., Charles, C., Ploeg, J., & McKibbon, K. (2015). Sampling in Qualitative Research: Insights from an Overview of the Methods Literature. *The Qualitative Report, 20*(11), 1772–1789.

Ghasia, B. A., Wamukoya, J., & Otike, J. (2017). Managing Business Records in Small and Medium Enterprises at Vigaeni ward in Mtwara-Mikindani Municipality, Tanzania. *International Journal of Management Research & Review, 7*(10), 974–986.

Gusau, M. A. (2020, January 25). *Polygamy Causing Poverty, Backwardness in North—Sanusi, Punch*. Retrieved from https://punchng.com/polygamy-causing-poverty-backwardness-in-north-sanusi/v.

Hamzat, Z. (2009, July 2–3). *Business Zakat Accounting and Taxation in Malaysia*. Paper presented at Conference on Islamic Perspectives on Management and Finance, Organized by School of Management, University of Leicester, UK.

Haniffa, R., Hudaib, M., & Mirza, A. M. (2008). Accounting Policy Choice Within the Shari'ahIslami'iah Framework. In M. D. Bakar & E. R. A. Engku Ali (Eds.), *Essential Readings in Islamic Finance*. Kuala Lumpur: CERT Publication.

Ibrahim, A. M. (2015). Evolutionary Trend, Spatial Distribution of, and Issues Associated with Markets in Kano Metropolis. *International Journal of Physical and Human Geography, 3*(2), 9–24.

Kano State Investor's Hand Book (KSIHB). (2013). Retrieved from www.kano. gov.ng.

Malaysian Accounting Standards Board. (2006). Technical Release *i*-1 (Accounting for Business Zakat).

Mohsin, M. I. (2015). Potential of Zakat in Eliminating Riba and Eradicating Poverty in Muslim Countries. *International Journal of Islamic Management and Business, 1* (1), 40–63.

Muhammad, I. N. (2010). Scholars, Merchants and Civil Society Imperative for Waqf-based Participatory Poverty Alleviation Initiatives in Kano, Nigeria. *Humanomics, 26*(2), 139–157.

Mustafa, D., Baita, A. J., & Adhama, H. D. (2020). Quantitative Economic Evaluation of Zakah-Poverty Nexus in Kano State, Nigeria. *International Journal of Islamic Economics and Finance, 3*(1), 21–50.

Mustafa, D., Baita, A. J., & Mamman, A. (2018). Zakah Institution and Poverty Alleviation Nexus in Kano State, Nigeria: A Structural Equation Model Approach. *Abuja Journal of Economics and Allied Fields, 9*(5), 156–171.

Mustafa, D., Baita, A. J., Sabo, M., & Adhama, H. D. (2017). Zakat System for Poverty Alleviation in Kano State, Nigeria: Pilot Study on the Validity and Reliability of Survey Instrument. *Bayero International Journal of Islamic Finance*, Bayero University, Kano.

Mustafa, D. A., & Idris, M. (2015). The Contributions of Islamic Economic Institutions to Modern Nigeria. *Journal of Islam in Nigeria, 1*(1), 36–58.

Mustafa, D., & Maiyaki, A. A. (2011).The Economic Significance of the Zakat System: An Exploratory Analysis of Its Fiscal Characteristics. *Elixir Finance Journal, 36*. Retrieved from www.elixirjournal.org.

Nadzri, F. A. A., AbdRahman, R., & Omar, N. (2012). Zakat and Poverty Alleviation: Roles of Zakat Institutions in Malaysia. *International Journal of Arts and Commerce, 1*(7), 61–72.

National Bureau of Statistics. (2019). *Internally Generated Revenue at State Level-Q1 & Q2.* Retrieved from https://www.nigerianstat.gov.ng/pdfupl oads/Internally_Generated_Revenue_At_State_Level_Q2_2018.pdf.

Nketsiah, I. (2018). Financial Recordkeeping Practices of Small Business Operators in the Sekondi-Takoradi Metropolitan Area of Ghana. *Asian Journal of Economics, Business and Accounting, 6*(3), 1–9. https://doi.org/10.9734/AJEBA/2018/39291.

Nor, S. M., & Hashim, N. A. (2015). CSR and Sustainability of Islamic Banking: The Bankers View. *JurnalPengurusan, 45, 73*–81.

Nyathi, K. A., Nyoni, T., Nyoni, M., & Bonga, W. G. (2018). The Role of Accounting Information in the Success of Small & Medium Enterprises

(SMEs) in Zimbabwe: A Case of Harare. *Journal of Business and Management, 1*(1), 01–15.

Okpala, L. I. (2017). Effect of Accounting Records on Financial Performance of Small and Medium Industries in Nigeria. *International Journal of Trend in Scientific Research and Development, 3*(4), 1120–1125.

Pavtar, A. A. (2017). Accounting Practices of SMEs: Challenges and Effects: A Survey of SMEs in Makurdi metropolis - Benue State—Nigeria. *World Journal of Finance and Investment Research, 2*(1), 16–29.

PM News. (2020, February 18). *Emir Sanusi: Northern Nigeria Will Destroy Itself*. Retrieved from https://www.pmnewsnigeria.com/2020/02/18/emir-sanusi-northern-nigeria-will-destroy-itself/.

Sahara Reporters. (2019, March, 21). *91.8 Million Nigerians Are Extremely Poor, Says World Poverty Clock*. Retrieved from http://saharareporters.com/2019/06/05/918-million-nigerians-are-extremely-poor-says-world-poverty-clock.

Saleem, M. Y. (n.d.). *Succession Planning of Family Businesses from an Islamic Perspective*. Retrieved from https://www.labuanibfc.com/.../Succession-Planning-of-Family-Businesses-from-an-Isl. Accessed 20 November 2017.

Shirazi, N. S. (2014). Integrating zakātand waqf into the Poverty Reduction Strategy of the IDB Member Countries. *Islamic Economic Studies, 22*(1), 79–108.

Solanke, A. A., Fashagba, P. F., & Okpanachi, J. (2016). Maintenance of Accounting Records and Business Growth Among Small and Medium Enterprises in North-Central Nigeria. *Journal of Accounting and Financial Management, 2*(1), 48–54.

Thaker, M. A. M. (2018). A Qualitative Inquiry into Cash waqf Model as a Source of Financing for Micro Enterprises. *ISRA International Journal of Islamic Finance, 10*(1), 19–35.

Thaker, M. A. M. T., & Thaker, H. M. T. (2015). Exploring the Contemporary Issues of Corporate Share waqf Model in Malaysia with the Reference to the waqaf An-Nur Corporation Berhad. *JurnalPengurusan, 45*, 165–172.

Umar, U. H. (2020). The Business Financial Inclusion Benefits from an Islamic Point of View: A Qualitative Inquiry. *Islamic Economic Studies, 28*(1), 83–100. https://doi.org/10.1108/IES-09-2019-0030.

Umar, U. H., & Haron, M. H. (2020). The Islamic Need for Investing Inherited Wealth and Accounting Treatments. *Presented at the Departmental Seminar Organized by the Department of Accounting, Yusuf MaitamaSule (Northwest) University, Kano-Nigeria*.

Umar, U. H., & Kurawa, J. M. (2019). Business Succession from an Islamic Accounting Perspective. *ISRA International Journal of Islamic Finance, 11*(2), 267–281. https://doi.org/10.1108/IJIF-06-2018-0059.

Umar, U. H., Ado, M. B., & Ayuba, H. (2019). Is Religion (Interest) an Impediment to Nigeria's Financial Inclusion Targets by the Year 2020?

A Qualitative Inquiry. *Qualitative Research in Financial Markets, 12*(3), 283–300. https://doi.org/10.1108/QRFM-01-2019-0010.

Umar, U. H., Kademi, T. T., & Haron, M. H. (2020). Integrating Waqf and Business: Ensuring Business Sustainability for the Welfare of Heirs and non-heirs. *International Journal of Economic, Management and Accounting, 28*(1), 191–213.

Vanguard. (2018, June 25). *Nigeria Overtakes India as World's Poverty Capital—Report*. Retrieved from https://www.vanguardngr.com/2018/06/nigeria-overtakes-india-as-worlds-poverty-capital-report/.

World Economic Forum. (2019). *Three Things Nigeria Must Do to End Extreme Poverty*. Retrieved from https://www.weforum.org/agenda/2019/03/90-million-nigerians-live-in-extreme-poverty-here-are-3-ways-to-bring-them-out/.

Zaid, O. A. (2000). Were Islamic Records Precursors to Accounting Books Based on the Italian Method? *The Accounting Historians Journal, 27*(1), 73–90.

Zotorvie, S. T. (2017). A Study of Financial Accounting Practices of Small and Medium Scale Enterprises (SMEs) in Ho Municipality, Ghana. *International Journal of Academic Research in Business and Social Sciences, 7*(7), 29–39. https://doi.org/10.6007/IJARBSS/v7-i7/3075.

CHAPTER 12

The Role of Islamic Ethical Wealth in Strategically and Technically Supporting 'No Poverty'-SDGs 1

Mustafa Omar Mohammed, Mohamed Cherif El Amri, and Ayman Bakr

INTRODUCTION

Nu'man bin Bashīr (may Allah be pleased with them) reported that the Messenger of Allah (ﷺ) said,

> The believers in their mutual kindness, compassion, and sympathy are just like one body. When one of the limbs suffers, the whole body responds to it with wakefulness and fever. [al-Bukhārī and Muslim – narrated by Muslim - Riyāḍ al-Ṣāliḥīn 224]

M. O. Mohammed
Department of Economics, International Islamic
University Malaysia [IIUM], Gombak, Malaysia
e-mail: mustafa@iium.edu.my

M. C. El Amri (✉) · A. Bakr
Islamic Economics and Finance, Sabahattin Zaim University, Istanbul, Turkey

© The Author(s), under exclusive license to Springer Nature
Switzerland AG 2021
M. M. Billah (eds.), *Islamic Wealth and the SDGs*,
https://doi.org/10.1007/978-3-030-65313-2_12

241

The afore-mentioned ḥadīth clearly shows the kind of relation that binds all the believers together. It provides the basis for strongly connected communities and societies. From such relationships stem the highest form of social solidarity. While Muslims owe each other social rights, the Sharī'ah has not limited it to them only, but has also recommended for Muslims to deal in good manners with non-believers. Mujāhid narrated that Abdullah bin Amr bin al-'Āṣ (may Allah be pleased with them) said that the Prophet [May Peace be upon him] had a sheep slaughtered for his family, so when he came, he said:

> Have you given some to our neighbor, the Jew? Have you given some to our neighbor, the Jew? I heard the Messenger of Allah saying: "Jibril continued to advise me about (treating) the neighbors so (kindly and politely), that I thought he would order me (from Allah) to make them heirs." [Jāmi'al-Tirmidhi 1943]

These great ethical values are the basis of many other values including those that are related to financial matters and poverty. For instance, Islam forbids charging interest (ribā) over loans (qarḍ). Qarḍ is also sometimes referred to as qarḍ ḥasan to differentiate it from loans that charge interest. Islam teaches that borrowers should not be overburdened with additional amount of loan and he or she is only expected to repay the loan at par. Islam also encourages ease (postponement of repayment period) of those who are in financial hardship and have defaulted their loan repayments:

> And if someone is in hardship, then [let there be] postponement until [a time of] ease. But if you give [from your right as] charity, then it is better for you, if you only knew. [Qur'ān 2:280]

Furthermore, Islam encourages the circulation of wealth and discourages any form of its concentration in the hands of a few affluent. This is clearly demonstrated in the Qur'ān [59:7] where Allah details the distribution of the spoils to avoid its perpetual distribution among the rich. This measure is not limited to spoil or booty allocations but extended to other financial transactions to ensure that wealth circulates and is transferred from the rich to the poor. Islam has prescribed charitable institutions such as general charity (ṣadaqah), alms (zakāh), and endowments (waqf) to facilitate income and wealth redistribution.

There are several Qur'ānic verses that encourage people to do charity; for instance, these verses in Sūrat al-Baqarah—Qur'ān [2:261–262, 265, 267, 270–274]. The verses have also explicitly mentioned the great rewards from Allah that accrue from charity giving. These include forgiveness of sins, multiple repayment, and high level of paradise. One of the important charity institutions is Zakat, which is one of the significant pillars of Islam. Ibn 'Umar reported God's messenger as saying,

> Islam is based on five things: the testimony that there is no god, but Allah and that Muhammad is His servant and messenger, the observance of the prayer, the payment of zakāh, the Pilgrimage, and the fast during Ramadan. [al-Bukhārī and Muslim – Mishkāt al-Maṣābīḥ 4]

Zakat is so significant that it is frequently mentioned in the various verses of the Quran and hadith along with prayer (ṣalāh). In the afore-mentioned ḥadīth, zakāh comes right after ṣalāh. In the examples of verses in the Qur'ān mentioned below, Zakat is mentioned along with ṣalāh:

> Indeed, those who believe and do righteous deeds and establish prayer and give zakah will have their reward with their Lord, and there will be no fear concerning them, nor will they grieve. [Qur'ān 2:277]

> ... So, establish prayer and give zakāh and hold fast to Allah. He is your protector; and excellent is the protector, and excellent is the helper. [Qur'ān 22:78]

> ... So, recite what is easy from it and establish prayer and give zakāh and loan Allah a goodly loan. And whatever good you put forward for yourselves - you will find it with Allah. It is better and greater in reward. And seek forgiveness of Allah. Indeed, Allah is Forgiving and Merciful. [Qur'ān 73:20]

Zakāh helps to alleviate poverty; it is a prescribed amount of wealth (usually determined as 2.5%) that each Muslim needs to give to the poor and needy often every year. However, the beneficiaries of zakāh are limited only to the eight types declared in one verse in Sūrat al-Tawbah:

> Zakāh expenditures are only for the poor and for the needy and for those employed to collect [zakāh] and for bringing hearts together [for Islam] and for freeing captives [or slaves] and for those in debt and for the cause

of Allah and for the [stranded] traveler - an obligation [imposed] by Allah. And Allah is Knowing and Wise. [Qur'ān 9:60]

Waqf is another important institution that helps in the distribution and circulation of wealth and alleviation of poverty. We have a plethora of evidence in the Qur'ān and Sunnah that explain waqf. The ḥadīth reported by Abū Huraira (may Allah be pleased with him) is one example of a clear evidence explaining Waqf. He reported Allah's Messenger (ﷺ) as saying:

> When a man dies, his acts come to an end, but three, recurring charity, or knowledge (by which people) benefit, or a pious son, who prays for him (for the deceased). [Ṣaḥīḥ Muslim 1631]

The perpetual charity, or ṣadaqah jāriyah, suggests a sustainable benefit to the community. In fact, scholars regard perpetual charity, ṣadaqah jāriyah, as referring to waqf. In the Qur'ān it is mentioned that in order to attain to true piety, one should expend from his properties that he cherishes the most:

> [But as for you, O believers,] never shall you attain to true piety unless you spend on others out of what you cherish yourselves; and whatever you spend - verily, Allah has full knowledge thereof. [Qur'ān 3:92]

Waqf forms an integral part of the Islamic economy's third sector. Such a philanthropic institution has constantly provided support for people throughout history. Its fundamental role in alleviating poverty, developing the non-profit non-governmental organizations, and contributing to the socioeconomic welfare of the society has been acknowledged by many researchers (Dogarawa 2010, p. 1; Haneef et al. 2015, p. 250; Kahf 1998, p. 9; 1999, p. 39). Waqf establishment proliferated during the Ottoman caliphate and soon every facet of life was enjoying the benefits of waqf: Educational and religious institutions and infrastructural services (sidewalks, bridges, etc.) were funded (Bulut and Korkut 2019, p. 8); schools, hospitals, orphanages, and libraries were built; scholars, students, poor, needy, and orphans were supported; graveyards and cemetery ceremonies were financed (Dogarawa 2010). Even feeding and caring for animals was reported like the waqf for cats and waqf of unwanted animals, both in Damascus (Kahf 2003).

Despite these tremendous contributions, there is no clear definition on the scope of Islamic ethical wealth. Whereas it is true to think of it as something full of ethics, values, morals, and principles, in this context it is also equally true to see it as a mechanism of wealth circulation that is motivated by Islamic ethics and principles. To this end, there is a need to propose an operational definition that will minimize the ambiguity of the term 'Islamic ethical wealth.' Hence, Islamic ethical wealth can be defined as: "All the institutions and tools provided by Islam that contribute to the elimination of wealth concentration in the hands of the few affluent and redistributing this wealth to the less privileged members of the society such as the poor, needy, indebted, etc. with the ultimate goal of alleviating poverty and hardship." Such a definition is broad to include institutions such as waqf and zakāh, and all other forms of charity like ṣadaqah and qarḍ.

REVIEW OF RELATED LITERATURE ON ISLAMIC ETHICAL WEALTH AND SDGS

There are several works about poverty and about Islamic wealth management. There are also numerous studies on SDGs from various dimensions and perspectives. However, there is a dearth of literature that combines poverty, Islamic wealth management and SDGs. The few studies that integrate Islamic ethical wealth, poverty, and SDG are largely descriptive and general. These studies comprise two categories: those that have tried to argue for the agricultural sector as one of the avenues to achieve the 'No Poverty SDG,' and those that have discussed the role of Islamic wealth management toward achieving 'No Poverty SDG.' Feliciano (2019), citing the World Bank, said growth and development of agriculture is a significant determinant for escaping poverty traps. This view is supported by a couple of researchers who recognize the development of the agricultural sector for addressing the 'No Poverty' SDG (Abayomi-Alli et al. 2018; Ali Hudaefi 2020; Feliciano 2019). Their approaches are different though. While Feliciano (2019) argues for crop diversification as a strategy for poverty alleviation, Ali Hudaefi (2020) and Abayomi-Alli et al. (2018) looked at the use of technology to support agriculture. Ali Hudaefi (2020) acknowledges that the use of technology to accelerate the achievement of SDGs has been intensive in Indonesia. He explored the role of the FinTech firms and found that they are instrumental in promoting financial inclusion through Islamic social funds

[Islamic ethical wealth]. For example, such funds mobilized through FinTech are used to finance underdeveloped sectors such as agriculture and small-to-medium enterprises (SMEs). Yet, Feliciano (2019) notes that poverty alleviation should not be assessed based on income alone but should include other dimensions in order to determine the best strategy for achieving SDG 1.

The use of Islamic social funds [Islamic ethical wealth] to alleviate poverty is not something new. Khan and Hassan (2019) maintain that zakāh and waqf institutions have jointly played an important role in socioeconomic development of Muslim societies and that they are still capable of offering a universal solution to achieve SDGs (Ali et al. 2019). Some researchers focused on waqf. For instance, while Khan and Hassan (2019) discuss the use of waqf to cater for the social development goals like education, Al Zobair and Hoque (2019) provide a seven-point strategic model to mobilize waqf resources under the seven targets of SDG 1 (Ali et al. 2019). On the other hand, Muhamat et al. (2019) discussed the significance of waqf for supporting several SDGs including SDG 1. Notwithstanding, they focused on the readiness of Takaful operators in integrating waqf into a new Takaful insurance policy product. There are comparatively few studies on waqf to support SDGs, and even those lack an in-depth coverage on how this can be achieved.

In contrast, interest in the use of zakāh to alleviate poverty has been increasing (Joan et al. 2019; Kidwai and Zidani 2020; Mohammad et al. 2020). This is not surprising. Based on the UNHCR Zakat Program: 2019 Launch Report, the actual Zakat collection globally in 2018 was US$76 billion. This figure of actual collection was far behind the full potential of Zakat, which was estimated as high as US$ 356 billion, assuming that proper Zakat governance was in place (UNHCR 2019). As such, Kidwai and Zidani (2020) see that there is a strategic alignment between zakāh principles and humanitarian goals since large part of the dramatic funding gap toward SDGs and humanitarian assistance will be used in the Muslim world. Therefore, many researchers investigated the use of zakāh for contributing toward SDG 1. For example, Joan et al. (2019, p. 138) explored how access to microcredit with guaranteed productive zakāh can help poor fishermen both in the capture fisheries and aquaculture sectors in order to develop their businesses.

However, Kidwai and Zidani (2020) criticize the bureaucracy in Muslim countries and call for review of zakāh management, one that should be commensurate with the contemporary challenges. They argue that new and more efficient ways to manage the needs of those eligible to receive zakāh must be explored and supported. Perhaps the zakāh and qarḍ platform developed by Mohammad et al. (2020, p. 358) can contribute to that call. In their platform, Mohammad et al. (2020, p. 358) used machine learning, natural language process (NLP), and digital image processing (DIP) for the analysis and verification of the recipients of loan or Zakah assistance.

Several studies have explored the issues related to the Islamic ethical wealth in alleviating poverty. These issues can be classified into two. Firstly, issues of limitations or obstacles that the philanthropical institutions might have or face. Secondly, issues of practice including issues concerning willingness of implementation, issues pertaining to proper implementation and misconduct, and issues related to effectiveness and efficiencies.

While Islamic philanthropical institutions are capable of alleviating poverty, Muslims need to put more seriousness in implementing them (Abdul-Majeed Alaro and Alalubosa 2019, p. 118). Until the beginning of the Ottoman caliphate, zakāh collection and distribution were carried out by the state. However, by the end of the Ottoman caliphate, this noble act started declining until it eventually flickered (varying from one Muslim country to the other) depending on whether Zakah is managed by the state or zakāh agency, or managed by individuals (Lessy 2013). Since then, zakāh was left to individuals to pay it whenever and however they wished. This decentralization of zakāh payment lessened the amount of Zakah in circulation from the estimated amount also it led to unbalanced distribution. The former occurred due to excessive freedom given to individuals, many of whom became affluent, negligent, and stopped the practice. The latter was caused by the focus of the zakāh payers on certain beneficiaries while neglecting others.

Abdul-Majeed Alaro and Alalubosa (2019, p. 119) explained that zakāh is established to eliminate interest (ribā) and eradicate poverty at the micro- and macro-levels if the state played its role. To support their argument, the authors described two instances in history where poverty was totally eradicated when zakāh was effectively collected and efficiently dispersed; the first was at the time of the caliph 'Umar bin al-Khattab while the second was at the time of his great-grandchild caliph 'Umar bin 'Abd al-'Azīz. Yet, loss of confidence in the state or the Zakāh agency affected the willingness of the zakāh payers to allow the zakāh collector, whether the state or an agency, to conduct it on their behalf (Owoyemi

2020, p. 498). Deficiency in Zakah collection would in turn limit the potential of funds for poverty alleviation.

The other issue is that Zakāh is highly regulated as it is prescribed only to the eight categories of recipients mentioned in the Qur'ān [9:60]. This limits the scope of maneuvering Zakāh funds for purposes beyond the eight categories. Issues of restriction are also found in waqf. Some waqf are restricted to certain beneficiaries limiting the way a waqf can be used to alleviate poverty. Hence, restricted waqf cannot be used for microfinancing or funding to other than the purpose determined by the donor (Abdul-Majeed Alaro and Alalubosa 2019).

Today, waqf institutions also face great challenges. Following the fall of the Ottoman caliphate, waqf institutions suffered excessive and continuous deterioration. The reasons reported included underfunding (Bagby 2012, p. 24; Kahf 1998), legislative issues (Kahf 1998; Nawa 2015), aggression, and lack of governmental support (Abdullah Nadwi 2014, pp. 5–6; Dogarawa 2010), colonial neglect and confiscation—"by hook or by crook" (Abdur-Rashid 2020, p. 26), and mismanagement, misconduct, and corruption (Abdullah Nadwi 2014; Rashid 2012, p. 135). There is another issue of waqf pertaining to digression from its worldview that began some time during the Ottoman period. Today, we see many waqf institutions that have skewed toward investment models. Cash waqf is lent to microenterprises and microfinance participants with the goal of distributing any resulting profits to shareholders and waqf founders, neglecting the real beneficiaries. Mismanagement of corporate waqf is another issue where only a small amount of the profits go to Waqf related developmental projects while the huge chunk of waqf funds go into the pockets of the shareholders.

On reviewing the related literature of Islamic ethical wealth and the 'No Poverty' SDG, several gaps are identified. Firstly, poverty alleviation should not be assessed by income alone as this would fall short of evaluating its real contribution to SDG 1. Other dimensions must be included to determine the effective strategy for achieving SDG 1. Secondly, there is a need for further research on how waqf can support SDGs as the current studies lack in-depth. Thirdly, more research is required for evaluating the extent to which the adopted approaches have contributed to achieving SDG 1. Fourthly, Muslim countries must minimize bureaucracy and adopt innovative approaches to overcome contemporary challenges. Table 12.1 summarizes these research gaps.

Table 12.1 Gaps in the literature

No	Gaps
1	Lack of other dimensions besides income to assess the achievement of SDG 1
2	Lack of adequate research on waqf and SDG 1
3	Lack of sufficient research for evaluating the extent to which the adopted approaches have contributed to achieving SDG 1
4	Bureaucracy in Muslim countries and absence of innovative approaches to overcome contemporary Islamic ethical wealth and SDGs related challenges

SDG on Poverty

Sustainable Development Goals (SDGs) were adopted in 2015 by all United Nations member states. The SDGs were developed to ensure that all people enjoy peace and prosperity by 2030 (UNDP 2020a). To achieve these goals, the United Nations Development Programme (UNDP) was tasked to oversee their implementation in 170 countries and territories. In most of these 170 countries, poverty alleviation is at the forefront. It is an international concern and therefore UNDP's first goal—"No Poverty" (Feliciano 2019). Globally, it is reported that one in every ten persons is extremely poor, and that amounts to 736 million people (UNDP 2020b). Within the sustainable development agenda, the United Nations consider poverty more than the lack of income and productive resources. It also includes hunger and malnutrition, limited access to education and other basic services, social discrimination and exclusion, as well as the lack of participation in decision-making (United Nations, n.d.). UNDP (2020b) recognizes that there are new threats brought about by climate change, conflict, and food insecurity and, which would need greater efforts for getting people out of poverty. The UNDP has allocated seven targets to achieve the "No Poverty" goal as shown in Table 12.2.

Analysis of No-Poverty: Islamic Ethical Wealth vs SDG

In this section, the authors analyze the targets of SDG1 [Table 12.2] in relation to the features of Islamic wealth management. The findings from the analysis have justified the research gaps presented in Table 12.1 earlier.

Table 12.2 Seven targets of SDG-1 (United Nations 2020)

Code	SDG 1 targets
1.1	By 2030, eradicate extreme poverty for all people everywhere, currently measured as people living on less than $1.25 a day
1.2	By 2030, reduce at least by half the proportion of men, women, and children of all ages living in poverty in all its dimensions according to national definitions
1.3	Implement nationally appropriate social protection systems and measures for all, including floors, and by 2030 achieve substantial coverage of the poor and the vulnerable
1.4	By 2030, ensure that all men and women, in particular the poor and the vulnerable, have equal rights to economic resources, as well as access to basic services, ownership and control over land and other forms of property, inheritance, natural resources, appropriate new technology and financial services, including microfinance
1.5	By 2030, build the resilience of the poor and those in vulnerable situations and reduce their exposure and vulnerability to climate-related extreme events and other economic, social, and environmental shocks and disasters
1.A	Ensure significant mobilization of resources from a variety of sources, including through enhanced development cooperation, in order to provide adequate and predictable means for developing countries, in particular least developed countries, to implement programs and policies to end poverty in all its dimensions
1.B	Create sound policy frameworks at the national, regional, and international levels, based on pro-poor and gender-sensitive development strategies, to support accelerated investment in poverty eradication actions

Furthermore, the findings from the analysis have implications for evaluating these SDG 1 targets, and recommendations for their improvements relative to the needs of Islamic wealth management.

The targets of SDG 1 shown in Table 12.2 reveal several important points about the UNDP SDGs. Firstly, the last two targets (targets 1.A and 1.B) show that the concept of poverty alleviation should primarily rely on continuous assistance from the rich developed nations to the least developed and developing nations that are struggling. While this is desirable due to wide income and wealth disparity between the rich north and the poor south, targets built upon continuous dependency of the underdeveloped regions in the world on the developed counterparts have nevertheless proven counter-productive and unsustainable over the years. Perhaps lessons can be derived from Islamic ethical wealth that is built upon solidarity, win-win partnership, rights of the poor and obligation the rich rather than being a dependency relationship. The description of the believers as one body [al-Bukhārī and Muslim—Riyāḍ al-Ṣāliḥīn 224] only shows strong ties where one would not leave fellow brother or sister in hardship until he or she overcomes it through charity, Zakāh, Qarḍ ḥasan, rescheduling of repayment without any additional charges, and waqf, just to name a few.

In line with the above, Ali Hudaefi (2020) cites an argument which acknowledges that the concept of maqāṣid al-Sharī'ah promotes more comprehensive view of human development than SDGs. In analyzing the fundamental of Zakāh based Maqasid al-Sharī'ah, for example, one finds dimensions such as spiritual, moral, ethical, and religious that are not apparently expressed or integrated in the targets of SDGs, which are comparatively limited. The merits of relating SDG targets to Islamic philanthropic institutions like waqf and Zakāh lie in enhancing the effective and efficient implementation and development of these institutions that are hindered by several challenges. These challenges include corruption, mismanagement, misconduct, and lack of strong legislative protection and governmental support to guard the interest of these institutions. Therefore, this bureaucratic challenges and absence of in-depth studies on Islamic ethical wealth and SDGs provide fertile ground for future research to address gaps 2 and 4 from Table 12.1.

Evidence shows that the UN Millennium Development Goals (MDGs), which extended from 2000 to 2015, remained largely unaccomplished, including goal 1 concerning the elimination of absolute poverty and hunger (Khan 2019, p. 4). Most of the failure still remain in the IDB member countries who remained off-track as outlined in the IDB MDG target study (Bello and Suleman 2011). MDG failed to achieve its targets partly because the goals set were mostly ambitious and unrealistic. This comparatively seems to apply to SDG 1. The first five targets of SDG 1 (targets 1.1 through 1.5) seem to set unattainable, unrealistically ambitious numbers to be achieved by 2030. For example, target 1.2 states, "By 2030, reduce at least by half the proportion of men, women, and children of all ages living in poverty in all its dimensions according to national definitions," and target 1.3 attempts to achieve substantial social protection coverage of the poor and vulnerable by 2030 (United Nations 2020).

As a matter of fact, after 4 years since its implementation, the UNDP raises the alert that it is not on track toward achieving the 'no poverty SDG' in 2030, the same experience that MDG went through. "The financing gap is $2.5 trillion per year. Poverty is falling too slowly. Global hunger has risen for the third successive year. No country is on track to achieve the goal on gender equality. Biodiversity is being lost at an alarming rate. And with greenhouse-gas emissions still rising, we are moving closer and closer to a 3 to 5°C temperature increase, with all the devastation that science keeps warning us about. In short, we are not doing enough..." (UN Deputy Secretary-General 2019). The selective focus on certain sectors at the expense of others, for example, the use of agriculture and crop diversification or support for fisheries is clearly untenable. The indicators and targets of the SDG 1 need to be revised to incorporate other sustainability elements found in Islamic ethical wealth, which as stated earlier provides a comprehensive view on human development motivated by close ties and social solidarity. Therefore, there is room for more research to revise the targets and definitions of SDG 1 incorporating all the necessary variables. Research is also needed to examine more dimensions for the assessment of poverty alleviation that contribute to SDG 1. Moreover, research is required for developing methods and approaches that take realistic views in evaluating results relative to the situation under investigation. These numerous research would close the gaps 1 and 3 outlined in Table 12.1.

To sum up, the UNDP SDG program lacks important dimensions and targets specific to Islamic ethical wealth at the national and global levels. Furthermore, SDG has provided targets at the global level, but the extant literature lacks the analysis of these targets from Islamic ethical wealth perspective.

Conclusion

Although the Islamic philanthropic institutions are part of the Islamic ethical wealth, the way they are being managed is largely inefficient and ineffective. This is because these institutions are being managed without any consideration for the ethical aspects of the Islamic ethical wealth. The mismanagement of, corruption, and misconduct in these institutions (like waqf and zakāh), for instance, are not compatible with the values of close ties that connect the society together and the one body that symbolizes them [al-Bukhārī and Muslim – Riyāḍ al-Ṣāliḥīn 224]. These are the fundamentals of Islamic ethical wealth. Despite these drawbacks, the Islamic ethical wealth still possesses tremendous potential for poverty alleviation and for contributing to the SDGs in general, and to SDG 1 in particular.

On the other hand, it is evident that SDGs may not meet their targets by 2030. This, as discussed, is partly due to setting unrealistically ambitious numbers, and partly due to setting inadequate scopes of the definitions and dimensions of the SDGs. Furthermore, the UNDP SDG program still lacks effective methods and ways for evaluating the extent of achieving SDG 1 particularly in relation to Islamic ethical wealth. Moreover, while the SDG has provided targets at the global level, there is dearth of literature to analyze these targets from the lens of an Islamic ethical wealth. For example, extant works on supporting SDG via waqf are still limited in scope as they lack in-depth coverage on how Waqf can support SDG. Meanwhile, the UNDP SDG still lacks specific targets for Islamic ethical wealth as national and global agendas. Consequently, any research effort toward integrating into SDGs specific targets for an Islamic ethical wealth is very important and will have great potential to put make the SDG program more inclusive.

Suggestions and the Way Forward

The potential size of the annual zakāh fund has been estimated between US$200 billion and US$1 trillion (Rehman and Pickup 2018), waqf is valued at billions of dollars (Rashid 2012) as well. Consequently, both Zakah and Waqf have tremendous capacities to contribute to the socioeconomic development of the society. It is alarming to note that no country is on-track to achieving the SDGs, even those countries that manage zakāh and waqf institutions. This calls for a revisit to the whole system and processes of SDGs. Rather than focusing on how to raise enough funds or mobilize resources to support 'No Poverty' (SDG 1) with or without using zakāh, waqf, and/or any other Islamic philanthropic instrument, it is of utmost importance to remedy the issues and contemporary challenges that undermine the potential of these philanthropic institutions and instruments.

Once this is done, the benefits achieved from zakāh, waqf, and other Islamic philanthropic institutions will flow smoothly and have more than the desired effect on supporting SDG 1 and other SDGs. Although sit is important to investigate how to tap the potentials of zakāh, waqf, or both, there is also need for further research in understanding the reasons behind their inefficiencies and ways of overcoming them. This should be coupled by real intentions and efforts to implement suggestions and recommendations from the finding of these research if countries were to set their directions on-track to achieve the SDGs.

Moreover, countries should be realistic when setting the targets, which becomes unattainable when faced with unforeseen conditions, such as political conflicts, environmental degradation and social unrest, among others. These make the targets very ambitious. Policy makers and concerned committees need to revise the way SDG targets have been set. Additional research is required to include further dimensions that better describe how certain decisions and projects contribute to SDG 1 (and other SDGs as well).

REFERENCES

Abayomi-Alli, O., Odusami, M., Ojinaka, D., Shobayo, O., Misra, S., Damasevicius, R., & Maskeliunas, R. (2018). Smart-Solar Irrigation System (SMIS) for Sustainable Agriculture. In H. Florez, C. Diaz, & J. Chavarriaga (Eds.), *Applied Informatics* (pp. 198–212). Springer International Publishing. https://doi.org/10.1007/978-3-030-01535-0.

Abdul-Majeed Alaro, A. R., & Alalubosa, A. H. (2019). Potential of Sharī'ah Compliant Microfinance in Alleviating Poverty in Nigeria: A Lesson from Bangladesh. *International Journal of Islamic and Middle Eastern Finance and Management, 12,* 115–129. https://doi.org/10.1108/IMEFM-01-2017-0021.

Abdullah Nadwi, M. (2014). *Fate of Awqaf in India: A Critical Appraisal.* Ssrn, 1–8. https://doi.org/10.2139/ssrn.2384283.

Abdur-Rashid, K. (2020). *Financing Kindness as a Society: The Rise & Fall of Islamic Philanthropic Institutions (Waqfs).* Yaqeen Institute of Islamic Research, 1–27.

Al Zobair, M. A., & Hoque, M. A. (2019). Role of Waqf to Attain the "SDG-1: Ending Poverty" in Bangladesh. In *Revitalization of Waqf for Socio-Economic Development* (Vol. 2, pp. 15–34). Springer International Publishing. https://doi.org/10.1007/978-3-030-18449-0_2.

Ali Hudaefi, F. (2020). *How Does Islamic Fintech Promote the SDGs? Qualitative Evidence from Indonesia Qualitative Evidence from Indonesia.* Qualitative Research Financial Markets. https://doi.org/10.1108/QRFM-05-2019-0058.

Ali, K. M., Hassan, M. K., Ali, A., & Elrahman, E. S. (Eds.). (2019). *Revitalization of Waqf for Socio-Economic Development, Revitalization of Waqf for Socio-Economic Development* (Vol. I). Cham: Springer International Publishing. https://doi.org/10.1007/978-3-030-18445-2_1.

Bagby, I. (2012). *The American Mosque 2011: Activities, Administration and Vitality of the American Mosque.*

Bello, A., & Suleman, A. (2011). *The Challenge of Achieving the Millennium Development Goals in IDB Member Countries in the Post-Crisis World.* Jeddah.

Bulut, M., & Korkut, C. E. M. (2019). Ottoman Cash waqfs: An Alternative Financial System. *Insight Turkey, 21,* 91–112. https://doi.org/10.25253/99.2018EV.07.

Dogarawa, A. B. (2010). *Poverty Alleviaton Through Zakah and Waqf Institutions: A Case for the Muslim Ummah in Ghana.* Ssrn 1–27. https://doi.org/10.2139/ssrn.1622122.

Feliciano, D. (2019). A Review on the Contribution of Crop Diversification to Sustainable Development Goal 1 "No Poverty" in Different World Regions. *Sustainable Development, 27,* 795–808. https://doi.org/10.1002/sd.1923.

Haneef, M. A., Pramanik, A. H., Mohammed, M. O., Bin Amin, M. F., & Muhammad, A. D. (2015). Integration of waqf-Islamic Microfinance Model for Poverty Reduction: The Case of Bangladesh. *International Journal of Islamic and Middle Eastern Finance and Management, 8,* 246–270. https://doi.org/10.1108/IMEFM-03-2014-0029.

Joan, K., Pambudi, B. C., & Adjie, D. P. (2019). Blending Islamic Microfinance and Productive Zakat to Support SDGs in Fisheries Sector. *International Journal of Islamic Economics, 1,* 136–150. https://doi.org/10.32332/ijie.v1i02.1805.

Kahf, M. (2003). *The Role of Waqf in Improving the Ummah Welfare.* In Waqf as a Private Legal Body. Islamic University of Nother Sumatra, Medan.

Kahf, M. (1998). *Awqaf of the Muslim Community in the Western Countries: A Preliminary Thoughts on Reconciling the Shari'Ah Principles with the Laws of the Land,* 1–25.

Kahf, M. (1999). Financing the Development of Awqaf Property. *American Journal of Islamic Social Sciences, 16,* 39–68.

Khan, T. (2019). Reforming Islamic Finance for Achieving Sustainable Development Goals. *Journal of King Abdulaziz University Islamic Economics, 32,* 3–21. https://doi.org/10.4197/Islec.32-1.1.

Khan, F., & Hassan, M. K. (2019). Financing the Sustainable Development Goals (SDGs): The Socio-Economic Role of Awqaf (Endowments) in Bangladesh. In *Revitalization of Waqf for Socio-Economic Development* (Vol. 2, pp. 35–65). Springer International Publishing. https://doi.org/10.1007/978-3-030-18449-0_3.

Kidwai, A., & Zidani, M. E. M. (2020). A New Approach to Zakat Management for Unprecedented Times. *International Journal of Zakat, 5,* 45–54. https://doi.org/10.37706/ijaz.v5i1.207.

Lessy, Z. (2013). Historical Development of the Zakat System Implications for Social Work Practice. *EMPATI J. Ilmu Kesejaht. Sos, 2,* 1–16. https://doi.org/10.15408/empati.v2i1.9752.

Mohammad, H. S., Khan, S., Mustafa, R. R., & Thalassinos, Y. E. (2020). An Artificial Intelligence and NLP Based Islamic FinTech Model Combining Zakat and Qardh-Al-Hasan for Countering the Adverse Impact of COVID 19 on SMEs and Individuals. *International Journal of Economics Business Administration, VIII,* 351–364. https://doi.org/10.35808/ijeba/466.

Muhamat, A. A., Ahmad, S. Z., Roslan, A., Karim, N. A., & Azizan, N. A. (2019). The Readiness of Takaful Operators to Adopt Waqf (Endowment) as Additional Feature in Takaful Policy. *Journal of Academia, 7,* 72–81.

Nawa, F. (2015). *Internal Struggles at US Mosques Seep into Secular Courts* [WWW Document]. Reveal.

Owoyemi, M. Y. (2020). Zakat Management: The Crisis of Confidence in Zakat Agencies and the Legality of Giving zakat Directly to the Poor. *Journal of Islamic Accounting and Business Research, 11,* 498–510. https://doi.org/10.1108/JIABR-07-2017-0097.

Rashid, S. K. (2012). Measures for the Better Management of Awqaf. *IIUM Law Journal, 20,* 103–138.

Rehman, A. A., & Pickup, F. (2018). *Zakat for the SDGs* [WWW Document]. United Nations Dev. Program.

UN Deputy Secretary-General. (2019). *Citing $2.5 Trillion Annual Financing Gap during SDG Business Forum Event, Deputy Secretary-General Says Poverty Falling Too Slowly* [WWW Document]. United Nations Meet. Cover. Press Releases.

UNDP. 2020a. *Sustainable Development Goals* [WWW Document].

UNDP. 2020b. *Goal 1: No Poverty* [WWW Document].

UNHCR. 2019. *UNHCR Zakat Program: 2019 Launch Report.*

United Nations (n.d.). *Ending Poverty* [WWW Document]. United Nations.

United Nations. 2020. *Goal 1: End Poverty in All Its Forms Everywhere—United Nations Sustainable Development Goals* [WWW Document]. United Nations.

CHAPTER 13

How Islamic Ethical Wealth May Strategically and Technically Support 'Zero Hunger' Scheme?

Irfan Syauqi Beik, Randi Swandaru, and Priyesta Rizkiningsih

INTRODUCTION

According to Cambridge dictionary, wealth can be defined as a large amount of money or valuable possessions. In the Islamic perspective, wealth is not something that belongs to someone as it is essentially an *amanah* which should be accounted to God because human is a *khalifah* (vicegerent) of God in this world (Asutay 2007; Ibrahim et al. 2014). Therefore, in terms of wealth management, Islam demonstrates a balance manner where experiencing God's bounties without exaggerating or hoarding wealth (Ibrahim et al. 2014). One of the activities in Islam to

---

I. S. Beik (✉)
Department of Islamic Economics, Bogor Agricultural University (IPB), Bogor, Indonesia
e-mail: irfan_beik@apps.ipb.ac.id

R. Swandaru · P. Rizkiningsih
National Board of Zakat, Jakarta, Indonesia

© The Author(s), under exclusive license to Springer Nature Switzerland AG 2021
M. M. Billah (eds.), *Islamic Wealth and the SDGs*,
https://doi.org/10.1007/978-3-030-65313-2_13

257

distribute wealth among people is through zakat. Zakat is an obligatory alm in Islam which paid by those who meet a certain amount of wealth in a period of time to be distributed to the eight groups of zakat recipients (*ashnaf*). In addition, there are also a voluntary act to distribute wealth which are *infaq* and *sadaqa*. Zakat, infaq as well as sadaqa are distributed to those who are in need. In zakat distribution, the main focus is to fulfill the basic needs of underprivileged while infaq and sadaqa could be used for further empowerment.

Beside a balance manner in wealth management, Islamic value also upholds responsible consumption behavior. This act also portrays a principle to protect future generation as mentioned in the sharia objectives (*maqashid sharia*) which are to preserve faith (*diin*), soul (*nafs*), intellect (*aql*), progeny (*nasl*), and wealth (*maal*). In addition, the general principles of maqashid al shariah are to rise *maslahah* or well-being and reduce *mafsadah* or harm so that in Islam consumption must be maximized for the benefit of community and not only for their own means. A responsible consumption, which in a moderate level of consumption, also can protect the environment and reduce the possibility of hunger for the future generation. According to FAO, IFAD, UNICEF, WFP and WHO (2019), the number of people who suffer for hunger in the world is slightly increase amounted to 820 million. It has increased mostly in the middle-income countries where the economy is contracted. Economic downturn threaten food security and income inequality can increase the probability of severe food insecurity where the effect is 20% higher in low-income countries compared to middle-income countries. In Islamic point of view, Islamic social finance can be one of the procedures in Islamic wealth management to decrease the number of hungers by supporting basic needs for those who are in vulnerable condition. In addition, it also can be utilized to perform a food security scheme through increasing agricultural productivity. This section will elaborate more on how Islamic wealth management, particularly through Islamic social finance, support zero hunger.

ISLAMIC ETHICAL WEALTH MANAGEMENT

Wealth is a large amount of money or valuable possessions or it is also defined as an excess of income apart from regular and basic needs. Capitalism recognizes wealth as something which is scare and each individual has a freedom to obtain wealth for their personal satisfaction. In addition, in socialism perspective wealth is also noticed as a limited object which is obtained to achieve equality among workers. In the Islamic perspective, wealth is not scare and its bounties of God to humankind. Therefore, humankind should utilize their wealth in order to achieve falah (prosperity). Islam does not restrict someone to obtain wealth but must be in accordance with Islamic principles. Islam has its own guidance on wealth, how to obtained, the ownership, distribution as well as the social relationship in someone's wealth (Alam et al. 2017).

As Islamic worldview believes that there are two aspects of utilities function which are the present situation and the hereafter, therefore humankind should utilize and conserve wealth and resources in a responsible way in accordance with Islamic foundational axioms. According to Naqvi (1994), there are four ethical axioms in Islam which are: (1) Tawhid (God's unity and sovereignty); (2) Al-adl wal Ihsan (justice and equilibrium); (3) Ikhtiyar (free will); and Fard (responsibility). The most fundamental axiom is Tawhid which essentially differs Islam to the others. This axiom indicates the unity of God and implies that the ownership of universe and all the resources are belong to God, thus humankind should utilize all the resources in the responsible way. This axiom also provides a vertical dimension in Islamic ethical system where each individual is equal in the sight of God. Tawhid also provides freedom of actions to individuals but each of them will be accountable of what they have done.

Second axiom is al-adl wal ihsan which promotes justice and beneficence as well as promotes equal access to resources (Asutay 2007). In addition, this axiom also stimulate mutual good life among humankind. In addition, Islamic value through ikhtiyar also believes that each individual endowed with a free-will but must be responsible with any consequences attached. The last axiom, based on Naqvi (1994), is Fard or responsible. Further, Asutay (2007) explained that even though responsibility is voluntary, individuals, and society should preserve it as part of tawhid and because of they are God's vicegerent in the earth. In addition, it also implies that there is a social aspect in each of resource that owned or managed either by private or public institutions. This ethical system based on Islamic axiom considered to produce policies in order to enhance motivation, productivity, and transparency. It also can enhance an intra and intergenerational equity.

Islam as a way of life also preserves the five necessities or known as maqashid al-shariah which consists of the preservation of religion (deen), soul (nafs), mind and intellect (aql), progeny (nasl), and wealth or property (maal) (Asutay 2007; Ibrahim et al. 2014). In terms of wealth, Islam recognizes the ownership of wealth as an amanah (trust or custodianship) from God, hence in the utilization of wealth as God's blessings in this world must be without any waste (israf) as also stated in the holy Qur'an. Moreover, Ibrahim et al (2014) also emphasize that individual's pursuit of wealth and worldly pleasure should be done without being harm to others as Islam upholds justice. Hence, wealth management in Islam can be divided into four aspects which are wealth creation, enhancement, protection, distribution, and purification of wealth where all activities must be in accordance with Islamic principles. In wealth creation, each individual or company should ensure that every single income earned is from Islamic permissible activities. Second, wealth enhancement in order to achieve capital growth is allowed as long as all the wealth is spent in sharia compliant instrument which are free from riba (interest), gharar (uncertainty), and maysir (gambling) and free from haram (illegitimate) products. Furthermore, wealth enhancement is permissible in order to preserve accumulated wealth in an ethical manner. Islam also teaches to protect our wealth which can be fulfilled, for instance, through risk management and takaful or insurance. As there is also a stern warning for those who accumulate wealth, particularly in the form of unproductive resources, or do not utilize the wealth in the path of God which also includes service to humanity. Islam also advises individuals that wealth must not only circulate among wealthy people but also be distributed for all humankind as Islam upholds fair distribution of wealth and prevent unjust and inequality among society. This is the purpose of wealth distribution.

The Concept of Responsible Consumption and Production

Recent years the United Nation Sustainable Development Goals (SDGs) also focus in responsible consumption and production as depicted in SDGs number 12. This becomes important as worldwide consumption and production over the last decades have been accompanied by environmental degradation which, if not managed properly, would endanger the future. Thus, in order to ensure the sustainable consumption and production pattern, a change in our habit is fundamental to achieve the goal.

United Nations (UN) data shows that each year one-third of all food produced or equivalent to 1.3 billion tons which worth around USD 1 trillion are end up in trash bin or spoiling because of poor transportation and harvesting practice while almost 2 billion people are hungry and being undernourished. In terms of agriculture, it is claimed that the biggest user of water which counted to 70% of all freshwater for human use. On the other hand, the time that nature can replenish water is slower than human using it. In addition, the number of material footprints (the total amount of raw material extracted to fulfill the final consumption) is still high and become an urgent aspect to reduce in order to save the environment.

With a view toward responsible consumption and production, we can start a small initiative around our society for a better world such as reducing food loss and increasing food systems, refusing the use of plastics bags and start to use reusable bags, reducing the single use of straw as well as trying to buy products where the production process is more sustainable. Furthermore, government also have to prepare policy which pays more attention to sustainability. Hence, all aspects in a country can work together to make a more responsible consumption and production by concerning a higher quality of environment, not only for current generation but also for future generation.

In Islamic perspective, responsible consumption and production have been taught a long time ago as depicted in *maqashid al-sharia* as the purpose of sharia. Furthermore, Islamic value also encourages to bring maslahah (well-being) and reduce mafsadah (harm). Islam encourages to consume and produce or use the property in a moderate level which lies between stinginess and extravagance. The excessive consumption beyond a fair level considered as *israf* (waste). Moreover, Islam also prohibits to do *tubzir* or use the property in a wrong way. There are some consumption principles in Islamic perspective as follow:

1. The purpose of consumption

    Muslim consumption purposes not only to fulfill individual satisfaction but also to worship and please Allah. In addition, consumption in Islam also must be just and equal. Rush (2018) explains that the consumption must be maximized for the benefit of the community for regenerate and circulate the wealth.

2. The sources of consumption

Islam teaches humankind only to consume something that allowed by the principles of Islam such as only consuming halal (permissible) and thayyib (good) food.

3. The amount of consumption

Islam also teaches humankind not to spend their wealth beyond their ability, thus humankind is encouraged to spend in a moderate manner so that it does not reduce the circulation of wealth because of hoarding or weaken the economy because of increasing the amount of waste.

The same pattern also occurs in the production side. As a vicegerent of God, humankind should not greedy to exploit the nature for production activities instead to use it ethically. From above explanation, we can conclude that the Islamic values are actually embedded in the SDGs as Islamic values also offers great advantage for environmental conservation, protection as well as sustainability in society.

HUNGER: THE CASE OF INDONESIA

According to Food and Agriculture Organization (2019), the number of people who suffer for hunger in the world is slightly increase amounted to 820 million. According to Global Hunger Index (2019), Indonesia ranked 70th out of 117 countries with the score of 20.1 and categorized as serious level of hunger. However, this condition is still worse compared to another ASEAN countries which are Malaysia (57th), Myanmar (69th), Thailand (46th) and Vietnam (62nd). In addition, the trend in global hunger index in Indonesia is depicted in Fig. 13.1.

Global Hunger Index (GHI) score consists of four component indicators which are undernourishment, child wasting, child stunting, and child mortality. GHI score categorized into five categories, they are: low ($\leq$ 9.9), moderate (10.0–19.9), serious (20.0–34.9), alarming (35.0–49.9), and extremely alarming ($\geq$ 50).

As Indonesia is still in a serious level in the hunger, a prompt solution should be implemented such as the access to nutrition for the children as well nutritional food for the society. The case of hunger will be worsened in the location with higher level of poverty, thus there should be a comprehensive solution. The Indonesian government certainly has programs to reduce this level of hunger, but to accelerate its impact, assistance from other institutions are also needed. In this case, Islamic social

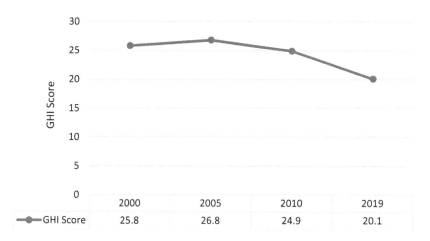

Fig. 13.1 GHI trend score for Indonesia (*Source* Global Hunger Index [2019])

finance can also be an alternative. As a part of Islamic wealth management, particularly in the distribution of wealth section, zakat, infaq, and sadaqa fund as well as waqf, could be utilized in such program to reduce the hunger cases in Indonesia.

In overcoming the problem of hunger, we do not only focus on short-term needs, but also ensure that in the long term this food demand can be fulfilled. Some programs for decreasing the number of hungers could be access to nutritional food for the short term and also a more environmentally friendly agriculture for a long term which also can lead to food security for the society.

Toward Zero Hunger by Utilizing Islamic Ethical Wealth

On the previous section we have discussed what Islamic Ethical Wealth is and how it is linked with the zero hunger initiatives. In this part, we will further scrutiny the application of Islamic Ethical Wealth for bolstering the SDGs with focus on achieving zero hunger target.

The study by UN SDSN and Human Act in 2018 on how closing the SDGs financing gap shows that we need 2–3 trillion dollar per year to achieve the SDGs. Hence, we need a more inclusive financial instrument to get more fund into the table. Having said that Islamic Social Finance as part of the Islamic Ethical Wealth has a potential to fill the gap. Bank Indonesia (2019) developed a model to integrate the Zakat dan Wakaf as part of the initiative to achieve SDGs (Fig. 13.2).

On the above model, Islamic Social Financing can directly boost the Islamic Financing Scheme or to be integrated with the Islamic Commercial Financing. Each has different advantage and benefit. Islamic social finance fund, i.e., zakat can be directly utilized for the Islamic financing scheme to serve the underserved community by providing low risk financing facilities under empowerment community development program and cover their basic needs. Meanwhile, integrating Islamic social finance fund, i.e., infaq and waqf with commercial transaction can enhance the size of the project while keeping the social benefit for the community. Figure 13.3 elaborates the role of zakat, infaq, and waqf in national economic development.

Having said that, the Islamic social finance sector, i.e., zakat, infaq, and waqf becomes more relevant to achieve zero hunger target as we can see on the 2019 Global Hunger Index, moslem populated countries are those who suffer on the list. This index measures each country under four main indicators. We can see on the list that Indonesia, Pakistan, and India as the biggest moslem populated countries rank in 70th, 94th, and 102nd, respectively. In this sense, the Islamic Social fund can be mobilized strategically to moderate this situation. On the following part we will discuss

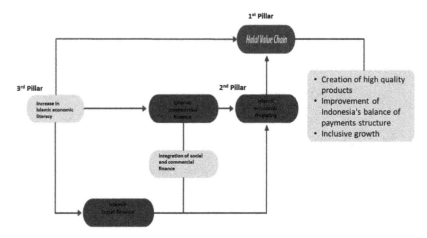

Fig. 13.2 Islamic social finance model (*Source* Bank Indonesia [2019])

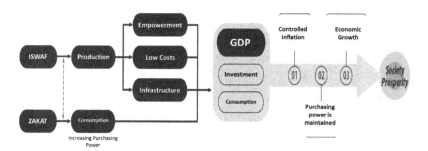

Fig. 13.3 The role of Zakat, Infaq, and Waqf in national economic development (*Source* Bank Indonesia [2019])

several initiatives on how this kind of funds are structured into various program to achieve Zero Hunger.

Zero Hunger Programs

To discuss further about this topic, we better understand several targets that have been defined by the United Nations on this second goal of SDGs. The official wording for this goal is 'end hunger, achieve food security and improved nutrition and promote sustainable agriculture.' This part will elaborate several programs funded by zakat fund that cover four out of eight targets to eradicate world hunger which are (1) universal access to safe and nutritious food; (2) reduction of all forms of malnutrition; (3) improvement of the productivity and incomes of small-scale food producers; and (4) sustainable food production and resilient agricultural practices.

The first target of zero hunger program, i.e., universal access to safe and nutritious food, requires access for all people especially the poor and vulnerable groups to safe, nutritious and sufficient food all year round. In this regard, the National Zakat Board of Indonesia (BAZNAS) has launched Bank Makanan (Food Bank) Program that becomes a bridge for food excess and the poor who do not have access to nutritious food. Under this scheme, BAZNAS has a cooperation with hotels to distribute excess food from their kitchen and dining to underserved community. The food excess in this program is a proper food which has been served but has not been consumed or touched by anybody. Under this program, within hours this food excess is identified prior to storing process and

Fig. 13.4 Food bank activities (*Source* BAZNAS [2020])

later on distributed to the community. Some foods are being processed and cooked by the staff prior to being distributed. The following Fig. 13.4 shows the food distribution activities under the food bank operation.

Since its launching in September 2019, this program has distributed 3,271 ton of food and impacted 6,790 families in Jakarta greater area. In this regard, BAZNAS has cooperation with three hotels which are Harrison Hotel in Ciledug, Arcadia Hotel in Mangga Dua, and Sofyan Hotel Cut Meutia. Besides, BAZNAS also has cooperation with Indonesian hotel and restoration association, Indonesia Halal Tourism Association, Indonesia Chef Association, etc. The following Fig. 13.5 represents the output of food bank program in 2019 and 2020.

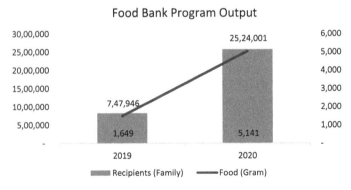

Fig. 13.5 Food bank program output (*Source* BAZNAS [2020])

The second target in zero hunger program is reduction of all form of malnutrition. In this regard BAZNAS has run a program called stunting prevention by giving additional nutritious food such milk, fruits, egg, VCO, etc. BAZNAS also does regular heath examination to the babies and kids in their targeted community to monitor the growth of the children (Republika 2020). The program educates parents to identify nutritious food and give their children the food in a sufficient amount. In addition, the community is also supported with training to cultivate their land and plant various nutritious food (Fig. 13.6).

In addition to this second target, BAZNAS also does water, sanitation, and hygiene (WASH) program as a complementary program to support malnutrition eradication. The WASH program is essential to avoid microbe or other microorganism that can cause diarrhea, dysentery, or other digestive diseases because no matter how good the food quality is, it will be vain if the water they consume is contaminated and caused diseases.

In February 2020, BAZNAS in collaboration with UNICEF and Bappenas (National Development Planning Agency) held a workshop on how to utilize zakat, infaq, and waqf fund to support SDGs especially for drinking water and sanitation. There are a lot of NGOs and local government involved in this workshop to learn how to integrate zakat, infaq,

Fig. 13.6 *Rumah Sehat* BAZNAS activities—monitoring children development (*Source* BAZNAS [2020])

and waqf as source of fund for the implementation of WASH program. Align with that, BAZNAS also has launched BAZNAS Index for Sustainability of Clean Water and Sanitation (Puskas 2019). This index measures the four main dimensions which are water facility, toilet facility, sanitation condition, and community behavior that represent sustainability of the clean water and sanitation in a community.

In addition to increase the protein consumption for preventing malnutrition, BAZNAS also develops several livestock centers across the archipelago that help breeder to raise better and sustainable livestock. During the qurban season, BAZNAS channels fund from urban area to rural area to buy local sheep or cows. By doing so, it helps the local breeder economically and gives better access for the poor to access a good quality of meat (Swandaru, How 'qurban' season can reduce inequality?, 2019). Outside the qurban season this livestock center provide various capacity building and assistantship for the breeder so that it gives a longer and sustainable impact.

The third and the fourth target of zero hunger goals, which are improvement of the productivity and incomes of small-scale food producers and sustainable food production and resilient agricultural practices, are covered by Sustainable Agriculture and Farmers Empowerment (SAFE) Program. In this program BAZNAS utilizes zakat fund for poor farmers so that they can increase their productivity by applying sustainable agriculture practices. The farmers group receive three main intervention namely, capital assistantship, production and capacity building, and market enlargement.

In the first intervention, the farmers group receive fund for purchase seed and supporting production equipment. They are also get financial literacy training so that they can manage the fund properly within their group. In the second intervention, the farmers group get access to prolific and excellent seed; involved in organic agriculture system and its application; and BAZNAS put a program supervisor who lives together with the farmers to maintain their motivation and give consultancy to the group. Lastly, BAZNAS also helps the farmers to enlarge their market by opening access to off takers and developing network for them. The following Fig. 13.7 illuminates the scheme of SAFE Program.

The study by Swandaru et al. (2020) shows that the implementation of organic farming system has increased the productivity of the farmers. This productivity increase is induced by three main factors which are incremental rice production, reduced operational cost, and increase of sales.

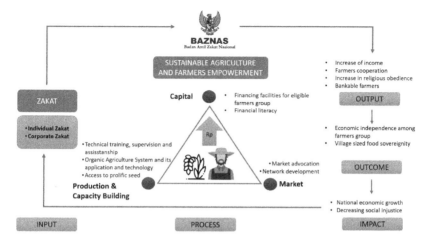

Fig. 13.7 Sustainable agriculture and farmers empowerment program (*Source* BAZNAS [2020])

The following Figure 13.8 elaborates the productivity increase during three consecutive season using organic farming in compare to the control (Season 0) that applying conventional farming.

In the beginning of the organic farming implementation, the rice production rate was lower than the conventional one. This was happened

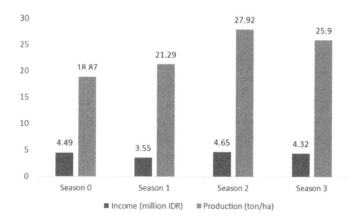

Fig. 13.8 Productivity of organic farmers (*Source* BAZNAS [2020])

due to not all of the farmers were discipline to use organic fertilizer and pesticide. However, in the season 2 and 3 the productivity rate has rebound to the conventional farming productivity rate. Secondly, the productivity increase of organic farming is induced by the lower production cost. The same study shows that 75% lower in compare to the conventional farming method. The most significant one is the none use of chemical fertilizer that is been substituted by organic fertilizer. Lastly, the productivity increase is induced by the higher sales due to higher price of end product.

CONCLUSION

In the Islamic perspective, wealth is not something that belongs to someone as it is essentially an *amanah* which should be accounted to God because human is a *khalifah* (vicegerent) of God in this world. Therefore, in terms of wealth management, Islam demonstrates a balance manner where experiencing God's bounties without exaggerating or hoarding wealth.

Islam also teaches that wealth must not only circulate among wealthy people but must also be distributed for all humankind as Islam upholds fair distribution of wealth and prevent unjust and inequality among society. This can be done through optimization of Islamic social finance. The 2019 Global Hunger Index shows that Moslem populated countries are those who suffer on the list. In this sense, the Islamic social fund, as one of the parts of Islamic wealth distribution, can be mobilized strategically to moderate this situation.

In the case of Indonesia, Islamic social fund has been utilized in several programs to reduce hunger, which are: (1) universal access to safe and nutritious food; (2) reduction of all forms of malnutrition; (3) improvement of the productivity and incomes of small-scale food producers; and (4) sustainable food production and resilient agricultural practices. A number of initiatives have been introduced by BAZNAS, as zakat authority in Indonesia, such as food bank program, development of livestock centers across the country, stunting prevention program, WASH program, and SAFE (Sustainable Agriculture and Empowerment Program) program. These programs are expected to be able to achieve zero hunger objective as highlighted in the SDGs.

References

Alam, N., Gupta, L., & Shanmugam, B. (2017). Islamic Wealth Management. *Islamic Finance: A Practical Prespective* (pp. 451–473). Switzerland: Palgrave Macmillan.

Asutay, M. (2007). A Political Economy Approach to Islamic Economics: Systemic Understanding for an Alternative Economic System. *Kyoto Bulletin of Islamic Area Studies, 1,* 3–18.

BAZNAS. (2020). *Laporan Pendistribusian dan Pendayagunaan Zakat Semester 1 (Internal Report).* Jakarta: BAZNAS.

BI. (2019). *Laporan Ekonomi dan Keuangan Syariah 2019.* Jakarta: Bank Indonesia.

FAO, IFAD, UNICEF, WFP, & WHO. (2019). The State of Food Security and Nutrition in the World 2019. *Safeguarding Against Economic Slowdowns and Downturns.* Rome, FAO.

Global Hunger Index. (2019). *Global Hunger Index 2019: Indonesia,* s.l.: Concern Worldwide and Welthungerhilfe.

Ibrahim, A. A., Elatrash, R. J., & Farooq, M. O. (2014). Hoarding Versus Circulation of Wealth from the Perspective of Maqasid Al-Shari'ah. *International Journal of Islamic and Middle Eastern Finance and Management, 7*(1), 6–21.

Naqvi, S. N. H. (1994). *Islam, Economics and Society.* London: Kegan Paul International.

Puskas. (2019). *BAZNAS Index for Sustainability of Clean Water and Sanitation.* Jakarta: BAZNAS.

Republika. (2020). *Republika.co.id.* [Online] Available at: https://republika.co.id/berita/qbgdtq423/baznas-gelar-layanan-kesehatan-cegah-stunting.

Rush, M. (2018). *Islam and Sustainable Consumption: A Literature Review.* Birmingham: Humanitarian Academy for Development.

Swandaru, R. (2019). How 'Qurban' Season Can Reduce Inequality? *The Jakarta Post,* p. 6.

Swandaru, R., Rizkiningsih, P., & Kuswanda, D. (2020). *Dampak Zakat Sebagai Instrumen Inklusi Keuangan Terhadap Produktivitas Pertanian Berkelanjutan.* Jakarta: Unpublished.

CHAPTER 14

Islamic Ethical Wealth and Its Strategic Solutions to 'Zero Hunger' Scheme

Aishath Muneeza and Zakariya Mustapha

INTRODUCTION

Islam is a comprehensive religion and a complete way of life that provides guidance not only in matters of ritual and worship but also mundane activities. Ethical principles, generally termed akhlaq, are embedded in Islam as important component of its guidance system for all dealings. Wealth in Islam is considered a trial, or a possession meant to try one's obedience to Allah (SWT). While one enjoys wealth, it is as well regarded as an endowed favour from Allah that embodies entitlements of poor and needy members of society. Appropriate disbursement of the entitlement due to the poor is an obligation that brings to light the issue of wealth as a trial, particularly on those who might not duly discharge it. Zakat, a third pillar of Islam, together with sadaqat and waqf are mechanisms designed to channel those entitlements from wealth of rich members of

A. Muneeza (✉)
INCEIF, Kuala Lumpur, Malaysia

Z. Mustapha
University of Malaya, Kuala Lumpur, Malaysia

© The Author(s), under exclusive license to Springer Nature Switzerland AG 2021
M. M. Billah (eds.), *Islamic Wealth and the SDGs*,
https://doi.org/10.1007/978-3-030-65313-2_14

273

the society to help the poor and needy who are poverty-stricken. Poverty is a prevalent global issue today which is said to be the reason for over 821 million people going hungry each and every day in some of the world's poorest communities (Islamic Relief, n.d.). Poverty is taking its toll on the economic and social aspects of the lives of the people such that in region such as Africa one out of four is undernourished. Globally, hunger kills a child in every ten seconds and 45% of under-five death among children is caused by poor nutrition. While women and girls constitute over 60% of the world's hungry, one-third of the total food produced world over end up not consumed or rather wasted. Climate change is continually resulting in floods and droughts that ravage crop production and harvests, thus affecting over 75% of the world's poorest people who only grow their foods (Muslim Global Relief, n.d.). In Islam, ensuring no one goes hungry in a society is sacrosanct. In this regard, Ibn Abbas reported that Prophet Muhammad (SAW) said, 'He is not a believer whose stomach is filled while the neighbor to his side goes hungry' (al-Sunan al-Kubraa 19049). Given the contemporary situation, lack of sufficient and nutritious food is a global issue that needs adequate solutions.

In 2015, a purposive collaboration among world leaders led by the United Nations (UN) culminated in the development of global agenda that hope to find solutions to address the menace of poverty and hunger. An agreement was therefore reached upon 17 global goals which are identified officially as the Sustainable Development Goals (SDGs). Through the SDGs, the global agenda aim to end poverty, curb inequality and address the urgency of change in climate by 2030 and create a better world. Zero hunger is Goal 2 of the UN SDGs. It was on 20 June 2012, at UN Conference on Sustainable Development otherwise known as Rio+20, that Mr Ban Ki-moon, the then UN Secretary General, launched Zero Hunger Challenge, an initiative aimed at ending hunger, eradicating malnutrition in all its forms and establishing a food system that is inclusive and sustainable (UN News 2012). The Zero Hunger Challenge variously stands for 100% opportunity to have sufficient food throughout the year, elimination of stunted growth among under two children, 100% growth of farmers' productivity and profits, sustainability of all food systems and elimination of food wastage (The Hunger Project 2014).

Islamic ethical wealth principles not only emphasize on acquisition and consumption of wealth in a *halal* manner but also the need for the wealthy to spend portion of their wealth on the poor as well. Waqf, sadaqat and zakat are social financing avenues that embody principles of Islamic ethical wealth and its management. While sadaqat and waqaf are voluntary mechanisms designed to ensure that those who are financially capable give back to the society in which they live, zakat is compulsory on those who are eligible by virtue of their wealth possession to be paid to certain recipients prescribed in the holy Quran. This chapter is a discourse on Islamic ethical wealth and sheds light on how it would strategically and technically support the 'zero hunger' scheme by exploring current application and future potential of Islamic finance for that purpose.

The chapter is divided into six sections. Section one is an introduction. Following the introduction, section two discusses the concept of Islamic ethical wealth, issue of hunger and food security in the world as well as zero hunger initiative. Section three briefly examines the idea of food security from Islamic perspective. Section four deals with Islamic ethical wealth in relation to its strategies and technics for food security and zero hunger. In this section, role of Islamic finance and Islamic social finance towards zero hunger initiatives and food security is accordingly discussed. Section five provides recommendations and proposes a model Islamic food banking for the promotion of zero hunger scheme. Finally, section six follows with a conclusion to the chapter.

Concept of Islamic Ethical Wealth

As a concept premised on Shariah, Islamic ethical wealth simply ordains that the ways to acquire and manage wealth are steered in accordance with Shariah parameters where ethics and morality are integral part thereof. In the same vein, ethical finance has been described as any enterprise involving investment that prioritizes well-being of people and environment. In other word, it is a financing decision and action that regards and gives support for social and environmental upliftment to those aspects of people's lives in relation to the environment where social exclusion is imminent. In ethical financing, funds are provided and allocated without considerations of ethnicity, gender, wealth and migration status in addition to regarding money as a means to an end (Palmisano 2014). Islamic finance is an ethical way of financing as it fulfils all the conditions and attributes of ethical finance. This is because Islamic finance encompasses an ethical system of administering and managing finances wherein responsibility and concern about results appear more prominent in all interactions. In cognizance of the use and role of finance materially speaking, it is subjected to higher overarching goals of Islamic law or *maqasid al-Shariah* that considers moral and ethical responsibility in due accomplishment of the said goals (Ahmed 2015). While it is generally said that wealth is a favour, it is at the same time a trial, by Allah (SWT) to test whether His servants obey His commandments regarding its acquisition and disposal. Accordingly, Islamic wealth management enumerates, administers and takes into account an individual's success in four financial pillars: accumulation, consumption, preservation and distribution of wealth (Hashim 2016). The governance of each of these pillars is defined by rules of Shariah.

As a matter of moral principles governing actions, ethics is defined as an esteemed notion of distinguishing right from what (Beekun 1996, p. 2). In this regard, several systems of ethics have been devised and adopted by secular societies in order to promote what is right and suppress wrong. These include relativism, a belief system based on the notion that no phenomenon is absolute but subject to circumstances and place as the determiners of the basis of human needs and self-interest; utilitarianism, a result-oriented system which determines what is ethical on the basis of a phenomenon resulting in greatest advantage for the greatest number of individuals; universalism, a notion of good for all based on intent of action and decision; right, a notion of ethics as upholding individual liberty in addition to ensuring freedom of choice; distributive justice, which, while emphasizing equitable disbursement of benefits, wealth and burden, focuses on justice in order to determine what is ethical; eternal law, which portrays ethical value as what has been ordained by revealed scriptures (Adebayo and Hassan 2013, p. 70). It is explicit that, from Islamic point of view, ethics is equitable and provides justice to the society as Islamic system is based on fundamental belief of Tawhid or oneness of Allah (SWT) where the commandments of Allah (SW) are given paramount consideration in all aspects of life. From the core primary source of Islam, the holy Quran, it is evident that man is a vicegerent of Allah (SWT) on this earth and man is given the responsibility to live and fulfil his responsibility as a trustee. Man is supposed to do what Allah (SWT) has permitted and avoid what Allah has forbidden. As such, the concepts of halal and haram are established standards integrated into all parts of human lives and thus all human actions, including consumption, shall be based on these criteria as essentials of Islamic ethical wealth.

Specifically, principles of Islamic ethical wealth call for and uphold elimination of riba as the most common dictate of Islamic law of transactions in addition to seeking the promotion of just, fair and halal ways of acquiring, spending, investing and distributing wealth. For Islamic redistribution of wealth, zakat, sadaqat and waqf play an integral role in channelling the rights and/or entitlements of the poor and needy people in the society which have also been considered a priority. These distributive mechanisms can establish social harmony through sharing of wealth. As such, the question one would rhetorically ask in all commercial activities would be: Am I engaging in an activity which is halal? If the answer is yes, then automatically one would know that whatever one is engaged in is ethical. The relationship between ethical and halal is positive as all ethical things are halal and all halal things are likewise ethical. Therefore, it would not be inappropriate to conclude that Islam as a way of life is inseparable from ethics (Mathkur 2019).

Overview of Hunger and Food Security Issue in the World

Goal 2 of the United Nations Sustainable Development Goals (UNSDGs) is 'zero hunger' which designates an objective as well as action plan based on global synergy to end hunger or, at best, alleviate its menace among affected global population by the year 2030. According to the official website of the UNSDGs, hunger is rising worldwide since 2015. Approximately, 821 million people were undernourished in 2017. Also, with over 12.9% of it as malnourished, most of the human population devastated by hunger is found in developing countries. The highest prevalence of hunger is in sub-Saharan Africa where its rate rose up to 23.2% in 2017 from 20.7% in 2014. In the same token, an increase was recorded in the number of undernourished people in the region in 2017 to be up to 237 million from 195 million recorded in 2014. The menace of hunger is alarming as its resultant poor nutrition has caused nearly half (45%) of under-5 children deaths, that is over 3.1 million children. It is reported that 144 million children under-5, corresponding to were chronically undernourished in 2019 (UNICEF 2020). Given the situation as such, food security and zero hunger initiatives become imperative.

On food security, according to the official website of the UNSDGs, agriculture is said to be agriculture remains the particular predominant employer all over the world which provides means of living to more than 40% of the world's population. It is accordingly the predominant source of employment and income worldwide most especially for rural households whose over 500 million farmlands, mostly dependent on rainwater, are responsible for almost 80% of the foodstuffs used in the larger and more developed parts of the world. Food security and nutrition can be enhanced among the poor people by investing in smaller entrepreneur farmers and improving their output for the local and global market. Nonetheless, it is been reported that from 1900s to date, about 75% of crop diversity is lost from farmlands. It has been observed that agricultural diversity and its proper usage contribute to production of nutritious diets, improved livelihood of rural communities and sustainably resilient farming system. It is further observed that had women farmers been given access to required resources as men, there would have been a great reduction in the number of hungry people in the world. Poverty of energy has also been a reason some people live in hunger. Nearly 840 people worldwide are reported to be living without access to electricity, mostly in the rural communities of developing countries. Lack of access to electricity has been a barrier to reduction of hunger and ensuring the world produces food enough to meet current demands and future exigencies.

Bearing in mind the background and issue of food security and hunger in the world, Goal 2 of the UNSDGs is set to achieve the following targets. To bring hunger to an end by 2030 and make sure sufficient, safe and nutritious food is made available throughout the year for all people most especially infants, the poor and those in vulnerable conditions. Also, by 2030, to bring to an end malnutrition in all its forms globally and, by 2025, end waste and stunting in under-5 children alongside addressing nutritional needs among girls, older women, lactating and pregnant women. Similarly, ensure productivity of agriculture and incomes therefrom are doubled by 2030 especially for women and family farmers, indigenous people, fishers and pastoralists through equality in access to farmland and other inputs as well as productive resources, markets, financial services, non-farming employment and value addition opportunities. Equally by 2030, sustainability in systems of food production would be ensured as well as implementing more adaptable practices in agriculture that will boost production and productivity, help in maintaining ecosystems, build up adaptation capacity with respect to change in climate and its attendant consequences in addition to progressive improvement in quality of land and soil. Moreover, by 2020, genetic diversity of cultivated plants, seeds, farm animals shall be maintained through robust and carefully managed plants and seeds banks at local and global levels. Likewise, as agreed internationally, opportunity shall be provided for sharing benefits that arise from utilizing genetic resources and related knowledge fairly and equitably. Also, within the same projected time span, investment shall be increased in extension services and agricultural research including rural infrastructural development through international synergy in order to improve production capacity in agriculture among least developed and developing nations. Again, corrective measures shall be undertaken to address and forestall agricultural markets distortions and restrictions in line with Doha Development Round. Similarly, measures would be adopted for the appropriate function of market for food commodities and reserves as well as access to timely information about the market to check volatility of food price (UNSDGs, N/A). These targets altogether form the blueprint aimed at guiding zero hunger initiatives.

Food Security from Islamic Perspective

It is important from the onset to understand food security from an Islamic perspective prior to discussion on potential Shariah compliant 'zero hunger' initiatives. As Islamic exegetists and scholars expound, by Quran 13:11, it is unarguably evident that Allah (SWT) does not change people' conditions and His bounties for them such as food availability, until people change their ways with respect to their comportment and compliances (Haddad 2012). In the same vein, it is also viewed that Islam refute the prediction of a global food crisis as Allah (SWT) has apportioned sustenance for all lives as it evident from Quran 41:10 where it is stated: 'And He placed on the earth firmly set mountains over its surface, and He blessed it and determined therein its [creatures'] sustenance in four days without distinction - for [the information] of those who ask' (Al-Qadi 2019). Accordingly, as Al-Qadi (2019) observed, food is available on earth to nourish all living beings. All that is required is to stimulate its production as well as distribution to ensure its availability where it is needed. This means that there is no basis to assert that people die as a result of water and agricultural lands scarcity due to population growth (Al-Qadi 2019). Growth in population does not automatically leads to scarcity of food resources. Then, going by this postulation, there would supposedly be no famine in low population regions but high population regions (Al-Qadi 2019). To further demonstrate this, Al-Qadi (2019) asserted that, China for instance, despite its more than a billion population, has not suffered food crisis, in contrast to some African countries where smaller populations that live on riverbanks and arable lands yet face interminable famine.

ISLAMIC ETHICAL WEALTH STRATEGIES AND TECHNICS FOR FOOD SECURITY AND ZERO HUNGER—ROLE OF ISLAMIC FINANCE AND ISLAMIC SOCIAL FINANCE

Islamic Financing of Agriculture for Food Security and Zero Hunger

As a type of financing which operates in accordance with rules of Islamic commercial jurisprudence, Islamic finance is an integral component of Islamic economic system. Basically, Islamic finance is governed by rules of Shariah that ordain dealing to be without an iota of interest (riba), excessive risk and uncertainty (gharar) and speculation or gambling (maisir) among other rules that ensure transactions are fair and ethical. Alongside these Shariah provides several agriculture-oriented financing strategies and technics that can be employed to support zero hunger scheme and promote food security. These, among others, include muzara'ah, musaqah, mugharasa, salam, musawamah, murabaha, istisna, ijarah, musharakah, etc.

1. *Musaqah* refers to an agricultural collaboration between owner of an orchard/trees and another person who will work as manger by cultivating the orchard such that all agriculture products turned out from the orchard/trees is shared based on an agreed ratio or percentage between the parties (Al-Zuhayli 2003; DAB Bank 2018). The essential elements of Musaqah contract are as follows. The share for both parties in the fruits/produce of the trees should be in percentage or ratio; the trees must be of the type that produces fruit during the period of partnership and the period must be determined. If the period expires before the production of fruits/produce, the contract will continue until the production and harvesting of the produce and the manager is given the permission to work on the fruits/trees (DAB Bank 2018).

2. *Mugharasah* is an agricultural partnership whereby owner of a piece of land enters into an agreement with another person (a cultivator) who will plant and maintain certain tree(s) so that both parties share the produce of the tree(s) based on an agreed ratio or percentage

(Al-Zuhayli 2003; DAB Bank 2018). The essential elements of Mugharasah contract are: the partnership must be on trees that last long such as date trees or olive trees and is not permissible on trees that are planted from time to time such as corn; the type of tree must be determined from the very beginning and the period of partnership must be sufficient to produce and harvest the particular produce (DAB Bank 2018).

3. *Murabaha* is a mechanism of sale transaction on the basis of either deferred or cash payment, where the seller discloses actual cost of goods to be sold with an additional profit margin (disclosed profit). With the cost of the goods known, the profit margin is determined by the agreement of both the seller and buyer.

4. *Musawamah* describes a sale transaction where the cost of services or goods to be sold is not revealed to the buyer. In contrast to murabaha, only the selling price is bargained by the parties. Basically, musawamah is applicable to spot transactions that are carried out instantaneously with tangible and consumable products as subject matter, not future transactions or yet to be manufactured, non-existent goods or services (Al-Zuhayli 2003).

5. *Musharakah* is a contractual partnership or a joint enterprise in which profit and loss are both shared between the parties. The sharing ratio is determined in accordance with the parties' respective contribution in the enterprise (Al-Zuhayli 2003).

6. *Istisna* is a sale contract where a purchaser puts an order based upon a predetermined price for the construction, building, manufacture or assembly of a specific product according to agreed specifications, to be delivered at an agreed future date (Al-Zuhayli 2003). Key validity elements of this type of contract are agreed product specification, price and payment mode, determination of place and time of delivery of the subject matter.

7. *Ijarah* is a contract for lease whereby an owner of an asset, apart from consumable, grants it or its usufruct to a party in exchange for an agreed consideration over a specified period. Ijarah also encompasses hiring the services of a person over a specified time span in exchange for a specified consideration (Al-Zuhayli 2003).

8. *Salam* is often described as a forward financing contract whereby an Islamic financial institution (a bank) pays in advance a predetermined price for a specified commodity whose delivery is deferred to a specified future date. At the execution of this transaction, the

seller (obligor), having received full payment, undertakes to supply the commodity as agreed. An Islamic bank often enters a back-to-back contract with another party to dispose of the commodity. This contract, known as parallel salam, is a measure to ensure mitigating the risk of holding the commodity by the bank so that the commodity could be disposed of immediately after receiving delivery from the obligor (BNM 2019).

Salam is an important instrument for financing agricultural production. It has been popular for such type of financing in countries such as Sudan and Pakistan from the 1990s even though its use in the recent years appears declining (Elhiraika 2003; Aburaida 2014). Salam is a major Islamic financing mechanism that enables farmers to obtain upfront cash that can be used to cover purchases of various agricultural inputs during farming season. It provides an opportunity for farmers to sell out their future crops and hedge against market uncertainties (Elhiraika 2003). Gradually, the practice of salam gave rise certain concerns as farmers began to express discontent about high cost of salam especially where harvest prices are higher in comparison with contract prices. Thus, *band al-Ihsan* (beneficence clause) was introduced as an option for compensation only where price of the salam commodity changes above 33% (Elhiraika 2003). Even though this clause was introduced by Islamic banks to hedge against fluctuation of price to provide an incentive (Ahmed and Khan 2007), it has become an issue that led salam begin to lose popularity (Elhiraika 2003).

9. *Muzara'ah* is generally a sharecropping contract or partnership for sharecropping or joint farming (Al-Zuhayli 2003; Yahuza 2019). In its technical sense, muzara'ah refers to a sort of partnership for agricultural production where parties agree to contribute factors of production and, on harvest, share the yield based upon a pre-agreed ratio (Yahuza 2019; Yaacob 2013). Muzara'ah contract is a farming technique that potentially provides opportunities of financing to local farmers where landowners offer their farmlands to tenant farmers. By employing the tenant farmers' labour, more lands are cultivated which in turn helps in alleviating poverty among local communities (Yahuza 2019).

From its Islamic origin, muzara'ah is a contract taught by the holy Prophet Muhammad (SAW) that could be applied to address problems related to farming and food production. It needs to be modernized due to its potential to develop the agricultural sector, a sector needed for the whole of human existence (Puspitasari et al. 2019). For all intent and purpose, the essential elements for the validity of Muzara'ah contract in Shariah are as follows: identifying the land and ensuring its suitability for farming; the type of plantation or seeds/seedlings shall be determined or left for the manager to choose as he seems fit, provided this is agreed in the contract; the type of plantation is compliant with Shariah; the share of each party in the crop shall be determined as a percentage or ratio proportionate to total crop production; the period of the partnership must be sufficient for the production of crop and harvesting same and parties may mutually agree on any period they wish (DAB Bank 2018). In this contract, it is important to determine between the parties who will provide the seeds or seedlings to be planted and the required equipment. In the event this is not agreed upon, recourse would be had to customary practice applicable to this arrangement (DAB Bank 2018). ... For practical application purpose, models and structures have been developed to base Islamic financing scheme thereon. In this regard, a proposed muzara'ah contract model has been put forward for agriculture financing (Shafiai and Moi 2015) as illustrated in Fig. 14.1.

Figure 14.1 illustrates three schemes of partnership that can be formed for muzara'ah financing. In the first scheme, be it muzara'ah or musaqah where piece of land and economic trees is, respectively, made available, the landowner additionally provides equipment, seeds or animals. The tenant farmer undertakes all works and management responsibility of farming. In the second scheme, be it muzara'ah or musaqah, the landowner makes available only the piece of land or the trees and the tenant farmer provides everything else. In the third scheme, seeds and land or trees are made available by the landowner while the farmer provides equipment/animals and labour. With Islamic banks serving as landowners, any of these schemes can be employed in financing agriculture over a specific period. This financing enables farmers to obtain basic farming inputs including fertilizers, pesticides, seeds/seedlings and equipment for irrigation, storage as well as marketing of the agricultural produce (Shafiai 2011).

Muzara'ah has been used to develop innovative financial product such as muzara'ah sukuk that could be used to provide financing for agriculture production. Muzara'ah sukuk are securities designed on contract of muzara'ah. They are presented as certificates of equal value evidencing

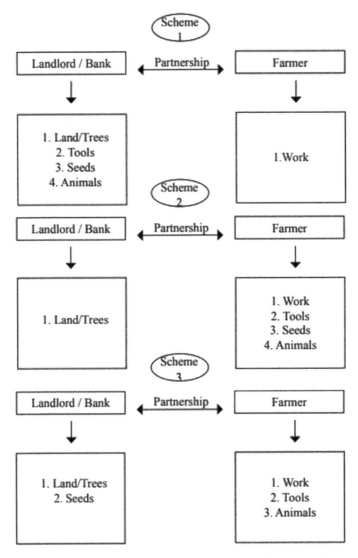

Fig. 14.1 A Muzara'ah agriculture financing scheme (*Source* Shafiai and Moi [2015])

subscription to funds mobilized to finance a muzara'ah project. Holders of the certificate own shares of the produce/commodities from that project in accordance with their subscription therein. Under this arrangement, the sukuk issuer purchases some arable land(s) using the mobilized funds from applicants. On behalf of the sukuk holders, the land is then transferred to farmer(s) who will undertake its cultivation and production of farm produce. At harvest, the farm produce are distributed among the sukuk holders. On the whole, the muzara'ah sukuk serve as deeds for the joint ownership of the land(s) among the sukuk holders who serve as landowners; the issuer serves as the sukuk holders' representative while the farmer(s) work as agent. Islamic financial institutions, most especially banks, can provide financing of working capital to farmers for certain activities. For instance, State Bank of Pakistan endorses and sanctions those strategies and technics for banks to provide financing services for the promotion of agriculture and fostering food security (State of Bank of Pakistan 2008).

It is noteworthy that the foregoing Islamic financing practices can be purposively and suitably employed Islamic banks to provide financing for the following agricultural activities: poultry and livestock farming, crop production, dairy farming, aquaculture or fish farming, maintenance of farms and equipment (State of Bank of Pakistan 2008). These technics and strategies can ensure not only the successful establishment of the stated agricultural activities but also their sustainability. From their contractual conception as highlighted above, these technics and strategies are being put into practice and/or employed to engage individual and corporate farmers on the one hand with governments, Islamic financial institutions or any corporate entities on the other hand for financing agricultural activities. For this purpose, thorough legal documentation is involved for the formalization and execution of contracts.

Concept of Islamic Social Finance—Its Governance and Role for Promoting Zero Hunger

Social finance refers to a technique of managing funds or assets and fund generated therefrom for the purpose of bringing about social dividend and/or ensuring social well-being. The concept of Islamic social finance is subsumed as a component of Islamic ethical wealth under an Islamic economic framework. Islamic social finance in this regard is constituted largely by financing via social enterprises for charitable and religious purposes which could be either voluntary or obligatory in fulfilment of religious devotion. These religious and charitable endeavours are obligatory zakat, sadaqat philanthropy and waqf endowment. Governance refers to the process through which an activity can be assured to be performed in accordance with applicable rules that uphold its workability, aims and ideals (Iqbal and Lewis 2009). Islamic ethical wealth is governed by rules that ensures purity of wealth, upholds sanctity of owner's right, warrants society's entitlement as well as the right of Allah (SWT) therein as dictated by Shariah. The governance of these charitable endeavours and their role in ensuring food security and zero hunger will be discussed in the subsequent part of this section.

As encompassed under the general purview of Islamic economic system, governance of Islamic ethical wealth as well as Islamic social finance has succinctly been outlined by the holy Quran which establishes the general framework and underpinning rules of Shariah. The holy Quran in addition to hadith of Prophet Muhammad (SAW) lay down general and specific rules applicable to running and managing Islamic charitable and social endeavours. Islamic social finance shall be based on the fundamentals of Islamic ethical wealth. So, from the onset, with regard to ethical wealth, the principal mechanism permitted by Allah (SWT) for wealth generation and acquisition is trade (Quran 2:275). Alongside this permission comes the prohibition against riba or interest. Therefore, the permissibility for wealth acquisition through trade and lawful exchange shall be subject to upholding the prohibition of riba in all its ramifications (Quran 2:275–276) and observance of other transactional ethics. Meanwhile, in accordance with Quran 2:277–281, muslims are enjoined to consider avenues for financial accommodation in their permissible trades so that not only market return is sought therefrom but also *infaq*, i.e. the act of giving to help those who are without means or incapable of participating in and taking the benefits of market. This is with view to please Allah (SWT) and earn His favour in one's soul and wealth. These avenues include advancing non-interest loan and postponement or writing off debt for distressed debtor.

In the same vein, while prohibiting riba or interest, Allah (SWT) enjoins muslims to engage in sadaqat and or charitable/philanthropic activities (Quran 2:276, 3:134). Hence, by the clear and unequivocal provisions of Quran 2:262–274, sadaqat which is a voluntary charity for philanthropy constitute another important Islamic mechanism for social finance to promote societal welfare next to obligatory zakat (Zulkhibri et al. 2019, pp. 34–35).

Zakat is a form of charity but obligation on people of zakatable means of specified quantity and an important pillar on which the Islamic economic framework is built (Quran 2:43, 9:60, 2:177, 2:273, 3:134). Zakat is paid annually and set as 2.5% of the one's net income that reaches a *nisab* threshold (zakatable minimum) as Allah (SWT) ordains it as an 'obligatory portion' of wealth in Quran 70:24. Qualifying wealth for zakat include money/cash, farm produce, livestock, incomes generated from assets, gold and silver among others.

Waqf or Islamic religious endowment is another Islamic charitable mechanism for social finance support and welfare of community generally. Waqf is sanctioned by the holy Prophet Muhammad (SAW) when he advised muslim to dedicate property or wealth inalienably and give proceeds from to charity. Waqf is also advised by the prophet when he enjoined people to engage in a 'continuing alms' as one of the things that survive and ensure rewards after a muslim's death. The instrument of waqf has been very formidable in terms of development finance and it is used to fund and finance construction and management of educational and health institutions among other charitable endeavours in several countries. On this note, it is proposed that a 'food security waqf' can be established to serve as an avenue for the allocation and organization of resources and capital to be invested in agriculture. In the same vein, essential activities for the advancement of agriculture and food security can be financed by the food security waqf. Such activities include research, innovation and transfer of technology in relation capacity building for agricultural production as well as income generation (Abdelhady 2012, p. 32). Therefore, Islamic ethical wealth can be mobilized and dedicated to the creation waqf instruments in order to support and promote food security as part of societal welfare.

Further, it must be ensured that any type and/or class of wealth to be invested for social finance is halal (lawful) and the means of obtaining, financing and facilitating its production or generation is halal as well. The concept of halal comprises not only of food or consumable materials as it is often portrayed but transcends to all actions and omissions likewise. In Islam generally, everything (including commission and omission) is said to be halal and permissible except those that are expressly made impermissible or haram (Zulkhibri et al. 2019). Accordingly, no amount of wealth shall be expended for indulgence in the consumption or production of impermissible foods (Quran 5:4–5, 6:145, 16:114–116), promiscuity (Quran 17:32), gambling, alcoholism and dealings in drugs and arms or any illicit business (Quran 5:93–94), unjust devouring and destruction of lives and property (Quran 4:29). These are Shariah standards to be observed for the establishment of a Shariah compliant financing activity including that of 'zero hunger' scheme. In essence, sadaqat, zakat and waqf are the main Islamic social financing mechanism, and from that dimension, they provide mechanisms and strategies that can be deployed to fund zero hunger and promote related initiatives.

It should be noted that, in addition to the foregoing rules of Shariah and depending on jurisdictions, Islamic social financing is subject to other laws and regulations that govern related subject matter with respect to administration, management and tax matters (Obaidullah 2016). At the same time, regulatory regimes have provided for the oversight of Islamic social finance endeavours by State Ministries of Awqaf or Islamic/Religious Affairs in several countries.

Islamic Social Financing Initiatives to Promote Zero Hunger

Several initiatives have been undertaken both by private and public entities using Islamic social financing technics to channel Islamic ethical wealth into funding zero hunger programmes. To a certain extent, zero hunger initiatives have been embarked upon by both governments and private not-for-profit entities in all countries of the world to achieve Goal 2 UNSDGs. Some of these initiatives are discussed below.

USA—In the United States of America for instance, there is Zakat Foundation of America (ZFA), an Islamic charitable body serving communities of needy through zakat. Under its programme for global food security financed via zakat funds, ZFA provides the hungry, undernourished and malnourished with an amazing ten million meals in a year, in addition to over ten million pounds of beef in forty-four countries (ZFA, n/d). However, such initiatives are said to be inadequate given the unprecedented and growing food insecurity the world is facing today where an estimated two billion people, approximately 1 in 4 persons on earth, live without adequate and nutritious diet. Among the affected people, an estimated 800 million thereof or 1 in 9 suffer real hunger due to acute food insecurity. The ZFA programme for this reason focuses on three main aspects of the food insecurity: availability of food and ensuring its adequate daily supply; accessibility to food by providing resources and making available suitable foods for nutritious diets; proper utilization of food via consumption of nutritious and healthy diet. In this regard, ZFA has undertaken the following important initiatives. Through partnership with similar charitable organizations (Mercy-Corps and Yemen Relief and Reconstruction Foundation), emergency materials and food items were provided to thousands of the poorest and internally displaced people on the verge of starvation in war-torn Yemen. In the same vein, ZFA financed training of hundreds of Yemenis in sesame cultivation in order to boost not only the availability of this staple food but also its quality and quantity with view to a lasting food resilience as solution to food insecurity. In the West African country of Ghana, ZFA established and automated two cooperatives of rural women for processing cassava, drought-resistant root crop rich in carbohydrate, into *gari* (local farina-like flour) which is a staple for producing bread and tapioca among other local diets. Another landmark initiative is ZFA's Animal Husbandry Program which started with initial limited number cattle pairs has today developed into a means of providing livelihood and financial independence to about 10,000 herders in over ten African and Asian countries (ZFA, n/d).

Sudan—Sudan is a country about one-third of whose GDP is accounted for by agriculture. Similarly, more than one-third of its national workforce has agriculture and agro-processing businesses as means of earning a living (FAO 2015). The Government of Sudan has provided for agriculture as an engine of development to ensure it gives effective contribution to its economic growth and export performance. The government seeks to all together improve livelihood of its citizens by reducing poverty, advancing food and nutrition security as well as developing and protecting its natural resources (FAO 2015). Sudan is a good example to illustrate the use of agriculture specialized banks to resolve financial constraints and increase food production. Also, Sudan has successfully implemented salam financing in a unique way that needs to be learnt by other jurisdictions that aspire to develop their agricultural sector in similar manner. In brief, how Sudan is able to achieve its agricultural development in this regard is stated as follows.

Sudan has converted its entire financial system into Islamic one and 60% of banks there do not impose any limit on farmers to obtain loan(s) from different financial institutions simultaneously regardless of farmers' repayment capability and risk of default. For *murabahah* transactions for instance, financing facility is considered as a default when a farmer is unable to pay for a month. For other kind of financing facilities, it is three months (Elhiraika 2003). For default cases, it is said that legal action has been taken against over 90% of farmers who have the ability to pay to realize defaulted payments. Recourse is often had to collateral and where farmers are genuinely unable to pay, the banks resort to rescheduling of advances (Elhiraika 2003). In case of *salam* financing, a process called 'Eqala' is adopted whereby a farmer is exempted from kind payment and only principal amount received by the farmer is postponed for repayment to coming seasons (Elhiraika 2003). With the exception of salam financing, in other types of financing arrangements where farmer is unable to pay, the farmers can get assistance from zakat department to pay off the debt (Elhiraika 2003).

UAE—The United Arab Emirates (UAE) has launched its National Food Security Strategy 2051 with the aim of achieving zero hunger. The strategy is an action plan set to provide and made available safe, nutritious and adequate food throughout the year. Lack of arable land and the pressure of population expansion strain the UAE's agricultural industry. Underpinned by Islamic financing, the strategy specially targets the implementation of agricultural practices that are resilient and boost productivity in addition to maintaining and preserving ecosystems (UAE Government 2020a). In order to establish a sustainably developed agriculture sector for food security, 'Ziraai' programme was launched to provide support for citizens employed in the agricultural production. The programme provides Islamic financing (via interest-free loan) of up to AED 1 million in addition to marketing services and training for each farmer. The programme has helped farmers and those in farming business improve their efficiency and profitability using cutting-edge technologies such as hydroponics systems that greatly reduce water consumption, enabling crop production without lands in furtherance of the zero-hunger drive (UAE Government 2020b).

India—Zakat Foundation of India (ZFI) is a private not-for-profit charity organization based in India. Its responsibility is largely collection, allocation, organization and utilization of zakat funds to finance charitable as well as philanthropic and socially beneficial activities. These activities include provision of feeding for the hungry among the poor and needy people, financing health and medical facilities, running schools and orphanages, and monetary assistance and scholarship for eligible people, management of waqf endowments. In addition to zakat, ZFI also collects, allocates and utilizes sadaqat and related charity in like manner.

In cognizance of Goal 2 UNSDs, ZFI has undertaken several projects aimed at food security through zakat funds such as its Hungry Person for Feeding. The project seeks out hungry persons and provide with food among other necessities of life. According to information available on its official website, individuals including hungry persons can fill a form made available therein to pride detailed personal information about hungry persons including their whereabouts. ZFI uses the information, find and reach out to the hungry persons with needed help and support (ZFI 2020).

Recommendation—Islamic Food Banking and Its Operations Guidelines

It is recommended to introduce Islamic food banking world widely. Each country can set up their own Islamic food banks following the guidelines of Islamic food banking with the common objective of eliminating hunger. As such, a uniform set of guidelines to regulate Islamic food banking need to be formulated. Food banking and establishment of food banks is not a new initiative in the world.

The food bank model is a unique concept meant to tackle the 'global paradox of hunger and food loss and waste'. As an environmentally beneficial initiative, food bank is considered a 'green' relief against hunger. It is non-profit, community-based solution that establishes and engages in a system of surplus recovery and redistribution. It procures surplus and healthy food that would otherwise be wasted or lost and redirects same to the feeding of the hungry via a network of home-grown charities and rural community organizations (The Global Food Banking Network 2019, p. 3). Wherever it operates, a food bank is said to epitomize a 'triple win' situation: provision of food to assist vulnerable and hungry people, reduction in food waste and protection of the environment. In addition, it strengthens grassroots civil societies through charities and humanitarian support (The Global Food Banking Network 2019). There are some global actions which the Global Food and Banking Network (2019) has prescribed in this regard which is provided in Table 14.1.

The proposed Islamic food banking model can be based on integration of Islamic finance and halal rules. Its basic principles will be derived from the reality of Islamic teaching where, as vicegerents of Allah (SWT), human obedience to Allah is at its apex. Additionally, Islamic ethical rules and practices such as prudence in consumption without wasting

Table 14.1 Actions for strengthening food banking by Global Food Banking Network

Party recommended to take action	Details
Government	• Quantify food loss and waste—support food recycling and redistribution • Establish public policies to encourage surplus food donation • Partner with food banks to expand the informal social safety net • Direct Official Development Assistance funding to support food banking expansion • Measure food insecurity using the Food Insecurity Experience Scale
Businesses	• Measure and manage food loss and waste • Develop and implement a global donation policy • Standardize date coding • Increase support and resources for local food banks
International Agencies & Multilateral Institutions	• Gather better data • Utilize food banks for logistics and storage to support in- kind emergency relief

Source The Global Food Banking Network (2019)

(israf) of food and helping each other constitute its core values to be complied with. There are some Muslim food bank initiatives among some muslim communities in the world. For instance, 'Muslim Food Bank and Community Services Society' (MFBCS) was formed on 6 July 2010 as a charitable, non-for-profit organization under Societies Act 2016 at Victoria, British Columbia, Canada (Muslim Food Bank and Community Services Society, N/A-1). The food bank initiative of MFBCS provides food bank programmes that serve the needs of clients with special dietary needs including halal, kosher, vegetarian and/or vegan (Muslim Food Bank and Community Services Society, N/A-2). MFBCS distributes food items for approximately 600 families monthly comprising of around 3,000 persons (Muslim Food Bank and Community Services Society, N/A-2). Muslim Welfare Canada (MWC) is another initiative which was pioneered as far back as 1993 by late Major Muhammad Abbas Ali (1921–2009) and his wife, late Sarwar Jahan Begum (1928–2013). It is a food bank that encompasses halal food and essential items and provides families and individuals with non-perishable food items as well as perishable such as meat (Muslim Welfare Canada, N/A). The commonest food items provided by NWC include rice/flour and meat, baby formula and diapers, pasta, milk, vegetables and fruits among others. MWC's database has over 9,900 families that registered with it and rely on the MWC's food bank for supplement to their daily food need (Muslim Welfare Canada, N/A). Another instance is Halal Food Bank of Melbourne, a philanthropic enterprise by Ansaar Project in Sydney. It is an initiative that provides an avenue for people who want to donate. People source and drop off food items for onward distribution to those in need in a bid to nurture giving and upholding Prophetic sunnah. Service and cash donations are accepted and utilized in essentials for inventory and packaging including tape, packing boxes, storage tubs and stickers (Halal Food Bank of Melbourne, N/A-2).

The existing notion of food bank is narrow in the sense that its main operation depends on receiving charity and providing food for needy. This narrow scope needs to be widened for sustainability of food banks initiatives. Accordingly, the idea of a full-fledge Islamic food banking is proposed in this chapter. Specifics of the proposed Islamic food banking are provided in subsequent paragraphs and the model is illustrated in a nutshell in Fig. 14.2. It is imperative to note that there could be some jurisdictions where applicable law would not allow the word 'bank' to be used except for banking in the traditional sense of the word. In those

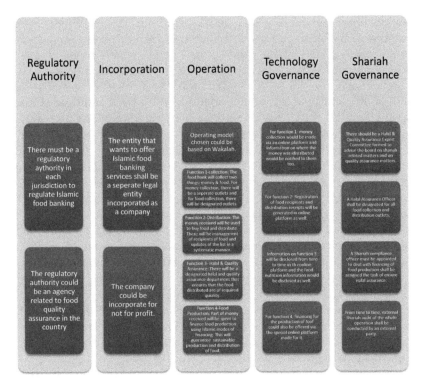

Fig. 14.2 Proposed Islamic food banking model (*Source* Author's Own)

instances, Islamic food bank could be called Islamic food house or such suitable term.

Each of the important aspects provided in Fig. 14.2 is explained.

Regulatory Authority

A regulatory authority is important to govern Islamic food banking in any jurisdiction to provide certainty, uniformity and confidence in terms of halal and quality assurance to the public and ensure that a sustainable bank is established to create a zero-hunger society. Without a watchdog, providing the required confidence for food or money contributors to the Islamic food banks would be difficult. As such, having a regulatory authority that establishes the required framework for the establishment of Islamic food banks will create the legal and regulatory framework required for it and simultaneously Islamic food banks will be backed by law. Now the probing question is: Who could be the best regulatory authority to regulate Islamic food banking in a jurisdiction? Should it be the central bank as it is called a bank, or could there be any other appropriate entity? To answer this question, one need to understand the functions of Islamic food banking that is not primarily focused on dealing with money, but on the food collection, production, distribution and financing of food production as well. Therefore, since food is the major component dealt under Islamic food banking, it could be much more appropriate to appoint a food regulation agency in the jurisdiction to be the primary regulatory authority and the financing part could be regulated by the central bank as well. Therefore, depending on the nature of the laws found in the respective jurisdiction that wants to adopt Islamic food banking, one may choose the appropriate regulatory authority or regulatory authorities. The important thing that needs to be understood is that definitely Islamic food banking shall be regulated by a single or multiple regulatory authorities.

Incorporation

Islamic food banking cannot be offered by individuals or by an unincorporated entity in a sustainable manner as corporate governance plays an integral role in the sustainability of the service provided in perpetuity irrespective of the demise of the natural persons involved in the incorporation of it at the inception stage. This is definitely something that should be considered in the incorporation of Islamic food banks and as such incorporation of Islamic food banks as a company could be much more suitable as companies are separate legal entities that is formed detached from its members or shareholders that has the legal right to hold movable or immovable properties under its own name; can be sued and can sue others and can run on its own in perpetuity without relying on the wishes of one single person which is also known from the landmark case on company law which is Salomon v. Salomon & Co. Ltd [1896] UKHL 1. However, depending on the national law of the respective jurisdiction, if incorporation of an Islamic bank as a company is unsuitable, then a more appropriate type of separate entity can be chosen. It would be also ideal to have a stake of the corporation taken by the government of the respective country and also some shares of the company could be given to the big food and beverage companies operating in the country. This way the cost of operation and know-how of the business will be known by the shareholders at the same time protecting the welfare of all the stakeholders including the contributors and recipients of the food. Since Islamic food banks are not profit-oriented entities, the government's role is important for the successful operation of it in a sustainable manner, at least from the onset.

Operation

There are four major functions proposed for the Islamic food banks. They are collection function, distribution function, halal and assurance function and food production function. Each of these functions is important for the sustainability of Islamic food banks and to ensure that zero-hunger objective in the society is achieved. The collection function of Islamic food banks includes establishing outlets or agents to collect money as well as food. In terms of money received, Islamic food banks can create three types of funds; zakat fund, cash waqf fund and sadaqat fund. The governance rules applicable to these three funds will be different though the point of collection could be uniform as it could be paid by cash to the outlets or via online payments via the special electronic platform formed by the Islamic banks. If the money is paid for zakat fund, then the money would be spent only to purchase food and then give it free to poor and needy which is a zakat recipient prescribed in Quran. There is no other way in which money received in zakat fund can be used. For the money received in cash waqf fund, the rules of cash waqf management will be followed and as such, investments will also be carried out from the fund and money will be managed in a way that the principal amount is not depleted. From cash waqf fund, money could be paid to purchase food or to finance food production activities without breaching principles of cash waqf. The final type of funds received, which is for sadaqat fund, the use of money received in this regard is more flexible as it could be either given to purchase food or food production as well. The rules applicable to each of these funds shall be publicly disclosed in the website of the Islamic food bank to inform contributors to enable them to make the best choice on where to use their funds. Furthermore, standard operating procedures for each of these funds must be developed separately and even in financial statements and disclosures, each of these funds shall be separately shown.

In this regard, an important question that needs an answer could be on how operational expenses of the bank could be financed if the bank is operated in as not-for-profit organization and the funds collected are used only for purchase of food or financing of food production. Therefore, an operational structure for the company could be used on wakalah or agency model whereby a fee could be charged as the wakeel or agent of the contributors who entrust the task of managing the food bank for them. As such, from every contribution made except for zakat fund, a small percentage could be determined as a wakalah (agency) fee and this could be put in a separate management account and should be separately handled from the contributor's funds. As for the money received from zakat fund, as the 'amil (collector) of zakat some amount of money could be used by properly publicly disclosing it and under the guidance of Shariah and Assurance Expert Committee of the respective Islamic food bank.

To boost up the amount of funds received, the Islamic food banks can form affiliations with other Islamic financial institutions operating in the jurisdictions whereby special financial products could be offered in association with each other for the consumers of the Islamic financial institutions. This way it will be easier to reach a wider audience and by leveraging on the customer base of the Islamic financial institutions, the Islamic food banks could receive funds in a sustainable manner.

As for the food collection, there will be an operational cost involved to keep them and store them without compromising the quality of it. As such, instead of financing the cost of having its own storage places for food keeping, it can form partnerships with big restaurants and food outlets in the nation whereby the food collection points will be these designated outlets and they will manage it. As a consideration for the tasks they conduct, these outlets could be paid a fee for their services or this could be a service maintained as part of their corporate social responsibility initiatives. By having these outlets, more people can reach out to Islamic food banks in a manner where each and every one obtaining service from the designated restaurants or food outlets could help the zero-hunger initiative. For instance, in the menu of the restaurant or food outlet, a bundle offer could be put whereby the option add a meal for a poor could be given or if food is left without use and falls the hygienic standards, then it could be given for charity. Not only this, but a subsidized food restaurant outlet for poor families to enjoy a meal could also be initiated. The assistance of food and beverage companies operating in the respective country could provide assistance to the growth and success of the Islamic food banks. If the shareholders of the companies are the government and the food and beverage companies, this task could become easy.

The distribution function of Islamic food banks would be to distribute the food received to those who need it in a convenient and sustainable way. As mentioned above, food distribution could be made by the designated restaurants and food outlets. However, for remote areas and places which are far away from the designated outlets, transportation of the food needs to be made. The difficult thing in this regard would not be the transportation of the food and the distribution of them in a frequent and sustainable manner, but to find the people who deserve it and update the list of deserved recipients in an effective manner so that the most deserve gets the benefit of it. Via technology, the registration of poor could be made easy. However, the question is whether the most deserved population are able to reach the technology-based platform to register. There could be regions where Internet is unavailable but mobile phone network is available. For those in these regions, registration via mobile phone could be made possible using USSD code or the classical way of contacting the village heads or head of those inhabitations and information collection and verification methods could be made. For this, more effort will need to be put as this would not be an easy task. The involvement of government as a shareholder and linking with the multilateral aid agencies also could be helpful in this regard. The cost of the operation of Islamic food bank and the effectiveness of its operation will also depend on this function. This is because, if the recipients of the food are not identified properly, then the purpose of creating Islamic food bank will be defeated.

The halal and quality assurance function is also an important function to provide best food for those who need food that is nutritious as well as beneficial to those who consume them. The Islamic food bank shall ensure that all distributed food by them or in affiliation with them shall be halal and is of quality prescribed by Shariah and Assurance Expert Committee of the respective Islamic food bank. Scheduled and ad hoc inspection and audit of food must be conducted to ensure this and also there must be put in place a research unit to research on how halal and quality food could be offered with technology and new innovations. Furthermore, review of whole operations of the Islamic food bank shall also be conducted in a periodic manner to improve the functions of the

Islamic food bank. Furthermore, training for those who need also will be managed under this function.

The food production is the final function of the Islamic food bank that emphasize on the sustainable production of food by providing funding to the producers of food with special emphasis on those living in remote areas with no financial access and a local market to sell them. The financing for this purpose would be made in a Shariah compliant manner and will be supervised by designated Shariah compliant officers under the guidance of Shariah and Assurance Expert Committee of the respective Islamic food bank. The board of the Islamic food bank will decide an equitable way of providing this service to those who need it and ensure that there is enough supply of food production.

Technology Governance

In this Industry 4.0 era, technology plays an important part in the lives of people. As such, in Islamic food banks, technology plays a vital role and its governance mechanisms need to be enacted properly to manage the risk properly. There are numerous types of technology that could be used to complement the operations of Islamic food banks. Blockchain technology, artificial intelligence and Internet of things could be used depending on the geographical location and the need. A virtual zakat shop can also be opened via technology so that any one in need could purchase things without a human intervention where there is no shame in obtaining any essential without being felt like begging.

Shariah Governance

Shariah governance is the heart of Islamic food bank as all of its operations shall be in compliance with Shariah. The prefix Islam in the name provides this assurance to all of its stakeholders and as such, it is imperative to put in place adequate mechanisms to ensure this. It would be mandatory to form a Shariah and Assurance Expert Committee to advise on the Shariah matters of the operation of the company to the board of directors of the company. The composition of the company shall include mostly Shariah qualified member and some members could be experts in food-related areas. Furthermore, a Halal Assurance Officer shall be designated for all food collection and distribution outlets and a Shariah compliance officer shall be appointed to deal with financing of food production shall be assigned the task of ensure halal assurance. From time to time, external Shariah audit of the whole operation shall be conducted by an external party and this arrangement shall be made by the respective Islamic food bank in a systematic manner.

CONCLUSIONS

From the foregoing discussion of this chapter, it is clear that there are many initiatives taken by different countries in the world to support 'zero hunger' schemes. However, a unification is required in this regard through institutionalization of the efforts. Accordingly, this chapter has proposed the idea and concept of Islamic food banking and demonstrates the need to pioneer as well as pilot its establishment to epitomize the required institutionalization. Islamic food bank is a strategic initiative that could be taken by respective countries of the world to support 'zero hunger'. A successful establishment of such an institution to deal with matter of food security could definitely help to resolve the issue of hunger in a sustainable way. It is anticipated that the recommendations offered by this chapter would assist relevant stakeholders including multilateral agencies to implement and institutionalize 'zero hunger' schemes under one roof of Islamic food banking. There is however the need for further research to understand and evaluate the feasibility of establishing such as an entity to support 'zero-hunger' initiatives.

REFERENCES

Abdelhady, H. (2012). Islamic Finance as a Mechanism for Bolstering Food Security in the Middle East: Food Security Waqf. *Sustainable Development Law & Policy, 13*, 1–29.

Aburaida, K. M. M. (2014). Rural Finance as a Mechanism for Poverty Alleviation in Sudan with an Emphasis on "Salam" Mode. *European Scientific Journal, 7*, 26–157.

Adebayo, R. I., & Hassan, M. K. (2013). Ethical Principles of Islamic Financial Institutions. *Journal of Economic Cooperation and Development, 34*, 1–63.

Ahmed, J. (2015). *Ethics in Islamic Finance: Embracing Duties and Consequences in the Post-Crisis Environment.* https://www.ifac.org/knowledge-gateway/building-trust-ethics/discussion/ethics-islamic-finance-embracing-duties-and. Accessed on 2 May 2020.

Ahmed, H., & Khan, T. (2007). Risk Management in Islamic Banking. In K. Hassan & M. Lewis (Eds.), *Handbook of Islamic Banking* (pp. 144–158). Cheltenham: Edward Elgar Publishing Limited.

Al-Qadi, A. (2019). *Food Security Under the Islamic Khilafah*. http://www.khilafah.com/food-security-under-the-islamic-khilafah/. Accessed on 1 May 2020.

Al-Zuhayli, W. (2003). *Financial Transactions in Islamic Jurisprudence* (Vol. 2, 4th ed.). Beirut: Dar al-Fikr Mouaser, 1447.

Bank Negara Malaysia. (2019). *Capital Adequacy Framework for Islamic Banks (Risk-Weighted Assets)* [BNM/RH/PD 029-3]. https://www.bnm.gov.my/index.php?ch=57&pg=137&ac=798&bb=file. Accessed on 1 June 2020.

Beekun, R. (1996). *Islamic Business Ethics*. Nevada: University of Nevada.

DAB Bank. (2018). *Agriculture Financing-Based Product Guide*. https://dab.gov.af/sites/default/files/2018-12/29AgricultureShariahParameterv3jfoerutoern121201612815170553325325.pdf. Accessed on 2 May 2020.

Elhiraika, A. B. (2003). *On the Experience of Islamic Agricultural Finance in Sudan: Challenges and Sustainability*. https://uaelaws.files.wordpress.com/2012/10/on-the-experience-of-islamic-agricultural-finance-in-sudan.pdf. Accessed on 2 May 2020.

FAO. (2015). *Sudan Plan of Action (2015–2019)*. http://www.fao.org/3/a-i4786e.pdf. Accessed on 2 May 2020.

Haddad, M. (2012). An Islamic Perspective on Food Security Management. *Water Policy, 14*, 121–135.

Halal Food Bank of Melbourne. (N/A-1). *About*. https://halalfoodbankmelburne.wordpress.com/donate/. Accessed on 4 May 2020.

Halal Food Bank of Melbourne. (N/A-2). *Donate*. https://halalfoodbankmelburne.wordpress.com/donate/. Accessed on 4 May 2020.

Hashim, M. A. (2016, August 2). Demystifying Wealth in Islam. *The Star*. https://www.thestar.com.my/opinion/columnists/ikim-views/2016/08/02/demystifying-wealth-in-islam-in-managing-his-wealth-a-muslim-must-strike-a-balance between-spiritual Accessed on 4 May 2020.

Iqbal, Z., & Lewis, M. K. (2009). *An Islamic Perspective on Governance* (p. 368). Cheltenham: Edward Elgar.

Islamic Relief. (n.d.). *Hunger No More*. https://www.islamic-relief.org.uk/about-us/what-we-do/food/. Accessed on 2 May 2020.

Mathukur, N. M. M. (2019). Business Ethics in Islamic Finance. *Archives of Business Research, 7*, 2–143.

Muslim Food Bank and Community Services Society. (N/A-1). *About Us*. https://www.muslimfoodbank.com/about/. Accessed on 4 May 2020.

Muslim Food Bank and Community Services Society. (N/A-2). *Food Bank Programs*. https://www.muslimfoodbank.com/food-bank/. Accessed on 4 May 2020.

302   A. MUNEEZA AND Z. MUSTAPHA

Muslim Global Relief. (N/A). *Feed the Hungry*. https://www.muslimglobalrel
ief.org/feed-the-hungry/. Accessed on 2 May 2020.

Muslim Welfare Canada. (N/A). *Halal Food and Essential Items Bank*. https://
www.muslimwelfarecentre.com/causes/halal-food-essential-items-bank/.
Accessed on 4 May 2020.

Obaidullah, M. (2016). A Framework for Analysis of Islamic Endowment (Waqf)
Laws. *International Journal of not-for-Profit Law, 18*, 54.

Palmisano, I. (2014). *Introduction to Ethical Finance and Responsible Investments*. https://ideasfactorybg.org/wp-content/uploads/2015/02/IntroFina
nceIng.pdf. Accessed on 2 May 2020.

Puspitasari, N., Hidayat, S. E., & Kusmawati, F. (2019). Murabaha as an Islamic
Financial Instrument for Agriculture. *Journal of Islamic Financial Studies, 5*,
1–43.

Shafiai, M. H. M. (2011). Crafting the Agricultural Product and Loss Sharing
(aPLS) in the Place of the Profit and Loss (PLS) for Islamic Agricultural
Finance. *Kyoto Working Papers on Area Studies: G-COE Series, 114*, 1–28.

Shafiai, M. H. M., & Moi, M. R. (2015). Fitting Islamic Financial Contracts in
Developing Agricultural Land. *Global Journal Al Thaqafah, 5*(1), 43.

State Bank of Pakistan. (2008). *Guidelines on Islamic Financing for Agriculture*. http://www.sbp.org.pk/guidelines/IslamicAgriculture/Guidelines-
Islamic-Financing-Agriculture-01-09-2008.pdf. Accessed on 2 May 2020.

The Global Food Banking Network. (2019). *Toward Zero Hunger: Food Banks
as a Green Solution to Hunger*. http://www.foodbanking.org/wp-content/
uploads/2019/03/GFN_WasteNot.pdf. Accessed on 3 May 2020.

The Global Goals for Sustainable Development. (N/A). *The 17 Goals*. https://
www.globalgoals.org/. Accessed on 2 May 2020.

The Hunger Project. (2014). *The Hunger Project and the Zero Hunger Challenge*. https://www.thp.org/the-hunger-project-and-the-zero-hunger-challe
nge/. Accessed on 3 May 2020.

The United Nations Sustainable Development Goals (UNSDGs). (N/A).
Goal 2: Zero Hunger. https://www.un.org/sustainabledevelopment/hun
ger/. Accessed on 26 May 2020.

The United Nations. (N/A). *Zero Hunger Challenge*. https://www.un.org/zer
ohunger/. Accessed on 4 May 2020.

UAE Government. (2020a). *National Food Security Strategy 2051*. https://u.
ae/en/about-the-uae/strategies-initiatives-and-awards/federal-governments-
strategies-and-plans/national-food-security-strategy-2051. Accessed on 2
June 2020.

UAE Government. (2020b). *Zero Hunger—Promoting Sustainable Agriculture*. https://u.ae/en/about-the-uae/leaving-no-one-behind/2zerohunger#
promoting-sustainable-agriculture. Accessed on 20 June 2020.

UNICEF. (2020). *Malnutrition.* https://data.unicef.org/topic/nutrition/mal nutrition/. Accessed on 2 June 2020.

United Nations (UN) News. (2012). *Rio+20: Secretary-General Challenges Nations to Achieve 'Zero Hunger'.* Retrieved from https://news.un.org/en/story/2012/06/413912.

Yaacob, H. (2013). Commercializing muzara'ah Model Contract Through Islamic Finance to Help Malaysian Aborigines. *International Journal of Business, Economics and Law, 2,* 3–69.

Yahuza, B. S. (2019). *Viability of Muzara'ah Contract on Agro-Financing in Alleviating Rural Poverty in Kano State, Nigeria.* https://www.researchgate.net/publication/330690756_Viability_of_Muzara'ah_Contract_on_Agro-fin ancing_in_Alleviating_Rural_Poverty_in_Kano_State_Nigeria. Accessed on 1 May 2020.

Zakat Foundation of America. (N/A). *Food Security.* https://www.zakat.org/en/what-we-do/food-security/. Accessed May 2, 2020.

Zakat Foundation of India. (2020). *Help ZFI Locate a HUNGRY PERSON for Feeding.* http://www.zakatindia.org/Hungry-Person-Feeding.html. Accessed on 30 June 2020.

Zulkhibri, M., Manap, T., Abdul, A., & Muneeza, A. (Eds.). (2019). *Islamic Monetary Economics and Institutions Theory and Practice.* Cham: Springer.

CHAPTER 15

Structures of Healthcare Waqf in Indonesia to Support SDGs

Ascarya and Hendri Tanjung

It is common knowledge that waqf will be able to increase the economic growth of a society/country. The philosophy of waqf that must not be reduced, it must even increase, shows that the economy will continue to grow with the existence of waqf. The economic growth is also sustainable. There are many best practices that can be seen, even the most phenomenal is a waqf from Usman bin Affan, a companion of the Prophet who died about 1,400 years ago. At present, a large and magnificent hotel is being built in Medina with its owner named Usman bin Affan. In Indonesia, there are many waqf assets that have not been optimized. There are 420 thousand hectares of waqf land that have not been maximally utilized (Ministry of Finance 2019). It is expected that with good governance, the large resources will become a power that can be enjoyed by the community. One of the allotments of waqf that can be enjoyed by the public is

---

Ascarya (✉)
Ibn Khaldun University, Bogor, Indonesia

H. Tanjung
International Institute of Islamic Economics, International Islamic University Islamabad, Islamabad, Pakistan

© The Author(s), under exclusive license to Springer Nature Switzerland AG 2021
M. M. Billah (eds.), *Islamic Wealth and the SDGs*,
https://doi.org/10.1007/978-3-030-65313-2_15

305

healthcare waqf. Physical pain is something that is undesirable. Nobody wants to get sick. However, if pain comes, then patiently deal with it and try to recover by treatment, is the right solution. Every Muslim is called upon to help the sick. For people who are sick, God tells us to seek treatment. Qur'an Surah As-Syu'ara, 26 verse 80 means: "If I am sick, then He is the one who healed me." Recovery is obtained by seeking treatment. Treatment can be done at the hospital.

HEALTHCARE WAQF

Healthcare waqf could be structured in various different models. Firstly, healthcare waqf could be structured as social waqf, where the healthcare facility is intended to provide free healthcare services for general public, especially the poor and near poor. Secondly, healthcare waqf could be structured as productive waqf to provide commercial medical services to general public. Lastly, healthcare waqf could be structured as integrated social-productive waqf to provide free healthcare services for the poor, as well as to provide commercial healthcare services for general public (Ascarya et al. 2020). The healthcare facility could be as small as a clinic up to as big as hospital or medical center.

Social Healthcare Waqf

The social healthcare waqf is a purely social waqf facility to provide free health services to the poor or mustahiq (zakat recipients) or the near poor vulnerable group that could not pay the health insurance. This social healthcare waqf could also serve general public for free or for small fees. The establishment of social waqf could be initiated by the waqif (waqf donor) that donate waqf assets (land, cash, etc.) to the nazir (waqf manager) to be managed for certain social activities, i.e., healthcare services, or it could also be initiated by the nazir who plan to build social healthcare waqf facility by collecting waqf (land, cash, etc.) from prospective waqif. Subsequently, nazir would sign a contract with the contractor or developer to build the social healthcare facility on waqf land that would be paid using cash waqf collected. Social healthcare waqf facility could then be run and managed by the nazir, or managed by the third-party professionals. The poor and the near poor could take advantage of this social healthcare facility (mauquf 'alaih) for free.

The characteristic of social waqf, like this social healthcare waqf, is the cost center, because it does not generate revenues, so the operational costs must be borne by other social funding sources, such as zakat and infaq collected by licensed zakat institution counterparts (see Fig. 15.1a). Zakat could be used to cover health service costs for the poor, while infaq could be used to cover health service costs of near poor or non-poor. The establishment of social waqf usually relies entirely on waqf collected by the nazir, especially direct cash waqf, and does not depend on commercial external financing.

In addition, social waqf, such as social healthcare waqf, could also be built and managed by social institution that acts as nazir of waqf and at the same time as amil of zakat, so that the waqf-zakat institution could collect waqf to build the social waqf facility, while it could also collect zakat and infaq to finance the operation and management of the social waqf, such as this social healthcare waqf. Moreover, in practice, the nazir

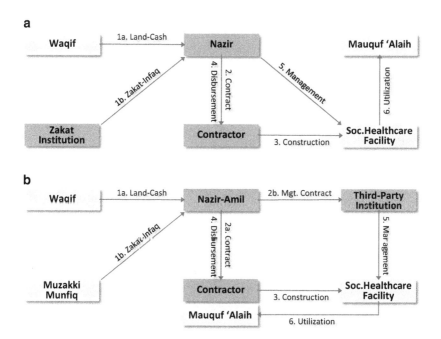

Fig. 15.1 General structure of social healthcare waqf (a) and (b)

does not really manage the healthcare facility by himself, but the nazir would establish or collaborate with new third-party institution specialized in healthcare management. This more applied version of social healthcare waqf can be illustrated in Fig. 15.1b.

Example of this type of social healthcare waqf was Rumah Sehat Terpadu—Dompet Dhuafa Hospital located in Parung, Bogor District, Indonesia, when it was established at the first time by Dompet Dhuafa Foundation.

Productive Healthcare Waqf

The productive healthcare waqf is a purely commercial waqf facility to provide paid health services to general public. However, even though this healthcare facility operates commercially, because it is built and financed using waqf and cash waqf, it could provide health services cheaper than market/standard costs, since there is no shareholder in this commercial waqf facility who ask for profits or returns.

Initially, the nazir of waqf institution plans to establish productive healthcare waqf facility, raises waqf, including land and cash, accordingly and builds the facility by hiring the contractor. In the meantime, the nazir establishes separate professional third-party institution (or collaborates with one) to manage the commercial healthcare facility to generate profits by providing health services to general public. The net profits received by the nazir would be used to finance various social programs needed by the general public, especially the poor (Fig. 15.2).

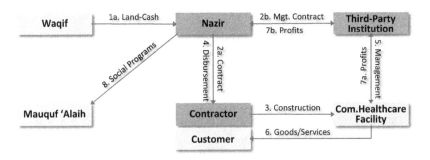

Fig. 15.2 General structure of productive healthcare waqf

There are plenty of productive healthcare waqf examples in Indonesia. Almost in every big city, there are Islamic hospitals built as productive waqf. Major Islamic organizations, such as Muhammadiyah, have focused their activities in providing education and health services based on waqf, so that they have established hospitals almost in every city for academic purpose, as well as for commercial purpose. Moreover, the ratio of hospital bed to the population in Indonesia is very low of only 1.21 bed per 1000 population, while the World Health Organization (WHO) standard is 5 bed per 1000 population. Therefore, the demand for health care in Indonesia has not been met by the supply, and productive healthcare waqf could be a solution to meet the demand with cheaper or more affordable costs.

Integrated Social-Productive Healthcare Waqf-1

Other type of healthcare waqf is integrated social-productive healthcare waqf, which combines social healthcare waqf and productive healthcare waqf, combining cost center waqf and profit center waqf to ensure the sustainability of social health services provided by social healthcare waqf needed by the needy, the poor, and the near poor. Therefore, commercial motivation is combined with social motivation, and profit orientation is combined with not-for-profit orientation. The idea of integrated social-productive waqf, such as integrated social-productive healthcare waqf, was originated from the need to establish social healthcare waqf to provide quality health services needed by the poor and the near poor people free of charge, which now have become increasingly commercially oriented, especially in Muslim-majority developing countries. To cover the operational costs of these health services, there must be a sustainable source of funds that could be met from the returns of productive waqf.

There are at least two integrated social-productive healthcare waqf models. First, two separate waqf facilities, where the social healthcare waqf facility serves the poor and the near poor (mauquf 'alaih) for free, while commercial waqf facility serves commercial customers, such as this free healthcare financed by real estate development, as shown in Fig. 15.3a. Initially, the waqf institution collects waqf, especially land and cash, to establish social healthcare waqf facility and commercial productive waqf facility, built by the contractor (it could be two different contractors). Upon the completion, productive waqf would generate returns, and these returns would be used to finance the social healthcare waqf.

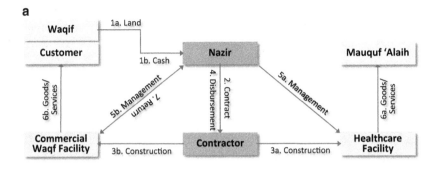

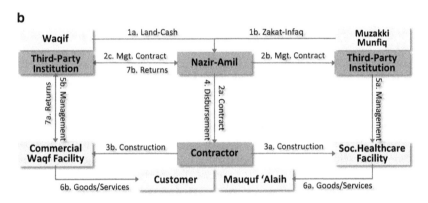

Fig. 15.3 General structure of integrated social-productive healthcare waqf-1 (a) and (b)

When the productive waqf could not generate enough returns, or it needs some time to generate significant returns to finance social healthcare waqf, the waqf institution could also register as zakat institution to be able to collect zakat and/or infaq to finance social healthcare waqf operational costs. Moreover, since healthcare provider should be managed by professionals, while the nazir has no competence in this area, this type of healthcare providers is managed by the professional third-party institution specialized in healthcare management. To ensure that the productive waqf would generate profits, the nazir will also collaborate with professional third-party institution to manage the productive waqf facility (see Fig. 15.3b).

This healthcare waqf model is highly needed by the poor in Indonesia, since many poor people are not officially registered as mustahiq (zakat recipients) or as social safety net recipients. Meanwhile, the zakat collection in Indonesia is still very low of only Rp10.1 trillion in 2019 (comprises of 60% zakat and 40% infaq and CSR), while newer zakat potentials are predicted to be around 1.74% of GDP or Rp275 trillion in 2019 (Asfarina et al. 2019). This means that the registered mustahiq will not receive sufficient zakat to cover all their basic needs, including health services. Therefore, many zakat-waqf institutions have established this type of social-productive healthcare waqf to serve the poor, including registered mustahiq and unregistered mustahiq.

Integrated Social-Productive Healthcare Waqf-2

The second model of a social-commercial healthcare waqf facility is designed to serve social customers (mauquf 'alaih) for free and to serve general customers commercially, because the products/services provided are exactly the same, i.e., the health services. First, the waqf institution collects land and cash waqf to build healthcare facility. After the contractor finishes the facility, the healthcare facility would be operated to serve the poor and the near poor for free, while simultaneously serve the general public commercially. The returns from productive healthcare waqf would be used to finance social healthcare waqf (see Fig. 15.4a).

Again, when the waqf institution lack funds to finance the operational costs of social healthcare waqf, it could collect zakat and infaq, as registered zakat institution, to finance the social healthcare waqf for the poor. Since the nazir has no competence in healthcare management, the nazir will establish or collaborate with professional third-party institution to manage the healthcare facility (see Fig. 15.4b). When income from commercial health services could not meet the needs to finance social health services, zakat and infaq would cover the difference. Conversely, when commercial health services generate plenty of profits, the profit share of nazir will be used to cover the costs of social health services, and may still have some profits left for the nazir to be used to finance other social programs or to be invested in other social-productive waqf.

This type of social-productive healthcare facility is also in high demand in Indonesia, not only to serve free health services for the poor or mustahiq, but also to serve non-poor general public with more affordable

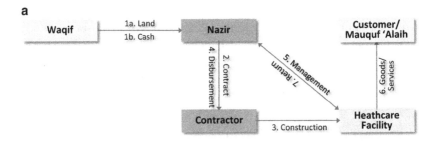

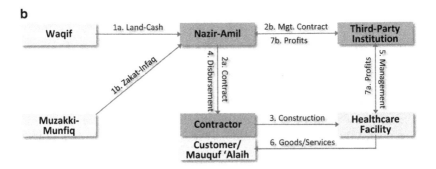

Fig. 15.4 General structure of integrated social-productive healthcare waqf-2 (a) and (b)

quality health services, since the demand of health services for general public has not been met by current healthcare providers.

Models of Healthcare Waqf in Indonesia

Healthcare waqf in Indonesia have been existed since the existence of Islamic organizations, such as Nahdlatul Ulama and Muhammadiyah, long before the independence of Indonesia. Healthcare waqf in Indonesia have adopted various models described in the previous section. Some organizations/institutions focus on establishing social healthcare waqf to help and serve the poor, especially zakat institutions, some focus on establishing productive healthcare waqf to serve general public and their members with affordable quality health services, especially Islamic organizations, while some others focus on establishing social-productive healthcare waqf to serve both, free for the poor and commercial for general public, with quality health services. All of these healthcare waqf would ensure that the Muslims' wealth would circulate among Muslims to improve the socioeconomic conditions of the ummah as a whole and to improve their well-being.

Social Healthcare Waqf

Dompet Dhuafa (DD) Foundation as reputable private zakat-waqf institution in Indonesia distributes its zakat collection to the mustahiq to fulfill their two types of basic needs, namely dharuriyat asasiyat (including clothing, food, shelter, and worship) and hajjiat asasiyat (including education, health, and transportation). To fulfill mustahiq's needs of health services, DD established Layanan Kesehatan Cuma-Cuma—Dompet Dhuafa (LKC-DD) Clinic in 2001. Initially, DD Foundation, through its waqf division Tabung Wakaf Indonesia (TWI), raises waqf (especially cash waqf) to build LKC-DD Clinic in certain location that has been surveyed for its feasibility, which will be built by DD Contractor. The LKC-DD Clinic will open for service, after completion, to serve the poor for free financed by zakat and infaq collected by zakat division of DD Foundation (see Fig. 15.5).

The LKC-DD provides free health services for the poor, including health promotive, preventive, and curative programs. Promotive program is intended to educate the public to care about their own health and the environment, through various campaign approaches to the importance of Healthy Clean Lifestyle (HCL), such as hand washing with soap, movement back to breast feeding, anti-tobacco campaign, reproductive health

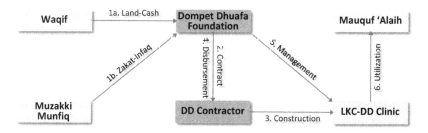

Fig. 15.5 Layanan Kesehatan Cuma-Cuma—Dompet Dhuafa (LKC-DD) Clinic

campaign, and Community-based Total Sanitation (CBTS). Preventive program is intended to prevent a disease by early detection/screening of non-infectious diseases and its first treatment, such as detection of blood sugar, if found diabetes is treated for control, so it does not fall into severe complications, hopefully not until hemodialysis, taught foot exercises, etc. For asthma, the patient would be taught and made group of asthma gymnastics so that the recurrence rate would decrease. For cancer, IVA tests would be performed on beneficiaries as early detection of cervical cancer, etc. Curative program is intended to provide treatment efforts from the first-level health services in the LKC clinic to referral to the referred hospital. For first-level health services, LKCs have been established in 13 locations spread from Aceh to Papua. The first-level health services provided by LKC-DD include: (1) general polyclinic; (2) dental polyclinic; (3) children polyclinic; (4) nutrition polyclinic; (5) laboratory; (6) pharmacy; (7) tuberculosis polyclinic; (8) integrated diabetes mellitus services; (9) lactation polyclinic; (10) emergency unit; and (11) ambulance services.

As time goes by, LKC-DD must deal with poor patients who need further specialist care, inpatient care, and surgery, so that existing service facilities are felt to be inadequate and need to be upgraded to the hospital level. To meet the growing needs of various advanced health services, DD Foundation decided to establish hospital. Once again, DD Foundation, through its waqf division Tabung Wakaf Indonesia (TWI), established social healthcare waqf named as Rumah Sehat Terpadu—Dompet Dhuafa (RST-DD) Hospital.

On behalf of the DD Foundation, TWI-DD collected waqf, including land and cash waqf, and then began to build a hospital building on a waqf area of 7,803 square meters through its subsidiary DD Contractor. Simultaneously, the DD Foundation formed the RST-DD Foundation which is responsible for operating and managing the hospital. RST-DD hospital inaugurated and started a full medical service in July 2012 free for the poor, funded by zakat and infaq funds collected by the zakat division of DD Foundation (see Fig. 15.6).

RST-DD Hospital provides full health services as type C hospital facilitated with a variety of modern health services including hemodialysis machines, 4-dimensional ultrasound, and cataract surgery (Phaco) machines. RST-DD Hospital is also equipped with health services including specialist polyclinic, intensive care unit (ICU), operating room, inpatient, 24-hour pharmacy, 24-Hour ER and MCU.

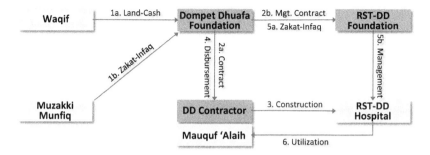

Fig. 15.6 Structure of Rumah Sehat Terpadu—Dompet Dhuafa (RST-DD) Hospital Social Healthcare Waqf, Early Model

Productive Healthcare Waqf

Sultan Agung Islamic Hospital (SA-IH) was initially established in 1971 by Sultan Agung Waqf Foundation (SA-WF) or Yayasan Badan Wakaf Sultan Agung (YBWSA) to provide general polyclinic and children polyclinic for general public, which in 1975 has been officially registered as general hospital and has been upgraded to become type B hospital in 2011 accredited/certified to provide 16 types of medical services. The featured medical services include: (1) lasik center; (2) oncology center; (3) medical rehabilitation center; (4) fertility center; (5) integrated clinic of specialist; (6) ent center; (7) urology center; (8) stoke center; (9) pain center; (10) cardiac center; (11) skin center; (12) eye center; and (13) diabetes mellitus center. SA-IH has also become education hospital for Sultan Agung University Medical School students since 2011. Initially, SA-WF that was established in 1950 affiliated with Muhammadiyah Islamic organization, raised land and cash waqf to establish Sultan Agung Islamic Hospital (SA-IH). Some 2.99 hectares of land located in Kaligawe Road, Semarang, next to the Sultan Agung University complex, were obtained and subsequently the hospital was built on that piece of land by a contractor. SA-WF, then, established SA-IH Management to manage the hospital inaugurated in 1971. The hospital started to provide medical services to general public, started with general polyclinic and children polyclinic to support family planning program. The hospital was expanded to 4.02 hectares to provide more complete medical services for dual purpose to serve general public and to become Islamic teaching hospital for medical students of Sultan Agung University. The profits from

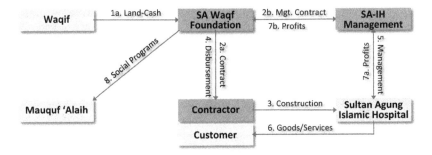

Fig. 15.7 Structure of Sultan Agung Islamic Hospital (SA-IH) productive healthcare waqf

the SA-IH would be used by SA-WF to finance various social programs, as well as to support the hospital development (see Fig. 15.7).

Furthermore, SA-IH has received Islamic Hospital certificate in September 2017, which made SA-IH as the first hospital certified as fully Islamic Hospital, so that it also became Islamic education hospital. There are 51 standard requirements and 173 assessment elements. For example, related to finance in this Islamic Hospital, they must also use Islamic contracts, such as Ijarah, Mudharabah, and Murabahah. The Islamic hospital has to have zakat collection unit (ZCU) that collects zakat and infaq from SA-IH stakeholders, especially medical workers and patients. Islamic hospital should not reject poor patients, and should be provided with medical services needed, while the service fee would become Qardh financing (benevolent loan) that must be paid by the patient later, or it could also be paid by zakat-infaq if the patients are proofed to be mustahiq (zakat recipients).

Integrated Social-Productive Healthcare Waqf-1

Rumah Bersalin Cuma-Cuma (RBC) or Free Maternity Hospital located in Bandung, which is managed by WakafPro99—Sinergi Foundation, is a free healthcare institution for poor mother and children, as is the mother and children hospital (RSIA). The operational costs of RBC are financed by zakat-infaq collected by the Sinergi Foundation (SF) zakat division and the profits of the productive waqf of the Ampera Restaurant, which is a business collaboration with the restaurant entrepreneur.

RBC first operated in October 2004 by renting a house. With land waqf and cash waqf from the community, finally RBC was built since September 2005 and completed in January 2007. RBC was built on 1400 square meters abandoned waqf land managed by the Attazmiyah Foundation, which was then collaborated with SF to build RBC by collecting cash waqf. The cost of building an RBC for the entire area was Rp1.7 billion and medical equipment was Rp. 0.5 billion. Upon the completion, WakafPro99-SF established RBC Management to manage RBC Maternity Hospital providing free medical services for the poor mother and children as Mauquf 'Alaih (benefit recipients) (Fig. 15.8).

During its 14 years in operation, RBC has assisted 8036 births of babies for free and has provided hundreds of thousands of maternal and child health services such as examination of pregnant women, family planning, mother-child health checks, immunizations, ultrasound, pregnancy exercises, RBC greets residents, and others. By 2019, RBC already had 9724 members who could access free medical services of RBC. As time goes on, the need for this RBC hospital to help the poor and underprivileged grows with costs that continue to grow too. Thus, SF has proposed its idea of creating a sustainable source of funding, which would later be a pillar of sustaining RBC medical services for the poor. One of the plans is the establishment of a productive healthcare waqf in the form of Mother and Children Waqf Hospital (RSWIA) that would be managed professionally and commercially, aimed at serving the upper middle-class community.

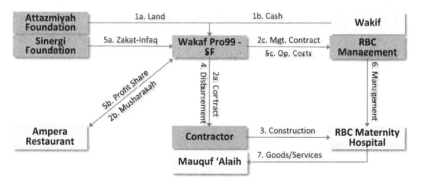

Fig. 15.8 Structure of RBC Maternity Hospital social-productive healthcare waqf

Integrated Social-Productive Healthcare Waqf-2

In January 2014, government health insurance (BPJS) was launched and the government required hospitals to accept patients holding BPJS, so that RST-DD also started accepting BPJS patients and generates income from these patients. Poor patients were then registered as BPJS holders who were paid by the DD Foundation using zakat and infaq collected, and still could receive free health services from RST-DD. This new scheme made RST-DD change from social waqf to integrated social-productive waqf generating waqf income for the RST-DD Foundation. An illustration of the RST-DD work flow can be seen in Fig. 15.9. The RST-DD hospital has become a leading hospital that provides professional and Islamic health services for the community, especially for the poor and needy or disadvantaged.

Every month RST-DD hospital provides health services for approximately 15000 patients, including the poor and general public. The costs of health services have become standardized by the BPJS. This new development in health insurance has made healthcare waqf become more competitive to compete with private hospitals. Therefore, waqf-zakat institutions have flocking to establish integrated social-productive waqf hospital. Another integrated social-productive healthcare waqf is Achmad Wardi Hospital located in Serang, Banten. Starting from an Islamic scholar in Banten, Achmad Wardi, who willed his children to endow a plot of land, which was located on Jl. Raya Taktakan Km. 1, Lontar Baru Sub-District, Serang District, Banten, covering an area of 1420.48 square meters, in order to build a mother and children hospital on it. Then, the land was donated as waqf to the Indonesian Waqf Board (BWI) as nazir.

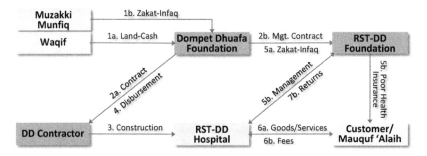

Fig. 15.9 Structure of RST-DD integrated social-productive healthcare waqf

So, BWI then collected cash waqf to build the hospital. After an interval of 7 (seven) years, the hospital construction process has been completed, but the process of becoming a hospital has stalled due to technical obstacles. Finally, BWI cooperated with Dompet Dhuafa waqf division, Tabung Waqf Indonesia (TWI-DD) to continue the hospital process and manage it. In just 2 (two) months, the building has been tidied up and the hospital has been activated as Achmad Wardi Eye Hospital since the beginning of 2018. This is the only eye hospital in Banten province, and the only waqf-based eye hospital that has a two-story building with a building area of 927.5 square meters (see Fig. 15.10).

This hospital equipment is on par with large eye hospitals in general that have "Vitreoretina" and "Cataract Center" services, which are free for the poor and inexpensive for the general public. In fact, for the general public who choose this hospital for eye care, it means that they also donor cash waqf which embedded within the fees/costs they paid. TWI-DD manages this eye hospital similar to the management of RST-DD, where the hospital could receive patients from the general public on a commercial basis (through BPJS health insurance or direct payment) but at a lower cost, while the hospital also welcomes poor or socially disadvantaged patients, free of charge, financed by infaq donors (munfiq) collected by TWI-DD (2c) and by profits of the hospital. The hospital often organizes free mass cataract surgeries for poor people on certain events/occasions, for example on the hospital birthdays and health days.

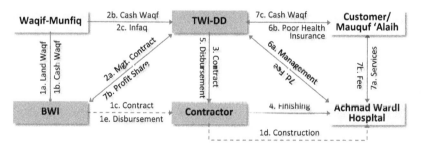

Fig. 15.10 Structure of Achmad Wardi Eye Hospital integrated social-productive healthcare waqf

Healthcare Waqf to Support SDGs

There are 17 goals of Sustainable Development Goals (SDGs). They are: (1) no poverty, (2) zero hunger, (3) good health and well-being, (4) quality education, (5) gender equality, (6) clean water and sanitation, (7) affordable and clean energy, (8) decent work and economic growth, (9) industry, innovation, and infrastructure, (10) reduced inequalities, (11) sustainable cities and communities, (12) responsible consumption and production, (13) climate action, (14) life below water, (15) life on land, (16) peace, justice, and strong institutions, and (17) partnership. There are two goals of SDGs that are directly correlated by this healthcare waqf, namely: good health and well-being, and clean water and sanitation. While other goals have an indirect relationship with healthcare waqf such as reduced inequalities. With this health waqf, the poor do not need to spend their money on health costs, because everything is borne by the waqf funds. As a result, poverty can be reduced, so that in the end, economic inequality can be reduced.

Good Health and Well-Being

In this 3rd SDG goal, there are several targets to be achieved by 2030. Some of these targets are (INFID, n.d.a):

- Reducing the ratio of maternal mortality to less than 70 per 100,000 births.
- Ending preventable deaths in newborns and toddlers, at least being less than 12 per 1000 births and under five deaths as low as 25 per 1000 births.
- End the AIDS epidemic, tuberculosis, malaria and other tropical diseases and fight hepatitis, waterborne diseases and other infectious diseases.
- Reducing one-third of premature deaths caused by non-communicable diseases, through prevention and treatment measures as well as improving mental health and well-being.
- Strengthening the prevention and treatment of abuse of dangerous substances, including narcotics abuse and dangerous use of alcohol.
- Ensuring universal access to sexual and reproductive health services, including for family planning, information, and education, and integrating reproductive health into national strategies and programs.

- Substantially reduce mortality and disease caused by hazardous chemicals and also pollution and contamination of air, water and soil.

To achieve the seven targets above, access to quality basic health services and access to medicines and vaccines that are safe, effective, quality, and affordable for all is needed. This is where the role of health waqf is very significant to help access to health services. For poor people, the expensive medical fees are the reason they don't want to go to the hospital. Even though BPJS already exists, not all BPJS medical expenses are also covered. Therefore, health waqf in all its forms (social waqf, as well as social and productive waqf integration) becomes important. Not only treatment is a concern, prevention is also very necessary. An ounce of prevention is worth a pound of cure. Disease prevention campaigns and healthy living campaigns require huge costs. The cost of this campaign can be taken from the benefits of managing this health waqf. One campaign that requires a lot of money is a campaign to use clean water and sanitation.

Water and Sanitation

The 6th goal of SDG is water and sanitation. The aim is to ensure the availability and management of sustainable clean water and sanitation for all. There are at least 7 targets to be achieved by 2030 (INFID, n.d.b):

- Achieve universal and equitable access to safe and affordable drinking water for all.
- Achieve access to proper and fair sanitation and hygiene for all and end open defecation, paying special attention to the needs of women and girls as well as those in vulnerable situations.
- Improve water quality by reducing pollution, eliminating waste disposal and minimizing the disposal of chemicals and hazardous materials, reducing half of the proportion of untreated wastewater and substantially increasing global recycling and safe reuse.
- Substantially increase the efficient use of water in all sectors and ensure sustainable clean water collection and supply to address water scarcity and substantially reduce the number of people experiencing water scarcity.

322 ASCARYA AND H. TANJUNG

- Implement integrated water source management at every level, including through inter-limited cooperation as appropriate.
- Increasing international cooperation and capacity building support to developing countries in activities and programs related to water and sanitation, including water harvesting, desalination, water efficiency, wastewater treatment, recycling technology and reuse.
- Support and strengthen the participation of local communities in improving water management and sanitation.

To achieve the seven targets, the Indonesian Ulema Council at the 2015 National Deliberation has set a fatwa no. 001/MUNAS-IX/MUI/2015 concerning Utilization of Zakat, Infaq, Alms & Waqf Assets for the Construction of Clean Water and Sanitation Facilities for the Community. This was done because of the limited funds for this health campaign. It is hoped that with the opening of waqf funds for clean water and sanitation facilities, many people will be helped by their health. The National Planning and Development Agency in March 2019 released that IDR 253.8 trillion was needed for equitable access to clean water in Indonesia. This is needed to help 33.4 million people lack clean water and 99.7 million lack access to good sanitation facilities.

The high demand for clean water, especially for consumption, has led the Global Wakaf-ACT to launch the Waqf Water Storage Program, Wednesday, December 18, 2019 (Global Wakaf 2019). The launch of the Waqf Water Reservoir was held at the Waqf Distribution Center, Kec. Singosari, Malang, East Java. Not only global waqf, Baitul Mal Aceh also did the same thing. Many other waqf institutions carry out this water and sanitation program.

The Way Forward

Health from an Islamic perspective is considered very important to be able to achieve the *Maqasid Shari'ah*. The objectives of the *Maqasid Shari'ah* such as safeguarding the faith (*Hifz al-Deen*), safeguarding the intellect (*Hifz al 'Aql*), and safeguarding the lineage (*Hifz al-Nasl*) cannot be achieved without being supported by good health (Khayat 1997). Therefore, health is considered as basic need for Muslim, which could be categorized as *hajjiyat asasiyat* or basic needs that complement the needs of human rights. Meanwhile, the health or medical services are usually provided by not-for-profit or for-profit healthcare provider, such as clinic and hospital, which could be built using waqf as not-for-profit social healthcare waqf, for-profit productive healthcare waqf or integrated social-productive waqf.

In the case of Indonesia, there is a need to increase the number of hospital beds to meet WHO standard ratio of 5 beds per 1000 population, while this ratio in Indonesia has just reached 2.1 beds per 1000 population. In the meantime, the new government health insurance (BPJS) has forced hospitals to be able to provide medical services at BPJS standard costs, which subsequently have forced hospitals to operate efficiently with minimum costs. In addition, based on data of Indonesian Waqf Board (BWI), there are 435.9 million hectares of waqf land waiting to be utilized for social and/or commercial waqf facilities, while the potentials of cash waqf have recorded to reach Rp77 trillion per year. Moreover, based on Charities Aid Foundation (CAF) World Giving Index 2018, Indonesia ranked number 1 (one) in the world as the most generous people.

All of these conditions have opened opportunities for waqf institutions to establish healthcare waqf, including social healthcare waqf, productive healthcare waqf, and/or integrated social-productive healthcare waqf to provide various medical services for all strata of the community, especially the Muslim community. Healthcare waqf possesses unique characteristics providing competitive advantages to compete with conventional healthcare providers, since healthcare waqf does not have shareholder or owner who ask for certain rate of profits, so that healthcare waqf could provide similar medical services with lower costs.

The drawback is that the overall Waqf Literacy Index (ILW) has reached only 50.48, which is considered as low category, consisting of a Basic Waqf Understanding Literacy Index of 57.67 and an Advanced Waqf Understanding Literacy Index of only 37.97 (BWI-BAZNAS-KEMENAG, 2020). Therefore, efforts must be made systematically and harmoniously by all main waqf stakeholders, especially BWI, waqf institutions, National Committee on Islamic Economic and Finance (KNEKS), Shariah Economic Community (MES) and universities, to educate Muslim society on waqf as their part of the Islamic way of live. The emergence of financial technology (fintech) and social media should be utilized optimally to educate Muslim society on waqf, to promote and raise waqf projects of waqf institutions and other social organizations.

REFERENCES

Ascarya, A., Sukmana, R., & Hosen, M. N. (2020). Integrated Social and Productive Awqaf in Indonesia (Chapter 19). In M. M. Billah (Ed.), *Waqf-Led Islamic Social Finance: Innovative Solutions to Modern Applications* (p. 2020). Abingdon-on-Thames, UK: Routledge.

Asfarina, M., Ascarya, A., & Beik, I. S. (2019). Classical and Contemporary Fiqh Approaches to Re-Estimating the Zakat Potential in Indonesia. *Journal of Islamic Monetary Economics and Finance, 5*(2), 387–418.

Bimaristan. (n.d.). Retrieved from https://en.wikipedia.org/wiki/Bimaristan#:~:text=The%20third%20and%20fourth%20Islamic,the%20first%20documen ted%20general%20hospital.

Global Wakaf. (2019). *Global Wakaf-ACT Luncurkan Lumbung Air Wakaf*. Retrieved from https://www.globalwakaf.com/id/berita/read/3314/global-wakaf-act-luncurkan-lumbung-air-wakaf.

INFID. (n.d.a). *Tujuan 03*. Retrieved from https://www.sdg2030indonesia.org/page/11-tujuan-tiga.

INFID. (n.d.b). *Tujuan 06*. Retrieved from https://www.sdg2030indonesia.org/page/14-tujuan-enam.

Khayat, D. M. (1997). *Health: An Islamic Perspective*. Cairo, Egypt: World Health Organization.

Ministry of Finance. (2019). *Potensi Aset Wakaf Rp2.000 Triliun, RI Butuh Database Nasional*. Retrieved from https://www.djkn.kemenkeu.go.id/ber ita_media/baca/12866/Potensi-Aset-Wakaf-Rp2000-Triliun-RI-Butuh-Dat abase-Nasional.html.

Mohsin, M. I. A. (2013). Financing Through Cash-waqf: A Revitalization to Finance Different Needs. *International Journal of Islamic and Middle Eastern Finance and Management, 6*(4), 304–321.

CHAPTER 16

How Islamic Ethical Wealth Manages the Risks That Threaten 'Good Health and Wellbeing' Mission?

T. O. Yusuf and I. A. Oreagba

INTRODUCTION

The current COVID-19 pandemic ravaging the whole world has revealed the fragility of the global health care delivery system. Surprisingly enough, the solution to contain the pandemic has been traced to two advices given by the Last Prophet for mankind as far back as the sixth century. These are quarantine and personal hygiene. More interestingly, the need and call for a holistic approach to health and wellbeing has become vociferous now than before. This has been accentuated by the unavailability of a vaccine to tackle the COVID-19 pandemic. This situation has now forced a shift in focus towards the Islamic alternative. One of the distinguishing features of the Islamic law is its comprehensiveness to address all multifarious issues of various dimensions; be it economic, social or

---

T. O. Yusuf (✉)
University of Lagos, Lagos, Nigeria

I. A. Oreagba
College of Medicine, University of Lagos, Lagos, Nigeria

© The Author(s), under exclusive license to Springer Nature Switzerland AG 2021
M. M. Billah (eds.), *Islamic Wealth and the SDGs*,
https://doi.org/10.1007/978-3-030-65313-2_16

325

political (Adebayo and Kabir 2013). This feature is characterized by what Imam Shatibi regards as the Maqaasid Shariah (objectives of the Shariah). The objectives are divinely set to actualize the (1) preservation of Deen (religion); (2) preservation of nafs (life); (3) preservation of aql (intellect); (4) preservation of posterity (Nasl); and (5) preservation of resources or wealth (Maal) (Ibrahim et al. 2019). The dilemma, today, then is how to adopt the above-stated objectives in addressing the Sustainable Development Goals adopted by the United Nations in 2015 as a new development blueprint that builds on the success of the Millennium Development Goals (MDGs). It was officially launched on 1 January 2016 with the recommendation to member countries to take ownership of the SDGs and establish national frameworks for the achievement of the 17 Goals (United Nations 2018). For want of space, we are skipping the listing of all the goals here.[1] This chapter is solely focussing on the third goal, namely ensuring the availability of health facilities and promoting well-being of the people through Islamic Ethical Wealth. But it stands to reason to firstly examine the state of human wellbeing prior to dwelling on the main thrust of the chapter.

Following this introduction, Sect. 2: "The Present State of Human Wellbeing" sets the stage with the presentation of the current state of human wellbeing. Section 3: "Islamic Ethical Wealth" presents the idea of Islamic Ethical Wealth (IEW); signposting its ethicality while delineating elements that vitiate it. Section 4: "Objectives" deals with the analysis of the objective of the paper while Sect. 5:"Methods and Analysis" discusses the methods adopted and the analysis. Section 6: "Islamic Ethical Wealth and Holistic Health and Wellbeing Model" extensively analyses the proposed model of Islamic Ethical Wealth and holistic health

---

[1] The seventeen (17) SDGs include: (i) eradication of poverty, (ii) ending hunger and malnutrition, (iii) ensuring health facilities and promoting wellbeing of the people, (iv) providing quality education to all and promoting lifelong learning opportunities for all, (v) promoting gender equality and working for empowerment of women, (vi) ensuring pure drinking water and sanitation, (vii) ensuring reliable, affordable modern electricity for all, (viii) ensuring economic growth by creating job opportunities for unemployed people, (ix) promoting industry, innovation and infrastructure, (x) reducing income inequality, (xi) creating safe, resilience and sustainable cities and communities, (xii) ensuring sustainable consumption and production of goods, (xiii) ensuring environmental sustainability, (xiv) protecting life below water, (xv) protecting life above land, (xvi) promoting peace, justice and strong institutions and (xvii) developing global partnership for sustainable development (Mukhtar et al. 2018).

and wellbeing. Section 7: "Conclusion" concludes with implications for policy and practice.

The Present State of Human Wellbeing

Of the 56.9 million deaths worldwide in 2016, more than half (54%) were due to the top 10 causes including ischaemic heart disease, stroke, chronic obstructive pulmonary disease, lower respiratory infections, Alzheimer's disease, trachea, bronchus and lung cancer, diabetes mellitus, lung injury, diarrhoeal diseases and tuberculosis. Ischaemic heart disease and stroke are the world's biggest killers, accounting for a combined 15.2 million deaths in 2016. These diseases have remained the leading causes of death globally in the last 15 years (Global health estimates 2016). Chronic obstructive pulmonary disease claimed 3.0 million lives in 2016, while lung cancer (along with trachea and bronchus cancers) caused 1.7 million deaths.

According to the world health statistics in 2019, it is estimated that about half of the world's 7.3 billion people cannot access essential health services. Even when people can access health care, the cost of paying for it is often catastrophically high. In 2010, over 800 million people spent at least 10% of their household budget on health care; nearly 100 million people fell below the poverty line as a result of their spending on health care.

Women often have limited decision-making power with respect to household resources, and there are critical inequities within households. The global shortage of health workers is also a serious concern. Around 40% of countries have fewer than 10 doctors per 10 000 people. By 2030, the world is estimated to be short of 18 million health workers, mainly in lower-income countries. A WHO document, *World Health Statistics* (2020) provides an annual summary of global trends and reports on the health and health-related Sustainable Development Goals (SDGs) and associated targets. As of 2019, five of the 43 SDG indicators are either not making progress or are in the negative direction. They include road traffic mortality, children overweight, malaria incidence, alcohol consumption and water (WHS 2020). With the foregoing, what can the Islamic Ethical Wealth (IEW) do to stem the tide in the downward trend of the global health care delivery system to achieve the SDG?

Islamic Ethical Wealth

Islamic Ethical Wealth is the wealth sourced and dispensed from lawful ventures that are approved by the Shariah (Islamic law). It is the wealth that does not entail unlawful means bothering on *'eating the resources of others unjustly* (Q4: 29). The objective of this idea is to establish justice and eliminate exploitation in business transactions. This is actualized by the prohibition of all forms of earnings bothering on interest, gambling, hoarding, excessive speculation and uncertainty (El-Melki and Ben Arab 2009).

Meaning of Ethics in Islam

The word 'ethics' and its adjective 'ethical' originated from the Greek word ethos, which means custom and usage (Borhan 1999). Its Latin equivalent 'moral' originated from the word 'more'. The two words are, therefore, sometimes used synonymously for each other (Borhan 1999). A morally right action is deemed to be ethical (Borhan 1999). Ethics, therefore, refers to a systematic attempt, through the use of reason to make sense of our individual and social moral experience, in such a way as to determine the rule that ought to govern human conduct and the value worth pursuing in life (Frankena 1973; Stephen 1882; Borhan 1999). It is a way to measure or assess human conducts with the view to judging their rightness or wrongness using specific standard of judgement known as code of ethics. Islam lays much emphasis on ethical behaviour in society; therefore, it is a code of life. This means that everything done by a Muslim is deemed to be Islamic and thus, ethical. Ethicality in the prism of Islam is divine in origin and nature and thus expected to be Shariah-compliant. The entire life of a Muslim is expected to be ethically inclined in form and substance in a manner that does not infringe on the rights of others. This is particularly stressed in economic transactions.

Ethical Dimension of Muslim Economic Transaction

In Islam, the dichotomy constructed between religion and wealth acquisition in the West does not exist. Wealth acquisition and dispensation are strictly governed by ethical conduct sanctioned in the Shariah. The basis of all legislations is permissibility except in cases where specific prohibitions have been mentioned by the Law-Giver. There are injunctions in the holy Qur'an and the traditions of the Prophet specifically condemning all unethical elements that may portend negative outcomes for parties in the contract of exchange. (Yusuf, 2010) Some of these are briefly mentioned below.

Riba

Riba or interest refers to the interest on loans; its prohibition essentially implies that the fixing in advance of a positive return on a loan as a reward for waiting, which is not permitted in Islam. It could also imply the excess over and above the loan paid in kind. It lies in the payment of an addition by the debtor to the creditor in exchange of commodities of the same kind (Akosile 2017). The Shari'ah wishes to eliminate not merely the exploitation that is intrinsic in the institution of interest, but also that which is inherent in all forms of unjust exchange in business transactions. The rationale for prohibiting interest the Islamic economic framework is to ensure that the risk-reward sharing would be more conductive to the realization of equity and the promotion of entrepreneurship.

Gharar

Gharar or ambiguity refers to a concept that literally means deceit, risk, fraud, uncertainty or hazard that might lead to destruction or loss. It is also hazard or uncertainty surrounding a commodity, its price, time of payment, time of delivery, quantity and so on. In Islam, it refers to any transaction of probable objects whose existence or description is not certain, which could be due to:

- information asymmetry among contracting parties,
- outright lack of information and knowledge of the ultimate outcome of the contract or the nature and quality of the subject matter of it
- However, small amount of gharar can be overlooked, the ones that may be humanly impossible to eliminate it (Akosile 2017).

Maysir

Maysir and Qimar are forms of gambling transactions that are considered totally inequitable in Islam. They are categorically and firmly prohibited in all their forms (Q2: 219) and (Q5: 90–91). Maysir refers to the easy acquisition of wealth by chance, whether or not it deprives the other's right. Qimar means the game of chance in which one gains at the cost of others. However, speculations based on analysis of a lot of economic and financial data and which involve the investment of assets, skills and labour are exempted. Rather, the prohibition is limited to effortless gain similar to a gambling scheme or activity (Akosile 2017).

Haram Items
Haram are things that have been prohibited by Allah and His Prophet (SAW) It also include dealing in all such transactions and properties that are prohibited in Islam. Consequently, trade in narcotics, wine, opium, heroin, cigarettes. dead animals, blood, swine pornography, arms and ammunition, or anything that have harmful and destructive effect to individuals or the society is forbidden (Akosile 2017).

OBJECTIVES

The focus of this chapter, hence, is to articulate how to deploy the Islamic Ethical Wealth to eradicate or at least, mitigate the risk factors that obstruct the attainment of good health and wellbeing of humankind. This being so, we examine the methodological approach.

METHODS AND ANALYSIS

The research is qualitative in nature, using content analysis to lay down the proposed model for Islamic Ethical Wealth (IEW) and the holistic health and wellbeing framework. Archival technique was employed in sourcing the required information from diverse materials, which include Qur'an, Hadith, online resources and scholarly articles on the subject matter. Our thesis is based on the assumptions that when Islamic Ethical Wealth is deployed to finance all the five dimensions of a human being and while avoiding the inimical risk factors, this results in a holistic health and wellbeing which ultimately results in the Maqaasid Shariah (objectives of the Allah-the Law-Giver). This is further depicted in the equation below (Fig. 16.1):

$$IEW + FDH - RF = HHW = MS$$

where IEW: Islamic Ethical Wealth
FDH: five dimensions of a human being—physical, biochemical, intellectual, emotional and spiritual bodies.

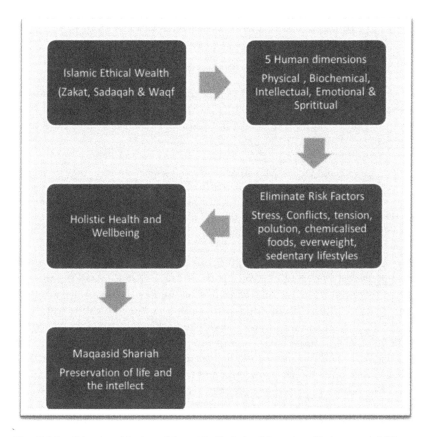

Fig. 16.1 Islamic ethical wealth and holistic health and wellbeing model (*Source* Authors)

RF: risk factors that are inimical or threats to the health and wellbeing of the five dimensions of human being mentioned above.
HHW: holistic health and wellbeing
MS: Maqaasid Shariah (Objectives of the Islamic Law)

ISLAMIC ETHICAL WEALTH AND HOLISTIC HEALTH AND WELLBEING MODEL

Islamic Ethical Wealth

The Islamic Ethical Wealth (IEW) is the most appropriate means of achieving holistic health and wellbeing (HHW) through conscious effort of funding all the requirements of a holistic approach to total health and wellness:

> Allah commands: O you who have believed, spend from the good things which you have earned and from that which We have produced for you from the earth. And do not aim toward the defective therefrom, spending [from that] while you would not take it [yourself] except with closed eyes. And know that Allah is Free of need and Praiseworthy. (Q2: 267)

The IEW is the resource sought from lawful sources and dispensed through lawful endeavours. Among these are Zakat (Charity), Sadaqah (Non-Obligatory charity) and Waqf (Endowments). These are wealth that meet certain criteria mentioned earlier to pass the ethicality test. For instance, Zakat must be paid from lawful and ethical investments or acquisition. The wealth must have been in the payer's possession for one lunar calendar year. And the amount deductible is the net of all earnings for that period which is 2.5%. The motive behind this obligation is clearly spelt out in the holy Qur'an '...so that it (wealth) may not circulate solely between the wealthy among you (Q59: 7). Sadaqah or non-obligatory charity has a more liberal status in the hands of the payer. The payer decides what, how, what, when, where to pay it. Waqf is more impactful though not obligatory as well. Individuals can endow their tangible and intangible properties for humanitarian and charitable purposes. The endowed properties are entrusted with credible trustees who manage it through lawful investment outlets with returns channelled towards charitable causes such as health, education, capacity building and rehabilitation (AAOIFI).

The socio-economic values of IEW have been utilized immensely for poverty eradication projects (Abdul Rahman 2015). The various financing modes in Islamic finance share risk-sharing elements that augur well for economic transformation of the economically active poor. Modes such as Qardul Hasan (interest-free loan), Murabahah (Mark-up) and Ijaarah (Equipment leasing) have great potentials for micro-entrepreneurs and the poor. Other participatory schemes such as Mudarabah (profit sharing) and Musharakah (equity) are veritable tools for middle-level entrepreneurs to ascend the prosperity ladder.

IEW offers the greatest potentials to health and wellbeing projects. The agricultural supply chain requires stupendous investment. This is the purview of Salam as a financing mode. Salam is the 'sale of a prescribed commodity for delivered delivery in exchange for immediate payment of the price' (AAOIFI-Shariah Standard No 10). Such capital can be invested in organic farming for the production of healthy crops that are not grown with pesticides and insecticides (Table 16.1).

Five Human Dimensions

The Islamic approach to health and wellbeing, unlike the conventional approach, is holistic by viewing man as a combination of five 'bodies (Ayad 2013). These are the physical, biochemical, intellectual, emotional and spiritual.

The Physical Body
The physical body consists of the muscle and bone structures in addition to other different functional systems and organs such as the heart, lungs and the digestive system. There are preventive and curative antidotes in the holy Qur'an and the traditions of the holy Prophet (S.A.W.). These are supposed to be followed to have a balanced, healthy physical body.

Biochemical Body
The biochemical body includes food and nutrition habits as well as the environmental conditions in which these are taken. All the two above—food and nutrition and the environment—are the two antidotes to enhance health and wellbeing in the biochemical body.

Intellectual Body
No religion expresses importance of learning for humankind as does Islam. This accounts for why the first revealed verse to the holy Prophet is 'Read'.

> Read: In the Name of your Lord who created. Created man from a clot. Read: And your Lord is the Most Generous. He who taught by the pen. Taught man what he never knew. (Q96: 1–5)

334 T. O. YUSUF AND I. A. OREAGBA

Table 16.1 Proposed Islamic ethical wealth deployment for holistic health and wellbeing

S/N Project	Focus	Objectives	Islamic Wealth Type (Funding)
1. Education	Education Establishment of specialized educational institutions addressing each of the human dimensions, i.e. educational institute on human intellectual development	Training of Muslim medical doctors, nurses and paramedical personnel	Zakat, Sadaqah, Waqf, Islamic Development Bank (IDB)
2. Health Institutions	Health Lack of Muslim hospitals and medical personnel; religious discrimination in employment and education of Muslim	Building of state-of-the-art hospitals across the geopolitical zones; training of more Muslim medical personnel;	Sadaqah, Awqaaf and Islamic Crowdfunding, IDB funds
3 Science and Technology	Science and Technology Little or lack of many Muslims who are skilled; little interest of Muslims in the area	Establishing of Universities or Colleges of Science and Technology across the Muslim world specializing on research development	Ju'alah, IDB Funds
4 Mass media	Few or absence of Muslim-owned global television, Radio and Newspapers; Misrepresentation of Islam and Muslims	Establishing Muslim-owned and controlled media and infrastructures to propagate HHW	Sadaqah, Awqaaf, Musharakah (Equity; Partnership)

(continued)

Table 16.1 (continued)

S/N Project	Focus	Objectives	Islamic Wealth Type (Funding)
5. The holy Quran Project	To eradicate lack of knowledge of the message of the Qur'an among the populace about holistic health and wellbeing in the holy Qur'an	Printing and translation of the Holy Qur'an into major international languages as well as its free distribution	Awqaaf (Endowments—Assets and Cash)
6. Agriculture Project	The establishment of organic farming in various continents of the world	Organic cultivation of the soil, animal husbandry, fishing in an environmental friendly manner	Salam, Musaqat (Irrigated partnership, Ju'alah
7. Pharmaceuticals	To establish pharmaceuticals that specialize in organic medicine or natural herbs and prophetic medicine	This includes training the personnel and supporting all the infrastructure that would make holistic approach realizable	Concession contracts, Mudarabah and Musharakah

Source Authors

The intellect is one of the greatest gifts of Allah to mankind. Its best nourishments are learning and meditation which stretches its elasticity. Man requires intellectual development to appreciate the wonders of creation in order to draw close to Allah. The food for intellectual wellbeing is numerous; cutting across different branches of knowledge. The most sublime of them all is the memorization and meditation of the holy Qur'an. Experts have observed a positive correlation between food nourishments and brain wellbeing. They have suggested switching to whole grains and cereals, eating the right kind of fats and protein as well as other micronutrients.

Emotional Body

The impact of mental and emotional stresses on the body tissues and secretions is amazing. The same can be said of destructive emotions like fear, resentment, worry, envy, boastfulness and egotism. How we deal with crisis, stress and problematic events have considerable impact not only on our psychology and emotions but also on the physical body and immune system (Ayad 2013, p. 259).

Spiritual Body

It is inconceivable to achieve holistic health and wellbeing (HHW) without a positive and strong connection with Almighty Allah, the sole creator of the universe. This is a universal belief in the nature of that One and Only Creator. Another source of concern is the obliviousness surrounding the nourishments of the soul in the modern time. Among some of the spiritual antidotes are Salat (Prayer), night prayer, pilgrimage, meditation and remembrance of Allah, fasting, Zakat, supplication and recitation of the holy Qur'an to mention the major few.

Elimination of Risk Factors

Traditional Reasons

Muslims are often lacking in knowledge concerning the relationship between food, nutrition, lifestyle, and health. Many of our physical problems stem from following the traditional methods of preparing and eating our foods. Altered tradition has most certainly played its part by changing the food from the manner in which Allah intended it to be consumed. (Q4: 119) Poisons are added to our food while it is being grown. Poisons are added to our foods during processing. Poisons are also added to our drinking water. Most of the nutrients in milk are destroyed during processing. During processing, flour not only has the nutrients removed, but then it is bleached and has artificial nutrients added.

During the deluge of the time of Prophet Nuh (A. S.), Allah destroyed most of His creation because man had changed things from the way He intended them to be. The Devil threatens:

> "And I will mislead them, and I will entice them, and I will prompt them to slit the ears of cattle, and I will prompt them to alter the creation of Allah." Whoever takes Satan as a lord, instead of Allah, has surely suffered a profound loss. (Q4: 119)

Drugs Dominance

We live in a drug-oriented society; even our water and food are drugged! We take drugs to cure the physical problems often brought on by the taking of devitalized, processed and drugged substances into our bodies. A drug, says Webster's dictionary, is a 'substance other than food intended to affect the structure or function of the body'.

The Qur'an warns us against the use of all drugs and the deception of drugs.

> O you who believe! Intoxicants, gambling, idolatry, and divination are abominations of Satan's doing. Avoid them, so that you may prosper. 91 Satan wants to provoke strife and hatred among you through intoxicants and gambling, and to prevent you from the remembrance of Allah, and from prayer. Will you not desist? (Q5: 90)

All drugs are poisons to our bodies (Hippocrates, c. 375 BCE). We cannot be drugged or poisoned into health! Health comes only when the body is provided with the proper materials to cleanse the poisons from the systems and rebuild new, living, strong, vital, vibrant cells. Allah made a body that is self-healing and will heal itself when given the opportunity!

Other Drugs

Tobacco, a narcotic drug, contains some 16 different poisons that coat the lungs and keep them from functioning properly and slowly kills the user and those around him. Coffee contains the drug caffeine, which can cause a multitude of physical problems. Tea, cola, soft drinks and chocolate all contain the drug caffeine, and all are extremely harmful to the body. Sugar, in the form of sucrose, is a drug that is very addictive and creates many of our physical and emotional and even social problems. Salt is a deadly poisonous drug and possibly the greatest killer of mankind (Colbert 2004) Fortunately, even after the body starts to break down, the body will usually respond and rebuild the damaged cells when we cooperate with it, stop abusing it, start cleansing it, and then properly feed our body, Allah's temple.

Sedentary Lifestyle

Allah made man to be physically active (18: 18). Man's primary physical activity was to be received through the labour necessary to grow his own food supply. Until recent years, most people raised their own food supply.

Convenience foods and the easy availability of food for purchase have dramatically reduced the amount of exercise the average person receives and has produced correspondingly increased physical problems (Malkmus, 2005).

Without daily, moderate exercise, tissue cells lose their elasticity. Without daily, moderate exercise, lymph cannot move adequately to cleanse and feed body cells. Without daily, moderate exercise, muscles atrophy ('decrease in size or waste away'—Webster).

Insufficient daily, vigorous exercise is one of the leading causes of why Muslims get sick (Malkmus, 2005).

Stress and Negative Emotions

Many Muslims experience emotional problems. There are only two kinds of emotions—positive and negative. Positive emotions contribute to happiness and health. Negative emotions produce unhappiness and physical problems. Physical problems contribute greatly to negative emotions. Drugs cause, rather than relieve, negative emotions.

Improving one's physical health through diet and vigorous exercise will lead to more positive emotion. Negative input can also produce negative emotions. We become what we program into our computer/brain.

> And the retribution for an evil act is an evil one like it, but whoever pardons and makes reconciliation - his reward is [due] from Allah. Indeed, He does not like wrongdoers. (Q42: 40)

The Quranic message is a positive message. The world needs to see a positive Muslim. Muslims ought to be the healthiest and happiest people on the face of the earth.

The Violations of Allah's Natural Laws

When Allah made man, He established natural laws to govern His creation. Allah's creation was perfect and His natural laws were designed to perpetuate that perfection.

> The Compassionate. Has taught the Quran. He created man. And taught him clear expression. The sun and the moon move according to plan. And the stars and the trees prostrate themselves. And the sky, He raised; and He set up the balance. So do not transgress in the balance. But maintain the weights with justice, and do not violate the balance.

Natural laws are impersonal. They apply equally to everyone, Muslim or non-Muslim. Sickness and disease are not natural but are the body's efforts to cleanse and heal itself after natural laws have been violated.

Holistic Health and Wellbeing: The Islamic Perspective

The core message of Prophetic medicine is the integration of spiritual with physical for the wellbeing of a person wholly. As Ibn Al Qayyim eloquently explains, 'Whenever the soul and the heart become stronger [spiritually], they will cooperate to defeat the illness' (Abd El-Qader 2003, p. 17).

Classification of Prophetic Medicine

Prophetic medicine has been described as advice by the Prophet (saw) to His followers with an objective to maintain health and wellbeing for their body and soul equally. The Prophet (saw) possessed a profound understanding of the connection between the human faculties, the body and soul, and the connection of those faculties with their Creator, Allah. Hence, the Prophet (ﷺ) embraced a wide definition of medicine, namely being therapy for one's body and soul, and not merely prescriptions which address one's illness alone. Al-Suyuti (born 849AH) divides Prophetic medicine into three classes:

(i) **Preventative Prophetic medicine**—The Prophet's (saw) teachings on moderation in food, exercise, toilet hygiene, personal hygiene, marriage and sexual relations, etiquette of drinking, quarantine for contagious diseases, specific herbal remedies to maintain explicit aspects of one's health (e.g. better hair), etc. All these teachings act as preventative measures with an overall objective of preserving one's wellbeing.

(ii) **Curative Prophetic medicine**—These include remedies which were prescribed by the Prophet (saw) with an objective to treat one's illness such as honey, olive oil, the black seed, milk as well as surgical treatments such as cupping and cauterization. Such remedies were prescribed for fever, bowel movements, headache, skin rashes, tonsillitis, heart disease, food poisoning, conjunctivitis, tumours, leprosy, fracture, dog bite, etc.

(iii) **Spiritual Prophetic medicine**—The teachings of the Prophet (saw) demonstrate that in conjunction with the treatment and recovery from an illness, the spiritual aspect of one's wellbeing must also be considered, as confirmed in the following verse,

> We send down in the Qur'an that which is a healing and a mercy to those who believe. (Q17: 82)

Whether one cultivates their spirituality through prayer, supplication, recitation of the Qur'an or remembrance of Allah, one's progression or regression of illness can essentially be affected by one's inner state.

It is thus important to note from the above classification that: Prophetic medicine possesses two unique features. On the one hand, Prophetic medicine provides numerous remedies as prescribed by the Prophet (saw), and on the other hand, it serves as a *system* which coalesces one's inner (spiritual) and outer (physical) wellbeing when treating an illness. Accordingly, the scope of Prophetic medicine is significantly broadened when considered beyond the remedies prescribed, and instead, appreciated in its entirety as a thorough system which provides a 'holistic approach' to medicine, addressing the complete person physically, spiritually and socially in the management and prevention of an ailment.

In his renowned book '*The Prophetic Medicine*', Ibn Qayyim describes Prophetic medicine as having 'a divine element to it' (Abd El-Qader 2003, p. 15), whereby the Prophet (saw) would provide remedies which concurrently address one's physical and spiritual wellbeing.

While Prophetic medicine offers limited remedies for specific illnesses, it nevertheless embraces a unique system in that it combines one's spiritual and physical wellbeing, thereby promoting a holistic approach to medicine. Accordingly, the scope of Prophetic medicine is largely broadened when considered as a comprehensive system rather than purely perceived as a catalogue for remedies. Contemporary physicians and organizations in the medical field are gradually acknowledging and adopting this holistic approach since there is a demand for the need to focus on the complete person in order to attain a superior level of wellness. Therefore, one may conclude by validly stating that this holistic approach in medicine, a system essentially established over fourteen hundred years ago by the Prophet (saw), has indisputably had implications on modern day medicine.

Then, to sustain this beautiful creation of Allah, there is the dire need to deploy ethical funds and resources approved by Islamic laws in abundant proportion. As widely known in Islamic parlance, *Allah is pure and He would not accept except that which is pure.*

Islamic Ethical Wealth is a means of actualizing all other essentials of life. To preserve religion, ethical wealth is needed to construct religion's institutions and infrastructures as well as remunerate the personnel. The preservation of the intellect cannot be sustained in isolation of financial resources to facilitate the necessary tools and mechanisms to sustain human intellectualism. Monetary resources are equally required to build the sustainable foundation for the continuity of life for the unborn generations. A solid economic foundation is non-negotiable for a viable economy that delivers prosperity and wellbeing of the populace.

Maqaasid Shariah (Objectives of the Islamic Law)

The realization of holistic health and wellbeing (HHW) is the desire of the Almighty for humankind. This is enunciated in several verses of the holy Qur'an. For instance He (S.W.T.) Mentions:

> Allah desires ease for you, and does not desire hardship for you…. (Q2: 186)

Allah is not capable of any harm against His creatures. Even when Ibrahim (A.S.) was eulogizing Allah, he never attributed his ailment to the Almighty:

> He who created me, and guides me. He who feeds me, and waters me. And when I get sick, He heals me. He who makes me die, and then revives me. (Q26: 78–81)

Prophet Ibrahim (A.S.) never attributed his sickness to Allah. He only hoped in His healing. This suggests that sickness only arises when man violates divine laws set by Allah. Divine laws are not to meant to create hardships or suffering in the life of man. He (S.W.T.) explains:

> We sent Our messengers with the clear proofs, and We sent down with them the Book and the Balance, that humanity may uphold justice. And We sent down iron, in which is violent force, and benefits for humanity.

That Allah may know who supports Him and His messengers invisibly. Allah is Strong and Powerful. (Q57: 25)

CONCLUSION

The chapter is devoted to proposing how Islamic Ethical Wealth (IEW) can be deployed to finance the SDG's goal on good health and well-being mission. Specifically, it is about proposing a framework/model for strategically and technically supporting good health and wellbeing for humankind through the Islamic Ethical Wealth. IEW meet divine principles and are therefore Shariah-compliant. A cursory look at the current targets set for the actualization of the SDG on good health and wellbeing suggests gross inadequacy when compared with the holistic approach of Islam presented above. The targets, to say the least, are barely addressing only about two bodies of the five dimensions identified by the Islamic holistic approach. The targets do not address the spiritual, intellectual and the emotional bodies of man. In addition, risk factors that threaten good health and wellbeing must be avoided. Hence, we propose a more holistic approach with suggested ethical funding type. Islamic Ethical Wealth (IEW) cannot be utilized to fund and finance projects that are inimical to the Maqaasid Sharia. Hence, a much more holistic approached is proposed through which IEW can be deployed.

IMPLICATIONS FOR PRACTICE AND POLICY

The implication of our proposal suggests both micro- and macro-approaches for implementation to achieve the maqaasid shariah. The micro-tier relates to retail and wholesale financing undertaken by Islamic financial institutions. The macro-tier belongs to the purview of the legislative and regulatory authorities. There are some of the projects that can be undertaken by IFIs such as the manufacturing and pharmaceuticals. For the macro-tier aspect, the need for governments' involvement is non-negotiable. In fact inter-government collaboration cannot be overlooked to begin with, in the areas of holistic health curriculum development. As time goes on, a global approach from the international levels of Organisation of Islamic Countries (OIC) would emerge to seize the initiative.

References

Abdul El-Qader, A. (2003). *Ibn al-Qayyim, The Prophetic Medicine; (Al-Tibb al-Nabawⁱ)*. Dār al-Ghadd al-Jadeed, al-Mansūrā, Egypt.

Abdul Rahman, A. R. (2015). *Islamic Microfinance: An Ethical Alternative to Poverty Alleviation*. Being Paper Presented at ECER Regional Conference 2008, UiTM Kelantan.

Adebayo, R. I., & Kabir, H. M. (2013). Ethical Principles of Islamic Financial Institutions. *Journal of Economic Cooperation and Development, 34*(1), 63–90. Viewed 15 June 2020. Available from: https://d1wqtxts1xzle7.cloudfront.net/60209190/149.

Akosile, T. (2017). *Islamic Finance History & Communication Skills (Gra 102) Lecture Slides*. Lagos: Institute of Islamic Finance Professionals (IIFP).

Ayad, A. (2013). *Healing Body and Soul*. Riyadh: International Islamic Publishing House.

Borhan, J. T. B. (1999). The Ethical Principles in Islam Commercial Transactions. *Journal Usuluddin, 9*, 97–112.

Colbert, D. (2004). *What You Don't Know May Be Killing You!*. Florida: Siloam A Strang Company.

El Melki, A., & Ben Arab, M. (2009). Ethical Investment and the Social Responsibilities of the Islamic Banks. *International Business Research, 2*(2). Viewed on 16 June 2020. Available from: http://citeseerx.ist.psu.edu/viewdoc/download?doi=10.1.1.1016.8071&rep=rep1&type=pdf.

Frankena, W. K. (1973). *Ethics* (2nd ed.). Englewood Cliffs, NJ: Prentice-Hall.

Ibrahim, A. H., Rahman, N. N. A., Saifuddeen, S. M., & Baharuddin, M. (2019). Maqasid al-Shariah Based Islamic Bioethics: A Comprehensive Approach. *Journal of Bioethical Inquiry, 16*(3), 333–345.

Malkmus, G. H. (2005). *Why Christians Get Sick*. Lagos: Lase Books.

Mukhtar, S., Zainol, Z. A., & Jusoh, S. (2018). Islamic Law and Sustainable Development Goals. *Tazkia Islamic Finance and Business Review, 12*(1), 81–99.

Stephen, L. (1882). *The Science of Ethics*. New York: Putnam's Sons.

World Health Organisation. (2020). *World Health Statistics 2019: Monitoring Health for the SDGs, Sustainable Development Goals* Viewed 18 June 2020. Available from: https://apps.who.int/iris/handle/10665/324835.

Yusuf, J. B. (2010). Ethical Implications of Sales Promotion in Ghana: Islamic Perspective. *Journal of Islamic Marketing, 1*(3), 220–230.

CHAPTER 17

The Role of Waqf in the Youth Empowerment to Attain the Quality Education in Kano for Sustainable Development Goals

Gwadabe Nura Abubakar and Asmak Ab Rahman

INTRODUCTION

Quality education tends to be more important for youth's earning ability, human development, and poverty alleviations (Murnane et al. 2001; Hanushek and Woessman 2008). Nigeria's economic and human development is tied with the countries' quality education development. The advancements in commerce, information technology, communication, science and technology have the direct relation to educational development of a state. Education signifies the knowledge, attitude, expertise, and skills possessed by human being. Qualitative education is defined as "A key element in improving a firm assets and employees in order to increase

G. N. Abubakar (✉)
Department of Islamic Studies, Yusuf Maitama Sule University Kano, Kano, Nigeria

A. A. Rahman
Department of Shariah and Economics, Academy of Islamic Studies, University of Malaya, Kuala Lumpur, Malaysia

© The Author(s), under exclusive license to Springer Nature Switzerland AG 2021
M. M. Billah (eds.), *Islamic Wealth and the SDGs*,
https://doi.org/10.1007/978-3-030-65313-2_17

345

productivity as well as to sustain competitive advantage" (Marimuthu et al. 2009).

The agitation for the inclusion and sustainable development was intensified since early twenty-first century. The nature of development differs from developed, developing, and underdeveloped nations; each of them has their own perspective of how nation is developed. But the main goal of sustainable development remains the same globally. Chapra (2008) argues that "There seems to be hardly any difference of opinion among all societies around the world that the primary purpose of development is to promote human well-being."

2017–2012 UNESCO's Report indicated that about 246 million school-aged youth and children are out of schools. Therefore, to actualize the United Nations Sustainable Developments agenda on education, the acquisition of qualitative education is paramount, that is to ensure all the youth are empowered with the qualitative education and this will promote the lifelong opportunities to the youth. Empowerment of the youth is a situation whereby youngsters were urged to assume responsibility of their lives. They do this by tending to their circumstance and afterward make a move with a specific end goal to improve their access to incomes and modify their knowledge via their beliefs, abilities, and mind-sets (Kar 1999). Educational empowerment helps in growing a person's intellectual ability, prosperity, and empowerment potentials. Education was considered as the absolute and most significant instrument of sociopolitical and economic change. Without legitimate training to all kids including young ladies, empowerments will not be feasible.

Awqaf institutions have played a vital role to the development of education in various Muslim communities to ensure that the youth acquired a qualitative education for all and at affordable rate. The institutions of Waqf have recorded in the History a tremendous success in the dissemination of knowledge and intellectual development of the people (Abattouy and Al-Hassani 2013). Sound and quality education develops human capital and increase the productivity of the youth toward building a better and peaceful society. Awqaf institutions have been proved to be reliable institution, for the attainment of quality education in the past, and can be used in the present day to achieve the desired need of human capital knowledge, skill, and abilities (Khan 2015).

The Concept of Waqf

Waqf emanated in the Arabic term "waqafa" that signifies to keep, grasp, or confine. Waqf refers to restricting or forbidden the movement, exchange or transporting something (Ahmad MD and Safiullah 2012). Waqf as an Arabic verb literally means to stop (al-sukun), to prevent (al-mana'a), and to suppress (al-ḥabs) (Ḥasān Ayyūb 1998). Technically, waqf means detainment of a particular thing by the proprietor or training that all the advantages derive should be given as a charity for the benefit of the less privilege once, for the sake of Allah and with intentions of getting rewards from Him. Kahf defines waqf as "holding a Maal (an asset) and preventing its consumption for the purpose of repeatedly extracting its usufruct for the benefit of an objective representing righteousness or philanthropy" (Khaf 1999). Lahsasna defines the waqf as conferment of assets, mobile or fixed form the originator (waqif) to the enthusiasm of its usufruct in permanence for the well-being of society. He further laments that the common idea of waqf is built on the above. Although the idea of cash waqf was designed for the welbeing of the people and to enhance the economic growth of the society (Lahsasna 2010).

Although there are variant definitions of terms, the essential legitimate significance of waqf is concurred all through the Muslim world as the devotion of a property for religious philanthropy and for the benefits of the society (Mahamood 2006). A divergent view of these interpretations of the meaning of these key economic-related concepts in Islam was not an issue of concern, provided they do not contradict or go against the instructions from the Qur'an and Hadith (Haneef et al. 2011).

Kinds of Waqf

There are three kinds of waqf which will be explained as follows:

i. Religious Waqf. These are kinds of awqaf which are endowed to provide religious needs of the people and help in reducing the direct cost and expenses of religious services to the people. Most of the Mosques and madarasa were managed and funded by these religious awqaf (Salarzehi et al. 2010).
ii. Philanthropic Waqf. This is a kind of waqf which endures purposely to cater for the societal needs and reduce the suffering of the people. These awqaf provides the basic needs to the poor and

less privileged in the society such as establishing schools, libraries, financing research, scholarships, health care services, educational services, entrepreneur development, and many more. An example of this act is the case of Umar who ask the Prophet regarding His farmland located at Kyabar, thus the Prophet advise him and said: "Give it in charity (i.e. as an endowment) with its land and trees on the condition that the land and trees will neither be sold nor given as a present, nor bequeathed, but the fruits are to be spent in charity" (Al-Bukhari).

iii. Family Waqf: Family waqf is a kind of waqf where property of cash endowed as waqf for the benefit of the family members. This kind of waqf gives a wealthy individual member of the family to dedicate some assets or property as waqf for their family members, some purchases a house, shop lots, and the rent acquired should be used to finance a specific need of the family. This kind of waqf was in practice during the time of the companions of the Prophet, Jabir bin Abdullah said when the Caliph Umar wanted to document his waqf land at Khaibar he invited the Sahaba, and when the news reached them every real estate owner made such waqf.

The Concept of Sustainable Development

Sustainable development can be defined as the development that fulfills the desire needs of the present day without conceding the needs of the next coming generation (Brundtland). Sustainable development has to do with what can be termed as essential items or commodities that are needed by human beings for their day-to-day survival and advancement such as quality education.

SDGs as described by the United Nation are: "The Sustainable Development Goals (SDGs), otherwise known as the Global Goals, are a universal call to action to end poverty, protect the planet and ensure that all people enjoy peace and prosperity. These 17 Goals build on the successes of the Millennium Development Goals, while including new areas such as climate change, economic inequality, innovation, sustainable consumption, peace and justice, among other priorities. The goals are interconnected – often the key to success on one will involve tackling issues more commonly associated with another" (UNDP Report). Sustainability Studies has become attractive area of study, as sustainable development is a necessity and uncompromised for the present and future generations in the socio-ecconomic, enviromental and other aspects of human endevour. The report has predicted the sustainable development as uncompromising needs of present and future generations' economic, social, and environmental aspects of life (Brundtland 1987). The concept of sustainable development can be interpreted in many ways, but at its core is an approach to development that looks to balance different, and often competing, needs against an awareness of the environmental, social, and economic limitations we face as a society. "Sustainable Development that meets the needs of the present, without compromising the ability of future generations to meet their own needs."

Quality Education for Sustainable Development

Education for Sustainable Development (ESD) is largely synonymous with quality education but requires far-reaching changes to the way education functions in modern society. How to structure and implement quality education for sustainable development is a key challenge. Another challenge is that systematically assessing the effectiveness of learning performance from ESD practices remains elusive, especially how effective learning performance contributes to sustainability.

Education for Sustainability (EfS) is an educational approach that aims to develop students, schools and communities with the values and the motivation to take action for sustainability—in their personal lives, within their community and also at a global scale, now and in the future. Quality education for sustainable development, which has been described by UNESCO, 2014. Education for Sustainable Development gives the youth opportunity to acquire the knowledge, expertise, skills, ability, attitudes, and moral values needed for the sustainable future. Education is one of the significant factors of development; the people's ability and productivity depends on their level of education; education helps in promoting technological advancement, social and economic growth, and entrepreneurial development toward improving the income generation.

Quality education is an avenue to give the youth the needed knowledge and skills that will enable them to understand and manage the social, economic, and environmental challenges that may occur in future. Youth need to get the proper understanding and to know how human can live in his environment. "*A quality education has the power to transform societies in a single generation, provide children with the protection they need from the hazards of poverty, labour exploitation and disease, and give them the knowledge, skills, and confidence to reach their full potential,"* said Audrey Hepburn, the iconic American.

Waqf as a Mechanism for Sustainable Development

Awqaf institutions have been a streamline for the SDGs in its aim of aid provisions. SDGs were aimed at assisting and funding the development programs in order to create a balancing paradigm of funding (Sachs 2012). It was argued that the success of the SDGs depends on the philanthropic, private, and public sector contributions and active involvement. The role of philanthropic (Waqf institutions) was indispensable in achieving the sustainable development goals (UNSDSN 2012). The SDGs agenda offers a potential role for the management of waqf institutions to demonstrate the roles of awqaf to the various communities by contextualizing the approach and orientation of waqf to achieve the required development goals. This can be actualized by adopting the different models of waqf-based development in line with the SDGs.

The role of waqf has been instrumental in developing societies in the past, and potentially it can be a catalyst in resolving the menace of underdevelopment in the contemporary times (Singer 2008; Yalawae and Tahir 2008; Sadeq 2002; Cizakca 1998). Waqf institutions in the history have recorded giant strides in the provision of social welfare and societal development, and it is a better means to be used to develop the society through philanthropic services (Hassan 2015). Waqf has the potentials and has the requisite needed for the philanthropic institutions, therefore, it can serve as a mechnism for youth empowerment to attain quality education for sustainable development (Shirazi 2014).

The Importance of Education in Islam

Islam has given much emphasis on the development of human capital in terms of knowledge and skills acquisitions. Islam has made seeking of knowledge obligation upon every Muslim be it male or female; the comprehensive understanding of Islam would not be achieved without proper knowledge. Islam has contributed to the human capital development through the instruction and obligation of knowledge acquisition by the people. As mentioned by the International Islamic Jurisprudence Academy (2007) "that development of human being to establish the comprehensive development in Islamic understanding will not be fulfilled except the means of education, teaching and training." Various Qur'anic texts and the Prophetic traditions have reiterated the importance of knowledge acquisition. Allah says in the Qur'an: "Allah will increase the status of the people who believe in Him and acquire knowledge. He said: (Allah will rise up, to (suitable) ranks (and degrees), those of you who believe and who have been granted (mystic) knowledge. and Allah is well-acquainted with all ye do.)" Q58:11.

Similar Qur'anic verse emphasis on the importance of knowledge to mankind, thus Allah said:

Allah questioned that the knowledgeable persons and the ignorant cannot be the same. He said: Say: *"Are those equal, those who know and those who do not know? It is those who are endued with understanding that receive admonition."* Q 39:9 the Messenger of Allah (PBUH) expresses the virtues of Knowledge, He said: *"Whoever seeks a path in search of knowledge, Allah would make easy for him a path leading to paradise."* (Al-Tirmidhi 1980, no. 2570)

THE ROLE OF MUSLIM COMMUNITIES TO THE ATTAINMENT OF QUALITY EDUCATION FOR SUSTAINABLE DEVELOPMENT

Societal development cannot be attainable with only government efforts; therefore, it's a duty and responsibility of the society to support government endeavors in order to achieve the desired goals of sustainable development; wealthy individuals waqf institutions and organization have to support their communities with the basic needs and organize appropriate means for sustaining them.

The Muslim Ummah especially the wealthy people have a great contributions to upper for the attainment of quality education in their localities, and it's a duty of individuals, institutions, and organizations to contribute to the development of human capital to ensure every child get access to quality education and required skills for sustainable development goals. In line with the above, the Hadith of the prophet emphasized that: "Muslim should teach his neighbour and a Muslim should learn knowledge from his neighbour so that knowledge spread out in the society. It is also mentioned in this Hadith that one should advise his neighbour for good work and prohibit him from bad work."

Methodology

Qualitative research method was adopted where two methods of data collections were used, primary data collection which includes literature review from documented articles, books and secondary data that comprise the semi-structured interview questions.

The data collection was done through semi-structured face-to-face interview which allows pragmatic approach toward the exploration of the subject matter, allowing the participants ability and subjectivity to query the emerging themes (Corbin and Morse 2003). The duration of the interview ranges from 30 min to one hour, with the strict adherence to interview guides. The questions proved the participants knowledge and experience in the waqf administration, educational development, and Youth Empowerment. Interview was conducted in English language and transcribe verbatim. The interview respondents comprise the expert scholars in waqf and Islamic finances, philanthropist, and officials of Kano Zakat and Waqf Commission. The respondents are coded here as P1, P2 up to P17.

The Role of Waqf in Attaining Quality Education in Kano

Awqaf institutions have been proved to be reliable institution, for the attainment of high level of human capital in education and healthcare services in the past, and can be used in the present day to achieve the desired need of human capital knowledge, skill, and abilities (Khan 2015). Sound and quality education develops human capital and increases the productivity of the youth toward building a better and peaceful society.

The institutions of waqf have helped in establishing schools, libraries, hostels, research centers, teachers' residential quarters, and many more just to encourage and facilitate better teaching and learning in the different Muslim areas. Also, with the support of waqf funds many scholars translate or wrote books and conduct a scientific research for the benefit of the society (Mannan 2005).

Studies found that waqf funds have be utilized mostly in three areas which include social and human development, education, and healthcare services. It was asserted that due to the importance attached to the education in Islam many awqaf organizations give much emphasis to education. Al Azhar University in Egypt was among the educational institutions that was established and maintained with the waqf resources. Madarasah, educational centers were established and financed by the waqf funds (Ahmad and Hassan 2015).

Steps for Achieving Quality Education in Kano

There are four steps as designed by sustainable development agenda that will aid the achievements of quality education, whereas waqf institutions have the potential roles and capability of actualizing these steps; the steps are as follows:

1. Establishing Effective Learning Environment

For the better effective teaching and learning environment, waqf institutions in Kano have provided various infrastructural and material supports in various communities which include:

Waqf-Based Primary and Secondary Schools in Kano

There are many primary and secondary schools established in Kano and administered by various awqaf institutions, these schools have been the places for knowledge acquisition to many youth in the state which includes orphans, less privileged, and other peoples in various communities. Qualitative teaching and learning are taking place in these schools and at affordable fees. One of the interview participants reiterated that:

> There are several waqf- based primary and secondary schools in the city of kano, which gives the Education to the youth and children in various communities as well as providing job opportunities to the youth as teachers and other supporting staff of the schools. Among the famous waqf based schools in kano are Darul- Hadith Foundations (Primary and Secondary schools), Alfur'qan, Alu Avenue Schools, Da'awah group of Schools, Markaz Usman Bu Affan, Gadon Kaya Kano and numerous awqaf schools in the city. (PT13)

The establishment of waqf-based primary and secondary schools at various communities has helped in the enrolment and attendance of many pupils in the schools, as most of the parents cannot afford to send their child to privately owned schools due to the fees charged and the government-owned schools cannot accommodate the large number of applicants. In this regard, an interview respondent maintains that:

High number of youth dropout of schools and engage in hawking, petty trading and some engage in one crime or the other because of their parent's inability to cater for their schools' expenses. But with the Waqf based schools, youth can be empowered educationally, can go back to schools and study with a little fee, certainly these schools helped the youth in accessing quality education at their doorsteps.

Waqf-Based Higher institutions of learning in Kano

There are few higher institutions of learning which operate under any waqf institutions, the institutions provide various post-secondary educations in different disciplines, and the data gathered from the interview show that;

> Da'awah institute of Islamic Education established a waqf based Higher institution of learning, whereas, Youth can obtain the Diploma certificate and NCE in the various fields of studies, the institutions operate part time programs which will give the opportunity to many people to study at their convenient times. (PT2)
>
> Annur Institute of Islamic Education, Hausawa, Kano Was Waqf based institution which offers programs for the award of certificates for Diploma and Teaching Certificates in related Arabic and Islamic Studies disciplines, the institutions are giving the opportunities to the Youth who are unable to study earlier due to one reason or the other, with this Waqf initiative, many Youth can get the quality education and subsequently contributed to the nations development. (PT4)

Waqf-Based Students Accommodations

Accommodations are very essential in the quest for quality education. Students that are coming from rural areas and far places to the Kano city in the quest for knowledge are finding it difficult to get shelter in the city, and this has become a long-time challenge to the desiring students. In the absence of students' accommodations or hostels, it is difficult for a student to have the conducive atmosphere of accessing the quality education. In the interview conducted, the researcher gathered that:

> There are sixty (60) housing units built as a waqf in Kano by Khalifah Ishaq Rabiu for the use of the memorizers of the Holy Qur'an and a hostel for the students who came from far places in the quest for learning Qur'an at kofar Waika Querters in the Kano metropolis. (PT11)

Dangote was said to have acquired land to build a 500 students capacity Hostels for the students of the Kano State University of Science and Technology, Wudil.

2. Improving Quality of Teaching

Kano state was blessed with many wealthy individuals who are willing to spend their wealth as sadaqatul jariya especially in the educational development. Many wealthy individuals have contributed in the educational sector in order to achieve the desired goals of quality education for sustainable development. The respondents of the study interview assert that:

> In his gesture to improve the quality of education and produce qualified human resource in kano state, Kano based philanthropist, Alhaji Aliko Dangote has rented the services of 15 qualified and renown foreign professors in the fields of science and technology to give their contributions in the state own University of science and technology Wudil, he promise to take care of their salaries and other expenses for 8 year starting from 2018
>
> Aliko Dangote donated a N1.2 billion ultra-modern business school edifices to the Bayero University, Kano, (BUK), first of such in the northern part of the country. the new structure comprises 650 seating capacity auditorium, two theaters, four lecture halls, two libraries, incubation center, two cafeterias, 800kva soundproof generator and borehole among others.
>
> Alhaji Aminu Dantata Kano based philanthropist has contributed immensely to the development of education in the state in various capacities, he has donated ₦50 million, 10 blocks of toilets and 5 boreholes to Girls Secondary School, Dala in order to enhance girl child education in the state.

3. Inspiring Transformative learning

There are high numbers of philanthropists who dedicated part of their wealth in assisting the less privileged youth who secure admission into any higher institutions and they could not afford tuitions fees or any other school expenses. Among them are Alhaji Kabiru Sani Kwangila, Alhaji Auwalu Rano, and many more.

The data obtained from the interview revealed that:

Some wealthy individuals in Kano established foundations, and these foundations allocate some of its resources in providing educational assistance such as building classrooms, libraries and giving scholarship and financial assistance to the deserving students studying in any Nigerian higher institutions. The notable among these foundations are Dangote Foundation and A.A. Rano Foundations. (PT.8)

In kano state, there are many people that has established family awqaf in their various families, these awqaf give financial assistance to their immediate family members especially the youth that want to further their studies in the higher institutions of learning. Some of this wealthy people buy a bus and set it for commercial purpose, and the profit generated will be used to finance their close family in their educational pursuit. (PT.4)

CONCLUSION

The importance of waqf institutions in a Muslims community particularly in Kano state will not be over emphasis. Waqf institutions have played a vital role in the socioeconomic well-being of different communities in the Islamic history, and it has provided the basic services to the societies at no cost from the governments. The waqf institutions in the state have provided various educational empowerment for the attainment of quality education among the citizens, which includes schools establishments, infrastructures, scholarships, accommodations, and other financial assistance. Therefore, the waqf institutions must be established in the state in order to take care of the societal needs of Youth Empowerment for peace to reign in the state. There are a lot of societal problems ranging from unemployment, drug addicts, school dropout, hawking, prostitutions, among others; all these accord as a result of negligence from the part of the government and wealthy individuals to provide the empowerment programs for the teeming youth in the state in the areas of education and vocational skills.

REFERENCES

Abattouy, M., & Al-Hassani, S. T. (2013). *The Role of Awqāf in Developing Islamic Civilisation: Definition, History, Functions and Articulations with Society. Article Contributed by the Foundation for Science*. Chicago.

Ahmad, M., & Hassan, Y. B. (2015). Funding the Sub-Saharan African Education Sector with Waqf: Experiences from Al-Azhar University and Selected Universities in Malaysia. *Journal of Creatuve Writing| ISSN 2410–6259, 1*(02), 40–54.

Ahmad, M. M., & Safiullah, M. (2012). Management of Waqf Estates in Bangladesh: Towards a Sustainable Policy Formulation. *Waqf Laws and Management*(with special reference to Malaysia). 229–262.

Brundtland Report. (1987). *Sustainable Development.* https://www.iisd.org. Accessed 18 May 2020.

Chapra, M. U. (2008). *The Islamic Vision of Development in the Light of maqasid al-shariah* (Occasional Paper). London: The International Institute of Islamic Thought.

Cizakca, M. (1998). Awqaf in History and its Implications for Modern Islamic Economies. *Islamic Economic Studies, 6*(1).

Corbin, J., & Morse, J. M. (2003). The Unstructured Interactive Interview: Issues of Reciprocity and Risks when Dealing with Sensitive Topics. *Qualitative Inquiry, 9*, 335–354.

Haneef, R., Kunhibava, S., & Smolo, E. (2011). Musharakah Mutanaqisah and Legal Issues: Case Study of Malaysia. *ISRA International Journal of Islamic Finance, 3*(1), 91–122.

Hanushek, E. A., & Woessmann, L. (2008). The Role of Cognitive Skills in Economic Development. *Journal of Economic Literature, 46*(3), 607–668.

Ḥasān Ayyūb (1998). Fiqh al-Muʿāmalaāh al-Mālīyahfī al-Islāmī, c.1, j. 2, Lubnān: Bayrūt Page 9, 611.

Hassan, S. (2015). *Philanthropy and Human Security: Islamic Perspectives and Muslim Majority Countries Practices.* New York, NY: Springer.

Kahf, M. (1999). Towards the Revival of Awqaf: A Few Fiqhi Issues to Reconsider, available at http://monzer.kahf.com/papers/english/FIQHI_ISSUES_FOR_REVIVAL_OF_waqf.pdf.

Kar, P. (1999). Chickering, & Medicine.

Khan, T. (2015). Introduction. In H. A. El-Karanshawy, A. Omar, T. Khan, S. Ali, H. Izhar, W. Tariq, K. Ginena, & B. Quradaghi (Eds.), *Access to Finance and Human Development-Essays on Zakah, Awqaf and Micro Finance.* Doha: Bloomsbury Qatar Foundation.

Lahsasna, A. (2010). The Role of Cash Waqf in Financing Micro and Medium Sized Enterprises (MMEs). In *Seventh International Conference-The Tawhidi Epistemology: Zakat and Waqf Economy* (pp. 97–118).

Mahamood, S. M. (2006). *Waqf in Malaysia: Legal and Administrative Perspectives.* University of Malaya Press.

Mannan, M. A. (2005). The Role of Waqf in Improving the Ummah Welfare. In *Presentation at the International Seminar on Islamic Economics as Solution, organised by Indonesian Association of Islamic Economists and Muamalat Institute, Jakarta Medan, Indonesia* (pp. 18–19).

Marimuthu, M., Arokiasamy, L., & Ismail, M. (2009). *Human Capital Development and its Impact on firm Performance: Evidence from Developmental Economics.*

Murnane, R. J., Willett, J. B., Braatz, M. J., & Duhaldeborde, Y. (2001). Do Different Dimensions of Male High School Students' Skills Predict Labor Market Success a Decade Later? Evidence from the NLSY. *Economics of Education Review, 20*(4), 311–320.

Sadeq, A. M. (2002). Waqf, Perpetual Charity and Poverty Alleviation. *International Journal of Social Economics.*

Sachs, J. D. (2012). *From Millennium Development Goals to Sustainable Development Goals.* Available at: www.thelancet.com/journals/a/article/PIIS0140-6736%2812%2960685-0/fulltext.

Salarzehi, H., Armesh, H., & Nikbin, D. (2010). Waqf as a Social Entrepreneurship Model in Islam. *International Journal of Business and Management, 5*(7), 179.

Singer, A. (2008). *Charity in Islamic Societies.* Cambridge: Cambridge University Press.

Shirazi, N. S. (2014). Integrating Zakat and Waqf into the Poverty Reduction Strategy of the IDB Member Countries. *Islamic Economic Studies, 22*(1), 79–108.

Sustainable Development Goals, United Nation Development Programme. https://www.undp.org. Accessed 8 May 2020.

UNSDSN. (2012). *A Framework for Sustainable Development.* Available at: http://unsdsn.org/wpcontent/uploads/2014/02/121220-Draft-Framework-of-Sustainable-Development1.pdf.

Yalawae, A. and Tahir, I. M. (2008, September 10–13). *The Role of Islamic Institution in Achieving Equality and Human Development: Waqf or Endowment.* Paper Presented at the 5th Annual Conference of the HDCA, New Delhi.

CHAPTER 18

How Islamic Ethical Wealth May Strategically and Technically Support "Reduced Inequality" Mission?

Irfan Syauqi Beik, Mohd Hasbi Zaenal, and Abdul Aziz Yahya Saoqi

INTRODUCTION

Inequality in economic and social aspects is a severe problem faced by various governments in various countries. The condition makes developing countries facing hardships economic to transform them into developed countries. According to the data from the World Bank, the average inequality ratio in the world reaches 0.38, which indicates that there are 38 out of 100 people who have low or below average income or wealth averagely (World Bank 2018). This fact also strengthens by the study, which found that one percent of the adult population on earth presently

---

I. S. Beik (✉)
Department of Islamic Economics, Bogor Agricultural University (IPB), Bogor, Indonesia
e-mail: irfan_beik@apps.ipb.ac.id

M. H. Zaenal · A. A. Y. Saoqi
BAZNAS Center of Strategic Studies, Jakarta, Indonesia

© The Author(s), under exclusive license to Springer Nature
Switzerland AG 2021
M. M. Billah (eds.), *Islamic Wealth and the SDGs*,
https://doi.org/10.1007/978-3-030-65313-2_18

359

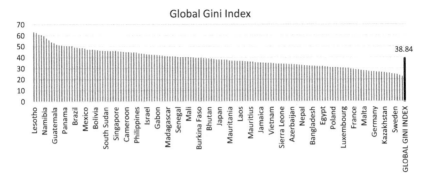

Fig. 18.1 The latest global Gini index (*Source* World Bank [2018])

occupies over 44% of household wealth (Credit Suisse Research Institute 2019) (Fig. 18.1).

However, to overcome inequalities in various aspects requires cooperation from multi-stakeholders; this is because inequality is a multi-dimensional problem caused by various factors. Hence, governments in various countries have tried and cooperated in anticipating this by issuing relevant policies to counter inequality issues together. In 2015, members of the countries of the United Nations had agreed to formulate a global blueprint called the Sustainable Development Goals (SDGs), which consist of 17 goals. Generally, the purpose of the formation of SDGs is to end poverty and its derivatives, but also hand-to-hand it can improve the level of health, education, economic growth, and the preservation of nature by the end of 2030 (United Nations 2015). However, the forming of the SDGs seems to be a proper action if stakeholders could not identify the main problems of inequality. Hence, they need to detect the causes of inequality. According to the World Bank, in general, at least four factors cause inequality facing every developing country, namely inequality of opportunities, labor market inequality, inequality in a resilient capacity toward economic shock, and inequality of wealth accumulation (World Bank 2015). Hence, any policies addressed to overcome the inequality problems should make these points as primary references (Fig. 18.2).

On the other hand, scholars argue that the lack of ethics implementation in managing the economy or wealth will raise inequality (Simpson 2009). The term ethical wealth is defined as implementing norms,

Fig. 18.2 The factors of inequality (*Source* World Bank [2015])

morals, and ethics in dealing with economic activities, including wealth management (Donaldson 2001). Presently, the economic system which persistently promotes the implementation of norms and justice in the theoretical and practical aspect is the Islamic economy (Kuran 1989). The five primary goals of Islamic law or known as *Maqasid al-Shariah*, which consist of safeguarding the religion, the life, the intellectuality, family, and wealth, are the main framework in establishing the Islamic economic system nowadays (Lahsasna 2009). In the context of the inequality discussion, the fifth goal in Maqashid al-Shariah seems to be more relevant to discuss and elaborate on how the concept of safeguarding wealth contributes to declining inequality. Hence, the paper aims to investigate how the Islamic ethical wealth in the management perspective may technically and strategically contribute to eradicating social and economic inequality (Fig. 18.3).

The Concept of Islamic Wealth Management

The existence of safeguarding wealth in *Maqasid al-Shariah* indicates that discussion of wealth management is one of the essential topics in the Islamic perspective because, in Islam, basically, private property, including wealth, is a temporary and the real owner is God. Hence, the utilization of

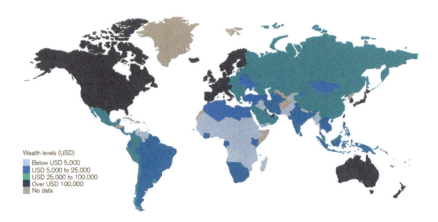

Fig. 18.3 World wealth map 2019 (*Source* Credit Suisse Research Institute [2019])

property will be asked its accountability hereafter; thus, the management of wealth must be appropriately done following the principles of *Maqasid al-Shariah* (Lokanathan 2018). Nevertheless, in the context of modern finance as it is today, many scholars have been widely discussing the implementation of Islamic law in wealth management. Thus, this chapter will elaborate further regarding the definition and concept of Islamic wealth management, the current practice of Islamic wealth management, and the concept of wealth distribution in the Islamic perspective.

Definition and Concept

Wealth management is known as the management of wealth based on financial and non-financial advisory to achieve particular objectives of wealth by utilizing relevant instruments. Nonetheless, Islamic wealth management is defined as the wealth administration driven by the principle of *Maqasid al-Shariah* (Five Islamic Goals Objective) in every circle of wealth management (Suryamukti 2016). Thus, the activity in wealth management should not contradict with Islamic principles. In the process of wealth management, both conventional and Islamic have different processes. In the conventional system, the process of managing wealth consists of four aspects, namely wealth accumulation, wealth protection, turning wealth to income, and transferring wealth (Brown). Conversely, Islamic wealth management has unique and different characteristics in the process of wealth management compared to the counterpart. Islamic wealth management has five wealth management processes: wealth creation, wealth protection, wealth accumulation, wealth purification, and wealth distribution (Shafii et al. 2013) (Fig. 18.4).

A. **Wealth Creation**

The stage of wealth creation is one of the crucial phases in Islamic wealth management. A Muslim must ensure that the property is *halal* (lawful) according to Islamic law both from its essence and from how to obtain it. From the aspect of wealth essence, a Muslim must assure that

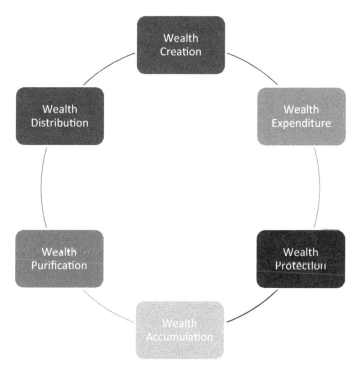

Fig. 18.4 The Islamic wealth management process (*Source* Shafii et al. [2013])

the wealth does not contain any *haram* (unlawful) elements as determined by Islamic law. Moreover, from the aspect of how to obtain it, a Muslim must also safeguard that in the process of wealth creation or income should avoid any practices of usury, wild speculation, and gambling in wealth creation because those kinds of practices will reduce productivity (Iqbal and Wilson 2005).

B. Wealth Expenditure

Wealth expenditure is a process of wealth spending both on consumptive and productive purposes. From the Islamic perspective, the activity of wealth spending should concentrate on three essential aspects: halal and good, moderation, and balance (Amanda et al. 2018). Thus, the wealth spending activities should allocate only on halal and good things permissible by Islamic law. Moreover, the way of wealth spending also should conduct in a moderate and balanced approach.

C. Wealth Protection

The protection of wealth is one of the essential aspects of Islam. The issue is included in *Maqashid al-Shariah's* goals, which encourages every Muslim to preserve their wealth as what Anas bin Malik narrated that a man said: "O Messenger of Allah! Shall I tie it and rely (upon Allah), or leave it loose and rely(upon Allah)?" He said: "Tie it and rely (upon Allah)" (Al-Asqalani 1971). The hadith explicitly explained that we are responsible for assuring our property from any harmful things.

D. Wealth Accumulation

Wealth accumulation is a process of income accumulation by utilizing relevant financial instruments. Shariah law legitimates the process which aims to preserve the wealth for long-time purposes as long as the activity does not contravene with shariah laws. The Holy Quran and Hadith encourage the activity so that we do not leave the generation in poor condition as Allah the almighty said in the Holy Quran "..And let every soul look to what it has put forth for tomorrow.." (The Holy Qur'an, 59:18) and "And let those (guardians) fear as if they had left weak offspring behind and feared for them" (The Holy Qur'an, 04:09). The two verses of the Holy Quran gave a legal judgment for the Muslim for having long-term preparation in many aspects, including in the financial aspect.

E. Wealth Purification

The wealth purification phase is a process of purifying wealth by re-allocating the wealth by giving it to people in need. The concept of wealth purification is not owned by conventional wealth management (Suryamukti 2016), so this is the difference between Islamic wealth management and conventional. The mechanism of wealth purification in Islamic wealth management is carried out by paying Zakat 2.5% of the assets or wealth obtained and distribute it into eight groups that have been determined by Shariah.

F. Wealth Distribution

Wealth distribution is the process of asset distribution through a particular mechanism. The Islam strongly encourages the concept of wealth distribution in aiming to circulate the wealth among the community and economy, as the Qur'an states, "..So that it will not be a perpetual distribution among the rich from among you.." (The Holy Qur'an, 59:08). The concept of wealth distribution in Islam is unique and different from the conventional distribution concept. In Islam, there are two general types of assets distribution instruments, namely mandatory instruments and voluntary instruments (Fadilla 2016). The mandatory instrument consists of Zakat, kafarat, and fidyah, while the voluntary part is including sadaqah, infaq (alms), and Waqf (endowment) (Suryamukti 2016).

The Role of Islamic Wealth Management In Reducing Inequality

The spirit in Islamic wealth management is *Maqashid al-Shari'ah's* values, which has five main objectives which are safeguarding of faith, life, intellectuality, offspring, and wealth. The objectives of *Maqashid al-Shari'ah* have similar purposes that are providing benefits and eliminate damages. Hence, every Islamic wealth management process must be based on the principle of benefits and eliminate damages, including economic and social inequality (Fig. 18.5).

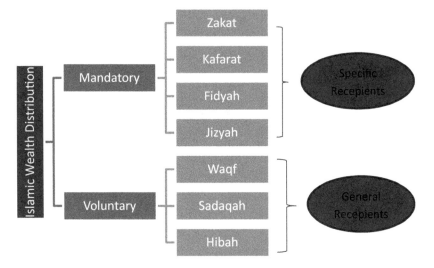

Fig. 18.5 The instruments of wealth distribution in Islam (*Source* Author's Document)

Furthermore, in the six processes of Islamic wealth management, there is one aspect that is crucial and has a very significant role in reducing the economic and social inequality of society, namely the process of wealth distribution. In its character, the Islamic wealth distribution has two main characteristics, namely mandatory and voluntary distribution of wealth.

In terms of mandatory wealth distribution, four instruments must be carried out by a Muslim with a specific time, amount, given to certain groups that have been determined in sharia law. The instrument consists of Zakat, *Kafarah* (expiation), *Fidyah*, and *Jizyah*. Furthermore, the voluntary instrument consists of Waqf, Infaq, Alms, and Grants. Unlike the mandatory instrument, the voluntary instruments do not have any specific provisions regarding the amount of charity issued or the group characteristics recipient that receives charity from this instrument. Eventually, the objective of wealth distribution in Islam is beyond its counterpart. Unlike conventional, Islamic wealth management has a specific system and instrument for redistributing wealth (Ariff and Mohammad 2017). The mandatory and voluntary system in Islamic wealth distribution strives to boost circulating wealth simultaneously, which reduces economic and social inequality consistently. Thus, it can claim that strategically the

Islamic wealth management system could reduce economic and social problems, notably inequality matters.

The Role of Zakat and Waqf in Inequality Elimination

Introduction

Zakat, Waqf, and other religious charities have great concern from the Islamic point of view. These instruments are part of worship for Muslims, but beyond that, the instruments have a significant impact on economic and social activities. The Zakat and Waqf are purposively designed to become economic stabilizers from unfairness and instability. This chapter elaborates further conceptually and technically the role of Zakat and Waqf in reducing inequality among the communities.

The Role of Zakat in Eliminating Inequality

Inequality is the extreme disparity of the income distribution with a high concentration of income, usually in the hands of a small part of the population. When inequality occurs, there is a large gap between one segment of the population and other segments. Zakat is a kind of compulsory transfer. In short, it acts as a transfer mechanism that enables the rich to help the needy and poor in society, thus paving the way to an efficient, fair, and equitable distribution of resources. It is also considered a kind of welfare assistance. Zakat distribution will be carried out to reduce inequality in income distribution and loss of community welfare. In other words, zakat distribution is hypothesized to contribute to increasing income distribution and social welfare positively (Ariff and Mohammad 2017). Zakat-distribution projects in areas such as economic empowerment, education, medical care, social welfare, and emergency need response will increase the productivity of the poor by meeting the basic needs of life. The income of the poor is expected to increase as a result of their higher productivity. Some evidences show that Zakat can reduce inequality and other effects in improving people's welfare. Mannan et al. (1989) observe the role of Zakat on increasing living standards, income levels, and wealth disparities through the multiplier effect of Zakat.

368   I. S. BEIK ET AL.

Jehle (1994) observed the impact of Zakat on income inequality in Pakistan. The results show that Zakat does reduce income inequality in Pakistan. Ayuniyyah et al. (2018) present a case study of 1,309 zakat recipients managed by The National Board of Zakat (BAZNAS) in various cities and districts. The result is the distribution of Zakat in poverty alleviation and reduction of income inequality between groups in urban and rural areas in Indonesia and has proven successful. Ibrahim (2006) shows that based on the positive measurement of the Lorenz curve and the Gini coefficient, the distribution of Zakat in Malaysia has increased the income distribution, reducing income inequality as well as the loss of social welfare decreases along with the distribution of Zakat in society.

The Role of Waqf in Eliminating Inequality

In the terminology aspect, Waqf originated from the Arabic language, namely *wa-qa-fa* means to stop, stay, still, or hold (Isfandiar 2008). From the Islamic law point of view, the definition of Waqf is an asset that is voluntarily given to hold the wealth of the property and preserve the benefits for social purposes (Isfandiar 2008). Furthermore, the hadith narrated by Ibn Umar about the endowments of Umar over the land of Khaibar is as follows:

> Umar said: O Messenger of Allah, I have gained a part of the land in Khaibar, I have never acquired such a good wealth, so what did you order me to do? The Prophet said: if you like, you hold (the main) land, and you give (the benefit of the land). Then Umar performed Waqf, it was not sold, was not granted, and was not inherited. Ibn Umar said: Umar offered it to the needy, relatives, slaves, who in the way of Allah, ibn sabil and guests. Moreover, he is allowing for those who control the waqf land to eat from the benefit and good result correctly with no intention to accumulate the wealth. (Al-Asqalani 1971)

The hadith delivers a broad explanation of Waqf both from the terminology aspect and from the practical aspect. In the terminology aspect, the hadith explained that Waqf is an asset that retains the asset physically and takes out the benefits for public purposes. On the side of practical aspects, the hadith also explained the requirements of Waqf, such as the availability of Waqf donator (Waqif), Waqf manager (Nadzir), the asset and initiates to endow the Waqf asset. If those requirements have been fulfilled, the waqf transaction is valid under Islamic law. In the modern context, generally, the Waqf asset consist of two crucial part, the social asset and the commercial asset. The social asset is addressing benefits directly to the beneficiaries and societies such as Mosques, free schools, and free hospital, whereas a commercial asset is a form of Waqf asset which circulates the asset into commercial things such as hotel, hospital, commercial buildings, agriculture land, and so on, which is aiming to result in a sustained profit; hence, the beneficiaries will gain the benefit in the long term.

Speaking on poverty and inequality, there are many empirical shreds of evidence of the implementation of the Waqf instrument, which successfully reduced the poverty rate and inequality among communities. Corporate Waqf has become the best example of how Waqf contributed significantly to declining the rate of inequality. The corporatization of Waqf Asset is an effort to manage waqf assets professionally by involving the asset manager to boost the profit from the asset; hence, the asset of Waqf can provide benefits with a large amount and broad coverage of the beneficiaries. Figure 18.6 explains the flow of how Waqf corporate works from the beginning of Waqf donation, the process of Waqf corporate by involving asset manager to maximize the asset profit appropriately and then give the benefit of the Waqf asset to beneficiaries or societies who are in need (Fig. 18.7).

Eventually, the discussion has briefly explained that Waqf, as a part of the instrument of Islamic wealth, has a significant role in reducing poverty and inequality in various ways. In the modern era, the concept of Waqf corporate has been implemented widely due to the greater benefits gained from the Waqf Asset to the beneficiaries, which also allows Waqf asset to contribute significantly to reducing poverty and inequality among the communities.

Fig. 18.6 Division of Waqf asset (*Source* Author's Document)

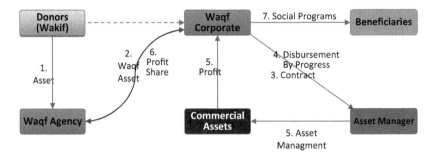

Fig. 18.7 The model of corporatization of Waqf asset (*Source* Author's Document)

Conclusion and Recommendation

Economic and social inequality is a classic problem that is facing every modern country nowadays. The study found that in 2019 1% of the world's population controls nearly 50% of world wealth. It shows that inequality is still a real problem. Scholars argue that inequality reflects the lack of implementation of ethics and morals in the economy. Besides, the current conventional economic system does not have clear structures and instruments to reduce inequality. The Islamic ethical wealth system, which is based on moral and ethical values in the *Maqasid al-Shari'ah* (the five Islamic objectives), has an applicative solution that can reduce inequality through the concept of Islamic wealth distribution. Mandatory and voluntary instruments, particularly Zakat and Waqf, are the most suitable and powerful instruments which strategically and technically may reduce inequality. Moreover, some relevant studies have demonstrated that Zakat and Waqf have a significant impact on declining poverty and inequalities. Eventually, this article recommends to the relevant stakeholders to explore the issue and utilizing these capable instruments to reshape the related-policies in order to attain the goal of the community welfare and make life better.

References

Al-Asqalani, I. I. (1971). *Attainment of the Objective in Conformity with Evidence of the Legal Judgments*. Beirut: Dar al-Kotab al-Ilmiyah.

Amanda, F., Possumah, B. T., & Firdaus, A. (2018). Consumerism in Personal Finance: An Islamic Wealth Management Approach. *Journal of Islamic Economics, X*(2), 325–340.

Ariff, M., & Mohammad, S. (2017). *Islamic Wealth Management: Theory and Practice*. Northampton: Edward Elgar Publishing.

Ayuniyyah, Q., Pramanik, A. H., Saad, N. M., & Ariffin, M. I. (2018). Zakat for Poverty Alleviation and Income Inequality Reduction. *Journal of Islamic Monetary Economics and Finance, 4*(1), 85–100.

Brown, R. F. (n.d.). *The Wealth Management Process*. Retrieved July 17, 2020, from https://us.rbcwealthmanagement.com/robertf.brown/the-wealth-management-process.

Credit Suisse Research Institute. (2019). *GLobal Wealth Report 2019*. Bern: Credit Suisse.

Donaldson, T. (2001). Te Ethical Wealth of Nations. *Journal of Business Ethics, 31*(1), 25–36.

Fadilla, Z. N. (2016). The System and Mechanism of Wealth Distribution in Islamic Perspective. *Iqtishodia Journal, I, 2*, 45–56.

Ibrahim. (2006). *Economic Role of zakat in Reducing Poverty and income Inequality*. Sri Kembangan: Universiti Putra Malaysia.

Iqbal, M., & Wilson, R. (2005). *Islamic Perspectives on Wealth Creation* (1st ed.). Edinburgh: Edinburgh University Press.

Isfandiar, A. A. (2008). Tinjauan Fiqh Muamalat dan Hukum Nasional tentang Wakaf di Indonesia. *La Riba Islamic Economics Journal, II*(1), 51–73.

Jehle. (1994). Zakat and Inequality: Some Evidence From Pakistan. *Review of Income and Wealth, 40*(2), 205–216.

Kuran, T. (1989). On the Notion of Economic Justice in Contemporary Islamic Thought. *International Journal of Middle East Studies, 21*(2), 171–191.

Lahsasna, A. (2009). *Maqasid al-Shariah in Islamic Economics and Finance*. Kuala Lumpur: National University of Malaysia.

Lokanathan, V. (2018). *A History of Economic Thought* (10th ed.). New Delhi: S. Chand Publishing.

Mannan, M. A., Imtiazi, I. A., Niaz, M. A., & Deria, A. H. (1989). *Management of Zakat in Modern Muslim Society*. Jeddah; Islamic Research and Training Institute, IDB.

Shafii, Z., Yusoff, Z., & Noh, S. M. (2013). *Islamic Financial Planning and Wealth Management*. Kuala Lumpur: IBFIM.

Simpson, B. P. (2009). Wealth and Income Inequality: An Economic and Ethical Analysis. *Journal of Business Ethics, 89*(4), 525–538.

Suryamukti, W. (2016). *Islamic Wealth Management: Planning and Managing Wealth Accordance with Shariah Law*. Retrieved July 13, 2020, from https://www.researchgate.net/publication/319257028.

United Nations. (2015). *Sustainable Development Goals*. Retrieved July 13, 2020, from https://sustainabledevelopment.un.org/sdgs.

World Bank. (2015). *Indonesia's Rising Divide*. Retrieved July 13, 2020, from https://www.worldbank.org/en/news/feature/2015/12/08/indonesia-rising-divide.

World Bank. (2018, July 13). *Gini Index (World Bank Estimate)*. Retrieved from World Bank Website: https://data.worldbank.org/indicator/SI.POV.GINI?end=2018&start=2018&view=map.

PART III

How is the Strategic Mechanism of 'Zakat' to Support SDGs?

CHAPTER 19

Zakat on Wealth and Asset: Lessons for SDGs

Mustafa Omar Mohammed, Mohamed Cherif El Amri,
and Ramadhani Mashaka Shabani

INTRODUCTION

Zakat is one of the five pillars of Islam levied on Muslims with wealth in excess of their needs to be transferred to the eight categories of beneficiaries specified in the Quran [9:60]. Zakat is a compulsory religious duty collected from all Muslims who are free and have the right to their wealth, sane and possess the Nisab (Basri and Khali 2014). Nisab is the fixed amount of property upon which Zakat becomes due. Zakat is divided into two: Zakat al-Fitr, which is paid during the month of Ramadan, and Zakat on the property that is paid on the various kinds of Zakatable assets. The property should be possessed and fully owned, generates income, a

M. O. Mohammed
Department of Economics, International Islamic University Malaysia, Gombak, Malaysia
e-mail: mustafa@iium.edu.my

M. C. El Amri (✉) · R. M. Shabani
Department of Islamic Economics and Finance, Istanbul Sabahattin Zaim University, Istanbul, Turkey

© The Author(s), under exclusive license to Springer Nature Switzerland AG 2021
M. M. Billah (eds.), *Islamic Wealth and the SDGs*,
https://doi.org/10.1007/978-3-030-65313-2_19

375

growing property, attains nisab, free from debt and fulfilled the one year condition (Al-Qardawi 1999; Hasan 2016).

Zakat is a very important institution for the spiritual and material development of the majority of Muslims. Spiritually [Surah Al-Tawbah, 9:103], Zakat helps the Muslims purify their soul from greed and excessive love for wealth. Materially, Muslims have benefitted from Zakat for enhancing their social and economic development. Zakat revenue can be transferred from one city or country to another whenever the need of that city or country transferring Zakat revenue are fulfilled. In countries such as Yemen, Saudi Arabia, and Sudan, their governments assume the responsibility of collecting and distributing of Zakat while in the cases of countries like Egypt, Tunisia, Lebanon, and Morocco, Zakat is managed by charitable organizations and the payment is made voluntary and in some countries, Zakat is given directly to the respective groups (Owoyemi 2020). The growth of Zakat collection has been growing over the years and shows impact on the society. For example, the most populous majority Muslim country like Indonesia has recorded a high growth of Zakat collections and distributions in 2018. Figure 19.1 shows Zakat

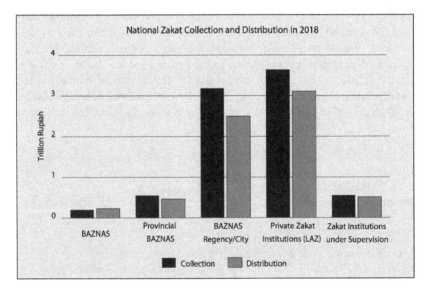

Fig. 19.1 Zakat collection and distribution in Indonesia in 2018 (*Source* BAZNAS [2020])

collection and distribution in Indonesia for the year 2018. The total collection reached 8.11 trillion Rupiah compared to 6.22 trillion Rupiah (BAZNAS 2019, 2020).

Zakat has played significant role throughout Islamic history toward the socioeconomic development of Muslim societies. The salient roles of Zakat included, among others, poverty alleviation, hunger relief, debt relief, job creation for Zakat managers, education, income and wealth redistribution, and of recent, financial assistance to refugees in a UNHCR Zakat program launched in late 2016 (Kidwai and Zidani 2020). These Zakat contributions have much relevance to the recently mooted United Nations' Sustainable Development Goals (SDGs). Areas of commonality between Zakat and SDGs include poverty, hunger, global health and well-being, quality education, decent work, economic growth, and income inequality (Ismail and Shaikh 2017a).

There is increasing interest among researchers on studies relating Zakat to SDGs. Most of these studies have focused on how Zakat funds can be used to finance SDGs-related projects. Yet there is hardly any works that has tried to examine the extent to which the dimensions of SDGs are relevant to the dimensions of Zakat, whose objectives preceded SDGs and seems to embody wider dimensions of objectives or goals than SDGs.

Overview on the Role of Zakat Toward Socioeconomic Development

This section discusses the concept of Zakat, and the role of Zakat toward socioeconomic, moral, spiritual, and religious development.

Concept of Zakat

The word "Zakat" is a derivative word from Arabic which literally means increase and growth. The origin of the word means purity, growth, blessing, and praise (Al-Qardawi 1999). The word also means purification, blessing, and commendation (The Zakat Foundation of America 2017). Technically it refers to the determined share of wealth prescribed by God and shared to the groups that deserve it (Al-Qardawi 1999). Zakat wasn't a new thing during the Prophet (Pbuh) period. The evidence of how Zakat was imposed during the preceding Prophet era is shown in various verses in the Quran. Surah Mariam (19:54–55) performs Ismael's Zakat, Surah Al-Baqarah (2:83) reveals Zakat of the Jews, Surah

Al-Anbiyaa (21:73) reveals Zakat in Surah Maryam (19:30–31) to the descendants of Prophet Ishaq and Zakat of Prophet Isa.

During the time of Prophet (Pbuh) at Makkah, the payment of Sadaqat was left to the people to decide how much to pay. Surah Al-Ma'arij (70:24–25) recommends *"And those within whose wealth is a known right. And those within whose wealth is a known right."* Zakat became mandatory after the Prophet (Pbuh) arrived in Madinah during the eighteen months, the second year of Hijrah. The Prophet (Pbuh) appointed workers to collect and distribute Zakat. The Quran did not give the direct definition for the property which is subjected to Zakat other than the general definition in some verses. Surah Al-Taubah (9:34), the silver and gold Zakat. Zakat Surah al-An'aam (6:141) and trade won Zakat Surah al-Baqarah (2:267).

The existence of Zakat is the same as the prayer because both complete the five pillars of Islam. Comparing to Salaat which is the form of worship in which is performed by the body, Zakat is also the form of worship which involves wealth and the form of performing the worship is monetary. Zakat's first objective is to purify (Surah Al-Taubah 9:103) means that Zakat cleans the wealth and sin as the prayer doing. Another reason is to resolve the inequality of society. The basis of payment and distribution is based on wealth than the income.

A Muslim with sanity and age of majority (Puberty) and nisab is obliged to pay Zakat (The Zakat Foundation of America 2017). The property that entitled to the payment of Zakat should be the one which generates income and the property which are growing. The property owned for personal consumption like house and car is not subjected to Zakat. Also, the property should be possessed and fully owned by the person, property for rent is not included (Hasan 2016). This shows that Zakat is the tax of excessive wealth (Ismail and Shaikh 2017a). The percentage rate of the amount of Zakat to be paid is prescribed as 2.5% of the wealth from the capital income (Hasan 2016). For the crops, 10% for the crop grown from the rainfall and 5% grown from irrigation while for the found treasure is 20% (Al-Qardawi 1999).

Zakat is payable upon the passage of lunar year for capital income. The jurists have different opinions about the time of nisab for Zakat. According to Shafii and Hanbal school, they opine that nisab should be present in a constant amount during the year. According to Hanafi school, the nisab should be present at the beginning and the end of the year. Maliki school opine that the nisab should be determined at the end of the year (Haneef 2008). The property which subjected to Zakat payment should be fully owned and should be under the person responsible for Zakat. This condition is not including the asset owned but does not generate income as well as an asset with divided ownership (Al-Qardawi 1999). Zakat expenditures are given to the different groups including poor and needy, employers in the collection of Zakat, and those whose reconciled to the truth. Also, Zakat is given to freeing slaves, for those owed while trying to fulfill their basic needs, those fighting for religion, and the traveler who cannot arrive at their destination without help (Surah Al-Taubah 9:60).

Non-Muslims are not entitled to Zakat, but if non-Muslims pay Zakat, they will be paid for his purpose (Surah Al-Tawbah 9:97–98). There are three reasons why disbeliever is exempted for paying Zakat. The first reason is Zakat is a social duty to the needy and destitute. This is the payment of tax in finance, which God obliges to distribute to the poor in the right of fraternity, the right of society, and the right of God. The second reason is that Zakat is the type of worship which constitutes the affirmation of Islam's confidence in the inclusion of other Islamic pillars. The third reason is part of Zakat proceeds are used in Islam to raise the spirit of Islam and reconciliation hearts with Islam (Al-Qardawi 1999).

The Socioeconomic and Religious Role of Zakat Toward Development

In economic terms, Zakat aims to achieving positive effects on consumption, savings and investment, labor supply and capital, poverty alleviation, and economic growth (Wahab and Rahman 2011). Zakat is a fair way to redistribute wealth because it is taken from the excessive wealth and not the actual income like government tax. It provides social security by solving the problem of society to raise and refine social welfare. It presents social responsibility and saves the Muslim from misfortune and it generates self-spiritual reformative system (Hasan 2016). These objectives and benefits encompass all aspect of human beings such as religion, life, oneself, intellect, and wealth.

Zakat increases the consumption of the basic goods and changes the consumption from luxury goods to the staple goods that are necessary for both the rich and the poor (Suprayitno 2019). Zakat funds play an essential role in economic development like eradication of poverty, illiteracy, diseases, and epidemics. Many countries try to alleviate poverty by applying different conventional policies such as price policies, income and wage policies, labor market and production policies and other policy packages such as structural and stabilization policies to alleviate poverty and achieve income equality (Abdelbaki 2013). The policies are different and not universal to apply to all problems. Zakat becomes the way out toward poverty alleviation without causing any extra problem. Zakat is efficient in eradicating poverty in Muslim communities and helps in achieving just distribution of income and wealth (Abdelbaki 2013).

Zakat shows the potential impact on individual sectors. The different impact is shown according to the priority. The countries like Sudan where the government enforces the payment of Zakat bring a significant impact in financing social protection like education health and poverty alleviation (Machado et al. 2018). Another study of Triyowati et al. (2018), in the comparison between Zakat, Infaq, and Sadaaq, found that Zakat has a great impact than other funds. Zakat showed a benefit to social development as well as benefits on the economy. In Bangka, Belitung Zakat contributes to per capita income and resolving the problem of unemployment (Fitriyanti et al. 2019). Overall the main aspect of development like economic growth, consumption, and investment cannot deny the contribution of Zakat (Suprayitno 2019). To solve the problem of hunger, Zakat is used for establishing food banks. The model of food banking enables the asnaf to access enough food in Malaysia (Zainal et al. 2019). In the study of Machado et al. (2018) in social protection between Sudan, Palestine, and Jordan, Zakat provides food, education services, and helping the poor to access health services, although the effective collection system was recommended to improve the amount of fund and reach many people in need. In the city of Jambi, Indonesia, Zakat management to support education plays a vital role in helping the poor household to access education (Ibrahim 2015). According to Hassan and Khan (2007) in their study of Zakat, external debt and poverty reduction strategy in Bangladesh, they found that Zakat is efficient when it is included in the government budget and used to finance projects which is related to the production activities such as agriculture and those related to the physical infrastructure such as rural read, electricity irrigation and embankment.

The funds mobilized from the collection of Zakat are not only subject to consumption. It is recommended to invest some of the funds so that it enhances economic growth. There are many areas in which Zakat fund can be used for investment. Atah et al. (2018) suggest that modern communication in the form of an e-community-based manifesto for information on the investment of Zakat fund in Mudarabah form. The Malaysian model of Zakat is found to be good in managing fiscal policy and macroeconomic determinants. Countries are encouraged to adopt this model because of its great impact on short and long-run (Suprayitno et al. 2017; Suprayitno 2019). In Indonesia, they establish SMEs for the mustahik (recipients) for the investment of Zakat fund with the view of helping those SMEs to grow bigger and contribute to the development and make them muzak (Zakat donors) (Harahap 2018). The same study was conducted by Meerangani (2019) on the role of Zakat in human development in Malaysia. The study shows how Zakat is practiced. The Islamic Religious Council that is responsible for managing Zakat fund provides a different project that empowers the society to engage in their own business. The project like entrepreneurship courses, catering, and sewing was provided. Gafoordeen et al. (2016) added that for the investment of Zakat fund, the investors should consider Shari'ah compliance toward investment and ensure that the investment is conducted in a halal way.

The UN Sustainable Development Goals (SDGs)

The Sustainable Development Goals (SDGs) developed by the U.N. Development Program (UNDP) focused on stimulating world growth. The 17 goals are set in 2016 with the target to achieve up to 2030. These goals are established with the statement *"the needs of the present without compromising the ability of future generations to meet their own needs."* The SDGs are proposals to create a more prosperous and safer future for everyone against the world's global challenges including inequality, poverty, climate change, environmental problems, peace, and justice. The objectives address the four key areas of the world, namely people, prosperity, the planet and peace and justice.

People

This focuses on the causes of poverty in many countries that make people fail to access the basic need for daily life. Removing poverty of all forms, promoting agriculture for nutrients and food security, promoting well-being and ensure healthy living by accessing health services and education for both boys and girls and clean water and sanitation. Goal 1: No Poverty, Goal 2: Zero Hunger, Goal 3: Good Health and Well-being,

Goal 4: Quality Education, Goal 5: Gender Equality, and Goal 6: Clean Water and Sanitation.

Prosperity

Investment in business and industries needs a conducive environment to support economic growth. Availability of electricity and water which is still a problem in many countries in Africa will foster investment in the new industrial sector and innovation. This will provide jobs and reduce income inequality, production and consumption will be enhanced. Goal 7: Affordable and Clean Energy, Goal 8: Decent Work and Economic Growth, Goal 9: Industry, Innovation, and Infrastructure, Goal 10: Reduced Inequality, Goal 11: Sustainable Cities and Communities, and Goal 12: Responsible Consumption and Production.

Planet

The planet is the dwelling place for all living organisms, and thus for their survival it is important to preserve the ecosystem for the survival of these organisms. Destruction of the environment endangers life on the planet. Goal 13: Climate Action, Goal 14: Life Below Water, and Goal 15: Life on Land.

Peace and Partnerships

Walking together is the key to success. To achieve the goals, nation and international cooperation are encouraged. Harmonization of international organizations such as the World Trade Organization (WTO) and the World Customs Organization (WCO) is recommended Goal 16: Peace and Justice Strong Institutions and Goal 17: Partnerships to Achieve the Goal.

The objectives set are intended to be funded in various ways by taking into account the respective country's economic condition through the use of domestic public resources, domestic and foreign private sector and finance, international development cooperation, international trade as a growth driver and debt sustainability (UN 2020).

Developing Zakat-SDGs Framework

Zakat and SDGs have significant relevance in the development of the community. Zakat has socioeconomic, religious, moral, and spiritual dimensions, among others, for the development of Muslim societies. On the other hand, SDGs embodies only three dimensions: economic, social, and environment. Hence, SDGs can be used as references to measure the results of certain objectives of Zakat (Nurzaman and Kurniaeny 2019). Handi Khalifah et al. (2017) tried to measure the Grand Programs of BAZNAS on 17 Goals of SDGs. They found that apart from the collaboration of all that programs, Zakat outweighs other variables. Zakat ensures the growth of economic in society and distributive justice of wealth. Another study was conducted by Asmalia et al. (2018) by employing the Theory of Planned Behavior to investigate how the population perceive the contribution of Zakat to SDGs. The findings show that the majority of the population believe that Zakat can finance SGDs and they focused mostly on poverty reduction, education, and improving the health sector. The mass collection and distribution would help to achieve the goals at the highest level (Noor 2017). With regard to SDGs, Zakat plays important role in goals like poverty, hunger, global health and well-being, quality education, decent work, economic growth, and income inequality (Ismail and Shaikh 2017a). On the other hand, Ismail and Shaikh (2017b) in their study on how Zakat can meet the development challenges. They suggest that since the objectives of SDGs are limited in time, then it is important that all necessary efforts involving different institution should be taken to make the largest dive onward.

Based on the findings from the literature reviewed above, the researchers have limited the scope of the performance of Zakat. They have not explored the other benefits available in Zakat. They measured the role of Zakat in one perspective only, as a financing instrument because SDGs need the money. The analysis of SDGs and Zakat shows only the success of SDGs but the success of Zakat is not fully examined. The researchers have not addressed the broad benefit of Zakat in financing beyond the SDGs, given that the dimensions of Zakat are broader than the dimensions of SDGs. This present chapter analyzes the extent to which SDGs can adequately measure the roles of Zakat and the reforms that SDGs need to undertake to do justice in measuring the performances of Islamic social finance institutions such as Zakat. To do this, the chapter has developed a Zakat-SDGs framework.

384 M. O. MOHAMMED ET AL.

On the other hand, there are researchers who have examined Zakat from the SDGs perspective. It is a common knowledge that the 17 SDGs is a global agenda with a motto of to "leave no one behind". To achieve this, it is necessary to reduce inequalities, end poverty, and fully incorporate social goals, environmental goals, and sustainable economy. These goals are not far from the objectives of Zakat. The first goal is no poverty. Comparing to Zakat, it relates to the rich people paying their due and distributing it to the poor and needy (Suprayitno 2019). The second goal is no hunger. The greater part of Muslims in Asia and Africa suffer from the problem of hunger. Zakat plays a very important role in solving the problem of hunger (Ismail and Shaikh 2017a). Another goal is good health and well-being. When health is improved then life will be saved. Education quality is another goal, for the improvement of intellect and innovation, education is very important. Up to 2012, about 78% of children entered school but many children from poor households are still not in school (UNDP 2020). To ensure equality in education, work distribution, and ownership of property, UNDP sets gender equality as another goal to ensure the balance of productivity in different sectors (Banham and Anhern 2016). Reduced inequalities are the goal established to reduce the income inequality between those who have and those who have not. This is because currently the wealth is owned by a small number of people. Zakat can encourage the consumption of basic goods and reduce luxury goods, and this will help the distribution of income to the poor (Suprayitno 2019). Conflict is the problem that hinders development in addition to corrupt institutions in many countries especially in Africa and the Far East. UNDP sets peace, justice, and strong institutions' goal to ensure peace and the strength of countries toward development. These goals can be achieved through Zakat, which under the guiding principles of Shari'ah would require commitment and sincerity as the way forward (Anonymous 2019). The framework with SDGs dimensions is not enough to utilize all the benefits of Zakat, while the framework with Zakat dimensions can be used to go beyond the objectives of SDGs. Figure 19.2 shows Zakat-SDGs framework based on their dimensions.

From the Fig. 19.2, the dimensions of Zakat are 6, all inside the red box. The three dimensions that are specific to Zakat [Religious, Spiritual, and Moral] plus the other three dimensions that are shared with SDGs, namely economic goals, social goals, and environmental goals. The subsequent section provides the analysis of the Zakat and SDGs dimensions embodied in the framework. Figure 19.2 compares between

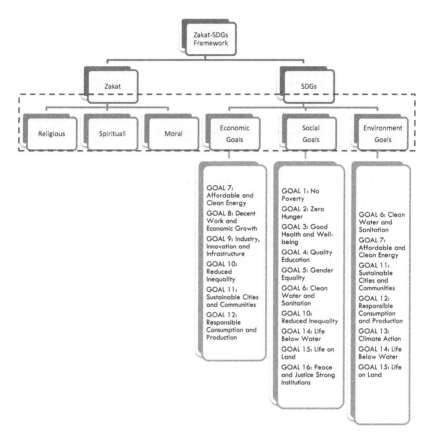

Fig. 19.2 Zakat-SDGs framework based on their dimensions

Zakat dimensions and SGDs dimensions with 17 SGDs. Zakat with 6 dimensions embodies all the 3 dimensions of SGDs which is social, economic, and environment goals. The social goals/dimension comprise the following goals: 1, 2, 3, 4, 5, 6, 10, 14, 15, and 16 which are related to no poverty, zero hunger, good health and well being, quality education gender equality, clean water and sanitation reduced inequality, life below water, life on the land and peace and justice strong institutions. Economic goals consist of the following goals: 7, 8, 9, 10, 11, and 12 goals, which are related to affordable and clean energy, decent work

386 M. O. MOHAMMED ET AL.

and economic growth, industry innovation and infrastructure, reducing inequality, sustainable cities and communities and responsible consumption and production. The last dimension of environment embodies the following goals: 6, 7, 11, 12, 14, and 15 which is concerned in clean water and sanitation, affordable and clean energy, sustainable cities and communities, responsible consumption and productions, climate action, life below the water and life on the land. The 17 goals [Partnerships to achieve the Goal] are established to focus on how those other goals are achieved.

ANALYSIS OF THE ZAKAT-SDGs FRAMEWORK

From the literature study, there is evidence that the dimensions and some objectives of SDGs are related to the dimensions and objectives of Zakat, yet the dimensions and objectives of Zakat are beyond the dimensions of SDGs as shown in Fig. 19.2. Zakat has six dimensions namely religious, spiritual, moral, social, economic, and environment. SDGs have three dimensions, namely social, economic, and environment. The objective of Zakat includes the three objectives of SDGs while SDGs do not have the other three dimensions of Zakat.

Dimensions of SGDs Related to Zakat

Zakat and SDGs share three dimensions, which are social, economic, and environment. The social dimension in Islam has an impact on both the collection and distribution of Zakat fund. The poor and the needy is the first group of Zakat recipients. Distribution of Zakat increases the consumption of the basic goods and will change the consumption from luxury goods to the staple goods that are necessary for both the rich and the poor (Suprayitno 2019) hence helping in reducing poverty. Through Zakat the community enhances their generosity by thinking not only of self-interest but also the interests of other. Some of the values embedded in this social dimensions that are achieved include Sincerity of Faith in the calculation and provision of one's wealth, Social Harmony and Justice by avoiding the accumulation of wealth in few hands, Social Security by providing solution to the monetary problem of the society and Circulation of Wealth (Abdullah and Suhaib 2011). To ensure the social development, the UN establishes goals which emphasize the improvement of the societies. These goals include alleviation of poverty and zero hunger which is a great problem to those with low income. Clean water and sanitation, good health and well-being goals are also established to ensure that people have safe and healthy access to their needs. Other goals are quality education and gender equality established to ensure access to quality education for both boys and girl. Also, the goals aimed at reduced inequality among society in accessing social services by empowering them with the means of earning income which will be used to pay for different services. Human life depends much on the ecosystem and peace. To ensure the human life is not ruined they establish life on land, life below the water and peace and justice strong institutions goals. All these goals are related to the objectives of Zakat toward society.

The economic dimension of Zakat embodies the overall Islamic economic. It includes the behavior of a man in the economic activities, his likes and dislikes, and how it is impacted by the economy which starts from the scarcity of accessing resources (Rosly 2005). The choice of action depends on disposable income available. The choice of consumption of the people with high income is different from the choice of people with low income The circulation of wealth is important for economic transfers from the rich to the poor. Zakat plays the role of countering inflation and deflations problem because it prevents the accumulation of wealth among few people (Ridwan et al. 2019). Zakat aims at achieving the positive effects on consumption, savings and investment, labor supply and capital, poverty alleviation, and economic growth (Wahab and Rahman 2011). Zakat has an impact on consumptions and productions. The producers who produce goods or services are required to pay Zakat only when they reach the nisab. This leaves the producers with enough resources to continue with their products and those who do not reach the nisab will not be obliged to pay Zakat. In the collection of Zakat, it employs those responsible for collection whether the task is institutionalized to the charitable organization or by the government. Islam encourages reforming the individuals who constitute part of the community. The UN goals in economics are related to these goals of zakat. For example, the goal related to the establishment of affordable and clean energy which aims at providing energy for industries and different production activities. Similarly, the goals related to decent work and economic growth focus on providing job opportunity coupled with reduced inequality goal to enable people to generate income and wealth circulation. These goals are established to improve not only the individual economic level but the development of the whole cities, countries, and the world. They establish goals related to infrastructure, innovation on the industries which will be used to add value to the products, sustainable cities and communities and responsible consumption and production goals which is directly related to the economic activities.

The environmental dimension focuses on climate changes and the balance of the ecosystem. The productions and consumptions contribute largely to environmental degradations. Human activities like farming, industrial and constructions activities are accompanied with digging the ground, cutting down trees and impurities to the water bodies and air. The distribution of Zakat provides the proper ways of human activities. For example, the distribution of Zakat will enable the people to access affordable energy and reduce the use of firewood and charcoal. The UN also focuses on the objectives by establishing goals relating to the environment which is clean water and sanitation, affordable and clean energy, sustainable cities and communities, responsible consumption and production, climate action, life below water and life on land. These seven goals ensure access to energy which is affordable for home consumption and industrial activities. Water and sanitation are important to the environment and help in preventing disease. Minimal production and consumption also will help to reduce the environmental impacts by not touching the unnecessary resources thereby reducing pollution. This will enable the protection of living organism on the land and under the water.

Dimensions of Zakat Not Included in SDGs

Religion is an important dimension of humanity which includes all information and system of life like reducing human neglect and criminal activities (Freeman 1986). In Islam, religion means in Arabic word means voluntary submission to God (Lewis and Churchill 2009). Religion in Islam is established based on five pillars which require the Muslims to live by the guideline from God and His Messenger. The five pillars include Zakat as the third pillar which is important in ensuring the strength and essence of the religion. Besides the other pillars, Zakat plays wealth-related role for human development.

The spiritual dimension is related to oneself belief or faith to Allah and religion. This belief acts based on perceptions about the purpose of this worldly life, and their ultimate destination after death (Farooqi 2017). Also, the belief is based on six pillars which are **Belief in Allah, the only**

God, Belief in Angels, Belief in the Holy Quran, Belief in Prophets of Allah, Belief in the Judgement Day and Belief in God's predestination (Qada and Qadar). Also, Surah An-Nisa' (4:136) provides that "O you who believe, Believe in Allah and His Messenger, and the Book which He revealed upon His Messenger and the Book which He revealed before. And whoever disbelieves in Allah and His Angels, and His Books, and His Messengers and the Day the Last, then surely he (has) lost (the) way, straying far away." The ability of someone to declare his true wealth and sacrificing a portion of one's wealth to solve the problems of brothers and sisters is a sign of spiritual belief. This creates stronger community bonds, removes hardships, and promotes brotherhood and compassion in the community (Farooqi 2017).

Morality is another important dimension in Zakat. The poor and illiterate society is sometimes forced by circumstance to compromise their moral value. Such circumstance can be adverse in extreme cases. So they are bound not to sustain their morality. The moral values inculcate mutual respect, cooperation, and sympathy among the members of society. Such noble traditions and great human standards are more often compromised due to the extreme situations of the poor and illiterate people (Abdullah and Suhaib 2011). Zakat contributes to the poor in alleviating poverty and enhance education which helps to increase the morality of such under privilege members of the community (Machado et al. 2018).

CONCLUSION AND THE WAY FORWARD

The objectives of this chapter are primarily to analyze the role of Zakat and its dimensions in relation to the dimensions and objectives of SDGs. Zakat has six dimensions while SDGS have three dimensions. The dimensions and objectives of Zakat encompass all the important spheres and needs of the human life, religious needs, spiritual needs, moral needs, social needs, economic needs, and environmental needs. The dimensions of SDGs are limited only to the social, economical, and environmental needs. This shows that the dimensions of Zakat are beyond SDGs. Therefore, Zakat is capable of fulfilling the SDGs goals, and beyond in terms of fulfilling the inner spiritual and moral needs of the society. The novelty of this chapter lies in proposing a framework for analyzing the roles of Zakat in relation to the SDGs. Future studies could expand the study by enriching the model, identifying detail variables, targets and indicators for robust analysis. Findings from such studies could provide recommendations to UNDP to benefit from the additional four dimensions of Zakat in formulating future goals related to Islamic social finance.

REFERENCES

Abdelbaki, H. H. (2013). The Impact of Zakat on Poverty and Income Inequality in Bahrain. *Review of Integrative Business and Economics Research, 2*(1), 133–154.

Abdullah, M., & Suhaib, A. (2011). The Impact of Zakat on Social Life of Muslim Society. *Pakistan Journal of Islamic Research, 8*, 85–91.

Al-Qardawi, Y. (1999). Fiqh Al Zakah, *A Comparative Study of Zakah, Regulations and Philosophy in the Light of Qur'an and Sunnah.*

Anonymous. (2019). *Revitalization of Waqf for Socio-Economic Development, Volume I*. Springer International Publishing.

Asmalia, S., Kasri, R. A., & Ahsan, A. (2018). Exploring the Potential of Zakah for Supporting Realization of Sustainable Development Goals (SDGs) in Indonesia. *International Journal of Zakat, 3*(4), 51–69.

Atah, U. I., Mohammed, W., Nasr, A., & Mohammed, M. O. (2018). The Role of Zakat as an Islamic Social Finance Towards Achieving Sustainable Development Goals: A Case Study of Northern Nigeria. In *e-Proceedings of the Global Conference on Islamic Economics and Finance 2018.*

Banham, L., & Anhern, M. (2016, February). Advancing Gender Equality in Education Across GPE Countries. *Global Partnership for Education*, 1–14.

Basri, E. H., & Khali, J. (2014). Payment of Zakat to Non-Muslims in the Light of Islamic Shariah. *Al-Idah, 29*(29), 91–106.

BAZNAS. (2019). *Indonesia Zakat Outlook.*

BAZNAS. (2020). *Indonesia Zakat Outlook.*

Farooqi, S. (2017). Zakah—The Spiritual Dimension | About Islam. *About Islam.*

Fitriyanti, E., Putri, A. K., & Valeriani, D. (2019). Zakat and Economic Development Analysis of Bangka Belitung Towards Sustainable Development Goals 2030. *Αγαη, 8*(5), 55.

Freeman, R. B. (1986). Who Escapes? The Relation of Churchgoing and Other Background Factors to the Socioeconomic Performance of Black Male Youths from Inner-City Poverty Tracts. *The Black Youth Employment Crisis*, 353–376.

Gafoordeen, N., Nayeem, M. M., & Aslam, A. M. (2016). Zakat Investment in Shariah.

Harahap, L. R. (2018). Zakat Fund as the Starting Point of Entrepreneurship in Order to Alleviate Poverty (SDGs Issue). *Global Review of Islamic Economics and Business, 6*(1), 063–074.

Hasan, Z. (2016). *Islamic Lawa of Property: Conceptual Framework of Zakat.*

Hassan, M. Kabir, & Khan, J. M. (2007). Zakat Is One of the Most Powerful Poverty Alleviating Instruments Available: Unfortunately, It Has Long Been Ignored by Westerners and *. *The Muslim World, 4,* 1–37.

Ibrahim, S. M. (2015). The Role of Zakat in Establishing Social Welfare and Economic Sustainability. *C, 3*(1), 437–441.

Ismail, A. G., & Shaikh, S. A. (2017a, February). Role of Zakat in Sustainable Development Goals Role of Zakat in Sustainable Development Goals. *International Journal of Zakat, 2*(2), 1–9.

Ismail, A. G., & Shaikh, S. A. (2017b). Where Is the Place for Zakat in Sustainable Development Goals? *IESTC Islamic Economic Studies and Thoughts Centre* (Working Paper No. 4, pp. 1–11).

Khalifah, M. H., Nurzaman, M. S., & Nafis, M. C. (2017). Optimization of BAZNAS Programs on Sustainable Development Goals (SDGs): Analytic Network Process Approach. *International Journal of Zakat, 2*(2), 71–83.

Kidwai, A., & Zidani, M. E. M. (2020). A New Approach to Zakat Management for Unprecedented Times. *International Journal of Zakat, 5*(1), 45–54.

Lewis, B., & Churchill, B. E. (2009). *Islam: The Religion and the People.* Wharton School Publishing.

Machado, A. C., Bilo, C., & Helmy, I. (2018). *The Role of Zakat in the Provision of Social Protection: A Comparison Between Jordan, Palestine and Sudan* (168).

Meerangani, K. A. (2019). The Role of Zakat in Human Development. *SALAM: Jurnal Sosial Dan Budaya Syar-I, 6*(2), 141–154.

Noor, Z. (2017). *The Role of Zakat in Supporting the Sustainable Development Goals Brief.*

Nurzaman, M., & Kurniaeny, F. (2019). Achieving Sustainable Impact of Zakāh in Community Development Programs. *Islamic Economic Studies, 26*(2), 95–123.

Owoyemi, M. Y. (2020). Zakat Management: The Crisis of Confidence in Zakat Agencies and the Legality of Giving Zakat Directly to the Poor. *Journal of Islamic Accounting and Business Research, 11*(2), 498–510.

Ridwan, M., Asnawi, N., & Sutikno. (2019). Zakat Collection and Distribution System and Its Impact on the Economy of Indonesia. *Uncertain Supply Chain Management, 7*(4): 589–598.

Rosly, S. A. (2005). *Critical Issues on Islamic Banking and Financial Markets: Islamic Economics, Banking and Finance, Investments, Takaful and Financial Planning.* Kuala Lumpur: Dinamas Publishing.

Haneef, S. S. S. (2008). *Issues in Fiqh Al-Zakat: Implications for Islamic Banking and Finance* (pp. 1–25).

Suprayitno, E. (2019). Zakat and SDGs : The Impact of Zakat on Economic Growth, Consumption and Investment in Malaysia. In *Proceedings of the 2018 International Conference on Islamic Economics and Business (ICONIES 2018).* Paris, France: Atlantis Press.

Suprayitno, E., Aslam, M., & Harun, A. (2017). Zakat and SDGs: Impact Zakat on Human Development in the Five States of Malaysia. *International Journal of Zakat, 2*(1), 61–69.

The Zakat Foundation of America. (2017). The Zakat Handbook, A Practical Guide for Muslims in the West.

Triyowati, H., Masnita, Y., & Khomsiyah Ak, C. A. (2018). Toward 'Sustainable Development' Through Zakat-Infaq-Sadaqah Distributions—As Inclusive Activities—For the Development of Social Welfare and Micro and Small Enterprises. *Australian Journal of Islamic Studies, 3*(2), 39–52.

UN. (2020). *Sustainable Development—Sustainable Development Fund.*

UNDP. (2020). Sustainable Development Goals.

Wahab, N. A., & Rahman, A. R. A. (2011). A Framework to Analyse the Efficiency and Governance of Zakat Institutions. *Journal of Islamic Accounting and Business Research, 2*(1), 43–62.

Zainal, H., Mustaffa, M. F., & Othman, Z. (2019). Zero Hunger and Sustainable Development Goals: Model of Food Bank Centre By Lembaga Zakat Negeri Kedah. *UMRAN-International Journal of Islamic and Civilizational Studies, 6*(2-2).

CHAPTER 20

Bridging Zakat Impacts Toward Maqasid Shariah and Sustainable Development Goals (SDGs), Influence of Corporatization and Experiences on COVID-19

Muhammad Iqmal Hisham Kamaruddin and Mustafa Mohd Hanefah

INTRODUCTION

Most Islamic institutions that run charity or voluntary activities undertake their activities to serve the needs of the society and community in which they operate closely linked with the society and community needs. As such, it is not uncommon for these institutions to receive large amount of funds such as *zakat*, *waqf*, and *sadaqah* from the public. For instance, Alterman et al. (2005) estimated the Muslims' contribution in terms of Islamic charity funds is within USD250 billion to USD1 trillion per year. Meanwhile, Obaidullah and Shirazi (2015) stated that

M. I. H. Kamaruddin (✉) · M. M. Hanefah
Universiti Sains Islam Malaysia, Nilai, Malaysia

M. M. Hanefah
e-mail: mustafa@usim.edu.my

© The Author(s), under exclusive license to Springer Nature   393
Switzerland AG 2021
M. M. Billah (eds.), *Islamic Wealth and the SDGs*,
https://doi.org/10.1007/978-3-030-65313-2_20

there are excess of about USD600 billion of *zakat* from the Organisation of Islamic Cooperation (OIC) member state countries, which may be annually distributable for humanitarian actions. However, there are several accountability issues regarding abuse and misconduct practices of Islamic funds including in Malaysia for instance, the 39 reports on manipulation and misappropriate of using *sadaqah* funds during flood crises in 2015 (*Astro Awani* 2015); the cancellation of contributions from 32,934 regular donors to Yayasan Pembangunan Ekonomi Islam Malaysia (YAPIEM) due to negative perception of YAPIEM spending method (Teng 2016); accusation of Malaysian Islamic organization being involved in terrorism financing (Kamaruddin and Ramli 2018; Othman and Ameer 2014); and the latest, the arrest of *zakat* institution's top management for embezzlement case (Hassan 2017). These are among the issues that lead to inquiries regarding institutions accountability to the public.

Similar to any institutions entrusted with managing public funds, *zakat* institutions (ZIs) are also subject to this accountability and trust issues from the public (Keating & Frumkin, 2003). Malaysian ZIs are religious-based non-profit organizations authorized by the government to manage Muslim's *zakat* fund. ZIs should be accountable to several stakeholders including *zakat* payers, *zakat* beneficiaries (*asnaf*), and the state government. Since ZIs depends on the Muslim zakat payers to collect zakat voluntarily, good governance and accountability is very important to gain their confidence (Saad et al. 2014). Wahid et al. (2010) revealed that one of the factors that dissatisfy the public toward ZIs is the lack of information about the impact of *zakat*. Thus, if the issue on the impact of *zakat* can be dealt with, more *zakat* contributors would be attracted to ZIs due to better discharge of accountability and preserve the image of Islam for sustainability by gaining trust from all Muslims (Masruki et al. 2018). In this millennium era, the distribution and the impact of *zakat* have led to a new level of measurement. Previously, the public were concerned about the collection and distribution of *zakat* funds (Ab Rahman et al. 2012; Lateff et al. 2014; Rahmatya and Wicaksono 2018; Rosli et al. 2018; Wahid et al. 2010). This includes on what types and how much the *zakat* funds collected and distributed to help *asnaf*. However, as time flies, the public nowadays are more concerned on the impact of the *zakat* especially for social and economic development (Bakar and Abd Ghani 2011; Kamaruddin et al. 2020; Nurzaman 2016; Suprayitno et al. 2013). Therefore, there is a need to examine the impact of the *zakat activities and programs*. Nevertheless, to this moment, there has not been a systematic study that has used proper measurements to study the impact of ZIs.

Notably, some of ZIs were restructured as a corporate entity owned by the state government, moving on from its previous legal establishment as a public entity owned and managed as a department by the state government. The changes in the legal structure were made for several purposes including to enhance the effectiveness and efficiency of the *zakat* management practices (Ahmad Shahir 2007; Ahmad Shahir and Adibah 2010). It would be interesting to know if the corporatization of some of these ZIs in improving its activities, and its impact on the program. So far, the effect of corporatization has not been studied systematically. Accordingly, the purpose of this study is to examine the socioeconomic impact practices of Malaysian ZIs toward both *maqasid shariah* and SDGs. This includes identifying and analyzing *zakat* activities and programs in order to access its impacts. Second, this study will compare the *zakat* activities and programs' impact between corporatized and non-corporatized Malaysian ZIs in order to evaluate whether the restructuring has an influence on *zakat* activities and programs' impact of the ZIs. Finally, this study also will identify significant impact of *zakat* impacts by Malaysian ZIs in responding COVID-19 pandemic recently, which also contribute to *maqasid shariah* and SDGs.

This paper is organized as follows. The next section overviews and discusses on the governance of Malaysian ZIs, *zakat* socioeconomic impacts and its relations with both *maqasid shariah* and SDGs. Following this, an outline of the research methodology including the sample selection and research design is presented. Discussion on research findings is then reported. Finally, the paper concludes the study, discusses the limitations, and suggests new area for future research.

LITERATURE REVIEW

Governance of Malaysian Zakat Institutions (ZIs)

Administration of the *zakat* fund in Malaysia is the responsibility of the State Religious Islamic Council (SRIC) of each state in the country. There are 14 Islamic Councils, one for each of the 13 states and one for the Federal Territory Wilayah Persekutuan of Kuala Lumpur. ZIs that were established under SIRC are given the authority to manage the *zakat* systems that include the collection and distribution of *zakat* (Abidin et al.

2014). Placing the *zakat* management authority under state governments as practiced by Malaysia is in line with the suggestion made by Al Qardawi (2000). Al Qardawi (2000) stated that as long as the government does not reject Islam, enforce *shariah* laws and its social structure is according to Islam, the authorized government should monitor the *zakat* collection and distribution due to several reasons.

- *There are Muslims who do not perform zakat obligation. Therefore, without authorized intervention, there are possibilities for zakat funds will not reach the asnaf;*
- *Zakat distribution by government can maintain and preserve the asnaf dignity compared to when the zakat donor gives directly to asnaf;*
- *Muslims who directly perform zakat obligation may be driven by their personal interests, and not performing zakat distribution according to accepted distribution concept;*
- *Several asnaf categories such as muallaf (new converts into Islam) and fi sabilillah (people who performing Islamic objectives) are only best recognized by the government; and*
- *Zakat is known as source of income for Muslim community.*

Albeit Islam is the official religion in Malaysia, the current structure of *zakat* management does not permit direct control by the Federal Government. Thus, we may expect differences in management styles according to states' requirement. Additionally, in the 1990s, with the changes in institutional environment, several state governments corporatized the *zakat* collection process while maintaining the *zakat* distribution function directly under the SIRC management. Meanwhile, several other state governments corporatized both *zakat* collection and distribution functions into a single corporate entity. Other ZIs practiced the traditional *zakat* management where both *zakat* collection and distribution functions operated directly under the SIRC (Ahmad et al. 2006). The corporatization reformation of ZIs in Malaysia was done to achieve several objectives (Ahmad Shahir 2007; Ahmad Shahir and Adibah 2010), which are:

- *To have an effective and efficient zakat management;*
- *To smoothen both collection and distribution processes of zakat funds;*
- *To minimize cost;*

- *To give a new image of ZIs; and*
- *To increase public confidence in ZIs.*

It is expected that the adoption of a more business-like practices through corporatization shall improve the performance of an organization. However, whether the expectation will prevail in the Malaysian ZIs is not well studied. In ZIs, attaining its socioeconomic objectives through successful *zakat* fund management can be portrayed through the utilization of *zakat* funds into *zakat* activities and programs. Accordingly, in this paper, the expectation is studied through the corporatization effects and impact of ZIs toward *maqasid shariah* and SDGs based on *zakat* activities and programs.

Zakat *Impacts*

It is undeniable that the main objective of *zakat* is to achieve socioeconomic justice. With respect to the economic dimensions of *zakat*, it is aimed to achieve the favorable effects on several dimensions such as aggregate consumption, savings and investment, aggregate supply of labor and capital, poverty eradication and economic growth (Abdul Wahab and Abdul Rahman 2011). Based on literature, there are quite intensive discussions based on findings on the impact of ZIs. For instance, Shehata (1994) mentioned that *zakat* funds can be used on socioeconomic infrastructure activities and programs such as providing education for the poor, the establishment of schools, vocational training and rehabilitation for *zakat* recipients to make them more productive, establishment of agriculture and cottage industries, provision of fixed assets and equipments to small business projects, provision of working capital, building of low-cost housing, providing medical treatment and health care, etc. Another research by Wahid et al. (2004) found that *zakat* has a significant effect toward the quality of life of the *usnaf* (beneficiaries of *zakat*) especially *al-fuqara'* (the poor) and *al-masakin* (the needy) in terms of education and social engagement.

Meanwhile, Olanipekun et al. (2015) stated that *zakat* will be able to promote a sustainable economy development as *zakat* is able to help the poor, circulate wealth and helping the causes of Allah. Moreover, the disbursement of *zakat* also has the ability to impact on consumption in the economy since the marginal propensity to consume of the *zakat* payer is lower than the *asnaf*, so that increasing the purchasing power parity of the *asnaf* (Kusuma and Sukmana 2010). Similarly, Suprayitno et al. (2013) found that *zakat* has a positive impact on aggregate consumption. However, the impact is small and short run. Hence, they recommend that *zakat* distribution should not be limited to the fulfillment of consumable needs only, but should also cover other forms of monetary aid that can generate a continuous flow of income for *asnaf*. In addition, Hossain (2012) opined that *zakat* has a number of positive impacts on the society. First, it is for the welfare of the unprivileged people of the society. Second, it is the blessing of Allah (SWT) for the giver as well as for the receiver, as it improves the total economy of the nation. Third, it establishes a society on a humanitarian ground. Fourth, it removes the economic hardship for *al-fuqara'* and *al-masakin* and reduces the inequality among different groups of people from the society. Finally, it satisfies the *asnaf* needs and alleviates their financial as well as mental sufferings.

Besides, *zakat* also has an impact in reducing poverty and inequality among people. In this case, Abdelmawla (2014) found that by increasing the distribution to the *asnafs* is statistically significant with reducing the poverty and inequality in Sudan. Similar study was also conducted in Malaysia by Mohsin (2015), and he observed that the current practice of the collection of *zakat* from monthly salary in Malaysia provides evidences that *zakat* has huge impact on the reduction of total poverty. Another study conducted in Bangladesh by Anis and Kassim (2016) indicates that the effectiveness of *zakat* programs has significant nominal and real increase in average monthly income, increase in fixed assets and an increase in monthly average household expenditure before and after receiving zakat money. On the other hand, *zakat* also has an impact on balancing the economic growth. In this regard, Aziz (2012) explained that income support provided to *al-fuqara'* and *al-masakin* would result in a measured increase of the money supply in the economy causing upward shift in demand for goods and services. To support this upward shift in the demand for necessities of life such as food, clothing, and shelter, the production facilities would gradually expand and begin to absorb the idle capital. In order to support the increased production, the economy would generate more jobs and new employment opportunities. This added employment in turn would generate more demand for goods and services, more room for additional investments, and finally, the growth cycle based on balance consumption would contribute to a balanced economic growth.

Finally, Nurzaman (2016) stated that *zakat* has huge impacts on socio-economy as *zakat* is levied on a broad base and includes a variety of economic activities. This is because *zakat* is levied on agricultural products, pets, gold and silver deposits, commercial activities, commercial and mining goods taken from the earth. Besides, *zakat* is also imposed on all revenues generated from the physical and financial assets and expertise of workers. Moreover, the acceptance of *zakat* fund is relatively stable as *zakat* is a spiritual tax paid by every Muslim under any circumstances. This will ensure the sustainability of *zakat* activities and programs in order to achieve its goals and objectives.

In short, *zakat* has huge impact on various aspects. By helping *asnaf*, it not only reduces the financial burden among them, but indirectly promotes a more decent quality of life. Besides, having more income among these *asnaf* also encouraging them to increase their spending and the impact of such spending can also stimulate the economic growth, while at the same time reducing inequality in economy. Moreover, the introduction of self-sustained programs via *zakat* funds for asnaf also will lift the poverty and increase their living standard (Bakar and Abd Ghani 2011). Thus, this kind of *zakat* programs will give greater impact on poverty eradication than the consumptive *zakat* in the long term (Nurzaman 2016; Yaacob et al. 2013).

Linkage Between Zakat *Impacts,* Maqasid Shariah, *and SDGs*

In general, *maqasid shariah* or Islamic objectives are used widely to guide legal decisions, especially when there are dynamic changes in the society that perhaps do not exist in the past (Muhamed et al. 2018). *Maqasid shariah* aims to realize goodness and prevent harm among humans, and thus guide humans in the best way (Laldin 2006). As has been highlighted by Ibn Ashur, the *maqasid shariah* is the acquisition of what is good and beneficial (*jalb al-masalih*) and the rejection of what is evil and harmful (*dar' al-mafasid*). Al-Shatibi defines *maslahah* as a principle that concerns the subsistence of human life, the completion of one's livelihood, and the acquisition of what his/her emotional and intellectual qualities requires of him/her in an absolute sense (Dusuki and Abdullah 2007). The concept of *maslahah* is further constructed into three elements of *dharuriyyah* (essentials), *hajiyyah* (complementary), and *tahsiniyyah* (embellishments). Al-Ghazali and extended by al-Shatibi (Ghazanfar and Islahi 1997; Chapra 1992) outlined five elements under the *dharuriyyah* (essentials): (i) preservation of faith (*hifz-ul-din*); (ii) preservation of life (*hifz-ul-nafs*); (iii) preservation of intellect (*hifz-ul-aqal*); (iv) preservation of posterity (*hifz-ul-nasl*); and (v) preservation of wealth (*hifz-ul-mal*).

As for *zakat*, the Muslim economists such as Chapra (1992) and Siddiqi (2004) rightly assert that the *maqasid shariah* should be viewed from a larger context by interrelating it with justice and equity through flows of distribution of wealth among different levels of society. Chapra (1992) goes further in depth by proposing that the rich should give away some portion of their wealth to help the poor obtain their needs at least at the *dharuriyyah* level. Besides, Islam defines poverty based on an individual failure to fulfill any of the five basic human requirements of life, which is based on *maqasid shariah* elements (Hassan and Ashraf 2010). Therefore, by aiding *asnaf* through *zakat*, it will fulfill these five *maqasid shariah* elements. On the other hand, SDGs represent a broader intergovernmental agreement to foster action on broad-based development encompassing economic development, human development, and environmental sustainability (Shaikh and Ismail 2017). There are 17 broad goals in which several targets had been set which are to be achieved by 2030. These SGDs include: (i) no poverty; (ii) zero hunger; (iii) good health and well-being; (iv) quality education; (v) gender equality; (vi) clean water and sanitation; (vii) affordable and clean energy; (viii) decent work and economic growth; (ix) industry, innovation, and infrastructure; (x) reduced inequality; (xi) sustainable cities and communities; (xii) responsible consumption and production; (xiii) climate action; (xiv) life below water; (xv) life on land; (xvi) peace and justice strong institutions; and (xvii) partnerships to achieve the goal.

There are some striking commonalities between the impact of *zakat*, *maqasid shariah*, and SDGs. Basically, much of what is in the SDGs reflects Islamic values or *maqasid shariah*. For instance, poverty and destitution can make a person vulnerable in faith and may engender the perception that his/her way out of poverty is dependent on others. A person facing poverty may be less able to exercise free will (Shaikh and Ismail 2017). Besides, this vulnerability is also aligned with SDGs 1, 2, 3, 6, and 10 on poverty, health, water, hunger, and inequality (Noor and Pickup 2017). These SDGs are fundamentally about reducing vulnerability, equipping people with the capacities and resources they need, and ensuring that institutions are accountable for providing services to which people are entitled so that people are empowered to make choices in their best interests. Therefore, if *zakat* can help in alleviating poverty, then it can contribute in promoting both *maqasid shariah* under *hifz-ul-din* and the above-mentioned SDGs.

Moreover, poverty also can result in loss of life from lack of essential nutrition, clean water and sanitation, life-saving medication, and ill health (Shaikh and Ismail 2017). Thus, ensuring healthy lives and promoting well-being are essential to sustainable development. These factors are also aligned with SGDs 2, 3, 6, 8, and 11 (Noor and Pickup 2017). SGD 2 is about eradicating hunger and food insecurity and developing sustainable agricultural systems. Goal 3 seeks to fully eradicate a wide range of diseases and address many different persistent and emerging health issues. By tackling water scarcity, poor water quality and inadequate sanitation, SGD 6 sets out to save lives and livelihoods of the poor. SGD 8 ensures decent work and income growth for all including the poor, while SGD 11 is about making cities safe, sustainable and upgrading slum settlements. Therefore, if *zakat* helps a person purchase essential foods, life-saving medicines, access clean water and health, then it can help to save lives, which is part of *maqasid shariah* under *hifz-ul-nafs* and at the same time to support the above-mentioned SDGs.

Furthermore, poverty, poor health, and food insecurity can cause stunting, poor schooling and affect intellectual capabilities (Shaikh and Ismail 2017). These effects are aligned with SDG 1, 2, 4, and 9 (Noor and Pickup 2017). In this case, children need to have access to education and nutritious food to build their human capital. Meanwhile, people can be supported through enhancement of skills and capacities to increase their earnings potential and productivity, while economic and financial institutions can support people's economic enterprise and local economic development. Therefore, if *zakat* can facilitate access to healthy nourishment, quality education and make them more productive in the future, then it can achieve *maqasid shariah* under *hifz-ul-aqal* and the above-mentioned SDGs.

On the other hand, war and conflict, climate change, environmental disasters, and infectious diseases can cause epidemic or large-scale loss of life that endangers the survival of entire communities and other species affected by their environment. Similarly, fear of poverty can result in desperation, vicious spirals deeper into poverty affecting future generations and terminally destroying the environment (Shaikh and Ismail 2017). These issues are in line with SDGs 3, 5, 7, 11, 12, 13, 14, 15, and 16 (Noor and Pickup 2017). There are disturbing trends in the way humans destroy the environment, exploit natural resources, and are irreversibly changing the climate for future generations. Besides, conflicts within and between societies and economic and financial crises threaten communities. Therefore, if *zakat* helps people escape the poverty trap, promoting peace and protecting the environment is consistent with human progeny, then it will be promoting *maqasid shariah* under *hifz-ul-nasl* and the above-mentioned SDGs.

Finally, when a person fulfills the obligation to pay *zakat*, he/she is able to purify his/her wealth (Shaikh and Ismail 2017). From SDGs' perspectives, this aligns with SDGs 1, 3, 8, and 10 (Noor and Pickup 2017). In this case, *zakat* has inbuilt wealth transfer, which is reflected in SDG 10 on reducing inequality. Besides, it also supports SDG 8 which is to create job opportunities and decent work conditions that support economic growth and are good for the environment. Therefore, *zakat* will help in wealth circulation which benefits everyone by generating economic activity and a social safety net, thus promoting *maqasid shariah* under *hifz-ul-mal* and the above-mentioned SDGs.

Based on the above discussions, Table 20.1 summarized the relationship between impact of *zakat* with *maqasid shariah* and SDGs.

At present, there are only limited studies have been conducted that aligns between *zakat* impacts with *maqasid shariah* and SDGs. This includes a study by Zakaria (2014) on *zakat* distribution effectiveness and *maqasid shariah*; a study by Shaikh and Ismail (2017) on the roles of *zakat* on SDGs; a study by Khalifah et al. (2017) on *zakat* activities and programs on SDGs in Indonesia; and a study by Noor and Pickup (2017) on the role of zakat in supporting SDGs.

Based on these studies, Zakaria (2014) examines the relationship between *maqasid shariah* with *zakat* distribution effectiveness and found that all five *maqasid shariah* elements positively influenced the effectiveness of *zakat* distribution. Meanwhile, study by Shaikh and Ismail (2017) on *zakat* wealth distribution based on socioeconomic indicators, which are economic, education, and health and suggests that *zakat* can play an important role in meeting SDGs related to poverty, hunger, global health and well-being, quality education, decent work and economic growth and income inequality. While, Khalifah et al. (2017) measured the priority of the seven grand programs of a ZI in Indonesia on 17 SDGs and indicate that there is high agreement by respondents that there is a significant impact of zakat activities with SDGs. Finally, Noor and Pickup (2017) investigated on the relationship between ZI activities and programs and

20 BRIDGING ZAKAT IMPACTS TOWARD MAQASID SHARIAH ... 403

Table 20.1 Relationship between *Zakat* impacts, *Maqasid Shariah*, and SDGs

Zakat *impacts*	Maqasid Shariah	*SDGs*
Alleviate poverty	*Hifdh-ul-din*	SDG 1: No poverty SDG 2: Zero hunger SDG 3: Good health and well-being SDG 6: Clean water and sanitation SDG10: Reduced inequality
Provide essential foods, life-saving medicines, access clean water and health	*Hifdh-ul-nafs*	SDG 2: Zero hunger SDG 3: Good health and well-being SDG 6: Clean water and sanitation SDG 8: Decent work and economic growth SDG 11: Sustainable cities and communities
Facilitate access to healthy nourishment, quality education, and productivity	*Hifdh-ul-aqal*	SDG 1: No poverty SDG 2: Zero hunger SDG 4: Quality education SDG 9: Industry, innovation and infrastructure
Escape the poverty trap, promoting peace and protecting the environment	*Hifdh-ul-nasl*	SDG 3: Good health and well-being SDG 5: Gender equality SDG 7: Affordable and clean energy SDG 11: Sustainable cities and communities SDG 12: Responsible consumption and production SDG 13: Climate action SDG 14: Life below water SDG 15: Life on land SDG 16: Peace and justice strong institutions
Wealth circulation and social safety net	*Hifdh-ul-mal*	SDG 1: No poverty SDG 3: Good health and well-being SDG 8: Decent work and economic growth SDG10: Reduced inequality

SDGs and found that several SDGs were prioritized such as SDG 1, 2, 3, 4, 6, 8, and 11.

Thus, this study will extend the scope of the above studies by measuring the interlinkage between *zakat* impacts from *zakat* activities and programs with both *maqasid shariah* and SDGs.

METHODOLOGY

Data Collection

The main purpose of this research is to examine the *zakat* impact of Malaysian ZIs toward both *maqasid shariah* and SDGs. Besides, this study also compares the *zakat* impact practices between corporatized and non-corporatized Malaysian ZIs in order to evaluate whether the restructuring has any influence on *zakat* practices of the Malaysian ZIs. There are 17 ZIs from 14 states in Malaysia. As mentioned earlier, management of the ZIs in some states separated the collection and distribution functions. Due to the scope of this study that focuses on *zakat* impacts based on the distribution of *zakat* through its activities and programs, three (3) Malaysian ZIs that have only collection functions are excluded from the sample. Therefore, the remaining 14 Malaysian ZIs were used as sample for this study.

Table 20.2 presents the list of 17 ZIs in Malaysia and its structure and functions. By excluding three (3) ZIs, the list indicates that five (5) institutions have been corporatized and the remaining nine (9) ZIs are non-corporatized. Specifically, categorization of the ZIs is based on its structure as follows:

- *Traditional—both zakat collection and distribution functions under the same entity that not been corporatized (Johor, Kedah, Kelantan, Perak, Perlis and Terengganu);*
- *Semi-corporatized—separate between zakat collection and distribution functions into different entities where zakat collection entity is corporatized and zakat distribution entity are not (Melaka, Pahang, and Wilayah Persekutuan); and*
- *Corporatized—both zakat collection and distribution functions under the same entity that had been corporatized (Negeri Sembilan, Penang, Sabah, Sarawak and Selangor).*

Table 20.2 ZIs in Malaysia

No	State	Zakat *institution*	*Structure*	*Function*
1	Johor	Majlis Agama Islam Johor (MAIJ)	Non-corporate	Collection and distribution
2	Kedah	Lembaga Zakat Negeri Kedah (LZNK)	Non-corporate	Collection and distribution
3	Kelantan	Majlis Agama Islam Kelantan (MAIK)	Non-corporate	Collection and distribution
4	Perak	Majlis Agama Islam dan Adat Istiadat Melayu Perak (MAIPk)	Non-corporate	Collection and distribution
5	Perlis	Majlis Agama Islam dan Istiadat Melayu Perlis (MAIPs)	Non-corporate	Collection and distribution
6	Terengganu	Majlis Agama Islam dan Adat Istiadat Melayu Terengganu (MAIDAM)	Non-corporate	Collection and distribution
7	Melaka	Majlis Agama Islam Melaka (MAIM)	Non-corporate	Distribution
8	Pahang	Majlis Ugama Islam dan Adat Resam Melayu Pahang (MUIP)	Non-corporate	Distribution
9	Wilayah Persekutuan	Majlis Agama Islam Wilayah Persekutuan (MAIWP)	Non-corporate	Distribution
10	Negeri Sembilan	Perbadanan Baitulmal Negeri Sembilan (PBMaINS)	Corporate	Collection and distribution
11	Penang	Zakat Pulau Pinang	Corporate	Collection and distribution
12	Sabah	Pusat Zakat Sabah MUIS (PZS-MUIS)	Corporate	Collection and distribution
13	Sarawak	Tabung Baitulmal Sarawak (TBS)	Corporate	Collection and distribution
14	Selangor	Lembaga Zakat Selangor (LZS)	Corporate	Collection and distribution
15	Melaka	Pusat Zakat Melaka (PZM)	Corporate	Collection
16	Pahang	Pusat Kutipan Zakat Pahang (PKZP)	Corporate	Collection

(continued)

406 M. I. H. KAMARUDDIN AND M. M. HANEFAH

Table 20.2 (continued)

No	State	Zakat *institution*	*Structure*	*Function*
17	Wilayah Persekutuan	Pusat Pungutan Zakat MAIWP (PPZ-MAIWP)	Corporate	Collection

*Research Design—*Zakat *Impacts,* Maqasid Shariah, *and SDGs*

In order to examine the *zakat* impacts, *zakat* activities and programs provided by ZIs for *asnaf* were analyzed. In general, there are eight (8) *asnaf* categories based on Surah at-Taubah verse 60, as follow: (i) *al-fuqara'* (the poor); (ii) *al-masakin* (the needy); (iii) *amil* (*zakat* manager); (iv) *muallaf* (the reverts); (v) *riqab* (the slave); (vi) *gharimin* (the debtor); (vii) *fisabilillah* (the one who fight in the name of Allah); and (viii) *Ibnu sabil* (the distant traveler). Meanwhile, for *maqasid shariah* and SDGs, all five (5) *maqasid shariah* elements and 17 SDGs goals identified were used in the analysis process. Table 20.3 lists all the *maqasid shariah* elements and SDGs goals adopted in this study.

Next, it is known that *zakat* activities and programs vary for each ZI. Therefore, to evaluate the significance of *zakat* impacts with both *maqasid shariah* and SDGs, a binomial logic as suggested by Ramli and Kamaruddin (2017) was used. For this, each *zakat* activities and programs are evaluated by analyzing its impact toward both *maqasid shariah* elements and SDGs goals. Based on all *zakat* activities and programs conducted for each ZI, one (1) will be assigned to each *maqasid shariah* elements and SDGs goals impacted by those collective *zakat* activities and programs and zero (0) will be assigned if those *maqasid shariah* elements and SDGs goals are not impacted. The total score for each *maqasid shariah* and SDGs then calculated at the end of the process to identify the total score of the *zakat* impact on both *maqasid shariah* and SDGs for Malaysian ZIs. The formula for this *zakat* impact for each ZI is as follow:

$$Zakat \text{ Impacts (22 Scores)} = Maqasid\ Shariah\ (5\ \text{Scores}) + \text{SDGs (17 Scores)}$$

Based on the formula, if any ZI have *zakat* activities and programs that affects all five (5) *maqasid shariah* elements and 17 SDGs goals for

Table 20.3 *Maqasid Shariah* elements and SDGs goals

Types	Items
Maqasid Shariah	*Hifz-ul-din* (protection of religion)
	Hifz-ul-nafs (protection of life)
	Hifz-ul-aqal (protection of intellect)
	Hifz-ul-nasl (protection of posterity)
	Hifz-ul-mal (protection of wealth)
SDGs	SDG 1: No poverty
	SDG 2: Zero hunger
	SDG 3: Good health and well-being
	SDG 4: Quality education
	SDG 5: Gender equality
	SDG 6: Clean water and sanitation
	SDG 7: Affordable and clean energy
	SDG 8: Decent work and economic growth
	SDG 9: Industry, innovation, and infrastructure
	SDG 10: Reduced inequality
	SDG 11: Sustainable cities and communities
	SDG 12: Responsible consumption and production
	SDG 13: Climate action
	SDG 14: Life below water
	SDG 15: Life on land
	SDG 16: Peace and justice strong institutions
	SDG 17: Partnerships to achieve the goal

each *asnaf* category, a score of 22 will be assigned. Accordingly, if all ZIs have *zakat* activities and programs that affect all five (5) *maqasid shariah* elements and 17 SDGs goals for each *asnaf* category in this study, a total score of 308 (14 ZIs × 22 scores) will be given.

RESULTS

The following section discusses the findings on *zakat* impacts on both *maqasid shariah* and SDGs. Next, comparison on *zakat* impacts between ZIs specifically between corporatized and non-corporatized ZIs is discussed. Finally, findings on ZIs responds on COVID-19 and its impact on both *maqasid shariah* and SDGs was also discussed.

Findings on Zakat Impacts on Maqasid Shariah and SDGs

Items for measuring *maqasid shariah* include: (i) *hifz-ul-din* (protection of religion); (ii) *hifz-ul-nafs* (protection of life); (iii) *hifz-ul-aqal* (protection of intellect); (iv) *hifz-ul-nasl* (protection of posterity); and (v) *hifz-ul-mal* (protection of wealth). For instance, if any ZI's activities and programs are carried out with the aim to affect *hifz-ul-din*, a score of 1 is given. If five (5) ZIs' activities and programs are carried out with the aim to impact *hifz-ul-din*, a score of five (5) is given to *hifz-ul-din* element. Based on the analysis, all five *maqasid shariah* elements are being impacted via all 14 ZIs' activities and programs. Therefore, from the total of 70 scores (14 ZIs × 5 *maqasid shariah* elements) for *maqasid shariah* elements affected from *zakat* impacts, the *maqasid shariah* elements scores are 70 (14 scores + 14 scores + 14 scores + 14 scores + 14 scores). Figure 20.1 shows result of the analysis on *maqasid shariah* elements affected by ZIs' activities and programs.

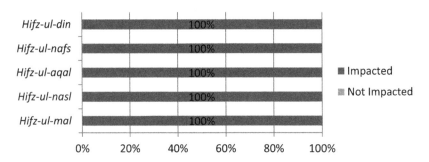

Fig. 20.1 *Zakat* impacts on *Maqasid Shariah* elements in Malaysian ZIs

The analysis indicates that all Malaysian ZIs have activities and programs that affect all *maqasid shariah* elements. It means that a combination of all *zakat* activities and programs by each Malaysian ZIs will able to fulfill all five *maqasid shariah* elements. This is not surprising due to the role of ZIs itself as social welfare based on Islamic principles. Besides, this finding also proved that one of the major distinguished characteristics between Islamic-based organizations like ZIs with other organizations is ZIs are based on Islamic objectives (*maqasid shariah*) (Kamaruddin and Auzair 2018). In addition, each *zakat* activities and programs have different impact in achieving *maqasid shariah* elements. For instance, under *zakat* activities and programs for education purposes, it has impact on *hifz-ul-aqal*. Meanwhile, *zakat* activities and programs for *al-fuqara'* and *al-masakin* on their survival have impacts on *hifz-ul-din*, *hifz-ul-nafs* and *hifz-ul-nasl*, while *zakat* activities and programs which focus in preparing *asnaf* with adequate business knowledge, skills, and even startup capital for business have impacts on *hifz-ul-aqal* and *hifz-ul-mal*. In addition, *zakat* activities and programs for health purposes, it able to impact *hifz-ul-din*, *hifz-ul-nafs*, *hifz-ul-aqal* and *hifz-ul-nasl*. However, *zakat* activities and programs that aim to help people who have been in debt especially on basic needs have impact on all *maqasid shariah* elements. This also goes to *zakat* activities and programs for disaster causes including COVID-19. These kinds of activities and programs are conducted by almost all Malaysian ZIs. Therefore, it answers the reason why *zakat* activities and programs by Malaysian ZIs are scoring the maximum 100% impact on *maqasid shariah*.

For *zakat* impacts on SDGs, items for measuring SDGs include: (i) SDG 1: no poverty; (ii) SDG 2: zero hunger; (iii) SDG 3: good health and well-being; (iv) SDG 4: quality education; (v) SDG 5: gender equality; (vi) SDG 6: clean water and sanitation; (vii) SDG 7: affordable and clean energy; (viii) SDG 8: decent work and economic growth; (ix) SDG 9: industry, innovation, and infrastructure; (x) SDG 10: reduced inequality; (xi) SDG 11: sustainable cities and communities; (xii) SDG 12: responsible consumption and production; (xiii) SDG 13: climate action; (xiv) SDG 14: life below water; (xv) SDG 15: life on land; (xvi) SDG 16: peace and justice strong institutions; and (xvii) SDG 17: partnerships to achieve the goal. Based on the analysis, it was found that both SDG 14: life below water and SDG 15: life on land were the only SDGs goals that had not been achieved by any of ZIs based on their activities and programs. A number of SDGs goals are fully achieved by all 14 ZIs based on their *zakat* activities and programs including SDG 1, SDG 2, SDG 3, SDG 4, SDG 5, SDG 6, SDG 7, SDG 10, SDG 11, and SDG 16. Meanwhile, SDG 9 becomes the second highest score with 85.71% (12 out of 14). While, other SDGs goals such as SDG 8, SDG 12, SDG 13, and SDG 17 are scoring 78.57% (11 out of 14). Therefore, from the total 238 scores (14 ZIs × 17 SDGs) for SDGs goals affected from *zakat* impacts, the SDGs goals scores are 190 (17 scores + 17 scores + 17 scores + 17 scores + 17 scores + 17 scores + 17 scores + 11 scores + 12 scores + 17 scores + 17 scores + 11 scores + 11 scores + 0 score + 0 score + 17 scores + 11 scores). Figure 20.2 shows result of the analysis on SDGs goals affected by ZIs' activities and programs.

Results of the analysis indicate that *zakat* activities and programs by Malaysian ZIs have high impacts on almost all SDGs goals. This is a surprising fact as the coverage of SDGs goals are much wider and *zakat* activities and programs are able to achieve these SDGs objectives. Although a number of *zakat* activities and programs have no impact on SDGs, the number is quite low. In addition, no *zakat* activities and programs by Malaysian ZIs are related to SDG 14 and SDG 15. This is due to the nature of *zakat* activities and programs itself, which are more focused on the benefits of *asnaf* as compared to the environment. Similar to *maqasid shariah* elements, each *zakat* activities and programs have different impact in achieving SDGs goals. For instance, under *zakat* activities and programs for education purposes, it has impacts especially on SDG 1, SDG 4, SDG 5, SDG 10, and SDG 11. Meanwhile, *zakat* activities and programs for *al-fuqara'* and *al-masakin* on their survival have impacts on SDG 1, SDG 2, SDG 3, SDG 6, SDG 7, SDG 10, and SDG 11, while *zakat* activities and programs that focused in preparing *asnaf* with adequate business knowledge, skills, and even startup capital for business have impacts more than half SDGs goals including SDG1, SDG 2, SDG 3, SDG 8, SDG 9, SDG 10, SDG 11, SDG 12, and SDG 17. This is also similar for *zakat* activities and programs that aim to help people who have been in debt especially on basic needs which able to impact SDG 1, SDG 2, SDG 3, SDG 6, SDG 7, SDG 10, SDG 11, and SDG 16. In addition, for *zakat* activities and programs for disaster causes, they do impact SDG 2, SDG 3, SDG 6, SDG 7, SDG 11, SDG 13, and SDG 16. Last but not least, *zakat* activities and programs for health purposes also affect SDG 3 and SDG 11 to certain extent. These kinds of activities and programs are undertaken by almost all Malaysian ZIs. Therefore, it answers the reason why *zakat* activities and programs

20 BRIDGING ZAKAT IMPACTS TOWARD MAQASID SHARIAH ... 411

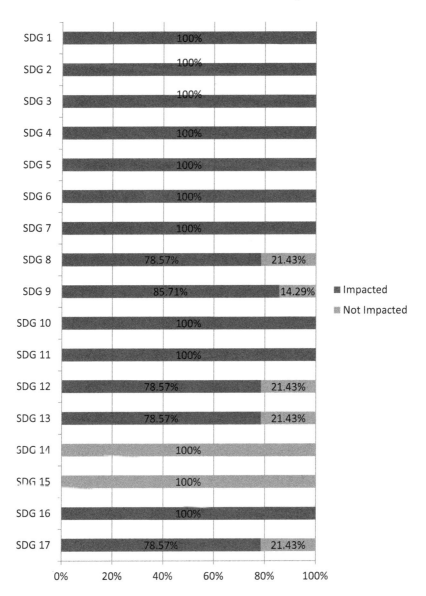

Fig. 20.2 *Zakat* impacts on SDGs goals in Malaysian ZIs

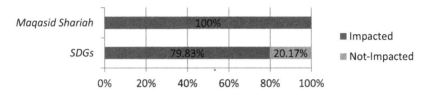

Fig. 20.3 *Zakat* impacts on *Maqasid Shariah* and SDGs by Malaysian ZIs

by Malaysian ZIs are scoring high on SDGs goals. Based on the above findings, the following Fig. 20.3 shows summary findings on ZIs impacts on both *maqasid shariah* and SDGs.

Figure 20.3 shows that all *maqasid shariah* elements are impacted from *zakat* activities and programs conducted by ZIs (100%, 70 out of 70 scores). Besides, SDGs goals are also highly impacted from *zakat* activities and programs conducted by ZIs (79.83%, 190 out of 238 scores). Overall, the Malaysian ZIs activities and programs have an impact on *maqasid shariah* and SDGs—84.42% or 260 scores (70 scores + 190 scores) from total *maqasid shariah* elements and SDGs goals scores.

Comparison of Zakat *Impacts Between Corporatized and Non-corporatized ZIs*

Zakat impacts for all ZIs were then compared between corporatized and non-corporatized institutions. Table 20.4 displays the findings of the analysis.

Table 20.4 Comparison between corporate and non-corporate ZIs in Malaysia based on *Zakat* impacts

	Corporate ZIs				Non-corporate ZIs			
	Impacted		Not impacted		Impacted		Not impacted	
	No.	%	No.	%	No.	%	No.	%
Maqasid Shariah	25	100%	0	0%	45	100%	0	0%
SDGs	66	77.6%	19	22.4%	124	81.05%	29	18.95%
Total	91	82.73%	19	17.27%	169	85.35%	29	14.65%

Table 20.4 shows the comparison on *zakat* impacts between five (5) corporatized and nine (9) non-corporatized ZIs. The data indicates that all *maqasid shariah* elements are fully affected by ZIs activities and programs regardless of whether they are corporatized or not. Specifically, the corporatized ZIs' activities and programs impact on *maqasid shariah* elements 100% (25 out of 25 scores), similar to the non-corporatized ZIs' activities and programs impact on *maqasid shariah* elements 100% (45 out of 45 scores). It shows that corporatization of ZIs do not have an influence on *maqasid shariah*. Regarding SDGs goals, the corporatized ZIs' activities and programs impact on SDGs goals 77.6% (66 out of 85 scores) while the non-corporatized ZIs activities and programs have impact on SDGs goals 81.05% (124 out of 29 scores). Interestingly, the findings show that the non-corporatized ZIs have greater impact on SDGs goals compared to corporatized ZIs.

Overall, about 82.73% (91 out of 110 scores) from both *maqasid shariah* elements and SDGs goals are impacted through *zakat* activities and programs by all five (5) corporatized ZIs while the non-corporatized ZIs' activities and programs impact on *maqasid shariah* elements and SDGs goals are 85.35% (169 out of 198 scores). Analysis of the data reveals that the non-corporatized ZIs have a slightly higher *zakat* impacts on *maqasid shariah* and SDGs, compared to the corporatized ZIs. Thus, at this moment, it cannot be concluded that the corporatization of ZIs in Malaysia has any significant influence in impacting more *maqasid shariah* elements and SDGs as compared to non-corporatized ZIs.

Prior studies (Ahmad Shahir 2007; Ahmad Shahir and Adibah 2010) have claimed that corporatization of the ZIs shall enhance their performance; nevertheless, findings from this study do not appear to support the claim with regard to ZIs impacts. They claimed that corporatization of ZIs will make them more effective and efficient in their operations and activities. Instead, the findings still indicate that corporatized ZIs have lower impact on both *maqasid shariah* and SDGs, compared to non-corporatized ZIs.

Zakat *Impacts on COVID-19 and Its Relationships with* Maqasid Shariah *and SDGs*

In the early discussions on findings, it is noted that one of *zakat* activities and programs conducted by Malaysian ZIs is for disaster causes. This includes for normal natural disasters such as floods, landslides, plagues, and fires. Besides, although Malaysia geography is located outside from volcanoes and earthquake circles, sometimes the impact from neighboring natural disasters also gives a little impact to Malaysia. This includes such as small scale of earthquakes and the biggest one is tsunami tragedy in 2004. For all these natural disasters tragedies, Malaysian ZIs play active roles especially to cater *asnaf* who are impacted from these natural disasters affect which causing them to lose such as houses, belongings and also business disruption especially in agricultural sectors and fisheries. Recently, world is facing a new virus which is known as Coronavirus-19 (COVID-19). This new pandemic crises started from Wuhan, China and now is spreading globally including Malaysia. Until 30 March 2020, about 785,777 cases with 37,815 casualties are reported due to this COVID-19. For Malaysia, this COVID-19 already recorded about 2,626 positive cases with 37 casualties (Worldmeter 2020). Besides, COVID-19 is also affecting economically especially where many industries are shutdown temporarily as part of quarantine processes, which affect a lot of supply and demand of goods and services in the market. This leads to job losses, and many persons becoming unemployed and do not have enough money to buy necessities like food and water.

In order to overcome such impact, Malaysian government already announced a stimulus economic package with amounting RM250 billion at 27 March 2020. Besides, each state government is also announcing their separate stimulus economic package to help for those who directly affected from COVID-19. Not forget to be mentioned, Malaysian ZIs also announcing their immediate *zakat* allocation funds specifically on this COVID-19 crisis. The detail on each Malaysian ZIs *zakat* allocation funds on COVID-19 is shown in the following Table 20.5.

Based on Table 20.5, total *zakat* allocation funds announced by Malaysian ZIs specifically for COVID-19 crisis as at 30 March 2020 was RM118.44 million. These allocations were targeted to benefits about 691,740 persons. On the distribution mechanisms, there are several *zakat* activities and programs identified. This includes financial and foodstuffs aids for individuals who their income was affected due to COVID-19. Besides, there is also allocation for COVID-19 frontliners such as doctors, nurses, polices, and soldiers where allocation was given in terms of cash and foods. In addition, there is also allocation for medical equipments such as face masks, medicines, gloves, personal protection equipments, ventilators, and others. Moreover, there is also allocation for hawkers and small business that are mostly affected by COVID-19. Furthermore, there

Table 20.5 Malaysian ZIs' Zakat allocation funds for COVID-19

No	State	Zakat institution	Zakat allocation funds	Asnaf beneficiaries
1	Johor	Majlis Agama Islam Johor (MAIJ)	RM5.7 million	20,000 persons
2	Kedah	Lembaga Zakat Negeri Kedah (LZNK)	RM16.7 million	520,000 persons
3	Kelantan	Majlis Agama Islam Kelantan (MAIK)	RM1 million	10,000 persons
4	Melaka	Majlis Agama Islam Melaka (MAIM)	RM3.54 million	8,929 persons
5	Negeri Sembilan	Perbadanan Baitulmal Negeri Sembilan (PBMaINS)	RM4.3 million	4,594 persons
6	Pahang	Majlis Ugama Islam dan Adat Resam Melayu Pahang (MUIP)	RM2.78 million	12,694 persons
7	Penang	Zakat Pulau Pinang	RM5 million	n/a
8	Perak	Majlis Agama Islam dan Adat Istiadat Melayu Perak (MAIPk)	RM11.95 million	n/a
9	Perlis	Majlis Agama Islam dan Istiadat Melayu Perlis (MAIPs)	RM4.43 million	22,857 persons
10	Sabah	Pusat Zakat Sabah MUIS (PZS-MUIS)	RM5.93 million	41,470 persons
11	Sarawak	Tabung Baitulmal Sarawak (TBS)	n/a	n/a
12	Selangor	Lembaga Zakat Selangor (LZS)	RM15 million	n/a
13	Terengganu	Majlis Agama Islam dan Adat Istiadat Melayu Terengganu (MAIDAM)	RM17 million	27,000 persons
14	Wilayah Persekutuan	Majlis Agama Islam Wilayah Persekutuan (MAIWP)	RM25.11 million	24,196 persons
	Total		RM118.44 million	691,740 persons

n/a = not available

No. of zakat allocation funds and asnaf beneficiaries announced by Malaysian ZIs as at 30 March 2020 is also rent exemption for those asnaf who rent ZIs premises for their business. Finally, there is also allocation for mosques and some of mosques are funded to perform disinfect process.

In reference to the above *zakat* activities and programs specifically for COVID-19, it is targeted that these *zakat* activities and programs are able to impact *maqasid shariah* elements such as *hifz-ul-din*, *hifz-ul-nafs*, *hifz-ul-nasl* and *hifz-ul-mal*. Besides, in terms of SDGs goals, these *zakat* activities and programs are able to impact SDG 1, SDG 2, SDG 3, SDG 6, SDG 7, SDG 8, SDG 10, SDG 11, and SDG 13. Therefore, it can be concluded that Malaysian ZIs play important roles including in facing COVID-19 crisis and their contributions are significant toward both *maqasid shariah* and SDGs.

CONCLUSION

This study examines *zakat* impacts on *maqasid shariah* and SDGs for Malaysian ZIs. The impact of *zakat* activities and programs toward both *maqasid shariah* elements and SDGs goals was analyzed and compared between corporatized and non-corporatized ZIs. Besides, this study also investigates on Malaysian ZIs experiences and their significant contributions in facing COVID-19 toward *maqasid shariah* and SDGs. In sum, the findings indicate both *maqasid shariah* elements and SDGs goals through *zakat* impacts are high, and corporatizations of ZIs do not appear to affect *zakat* impact on *maqasid shariah* and SDGs. Besides, Malaysian ZIs were also found to play important roles in facing COVID-19. Thus, the findings probe further question as to whether corporatization of the institutions plays any role in enhancing their management efficiency. In ZIs, attaining its socioeconomic objectives through successful *zakat* fund management can be portrayed through the management's effectiveness and efficiency in delivering and utilizing of resources. Various stakeholders exist and *zakat* impact can be a good indicator to evaluate the effectiveness and efficiency of *zakat* activities and programs. As *zakat* impacts present the significant contribution made by ZIs, a practical implication of this study is for the ZIs management to plan carefully their activities and programs in the future. Although the main objective of *zakat* distribution is to help *asnaf*, notably, other criteria such as *maqasid shariah* and SDGs also can be used to measure *zakat* impacts besides its significance on *asnaf*.

The fact that non-corporatized ZIs have higher *zakat* impacts on *maqasid shariah* and SDGs signals a crucial point toward effectiveness of the ZIs restructuring. While good management practices can measure effectiveness, there are also other factors that could contribute to ZIs success. Thus, it is not conclusive that the corporatization reformation is not fully achieving its objectives. Future research may conduct an in-depth analysis toward public perceptions on ZIs role and achievement toward their intended existence objectives.

REFERENCES

Ab Rahman, A., Alias, M. H., & Omar, S. M. N. S. (2012). Zakat Institution in Malaysia: Problems and Issues. *Global Journal of al-Thalaqah, 2*(1), 35–42.

Abdelmawla, M. A. (2014). The Impacts of Zakat and Knowledge on Poverty Alleviation in Sudan: An Empirical Investigation (1990–2009). *Journal of Economic Cooperation and Development, 35*(4), 61–84.

Abdul Wahab, N., & Abdul Rahman, A. R. (2011). A Framework to Analyse the Efficiency and Governance of Zakat Institutions. *Journal of Islamic Accounting and Business Research, 2*(1), 43–62.

Abidin, S., Saad, R. A. J., & Muhaiyuddin, N. M. M. (2014). Evaluating Corporate Reporting on the Internet: The Case of Zakat Institutions in Malaysia. *Jurnal Pengurusan, 42,* 19–29.

Ahmad, S., Wahid, H., & Mohamad, A. (2006). Penswastaan Institusi Zakat dan Kesannya Terhadap Pembayaran Secara Formal di Malaysia. *International Journal of Management Studies, 13*(2), 175–196.

Ahmad Shahir, M. (2007). Paradigma Pengurusan Institusi Zakat: Pengalaman Lembaga Zakat Selangor (MAIS). In *Persidangan Cukai & Zakat Kebangsaan,* 22–24 May. Kuala Lumpur, Malaysia.

Ahmad Shahir, M, & Adibah, A. W. (2010). Pengurusan Zakat di Negeri Selangor: Isu dan Cabaran. In *Prosiding Konvensyen Kebangsaan Perancangan & Pengurusan Harta dalam Islam,* 14 July. Selangor, Malaysia.

Al Qardawi, Y. (2000). *Fiqh al Zakah.* Jeddah· King Abdulaziz University.

Alterman, J. B., Hunter, S., & Phillips, A. L. (2005). *The Idea and Practice of Philanthropy in the Muslim World.* US Agency for International Development.

Anis, F. M., & Kassim, S. H. (2016). Effectiveness of Zakat-Based Programs on Poverty Alleviation and Economic Empowerment of Poor Women: A Case Study of Bangladesh. *Journal of Islamic Monetary Economics and Finance, 1*(2), 229–258.

Astro Awani. (2015). SPRM Terima 286 Aduan Diterima Libatkan Penyelewengan Dana Banjir - Mustafar, *Astro Awani,* May 10. Available at http://www.astroawani.com/berita-malaysia/sprm-terima-286-aduan-diterima-libatkan-penyelewengan-dana-banjir-mustafar-59656. Accessed 18 March 2016.

Aziz, M. R. A. (2012). *Introduction to Islamic Institutions in Economics and Finance*. Negeri Sembilan: USIM Press.

Bakar, M. H. A., & Abd Ghani, A. H. (2011). Towards Achieving the Quality of Life in the Management of Zakat Distribution to the Rightful Recipients (The Poor and Needy). *International Journal of Business and Social Science, 2*(4), 237–245.

Chapra, M. U. (1992). *Islam and the Economic Challenge (No.17)*. Virginia: International Institute of Islamic Thought (IIIT).

Dusuki, A. W., & Abdullah, N. I. (2007). Maqasid al-Shari'ah, Maslahah, and Corporate Social Responsibility. *The American Journal of Islamic Social Sciences, 24*(1), 25–44.

Ghazanfar, S. M., & Islahi, A. A. (1997). *Economic Thought of Al-Ghazali*. Jeddah: Islamic Economics Research Center.

Hassan, H. (2017). Pegawai Kanan Zakat Pulau Pinang Ditahan, *Harian Metro*, May 9. Available at http://www.hmetro.com.my/utama/2017/05/228036/pegawai-kanan-zakat-pulau-pinang-ditahan. Accessed 13 May 2017.

Hassan, M. K., & Ashraf, A. (2010). An Integrated Poverty Alleviation Model Combining Zakat, Awqaf and Micro-Finance. In *7th International Conference—The Tawhidi Epistemology: Zakat and Waqf Economy*, pp. 261–281, 6–7 January, Bangi, Malaysia.

Hossain, M. Z. (2012). Zakatin Islam: A Powerful Poverty Alleviating Instrument for Islamic Countries. *International Journal of Economic Development Research and Investment, 3*(1), 1–11.

Kamaruddin, M. I. H., & Auzair, S. M. (2018). Classification of Islamic Social Enterprises (ISEs) in Malaysia Based on Economics Sectors. *Management and Accounting Review, 17*(2), 17–42.

Kamaruddin, M. I. H., & Ramli, N. M. (2018). The Impacts of Internal Control Practices on Financial Accountability in Islamic Non-Profit Organizations in Malaysia. *International Journal of Economics, Management and Accounting, 26*(2), 365–391.

Kamaruddin, M. I. H., Hanefah, M. M., & Masruki, R. (2020). Empirical Investigation on Awqaf and Its Socio-Economic Impact in Malaysia. In *Awqaf-Led Islamic Social Finance*, pp. 218–233, Routledge.

Keating, E. K., & Frumkin, P. (2003). Reengineering Nonprofit Financial Accountability: Toward a more Reliable Foundation for Regulation. *Public Administration Review, 63*(1), 3–15.

Khalifah, M. H., Nurzaman, M. S., & Nafis, M. C. (2017). Optimization of BAZNAS Programs on Sustainable Development Goals (SDGs): Analytic Network Process Approach (ANP). *International Journal of Zakat, 2*(2), 71–83.

Kusuma, D. B. W., & Sukmana, R. (2010). The Power of Zakah in Poverty Alleviation. In *7th International Conference—The Tawhidi Epistemology: Zakat and Waqf Economy*, pp. 409–434, 6–7 January, Bangi, Malaysia.

Laldin, M. A. (2006). *Islamic Law: An Introduction*. Kuala Lumpur: International Islamic University Malaysia.

Lateff, E. E. A., Patil, M. R., & Hassan, M. S. (2014). Prestasi Kecekapan Agihan Kewangan dan Bukan Kewangan di Kalangan Institusi Zakat di Malaysia. *Jurnal Ekonomi Malaysia, 48*(2), 51–60.

Masruki, R., Hussainey, K., & Aly, D. (2018). Mandatory Reporting Issues in Malaysian State Islamic Religious Councils (SIRC): Evidence from Interviews. *Journal of Engineering and Applied Sciences, 13*, 2092–2097.

Mohsin, M. I. A. (2015). Potential of Zakat in Eliminating Riba and Eradicating Poverty in Muslim Countries. *International Journal of Islamic Management and Busines, 1*(1), 40–63.

Muhamed, N. A., Kamaruddin, M. I. H., & Nasrudin, N. S. (2018). Positioning Islamic Social Enterprise (ISE). *Journal of Emerging Economies & Islamic Research, 6*(3), 28–38.

Noor, Z., & Pickup, F. (2017). The Role of Zakat in Supporting the Sustainable Development Goals. *BAZNAS and UNDP Brief Series*, Indonesia.

Nurzaman, M. S. (2016). Evaluating the Impact of Productive Based Zakat in the Perspective of Human Development Index: A Comparative Analysis. *Kyoto Bulletin of Islamic Area Studies, 9*(29), 42–62.

Obaidullah, M., & Shirazi, N. S. (2015). *Islamic Social Finance Report 1436H*. Jeddah: Islamic Research and Training Institute (IRTI).

Olanipekun, W. D., Brimah, A. N., & Sanusi, H. B. (2015). The Role of Zakat as a Poverty Alleviation Strategy and a Tool for Sustainable Development: Insights from the Perspectives of the Holy Prophet (PBUH). *Arabian Journal of Business and Management Review (Oman Chapter), 5*(3), 8–17.

Othman, R., & Ameer, R. (2014). Institutionalization of Risk Management Framework in Islamic NGOs for Suppressing Terrorism Financing: Exploratory Research. *Journal of Money Laundering Control, 17*(1), 96–109.

Rahmatya, M. D., & Wicaksono, M. F. (2018). Model of Receipt and Distribution of Zakat Funds Information System. *IOP Conference Series: Materials Science and Engineering, 407*(1), 012071.

Ramli, N. M., & Kamaruddin, M. I. H. (2017). Disclosure of Web-Based Accountability: Evidence from Zakat Institutions in Malaysia. In *5th South East Asia International Islamic Philanthropy Conference 2017 (SEAIIPC 2017)*, pp. 664–678, 14–16 February. Melaka, Malaysia.

Rosli, M. R. B., Salamon, H. B., & Huda, M. (2018). Distribution Management of Zakat Fund: Recommended Proposal for Asnaf Riqab in Malaysia. *International Journal of Civil Engineering and Technology, 9*(3), 56–64.

Saad, R. A. J., Aziz, N. M. A., & Sawandi, N. (2014). Islamic Accountability Framework in the Zakat Funds Management. *Procedia-Social and Behavioral Sciences, 164*, 508–515.

Shaikh, S. A., & Ismail, A. G. (2017). Role of Zakat in Sustainable Development Goals. *International Journal of Zakat, 2*(2), 1–9.

Shehata, S. I. (1994). Limitations on the Use of Zakah Funds in Financing Socio-Economic Infrastructure. *Islamic Economic Studies, 1*(2), 63–78.

Siddiqi, M. N. (2004). *Riba, Bank Interest and the Rationale of Its Prohibition.* Jeddah: Islamic Research and Training Institute (IRTI).

Suprayitno, E., Abdul Kader, R., & Harun, A. (2013). The Impact of Zakat on Aggregate Consumption in Malaysia. *Journal of Islamic Economics, Banking and Finance, 9*(1), 39–62.

Teng, L. H. (2016). Why 32,934 Donors Cancelled Contributions to YAPEIM. *Malaysiakini*, April 5. Available at https://www.malaysiakini.com/news/336522. Accessed 23 August 2016.

Wahid, H., Ahmad, S., & Mohd Noor, M. A. (2004). Kesan Bantuan Zakat Terhadap Kualiti Hidup: Kajian Kes Asnaf Fakir dan Miskin. *The Journal of Muamalat and Islamic Finance Research, 1*(1), 151–166.

Wahid, H., Ahmad, S., & Kader, R. A. (2010). Pengagihan Zakat oleh Institusi Zakat kepada Lapan Asnaf: Kajian di Malaysia. *Jurnal Pengurusan JAWHAR, 4*(1), 141–170.

Worldmeter. (2020). Covid-19 Coronavirus Pandemic (Update). *Worldmeter.* Available at https://www.worldometers.info/coronavirus/#countries. Accessed 30 March 2020.

Yaacob, A. C., Mohamed, S., Daut, A., Ismail, N., Ali, M., & Don, M. (2013). Zakat Disbursement via Capital Assistance: A Case Study of Majlis Agama Islam Johor. *Journal of Emerging Economics and Islamic Research, 1*(2), 1–20.

Zakaria, M. (2014). The Influence of Human Needs in the Perspective of Maqasid al-Syari'ah on Zakat Distribution Effectiveness. *Asian Social Science, 10*(3), 165–173.

CHAPTER 21

How Far Corporate Zakat May Contribute to Sustainable Development Goals?

Suhail Ahmad and S. Ghiasul Haq

INTRODUCTION

Poverty is one of the most difficult challenges facing humanity. Poverty is fundamental not reaching the minimum standard of living and not enough money to buy important necessities of life such as food, clothing, shelter, basic education, health, and many others. The poor are those who do not have enough income or consumption to earn beyond a minimum social welfare do not have now it is not only considered an economic problem but it is also recognized globally and socially (World Bank 2001a). Because poverty is more or less the same in almost all countries of the world and each community tried to address this issue with its own resources and methods. Other than that World Bank, International Monetary Fund (IMF), International Labor Organization (ILO), States United Nations (UN), United Nations Educational, Scientific and Cultural Organization (UNESCO), United Nations International Emergency Fund for Children (UNICEF), United Nations Development Program (UNDP),

S. Ahmad (✉) · S. Ghiasul Haq
Sarhad University of Science and Information Technology, Peshawar, Pakistan

© The Author(s), under exclusive license to Springer Nature Switzerland AG 2021
M. M. Billah (eds.), *Islamic Wealth and the SDGs*,
https://doi.org/10.1007/978-3-030-65313-2_21

421

Asian Development Bank (ADB) and various other organizations and institutions are also allocating funds for this purpose (World Bank 2001b).

Pakistan is a developing country and their per capita income is very low there is no literacy rate they have made significant progress in the last seven decades. Poverty is on the rise in Pakistan day to day; in 2012, one-third of households in Pakistan were below the poverty line and 21% were very poor (Naveed and Ali 2012). Pakistan ranks 146 out of 187 countries with Human Development Index (HDI) 0.515. The report shows a gradual increase in the HDI value of 0.504 in 2011 and 0.503 in 2010, although Pakistan's range decreased slightly during 2012 is at the bottom. Adjusted Human Development Index (IAHDI) for inequality multidimensional poverty index (MDI) and gender inequality index (GII) for Pakistan stood at 0.356, 0.264, and 0.567, respectively (Human Development Report 2013). These indicators show the dimensions of inequality and non-profit income Pakistan ranks 123rd in terms of gender inequality and reported that 49% of Pakistan's population lives in multiculturalism poverty; the lowest rate in the region (Bangladesh) 58%. According to the report, the severity of deprivation is 50% in Bangladesh and 53% in Pakistan (UNDP 2013).

The political problem exists in almost all societies of the world regardless of their economic condition. It has become an important humanitarian issue that goes beyond economic, political, social, and economic maybe even cultural and religious issues. Poverty is a multi-faceted problem today and only it depends on the availability of resources, the size of the population, and the economic profile of the country. A review of the literature reveals that there is a problem of poverty and its eradication along with the secular point of view; it is also being given much importance in Islamic literature point of view.

Several studies have explained the potential effects of Zakat on various Sustainable Development Goals (SDGs) such as poverty (SDG1), zero hunger (SDG2), good health (SDG3), quality education (SDG4), clean water and sanitation as well as low inequality (SDG10) (Nurzaman et al. 2018). The SDGs encourage humanity to work together to achieve the 17 SDGs. The United Nations global investment report shows that this cooperation is necessary as there is an average investment gap of $2.5 trillion for developing countries. This gap can only be filled if more funds are received from existing donors and new areas of social finance are utilized (UNCTAD 2014).

Eradicating poverty and inequality is one of the biggest challenges from the current decade to the next. Different societies and non-governmental organizations (NGOs) face these challenges in the society. These organizations depend on their work or public funding; although the amount of charitable donations has increased in recent years (Stirk 2015). There is still a gap between need and financial support and the gap could widen as public distrust of charities grows. Islamic finance a branch of Islamic social finance includes a number of tools, both mandatory and voluntary that can be used to reduce inequality and achieve social and economic justice (Charity Commission 2018).

Many studies have been done in which the role of different has been discussed and explained Islamic measures to eradicate poverty (Akhtar 2000; Yasin and Tahir 2002; Iqbal 2002; Ahmad 2004; Iqbal 2005; Naumani 2007; Khattak 2013; Siddiqui 2013). All past studies have done a lot on the theoretical aspects of Islamic poverty alleviation measures they introduced Zakat system in poverty alleviation.

Islam is the religion of all time and an institutional approach is used for itself throughout the region distribution scheme for poverty alleviation. The market is allowed to play a role as an institution role through other institutional arrangements to correct market imbalances. In other institutions, family, Zakat, endowment, Sadaqah al-fitr, animals for happiness, animal sacrifice to Allah, anqat al-af (excess charity), inheritance elimination of (inheritance) and usury. In addition, all forms of exploitation (including violations of fundamental human rights) are strictly prohibited in the *Shari'ah*.

Importance of Zakat

Zakat's purpose is only to help and bring the poor and needy and wealth is in circulation but as an essential act of worship it also purifies the heart and soul which transform man into a sincere and obedient servant of Allah. Zakat is an expression of gratitude for the reward of Allah Almighty. Zakat's institution eliminates disorder, greed; it breeds selfishness, enmity, jealousy, insensitivity, and exploitation in the society and gives birth to the soul in it such as love, bigotry, welfare, sincerity, consideration, cooperation, brotherhood, and friendship.

Allah Almighty has clearly mentioned those who are entitled to receive Zakat; "In fact, the collection of Zakat is only for the needy and the poor and for those who have a job to collect them and for those who must win their hearts and for the salvation of slaves and the help of debtors and for the cause of Allah and hospitality this is the duty of Allah to the travelers of the road; And Allah is All-Knowing, All-Wise" (Al-Tawbah, 60).[1] This verse describes the eight expenses of Zakat and its main objectives are poverty alleviation, economic empowerment as well as social development which are the core principles of SDGs.

Zakat is a monetary form of worship in Islam that has been declared obligatory and this is the cornerstone of the Islamic economic system for Muslims and it is one of the five pillars of Islam also declared Zakat obligatory. Salah and Zakat in the Qur'an are mentioned in thirty-two places together and a strong command is given Zakat at 22 places. Establishment of a system of Zakat is one of the basic responsibilities of an Islamic state. In Surah Al-Hajj, Allah Almighty Says: "These are the people who, if We give them power over the earth, will establish Salah and Zakat. They enjoin what is right and forbid what is wrong (Al-Hajj, 41)[2] Every Muslim who a certain amount of wealth must give a certain amount of his wealth according to the *Shari'ah* those who are entitled to receive Zakat in the eyes of *Shari'ah*."

There are different types of wealth on which Zakat get together among the animals for which Zakat is obligatory are camels and cows (including oxen and buffaloes) and goats. Zakat is also necessary in gold and silver. There are many traditions of the Prophet (peace and blessings of Allah be upon him) that describe this responsibility; the Zakat on gold is 7.5 tola and that of silver is 52.5 tola. Zakat in trade mandatory too; goods and commercial property includes all property that is sold and purchased for profit.

Corporate Zakat

Corporate Zakat is an essential charity that comes from business wealth whether it is based on manufacturing, mining, fishing, shipping, supplies, agriculture, services, etc., for commercial purposes, whether in private business, Muslims or associations between non-Muslims, companies of all kinds, cooperatives or stocks (Noor 2017). As a result, the requirements that are met in all types of business related to goods or services are

---

[1] Surah Al Tawbah, 60 of the Holy Book Qur'an.
[2] Surah Al Hajj, 41 of the Holy Book Qur'an.

subject to Zakat (Jawhar 2008). The legal requirement to pay commercial Zakat pay in Malaysia has been determined by the Business Zakat Fatwa (Consultative Opinion) in the Fatwa National Council of Malaysia. The meeting was held on December 9, 1992, to discuss the Zakat upon company. The Dialogue has decided that the companies must pay Zakat as per the conditions.

The National Fatwa Council of Malaysia established the conditions for the corporate Zakat which a company must be freely owned and fully owned, the curriculum threshold (minimum amount), full transportation (one year or 354.3 days), and the company must have a rate of Zakat of 2.5%, and for these companies owned by Muslims and non-Muslims. Zakat is equal to the number of shares of Muslims based on the net income obtained so paying Zakat is an obligation that is fulfilled as part of religious obligations. Zakat is not a barrier to trade but a factor that improves self-sufficiency in pursuit of blessings.

Zakat paid by commercial entities is mandatory although some companies in Indonesia have studied it despite ambiguity in Islamic jurisprudence and Indonesian law. This includes corporate Zakat in Islamic banks in Indonesia. Attention will be paid to compliance and it will also determine whether moral, religious, or secular values have compelled banks to comply with corporate Zakat with to determine whether Islamic charitable and corporate social responsibility in Indonesia is a *Shari'ah* business. To use the case study as an investigative method and thus to multiply the various sources and structured files of the interview evidence (annual, financial, and corporate governance reports); in their decision on whether or not to pay Zakat the study found that Islamic commercial banks' views on the legitimacy of regulating corporate Zakat in Indonesia are influenced by a combination of two or three factors, i.e., type of trade (how *Shari'ah* related industry), Zakat in Islam. Its attitude toward the principles of, its size (the amount of earnings deemed eligible to pay Zakat pay) and benchmarking for other competitors. Factors number one and a combination of two become the most important factors (Alfitr and Samarinda 2017).

Islam's institutional approach uses Zakat as a tool to distribute solutions for many economic and social problems (categorized by 17 SDGs goals) among them; this tool can also be used. It is very effective in reducing and ultimately eradicating poverty in the society because it is a multipurpose strategy used not only to alleviate poverty and inequality but also its purpose is to achieve other goals of the Islamic system. Islam uses mandatory classification and voluntary, permanent and temporary measures, which give flexibility to the system, such as Zakat, as Islam is not limited to the eradication of poverty but to the eradication of all forms social problems.

Zakat and Sustainable Development Goals

The literature of Islamic economics is rich in highlighting the welfare potential of Zakat, but very few empirical studies have studied Zakat. Zakat is considered a means of "fighting poverty." According to Bastian (2009), the fight against poverty is one think about how to reduce poverty by targeting poor people in a specific area. This has the potential to develop effective economic activity in which the anti-poverty system guarantees that people can achieve basic needs. Zakat has fundamental differences from other pillars of Islam. It allows the poor to participate in and create economic activities useful as part of the community.

Dinamika (2009) stated that the Zakat is logically affected and has a significant level of negative correlation. This is because the discussion on Zakat only focuses on the mechanisms involved, social groups that issue Zakat (Mawzaki) are in fact a very dominant group in this regard charity is those who receive Zakat in which their consumption rate depends on the connection and distribution of Zakat. Zakat consumption has a positive correlation with consumption and number of investments and the economy will grow due to the fair and proper Zakat management and disbursement mechanism.

It estimates the potential reserves of Zakat to find the welfare capacity of the institution of Zakat institution at the level of the whole economy. And also trying to estimate the accumulation of Zakat stock in the economy which includes agricultural products, livestock value, marketable inventory, currency circulation, foreign exchange reserves, gold and silver reserves estimates, and financial assets such as national savings system involves investing. Bank reserves in investment funds, market capitalization, pension schemes, and compensation. Our estimates show that Zakat is almost in Pakistan. The total could reach 7% of the total GDP and it is enough to fill the poverty gap in Pakistan. It also discussed how the Zakat system can have a positive impact on investment flows, promoting business culture and making capital and real estate markets more competitive. At the economic level, we also discussed the role of the institution of Zakat as a stabilizer (Shaikh 2016).

The General Economic Division (GED) of the planning commission says that Bangladesh has made significant progress on a number of MDG targets in terms of food security, health, education and poverty alleviation. However, due to lack of funds from local and foreign sources, the country still faces several challenges in achieving other MDG targets. Similarly, determining the availability of funds will be the biggest challenge for Bangladesh to achieve the SDGs. Bangladesh needs massive infrastructure developments such as roads, bridges, amusement parks, schools, colleges, universities, religious, and cultural institutions. Raising resources through taxes, fees, or tolls is not enough to finance these much-needed public goods. Therefore, financial support from individuals as well as institutions, such as private, governmental NGOs is essential[3].

Historically, it is clear that Zakat and Awqaf together played a major role in the socio-economic development of Muslim societies. These organizations are still able to come up with comprehensive solutions to achieve SDGs. In particular, the endowment has the potential to serve as an effective third sector (excluding the private and public sector) as a vehicle for SDGs. Based on the book documentary survey and secondary statistics, the study explores the socio-economic role of endowments in financing SDGs in Bangladesh (Khan and Hassan 2019). An overview of the Islamic perception of poverty and its strategies for poverty alleviation presented and described the system of Zakat in Islam as a cooperative society, insurance company, and Muslim provident fund[4]; whereas the institution of Zakat has played a very effective role in the Muslim community of all ages.

Yasin and Tahir (2002) have discussed Zakat application for elimination of interest and inequality in income and alleviating poverty within the framework of general balance. In contrast, the economy will do better in eliminating poverty and income distribution partial plans. Iqbal (2002) concludes his findings and the view of an Islamic system which demands the fulfillment of the basic needs of all and this situation leaves much to be desired. Now is the time for Islamic scholars and governments to work together, design, and implement a policy package that can reasonably address this issue.

---

[3] General Economic Division of Bangladesh
[4] Maududi (1984), Islamic Scholar.

Zakat on income discussed the effects of the new distribution groups and regions in Pakistan using data collected from integrated economy homes survey 1996–1997. It concluded that the possible addition and subtraction of Zakat were significant impact on household income in the low-income group ranging from 10.63 to 29.23%; therefore, Zakat has its potential role but it requires serious government efforts.[5]

The poverty reduction strategy paper (2003) states that it is an important tool for society rehabilitation and reducing the risk of external shock is Zakat's new system and it not only provides funds to the beneficiaries to meet basic needs but also for permanent rehabilitation. Ahmad (2004) describes Zakat as a fifth pillar of Islam and *Shari'ah* which has direct economic implications and can be solved poverty and social injustice and inequality by Zakat and Waqf institutions. They suggest that Zakat and Awqaf (endowments) should be included in poverty reduction strategies adopted by developing countries. If used effectively, they can play an important role in the distribution of assets that enables the poor to be productive.

It is estimated the lack of resources and reported that some low-income Muslims countries with potential Zakat can fill the gap in their resources below international poverty index.[6] The strategy adopted by the government of Pakistan for poverty he says almost all of these programs failed to achieve their financial goals. Appreciate the success of the Zakat system especially in rural areas and advise the government that improves the resources provided under the Zakat system but only after correcting the failures.[7] A study investigates the role of Zakat in alleviating poverty in the context of Selangor in Malaysia experimental results indicates a positive contribution of Zakat distribution to reduce income inequality. Their study show that the distribution of Zakat can be reduced poverty incidence reduces the extent of poverty and reduces the severity of poverty.

Siddiqui (2013) stated that Zakat at Islam is a system of social protection. Because it is a permanent and direct transfer of resources from rich to poor the incidence of poverty is rapidly declining. Currently, many Islamic states like Saudi Arabia, Sudan, Pakistan, Jordan, Libya, Kuwait,

---

[5] Shirazi (2003).

[6] Shirazi (2006).

[7] Arif (2006)

Malaysia, Indonesia, Iran, and Bangladesh; These countries deals Zakat at the state level and meeting the needs of people who deserve it.

Shapes of social empowerment through the use of by business waste Nusa Tenggara province are; (i) empowering individuals in the field of education to help those in need and failure to improve quality in the future, which affects an individual's productivity and the realization that educated people are more productive than illiterate people, (ii) empowering groups in the fields of economics to maintain the clause in the way of maintaining property because when they occur able to retain property, which will hinder disbelief in order to improve their standard of living make those who benefit financially and empowered more productive and economically free, and (iii) empowering people in the health sector to meet the basic needs of the poor in the case of access to people in need to maintain and improve the quality of medical care, because health is a condition A body and soul that enables the poor and homeless to live socially and economically productive lives. Barriers to relocation in the western province of Nusa Tenggara are a social factor and a lack of transportation.[8]

NGOs Which Active in the Zakat and SDGs in Pakistan

Al-Khidmat Foundation

Alkhidmat foundation is established in 1990 in the country and very active in the welfare and societal activities across the country. Especially they are practicing various activities in the country such as food and nutrition, education, health, shelter, climate and environmental aspects of the society and other harmony and social justice through several welfare and support to the individuals in the country. About all, it is the best in true sense ramping toward the sustainable development goals of united nation in Pakistan.

Transparent Hand

Pledges to provide free surgery to those who cannot afford; *Transparent Hand* is a non-profit organization that is addressing this important health

---

[8] A study in Nusa Tenggara Timur—NTT is the southernmost province of Indonesia.

issue in Pakistan with the help of fundraising through its exclusive crude funding platform. Transparent hands, with the help of donations and charities, perform deserving surgeries for free in private hospitals. If they want to donate, donors around the world can use our online crowd-funding web portal. You can select any patient, fund the surgery, and receive regular feedback and updates, until the patient is fully recovered.

Online fundraising is easy to use;

(i) *Choose the patient for whose surgery you want to finance.*
(ii) *Choose from a variety of payment methods at your convenience.*
(iii) *Donate to this patient and get a tax deduction.*
(iv) *Get regular updates from this patient until you are fully recovered.*

You want to save people's lives by donating money for surgical treatment. You need full transparency about where your donation/charity are going. Donors can trust us completely with their donations and charities. There are many people in Pakistan and around the world who want to spend their money on trusted organizations, but we are not sure who we should donate to. To ensure complete transparency, transparent hands load all documents with patient success stories, so donors can see that their money is being spent on a good cause[9]

Shaukat Khanum Cancer Hospital

Shaukat Khanum Cancer Hospital is one of the largest charities in Pakistan founded by Imran Khan[10]. At its inception, the historic hospital was the only healthcare provider for cancer patients. With its successful operations in Lahore and Peshawar, Shaukat Khanum Cancer Hospital has used state-of-the-art technology and state-of-the-art machinery to detect and treat various types of cancer. The training includes the services of qualified doctors who care for people who cannot afford cancer treatment. The hospital does not charge a single penny and transforms the victims into a better life from the brink of death (Table 21.1).[11]

---

[9] https://www.transparenthands.org/list-of-top-10-zakat-accepting-organizations-in-pakistan/.

[10] Currently Prime Minister of Pakistan.

[11] https://www.transparenthands.org/list-of-top-10-zakat-accepting-organizations-in-pakistan/.

Table 21.1 Four years campaign and details of Shaukat Khanum Cancer Hospital

S. No.	Zakat campaign year	Objectives and outcome
1.	2017	1. Many cancer patients to Shaukat Khanum Hospitals in Lahore and Peshawar in the hope of getting free cancer care 2. Its Zakat allows us to support the treatment of 75% of our patients 3. This year we have Rs. 5.5 billion to help more patients of this nature
2.	2018	1. Many mothers' children are fighting for their lives against cancer. They rely on their Zakat, charity, and donations to continue their fight 2. Shaukat Khanum Hospital is providing free treatment to more than 75% of its cancer patients 3. This year, we need Rs. 6.5 billion to help treat thousands of patients completely free every year
3.	2019	1. You're Zakat and donations help us to treat 75% of the patients receiving free treatment at Shaukat Khanum Hospitals in Lahore and Peshawar 2. This year, we need to help 8.5 billion cancer patients overcome cancer and win the biggest battle of their lives
4.	2020	1. Shaukat Khanum Memorial Cancer Hospital is a specialized cancer center, however, given the current situation, we are well aware of its role as a leading care institution in the country and they have found themselves fighting the dual battle of cancer. Prepared for coronavirus we have already taken extraordinary steps to make every effort to help in this time of national crisis and we hope that you will open your hearts and provide unparalleled support so that we can do it 2. Shaukat Khanum Hospitals in Lahore and Peshawar are providing free treatment to more than 75% of all patients 3. This year we need Rs. 11 billion to help these patients. Give your Zakat to Shaukat Khanum Hospitals so that we can save thousands of mothers for their children

Source www.skmh.org.pk

Edhi Foundation

The Edhi Foundation is the most internationally acclaimed foundation. The foundation was founded by Abdul Sattar Edhi in 1951. The foundation provides 24-hour emergency services across the country. It has about 300 operating centers. Services offered include housing for the homeless, disabled, and orphans. It also offers free medical care and hospital services, along with national and international aid, drug rehabilitation, education, blood and drug banks, medical care, coastal and maritime services, and air ambulance services. The foundation has helped change the lives of hundreds of people and donations or Zakat can be accepted through credit cards, banks, or PayPal.[12]

Chhipa Welfare Association

The Chhipa Welfare Association is one of the most effective charities in Pakistan. It was founded by Ramzan Chippa in 2007. Its activities include an ambulance service and free or low-cost meals for low-income people. The association is based in Karachi and operates throughout the city. The Hidden Welfare Association is a completely non-profit NGO that serves humanity without distinction of race or caste.[13]

Ehsas

EHSAS is an NGO based in Chakwal and Islamabad. Its plans target a wide range of areas, including poverty alleviation, health care, education, and social development. EHSAS has several ongoing efforts, including the EHSAS Library, the EHSAS Blood Bank, the EHSAS Hepatitis Vaccination and Awareness Program, the EHSAS Horticulture Development Program, and the EHSAS Good Governance Program.[14]

The Rising Sun

The idea for "The Rising Sun" was developed by Mr. and Ms. Abdul Tawab Khan in 1984, and the journey began at that time, with only

[12] Ibid.
[13] Ibid.
[14] Ibid.

two special children. It now cares for about 415 registered children and about 68 children through its home rehabilitation services. It is one of the largest institutions in Pakistan providing services such as physical therapy and speech therapy to children such as education, physical therapy, speech therapy, sensory integration and hydrotherapy, mental retardation, cerebral palsy and autism, and vocational training.[15]

The Citizen Foundation

The Citizen Foundation is one of the largest non-profit organizations in the field of education. It was established in 1995. According to records compiled in April 2014, the organization has about 1,000 operating schools serving more than 145,000 students in different parts of the nation. The organization has also partnered with 141 schools to achieve its goals and build 141 TCF schools in different parts of Pakistan.[16]

Care Pakistan

Care Pakistan was founded by Seema Aziz in 1988. The first school attracted about 250 students on the first day and they are now serving in different parts of the country. The name now has about 2,352 schools, each providing quality education to more than 180,000 students. It now offers an English program that provides high-quality English education to approximately 2991 students. The organization aims to educate 1/9 million children.[17]

The Sindh Institute of Urology and Transplantation

The Sindh Institute of Urology and Transplantation, also known as SIUT, began its journey almost four decades ago with an eight-bed ward in the burn unit of Karachi Civil Hospital. It now has more than 500 beds and the facilities and services offered are more than 400,000 square feet long.

[15] Ibid
[16] Ibid.
[17] Ibid.

Regionally well-known as a center for kidney transplantation and related diseases, the institute is highly respected.[18]

CONCLUSION

In order to increase the rate of payment of commercial Zakat of institutions should be given additional coverage on Zakat so that they understand the obligation to pay Zakat to which is a rule of Islam and binds traders and needy and deserving segment of the society. Company's business record (net cash flow) estimating the annual income of Zakat. Therefore, this study will definitely play an important role in raising awareness in business especially regarding the obligation to pay Zakat pay in businesses, in fact it may increase the rate of collection of commercial Zakat in Pakistan and will spent on the welfare and humanitarian objective of the country and toward the SDGs of 2030. The literature of Islamic economics is rich in describing the potential for the welfare of Zakat but in very few experimental studies. Zakat thought is an economic act of worship that reminds Muslims that they have certain responsibilities not only to their family, relatives, or friends, but also to their community and people. If we take a closer look at Pakistan today, we can understand how important Zakat really is for the betterment of our society. According to the online magazine Bourgeois Project, about 35% of the country's population lives below the poverty line and is heavily dependent on the wealth of wealthy families. Poverty has also increased the country's child labor rate and hinders their education. Out of 40 million Pakistani children, 3.8 million works to support their families at an early age and 11 million of them work in factories in dangerous conditions.

Today's children are tomorrow's leaders but what are we giving them? We have given them nothing but unhealthy and poor childhood with zero education which will eventually take them nowhere. Even in the future, they will be trapped in this vicious circle of poverty and will live a meaningless life just like their poor parents. Many Pakistanis are living in poverty because the country's wealth is concentrated in a few wealthy families. Islamic history of the past and Pakistan's Zakat system experience implementation in 1980 shows that the trend of Zakat is to eradicate poverty. During the first decade after the introduction of the

[18] Ibid

Zakat system, Pakistan has seen a decline in poverty. However, later this system did not produce the same results as seen earlier decade. Zakat provisions due to nepotism, corruption in political influence formation of Zakat committees and provision of Zakat through these Zakat committees. Behind these problems is the lack of an effective monitoring system.

RECOMMENDATIONS

Pakistan's wealthiest corporations, landlords, and institutions have been reluctant to pay government taxes and pays annual Zakat, leading to higher rates of poverty, hunger, and illiteracy. Zakat is a great way to generate income for the welfare of the poor when big landowners, capitalists, industrialists, and other wealthy people realize its importance and move forward to fulfill their religious obligations. Every wealthy Muslim family has to commit to the welfare of Pakistan by giving annual Zakat. We can donate our Zakat money to deserving charities or non-profits that are fighting poverty and working to improve our country's education, employment, and healthcare sectors. When people with strong morals come together to make small sacrifices for the welfare of the country, social changes will surely take place. Give your Zakat with sincerity and honesty for the good of the people and see that something magical happens to both the donor and the recipient. A comprehensive approach should be adopted for the implementation of Islamic education in all fields' of life to get the best results and save people in this world from the difficulties that come in their lives after this the constitution of Pakistan suggests that no legislation can be passed against it in Pakistan. This will not only improve economic activity in the region useful in the country but also in a vast collection of Zakat and therefore in the eradication of poverty, inequality and ensure harmony and social justice in the society.

In addition to acknowledging the Lord of the worlds and self confidence in addition to a sense of responsibility pursuing the people for livelihood by adopting respectable means. The government must guarantee free and compulsory education and health to all children and youth. It is also recommended that people establish technical and professional institutions in remote areas together with urban areas as a priority. It will be helpful to get rid of poverty in urban as well as rural areas. Here is another reason observed that most people do not want to pay Zakat through the government lack of trust in government agencies. That is why there are no Zakat procedures consistent with the growth of people's income and wealth. It is important that a large-scale system does not fail the shortcomings of this system need to be addressed so that society can once again enjoy it.

REFERENCES

Ahmad, H. (2004). *Role of Zakat & wqaf in poverty alleviation*. Jeddah: Islamic Research & Training Institute.

Akhtar, M. R. (2000). Poverty Alleviation on a Sustainable Basis in the Islamic Framework. *Pakistan Development Review, 39*(4), 631–647.

Alfitr, A., & Samarinda, I. (2017). Why Do Companies Pay Their Alms Tax (Zakat)? Case Studies of Compliance with Corporate Zakat Obligation in Islamic Commercial Banks in Indonesia. *Advances in Social Science, Education and Humanities Research, 162*, 23–26.

Bastian, D. (2009). Pengaruh Program Anti Kemiskinan Dan Peningkatan Pendapatan Petani: StudiKasus Di Kelompok Tani Karya Makmur Kabupaten Pacitan. *Journal of Indonesian Applied Economics, 3*(2), 121–133.

Charity Commission. (2018). *Trust in Charities (Charity Commission for England and Wales)*. Wales.

Dinamika, Z. (2009). *Penggalangan Dana Zakat Bagi Pembangunan: Studi Dengan Pendekatan Kualitatif Di Desa Putukrejo Kecamatan Gondang Legi Kabupaten Malang*. Indonesia: Doctorate Program in Economic Science, Brawijaya University.

HDR. (2013). *Human Development Report 2013*.

Iqbal, M. (2002). *Islamic Economic Institutions and the Elimination Of Poverty*. Leicester: The Islamic Foundation.

Iqbal, M. (2005). *Poverty Elimination in Islamic Perspective: An Applied General Equilibrium Approach*. Islamic Institutions.

Jawhar. (2008). *Manual Pengurusan Pengiraan Zakat*. Kuala Lumpur, Malaysia: JAWHAR.

Khan, F., & Hassan, M. K. (2019). *Financing the Sustainable Development Goals (SDGs): The Socio-Economic Role of Awqaf (Endowments) in Bangladesh*. Cham: Revitalization of Waqf for Socio-Economic Development, Volume II. Palgrave Macmillan.

Khattak, N. (2013). *Poverty Alleviation: An Aim of Islamic Economics*. Retrieved from www.islamichouse.com.

Maududi. (1984). *Sayyid Mawdudi's Contribution Towards Islamic Revivalism*. Lahore: Idarah-i Ma'arif-i Islami.

Naumani, S. (2007). *Al-Farooq*. Lahore: Maktaba Islamia.

Naveed, A., & Ali, N. (2012). *Clustered Deprivation: District Profile of Poverty in Pakistan*. SDPI.

Noor, M. S. (2017). Indicators of Business Zakat Amongst Small Business: Concept and Contemporary Need. *International Journal of Academic Research in Business and Social Sciences, 7*(6), 1142–1157.

Nurzaman, M. S., et. al. (2018). *The Role of Zakat in Sustainable Development Goals for Achieving Maqashid Shari'ah.* Indonesia: Centre for Strategic Studies, BAZNAS.

Shaikh, S. A. (2016). Welfare Potential of Zakat: An Attempt to Estimate Economy wide Zakat Collection in Pakistan. Online at https://mpra.ub.uni-muenchen.de/68752/, MPRA Paper No. 68752, 14-53.

Shirazi, N. S. (2003). Distributive Effects of Zakat in Pakistan: Some Empirical Evidence. *KENMS Occational Paper No.1.* Malaysia: International Islamic University.

Shirazi, N. S. (2006). Providing for the resource shortfall for poverty elimination through the institution of Zakat in low-income Muslim countries. *International Journal of Economics, Management and Accounting, 14*(1), 1–27.

Siddiqui, S. (2013). *Islamic Economic System and Poverty Reduction.* Retrieved from www.pta.yogyakarta.go.id.

Stirk, C. (2015). *An Act of Faith: Humanitarian Financing and Zakat.* Global Humanitarian Assistance.

UNCTAD. (2014). World Investment Report 2014—Investing in the SDGs: An Action Plan. *United Nations Conference on Trade and Development, 2014.*

UNDP. (2013). *Human Development Report 2010.* New York: United Nations Development Programmeme.

World Bank. (2001a). *Poverty in the Developing World.* World Bank.

World Bank. (2001b). *World Development Report 2000–01 Attacking Poverty.* New York: Oxford University Press.

Yasin, M. H., & Tahir, S. (2002). *Poverty Elimination in Islamic Perspective: An Applied General Equilibrium Approach.* Leicester: The Islamic Foundation.

CHAPTER 22

Global Zakat Cooperation Chain to SDGs: How Shall Mechanisms and Master Plan Be?

Fauzia Mubarik

INTRODUCTION

And establish prayer and give Zakat, and whatever good you put forward for yourselves – you will find it with Allah. (2:110, Qur'an)

COVID-19 where brought in the disastrous era in the existing world, at the same time brought some utmost bright opportunities of the concept of digitized economies worldwide. The opportunity of digitized economies has become prominent because of the shrinking of economies as made vulnerable by the pandemic of COVID-19. The sufferings of the "well-established" conventional businesses were backfired because of the evil of debt backed financing; an evil that brings injustice and inequality in the society. A sin that is strongly discouraged in Islam; who actually believes in equality, distributive justice, and collectivism. If Islam believes on this notion of equality, distributive justice and collectivism, then a

---

F. Mubarik (✉)
National University of Modern Languages (NUML), Islamabad, Pakistan
e-mail: fmubarik@numl.edu.pk

© The Author(s), under exclusive license to Springer Nature Switzerland AG 2021
M. M. Billah (eds.), *Islamic Wealth and the SDGs*,
https://doi.org/10.1007/978-3-030-65313-2_22

439

Muslim whose belief is Islam cannot ignore it rather considers it as a fundamental of belief and practice. A fundamental that 1400 years before was revealed to our Holy Prophet (P.B.U.H) as a Pillar of Islam, Zakat.

Zakat is the third fundamental of Islam who believes in the equal distribution of wealth in the society to provide the basic necessities of life to the human beings. It is an obligatory fundamental of Islam that contributes to provide relief in the economic and the social activities of a society. Zakat is found to be the most fundamental Corporate Social Responsibility (CSR) activity among the Muslim Ummah. According to AAOIFI standard 7, the CSR funds are comprised of Zakat, Charity and Qard-ul-Hasan among which Zakat is the compulsory fundamental of Islam which needs to be furnished if the individual falls within a certain criterion. However, Zakat is a right not charity which makes it compulsory for a Muslim if the total wealth reaches to a level defined in "nisab,[1]" according to the Financial Accounting Standards 9 (FAS 9) of AAOIFI framework.

Many Islamic financial institutions include Zakat and charity in the CSR activities. The Zakat and charity are among the 85% of the disbursed funds reported and disclosed by the Islamic financial institutions whereas the Qard-ul-hasan and Waqf items are the least disclosed items, respectively. Three years back, a total amount of Corporate Social Responsibility (CSR) funds of US $518 million were disbursed by 253 Islamic financial institutions worldwide whereas the CSR disclosure index reached to 3.12 in the year 2017 from 2.61 from the previous year, respectively. The CSR development worldwide is currently being vigorously addressed by the United Nations' 17 Sustainable Development Goals on the areas of poverty, health, education, human rights, and the climate. The Islamic banks have shown keen interest to address these same goals because Islamic finance model is similar to these goals which is built on the ethical practices taking into account the welfare of the society. The Islamic financial institutions worldwide cover at least these five CSR activities on average, with Saudi Arabia and the United Arab Emirates at the highest rank of disbursing huge amounts of CSR funds, respectively.

A conference of World Zakat Forum held in Bandung, West Java in the year 2019, showed grave concern of the inefficient allocation of

---

[1] Nisab is calculated on the basis of gold or silver. In case of gold standard, the nisab is based on 3 ounces of gold or its cash equivalent. In case of silver, the nisab is based on 21 ounces of silver or its cash equivalent. https://www.islamic-relief.org/Zakat/nisab/.

Zakat Fund to the poor Muslim countries because of the poor channel-ization and ineffective strategic planning. A report[2] generated by World bank and Islamic Research and Training Institute (IRTI) of the Islamic Development Bank (IDB), an amount of $550–$600 billion of world Zakat fund is collected but still Muslim population in some countries live below the poverty line. According to the Executive Secretary of the World Zakat Forum, Irfan Syauqi Beik, there is a lack in the transparency of the allocation of Zakat Fund among the Muslim communities which creates obstruction in the well-in-time welfare assistance to the respective communities. Most of the Muslims worldwide prefer to pay the Zakat directly without involving any financial intermediary which creates the imbalance in the allocation of the right amount of Zakat Fund to the right Muslim population. It is because that most of the Muslim countries do not have a well-managed Zakat institution. According to the Executive Secretary of the World Zakat Fund, only in 1/3 of the member countries of the World Zakat Fund, the Zakat laws prevail.

As a Sustainable Development Goal (SDG) of poverty reduction, the World Zakat Fund has planned to digitize the Zakat allocation of funds to reach the right Muslim population to enhance transparency in the receipt and distribution of the Zakat Fund, respectively. One prominent land-mark is made by the Zakat Foundation of India where the Zakat payment and distribution are digital and the Zakat report of the reception and transmission immediately becomes available on the smartphones of the officers. Because of its transparency, the Muslim population amiably pays Zakat online as it uplifts trust among them about the effective recep-tion and distribution of the respective fund. Similarly, Baznas in Indonesia has also endeavored to digitize the Zakat payment system but still it's a long journey to bring the Muslim communities on one digital platform for an effective and efficient utilization of the Zakat Fund. The main purpose of this chapter is to strategically analyze and ascertain the role played by artificial intelligence in the Zakat Fund Mechanism, a Sustain-able Development Goal identified by the Islamic financial institutions as the need of today's time. This chapter primarily analyzes and model crowdfunding effectively operative through blockchain digital technology. Crowdfunding is based on peer-to-peer networking that amiably acknowl-edges blockchain technology because of the technical resemblance of the

[2] https://www.aa.com.tr/en/middle-east/world-Zakat-forum-optimizing-funds-to-red uce-poverty/1640107.

442 F. MUBARIK

former and the latter activities of transmission of the data (funds) from one user to the other user.

DIGITIZED ZAKAT MECHANISM

The Islamic financial institutions keeping the fast pace in the race with the conventional financial institutions in this pandemic have maneuvered their footprints in the digitized mode of operations. A report published by PwC (2018)[3] large numbers of digital banks has evolved named as the disruptor banks possessing no physical existence. To keep up the vigilant pace, nonetheless, according to a published report (2018),[4] the Islamic financial institutions have revolutionized to effective digital subsidiaries as well as the completely new digital (disruptor) Islamic banks, respectively. For sustainability and the continuous process improvement, the Shariah compliant boards are playing a key role for the approval and retention of the digital instruments and services by the Islamic financial institutions to compete in the global financial market. The significant digitized advancement of the Islamic financial institutions in the Gulf countries (see Fig. 22.1) specifically that of Bahrain and the United Arab Emirates such as the Dubai Internet city and Dubai Silicon Oasis, Meem Digital Retail Banking segment of Gulf International Bank owned by six Gulf Cooperation Council (GCC) countries primarily with the major shareholding of Saudi Arabia, Insha, a digital service provider on Islamic principles by the Turkish subsidiary of Albaraka in Germany has opened the prospect chance of the financial technology to penetrate in these countries through sophisticated regulations of computer security systems formally known as sandboxes. Nonetheless, the enlightenment of the digital Islamic banking services and instruments in the regions of Europe and Africa such as Morocco, Nigeria, and UK have also given a ray of hope for the Muslims communities worldwide to effectively utilize the Islamic services living at any place at any time specifically in the Non-Muslim majority regions, respectively.

As documented earlier, the need of today's time has created keen interest among the global stakeholders of artificial intelligence in the

---

[3] https://www.globenewswire.com/news-release/2019/03/20/1758003/0/en/Global-Islamic-Finance-Markets-Report-2019-Islamic-Banking-is-the-Largest-Sector-Contributing-to-71-or-USD-1-72-Trillion.html.

[4] https://ceif.iba.edu.pk/pdf/Reuters-Islamic-finance-development-report2018.pdf.

22 GLOBAL ZAKAT COOPERATION CHAIN TO SDGS ... 443

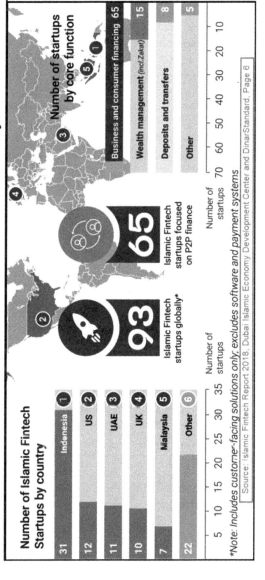

Fig. 22.1 Outlay of the global islamic financial technology industry

form of various information technology models such as crowdfunding, cryptocurrencies, blockchain, and the Rob-advice to name few. The world's first digital Islamic consortium on financial technology between Dubai International Financial Center (DIFC) of Dubai and ALGO of Bahrain received worldwide appraisal and recognition. Similarly, Fintech Bay launched in the Gulf and the regulations on the new sandbox issued are applauded worldwide. A Muslim community worldwide with strength of 1.8 billion Muslims wordwide[5] can play an active role to strengthen the digitized Zakat Mechanism worldwide into one common pool for the whole Muslim Ummah through crowdfunding.

As depicted in Fig. 22.1, the thrive of the Islamic financial institutions to collaborate with the small and medium enterprises by engaging into the digitized blockchain financial projects could earn to be a fruitful initiative to be more competitive at least in the rigorous reception and distribution of the Zakat Fund.

LITERATURE REVIEW

Few studies are added in the chapter to show the role of the Information technology on the disbursement of the Zakat Fund, respectively. Yahaya and Ahmad (2019) aims to investigate the factors affecting Zakat acceptance rate in approving mobile banking for Zakat distribution with the help of UTAUT model. The authors analyze the empirical data which is collected from Selangor, state of Malaysia. The authors suggested that there is still a lot which can improve Zakat distribution with the help of financial technology. Utami (2019) address the two main issues regarding the use of financial technology for Zakat payment. First is about the Shariah methods adopted for Zakat payment through financial technology. Second, is about the implementation methods of using financial technology for Zakat payment management system. Authors used exploratory research methodology for the study and concluded that as long as the financial technology does not harm and conflict with Shariah principles it is legally acceptable. Moreover, authors also suggest that if the institutions apply principles of Zakat payment for using financial technology then it can create good corporate governance system.

[5] https://www.pewresearch.org/fact-tank/2019/04/01/the-countries-with-the-10-lar gest-christian-populations-and-the-10-largest-muslim-populations/.

Friantoro and Zaki (2018) examined the positive and negative impact of using financial technology for Zakat collection in Indonesia. The author draws observations by analyzing the theories proposed by other scholars. The author concluded that there are opportunities where Zakat can be collected through financial technology whereas there are some weaknesses and threats regarding the use of financial technology for Zakat collection. Study by Saksonova and Irina (2017) proposed that there is large risk associated with the use of financial technology for Zakat collection as compared to traditional methods. In contrary, Al Azizah and Choirin (2018) study the issues regarding financial technology application for Zakat distribution in Indonesia. The authors analyzed the literature of numerous studies and concluded that Islamic finance and technological and factors play an important role in economic growth. Moreover, authors find that countries encourage more digital finance startup formation when Zakat institutions are deep well developed and latest technology is available. King and Levine (1993) proposed that country improves its productivity and generate high profits through high quality of Zakat distribution along with the development of financial system.

Ulya (2018) attempted to investigate legal protection of crowdfunding donation-based Zakat on financial technology in Indonesia which is caused by large spreading of startup with Zakat fund. Author finds no evidence of legal protection regulation in Zakat on donation-based crowdfunding. Kurnia and Hidayat (2008) proposed that the authorized basis for Zakat is one of the words of ALLAH SWAT an-Nur 56: Meaning: And establish prayer, give Zakat, and obey the apostle, that you may be given mercy. According to Basuki and Husein (2018), Imanuel Adhitya (2017), and Tsourela et al. (2007), the payment and collection of Zakat through financial technology plays an important role in the ease and faster transaction process as compared to the traditional way.

Rachman and Salam (2018) study the developments and innovations created in the integrated Zakat management system. The results of the study suggest that establishment of Zakat management should be gone through strategic steps including accountability, Shariah compliance, and legal compliance. These can be achieved by education, technology development systems and standardization. Another study proposed that efficiency level of Zakat management is examined by using an information management system by Bayu (2015). Widarwati et al. (2016) describe that upper middle class in Indonesia are known as muzakki who have capability of fulfillment of Zakat payment. The authors study numerous literatures and stated that behavior of muzakki plays an important role in the optimization of Zakat collection therefore Zakat institutions should maintain good relations with muzakki.

Ahmad et al. (2015) stated that regardless of technology advancement, word of mouth is considered to be the main source used to get Zakat information however, by increasing an efficiency level of Zakat management system; Zakat institutions can meet the needs of recipients. Wahab and Rahman (2011) examine the governance and efficiency model of Zakat institutions consists of collecting, handling, and allocating Zakat in Malaysia. Authors analyze the literature of various studies and proposed that effectiveness and efficiency of Zakat institutions can only be achieved if proper distribution of wealth is ensured. Similar study by Rahman (2007) specified that a proper performance measurement system should be developed in order to integrate Zakat into common Islamic financial system in Malaysia.

Pradja (2012) conducted study to examine an impact of using financial technology for Zakat payment. The author stated that Zakat institutions can use various approaches to understand historical, philosophical, theological and Islamic culture in order to integrated financial technology for Zakat payment. According to Brooks and Dunn (2012), Ng and Kwok (2017), Zakat institutions should have training and development of cybersecurity in order to use financial technology for Zakat payment. Moreover, Zakat institutions should also create awareness of fraud risks associated with human integrity and ethics.

DIGITIZED ZAKAT FUND MECHANISM AND CROWDFUNDING

The digital innovation in the form of crowdfunding is projected to be the most important and need of the time artificial intelligence product that may prove to be effective in penetration, regulation and control mechanism of the global Zakat Mechanism, respectively. It is one of the today's time Sustainable Development Goals among the Muslim community to strengthen the Zakat distribution mechanism from the rich to the poor and this is conveniently possible through the implementation of the robust model of technology. Figure 22.2 clearly depicts that the Islamic financial technology landscape majorly comprises of crowdfunding. It

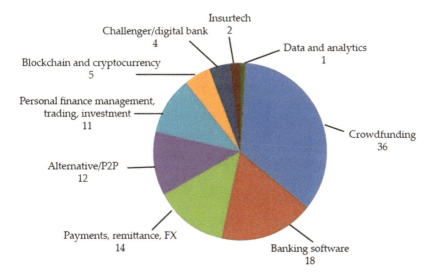

Fig. 22.2 Islamic financial technology landscape

indicates the reliance of the Islamic financial institutions on crowdfunding for the reception and distribution of funds.

Saiti et al. (2019) explain four forms of crowdfunding labeled as the rewards-based crowdfunding, donation-based crowdfunding, equity crowdfunding and the debt crowdfunding. Because, Islam discourages debt, therefore the other forms of crowdfunding can be strategically workable to attain the Sustainable Development Goals by making Zakat Fund an integral player of crowdfunding. The Shariah supervisory boards can play a key role in analyzing the concrete allocation of funds through Zakat acting as the key stakeholder of the crowdfunding artificial intelligence platform. The transparency of the disbursement of Zakat Fund by the respective Islamic financial institutions can be ensured by the Shariah boards, respectively.

Moreover, different forums can be utilized to vigorously work for the channelization of the Zakat Fund, specifically bringing the financial technology aspect into it. The Organization of Islamic Cooperation comprising of 57 Muslim countries, the Islamic Relief worldwide, World Zakat Forum, United Nations Children's Fund, United Nations Development Program, and the banks could collaborate digitally to create one platform of the Zakat Fund Mechanism through crowdfunding. In a strategic endeavor, the Zakat Fund through crowdfunding can be utilized to facilitate several corporate responsible projects on social finance, governmental projects, socially responsible micro-finance institutions for example, Ethis Venture, a Singaporean group operating in Malaysia is endeavoring to raise funds in the areas of real estate, health and education, as well as the small businesses. Managed electronically, therefore the audit of the fund could be ensured. The only thing needed is "will." A determination needed by the Muslim Ummah worldwide to collaborate for the digitized Zakat Fund to uplift the poor and the needy among the Ummah.

CONCLUSION

This chapter attempts to strategically analyze and ascertain the role played by artificial intelligence in the Zakat Fund Mechanism. As a need of today's time, the World Zakat Forum has recognized the digitized Zakat Fund Mechanism as a strategic Sustainable Development Goal to uplift the poor and the needy Muslim Ummah worldwide. The major agenda behind the digitization of the Zakat Fund by the World Zakat Forum is the appropriate reception, distribution, and transparency of the fund that reach the right person at the right time. This chapter has primarily focused on crowdfunding effectively operative through blockchain digital technology. The digital innovation in the form of crowdfunding could be projected to be the most important and need of the time artificial intelligence product that may prove to be effective in penetration, regulation, and control mechanism of the global Zakat management system. The Islamic finance landscape majorly relies on crowdfunding. Therefore, the World Zakat Forum can play a pivotal role to bring worldwide Islamic financial institutions into a peer-to-peer network crowdfunding to make the digitized Zakat Fund Mechanism more robust and peer centric.

REFERENCES

Adhitya, I. (2017). Analisis SWOT implementasi teknologi finansial terhadap kualitas Layanan Perbankan Di Indonesia. *20*(1), 137–148.

Ahmad, R. A., Othman, A. M., & Salleh, M. S. (2015). Assessing the Satisfaction Level of Zakat Recipients Towards Zakat Management. *Procedia Economics and Finance, 31,* 140–151.

Al Azizah, U. S., & Choirin, M. (2018). Financial Innovation on Zakat Distribution and Economic Growth. In *International Conference of Zakat*.

Basuki, F. H., & Husein, H. (2018). Analisis SWOT Financial Technology pada Dunia Perbankan di Kota Ambon. *Jurnal Manis, 2*(1), 60–74.

Bayu, M. R. (2015). *Penerapan sistem informasi manajemen pada badan amil Zakat nasional (BAZNAS) dalam peningkatan akuntabilitas dan mutu pengelolaan Zakat, infaq dan sedekah* (Thesis).

Brooks, L. J., & Dunn, P. (2012). *Business and Professional Ethics for Directors, Executives and Accountants*, 6th ed. Mason City: South-Western Cengage Learning. books.google.co.id.

Friantoro, D., & Zaki, K. (2018). Do We Need Financial Technology for Collecting Zakat? In *International Conference of Zakat*.

King, R. G., & Levine, R. (1993). Finance and Growth: Schumpeter Might Be Right. *The Quarterly Journal of Economics, 108*(3), 717–737.

Kurnia, H., & Hidayat, A. (2008). *panduan pintar Zakat*. Jakarta: Qultum Media.

Ng, A. W., & Kwok, B. K. (2017). Emergence of Fintech and Cybersecurity in a Global Financial Centre: Strategic Approach by a Regulator. *Journal of Financial Regulation and Compliance, 25*(4), 422–434. Available at: https://doi.org/10.1108/jfrc01-2017-0013.

Pradja, J. S. (2012). *Sharia Economic*. Bandung: CV. Pustaka Setia.

Rachman, M. A., & Salam, A. N. (2018). The Reinforcement of Zakat Management Through Financial Technology Systems. *International Journal of Zakat, 3*(1), 57–69.

Rahman, A. R. A. (2007). Pre-requisites for Effective Integration of Zakah into Mainstream Islamic Financial System in Malaysia. *Islamic Economic Studies, 14*(1–2), 91–107.

Saiti, B., Musito, M. H., & Yucel, E. (2019). *Islamic Crowdfunding: Fundamentals, Developments and Challenges* (Conference Paper).

Saksonova, S., & Irina, K. M. (2017). Fintech as Financial Innovation—The Possibilities and Problems of Implementation. *European Research Studies Journal, 20*(3A), 961–973.

Tsourela, M., Paschaloudis, D., & Fragidis, G. (2007). SWOT Analysis of Service e-Business Models. In *Proceedings of 13th Annual MIBES International Conference Western Macedonia University of Applied Sciences, School of Business and Economy*, Greece.

Ulya, N. U. (2018). Legal Protection of Donation-Based Crowdfunding Zakat on Financial Technology: Digitalization of Zakat Under Perspective of Positive Law and Islamic Law. In *International Conference of Zakat*.

Utami, P. (2019). Management of Zakat Payment Based on Fintech for the Good Corporate Governance Improvement. *Eastern Journal of Economics and Finance, 4*(2), 41–50.

Wahab, N. A., & Rahman, A. R. A. (2011). A Framework to Analyse the Efficiency and Governance of Zakat Institutions. *Journal of Islamic Accounting and Business Research, 2*, 43–62.

Widarwati, E., Afif, N. C., & Zazim, M. (2016). Strategic Approach for Optimizing of Zakah Institution Performance: Customer Relationship Management. *Al-Iqtishad: Jurnal Ilmu Ekonomi Syariah, 9*(1), 81–94.

Yahaya, M. H., & Ahmad, K. (2019). Factors Affecting the Acceptance of Financial Technology Among Asnaf for the Distribution of Zakat in Selangor-A Study Using UTAUT. *Journal of Islamic Finance, 8*, 035–046.

PART IV

How Potential of 'Awqaf' in Supporting SDGs?

CHAPTER 23

Not Yet Fully Understood Divine Status of Waqf and Its Social Welfare Role

Syed Khalid Rashid

COEXISTANCE OF THE QURAN AND CHARITY

In my forty-seven (47) years of teaching law in four universities of three countries and interaction with the law students and teachers in many English-speaking countries, I found to my utter surprise their ignorance of the Quranic roots of waqf, which they attributed to the Muslim law books in the English-medium universities and Law Schools. I myself have gone through the law books written by Ameer Ali,[1] Abdur Rahim,[2]

---

[1] Syed Ameer Ali, *Muhammadan Law* (1884), Tagore Law Lecture (4th ed. Calcutta, 1912), Vol. 1, (5th ed. Calcutta, 1929), Vol. 2.

[2] Abdur Rahim, *Muhammadan Jurisprudence*, Tagore Law Lecture, 1907 (Madras, 1911).

S. K. Rashid (✉)
International Islamic
University, Kuala Lumpure, Malaysia

© The Author(s), under exclusive license to Springer Nature   453
Switzerland AG 2021
M. M. Billah (eds.), *Islamic Wealth and the SDGs*,
https://doi.org/10.1007/978-3-030-65313-2_23

454   S. K. RASHID

Tyabji,[3] Fyzee,[4] Mulla,[5] Baillie,[6] Anderson,[7] Schacht,[8] Macnaghten,[9] *Hedaya*,[10] *Fatawa Alamgiri*,[11] Wilson,[12] Saksena,[13] Verma,[14] and the list goes on and on, and in none of these, there is even a passing remark about Quranic relationship with waqf. The same is true in case of judicial pronouncements of even superior courts.[15] It is surprising how everyone has missed fifty-nine (59) verses of the Quran which mentions in every possible manner the basic spirit of waqf. Twenty-one (21) verses are cited here in full, while thirty-eight (38) are cited in the footnote.[16]

Quranic verses cited in full, (operative parts only):

Surah Al-Baqarah (2), ayat 177,	"It is not righteousness that ye turn your faces East or West; but it is righteousness...to spend of your substance, out of love for Him, for your kin, for orphans, for the needy, for the wayfarer, for those who ask, for the ransom of the slaves...",

---

[3] Badruddin Tyabji, *Muhammadan Law*, 3rd ed. (Bombay, 1940).

[4] A. A. A. Fyzee, *Outlines of Muhammadan Law*, 3rd ed. (London, 1964).

[5] D. F. Mulla, *Principle of Mahomedan Law*, 15th ed. (Calcutta, 1961).

[6] N. B. Baillie, *Digest by* Muhammadan Law, Part 1 (London, 1875).

[7] J. N. D. Anderson, *Islamic Law in Africa* (London, 1954).

[8] J. Schacht, *Origins of Muhammadan Jurisprudence* (Oxford, 1950).

[9] W. H. Macnaghten, *Principles and Precedents of Moohummudan Law*, 1825).

[10] *Hedaya* of al-Marghinani, Tr. by Charles Hamilton (London, 1870).

[11] *Fatawa Alamgiri* (or *Fatawa al-Hindiyya*), Urdu tr. by S. Amir Ali, in ten vols (Hamid & Co., Delhi, 1988).

[12] R. K. Wilson, *Anglo-Muhammadan Law*, 6th ed. (London, 1930).

[13] K. P. Saksena, *Muslim Law As Administered in India and Pakistan*, 4th ed. (Lucknow, 1963).

[14] B. R. Verma, *Muhammadan Law*, 6th ed. (Lucknow, 1991).

[15] (Privy Council) *Vidya Varuthi Thirtha Swamigal v Balasami Ayyer* (1920–1921) 481.A.302.

[16] Quranic verses not cited in full for space constraint: **2**: 3, 4, 5, 83, 195, 219, 254; **4**: 8, 36; **9**: 60, 79, 98, 99, 111; **13**: 22, 23; **16**: 90; **28**: 54; **35**: 29; **42**: 38; **58**: 12; **61**: 10, 11; **64**: 17; **76**: 8, 9, 10, 11; **90**: 13, 14, 15, 16, 17: **93**: 9; **107**: 1, 2, 3, 7 [Total: 38].

Surah Al-Imran (3), ayat 92,	"By no means shall ye attain righteousness, unless ye give of that which ye love…",
Surah Al-Maidah (5), ayat 12,	"Practice regular charity and loan to Allah a beautiful loan."
Surah Al-Anfal (8), ayat 3–4,	"Who establish regular prayers and spend (freely) out of the gifts We have given them for sustenance; such in truth are the believers…",
Surah Al-Ibrahim (14), ayat 31,	"Speak to my servants who have believed, that they may establish regular prayers and spend (in charity) out of the sustenance We have given them…",
Surah Al-Isra (17), ayat 26,	"And render to the kindreds their due rights as (also) to those in want and to the way-farer…",
Surah Al-Hajj (22), ayat 35,	"To those… who… keep up regular prayer and spend (in charity) out of what We have bestowed upon them",
Surah Al-Furqan (25), ayat 67,	"Those who when they spend, are not extravagant and not niggardly, but hold a just balance between these two extremes",
Surah Al-Sajdah (32), ayat 16,	"…and they spend (in charity) out of the sustenance which We have bestowed on them."
Surah Ya Sin (36), ayat 47,	"And when they are told, spend ye of (the bounties) with which Allah has provided you," the unbelievers say to those who believe: Shall We then feed those whom, if Allah had so willed, He would have fed (Himself?), ye are in nothing but manifest error.",
Surah Al-Dhariyat (51), ayat 19,	"And in their wealth and possessions (are) the right of the needy, him who asked, and him whom (for some reason) was prevented (from asking)",

Surah Al-Hadid (57), ayat 7, and 10	"and spend (in charity) out of the substance whereof He has made your heirs, For, those of you who believe and spend (in charity)-for them is a great reward."
	"And what cause have ye why he should not spend in the cause of Allah?- For to Allah belongs the heritage of the heavens and the earth..."
Surah Al-Munafiqun (63), ayat 10,	"And spend something out of the substance which We have bestowed on you, before death should come to any of you and he should say 'O my Lord! why didst thou not give me respite for a little while? I should then have given in charity and I should have been one of the doer of good",
Surah Al-Taghabun (64), ayat 16,	"And spend in charity for the benefit of your own soul...",
Surah Al-Talaq (65) ayat 7,	"Let the man of means spend according to his means, and the man whose resources are restricted, let him spend according to what Allah has given him."

In addition to the above-quoted verses, Quran continues to adopt the repetitive mode of narration when in verse after verse it keeps on promising blessings on those who give in charity. For example, look at the repeated reminder of Allah in the following four verses, which He could have given in one verse only. Look at the repeated promises He is making of rewards, whereas His one promise would have been more than enough.

Surah Al Hadid (57), ayat 18,	"For those who give in charity, men and women, and loan to Allah Qarz e Hasna (Beautiful loan), it shall be increased manifold (to their credit)

	and they shall have (besides) a liberal reward";
Surah Al Rum (30), ayat 38,	"So give what is due to kindred, the needy, and the wayfarer. That is best for those who seek the countenance, of Allah, and it is they who will prosper"; and
Surah Al Baqarah (2), ayat 274,	"Those who (in charity) spend of their goods at night and by day, in secret and in public, have their reward with their Lord: On them shall be no fear, nor shall they grieve".
Surah Al Baqarah (2), ayat 215,	"They ask thee what they should spend (in charity)-Say: Whatever ye spend that is good, is for parents and kindred and orphans and those in want and for wayfarers, and whatever ye do that is good Allah is aware."

It proves that a very close relationship exists between charity and Quran, that is, between waqf and Quran. This, however, was never highlighted sufficiently by the jurists.

What Is the Outcome of All the Above-Quoted Verses?

Now, if what is meant by waqf is helping the poor and those in need, providing sustenance to parents, kith and kin and meeting the societal needs, and so on, would it not be correct to say that the above-quoted Quranic verses refer to waqf, not by name but in their meaning both implied and direct This being so, how illogical and incorrect would it be to say that there is no mention of waqf in the Quran. It would be the same kind of ignorance if we say that in 99 names of Allah, Allah is mentioned even once! Why then we still call these as 99 names of Allah!

Through these verses, Allah wishes to create a mindset among Muslims to practice charity which is called "*Infaq*". The motivation behind charity is not created by waqf. Waqf is the name of a "procedure" of tying up of the corpus' (*habbis asla*) incompliance with the rules of perpetuity, inalienability and irrevocability. It does not require, as a compulsory necessity, that an object must be mentioned for the waqf to be valid.

In such a case, the object is presumed to be *fi sabil Allah*, and the *mutawalli* or the *qadi* may name the object with the help of the Quran and needs of the case. However, if the characteristics of "habbis asla" (tie up the corpus) are missing in a dedication, it cannot be a waqf. Here waqf is the body and Quranic concept of charity is the soul without which waqf cannot exist.

Repeated mention of numerous heads of charity in the Quran shows that a very close relationship exists between waqf and the Quran. The culture of Islam aims at a harmonious blending of *huquq Allah* with *huquq al Ibad*, or obligation to self with the obligation to society. They are placed side by side to form integral parts of one's activity in life. Prof. Syed Abdul Latif in his well-known book: *The Mind Al-Quran Builds* says that the Quran gives a wide interpretation to *amal al-Salih* (righteous action) to mean discharging dual responsibility: one to himself and the other to his external world.

Life thus viewed, every action of man assumes a spiritual significance.[17]

The reason the intimate relationship of waqf and the Quran was never fully acknowledge may be attributed to the failure of the early Quranic commentators (*Mufassirins*) to do so. Syed Abdul Latif is right in asserting:

The dismal failure on the part of our early doctors of religion (was that their primary attention) was not *Sunnah* of Allah but another *Sunnah* of the Muslim Arab community, their customs and usages, modelled on what they believed to be the practice of the Prophet. So obsessed were they with this task that they could not give adequate attention to this study and exposition of the *Sunnat Allah* or *Fitrat Allah* or *Khalq Allah*.[18]

Another very prominent Quranic scholar Abul Kalam Azad also felt in nearly the same way and says:

[17] Syed Abdul Latif, *The Mind Al-Quran Builds*, 1st published in 1952, new ed. by Islamic Book Trust, Kuala Lumpur, 2002, reprinted 2004, pp. 64, 67.

[18] Id. at 46.

The first generation of people among whom the Quran was delivered were not a sophisticated race. Their mind was not cast in any artificial or conventional mould. It was content to receive a simple thought in its plain simplicity. That was why the Quranic thought simple as it was, sank easily into their hearts. No one at the time felt it difficult to catch its meaning. The moment the companions of the Prophet heard a verse recited to them, they forthwith caught its meaning.[19] Azad was the first eduction minister of free India and was recognized Muslim Scholar.

According to Fyzee the simple character of Muslims made it easy for them to understand the spirit of charity preached by Islam. There came a flood of waqf in the Muslim world. Three-fourth of arable lands in Turkey, one half in Algeria, one-third in Tunisia, and one-eighth in Egypt stood dedicated as waqf. Alarm bells started to ring in the corridors of the governments as it was treated not only as a major drain of land revenue but also a shift of influence and power from the state to religious leaders controlling *awqaf* and their administrators. On the other side, the Western orientalists started calling waqf "Dead Hand" to cast aspersion on its perpetual aspect. So, many Muslim states, both in pre- and post-colonial eras, were either goaded or acting on their own, abolished *awqaf*. French colonial government did this in 1830 in Algiers and Morocco, followed by Turkey and Egypt, Russia and British India.[20]

This story started hundreds of years ago is still continuing in nearly the same way. The state continues to be the hero, the saviour, while waqf administrators are branded as the villain.

Family Waqf was branded as non charitable, ignoring its social welfare potential

It is nothing less than academic dishonesty of the english jurists to call family waqf "non-charitable purpose trust". This interpretation becomes derogatory when it alleges that family waqf aims at preserving the family property from division under the law of inheritance. However a waqf

---

[19] Mawlana Abul Kalam Azad, *Tarjuman Al-Quran* (Urdu 1st ed. 1930, 2nd ed. 1945), Eng. tr. by Syed Abdul Latif, *Tarjuman Al-Quran*, 1st ed. 1968, reprinted 1976, Sind Sagar Academy, Lahore, n.d.), pp. x–xi.

[20] See, A. A. A. Fyzee, *Outlines of Muhammadan Law*, 3rd ed. (Oxford University Press, 1964), pp. 266–267. See also, Syed Khalid Rashid, *Waqf Administration in India: A Socio-legal Study* (Vikas Publishing House, New Delhi, 1978), pp. 11–36.

created with the intention of saving the family property from division among the heirs from creditors, is no waqf and this is very clearly stated in all the books on the law of waqf.

Giving In islam giving to one's own kith and kin is charity and a social welfare act. Both Quran and *hadith* establish this, as seen in *surah-Al-Baqarah (2), ayat 177* and *surah Al-Isra (17), ayat 26; Sahih Bukhari, Kitab Zakah, hadith no. 24*, Eng. tr. by Mohsin Khan (*Maktaba Dar-es- Salam, 1994*), p. 367; *Sahih Bukhari, Kitab al-Shurut, hadith no. 52*, Eng. tr. p. 576; and *Sunan-al-Nisai, Kitab Al- Ahbas, hadith no. 3541.*

In the presence of proofs from the highest sources of *Shariah*, regarding the sanctity and validity of family waqf, it is not surprising to see its instant popularity among Muslims. It was never seen as a method to safeguard family property from the effects of inheritance law or to save it from prodigality of wayward offsprings.

The only point which deserves attention is that with the passage of time the number of beneficiary descendants in a family waqf could increase to an extent where their individual share may get reduced to a negligible amount. It would be the end of such family waqf property because no beneficiary would be willing to waste his time in maintaining such a property.[21]

This is really a serious problem, deserving our attention. Instead of finding a viable solution, the states have abolished it, without bothering even in the least about its Quranic and *hadith* moorings and its social welfare potential.

Anti-waqf *ahli* laws did not take time to come in quick succession. First Egypt did it through Law No. 48 of 12 June 1946 which initially made waqf *ahli* temporary and then in 1952 abolished it altogether (Law 180 of September 1952).

Lebanon copied Egypt (Law 8 of 1947 and No. 9 of 1949). Syria followed suit (Decree 97 of 26 Nov. 1949), so also Tunisia (1958), Libya (1973), UAE (1980), and Kuwait (1951).

Siraj and Lim are right in saying that—

---

[21] Lucy Carroll, "Life Interests and Inter-Generational Transfer of Property: Avoiding the Law of Succession", *Islamic Law and Society*, 8, 2. (2001). See also, Syed Khalid Rashid, *Waqf Administration in India: A Socio-Legal Study* (Vikas Publishing House, New Delhi, 1978), pp. 127–148.

This abolition of the waqf or its nationalization by postcolonial Muslim States is ironical. It was welcomed in the West as a move towards land market economies and private property.

State's efforts to control awqaf as a means of extending their power have been evident throughout Islamic history, although such efforts have met with resistance.

In modern times State's main justifications for interference were public interest, in that the waqf did not serve the purposes for which it was originally intended and the State was better positioned to administer them efficiently.[22]

This is, however, a statement not supported by the realities on the ground. Siraj himself is of the opinion that "*The State in most Muslim countries has failed to live up to the welfare support standards evident in Western countries. There is an impetus towards 'releasing' waqf properties now controlled by the State*".[23]

The social welfare role of *waqf ahli* cannot be fully understood unless we remind ourselves of the vast meaning Islam gives to charity. Giving to one's own children amounts to charity in Islam, but not in English Law, and applying this rule to family waqf the Privy Council's judgement given by Lord Hobhouse in *Abul Fata's case* (1894) 22 1A76 set a trend of disregarding the divine and charitable nature of family waqf. The then colonial powers subjected the family *awqaf* to all the direct and indirect taxes, even Estate Duty and land reform Laws during post-colonial era also, making the extinction of family waqf a virtual certainty in due course of time.

Justification for family *awqaf* consisting of agricultural lands was sought on rejection on the ground that doing so in perpetuity would be unproductive, as the beneficiaries might lack expert knowledge of agriculture and total dependence on tenants to do the job might not be the best option.

Problems confronting family *awqaf* are not insurmountable, provided there is a political will to find solutions, which include making these *awqaf* exempt from perpetuity and restrictions may be imposed on the dedication of agricultural lands in favour of a family waqf, total or partial

---

[22] Siraj Sait and Hilary Lim, loc cit at 164.

[23] Ibid.

exemption from direct and indirect taxes, subjecting these *awqaf* to proper administrative infrastructure already existing for *waqf Khairy*, etc.

Notwithstanding the negative atmosphere against family *awqaf* in many countries of the world, these *awqaf* have a lot of positive attributes to offer and deserve a fairer deal.

What has been done to them is simply unjust and imprudent. If a public opinion poll is conducted today in the countries where these *awqaf* stand condemned asking the question whether waqf *ahli* should be revived, a majority would surely say "yes", because of its Quranic origin.

Family *awqaf* have helped many families to survive the vicissitudes of misfortune, and they still may do so. Their abolition or curtailment amounts to a blow to social welfare capability of the Muslim societies.[24] Let us hope that we will soon see the re-emergence of family *awqaf* in its reformed avatar.

Cash Waqf and its Soial Welfare Potentiality

The on-going redesigning of cash waqf has opened up a lot of new avenues of investment which a few years back were simply un-imaginable. The main area where things are happening is Islamic banking and finance. Those folklore days have gone when Imam Zufar's *Mudarabah* mode of financing was the only option available for cash waqf investment. Investments are now possible in equity shares, micro- and macro-financing, low-risk debt financing, participation in banking and finance partnership business, and so on.

Some examples are available of the utilization of cash waqf in the social welfare sector, where Bangladesh has taken a lead. The Social Investment Bank Ltd, established in 1995, started issuing Cash Waqf Certificates. Anyone could buy these certificates for any amount, according to his financial capability. This opened up the market to the entire population of the country, irrespective of the caste, creed and religion. The funds so pooled were used for financing numerous social welfare financing schemes in education, health, poverty eradication, etc. According to the annual

---

[24] A useful and informative discussion on family waqf, may be seen in Muhammad Abdurrahman Sadique, "Re-assessment of Family Waqf", in Syed Khalid Rashid (ed.), *Waqf Laws and Management* (International Islamic University Press, Kuala Lumpur, 2017), pp. 24–45, and in the same volume, Magda Ismail Abdel Muhsin, "Past, Present and Future of Family Waqf", pp. 46, 56.

reports for the years 1998 to 2006 of the Social Investment Bank, as many as thirty-two (32) project areas were identified for the utilization of Cash Waqf Fund. The 32 projects areas were divided into four (4) sectors, namely: Family Empowerment; Education and Culture; Health and Sanitation; and Social Utility Services. In 2007, there were 3042 cash waqf account holders, with total deposit amount of Taka 14513000.00.[25]

Cash waqf in Turkey emerged in the fifteenth and sixteenth centuries. Money was dedicated for social and pious purposes, and also to provide credit and other financial services. Cash awqaf in Bursa during the period 1555–1823 were engaged in education, food, family, mosques, repairs of roads, public baths, etc.

Cash *awqaf* in Turkey provided social security. Many cash *awqaf* were established under the name of *Orta Sandıgı Middle Fund for the members of the Yeniceri Ocagi (Janissary Barrack) to provide mutual aid and social security services to the members.*

Foundations like *Eytam Sandiklari* (Fund for Orphans) and *Memlekat ve Menafi Sandiklari* collected money for burial services, food and cloth distribution among unemployed, helping people affected by natural disasters. The collected money, held as cash waqf, was also used for-

- loaning money to poors on *qarz-i-hasan* basis;
- giving financial support to people having capital raising problems; and
- giving gratuitous aid to poors.

Avariz Awqaf gave financial support to people of a village who could not fulfil their civil or municipal obligations.[26]

The Ottoman cash waqf was virtually destroyed in 1954 by being incorporated into the bank of *Waqf-Vakiflar Bankasi*. But like a phoenix,

---

[25] M. A. Mannan, "Beyond the Malaysian Twin Towers: Mobilization Efforts of Cash Waqf Fund at Local, National and International Levels for Development of Social Infrastructure of the Islamic Ummah and the Establishment of the World Social Bank", Paper presented at the International Seminar on Awqaf 2008, organized by JAWHAR; Institute of IUM; Kumpulan Waqf, Johor Bahru, 11–12 August 2008.

[26] Murat Cizakca, "Waqf in History and the Its Implications for Modern Islamic Economies", in Dr. Monzer Kahf and Dr. Siti Mashitoh Mohamood (eds.), *Essential Readings in Contemporary Waqf Issues* (Centre for Research & Training, Kuala Lumpur, 2011), pp. 36–37.

it was reborn in a dramatically different form: Diyanet Vakfi—a waqf creating a multitude of companies, providing equity finance to already established companies. While Koc Foundation provides an example of a huge conglomerate creating its own Waqf-Koc foundation, which specializes in education and finance, a highly ambitious secondary high school and a major university. Diyanet Vakfi, also operates like Tabung Haji of Malaysia, organizing Umrah and Hajj trips. It has 700 local branches in Turkey, with 90,000 membership.

Pooling of resources of many cash waqf institutions to formulate a Cash Waqf Bank is something waiting to be taken up.

Crossing the Hurdle of Perpetuity If It Detracts the Social Welfare Role of Family Waqf or Cash Waqf

Virtually the whole of the law of waqf is jurist made. There appears an apparent agreement, though not unanimous, on the perpetuity as well as temporality of waqf. Once the jurists agreed on the validity of waqf of things like buildings, trees, horses, books, etc., it became apparent that these items even though non-perpetual in their nature are considered perpetual. Hence, in case of waqf, it could safely be said, "perpetuity" means—"as long as the property lasts".

Hence, we should not be struck with fear when the issue of perpetuity is raised in case of family waqf or cash waqf. In both of these *awqaf*, perpetuity has always been regarded as virtual killer. However, if we see the stand that was taken on this issue by Imam Abu Hanifa and Imam Malik, perpetuity becomes a non-issue, as both the jurists regarded the ownership of waqf property to continue with the *waqif* even after the waqf's creation. So in case of cash waqf, "as long as the cash lasts" rule will apply. Whereas in case of family waqf, the *waqif* may set an age limit on the waqf. This is what was done in Egypt.

Section 40 of the Egyptian Waqf Act, 1946 provides:

i. A family waqf may not last for more than two generations or sixty (60) years from the time of *waqif's* death, after which it will become the absolute property of the *waqif's* heirs;
ii. Creation of waqf for a limited duration is possible;
iii. A waqif may revoke his waqf, whether or not he has reserved this right at the time of creating the waqf; and
iv. A waqf may be divided among the beneficiaries if they so like.

The nearly mandatory rule of perpetuity of waqf seems to be losing ground to temporality. Presently Muslims like to see waqf as a life tenure depending on the *waqif's* wishes.

In Malaysia, a trust named *Hiba Harta*, advertised as a virtual waqf by a bank, became very popular because of its revocability and limited life span. Probably, its popularity among Muslims is an indirect endorsement of non-perpetual waqf concept. For social welfare, it may prove to be an idea worth serious consideration.

Probably, the time has come to accept the fact of revocable non-permanent waqf co-existing with the perpetual waqf. It may give a big boost to social welfare initiatives through waqf.

Waqf Has Still Enough Potential to Play a Role in Social Welfare Initiatives

There used to be a time in early Islamic history that social welfare role played by *awqaf* made it virtually the Third Arm of the State. Nearly every segment of the society received a benevolent patronage from *awqaf*. We have evidence of Ibn Battutah, who visited Baghdad in 726 AH (1327 AD), that the variety of *awqaf* there was mind-blowing. There were *awqaf* to sponsor pilgrimage to Makkah; wedding gifts for poor girls; for freeing of prisoners; for travellers' food, clothing and travel expenses; paving of streets and lanes; and so on. Ibn Battutah tells his personal experience of witnessing an incident in Damascus:

> I saw a young slave boy who dropped a Chinese porcelain dish, which was broken to bits. A number of people collected round him and one of them said to him, collect the pieces and take them to the 'Custodian of Endowment for Utensils'. He did so, and the man went with him to the custodian, where the slave boy showed the broken pieces and received a sum sufficient to buy a similar dish. This is an excellent institution, for the master of the slave boy would have undoubtedly beaten him, or at least scolded him, for breaking the dish, and the slave would have been heartbroken and upset by the accident. This benefaction is indeed a matter of hearts-may Allah richly reward him whose zeal for good work rose to such heights.[27]

---

[27] Ibn Battutah, *Travels in Asia and Africa*: 1325–1354 AD, Eng. tr. by H. A. Hardy Gibb (London, 1929), pp. 69–70.

In the eleventh-century Baghdad, *awqaf* provided funds and facilities in the field of education, social welfare, health and religion.[28] The economic potential of waqf however went down slowly under the impact of nationalization and neglect of the religious leaders to emphasize the religious sanctity of waqf based on its Quranic roots. The Muslim public opinion was not reminded of the divine status of waqf, and the role of *Ummah* in social welfare initiatives. Waqf is an embodiment of the principles of self-sufficency, egalitarianism and learning that mark Muslim societies. The recent rise of Islamic finance and banking provides a good environment for the renovation and reinvigoration of waqf.

Several Islamic Institutions such as OIC, KAPF, IDB and General Directorate of Foundations, Turkey, to name a few, are playing a major role in socio-economic upliftment of the *Ummah*. Islamic University in Uganda and Model Waqf legislation for Muslim countries are OIC initiatives.[29] Under its direct Project Financing, IDB funded the Urban Waqf Land Development Project; *Awqaf* commercial complex Project; Technical Assistance Projects, establishing Islamic Universities in several Asian and African countries[30]; Kuwait *Awqaf* Public Foundation (KAPF) established Waqf Funds for handicapped, for academic development; for family care, for environmental protection, for health development, for care of mosques, for community development, etc.[31] In Turkey, 1023 new *awqaf* are created for education, 244 to provide health services, and 1305 to provide a wide variety of other social services.[32]

Elsewhere also, positive developments are visible in India, Malaysia, and Nigeria, to name only a few. In India, the 2013 amendment to the

---

[28] George Makdisi, *The Rise of Colleges: Institutions of Learning in Islam and the West* (Edinburgh University Press, 1981, p. 281 ff, citing Ibn-al-Jauzi. *Al-Muntazam fe Tarikh al-Muluk Wal-Umam*, Vol. 6, p. 133 ff. (Hyderabad, 1938).

[29] OIC (2000), 'Promoting Waqfs and Their Role in the Development of Islamic Societies,' Report of the Secretary-General to the Twenty-Seventh Session of the OIC Conference, Kuala Lumpur, Malaysia, 27–30 June, 2000.

[30] Mahmoud A. Mahdi, "Enhancing the Growth and Performance of Awqaf: The IDB Experience", in Syed Khalid Rashid (ed.), *Awqaf Experiences in South Asia* (IOS, New Delhi, 2012), pp. 231–247.

[31] Abdul Mohsen M. Ali Othman and Dahi Al-Fadhli, "Role of Kuwait *Awqaf* Public Foundation in Promoting *Awqaf*", in Syed Khalid Rashid (ed.), *Awqaf Experiences in South Asia* (IOS, New Delhi, 2012), pp. 249–262.

[32] Ahmat Ihsan Eryilmaz, "Awqaf and Their Structure in Turkey", in Syed Khalid Rashid (ed)., *Awqaf Experiences in South Asia* (IOS, New Delhi, 2012), pp. 263–269.

Waqf Act, 1995 has made corruption of Mutawallis a penal offence and inclusion of females in waqf administration as mandatory. In Malaysia, the number of States having their own waqf enactment has grown to six (Selangor, Malacca, Negeri Sembilan, Johor, Perak and Terengganu), and in Nigeria, whereas none of the State had its waqf enactment, their number is now eight (8) (Bauchi, Borno, Jigawa, Kano, Kebbi, Niger, Yobe and Zamfara).[33] It is to be accepted that State intervention in waqf is not a bad thing in itself if things are done in the right spirit and way.

However it is observed that once the State took over the social welfare function that used to be in the domain of waqf, it was thought things were to improve. But soon it became apparent that State is unable to deliver speedy aid and humanitarian support to vulnerable groups, whose number exceeded all approximations. So now it appears waqf has to play once again the role they played during centuries past. This opportunity should also be used to learn from the mistakes of the past and to construct a modern legal and administrative framework.

> The increasing popularity of the waqf does not necessarily imply a nostalgic return to a traditional model. Modernization of the waqf can deliver a transparent and responsive institution with modern management structures, like microfinance and other initiatives. This may well be an opportunity to facilitate the development of indigenous models based on modern benchmarks and capable of responding to contemporary challenges.[34]

---

[33] Information about India and Malaysia are based on personal knowledge of the author, while information about Nigeria is based on Umar A. Oseni, " The Need for an Effective Legal and Regulatory Framework for waqf in Nigeria," in Syed Khalid Rashid (ed.), *Waqf Laws and Management* (IIUM Press, 2017), pp. 240–270.

[34] Siraj Sait and Hilary Lim, *Land, Law & Islam: Property and Human Rights in the Muslim World* (Zed Books, London, 2006), p. 173.

CHAPTER 24

Analysis of Global Ethical Wealth Based on Maqasid al-Shari'ah: The Case of Waqf

Suheyib Eldersevi, Mustafa Omar Mohammed, and Mohamed Cherif El Amri

INTRODUCTION

Islamic Shari'ah has constituted the ethical system of the entire life of the human. According to Islam, whatever leads to welfare of the individual or society is morally good and whatever is injurious is morally bad. Considering the Islamic financial services industry, it can be noticed that the ethical considerations from Shari'ah law are obvious in its directives. The

---

S. Eldersevi
Department of Islamic Economics and Finance, Istanbul Sabahattin Zaim University, Istanbul, Turkey

M. O. Mohammed
Department of Economics, International Islamic University Malaysia [IIUM], Gombak, Malaysia
e-mail: mustafa@iium.edu.my

M. C. El Amri (✉)
Department of Islamic Economics and Finance, Istanbul Sabahattin Zaim University, Istanbul, Turkey

© The Author(s), under exclusive license to Springer Nature Switzerland AG 2021
M. M. Billah (eds.), *Islamic Wealth and the SDGs*,
https://doi.org/10.1007/978-3-030-65313-2_24

469

ethical system prescribed in Islam is eternally divine and forms the foundation of an Islamic society (Mohammed 2013). Global ethical wealth refers to the different forms of Sadaqat that were established by Prophet Muhammad (PBUH). In Islamic terminology, Sadaqah has been defined as an act of giving something without seeking a substitute in return and to please Allah. Prophet Muhammad (PBUH) says "When a man dies, his deeds come to an end except for three things: Sadaqah Jariyah (perpetual charity); a knowledge which is beneficial, or a virtuous descendant who prays for him (for the deceased)" (Sahih Muslim: 3/1255).

Global ethical wealth is categorized into two groups. The first group is the obligatory charity such as Zakat and Sadaqah al-Fitr, while the second group is voluntary charity such as Waqf (Islamic endowment), Qard Hassan (benevolent loan). The aim which all global ethical wealth forms try to achieve is the elevation of poverty. Currently, non-government organizations (NGOs) and other civil society organizations are all striving to combat poverty (Mohammed 2013). However, considering the social dimension of global ethical wealth categories, it can be noticed that the ultimate aim is to maintain equality and social welfare in society and provide for those who can't provide for themselves. Global ethical wealth serves to purify one's wealth and helps to establish a flow of wealth in society. Muslims are bonded together by not only the good deeds of Sadaqah but also the economic stability that flows through society with the distribution of wealth. Hence, Muslims are instructed by Allah to try to give Sadaqah for His sake and spread generosity in society.

Considering the role of Waqf during the glorious days of Islam, it can be noticed that Waqf played a considerable role in Islamic society. Thus, this study chose Waqf among the forms of global ethical wealth to be studied and analyzed. The principle of Waqf has been in practice since the time of the Prophet (PBUH) and the companions although the term Waqf does not appear even for a single instance in the Qur'an. It is observed in the religious, social, economic, and environmental aspects of life. The type of Waqf varies according to the needs of the era, as Waqif (Waqf giver) seeks to provide what is needed through the Waqf system. For instance, schools were built when there was a need for it, while in other cases wells were built when there was a lack of water in the society (Al-Saad 2009). Considering the religious dimension of Waqf, it is observed that mosques played an important role in bringing Muslims together to teach them Islamic sciences. It is obvious in the case of al-Masjid al-Nabawi when the Prophet Muhammad built it to use it as a place for Muslims to gather and learn from Prophet (PBUH). From a social dimension, there have been many social activities that had a major impact on the Muslim community, such as orphanages, nursing homes, and other places prepared as housing for the poor. Also, the well of Rumah that Uthman bin Affan (PBUH) made it as Waqf is a great example that proves the social dimension of Waqf. Moreover, from the economic dimension, Waqf could divert funds and other resources from current consumption and investing them into productive and prospective assets which generate revenues for future consumption by individuals or society at large. Finally, in the environmental dimension, Waqf can play an important role in building and cleaning the environment, the Waqf funds could be used to pave roads, build parks, clean the cities (Tarkawi 2014).

Starting with the belief that all practices of Prophet Muhammad were seeking to bring welfare and prosperity to Muslim society, it automatically proves that all types of Awqaf would achieve different Maqasid al-Shari'ah (objectives of Shari'ah). For instance, the creation of a mosque would fall under the preservation of religion which is one of the al-Maqasid al-Daruriyyat (essential Shari'ah objectives). From a social dimension perspective, Waqf which aims to give a hand to the needy is related to the preservation of life; while from an economic dimension perspective, it can be argued that Waqf which aims to divert funds from current consumption and investing them generate revenues is related to the preservation of wealth or property. Finally, from the environmental dimension perspective, it can be said that Awqaf which aims to improve the environment are related to the complementary objectives of Shari'ah or what is called Maqasid Hajiyyah (Tarkawi 2014).

REVIEW OF THE RELATED WORKS ON WAQF

This section reviews the extant literature on three main themes, starting with the concept and role of Waqf, followed by the concept and theory of al-Maqasid, and concluding with Waqf and al-Maqasid.

The Concept and Role of Waqf

Scholars provided different definitions of Waqf. Imam Abu Hanifa defined it as "withholding property, according to the judgment of its owner, and providing charity from its revenues." It means that the ownership of property will remain continuously under the ownership of its custodian

(Abideen 2003). Maliki says that Waqf is: "the devoting of profit of some property as long as it exists, provided that it shall be owned by the benefactor even if by name" (Khurshi 2010). Shafi'i defined it as "keeping of money that may be benefited from the remaining of its property confined as well as devoting of its profit for charitable purposes" (Nawawi 1991) The Hanbali School says that "Waqf is the confinement of the property and the devoting of its profit for the charitable purposes for the sake of Allah's mercy" (Al-Bahuti 1983).

The validity of Waqf is derived from the general rulings of the Qur'an advising Muslims to be altruistic and benevolent toward the social causes. For instance, Allah S. W. T says *"They ask you, [O Muhammad], what they should spend. Say, Whatever you spend of good is [to be] for parents and relatives and orphans and the needy and the traveler. And whatever you do of good - indeed, Allah is Knowing of it"* (2:215). Also, Allah S. W. T says *"O you who have believed, spend from the good things which you have earned and from that which We have produced for you from the earth. And do not aim toward the defective therefrom, spending [from that] while you would not take it [yourself] except with closed eyes. And know that Allah is Free of need and Praiseworthy"* (2:267). Moreover, Prophet Muhammad himself urged his followers to create Awqaf, it can be noticed in the hadith in Sahih Muslim 3/1255, Abu Hurairah narrated that Prophet Muhammad (PBUH) said: "When a man dies, his good deeds come to an end except three: ongoing charity, beneficial knowledge, and righteous offspring who will pray for him." Thus, Waqf is a great example of an ongoing charity.

Considering the division of Waqf, most of the authorities divide Waqf into three types. (1) Religious Waqf, it refers to assets that are dedicated to be used for worship. The mosque is an example of this kind of Waqf. (2) Philanthropic Waqf refers to a type of Waqf whose proceeds are used to serve a specific group of individuals (beneficiaries) such as students. (3) Family Waqf, it is defined as an "Islamic charitable endowment dedicated to the family member of the waqif or founder." It started after the death of the Prophet (PBUH), during the reign of 'Ummar (PBUH) (Kahf 1998).

There is a great number of literature produced on the economic aspects of Waqf, to explore its role in the life of Muslims. Çizakça (1998) stated that Waqf has historically played a great function in the economic aspect. Waqf is a great part of the fundamental economic institution that can generate economic activities as well as ensuring that the benefits go to the certain parts of the society (Ibrahim and Ibrahim 2013). It is said that Waqf can reduce the government's burden and responsibility in the economy in the sense that Waqf can finance the social activities to enhance welfare, thus, the government, therefore, could make some savings in its budget and expenditure which initially planned for public interests. The saved amount could be used for other important development activities (Hassan 2010). Çizakça (1998) stated that the Waqf system can significantly contribute to a massive reduction in government expenditure. Hassan (2010) stated that Waqf institutions can play an important role to achieve a just distribution of wealth and income in the economy.

Considering the role of Waqf in the educational aspect, it is known that educational institutions are considered as a place where people get educated different sciences to lead society. Muslims need to be aware that Waqf is a crucial investment to prepare leaders who should lead the community (Azha et al. 2013). Ahmad et al. (2012) studied several models that may develop higher education institutions through a Waqf. Considering the role of Waqf in healthcare services, Baqutayan and Mahdzir (2018) tried to analyze the success of Waqf as a source to support the healthcare services in Islamic history. They tried to analyze the provided services such as establishing hospitals in the Muslim world. Waqf and healthcare are linked for thousands of years when the first hospitals in the Islamic world. These hospitals were trying to give usual medical care to the poor and needy. From the above-mentioned studies, it can be understood that Waqf has played a very crucial role in Islamic society, it has supported economic activities, education, and health care. In nutshell, it is obvious that those Awqaf have achieved Maqasid al-Shari'ah, although they did not mention it.

The Concept and Theory of Al-Maqasid

Basic Concepts

Maqasid is the plural of "Maqsid." The literal meaning of Maqsid could be purpose, intent, objective, principle, goal, or end. Therefore, Maqasid al-Shari'ah can be defined as the objectives, purposes, intents, ends, or principles behind Islamic law or Islamic rulings (Ibn 'Ashur 2006). Al-Raisuni (1995) stated that Maqasid al-Shari'ah could be explained as the higher objectives of the lawgiver.

Shaikh ʿAllal Al-Fasi—prominent scholar—has defined Maqasid al-Shari'ah in his book Maqasid al-Shari'ah al-Islamiyyah Wa Makarimuha, he stated that "Maqasid al-Shari'ah depicts the objective and internal significance or mystery which is considered by the entity (Allah) while He imposes it upon His servant" (Al-Fasi 1993).

It is stated by Imam al-Ghazali that the objectives of Shari'ah are five for creatures. Shari'ah desires to protect Deen (Religion), Nafs (Life), Aql (Intelligence), Nasl (Generation), and Mal (property). Maslahah includes the protection of these five fundamentals (Al-Ghazali 2004). Imam Al Ghazali also mentioned that attaining welfare and removing harm is the main objective of the Shari'ah (Al-Ghazali 2004).

Imam al-Tahir Ibn Ashur stated that "the universal Maqasid of the Islamic law is to maintain orderliness, equality, freedom, facilitation, and the preservation of pure natural disposition (*fitrah*)" (Auda 2007). Shaikh Yusuf al-Qaradawi also surveyed the Qur'an and concluded the following universal Maqasid: "Preserving true faith, maintaining human dignity and rights, calling people to worship God, purifying the soul, restoring moral values, building good families, treating women fairly, building a strong Islamic nation and calling for a cooperative world" (Auda 2007).

However, Maqasid al-Shari'ah is normally classified according to levels of Maslahah. Ibn 'Ashur (2006) in his comprehensive book pertaining to Maqasid al-Shari'ah classified Maslahah into Maslahah Daruriyyat (Maslahah for essentials) which consists of the preservation of the five objectives, namely the protection of religion, life, mind, lineage, and property. The second type is Maslahah Hajiyyah (Maslahah for complementarities), which is below the Daruriyyat level, which is like the supplementary actions which must be taken to protect the Daruriyyat. The last type is Maslahah Tahsiniyaat (Maslahah for embellishments), which completes the life of a Muslim. Maqasid has also been classified according to their goals, to include definitive goals (al-Maqasid al-Qat'iyyah) and speculative purposes (al-Maqasid al-Zanniyyah) as well as general purposes (al-Maqasid al-Ammah) and particular purposes (al-Maqasid al-Khassah) (Al-Raisuni 1995).

Classification of Maqasid al-Shari'ah

Muslim scholars classified Maqasid al-Shari'ah differently. Majority of scholars classified them into three main categories: Daruriyyat (essentials), Hajiyyat (complements), and Tahsiniyaat (embellishments). The Daruriyyat are particulars that people's lives depend on so that if they are missed, the system of life will be disturbed. They are considered as vital for the founding of well-being in this world and the Hereafter. The essential Daruriyyat is divided into five: Preservation of faith/religion (Deen); Preservation of the life (Nafs); Preservation of lineage/descendants/ (Nasl); Preservation of property (Mal); and Preservation of intellect/reason ('Aql) (Al-Ghazali 2004)

Embracing the mentioned values is obligatory to ensure the normal functioning of society and the welfare of individuals. The Shari'ah seeks always to improve the lives of its followers; it seeks to eradicate the poverty and the hardship of individuals and the community. The aim is to ensure a great life for Muslims (Al-Yusuf 2007). The Hajiyyat serve as complementary to the essentials. Without the needs, people will face hardship. However, the non-existence of the needs will not create a complete disruption of the normal order of life as is the case with the essentials (Ibn 'Ashur 2006). The Tahsiniyaat relates to matters which grant enhancement in the society and guide to an improved life. The rationale of all these is the accomplishment of integrity and perfection in entire fields of a person's behavior. However, without these values, society will still be able to function and the normal life process will not be interrupted. The illustrations of these matters are voluntary (*sadaqah*), and ethical and moral rules (Ibn 'Ashur 2006).

Contemporary Studies on Maqasid al-Shari'ah
Considering past literature, which was conducted on the Maqasid al-Shari'ah, Benzeghiba (2008) conducted a study regarding Maqasid al-Shari'ah related to financial disposition. He discussed the wealth in Shari'ah and Maqasid al-Shari'ah behind the preservation of Wealth. Benzeghiba conducted his study based on two categories of Maqasid al-Shari'ah, the general Maqasid, and the specific Maqasid. Alshibany et al. (2019), studied the effect of Maqasid al-Shari'ah on Islamic transactions. The study found that Islamic law has considered several general purposes in the legislation of financial transactions in particular, and the economic system in general. And that the purposes of legitimacy have a great impact on rationalizing and guiding the fatwa, especially in ruling on the developments of financial transactions. And also urged scholars and researchers to apply the Maqasid al-Shari'ah of Islamic financial transactions and developments. Al Muqrin (1999) studied the linkage between Juristic opinions and Maqasid al-Shari'ah. He also studied the Maqasid behind the preservation of property and how the property could be maximized from Shari'ah point of view. The topic of Maqasid al-Shari'ah is a fruitful area that can be linked to different aspects of life. Moreover,

several conferences are being held, and there are now volumes of literature on al-Maqasid related studies. Therefore, it is interesting to conduct a study that brings the Waqf system and Maqasid al-Shari'ah to examine to what extent the Waqf has achieved Maqasid al-Shari'ah.

Al-Maqasid and al-Waqf

The topic of Maqasid al-Shari'ah and al-Waqf has gained the attention of some researchers. Al-Yusuf (2007) conducted a study regarding the Maqasid al-Shari'ah in the Islamic Waqf. The study analyzed the Waqf system based on the three levels of Maqasid, i.e., Daruriyyat, Hajiyyat, and Tahsiniyaat. This study focuses more on the legality of Waqf, types of Waqf, and the history of Waqf. Al-Saad (2009) also conducted a study on Maqasid and Waqf. He analyzed the relationship between the Waqf system and Maqasid al-Shari'ah. This study did not present the topic of Waqf precisely. Tarkawi (2014) also conducted a study regarding the Maqasid al-Shari'ah in the Islamic Waqf, his study was very comprehensive, but he did not include a proper introduction regarding the topic of al-Waqf.

Considering the past literature related to the subject of the Maqasid al-Shari'ah and Waqf, it is obvious that several studies were conducted. However, this study is dedicated to searching the role of Islamic Waqf based on Maqasid al-Shari'ah. It differs from other studies from two angles. (1) The study aims to go in-depth in both aspects of this topic, Waqf and Maqasid. (2) The study aims to present its analysis in a better way.

ANALYSIS OF THE ROLE OF WAQF IN ACHIEVING AL-MAQASID

Al-Maqasid al-Daruriyyah

Those are the essential objective of Shari'ah which cannot be neglected, they are as follow, preservation of religion, preservation of life, preservation of intellect, preservation of lineage, and preservation of property. Considering the preservation of religion which is one of the al-Maqasid al-Daruriyyah, it refers to the essential worships that need to be supported to be performed perfectly. However, throughout history, Waqf has an important role in the preservation of religion, it can be observed in both prayer and pilgrimage, for instance, Waqf of mosques and its maintenance. It is known that building mosques is an essential part of Islamic Waqf. The primary purpose of the mosque is to serve as a place where Muslims can come together for prayer. In the early seventh century, mosques and religious education constituted the largest portion of Waqf and voluntary contributions (El Basyoni 2011).

Allah S. W. T says "*The mosques of Allah are only to be maintained by those who believe in Allah and the Last Day and establish prayer and give Zakah and do not fear except Allah, for it is expected that those will be of the [rightly] guided*" (9:18). In this regard, Waqf has played a major role in supporting mosques and enabling them to deliver its message. However, those Awqaf could be general which means that it supports more than one mosque, and it can be a specific Waqf mainly for the maintenance of specific mosques, such as Masjid al-Haram, Al-Masjid al-Nabawi, and Al-Aqsa Mosque. Moreover, the prosperity of Waqf strengthened the religious sentiment among Muslims because those religious institutions were full of imams, preachers, jurists, teachers, and students (Ibn Jubayr 1984).

However, besides building mosques, Waqf played an important role in terms of offering resources for other facilities in the mosques. For instance, it contributed to the maintenance of microphones, lights, water dispensers, water closets, furniture, interior decorations, and paint. The aim is to offer a healthy and safe environment for worshipers in line with the principles of Islam and upkeep the houses of Allah. Moreover, Waqf played an important role in religious occasions since it provided food and sweets to the attendants (Qahwi 2015). Moreover, Waqf to facilitate the pilgrimage is considered as a Waqf which preserves the religion. The pilgrimage is one of the five pillars of Islam, it is greatly supported by the Waqf system, especially for Muslims who are unable to afford the cost of pilgrimage, although the pilgrimage is only imposed on those who can afford. Allah S. W. T says "And [due] to Allah from the people is a pilgrimage to the House - for whoever is able to find thereto a way" (3:97).

However, the strong religious feeling among Muslims made many people yearn to perform the duty, thus, the Waqf givers found that such assistance is great righteousness. Therefore, Awqaf institutions used to allocate some money each year to give a hand to these pilgrims, the aim is to warrant the comfort and safety of pilgrims and provide all the needs required for pilgrims to perform their Hajj rituals in the best manner possible. (Amin 2014).

Considering the preservation of life, it is achieved by providing the essential needs for the human to survive such as food, water, and clothing. Islam legalized the Waqf system to guarantee an ongoing charity system. Therefore, providing food and water through Waqf was recommended in Shari'ah and it was popular in Islamic history. For instance, Waqf to Feed Humans, this kind of Waqf is divided into three categories: (A) the first category is permanent feeding; it means that meals are provided on a daily basis. It exists in several places, for instance, the mosque of Shaikh Abdul Qadir Al-Kilani in Baghdad; (B) the second category is feeding on religious occasions such as Ramadan, the Day of Ashura, Eid al-Fitr, and Eid al-Adha. Awqaf were very active in those occasions till it became a tradition associated with these seasons; (C) the third category is to create a Waqf to use its proceeds to buy foodstuffs for poor, needy widows, and orphans (Salih 2001).

However, among the most famous and oldest Waqf is the Waqf of Tamim al-Dari in the Hebron region in Palestine, although it was not officially registered until the year 1096. The Waqf included four villages: Hebron, Maratoum, Beit Enoun, and Beit Ibrahim. The proceeds of this Waqf were usually used to provide soups, bread, and food to the needy and the elderly in the city of Hebron (Salih 2001). Moreover, Waqf to Provide Water Services is also a great example of Waqf which preserves life. Water is a necessity as the food, it is known as the spirit of life and the basis of every living creatures. Therefore, from the beginning, providing water was among the concerns of Muslims, this is proved through the practice of Othman bin Affan (PBUH) who bought the well of "Rumah," and made it as Waqf to serve drinking needs of the general public. From that time, providing water has become a common practice in Islamic cities (Al-Yusuf 2007). It was narrated from Sa'd bin 'Ubadah that his mother died. He said: "O Messenger of Allah, my mother has died; can I give charity on her behalf? He said: Yes. Sa'd asked: What kind of charity is best? Prophet responded: Providing drinking water, and that is the drinking-fountain of Sa'd in Al-Madinah" (Sunan an-Nasa'I, No: 3666).

Interestingly, Mrs. Zubaydah—the wife of Harun al-Rashid—realized when she went to perform pilgrim in 186 AH that people of Makkah suffer from the hardships of obtaining water, therefore, she sent to her treasurer to call workers across the country to build a water road below the rocks from Ain Hanin to the Masjid al-Haram, which relieved the pilgrims of the burden of thirst throughout the ages until today (Al-Yusuf 2007). Considering the preservation of intellect, the objective of preservation of intellect is to build an ideal Muslim who could be able to contribute to the Ummah and Serve the Muslim community. The Awqaf were made for schools and libraries. They helped in the spread of knowledge and promoted scientific research. As a result, great research scholars, philosophers, physicians, and scientists were born in an Islamic tradition.

For instance, Waqf of schools and scientific institutes. A unique experience of the Waqf role in supporting educational facilities is witnessed in Islamic history. The Waqf system used to serve all categories of the society the rich and the poor, the old, and the young. The Waqf allocations extended to the establishment of specialized schools to teach jurisprudence (Fiqh), medicine, and management. It served men and women.

The importance of Waqf in the educational field is realized when it is found that many of the most famous scholars have graduated from those Waqf schools. For instance, Imam al-Ghazali in his childhood with his brother Abi Al-Fotouh Ahmed attended one of those Waqf schools after the death of their father (Alqudah 2011). Moreover, the creation of Waqf over libraries started prior to the creation of Waqf over schools, those libraries have taken multiple names such as Khazanat al-Kutub, Dar al-'ilm, and Buyut al-Hikmah (Diab 1998). These Waqf libraries were the center for the development of many professions related to the culture, it used the scientific methods by developing the capabilities of science personnel and developing their specializations. In many cases, Waqf libraries not only provided books but all necessary requirements of a researcher, for example, pen paper, facilities for copying manuscripts, and even financial help if needed (Ibn Jubayr 1984).

Considering the preservation of lineage. It is observed that the preservation of lineage is one of the basic pillars of life and one of the factors of building the earth. Islam has concerned the protection of lineage and urging its continuity and multiplication, for instance, Waqf for orphan care. Islam has given a lot of concern to the orphans and their life to engage them with the society they live in, and with being able to perform the duties, and carries the responsibilities. However, the Orphanages were among the most prominent social institutions in Islamic cities. The philanthropists were creating Awqaf over orphans as well as educating them and providing food and clothing to them (Alwan 2007).

Moreover, Waqf to provide care to widows and divorced women is another example. The preservation of widows and divorced women was a priority in Islamic law. Prophet Muhammad (PBUH) guaranteed some

480   S. ELDERSEVI ET AL.

of Muslim children and widows who were martyred in the battles. The great companion Al-Zubair bin Al-Awam is the first creator of Waqf over widows and divorced women from his daughters. However, social work has evolved to serve this social segment. Several social institutions have been created in various parts of the Islamic state throughout Islamic history in Baghdad and Egypt, as well as in Morocco. The city of al-Fez was a shelter for poor women (Al-Yusuf 2007). Considering the preservation of property, Waqf enables the properties to remain and last for a long period as it is the idea behind Waqf (last for long, with repetitive benefits). The Waqf institutions work to achieve the goal or the objective of the Waqf, it is required from Waqf institution to protect, maintain, construct, and generate returns from the Waqf properties to support the various fields such as religious, health, educational, and social. The final result is growth and development in the entire economy (Al-Bahouth 1422H). Allah S. W. T says "And do not give the weak-minded your property, which Allah has made a means of sustenance for you" (5:4).

Al-Maqasid al-Hajiyyah

The Hajiyyat serve as complementary to the essentials. It is not important as much as the absolute necessities, yet it provides comfort to the human life. It consists of what is needed by the community for the achievement of its interest and the proper functioning of its affairs. If it is neglected, the social order will not collapse but will not function well. Likewise, it is not on the level of what is indispensable (Daruri). In this part, some of the Maqasid al-Hajiyyah will be mentioned. For instance, providing job opportunities, it can be noticed that throughout history, Waqf played an important role in providing job opportunities to individuals in the community. The nazir may create new businesses that provide public services, such as markets, hospitals, and universities. This generates more job opportunities to the society as well as it appropriately satisfies some people's basic needs. Waqf system contributes positively to the entire economy of the country as it provides jobs and creates values (Al-Saad 2009).

Moreover, a reduction in the financial burden of the state. It is another example of Waqf which serves al-Maqsid al-Hajiyyah. This objective is extremely important, as the state often goes to impose taxes as a primary resource to fund the treasury to implement its financial policy to spend on public projects. However, creating a Waqf over educational, health, defense, and infrastructure projects will assist the state in term of reducing the country's public spending, it means that the public budget may end up with some savings in its resources, and therefore, the saving could be used in other kinds of investment. The result would be a growth in the economy (Kahf 1999).

Al-Maqasid al-Tahsiniyaah

The Tahsiniyaat relates to matters which bestow enhancement in society and lead to a better life. Islam encourages its followers to achieve these purposes, nevertheless, Islam teaches its followers to pursue these goals in correct manners. In this part, some of the Maqasid al-Tahsiniyaah will be mentioned, for instance, the role of Waqf in the development of the regions. The managers of Awqaf used to build some businesses such as shops and farms beside the Awqaf property which are in most cases—schools, hospitals, and mosques. The idea was to generate some money from those businesses to support the Awqaf property. Hence, the establishment of Waqf in many regions led to development and prosperity. Interestingly, the availability of these Awqaf facilities led to the emerge of fifty cities in the Balkans during the Ottoman empire (Al-Saad 2009).

Moreover, the role of Waqf in manufacturing is another example of Waqf which serves al-Maqsid al- Tahsiniyaah. Throughout history, the Awqaf in all Islamic countries contributed to the emergence of new industries that had led to important growth in the economy. The masterpieces of the mosques and the various institutions received creativity in the forms of engineering (Al-Saad 2009).

Conclusion

This study argued that global ethical wealth such as Waqf, Zakat, and other forms are established to play important role in the society. The ultimate aim is to maintain equality and social welfare in society and provide for those who can't provide for themselves. Considering the role of Waqf, it is shown that Waqf can achieve different Maqasid al-Shari'ah (objectives of Shari'ah). For instance, the creation of a mosque falls under the preservation of religion which is one of the al-Maqasid al-Daruriyyat (essential Shari'ah objectives). From a social dimension perspective, Waqf which aims to give a hand to the needy is related to the preservation of life. However, from the environmental dimension perspective, it can be said that Awqaf which aims to improve the environment are related to the complementary objectives of Shari'ah or what is called Maqasid Hajiyyah. To sum up, Awqaf has varied according to their purposes and the interests they achieve. This study has shown that Awqaf played an important role in all levels of Maqasid, i.e., necessities, complements, and embellishment. Awqaf system provided self-financing to the community service institutions, it helped to graduate strong Muslim scholars, writers, and doctors. It also protected wealth from being lost in false entertainment; it was a force for society in parallel with the power of the state. Finally, the Waqf system is one of the systems that distinguish Islam from other religion and has immense socio-economic benefits. Therefore, this system has to be maintained and preserved by Muslims for the benefit of mankind.

REFERENCES

Abideen, M. A. S. B. (2003). *Raddul al-Muhtar Ala al-Dur al-Mukhtar*. Riyadh: Dar Alam al-Kutub.

Ahmad, A., Muhammad, S., & Kamaruzaman, M. A. S. (2012). Education Development Through Waqf. *3rd International Conference on Islam and Higher Education, 13,* 1–22.

Al-Bahouth, A. (1422). *al-Waqf wa al-Tanmiya al-Iqtisadiyyat*. Mecca: Umm Al Qura University.

Al-Bahuti, M. (1983). *Kashshaf al-Qina'*. Beirut: Dar Al-Kutub Al-Ilmiyyah.

Al-Fasi, 'Allal. (1993). *Maqasid al-Syari'ah al-Islamiah Wamakarimuha*. Rabat: Maktabatur Risalah.

Al-Ghazali, A. H. (2004). *al-Mustasfa min ilm al-Usul*. Riyadh: Dar al-Miman.

Al-Raisuni, A. (1995). *Nazariyyat al-Maqasid 'inda al-Imam al-Shatibi*. Egypt: Dar Al-Kalimah, Mansoura.

Al-Saad, A. (2009). Al-Maqasid al-Shar'iah lil al-Waqf. In *Third Conference on Waqf*. Madinah: Islamic University of Madinah.

Al-Yusuf, I. (2007). *Al-Maqasid al-Tashri'iyah lil Awqaf al-Islamiyyah*. Jordan: The University of Jordan.

Al Muqrin, M. (1999). *Maqasid al-Shari'ah fi hifz al-Mal wa Tanmiyatuhu*. Mecca: Umm Al Qura University.

Alqudah, M. (2011). *Ahkam al-Waqf - Dirasah Qanuniyyah Fiqhiyyah Muqaranah bayn al-Shari'ah wa al-Qanun*. Jordan: Dar Al Thaqafa For Publishing & Distributing.

Alshibany, A. M., Mat, M., & Shamsuddin, J. (2019). The Effect of Objectives of Shariah on Islamic Transactions. *Academic Knowledge, 2*(1), 87–106.

Alwan, A. (2007). *al-Takaful al-Ijtima'I fi al-Islam*. Cairo: Dar Al Salam.

Amin, M. (2014). *Al-awqaf wa al-Hayat al-Ijtima'iah fi Masir.* Cairo: Egyptian National Library and Archives.

Auda, J. (2007). Systems as Philosophy and Methodology for Analysis. *Maqasid al-Shariah as Philosophy of Islamic Law.* https://doi.org/10.2307/j.ctvkc6 7tg.8.

Azha, L., Baharuddin, S., Sayurno, Salahuddin, S. S., Afandi, M. R., & Hamid Afifah, H. (2013). The Practice and Management of Waqf Education in Malaysia. *Procedia—Social and Behavioral Sciences, 90*(InCULT 2012), 22–30. https://doi.org/10.1016/j.sbspro.2013.07.061.

Baqutayan, S. M., & Mahdzir, A. M. (2018). The Importance of Waqf in Supporting Healthcare Services. *Journal of Science, Technology and Innovation Policy, 4*(1), 13–19.

Benzeghiba, A. (2008). Maqasid al-Shari'ah al-Khasah bi al-Tasarufat al-Maliyyah. *Journal of King Abdulaziz University.*

Çizakça, M. (1998). Awqaf in History and Its Implications for Modern Ecoomics. *Islamic Economic Studies, 6*(1), 43–70.

Diab, H. A. (1998). *Al-Kutub wa al-Maktabat fi al-Andalus. Cairo: Quba House for Printing.* Publishing and Distribution.

El Basyoni, M. (2011). Revitalization of the Role of waqf in the Field of Architecture: Activation of Waqf to Improve the Function of Public Buildings. *WIT Transactions on the Built Environment, 118,* 129–140. https://doi.org/10.2495/STR110111.

Hassan, M. K. (2010). *An Integrated Poverty Alleviation Model Combining Zakat, Awqaf and Micro-Finance,* 261–281.

Ibn 'Ashur, M. al-T. (2006). *Treatise on maqasid al-Shari'ah.* Herndon: International Institute of Islamic Thought.

Ibn Jubayr, M. I. A. (1984). *Rihlat ibn Jubayr.* Beirut: Dar Beirut.

Ibrahim, D., & Ibrahim, H. (2013, September). Revival of waqf properties in Malaysia. *The 5th Islamic Economics System Conference (IECONS 2013),* 4–5.

Kahf, M. (1998). *Financing the Development of Awqaf Property,* 1–45.

Kahf, M. (1999). *Financial Politics Their Role and Restrictions in the Islamic Economics.* Beirut: Dar al-Fikr.

Khurshi, M. (2010). *Sharh Mukhtasar Khalil.* Beirut: Dar al-Fikr.

Mohammad, A. (2019). Reflection of Maqāṣid al-Sharī'ah in the classical Fiqh al-Awqāf. *Islamic Economic Studies, ahead-of-p* (ahead-of-print). https://doi.org/10.1108/IES-06-2019-0011.

Mohammed, J. A. (2013). The Ethical System in Islam—Implications for Business Practices. *Springer Science + Business Media B.V.,* 1–1581. https://doi.org/10.1007/978-94-007-1494-6.

Nawawi, Y. (1991). *Rawdah al-Talibin wa Umdat al-Muftin.* Al-Maktab al-Islami.

Qahwi, H. (2015). *Dawr al-Waqf fi taf'il Maqasid al-Shari'ah*. Kuwait: Kuwait Awqaf Public Foundation.

Salih, M. (2001). *al-Waqf fi al-Shari'ah al-Islamiyyah Wa "athruhu fi Tanmiat al-Mujtama"*. Riyadh: Imam Muhammad ibn Saud Islamic University.

Tarkawi, H. (2014). *Al-Maqasid al-Shari'iyyah lil al-Waqf*. Kuwait: Ministry of Awqaf and Islamic Affairs.

CHAPTER 25

Forms of Waqf Funds and SDGs

Hichem Hamza

INTRODUCTION

The welfare of Muslim societies is mostly based on the solidarity and philanthropy values that are embedded in the philosophy of waqf. In fact, the waqf is driven by the will of giving and charity which requires the implementation of waqf strategy to achieve the social goals. The waqf contributes to the coverage of the societal needs by following different strategies to mobilize and allocate waqf resources. Broadly, these strategies as practiced by many waqf institutions are based on different types of waqf funds given their flexibility and the succeeded experiences in many countries mostly in Kuwait, Saudi Arabia, and Malaysia in covering society's needs. This highlights the central role that waqf funds can play in achieving sustainable development goals. The development of waqf funds is essential for the sustainability of waqf assets and by consequence the sustainability of the waqf system. The resources of waqf funds are essentially mobilized through cash waqf as a Sharia-compliant waqf. In fact, cash waqf through its perpetual and temporary forms is increasingly the priority of the waqf institution in terms of financing and investment given its characteristics related to mobilization flexibility, investment choices,

H. Hamza (✉)
Islamic Economics Institute, King Abdulaziz University, Jeddah, Saudi Arabia

© The Author(s), under exclusive license to Springer Nature Switzerland AG 2021
M. M. Billah (eds.), *Islamic Wealth and the SDGs*,
https://doi.org/10.1007/978-3-030-65313-2_25

485

and liquidity. In this regard, the waqf funds could make waqf more attractive for all types of donors enabling the success of waqf to fulfill the SDG. Besides, as an essential component of waqf mobilization and investment mechanism, the waqf funds can take different forms each one of them meets the SDG regarding poverty, inequality, education, and health. Fundamentally, these forms include the pure investment waqf funds, the specialized waqf fund, and the Qard Hassan waqf funds. The design of waqf funds forms depends on the vision and commitment of waqf institution in achieving societal needs.

The allocation of waqf resources and returns to the charity activity or the direct awqaf (Kahf 2000) is the final objective of the waqf funds establishment. Indeed, the donors contribute to the redistribution of their wealth derived mainly from the profit sector by channeling a part of it to the non-profit sector (Hamza 2019, p. 110). The contribution of the donors to the charity waqf assets increases when they perceive that their funds are used effectively and with transparency to resolve societal issues for instance poverty, health, education, and inequality and by consequence achieving the SDG. Through the pure investment waqf funds or specialized waqf funds, the waqf institution is committed to ensure the sustainability of direct awqaf. The reason for the creation of investment waqfs fund is to serve the direct awqaf. In fact, the waqf institution looks for a balance between direct waqf assets and waqf investment assets to ensure the stability and sustainability of awqaf (Alarnaut 2018, p. 46; Hamza 2020, p. 156). Moreover, the allocation of donations to real and financial assets is beneficial to the financial system goals through the increase of financing sources. A successful waqf is a successful investment of assets (Alarnaut 2018, p. 46) which generates a return that is going to be affected to the direct awqaf. The rational allocation of investment waqf funds return under donor conditions and in compliance with Sharia is determinant for the realization of the waqf objectives. The example of waqf funds established and managed by the General Authority of Awqaf in Kuwait and Islamic Development Bank (IDB) illustrates the efficiency of these waqf funds in meeting the goals of sustainable development.

Another important form of waqf funds is the Qard Hassan waqf funds. In fact, the Islam through its prohibition of Riba has limited the role of Qard in the economy in a narrow scope which is the charitable scope (Siddiqi 2016, p. 289). The Qard Hassan waqf funds are under the Sharia umbrella of temporary waqf and can be channeled to a variety of individual, microfinance, and SME needs. The Qard Hassan waqf funds exhibit the economic role of waqf similarly to the investment waqf funds with some differences related to return and redemption of funds and therefore are the projection of the economic and social role of cash waqf. The beginning of some experiences of Qard Hassan waqf funds in Saudi Arabia and Malaysia deserves more attention in terms of objectives and impact on society.

This chapter examines the contribution of waqf funds in achieving the challenges regarding poverty, inequality, education, and health which is in convergence with the SDGs. The second section presents the convergence between the concept of waqf and the SDG concept and the importance of the waqf funds as an involvement of the society in the charity activities. The third section examines the forms of waqf funds and their role in achieving SDG with the particularity of the Qard Hassan waqf funds as an instrument for lending cash waqf free of interest to the needy people. The final section concludes by giving recommendations to policymakers for the development of waqf funds.

Convergence of Waqf with SDGs

The concept of waqf reflects multiple dimensions of solidarity and charity through continuous donations and benefits for the welfare of society. The waqf concept is based on the relationship between donor, waqf assets, and beneficiaries. The resources mobilization from donors ensures the sustainability of waqf assets and the achievement of the social goals or beneficiaries' needs. The waqf resources through cash waqf are characterized by the flexibility of mobilization and investment, the promotion of the collective donations, and the advantages of the liquidity (Hamza 2020, p. 156). Given the importance of cash waqf, several waqf institutions (Saudi Arabia, Kuwait, Bahrain, Turkey, and Malaysia) have adopted strategies to mobilize waqf resources within the framework of perpetual or temporary cash waqf (Hamza 2017, p. 124). Cash waqf gives opportunities for a much wider pool of donors to contribute to social good and reap eternal rewards than waqf restricted to immovable property (World Bank, INCEIF and ISRA 2019, p.vi). The cash waqf mobilization and investment can be performed through multiple instruments the most important of them are the waqf funds.

In fact, as a form of cash waqf, the permissibility of waqf funds is derived from the permissibility of cash waqf[1]. This permissibility allows waqf funds to be an important tool for financing waqf in order to achieve social objectives. The most important characteristic of waqf funds is their ability to promote the culture of popular participation in waqf projects. In fact, waqf funds allow all groups of society to participate in waqf and social development, it is also a transparent instrument that enables the private and governmental oversight of the waqf (Ali 2017). The waqf funds hold and invest the funds collected and spends their return on the waqf purposes specified in the donor condition or the participation document in the waqf funds in order to realize the benefit for individuals and society (Ali 2017). The strength of waqf funds lies in the ability to commercialize the waqf project and hence the ability to attract financial resources and urging donors to donate and contribute to the growth of the waqf funds resources. This requires an experience of the fund management in communicating with the donors (individuals, government, and institutions) in a correct manner and in full transparency (Al-Salahat 2014).

Waqf funds are an extension of the concept of investment funds[2] with important differences regarding the resources nature, the types of assets, which should be Sharia-compliant, and the allocation of the return to the charity activity instead of shareholders. In fact, waqf funds mobilize resources from the donors in order to allocate them in awqaf in investment or charitable nature. The role of waqf funds is to contribute to the sustainability and development of waqf assets in order to remain useful and productive within the framework of Sharia. In terms of resources mobilization and investment, the experiences in Kuwait, Saudi Arabia,

---

[1] In 2004, the Islamic Fiqh Academy of the Organization of the Islamic Conference (OIC) authorized the perpetual and temporary cash waqf in the resolution N° 140 (15/6) on investment in waqf and its yields and Rents—Fifteenth Session of the International Islamic Fiqh Academy, Muscat (The Sultanate of Oman) 14–19 Muharram 1425 AH, corresponding to 6–11 March 2004. The Accounting and Auditing Organization for Islamic Financial Institutions (AAOIFI) authorized the cash waqf, stocks, funds, and sukuk waqf in Sharia Standard N° 60 (amended), items N°. 2/4/13, 2/4/14 and 2/4/15 (AAIOFI 2019).

[2] The investment funds illustrate the collect of resources from individuals and institutions in order to invest them in different economic sectors and achieve returns for investment funds holders.

Malaysia, and Turkey are the best examples of waqf funds management and development.

The waqf specificities regarding perpetuity and utility continuity and by consequence the waqf funds are in some extent in convergence with the concept of sustainable development. In this regard, the waqf funds objectives square with the SDG which gives waqf an international dimension in resolving social and economic issues. In fact, The United Nations General Assembly adopted in 2015 the 2030 Agenda for Sustainable Development which includes 17 SDG's. These goals are integrated and indivisible and balance the three dimensions of sustainable development: the economic, social, and environmental.[3] From general view, these goals pertain to all issues essentially poverty, hunger, health, education, inequality, climate change, and environment protection. In this regard, the sustainable dimensions of waqf and waqf funds particularly are aligned with the dimensions of sustainable development and could contribute, with the efforts of governments, in reaching the SDG in compliance with the 2030 Agenda. It is important to ensure the convergence between the investment of waqf and the necessities of development through focusing on the developmental role of the waqf and linking it to the State's strategic development directions as long as it does not affect the investment return of the waqf (Al-Omar 2007, p. 276).

The waqf funds vary according to the strategy of the waqf institutions and can be divided in three principals' forms: pure investment waqf funds, specialized waqf funds, and Qard Hassan waqf funds (Table 25.1).

The multiplicity of waqf funds and their purposes leads to a diverse and integrated assortment of projects financed by these funds in all fields that serve a comprehensive sustainable development (Jaafar 2014, p. 160). The forms of waqf funds differ according to the goal that they seek to achieve, the internal conditions of the country, and the conditions of people and society, and cover many areas of religious, social, scientific, health, environmental, development, and economic life (Al-Zuhaili 2006). The choice of one or more forms of waqf funds by waqf institutions should be examined according to the waqf policy of the general waqf authority and the capacity of waqf institutions in respecting its commitments toward the society. In fact, each form of waqf funds has its own

---

[3] https://sustainabledevelopment.un.org/post2015/transformingourworld.

490   H. HAMZA

Table 25.1   Forms and impacts of Waqf funds

Waqf funds	Sustainable development impact	Funds' assets allocation	Returns' beneficiaries allocation
Pure Investment waqf funds	Economic, social and environmental	Housing, educational and health institutions, climate change, real estate, agricultural lands, Infrastructure, renewable energy projects	Poverty, health, education, unemployment
Specialized waqf funds		Holy Quran, mosques, scientific and social development, health development, educational and health institutions	
Qard Hassan waqf fund		Financial inclusion, microfinance	

characteristics and challenges in terms of funds mobilization, management and allocation of resources, and the social impact targeted. In fact, achieving the SDGs require mobilizing a vast amount of resources to fill the gaps (Ahmed 2017, p. 39). The existence of these forms in a balanced manner could contribute efficiently to the realization of SDGs. Similarly, waqf funds and SDG take into consideration the need and rights of the future generation regarding life conditions in terms of health, education, poverty, and climate. The realization of SDG from an Islamic perspective is potentially conditional to the existence of multiple waqf funds forms which can cover the economic, social, and the environmental dimensions through investment and Qard Hassan.

Role of Waqf Funds Forms in SDGs Realization

Waqf funds are a tool for mobilization of financial resources from donors, individuals, and institutions, through donations for the purpose of allocating these resources in waqf assets that generate benefits and returns that are disbursed to specific entities within the framework of the donor clause and Sharia, which benefits individuals and society and contributes to the preservation and development of waqf assets[4]. In this regard, waqf funds are an important mechanism of resources mobilization and assets investment allowing the realization of waqf objectives regarding needy parties. Therefore, direct or charity waqf assets use the returns of waqf investment assets to achieve their goals and both types of assets are generally managed separately to ensure economic efficiency. Globally, the waqf funds resources are composed of donations (individuals, institutions, firms, government) and returns of new and old investment waqf (real and financial assets). There are three principal forms of waqf funds, each one incorporates multiple dimensions of the SDG.

Pure Investment Waqf Funds

The waqf investment represents the process of selecting, managing, and developing the waqf assets represented by real and financial investments. The waqf investment gives the waqf an economic and developmental dimensions in addition to its charitable and social roles. The philosophy of waqf investment is to serve the charitable awqaf assets to ensure its continuity and historically, the development of the waqf forced the donor to build income-generating enterprises or waqf investment to ensure the continuation of charitable waqf (Alarnaut 2018, p. 40). The specificity of waqf and the nature and size of charitable waqf give an orientation to what should be the investment in terms of strategy to implement and return to realize. In this regard, the establishment and success of investment waqf funds as a form of investment waqf is highly tied to the trust of donors toward waqf institution and the responsibility of this institution in the investment and return management.

The establishment of investment waqf funds policy in accordance with SDG may enable waqf institution to have a global vision regarding waqf policy and to expand its activities by attracting more donations and reaching more social layers. The SDG may allow the development of investment waqf funds regarding the assets allocation which ensure more efficiency and stability of the waqf asset. The investment policy of waqf institution regarding investment waqf funds focus on the optimal investment assets according to the waqf specificities. The choice of real and financial assets in compliance with Sharia and with reasonable and stable

---

[4] Author definition.

return is the essential conditions given the specificities of the waqf and responsibilities toward the waqf beneficiaries. The investment waqf funds is a blend of investment thought and waqf thought and is considered as a special type of investment fund since they are under the law and procedures of investment funds (Al-Rached 2019, p. 224).

A successful waqf is a successful investment of assets (Alarnaut 2018, p. 46) given the importance and role of investment return to guarantee the continuity and sustainability of waqf benefits for future generations. The investment waqf funds follow a strategy based on diversifying assets and maintaining their sustainability and it seeks to achieve the goals of stabilizing the waqf returns by reducing the risks. The optimal management of waqf assets is based on diversification of a number of elements, the most important are the diversification of investment assets, investment sectors, investment areas, investment terms, and investment currencies in order to reduce risks, sustain returns and provide liquidity. In fact, as a result of waqf investment, the distribution of return to the beneficiaries is the core of the waqf philosophy and is determinant for the donor's commitment regarding the social impact of their donations.

The multiplicity of investment waqf funds in terms of assets allocation (economic sectors, financial assets, real assets) and returns allocation to the different need of the society (Health, poverty, employment, SME) is determinant for the realization of the SDG in accordance with the objectives of the government and the priority need of the society. The optimal choice of waqf investment assets and the level and stability of the waqf return is crucial for the realization of the social impact of waqf. The management of investment waqf funds should respect some conditions mostly the compliance with the Sharia and the avoidance of high-risk investment which could be harmful for the waqf assets and by consequence waqf beneficiaries. The western experience in investing waqf assets shows the importance of investing assets through low-risk mechanisms, even though their profits are reduced (Khafagy and Irfan 2012, p. 14). The investment waqf funds could be more useful if a part of funds are channeled to the necessary sectors and small and micro-enterprises leading to an economic benefit added to charitable benefits provided that reasonable and stable return is ensured. The success of the investment fund in meeting the SDG is a key motivation for the donors' continuous donations which may reinforce their trust and relationship with waqf institution.

The most important pure investment waqf funds are those established and developed by the (IDB). These investment waqf funds are closely converged with the SDG mainly regrading poverty alleviation, education and health. In fact, the IDB has established the first endowment fund in 1997 called "The Bank waqf Fund," which finances health, education, relief, and natural disaster. In addition, the IDB has established a "Waqf Property Investment Fund" in 2001 which finances waqf projects in the housing and trade sector generating benefit for education, religion institutions and health. This waqf fund is a profitable investment portfolio for the development of waqf properties. In 2005, the "Islamic Solidarity Fund" has been established, whose tasks include financing programs to combat poverty and diseases, reducing professional illiteracy, supporting microfinance, and establishing solidarity villages (Hamza 2019, p. 121). Among the "Islamic Solidarity Fund" priorities: human development, agricultural and rural development, infrastructure development. The resources of the fund are determined through fieldwork, identifying the needs of local communities, and the projects and programs necessary for IDB member states. The financial resources of this waqf fund consist of the fund's capital, immovable waqf, cash waqf, financial grants from IDB member states.

Specialized Waqf Funds

This form of waqf funds are based on a set of donations mobilized continually and allocated simultaneously to charity projects and investment assets. The charitable waqf fund is dedicated to the establishment and administration of charitable projects or what is called direct awqaf. These awqaf do not represent a capital of investment nature and are used directly by the society, where they provide direct and basic benefits or services to the needy people and the general public (Kahf 2000). The benefit of these awqaf is through their use by providing real benefits that represent their social contribution. Direct awqaf include mosques, wells, roads, orphanages, educational and health institutions. The decision to establish these funds and the choice of their fields depend on the social and economic needs. Moreover, given their nature, this form of waqf funds require continuity donations as a main source of funds mainly from individuals, institutions, and government.

The awareness of the importance of developing this form of specialized waqf funds explain the succeeded strategy followed by the General Awqaf

Authority in Kuwait which is the pioneer in this field. In Kuwait, the waqf funds are under a special law other than the investment fund law. The special law mentions that the waqf funds have among objectives an investment objective. These specialized waqf funds are under the organization and control of the general awqaf authority. The strategy and organization of the specialized waqf funds are fundamentally based on the realization of social objectives regarding the beneficiaries (Al-Rached 2019, p. 222). In fact, waqf funds have been chosen as a strategic choice in the development of waqf by the General Awqaf Authority in Kuwait. In this regard, four types of charitable waqf funds were established: The waqf fund of the Holy Quran and its sciences, the waqf fund for the care of mosques, the waqf fund for scientific and social development and the waqf fund for health development.[5] The waqf funds of the general authority of awqaf have a special importance, as financial waqf units specialized in a variety of charity activities. The financial resources of waqf funds are provided by the donors for the purposes sponsored by the fund, and of the funds allocated by the general authority of awqaf for each waqf fund (Ali 2017).

The identification of charitable projects through the knowledge and prioritization of the needs of the society complies with *Maqasid Sharia*. The prioritization could be tied to the major social issues for instance poverty, health, and education. The multiplication of the charitable waqf funds designed to multiple needs is able to cover large layers of the society. In this regard, the involvement of the waqf institutions in the attraction of donors through charitable projects is crucial and necessitate a waqf management with transparency and governance which are required by the general authority of awqaf.

The specialized waqf fund are financed by donations from general public, institutions, compagnies, government, and the awaqf general authority. These donations through cash or real assets are allocated to the spending and investment sections of the waqf funds. In fact, the waqf fund administration is divided on spending administration and investment administration both are separated and having different roles. The role of the spending administration is to serve the waqf beneficiaries or the waqf project by the realization of the social role of the fund. The role of investment administration is the realization of returns as new resources

---

[5] The General Authority of Awqaf in Kuwait (2001). The waqf funds and their role in the development of Kuwaiti society. Chapter 2 The Kuwaiti Waqf Bill.

serving the spending administration. The specialized waqf funds mechanism are based on a recurrent collect of donations allocated on one hand to charity projects initially established and in another hand to investment assets. The management of charity waqf funds and the investment waqf funds is separated which could make more efficiency in the realization of the waqf institutions objectives. The establishment of waqf fund has been based on allocation of amounts and waqf assets where its return is spent for the realization of waqf fund objectives (Al-Moutawa 2001, p. 503).

The multi-purpose of waqf funds and the diversity of their specializations in proportion to the needs of society have had a significant impact on the success of the waqf funds experience as a financier of sustainable development in Kuwait, and the evidence of their success is the increase of the waqf capital of these funds, and the increase in volume of financing to serve their various purposes in various fields of sustainable development (Jaafar 2014, p. 170)

Qard Hassan Waqf Funds

The Islamic Fiqh Academy of the Organization of the Islamic Conference (OIC) authorized cash waqf for Qard Hassan[6]. The Accounting and Auditing Organization for Islamic Financial Institutions (AAIOIFI) has authorized the cash waqf including the establishment of waqf funds whose purpose is to collect, develop, and loan funds[7] in form of Qard Hassan. In addition, the thirty-third Al-Barakah Symposium (2012) and the European Council for Fatwa and Research authorized the permissibility of the cash waqf for purpose of Qard Hassan and investment of the funds collected[8]. Historically, waqf for lending is proven in Morocco which was distinguished by a waqf fund for interest-free loan that was located in the city of Fez underlining the attention given for helping needy layers[9] (Hamza 2019, p. 73). The Qard Hassan waqf fund devotes

---

[6] The resolution N° 140 (15/6) on investment in waqf and its yields and Rents - Fifteenth Session of the International Islamic Fiqh Academy, Muscat (The Sultanate of Oman) 14–19 Muharram 1425 AH, corresponding to 6–11 March 2004.

[7] Sharia Standard N° 60 (2019) paragraph No. 13/4/2.

[8] The European Council for Fatwa and Research Resolution No. 1/20- at its twentieth session 1431 AH corresponding to 2010.

[9] This is what was mentioned by Professor Muhammad bin Abdulaziz bin Abdullah (1996) in his book "The Endowment in Islamic Thought."

the notion of solidarity toward a category of needy persons concerned by the financial inclusion and access to finance.

The origins of resources of Qard Hassan waqf fund are the donations with perpetual nature and the temporary cash waqf in form of Qard Hassan. The donors have the choice to donate cash waqf temporarily or perpetually. These donations are allocated in the form of Qard Hassan to the eligible persons for microfinance and entrepreneurship projects depending on their projects in terms of volume, duration, and solvency capacity. The allocation of Qard Hassan to the needy persons reinforces the financial inclusion and access to finance. Through the Qard Hassan waqf funds, the waqf institution endeavors to meet the needs of an important segment of society, especially microfinance, which supports the efforts of the state in achieving sustainable development goals.

The selection of projects is based on their economic and social feasibility which allow the grant of Qard Hassan to the persons that have suitable profitable projects, thus guaranteeing the repayment of the Qard Hassan at specific times according to the donors' conditions. Likewise, to manage liquidity risk, delays and non-payment of Qard Hassan by creditors, the fund management can take the necessary measures to counter these risks by taking the necessary guarantees and verifying the economic feasibility of the funded projects (Hamza 2017). Furthermore, the administration of Qard Hassan waqf funds follow-up the financing process until the repayment of the total Qard and manage the changes that can happen during the Qard Hassan period (project performance, deficit, death ...). The Qard Hassan waqf funds can encourage people for donating to constitute reserves useful for facing the non-performing Qard Hassan or the insolvency of the needy persons (Al-Gari 2015). Zarqa (2006) suggested a practical instrument for financing micro-projects for the poor, based on the Qard Hassan as a temporary cash waqf[10]. Zarqa (2006) pointed out that this instrument aims to provide temporary charitable financing to the poor, enabling them to finance a permanent livelihood with the necessity to find guarantors to avoid liquidity risk and insolvency.

The Qard Hassan waqf funds can be established from the investment waqf fund. In fact, Khalid (2014) indicates that the waqf institution can use a percentage of the income generated from investment waqf

---

[10] For instance, in the Kingdom of Saudi Arabia, the Sulaiman Bin Abdulaziz Al-Rajhi Foundation for the development finance is specialized in the Qard Hassan for microfinance.

to give interest-free loans to those in need using the Qard Hassan contract. Therefore, the potential establishment of Qard Hassan waqf funds through investment waqf funds will depend on the strategy of the waqf institution regarding the management of return distribution and also on the performance of the waqf return. As a result, the success of waqf investment is beneficial for the waqf institutions continuity, waqf beneficiaries and the creation of new waqf funds for instance the Qard Hassan waqf fund. Moreover, as mentioned above, Qard Hassan waqf funds could experience some financial difficulties regarding the insolvency of the Qard Hassan beneficiaries or non-performing Qard Hassan, in this case, the income of investment waqf funds can also be used to face these difficulties and ensure the financial sustainability of the Qard Hassan waqf funds.

CONCLUSION

The waqf funds are the most popular and efficient instrument of mobilization and investment of waqf resources. The experiences of the Awqaf General Authority in Kuwait and the Islamic Development Bank in Saudi Arabia are considered as the best model given their success in meeting the social needs. The success of these waqf funds is based on the involvement of waqf institutions and government in mobilization of resources and assets allocation to cover the beneficiaries need. The forms development of these waqf funds can fill the gap for reaching the majority of SDGs. The investment waqf funds initiated by the IDB and followed by other institutions and countries show the efficiency of this form of instrument in the SDG realization. The specialized waqf funds in Kuwait as a form of investment waqf funds constitute a successful example regarding the comprehensive realization of the SDG and can be expanded in other countries. Finally, the Qard Hassan waqf funds can complete and promote the role of waqf funds in society given its characteristics and the beneficiaries targeted. The Qard Hassan waqf funds need more attention and development from the authority and waqf institutions given its multiple social and economic benefits. The existence of these forms of waqf funds in a balanced manner can promote the waqf sector and contribute substantially to the SDGs.

REFERENCES

Accounting and Auditing Organization for Islamic Financial Institutions (2019). Waqf. Shari'a Standard n° 60 (amended). Item No. 2/4/13, 2/4/14 and 2/4/15 (AAIOFI, 2019).

Ahmed, H. (2017). *Contribution of Islamic Finance to the 2030 Agenda for Sustainable Development.* https://www.un.org/esa/ffd//high-level-confer ence-on-ffd-and-2030-agenda/wp-content/uploads/sites/4/2017/11/Bac kground-Paper_Islamic-Finance.pdf.

Alarnaut, M. M. (2018). Toward an Active Role of Awqaf in the Life of Contemporary Muslim Societies. *Journal of King Abdulaziz University: Islamic Economics, 31*(3), 33–58.

Algari, M. A. (2015). The waqf funds and their Sharia adaptation. http://www.elgari.com/?p=1467.

Ali, M. A. (2017). Waqf Funds in Islamic Countries. Islamic Conference for Awqaf. Speech of the Ali Mohamed Ahmed. 17 October 2017. Makkah.

Al-Moutawa, I. A. (2001). *Project of Kuwait waqf Law in the Framework of Investment and Development of waqf Resources* (1st ed.). Kuwait: General authority of Awqaf.

Al-Omar, F. A. (2007). *Investment of Funds of waqf (Economic Conditions and Development Requirements)* (1st ed.). Kuwait: Awqaf General Authority.

Al-Rached, S. B. S. (2019). Investment waqf Funds and Its Application in Kingdom of Saudi Arabia (In Arabic). SAEE for awqaf Development.

Al-Salahat, S. M. (2014). *The Waqf Between Authenticity and Modernity: Specialized Studies in the Balance of Institutional waqf Work.* Edition No. 1. Arab Science House Publishers.

Al-Zuhaili, M. (2006). *Contemporary Waqf Funds: Their Adaptation, Forms, Rulings, and Problems.* In Research Presented to the Second Waqf Conference at Umm Al-Qura University 18–25 Dhu Al-Qi'dah 1427 AH, p. 82.

Bin Abdulaziz bin Abdullah, M. (1996). The Endowment in Islamic Thought. Published by the Ministry of Endowments and Islamic Affairs, Kingdom of Morocco.

General Authority of Awqaf in Kuwait. (2001). The Waqf Funds and Their Role in the Development of Kuwaiti Society. Chapter Two. The Kuwaiti Waqf Bill.

Hamza, H. (2017). Financial Structure of Cash waqf. *Journal of King Abdulaziz University: Islamic Economics* (Arabic version), *30*(3), pp 123–141.

Hamza, H. (2019). Financing and Investment in Awqaf. Textbook. Islamic Economics Institute. King Abdulaziz University. KSA. ISBN: 978-603-8272-19-0.

Hamza, H. (2020). *Developing Awqaf Through Cash waqf. Handbook Waqf Led Islamic Social Finance Innovative Solutions to Modern Applications.* Routledge.

Jaafar, S. (2014). *Role of Waqf Funds in the Realisation of Sustainable Development: Comparative Study Between Kuwait and Malaysia.* Setif, Algeria: Farhat Abbes University.

Kahf, M. (2000). Al-Aaqf Al-Islami: Tatawwuruh, Idaratuh, Tanmiyatuh (The Islamic Endowment: Development, Administration, and Evolution). Dar al-Fikr Damascus.

Khafagy, R., and Irfan, A. (2012). Ihiaa Nidham Al-Waqf Fi Misr …Qiraa Fi Al-Namathej Al-Alamia (Reviving the waqf System in Egypt … Reading in International Models). John D. Gerhart Center for Philanthropy and Civic Engagement.

Khalid, M. (2014). Waqf as a Socially Responsible Investment Instrument: A case for Western-Countries. *EJIF—European Journal of Islamic Finance, 1.*

Siddiqi, M. N. (2016). Objectives of Sharia and contemporary life (Arabic version). Dar Al-Kalam. Damascus.

World Bank, INCEIF and ISRA. (2019). *Maximizing social impact through waqf solutions.* World Bank, INCEIF and ISRA report.

Zarqa, M. A. M. (2006). The Temporary Cash Waqf to Finance Micro Projects for the Poor—The Second Conference of Awqaf - 2006 - Umm Al-Qura University – Makkah.

CHAPTER 26

Contributions of Waqf Investments in Achieving SDGs

Barae Dukhan, Mustafa Omar Mohammed, and Mohamed Cherif El Amri

Introduction

Waqf is an Arabic terminology that means holding, or confinement. Technically, it means retaining the corpus of a property, whether movable or immovable, for the sake of certain beneficiaries—which could be individuals or institution, to serve certain objectives defined by the Waqf founder. The detailed definition and conditions of Waqf have been the subject of historical debate among classical Islamic Jurists who vary in their opinions over almost everything related to Waqf including its conditions, such as whether Waqf can be temporary or permanent, whether it must be immovable or it can be in cash, or whether the Waqf founder or

B. Dukhan · M. C. El Amri (✉)
Department of Islamic Economics and Finance, Istanbul Sabahattin Zaim University, Istanbul, Turkey

M. O. Mohammed
Department of Economics, International Islamic University Malaysia [IIUM], Gombak, Malaysia

© The Author(s), under exclusive license to Springer Nature Switzerland AG 2021
M. M. Billah (eds.), *Islamic Wealth and the SDGs*,
https://doi.org/10.1007/978-3-030-65313-2_26

501

owner has the right to cancel the status of Waqf property and use it for other purposes. According to (Shwaiki 2012), despite these variations in opinion on the definition of Waqf, the four Islamic schools of thoughts have unanimously agreed that Waqf is "retaining the corpus of the asset and utilize its usufruct for the beneficiaries."

Meanwhile, modern Islamic scholars have further added to the diverse definitions and conditions of Waqf. For example, Kahf (1998) defined Waqf as "retaining the corpus of Maal (an asset) and preventing its consumption for the purpose of perpetually utilizing its usufruct to serve righteousness or philanthropy objectives." On the other hand (Hallaq 2013) stated that Waqf can be defined as "a charitable endowment; usually, immovable property alienated and endowed to serve the interest of certain beneficiaries, such as members of a family, the poor, the wayfarers, scholars, mystics, the general public, etc.".

The need of social support in all societies and cultures has been covered through philanthropic and non-governmental institutions that play similar role which Waqf is playing in Islam. Institutions that are playing similar role of Waqf in non-Muslim countries can be found under different names, which are synonymous to Waqf. Some of these terms include: Endowment, Foundations, Philanthropy, Third sector, voluntarism, social capital, civil society, and non-profit organizations (NPO). However, the improvements introduced by Muslim scholars over these kind of institutions since the sixth century can be considered undeniably as the most substantial improvements both on the conceptual and theoretical field as well as in the practical field. In fact, Waqf institutions in Islamic history have played major roles in sustaining the societies and providing more independence from government control, while relieving the government from many forms of social support expenditures. It has been estimated that by the sixteenth century, nearly 50% of all real properties owned by Muslims were in fact Waqf properties (Hallaq 2013).

According to Islamic economists, Waqf institution is classified among the poverty alleviation institutions along with Zakat and Sadaqah (Sadeq, 2002). It works toward improving economic enabling tools and infrastructure such as education, cash, land, and other economic activities. Furthermore, it is seen to support societies through disaster relief programs, and health services. Moreover, its impact extends further to serve animals and the environment (Islamic Development Bank 2019). Due to its success, the Waqf institution model has been replicated by modern western organizations—especially universities, to benefit from the

Islamic experience of Waqf in developing their educational organizations and supporting them through Waqf like institution such as endowment (Awqaf Properties Investment Fund [APIF] 2019).

Looking at the system of Waqf investment more broadly across the world, we find that Waqf investment entities have relied heavily on tangible assets to avoid any risk of falling into interest through debt financial instruments. Nevertheless, Waqf institutions continue to explore new investment opportunities and vehicles or avenues to sustain their project needs. Such investment vehicles include financial service, securities such as stocks and Sukuk, Waqf investment funds, and Islamic banking investment accounts.

Waqf investment has been defined as: "diverting funds (and other resources) from consumption and investing them in productive assets that provide either usufruct or revenues for future consumption by individual or group of individuals" (Budiman 2011). Needless to say, such investment would require savings by Waqf institution. Investments enhance the perpetual feature of Waqf properties to sustain their objectives of providing usufructs to the beneficiaries throughout the life span of these properties. In order to generate a Shari'ah compliant revenue for the Waqf institutions, the Waqf properties need to be invested ethically, free from negative values such as interest. Investments can be in the product market as well as the service market, financial or otherwise. The product market includes trade in commodity, agriculture, real estate, or manufacturing. Whereas the service market includes education, health care, and securities, among others. Meanwhile investment in the financial service market includes Cash Waqf funds, Waqf sukuk and stocks. Sukuk are forms of investments to raise funds that are usually utilized to finance ethical projects identified by the Waqf manager. Another avenue for investment is "Cash Waqf" which comes in many forms including funds that provide cash for the needy people in form of Qard Hasan Loans. The capital of those funds is not completely consumed in the process of Loans. Rather part of the capital is invested to continue growing. The invested capital can be used to cover any loan default as well as overhead costs.

Traditionally, Waqf investment served as a decentralized pool of funding to support the provision of public goods and services such as health care, agriculture, and education, which are nowadays considered as part of the central government responsibilities. It is estimated that around one-third of inhabitable land ruled by the Ottoman Empire was designated as Waqf owned lands which was used to ensure food security, while its investment arm generated profits from the sale of its agricultural yields. Those profits were most likely used to support education and healthcare services for the society as whole (Babacan 2011). Funding by Waqf investment was not limited to education and health care. Other social services were also funded by Waqf investments including Mosques, restaurants, soup kitchens, cultural institutions, social welfare organizations, Jihad and military power (Babacan 2011). Although Waqf investments have greatly diversified over the years, the following areas remain vital vehicles and opportunities where Waqf capitals and properties are invested: Shari'ah compliant equity shares, education sector, construction and property sector, commercial sector, real estate, and Islamic banking and finance sector.

SUSTAINABLE DEVELOPMENT GOALS (SDGs) AND THEIR INVESTMENT AREAS

Since Waqf Investment Institutions focus on provision of finance, it is necessary to identify the financial needs of all the sustainable development goals (SDG). However, SDGs describe broad outcome objectives that require large numbers of inputs, which may contribute to more than one goal. For example, access to safe water contributes to GOAL 2: Zero Hunger, GOAL 3: Good Health and Well-being, and GOAL 6: Clean Water and Sanitation. Hence, it is impossible to organize SDG investment needs by goals since this would lead to double-counting of those investment needs. Attempts to solve this problem were undertaken by United Nations Conference on Trade and Development (UNCTAD) in 2014 and 2020, and by Guido Schmidt-Traub, the executive director of Sustainable Development Solutions Network (SDSN) in 2015. Below are brief explanations of each of those methodologies.

UNCTAD Sdgs Investment Areas

UNCTAD converted the 17 SDGs into 10 investment sectors in 2014 and enhanced them further in its 2020 report. Their Investment areas are identified in Table 26.1 along with the most relevant SDGs (United Nations Conference on Trade and Development 2014, 2020).

It can be noted in Table 26.1 that the proposed investment areas miss the following SDGs:

Table 26.1 UNCTAD SDGs investment areas

	Investment sector	Definition	Most relevant SDGs
1	Power	Investment in generation, transmission and distribution of electricity	GOAL 7: Affordable and Clean Energy
2	Transport Infrastructure	Investment in roads, airports, ports, and rail	GOAL 9: Industry, Innovation and Infrastructure GOAL 11: Sustainable Cities and Communities
3	Telecommunications	Investment in infrastructure (-fixed lines, mobile and internet)	GOAL 9: Industry, Innovation and Infrastructure
4	Water Sanitation and Hygiene (Wash)	Provision of water and sanitation to industry and households	GOAL 6: Clean Water and Sanitation
5	Food and Agriculture	Investment in agriculture, research, rural development, etc.	GOAL 2: Zero Hunger
6	Climate Change Mitigation	Investment in relevant infrastructure, renewable energy generation, research and deployment of climate-friendly technologies, etc.	GOAL 13: Climate Action
7	Climate Change Adaptation	Investment to cope with impact of climate change in agriculture, infrastructure, water management, coastal zones, etc.	GOAL 13: Climate Action
8	Ecosystems and Biodiversity	Investment in conservation and safeguarding ecosystems, marine resource management, sustainable forestry, etc.	GOAL 14: Life Below Water GOAL 15: Life on Land
9	Health	Investment in infrastructure, e.g., new hospitals, and R&D on vaccines and medicines	GOAL 3: Good Health and Well being
10	Education	Infrastructural investment, e.g., new schools	GOAL 4: Quality Education

Source Adopted from (United Nations Conference on Trade and Development 2014, 2020)

1. GOAL 1: No Poverty.
2. GOAL 5: Gender Equality.
3. GOAL 8: Decent Work and Economic Growth.
4. GOAL 10: Reduced Inequality.
5. GOAL 12: Responsible Consumption and Production.
6. GOAL 16: Peace and Justice Strong Institutions.
7. GOAL 17: Partnerships to achieve the Goal.

Guido Schmidt-Traub SDG Investment Areas

In 2015, Guido Schmidt-Traub attempted to identify the SDG invest-ment areas by adopting the same methodology that was used by the UN millennium project in 2005 to rearrange all interrelated inputs into sepa-rate investment areas with regard to the Millennium Development Goals (MDGs). He suggested that the 17 SDGs be translated into the following eight "SDG investment areas": (1) health, (2) education, (3) social protection, (4) food security and sustainable agriculture, (5) infrastruc-ture—including (a) energy access and low-carbon energy infrastructure, (b) water and sanitation, (c) transport infrastructure, and (d) telecom-munications infrastructure, (6) ecosystem services and biodiversity, (7) data for the SDGs, and (8) emergency response and humanitarian work (Schmidt-Traub, Investment Needs to Achieve the Sustainable Develop-ment Goals, 2015a). Schmidt-Traub list of investment areas, however, excluded GOAL 8: Decent Work and Economic Growth, and GOAL 17: Partnerships to achieve the Goal for no apparent reason. Besides, the final list of investments areas also excluded the investment area of "social protection" because its components overlap with other investment areas, particularly with health and education areas of investment. Table 26.2 shows Guido Schmidt-Traub SDGs Investment Areas.

Analysis and Consolidation of SDG Related Investment Areas

Both studies above agree with regard to excluding GOALS 8 and 17 from the list of SDGs that have investment needs. Schmidt-Traub investment model, however, is the one which has more coverage of the Sustainable development Goals in its investment areas. It is hence more logical to go with Schmidt-Traub investment model with its final form after removing the Investment Area 3 (social protection) from its list because of the immense overlap of this investment area with the

26 CONTRIBUTIONS OF WAQF INVESTMENTS IN ACHIEVING SDGS 507

Table 26.2 Guido Schmidt-Traub SDGs investment areas

	Investment area	*Most relevant SDGs*
1	Health	GOAL 3: Good Health and Well-being GOAL 12: Responsible Consumption and Production
2	Education	GOAL 4: Quality Education GOAL 12: Responsible Consumption and Production
3	Social Protection	GOAL 1: No Poverty GOAL 3: Good Health and Well-being GOAL 4: Quality Education GOAL 5: Gender Equality (No Data could be found) GOAL 10: Reduced Inequality GOAL 11: Sustainable Cities and Communities GOAL 12: Responsible Consumption and Production GOAL 16: Peace and Justice Strong Institutions.
4	Food Security and Sustainable Agriculture	GOAL 1: No Poverty GOAL 2: Zero Hunger GOAL 12: Responsible Consumption and Production
5	INFRASTRUCTURE: Covers the following sectors: Energy, Water, Transportation, and Telecommunication.	GOAL 7: Affordable and Clean Energy GOAL 6: Clean Water and Sanitation GOAL 9: Industry, Innovation and Infrastructure GOAL 10: Reduced Inequality GOAL 11: Sustainable Cities and Communities GOAL 12: Responsible Consumption and Production GOAL 13: Climate Action
6	Ecosystem Services and Biodiversity	GOAL 12: Responsible Consumption and Production GOAL 13: Climate Action GOAL 14: Life Below Water GOAL 15: Life on Land
7	DATA FOR THE SDGS: Covers production and dissemination of data to monitor progress toward operationalizing and achieving the SDGs	All GOALS (General requirement)

(continued)

508   B. DUKHAN ET AL.

Table 26.2 (continued)

Investment area	Most relevant SDGs
8 EMERGENCY RESPONSE AND HUMANITARIAN WORK	GOAL 12: Responsible Consumption and Production

Source Adopted from (Schmidt-Traub, Investment Needs to Achieve the Sustainable Development Goals—Supplemental material, 2015b)

rest of the seven remaining areas. To benefit from UNCTAD as well as Schmidt-Traub models, the authors have developed Table 26.3 to find common and unique investment areas for each of the models. It is clear in Table 26.1 that four of UNCTAD SDG investment areas are covered under the INFRASTRUCTURE Investment area proposed by Schmidt-Traub model. These are: Power, Transport Infrastructure, telecommunications, Water Sanitation and Hygiene (Wash), and Climate change Mitigation.

The other point that is worth highlighting here is that Schmidt-Traub model has added the following two areas for investment which need to be further understood in order to use them right (Schmidt-Traub, Investment Needs to Achieve the Sustainable Development Goals, 2015a):

1. DATA FOR THE SDGS: Achieving the SDGs and promoting sustainable development will require significant investments in data and monitoring systems—a genuine "data revolution" is required. According to the Asian Development Bank (ADB) Sustainable Development Goals 2020 report, governments in the Asia Pacific region should invest in improving statistical data quality and in better transparency in monitoring and accountability activity (Asian Development Bank 2020).

2. EMERGENCY RESPONSE AND HUMANITARIAN WORK: These are basically the humanitarian aids provided to victims of war, civil strife, and natural disasters in long-term humanitarian settings and short-term emergency forms.

The final list of SDG Investment Areas that we will be covered are the following:

Table 26.3 UNCTAD vs Schmidt-Traub SDG investment areas

		Schmidt-Traub SDG Investment areas							Extra Investment Area
		Health	Education	Food Security and Sustainable Agriculture	INFRASTRUCTURE (Energy, Water, Transportation, and Telecommunication)	Ecosystem Services and Biodiversity	Data for the SDGS	Emergency Response and Humanitarian Work	
UNCTAD SDG Investment Areas	Power				GOAL 7: Affordable and Clean Energy				No Extra Investment Area by Schmidt-Traub Model
	Transport Infrastructure				GOAL 9: Industry, Innovation and Infrastructure				
	Telecommunications				GOAL 9: Industry, Innovation and Infrastructure				
	Water, Sanitation and Hygiene (Wash)				GOAL 6: Clean Water and Sanitation				
	Food and Agriculture			GOAL 2: Zero Hunger					
	Climate Change Mitigation								
	Climate Change Adaptation					GOAL 13: Climate Action			

(continued)

Table 26.3 (continued)

Ecosystems and Biodiversity				GOAL 14: Life Below Water GOAL 15: Life on Land	
Health	GOAL 3: Health and Well-being				
Education		GOAL 4: Quality Education			
Extra Investment Area by Schmidt-Traub Model				Data for the SDGS	Emergency Response and Humanitarian Work

1. Health
2. Education
3. Social Protection
4. Food Security and Sustainable Agriculture
5. INFRASTRUCTURE: Energy, Water, Transportation, and Telecommunication
6. Ecosystem Services and Biodiversity
7. Data for the SDGS
8. Emergency response and Humanitarian Work.

WAQF-SDGs INVESTMENT AREAS

In 2015, the Asian Development Bank (ADB) estimated that annually over one trillion USD is needed to meet the financial needs of Sustainable Development Goals in the Asian pacific region (Kwa 2015). ADB estimated that seventy-five percent of those costs are needed to build infrastructure between 2010 and 2020 (Kwa 2015). In 2017, the UN Assistant Secretary General "Magdy Martínez-Solimán" stated that the financial investment needed to support the Sustainable Development Goals (SDGs) for the developing countries was approximately US$4.5 trillion per year, and that The Official Development Assistance (ODA) was not even close to support those needs (Martínez-Solimán 2017). Below are some of the important investment areas of Waqf that are related to SDGs investment.

Investment Area 1: Health

Waqf in the field of health care are as old as the idea of Waqf itself. Waqf investment entities use different models to ensure healthcare support of the needy people. For example, a healthcare Waqf entity that is targeting the needy people can have a commercial healthcare entity which serves as its investment arm. Another model in this field comes in the form of limiting the Waqf to the healthcare service, where the needy people benefit from this Waqf while the rich patients pay for their treatment as per the commercial market price, hence serving as the investment arm of the healthcare service Waqf.

512   B. DUKHAN ET AL.

Investment Area 2: Education

What has been said about healthcare Waqf investment forms can also be applied to education. Furthermore, Education Waqf entities are usually supported through many different investment arms such as research investments, fees, licensing, and patenting, as well as some services that are provided through their investment entities such as hospitals and factories.

Investment Area 3: Social Protection

This area is also considered as the indirect target of Waqf according to Islamic guideline, (Hoque 2019). Muslims who seek mercy and hope to be blessed by ALLAH are usually engaged in social Waqf activities which are usually sustained by their Waqf investment institutions.

Waqf investment institutions can support this Investment Area both in the short term, and the long term. However, it can be achieved through other Investment areas as well. For example, cash or financial support can be directly provided to extremely poor people, including women and children through micro-finance in order to enable them to invest in livestock, fishing agriculture, and handicraft to help them come out of poverty under the supervision of well-governed Waqf institutions whether government, NGO, or civil society. This action can be classified under the Investment Area 4: food security and sustainable agriculture.

Similarly, social protection can be achieved by providing financial support for poverty reduction enabling instruments including education (Investment Area 2: Education), infrastructure, and ICTs all of which fall under Investment Area 5: Infrastructure. It can be also achieved by expanding the social safety net capital through financial support obtained from Waqf investment institutions. Moreover, the government can use these financial resources to replace the Interest-based loans to support poverty alleviation projects.

Investment Area 4: Food Security and Sustainable Agriculture

This can be achieved by financing malnutrition combating projects through food feeding programs in areas that are poverty-prone, climate-hit, or war-affected. Many Waqf entities are already playing role in supporting this area through provision of long-term investment in agricultural activities.

Investment Area 5: Infrastructure

This is the costliest area as it covers infrastructure in the field of Energy, Water, Transportation, and Telecommunication. Major projects taken by governments to ensure provision of clean water and sanitation for their people get financed through many financial instruments including interest-based loans, bonds, Sukuk, BOT (Build Operate and Transfer) scheme. Such projects can be financed by revenue generated from Waqf investment institutions using direct cash, Waqf sukuk, engaging in Mudarabah contract with the Waqf, or any other means of financing between the project owner and the Waqf investment institution.

Investment Area 6: Ecosystem Services and Biodiversity

This area is usually supported through governments and international entities. It is not one of the classically known areas of Waqf investment and since it is not yet clear how much financial support this area get from Waqf investment entities, it is believed that it is one of the areas that can be considered as an opportunity for investment by Waqf investment entities.

Investment Area 7: Data for the SDGs

Since this is the least financially supported area, Waqf investment entities need to focus on governmental or civil projects for developing state of art data management system that focuses on acquiring, analyzing, and releasing reports with regard to the Sustainable Development Goals targets. The financial support that Waqf investment entities can provide does not limit only to the system, but it shall support the system management organizations and its human resources that are used to collect needed data, operate the system, and organizations that are responsible for monitoring and auditing the whole process.

514 B. DUKHAN ET AL.

Investment Area 8: Emergency Response and Humanitarian Work

This area is challenging to deal with from Waqf investment perspective because of its unpredictable nature. Waqf investments are usually developed to support continuous needs of beneficiaries. Emerging humanitarian needs are taken care of by specialized organizations whose scope is unique to those kinds of circumstances. Waqf investment entities can support those humanitarian aids organizations based on their operating models (Table 26.4).

Challenges of Waqf Investments and Some Suggestions
Throughout Islamic history, Waqf investment enterprises have played vital roles in supporting sustainable social projects. Despite these tremendous contributions of Waqf to SDG-related projects, the investment faces several challenges. Waqf investment lost its role after much of the Muslim governments abandoned the system. In many countries, Waqf investment entities are underdeveloped and underutilized because of many reasons. For example, a study in India on a sample of 32 Waqf properties showed that only six percent of those Waqf properties were developed, while the remaining ninety-four percent were undeveloped and at most underdeveloped. A study by World Bank showed that with an average investment of USD 660,896 in Waqf, with an average rate of return of more than 19%, expected income from it could be increased by USD 126,547 on annual basis (Ahmed 2015).

The major challenges that are faced by Waqf investment institutions can be classified as the following:

1. Role of the government in managing the Waqf investment enterprise: it is noted that government central control over Waqf entities has led to mismanagement and opened the role to lots of problems. In many Muslim countries, the Waqf investment enterprise manager (Nazir) is assigned by the government and gets his salary paid by the central government agency. There is lack of centralized institutions that can provide strategic and technical planning needed to help managing Waqf investment entities efficiently.

   Furthermore, in many countries, Waqf are not seen by governments as a source of financing projects that serve the public, and hence Waqf investments are not required to be registered,

26 CONTRIBUTIONS OF WAQF INVESTMENTS IN ACHIEVING SDGS   515

Table 26.4   Waqf-SDGs Investment Areas

	Investment Area	Estimated popularity in Waqf	Examples	Waqf investment Opportunity
1	Health	Popular	Healthcare Waqf investment arm Healthcare Waqf sukuk	New forms of healthcare services can be supported throughout Waqf investments
2	Education	Popular	Education Waqf investment arm Education Waqf sukuk	Needs to expand to new places and reach more people
3	Social Protection	Achieved through other Investment Areas	See other Investment Areas	See other Investment Areas
4	Food Security and Sustainable Agriculture	Popular	Waqf kitchens Agriculture lands and agriculture products provision	Establishment of food security Waqf
5	Infrastructure	Limited to small individual projects	Wells	Need to be directed toward financing mega infrastructure projects
6	Ecosystem Services and Biodiversity	New	New	Ecosystem supporting projects need to be supported by Waqf Investments
7	Data for the SDGs	New	New	Data analysis and research centers supporting centers funding.
8	Emergency Response and Humanitarian Work	New	New	Waqf investment entities need to collaborate with Humanitarian aids organizations

which opens the door for illegally occupied and underutilized Waqf investment entities.

2. Lack of community knowledge regarding the Waqf investment entities: With regard to compliance with Shari'ah, the services provided by those entities, and the relationship between those entities and the community in large. One of the issues that are faced by Waqf

investment institutions is the Shari'ah knowledge of the people. In India for example, Muslim communities are reluctant to deal with cash Waqf entities due to the controversial status of this practice according to the Hanafi jurisprudence school.

3. Lack of management skills of the Waqf investment entities: managers play strong role in developing those entities and allow them to play their role in the development of the sustainable objectives. Researchers identified the following management related challenges as major constraints for developing Waqf investment institutions: unskilled nazirs, lack of trained employees, poor information system, lack of accessibility, lack of trust, lack of asset maintenance, misuse of Waqf assets (Saad 2018).

4. Lack of proper legal and policy sources: In many Muslim communities Waqf investments have been hindered by lack of proper legal and policy sources. In some countries, there are no Waqf laws. In some others, there are no comprehensive definitions of Waqf. In many other countries, the institution of Waqf investment is not even recognized or regulated. Legal restrictions are even practiced by some governments. Such issues disincentivize adoption of Waqf investment rather than facilitating its development (Obaidullah 2014).

5. Absence of Islamic banking and finance infrastructure in minority Muslim countries: This issue has also formed a challenge in providing Waqf investment services to people who are in need of it. In India, for example, where all banks are interest-based banks, very small-sized Islamic banks which are situated in Kerala are not able to provide any worth mentioning Islamic banking facilities. Furthermore, Complexity of modes of utilizing cash Waqf resources adds to the difficulties faced by Waqf investment institutions to convince people to deal with them (Rashid 2018).

To remedy these challenges, the following are some of the proposed suggestions:

Role of government in managing the Waqf investment enterprise: The role of the central government should be to maintain needed tools and supervision for Waqf investment entities and leave it to the Waqf to be managed in a way similar to private companies. Muslim governments need to meet and agree on a set standard for managing Waqf entities in general and Waqf investment institutions in particular. Furthermore, the standard needs to be converted into a grading framework where authorized independent auditing and assessment bodies assess and publish annual reports with regard to Waqf investment institutions compliance with those standards. Such a solution can build trust in the Waqf investment arms and create competition between Waqf entities to increase their grading according to the standards.

Lack of community knowledge regarding the Waqf investment entities: As with other forms of non-conventional financing tools, Muslim communities first need to be fully aware of the efficient implementation of Waqf investment practices. This can be promoted through enough awareness programs.

Lack of management skills of the Waqf investment entities: as stated in the first point above, central government has a major role to play with regard to building needed institutional and management capabilities for Waqf investment entities starting with accountability and transparency as well as good governance. With those steps implemented, strong reputation of Waqf investment institutions will encourage wealthier individuals to participate in the cycle of Waqf development and sustainability.

Lack of proper legal and policy ground: Another point that needs to be solved is the provision of enabling environment. For example, government regulations need to facilitate and incentivize Waqf investment practices and encourage citizens to participate in it, while at the same time work as a guarantor for their participation in case of any defaults. Furthermore, taxation of transactions made through Waqf investment entities shall be exempted.

Absence of Islamic banking and finance infrastructure in minority Muslim countries: This issue is unique to each country, and it depends on the political and legal system of these countries, as well as the relationships between them and Muslim countries that are leading in the field of Islamic banking. Islamic banking and finance pioneering countries can play a great role in facilitating establishment of Islamic banking and finance entities through economic or diplomatic means.

Conclusion and Way Forward

The role of Waqf in supporting the 17 internationally recognized Sustainable Development Goals, has been the subject of lots of studies in the field of philanthropy recently. It is well-established that Waqf entities and activities add great value to the 2030 agenda as several goals are already embodied into Waqf dimensions since the birth of Islam. For the Waqfs to sustain the provision of their service to achieve their objectives, they need sustainable financial income. Such income comes in two forms: donation or investment. Two problems are associated with the financial donation. For one, it is not sustainable as it relies on the availability of donors. Moreover, it is susceptible to manipulation by the donors who can affect Waqf entity and can open door to corruptions. The form of financial support through investment is immune to those problems as they are more sustainable and have the privilege of keeping Waqf independent of any favor by the donors. The benefit of Waqf investment is that they can come in any form and scale such as Cash Waqf, Waqf Sukuks, financial forms of Murabaha, Mudarabah, Musharakah, and BOT.

This chapter has analyzed the relationship between Waqf investment and Sustainable Development Goals based on crystallizing the 17 SDGs into the following 8 SDG investment areas: (1) health, (2)education, (3) social protection, (4) food security and sustainable agriculture, (5) infrastructure; energy, water, transportation, and telecommunication, (6) ecosystem services and biodiversity, (7) data for the SDGs, (8) emergency response and humanitarian work.

It is concluded that Waqf investment entities are already strong in the Investment Areas of (1) health, (2) education, (3) social protection, and (4) food security and sustainable agriculture. As for the investment area number (5) infrastructure; energy, water, transportation, and telecommunication, it is found that there are lots of rooms for improvement. Waqf investments are usually limited to small scale infrastructure projects which directly affect the lives of the society. However, mega projects that are of long-term benefits can benefit from the investments provided by those Waqfs.

On the other hand, there are gaps in the following three areas: (6) ecosystem services and biodiversity, (7) data for the SDGs, (8) emergency response and humanitarian work. The latter one is unique because it is unpredictable and can be avoided by investing in other areas including infrastructure. As for investment areas number (6) and (7), they are areas that have not been considered by the classical literature of Waqf, hence they can be considered as major opportunities for Waqf investments. Apart from the investment opportunities in those areas of investments, Waqf investments need to consider different challenges that might face them. Firstly, the role of government might bring down the whole effort through excessive control of the Waqf investments, or totally ignoring their existence and leaving them without proper legislations strategic planning, education, or auditing and monitoring. The second challenge that Waqf investment might face is the lack of community knowledge regarding Waqf investment which can be solved by various awareness and educational initiatives regarding the status of Waqf investment tools that conform to Shari'ah. Thirdly, many Waqf investment entities fail because of lack of management skills by their managers and team. This can be overcome by compelling all management teams to achieve a minimum management certification in Waqf investment. If such certification programs do not exist, the Muslim world is called upon to develop an "International Waqf Investment Management" certification programs and make it a standard for any Waqf investment management teams. Finally, the lack of Islamic banking and financial infrastructure in many countries pose a major challenge for Waqf investments particularly in minority Muslim countries. Major Muslim countries and Institutions need to tackle this problem through political, diplomatic, and economic channels.

References

Ahmed, H. (2015). *On the Sustainable Development Goals and the Role of Islamic Finance* (Policy Research Working Paper).

Awqaf Properties Investment Fund (APIF). (2019). *The Development Impact of the Awqaf Properties Investment Fund a Model for Sustainable Development* Islamic Development Bank (IDB).

Babacan, M. (2011). Economics of Philanthropic Institutions, Regulation and Governance in Turkey. *Journal of Economic and Social Research*, 61–89.

Bank, A. D. (2020). *Sustainable Development Goals Trends and Tables Part I.* Asian Development Bank.

Budiman, M. A. (2011). The Economic Significance of Waqf: A Macro Perspective.

Hallaq, W. B. (2013). *The Impossible Stateislam, Politics, and Modernity's Moral Predicament.*

Hoque, M. A. (2019). Role of Waqf to Attain the "SDG-1: Ending Poverty" in Bangladesh. In K. M. Ali, *Revitalization of Waqf for Socio-Economic Development, Volume II* (pp. 15–32). Cham: Palgrave Macmillan.

Islamic Development Bank. (2019). *The Development Impact of the Awqaf Properties Investment Fund a Model for Sustainable Development.*

Kahf, M. (1998). *Financing the Development of Awqaf Property.* Paper Prepared for the Seminar on Development of Awqaf Organized by IRTI.

Kwa, M. (2015, August 4). *Financing Sustainable Development.* From New Strait Times: https://www.nst.com.my/news/2015/09/financing-sustainable-development.

Martínez-Solimán, M. (2017, March 3). *Islamic Finance: An Innovative Avenue for Financing the Sustainable Development Goals.* From huffpost: https://www.huffpost.com/entry/islamic-finance-an-innovative-avenue-for-financing_b_58b97c82e4b02eac8876cd83.

Obaidullah, M. (2014). *Islamic Social Finance Report 2014 Technical Report.* IRTI.

Rashid, S. K. (2018). Potential of Waqf in Contemporary World. *JKAU: Islamic Economics, 31*(2), 53–69.

Saad, M. S. (2018). Waqf Fundraising Management: A Conceptual Comparison Between Traditional and Modern Methods in the Waqf Institutions. *Indonesian Journal of Islam and Muslim Societies,* 57–86.

Sadeq, A. (2002). Waqf, Perpetual Charity and Poverty Alleviation. *International Journal of Social Economics, 29*(1–2), 135–151.

Schmidt-Traub, G. (2015a). *Investment Needs to Achieve the Sustainable Development Goals.* Sustainable Development Solutions Network (SDSN).

Schmidt-Traub, G. (2015b). *Investment Needs to Achieve the Sustainable Development Goals—Supplemental material.*

Shwaiki, A. (2012). *Haqiqat Al Waqf wa athar khilaf almathaheb alarbaa.* Hebron, Palestine: Hebron university.

United Nations Conference on Trade and Development. (2014). *World Investment Report.* United Nations.

United Nations Conference on Trade and Development. (2020). *World Investment Report.* United Nation.

CHAPTER 27

Corporate Waqf for Healthcare in Malaysia for B40 and M40

Khairul Fikry Jamaluddin and Rusni Hassan

INTRODUCTION

According to Kahf (2003), waqf means to hold a property and preserve it in order to benefit the beneficiaries and it is prohibited to be disposed of other than specified objectives detailed by the donor (waqif). The definition of waqf given by Kahf can be inferred that waqf is essentially a perpetuity philanthropic instrument where the benefit shall be extracted from it and disseminated to the beneficiaries. Its perpetuity can neither be relinquished nor decreased although the action of istibdal (exchange) is executed by the authority, in some cases, for public interest. Traditionally, waqf was practiced mainly through involvement of immovable properties such as land, mosque, and buildings. However, waqf is not only confined to such types of properties, but rather it also embraces movable properties such as books, livestock, shares, stocks, and cash.

K. F. Jamaluddin
International Islamic University Malaysia [IIUM], Gombak, Malaysia

R. Hassan (✉)
Institute of Islamic Banking and Finance, International of Islamic University of Malaysia (IIiBF/IIUM), Gombak, Malaysia
e-mail: hrusni@iium.edu.my

© The Author(s), under exclusive license to Springer Nature Switzerland AG 2021
M. M. Billah (eds.), *Islamic Wealth and the SDGs*,
https://doi.org/10.1007/978-3-030-65313-2_27

521

History of waqf in Malaysia is believed to have come into existence ever since more than eight hundred years ago. It was introduced by the Arab traders who came into Malay Land (Tanah Melayu) for trading purposes. At that time, Sultan Umar, who was the ruler of Terengganu developed the waqf system and it was evidenced by a waqf deed executed by him. The Sultan regarded waqf as an instrument to disseminate knowledge and promote education to the people (Yaacob 2013). During this era, waqf was executed through verbal communication between a man and a leader of village which was known as penghulu. Since it was only a verbal communication, problems would commonly occur especially in the event of penghulu's death. It rises due to the absence of records between the waqif and the nazir (trustee) (Yaacob 2013). After modernization took place in Malaysia, this country has developed more systematic laws governing the waqf administration. Federal Constitution, which is the highest law in Malaysia, has outlined matters pertaining to Islamic laws which are put under the jurisdiction of State List specifically in the Ninth Schedule List II of Federal Constitution. By virtue of the law, the King or the Yang Di Pertuan Agong becomes the head of religious affairs in every state. State Islamic Religious Council (SIRC) is established in every state in order to ensure the efficiency in administering Islamic law which includes waqf. The institution of SIRC will act as sole nazir in managing all the waqf assets in the interest of waqif specified in the foundation deed (Yaacob 2013).

POTENTIAL OF WAQF IN DEVELOPING THE SOCIO-ECONOMY OF NATION

Waqf has its own unique characteristic that resembles genuine social justice in distribution of wealth. This instrumental approach is in line with the maqasid (objectives) of Shariah and it addresses most of the Sustainable Development Goals (SDGs) which were introduced by United Nations (UN) back in 2015. Waqf is an established philanthropic instrument that can produce abundance of socio-economic benefit to the whole nation. The holistic nature of waqf allows its benefit to be enjoyed by Muslims and non-Muslims community as well (The World Bank Group, INCEIF and ISRA 2019).

Waqf is not considered as a simple charity such as zakah or sadaqah. It is perpetual in nature, where its benefits extend from generations to generations. World Islamic Economic Foundation (2017) also acknowledges that waqf is a multi-generational usage and multi-generational benefit. Waqf is embedded with integral components of piety, promoting innovation, social development, and providing kindness and justice. Undeniably, due to its distinguishing features, waqf offers great potential and positive impact towards public facilities in the fields of healthcare, education, religion, and social welfare in every nook and corner (Rashid 2018). In addition to that, waqf as a benevolent, non-governmental, and non-profit mechanism could fill in the gaps in the socio-economic system by engaging the piety of wealthy community (Zuki 2012).

During the period of Islamic civilization, waqf had played a crucial role throughout the centuries in flourishing the socio-economic life of people that come from different segments. Through waqf, the fortunate individuals share their wealth with the less fortunate (Rashid 2018), and eventually the issue of poverty will be eradicated in the society. Not only that, this act of kindness also contributes to the improvement of moral values and spirituality of Muslim nations (Mahat et al. 2015). By helping the needy one will not only fix the worldly life of the needy, but it also fixes the life of rich people in the hereafter. Hence, it can be seen that waqf could bring massive benefit to the people spiritually and physically.

It is an interesting fact to note that even crusaders who noticed the benefits of the waqf took the idea and concept of it and brought it back to Europe and introduced it to their society. Consequently, endowments institutions were established in Western countries to support the academic institutions such as Inns Court ad Merton's College of Oxford University in the United Kingdom (The World Bank Group, INCEIF, and ISRA 2019).

Other than that, Mahat et al. (2015) also mention that waqf has the capability in shining up the quality and quantity of public services and infrastructures. Tun Abdullah Ahmad Badawi, Malaysia's former Prime Minister, said that waqf as an inalienable religious endowment could support both social welfare and economic development of the nation. Its good values can be disseminated in the conservation and preservation of mosque, education, and healthcare services. Moreover, it can benefit the travelers by providing them guesthouses and water facilities through waqf fund. It is undeniable that waqf is a dynamic vehicle and catalyst for the expansion of economic and social welfare of community (World Islamic Economic Forum 2017).

Under the reign of Ottoman Empire, there were about 500 cash waqf established which gave opportunities for the small entrepreneur to get financing. In the World Islamic Economic Forum (2017), it reports that one-third of the state revenue under the Ottoman Empire were generated from the waqf endowment. That is why the Ottoman Empire could assist the citizens to get access to the medical services for free. Zuki (2012) mentions that under the Empire, the financing for healthcare and education were entirely dependent on waqf. The World Bank Group, INCEIF, and ISRA (2019), recognized that waqf sector was so advanced during the golden reign of Ottoman. It was described that every citizen during the reign went through life cycle within waqf ambience. A child was born under the roof of waqf property, receive education in waqf educational institutions, working in waqf enterprise, getting free access of medical treatment in waqf hospital, and buried in waqf land at death. Over and above, it is rather interesting to point up that the waqf system at that time was operated not only for Muslims and non-Muslims, but it also extends to well-being of animals. The vast benefits of waqf could be able to flood the nation due to its unique potential.

Furthermore, Zuki (2012) mentioned that waqf sector does not cost anything to the government. In fact, it significantly reduces the government expenditure and borrowing. During the reign of Ottoman Empire, the honour and benefits of waqf institutions had dominated the general public in every aspect of life, assisting the government in providing public goods and services (The Word Bank Group, INCEIF and ISRA 2019). Consequently, general public could be relieved from heavy tax that is imposed upon them and this will lead the public to save more and channel their savings more in private investment. This will also circulate the growth of the economy. Moreover, waqf sector can also redistribute resources justly and reduce inequality in society (Zuki 2012).

Waqf had successfully influenced the exaltation of the economic development in the previous Islamic civilization. The success stories of the past are the proof on the viability of waqf as a mechanism to solve the socio-economic issues faced by many countries at present. The abundance of waqf revenues would relieve the government expenditure and assist them to spend more on other crucial matters that are not supported by waqf sector such as tourism, investment, agriculture, and healthcare. In the context of Malaysia, a thoughtful alternative is essentially needed for Malaysia to develop better approach to increase the development and efficiency of waqf in order to reduce the burden of debt of this country. As at end of June 2019, the overall total debt and liabilities of Malaysia have escalated to RM1.17 trillion (The Edge Market 2019).

WAQF AND HEALTHCARE SECTOR

The link between waqf and healthcare can be traced from the history of Islamic civilization during the medieval age. Healthcare had been always accompanied by the support from the waqf sector. Islamic civilization previously had established many hospitals that gave excellent medical care and services to the citizens regardless of whether they are rich or poor. Unfortunately, in today's situation, the contribution from the waqf endowment to healthcare institutions is deficient (World Islamic Economic Forum 2017). Zuki (2012) also reports that the potential of waqf currently had eventually deteriorated. People can witness that the conventional philanthropic institutions especially in the west are more well organized as compared to waqf administration in Malaysia. Jafri and Mohd Noor (2019 state that the bulk of waqf assets are still tangible and immovable. Hence, this could lead to a phenomenon of overlooking the waqf assets that essentially have the potential to be developed for better usage. Unfortunately, immovable waqf property is always being associated with liquidity problem.

Waqf is also commonly understood by many people that it is a perpetual charity that only involves immovable properties such as lands and buildings. It is also reported by Jafri and Mohd Noor (2019) that Majlis Agama Islam Selangor (MAIS) records that 95% of the waqf assets in the state are categorized as immovable asset s/properties which are lands and buildings. Indonesia, which has the most number of Muslim population in the world, also faces similar circumstances. The immovable assets in that country cover 3.4 million square metres of lands, which can be regarded as the largest waqf in the world. Unfortunately, lots of the waqf land in the country are only being utilized for the purpose of education, building mosques and graveyards. It is displeasing to note that only 23% of waqf properties in Indonesia are productive, while the rest of it are non-productive.

Malaysia has a financing issue to establish more quality healthcare services in order to provide safety net for patients especially among the low-income group (Atan et al. 2017). Currently, since the COVID-19 epidemic has captured the lives of many people, the hospitals lack medical appliances to give the life support to those who are in need. In view of this, it is hoped that the waqf healthcare endowment account to be at par with waqf mosque account. If this goal can be made possible in the future, the escalation of the quality and quantity of healthcare services can be experienced by the masses. Hence, Muslims need to be educated that waqf does not only confine to the religious matter only. One of the challenges faced by the Muslims' mentality is that waqf is commonly related and confined to Islamic institutions such as development of madrasah for Tahfiz and mosques. On this ground, many of the money endowed by Muslims is usually channelled to the mosque account. Jafri and Mohd Noor (2019) report that this phenomenon happens due to the lack of public understanding on the flexibility or dynamic of waqf.

In order to water down the obnoxious scenario, Malaysia has arrived to a position to revive the waqf development through the incorporation of corporate waqf. Johor Corporation which is well known as JCorp is the pioneer and only institution in Malaysia that initiate the concept of corporate waqf. JCorp has launched waqf donation in the form of shares to its subsidiaries. As a result, the dividend that arise from it has successfully been channelled to clinics and hospitals in Johor (World Islamic Economic Foundation 2017). The clinics and hospitals are the chain of Waqf An-Nur under WAN Corp Berhad (Atan et al. 2017). The healthcare provided has offered excellent treatments to patients with nominal charge, regardless of their religion and ethnicity. The other corporations are advised to replicate the initiatives taken by JCorp in order to expedite the access to good healthcare to all segments of society irrespective of their races, religion, ethnicity, and social status (World Islamic Economic Foundation 2017).

Importance of Healthcare in Islam

One of the profound features embedded in the religion of Islam is "shumuliyah" (holistic) in nature. The concept covers the journey of an individual from before life to after death. Healthcare is not alienated from the feature because healthcare itself covers the part of one's journey from womb to tomb and from cradle to grave (Nawawi 2002). A good state of health is very important for every individual that lives on this earth. Life would be worthless and powerless if there is no proper healthcare provided for the individuals. Everybody is in dire need of perfect health because by having so, it can assist people to be more productive in exercising their daily routines.

In Islamic law, scholars in Islamic jurisprudence have classified five major fundamental rights that a person must preserve in order to attain goodness in life. Among them are protection of religion, life, mind, progeny, and wealth. Healthcare is closely related with life and progeny. Absence of good health will lead to insecurity, misery, and instability of a person's life (Baqutayan and Mahdzir 2018).

In analysing the fundamental rights outlined by Shariah, possessing good state of health could give impact to the preservation of the religion. A healthy Muslim would be able to maintain the acts of worships to The Creator. Good health is also closely related to protection of life. A good state of health could maintain the lifestyle of an individual and could encourage people to do work and activities to flourish the nation. This is closely related with protection of wealth, where individuals would be able to do transactions effectively which involve wealth such as money and property, provided that a good state of health is preserved. This can be proven in a recent unprecedented calamity strikes throughout the globe. Many countries that are affected by the invisible killer, which is the coronavirus ("Covid-19"), happen to suffer economically. The "twin crises" of health and economy have brought adverse effect to the businesses of individuals and Small and Medium Enterprises ("SME"). Furthermore, protection of progeny could also be linked with health. By having a good health, people would be able to raise up their children or family members without having spread of disease to the community. Healthy family would produce an excellent community. Lastly, the protection of mind is also related to health. Mental health such as depression is also an issue that has emerged in the society and it has become more common in recent years. Due to this tragic shortcoming, it will cause individuals to poor productivity in contributing to the economic behaviour. A study has proven that mental health can cause economic damage to the country. According to Relate Mental Health Malaysia, in 2018, the estimated business cost of metal health disorders incurred among employees was 1% of country's gross domestic product (GDP) (*The Star* 2018).

Aside from the above, it also important to note on the importance of health in Islam. Prophet Muhammad (saw) once said that Allah has not created a disease without creating a cure except old age. In another narration, the Prophet Muhammad (pbuh) said that Allah has sent down a disease and has also to brought down its cure (Baqutayan and Mahdzir 2018). Based on these two virtuous narrations, it can be construed that Islam encourages the nation to seek medical assistance if any sickness befalls an individual. Islam has taught the nation that medicine is part of the effort in order to gain healing from the Almighty. According to Baqutayan and Mahdzir (2018), the Prophet Muhammad (pbuh) used to instruct a doctor in his lifetime to treat all patients for free of charge. Numbers of sahabah (male companions of the Prophet) during the period of Prophethood received free treatment from doctors. It was recorded that sahaabiyat (female companions) also involved in a great humanitarian mission in the era of the Prophethood.

For the past centuries, the Islamic civilization has produced Muslim scholars that are experts in medical area, among them are Al-Biruni, Ibn Sina, Al-Razi, Ibn Rushd, and Ibn Srabiyun. They are all emerged from ninth to twelfth centuries and had contributed in modern medicine (Nawawi 2002; Baqutayan and Mahdzir 2018). It is reported that during the successive periods of Islamic civilization, hospitals used to treat all the patients without any payment, regardless of the religion, races, gender, and social status. The hospitals at the times were fully equipped with best services and facilities to cater the need of the patients. On top of that the healthcare architecture at that era was administered by princes and supervisors in order to ensure the stable health state of the citizens (Baqutayan and Mahdzir 2018). In fact, the health of citizen is important to produce blossoming community in a country. Hassan et al. (2012) mention that the state of health would be a fundamental element for the development of physical, psychological, and social lifestyle of humans.

Jalil and Kadir (2013) also put emphasis on health that it is vital for everyone to take care of. A healthy society would lead to a better development of oneself and prosperity of community in a country (Hassan et al. 2012; Jalil and Kadir 2013). It is undeniable that health is a crucial and fundamental matter for everyone without any exception. Health is definitely a valuable thing for each individual to survive in life. No amount of wealth would be able to compensate the value of good health. In view of the absence of good health, individual's life would become doom and gloom (Hassan et al. 2012). Therefore, it is pertinent to mention that healthcare of people must be taken care not only by people themselves, but also by the authority through providing excellent healthcare services. None of the human being wants their lives to be adversely affected with health issues, both physically and mentally. If good health could be sustained and preserved within one's society, favourable outcome of the country's well-being could be witnessed in long run. Indubitably, health does influence the external environment and the harmonization of a country. Wealth, fame, and status would be cease to become one's pleasure in the absence of health.

CHALLENGES OF B40 AND M40 IN ACCESSING GOOD HEALTHCARE SYSTEM IN MALAYSIA

The healthcare industry in Malaysia is currently experiencing an unpleasant scenario that is hardly to be avoided. The cost of medical expenses has been skyrocketing tremendously due to medical inflation that occurred in recent decades. Survey found that the global medical inflation rate in 2018 was 8.4%. However, it is unfortunate for the Malaysians to experience worse medical inflation rate which was at 15.3% in 2018. The rate resembles as the second highest in Asia. Another agony experienced by the citizen was between 1997 and 2006. During the period, data has revealed that healthcare expenditure had increased of more than 100%. In 1997, the total of health expenditure was RM8,604 million, whereas, in 2006, the expenditure value had increased to RM22,144. In addition, 2016 was a year that records a rapid escalation of total health expenditure doubled the amount to RM51,742.

M40 and B40 are among the vulnerable group that can be severely impacted by the high cost of medical expenses in Malaysia. B40 and M40 are the classification of household income in Malaysia. According to *The Star* (2018), B40 refers to the group that earns less than RM4,360 in monthly household income, whereas M40 refers to the group of people that earns income between RM4,361 and RM9,619 monthly household income. S. Shahar, H. Lau, S. E. W. Puteh et al. (2019) mentioned that the low-income group in Malaysia is struggling to gain access to health equalities. Concerning the B40 group, Tenth Malaysia Plan (10MP 2011–2015) claimed that there are about 2.4 million households of B40 segments, which comprises of 73% locals (bumiputeras) and 27% of non-locals (non-bumiputera). Meanwhile, during the Eleventh Malaysia Plan (11MP 2016–2020) declared that B40 segments consists of 2.7 million households, which comprises of 68% locals (bumiputeras) and 32% non-locals (non-bumiputera). It is admitted that the B40 and M40 have problem with health insecurity.

Therefore, great care and attention by community leaders, policy makers, politicians, corporate, and researchers towards the low-income and middle-income group should be upheld extensively for the betterment of society livelihood. The extensive care is vital to ensure the survival of people especially when facing economic and health crisis, for instance, in the midst of COVID-19 that has attacked global by storm. Thus, it is essential to propose alternative solution that can award assistance to the B40 and M40 group since the government has debt burden of RM1 trillion (The Edge Markets 2018). The Edge Markets (2018) also reported that for the past 15 years, with the exception on 2008 and 2010, the government had spent a lot of money to service government debt as compared to the allocation of funds to the Ministry of Health (MoH). Hence, the cooperation from other private sectors is required to alleviate the burden of the government in dealing with healthcare sectors. If this step could be taken in coming years, the government would be able to shift its focus to other sector for the betterment of the society.

THE PROPOSAL FOR E-WALLET CORPORATE WAQF FOR HEALTHCARE

As emphasized earlier, corporate waqf is one of the most advanced, acceptable and suitable innovative instruments to revive the waqf sector in Malaysia. Therefore, this research proposed to outline a new model of corporate health waqf that may be implemented by corporate entities, for the betterment of healthcare system in Malaysia. It is suggested that the Touch 'n Go Sdn Bhd ("Touch 'n Go") company might be one of the best companies that can be part of this philanthropic instrument model. It would be more significant when the collaboration can be spearhead by bumiputera (local) financial institutions such as Malayan Banking Berhad ("Maybank") and Commerce International Merchant Bankers ("CIMB"). The proposed model is illustrated in the below diagram.

The above diagram is explained as follows;

- Users of Touch 'n Go e-Wallet, CIMB Clicks and Maybank2u make donations to the TNG Corporate Health Waqf (Subsidiary Company of Touch 'n Go).
- Simultaneously, CIMB and Maybank could implement their CSR programme by donating CSR funds to the TNG Corporate Health Waqf.
- The accumulated funds to the TNG Corporate Waqf will be channelled into two categories which are Category A and Category B.

27 CORPORATE WAQF FOR HEALTHCARE IN MALAYSIA FOR B40 AND M40   531

- 50% of the funds will be channelled to Category A which consists of Shariah Compliant Investment (40%), State Islamic Religious Council (5%), and Nazir (5%).
- Meanwhile, another 50% will be channelled to Category B which will be distributed to the maintenance of the government hospitals/clinics (20%) and the remaining portion of 30% will be distributed for financing the medical cost of the patients, financing medical appliances for the hospitals/clinics and for campaign/advertisement to increase the awareness of waqf through TNG Corporate Waqf.

Touch 'n Go is a company that was incorporated in October 1996 and launched its services in March 1997. This company is a wholly owned subsidiary of CIMB Group Holdings Berhad ("CIMB Group"). The company has introduced and initiated an electronic payment system through a card named as Touch 'n Go card. It has successfully provided the users a convenient mode of payment to perform cashless transactions. It is also an easy mode of payment for the users to involve in numerous transactions without making any effort to bring physical cash to make payment. Unquestionably, cashless payment is much safer and more convenient to be used in this era. Recently, Touch 'n Go has also innovate its usage by introducing Touch 'n Go e-Wallet for payment services that can be enjoyed by its users across the nation. Touch 'n Go is chosen as the participative company for the philanthropic instrument because the company is a bumiputera company that has potential to develop more in coming years. As of 31 December 2017, Touch 'n Go recorded that there were about 7 million Touch 'n Go transactions are being done per day. It is also submitted that Touch 'n Go e-Wallet is the Malaysia's largest e-Wallet with over 6.8 million registered users and 120,000 merchants by the end of 2019 (The Edge Markets 2020). The CIMB's Annual Report 2017, which revealed that Touch 'n Go successfully generated RM32.53 million in pre-tax profit on revenue of RM122.03 million in 31 December 2017 (The Edge Markets 2018). This can also be amplified by the fact that Touch 'n Go e-Wallet remains to witness healthy volumes for essential services and online-based transactions despite of movement control order (MCO) imposed by the government (The Edge Market 2020).

Other than that, the outlined model also proposed the collaboration of CIMB and Maybank. It is undeniable that both of these institutions are the common banks that are engaged by majority of Malaysians.

Maybank is considered to be the largest bank in Malaysia by assets, deposits, loans, number of employees, and branches. Another unique feature that attracted the attention of the researchers about Maybank is the involvement of the company with community services through Corporate Social Responsibility (CSR). They implemented their social service programs through a special establishment of Maybank Foundation. This foundation is created for the purpose of enhancing quality of people's lives regardless of race, gender, or creed with an emphasis on the poor, needy, and marginalised segments of society (Maybank Foundation 2020). The Maybank Foundation also deals with six (6) main activities for CSR programmes, which are education, community empowerment, arts and culture, environmental diversity, healthy living, and disaster relief. Recently, during the pandemic COVID-19, Maybank has contributed RM4 million through MERCY Malaysia's COVID-19 Pandemic Fund to support COVID-19 Strategic Preparedness & Response Plan.

Meanwhile, CIMB Group Holdings Berhad is the second-largest banking group in Malaysia. It is one of the largest Islamic and investment banks in Asia. CIMB realizes its very own corporate responsibility through the establishment of CIMB Foundation. It mainly deals with education, sport, and community development project. This foundation is a philanthropic platform for the CIMB to support the growth of sustainable environments in which everyone prospers. Philanthropic involvement is part of the DNA of CIMB which can be proven through the disbursement funds which amounting nearly to RM76 million for education, sports, and community development programme (CIMB Foundation 2020).

Majority of Malaysians have at least an account with Maybank and/or CIMB and thus their outreach to the community is wider. Maybank and CIMB have been actively participated in social activities for the purpose of giving a brighter life to people particularly for the needy community. These two financial institutions have been contributing funds to achieve their target in delivering kindness to the masses. It is timely for these institutions to put their attention to healthcare services particularly for B40 and M40. Undeniably, absence of health can cause major trepidation to the nation particularly in its economic activity. Health and economy must always be taken care of side by side; otherwise, they can turn into a "twin crisis" that can cause alarming event to the country and even across the globe. Corporate health waqf is one of the platform that has the potential as an antidote to the healthcare problem in Malaysia. The corporate health waqf may not be able to operate in the absence of prestigious and lucrative corporations into the waqf sector. Hence, Maybank and CIMB are the best financial institutions to collaborate with Touch 'n Go company to participate in this philanthropic instrument, which is corporate waqf for healthcare services.

The three proposed participating companies are bumiputera local companies that are expected to give back to the people in the country. By incorporating these companies into the proposed structure, they can directly contribute to the economy through waqf. The investment through this Corporate Health Waqf can be part of the medium to circulate the wealth of the economy domestically. People can make waqf contributions through their respective Maybank or CIMB bank account or even Touch 'n GO e-Wallet. On top of that, Maybank Foundation and CIMB Foundation could channel their CSR funds for the Corporate Health Waqf to support the waqf healthcare projects.

Another justification for choosing Touch 'n Go company to support waqf is because its unique connection with government entity such as National Registration Department of Malaysia (Jabatan Pendaftaran Negara Malaysia). With the advancement of technology, the National Registration Identity Card (NRIC) of each Malaysian is embedded with Touch 'n Go function. In Malaysia, it is compulsory for every Malaysian citizen that has reached 12 years old and above to have NRIC. Touch 'n Go company may collaborate with Inland Revenue Board of Malaysia (LHDN) in order to determine qualified citizens who are categorized as B40 and M40. The NRIC card of B40 and M40 will automatically be registered as one of those is eligible to get the medical assistance for free of charge or minimal charge of RM2 (subject to the medical condition of the patients). In relation to the embedment of Touch 'n Go into the NRIC, it is proposed that the method of payment at the public hospitals and clinics in the future would be using the NRIC only without having to bring any physical cash. Practically, NRIC can be used as mode of payment for B40 and M40 to pay for their medical bills due to the fact that the card already been registered by LHDN and has the Touch 'n Go payment function. Therefore, the Touch 'n Go now can diversify its function not only confine to payment for food and beverages, convenience store, entertainment, and others but also to pay medical bills. In fact, the company can diverse its usage for other waqf related matters.

In order to ensure the efficiency of this model, a waqf deed is to be made to specify the channelling of the waqf funds and it is to be revealed to the donors. It is proposed that 50% of the waqf funds will be channelled to the first section of the division which is allocated for Shariah complaint investment (40%), State Islamic Religious Council (5%) and Nazir (5%). The TNG Corporate Health Waqf company as the nazir is part of the beneficiaries. Another 50% of the funds endowed will be channelled for the purposes of: (i) covering the medical cost for B40 and M40 patients, (ii) providing medical appliances for the hospitals/clinics, (iii) maintenance costs of the government hospitals/clinics; and (iv) activities to increase the awareness of waqf through TNG Corporate Health Waqf. The awareness activities can be done by giving the updates via emails, letters, and advertisement on the outcome of the waqf funds on healthcare matter. The advertisement can be done at the Touch 'n Go e-Wallet apps installed by the users. This measure will inspire the donors to keep on donating and convince them on the projects executed by the corporate waqf. This will convince more citizens to be part of this waqf donation.

Conclusion

Waqf is undeniably proven to be an instrument that can assist the society in mitigating their financial hardships in their lives. History in the golden age of Islamic civilization has proven that the blessings in waqf sector were successfully disseminated thoroughly to the beneficiaries throughout the golden era. It is irrefutable that waqf is an important institution that can blossom the economic development in an effective way. Historically, the outcome of waqf can be witnessed by the masses in many sectors such as education, health, religious-related matter, and many others. The blessings of waqf could be felt by each citizen that was living at the time of Islamic civilization. All of them experienced the life cycle of waqf. They were born in waqf hospitals, studied and worked in waqf educational and working institutions, respectively, and buried in waqf lands.

Despite of the countless benefits of waqf explained in the literature review, the outcomes may not be able to be realized in the absence of good administration from respective authorities. The waqf sector in Malaysia is construed as 'sleeping giant' where it actually has a huge potential to make the nation great again in economic sector. However, due to some internal problems occur in waqf institutions, the benefits of waqf could not be able to be felt by many people. Frustration arises when the news of waqf are not being managed properly due to, but not limited to, lack of funds and inefficient of waqf management. Ironically, there are abundance of waqf assets in Malaysia reported to be in idle state yet it has not met the ultimate outcome of waqf, which is to assist the beneficiaries. This adversely affects many sectors, inter alia, the healthcare sector.

Healthcare sector is one of the vital sectors that are needed to be paid attention to because it involves lives of people. The health is a sector that should be maintained by waqf institutions with the help from bumiputera companies. Medical expenses in Malaysia have been skyrocketed in recent years that cause the society especially B40 and M40 to suffer from getting the medical treatment. It is displeasing to highlight the hardship that these groups of people have to go through in solving their medical issues. Initiatives need to be taken to cater this problem from compounding in the future. The government cannot be the sole place to be relied upon to support the healthcare sector financially. This is because there are other equally important sectors as well that are needed to be maintained and supported by the government. Millions of ringgit had been spent by the government just to support the healthcare sector especially in the midst of the COVID-19 pandemic in the first half of 2020.

Due to the detrimental phenomena that happen in waqf and healthcare sector, a new corporate waqf model is proposed to mitigate the problem arises in waqf sector as well as healthcare sector in Malaysia. This paper had suggested that corporate waqf can mitigate the problem of healthcare sector that arises in this country. At least, the proposed structure can prevent the problem from getting multiplied in the future. With the technology of e-wallet waqf, it may help the development of waqf sector to be the beacon of light for the economic progress in Malaysia. It is hoped that the waqf sector in the future can blanket the planet with good values embedded in it. Hence, many steps and initiatives are needed to be taken into consideration to accomplish this mission. Collaboration from many parties is highly advisable and recommended to uphold the glory of waqf in the future, for the betterment of the country. The private sector may become the trustee for the waqf asset by collaborating with the state religious council, as initiative demonstrated by the Johor Corporation Berhad. Indeed, an innovative alternative is necessary to lighten up the effectiveness of waqf institutions.

References

Atan, N. A., Johari, F., & Zulkefli, Z. K. (2017). *The Importance of Reviving Waqf-Based Health Care Institutions In Malaysia.* 5th Soith East Asia International Islamic Philanthropy Conference 2017.

Baqutayan, S. M., & Mahdzir, A. M. (2018). The Importance of Waqf in Supporting Healthcare Services. *Journal of Science, Technology and Innovation Policy, 4*(1).

CIMB. (2020). *About Us.* Retrieved from CIMB: https://www.cimb.com/en/who-we-are/about-us.html.

CIMB Foundation. (2020). *What We Do.* Retrieved from CIMB Foundation: https://www.cimbfoundation.com/what-we-do/our-pillars.

Hassan, A., Yusooff, F., & Alavi, K. (2012). Keluarga sihat melahirkan komuniti sejahtera: Satu ulasan. *Geografia Malaysian Journal of Society and Space, 8*(5), 51–63.

Jafri, F. A., & Noor, A. M. (2019). Temporary Waqf Model for Islamic Private Retirement Scheme in Malaysia-A Proposal. *Journal of Islamic Finance, 8*(1), 023–035.

Jalil, M. H., & Kadir, F. A. A. (2013). Kepentingan Kesihatan Diri Dalam Pembangunan Insan: Analisis Karya Falsafah Hamka. *Jurnal Hadhari, 5*(2), 53–66.

Kahf, M. (2003). The Role of Waqf in Improving the Ummah Welfare. In *International Seminar on Waqf as a Private Legal Body* (pp. 6–7).

Mahat, M. A., Jaaffar, M. Y., & Rasool, M. S. A. (2015). Potential of Micro-Waqf as an Inclusive Strategy for Development of a Nation. *Procedia Economics and Finance, 31,* 294–302.

Maybank. (2020). *Maybank Overview.* Retrieved from Maybank: https://www.maybank.com/en/about-us/who-we-are/overview.page.

Maybank Foundation. (2020). *Who We Are.* Retrieved from Maybank Foundation: http://www.maybankfoundation.com/index.php/who-we-are.

Nawawi, N. M. (2002). Islamic Perspective to Healthcare Architecture—An Overview of the Medieval Islamic World with Case Study of Contemporary Healthcare Architecture in Malaysia.

Rashid, S. K. (2018). Potential of waqf in Contemporary World.

The Edge Markets. (2018, July 30). *CIMB Says No Touch 'n Go IPO Anytime Soon.* Retrieved from The Edge Markets: https://www.theedgemarkets.com/article/cimb-says-no-touch-n-go-ipo-anytime-soon

The Edge Markets. (2019, October 11). *Malaysia's Total Debt, Liabilities Rose to RM1.17 Tril as at End-June.* Retrieved from The Edge Markets: https://www.theedgemarkets.com/article/malaysias-total-debt-liabilities-rose-rm117-tril-endjune.

The Edge Markets. (2020, April 10). *MCO: CIMB Says Touch 'n Go eWallet Continues to See Healthy Volumes for Essential Services, Online-Based Transactions*. Retrieved from the edge markets: https://www.theedgemarkets.com/article/touch-n-go-digital-sees-more-cashless-payments-postcovid-19.

The Star. (2018, February 18). Mental Health Hurts Economy Badly. Retrieved from The Star Online: https://www.thestar.com.my/news/nation/2020/02/18/mental-health-hurts-economy-badly.

The World Bank Group, INCEIF and ISRA. (2019). *Maximizing Social Impact Through Waqf Solutions*. The World Bank Group, INCEIF and ISRA.

World Islamic Economic Forum. (2017, July 17). *The Role of Islamic Finance and waqf in Healthcare*. Retrieved from World Islamic Economic Forum: https://infocus.wief.org/role-isl-fin-waqf-healthcare/.

Yaacob, H. (2013). Waqf History and Legislation in Malaysia: A Contemporary Perspective. *Journal of Islamic and Human Advanced Research*, *3*(6), 387–402.

Zuki, M. S. M. (2012). Waqf and Its Role in Socio-Economic Development. *ISRA International Journal of Islamic Finance*, *195*(1014), 1–11.

CHAPTER 28

How Corporate Awqaf Can Support SDGs?

Rusni Hassan and Fatimah Mohamad Noor

INTRODUCTION

Sustainable Development Goals (SDGs) is a set of universal goals that aims to tackle the urgent crisis and challenges that we are facing today such as climate change, gender inequality, health deprivation, political and economic injustice and much more. It consists of 17 Goals interconnect, meaning success in one affect success for others (United Nation Development Program, n.d.). In response to this, the active involvement of the philanthropic sector in realizing these goals is indispensable (Abdullah 2018). In this sense, waqf institution as an Islamic charitable organization also could play a role in realizing the SDGs. The role of waqf institutions in contributing to the socio-economic development of the Muslim ummah in various fields such as education, health, social activities, and many others is also undeniable (Kahf 2003).

Despite the pivotal roles of waqf institutions in the socio-economic development of Muslim ummah, the waqf institutions also have experienced turbulences and failure. Over the centuries, there were vast idle

---

R. Hassan (✉) · F. Mohamad Noor
Institute of Islamic Banking and Finance, International of Islamic
University of Malaysia (IIiBF/IIUM), Gombak, Malaysia
e-mail: hrusni@iium.edu.my

© The Author(s), under exclusive license to Springer Nature   539
Switzerland AG 2021
M. M. Billah (eds.), *Islamic Wealth and the SDGs*,
https://doi.org/10.1007/978-3-030-65313-2_28

waqf properties due to the weak governance system of waqf institutions. The phenomena of lack of accountability among the waqf trustees are one of the noticeable governance issues that caused the mundane of waqf institutions (Ihsan et al. 2016). As the waqf trustees, they fail to demonstrate their accountability and always have been perceived negatively and are associated with dishonesty, corruption, and mismanagement. Abdul Latif et al. (2018) assert that inefficient management is among the impeding factors in the governance of waqf, which weaken the sustainability and development waqf. As a result of poor management of waqf institutions, the vast Muslim society has lost the benefits from waqf (Md Saad et al. 2013). On the other hand, in some countries, the management of waqf properties is not being given serious attention, with a vast amount of waqf properties being ill-managed and still lying dormant. However, those waqf properties have a high commercial value, and they are not being maintained regularly (Md Saad et al. 2013).

Concerning to the issues the lack of management, accountability and regulation that are associated with waqf institutions, it has given rise to the engagement of corporate bodies in managing waqf affairs in Malaysia (Ramli et al. 2018). The involvement of the corporate entity in managing waqf is meant to address the institutional weaknesses of the waqf institution by empowering Muslims' economy through waqf. As a highly regulated institution, corporate entities are obliged to adopt the best corporate governance practice and a high standard of transparency and accountability.

The involvement of corporate waqf has given a positive impact on the development of waqf properties. There some countries have experienced great development of waqf properties after the involvement of corporate entities in the management of waqf. As a result of effective and efficient management, the idle waqf properties could be developed through a creative and innovative instrument such as waqf shares, waqf bond, cash waqf and the like. All these instruments have been used to benefit to the poor and the needy but also as a strategy to finance the waqf development project.

LITERATURE REVIEW

Understanding Waqf and Its Objectives in Shariah

Waqf refers to 'holding certain property and preserving it for the confined benefit of certain philanthropy and prohibiting any use or disposition of it outside that specific objective' (Kahf 2003, p. 2). Meanwhile, Abu Zahrah (1971) stated that waqf is the prevention of a benefit-generating estate from corporal disposal but using its usufruct and benefit in charity, intended so at the time of creation and thereafter (Zahrah 1971). Meaning to say that once a person endowed or donated his or her property as waqf, he or she no longer owns the property and the ownership has been transferred Allah as his belongings eternally. While the benefits of waqf must be used for the philanthropy purpose, it must be in accordance with the principles of Shariah. This is to ensure the main objective of waqf to provide a lasting benefit while the principal of waqf is preserved.

Meanwhile Ibn Ashur (2006) defined *Maqasid Shariah* as 'the overall objective (*maqsad amm*) of Islamic legislation is to preserve the social order of the community and ensure its good progress by promoting the wellbeing and virtue (salah) of the human being. The salah of human being consist of the soundness of their intellects and the righteousness of their deeds, as well as the goodness of the thing of the world in which they live that are put at their disposal' (p. 87). Dusuki and Bouheraoua (2011) further elaborate that Shariah scholars have categorized *Maqasid Shariah* into two categories: general objectives (*maqasid ammah*) and specific objectives (*maqasid khassah*). General objectives may be referred to as what is beneficial and useful for the whole or most of the community and are not much concerned about individuals so far as they are its members of the whole (Ibn Ashur 2006). For instance, the implementation of justice improves the facilities of all human beings.

Additionally, *maslahah* can be referred to the term 'consideration of public interest' which means the 'utmost righteousness and goodness' (Ibn Ashur 2006, p. 96). Meanwhile, specific objectives of Shariah refer to anything that benefits the individuals. The main concern of the specific objectives of Shariah is the righteousness and goodness of individuals' acts as a means to the righteousness and wellbeing of the whole society to which they belong (Auda 2010). It covers the aspect of objectives of the Shariah, specifically in the rules and regulations of five protections (*dharuriyat khams*): protection of faith (din), protection of lives (*nafs*), protection of intellect (*'aql*), protection of posterity (*nasl*), and protection of wealth (*mal*) (Al-Ghazali 1973, pp. 139–140).

In view of general objective Shariah of waqf, Mohammad (2018) asserts that ensuring economic justice is one of the main objectives of waqf. For instance, the distribution of wealth from the rich to the poor represents the manifestation economic injustice. In this sense, redistribution of wealth is achieved waqf in which the wealth of the rich is distributed and disseminated among to needy and the poor. Regarding this, the Quran highlights the rights of others in wealth. The Quran says: '*Zakah expenditures are only for the poor and for the needy and for those employed to collect [zakah] and for bringing hearts together [for Islam] and for freeing captives [or slaves] and for those in debt and for the cause of Allah and for the [stranded] traveler - an obligation [imposed] by Allah. And Allah is Knowing and Wise*' (al-Tawbah, 9:60). In this verse, the poor and the needy have been mentioned first because they have more essential needs rather than other categories. According to Lasasna (2013), in the modern economy, the poor commonly refers to the people whose income is less than 50% of their essential needs while the needy refers to the people whose income is less than their basic needs such as food, clothing, and shelter. Apart from ensuring economic justice, the general Shariah objective of waqf also is to achieve development. It was supported by the historical evidence that portrays the pivotal role of waqf in socio-economic development. All resources such as land, cash money, goods and services that have been endowed into waqf help in achieving an inclusive development of the ummah (Mohammad 2018).

In the vein of the specific objective of waqf, it is believed that waqf has a special role to play in order to safeguard the five protections. Thus, the role of waqf to preserve those five protections is summarized in the Table 28.1.

The Concept of Corporate Waqf

The revitalization of waqf institution creates a need for waqf institution to resolve the issue of weakness of waqf institution in governance and management of waqf properties. It is, therefore, corporate waqf has been defined by Ismail Abdel Mohsin (2014) as 'the confinement of an amount of liquid money, shares, profit, dividends by the founders such as individuals, companies, corporations, organizations or institutions, and the dedication of its usufruct in perpetuity to the welfare of society' (p. 16).

28 HOW CORPORATE AWQAF CAN SUPPORT SDGS? 543

Table 28.1 The five protections and the role of waqf

	Description	The role of waqf
Protection of faith (din)	It refers to the obligation to propagate the teaching of Islam and protection of its applied systems and its followers. Meanwhile, al Ghazali (d. 505 AH) further explains that it may be achieved through belief in Allah, worshipping Him ('*Ubudiya*h), the performance of rituals and other obligations, learning and teaching, and educational centres are means of protecting Islam	Waqf assets can be used for the above purposes following the order of priorities according to the three types of Sharīah objectives. The building of a mosque, for instance, maybe viewed necessary (ḍururi), while its maintenance and appointment of imam and *mu'adhin* needed (ḥaji), and carpeting them, or lightning them may be considered good (taḥsiniyat)
Protection of lives (*nafs*)	This objective protects humans from death, individually, or collectively. This protection includes preventive measures and retributive penalties. The last is the weakest of all, despite fuqahā' emphasis on it. Other preventive measures include the provision of food, clothing, and place of abode or shelter; prevention of disease; and prohibition of participation in activities resulting in the death of the risk-taker (Ibn Ashur, p 303)	Waqf have provided for all preventive measures leading to the safety of humans and their lives and pursuits throughout the history of Muslims. These also include medical treatment, medicines, building hospital, etc.

(continued)

Ahmad (2017) argues that this definition does not reflect the whole range possibilities that abound in a corporate waqf, the definition only emphasizes on 'confinement of asset', but it does not distinguish between corporate waqf and non-corporate waqf. The author further argues that based on this definition, it seems like all those waqf financial assets such as money, shares and profit are also possible if it not incorporated. Additionally, Omar et al. (2018) assert that this definition also brings to the

544   R. HASSAN AND F. MOHAMAD NOOR

Table 28.1   (continued)

	Description	The role of waqf
Protection intellect (*'aql*)	The protection of the human mind may be achieved through education such as thinking, experimentation, the prohibition of intoxicants and penalizing those who commit this sin (i.e. assaulting their rational capacity by consuming intoxicants or other poisons)	Waqf, therefore, can be for schools and universities, knowledge of the religion and other sciences, books and facilities, for the wellbeing of humans
Protection of posterity (*nasl*),	The sanctity of human blood is the means to the protection of the human race and its sustained regeneration. Human regeneration will keep the earth and its resources developed and is also needed for the protection of the religion and security of humans. Marriage to be the means for protection of continuous regeneration of humans; commensurately, he underscored the prohibition of adultery	For the sustenance of one's children, charity on family as well as waqf on family is permitted
Protection of Wealth (*mal*)	Property is protected from loss, being used to harm others, and it has to be grown and enhanced. Sharī'ah prohibits the taking of property of others without just cause, which comprises prohibited dealings, wastage and irresponsible use of one's property, such as keeping it unproductive	Both waqf am (general waqf), and waqf khas (waqf for specified purpose or beneficiaries) can be created for the benefit of the poor and needy. Regardless of whether the waqf is in cash or immovable property, the proceeds of them after a *mu'amalah* (investment dealing) are distributed among the deserving individuals

Source Mohammad (2018)

idea that corporate waqf has its own legal rights and liabilities to perform a duty on behalf of the founders as well as to conduct business for either profit-seeking or not-for-profit in for societal wellbeing. Once it is registered, it will have a condition of limited liability. As a result, as a corporate entity is subject to the founders' conditions, and it must be controlled by a board of directors who were appointed by the founders.

Meanwhile, Jalil and Mohd Ramli (2014), therefore, have come out with more precise definition corporate waqf as 'the creation and management waqf asset and distribution of waqf proceed of by a corporate entity independently or collectively with other parties'. Based on this definition, the corporate entity as a waqf creator or 'waqif' makes a waqf by utilizing its own assets. The corporate entity in this sense functions as waqf trustee or '*nazir*' or '*mutawalli*' who is responsible for managing, maintaining as well as investing the waqf asset. The corporate entity is able to nominate itself as beneficiaries of the waqf proceed in order to gain flexibility in managing and utilizing the waqf. Furthermore, the establishment of corporate waqf is made by a private entity that involves some activities in order to generate income, such as trading and investment. Thus, the principles of corporate governance such as accountability, transparency, and professionalism must be applied in the entity for the purpose of accumulating and generating asset. Lastly, waqf proceeds created by the corporate entity could be established, managed, and distributed independently (Jalil and Mohd Ramli 2014).

The Significance of Corporate Waqf in the Development of Waqf Property

Corporate waqf is more than a charitable and philanthropic act by a business entity; it is an initiative to combine the waqf concept and apply it to achieve business and corporate objectives. Corporate waqf, consequently, intends to redefine the role and function of business organizations by 'giving back' to society and reaching out to the community (Hamid and Saleem 2017). The experience of Waqaf An-Nur Corporation (WANCorp) in managing assets and shares has shown positive growth in terms of the development of waqf asset. Approximately 3–4 million of money has been distributed every year to a general welfare fund as a result of 25% of dividend invested as waqf shares. Johor Corporation (JCorp) by using the formulae of 70:25:5. 70% of the benefit goes back to JCorp for reinvestment and human capital development, 25% goes to WANCorp for Fisabilillah, and 5% is distributed to the Islamic Religious Council of Johor. This formula gives an opportunity for the company to maintain its growth and maximize its contribution to society.

Meanwhile, the experience of Singapore in developing and administering the waqf sector has been quoted as a success story and best examples in many forums. The joint venture between Majlis Agama Islam Singapore (MUIS) and Warees Investment Pte Ltd (Warees) has successfully transformed a number of low yielding assets into high generating performers giving higher returns. Apart from this, another approach of raising financing for the development of waqf properties by this joint venture effort is through leveraging on the properties, for example, the waqf development projects in Bencoolen Street (Shinsuke 2016). The issuance of *musharakah Sukuk* for these two projects was 100% subscribed and managed to raise S$600 million with revenue escalated from S$19,000 in 1995 to S$5.3 million in 2006.

RESEARCH METHODOLOGY

This study will focus on selected corporate waqf institutions in Malaysia and Singapore. The corporate waqf institutions involved in the study includes three corporate waqf institutions, Wakaf An-Nur Corporation Berhad (WANCorp), Perbadanan Wakaf Selangor (PWS) in Malaysia while Warees Investment Pte Ltd (Warees) in Singapore. This study uses a qualitative research method in which library research skill was used to gather all data related to the selected corporate waqf institutions in Malaysia and Singapore. For this purpose, secondary data such as journal articles, books, annual report, bulletin were used to identify the model of corporate waqf and its contributions to society.

EXPLORING THE ROLES OF CORPORATE WAQF IN SUPPORTING SDGs: THE EXPERIENCES OF SELECTED CORPORATE WAQF INSTITUTIONS IN MALAYSIA AND SINGAPORE

Waqaf An-Nur Corporation (WANCorp)

In Malaysia, Johor Corporation (JCorp) has launched the idea of 'Corporate Waqaf' in 2006 which involved the transfer of 12.35 million unit shares owned by JCorp Kulim (M) Bhd, 18.60 million unit shares in

KPJ Healthcare Bhd and 4.32 million unit shares in Johor Land Bhd to Kumpulan Waqaf An-Nur Bhd as trustee (Jalil and Mohd Ramli 2014). Through its corporate waqf agenda, as reported in 2007, JCorp pledges to dedicate 25% of the annual dividend from the shares transferred into waqf. Thus, the dividend is channelled to charity programmes not only for Muslims but non-Muslims and any charitable and religious activities that benefit and fulfil the needs of the society as a whole (Ibrahim et al. 2016).

The establishment of WANCorp could be considered as the first corporate waqf model in Malaysia. WANCorp has been incorporated to manage the assets and shares of companies of JCorp which have been endowed in accordance with the principles of Shariah. WANCorp acts as an entity under JCorp. It is the core of the waqf corporate model practised by JCorp with the authorization from Majlis Agama Islam Johor (MAIJ). Based on the MoU between MAIJ and JCorp on 4th December 2009, MAIJ has agreed to appoint WANCorp as '*Nazir Khas*' for the endowed shares effectively from 11th July 2005. WANCorp acts as the Beneficiary, Manager and Administrator of waqf assets recognized by MAIJ. At the same time, WANCorp acts as (*mauqufun 'alaih*) for the assets endowed by the endowers. It also performs the Islamic Corporate Social Responsibility (CSR 'Islam') on behalf of JCorp (WANCorp 2018) (Fig. 28.1).

The sources of funds for WANCorp primarily come from the endowed shares of corporations. The endowments of shares are made by several subsidiaries of JCorp. The endowed shares could be further divided into listed and non-listed shares. The listed companies participating in this corporate waqf model include KPJ Healthcare Berhad, Kulim (M) Berhad and Al-Aqar KPJ REIT. The non-listed companies are Tiram Travel Sdn Bhd, Capaian Aspirasi Sdn Bhd and TPM Management Sdn Bhd (Mohd Ramli and Jalil 2013; Ibrahim et al. 2016; Jalil and Mohd Ramli 2014). Distribution of waqf proceeds is made based on the *Hujah Waqaf* document which regulates that 70% of them are distributed for reinvestment and human resource development, 25% is for *fisabilillah* purpose, and 5% is for Majlis Agama Islam Johor (MAIJ). 70% of the waqf proceeds are kept in two main forms:

i. Investment (fixed) deposits at Shariah-compliant financial institutions
ii. Purchase of 'Saham Dana Johor'.

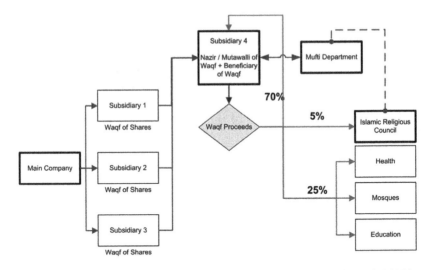

Fig. 28.1 Model of corporate Waqf WANCorp (*Source* Hanefah et al. 2011)

While the 25% portion of the waqf proceeds, it has been divided into three types of charity programmes accordingly:

i. Charity and Good Deeds (55%)
ii. Human Resource Development, Education and Entrepreneurship Capital (10%)
iii. Specific Projects (35%)

The category includes a contribution to health care, mosque, Islamic chapel, public societies, orphanage, bridged waqaf, and other types of CSR. The second category could include seminars, *mutawwif* training programme, books, non-interest loans, scholarships, etc. Specific projects are those projects that have been decided by WANCorp for that particular year that needs enormous contribution such as indigenous people improvement programme in 2011 and Imam al-Bukhari theatre in 2010. In 2011, RM718, 076 of the waqf proceeds or 5% had been distributed directly to MAIJ (Jalil and Mohd Ramli 2014).

Perbadanan Wakaf Selangor (PWS)

For the banking and financial institution model of corporate waqf, the waqf programme by Perbadanan Wakaf Selangor (PWS) and Bank Muamalat Malaysia Berhad (BMMB) could provide a sample framework as an established banking model. Figure 28.2 shows the model banking of corporate waqf.

This figure indicates that there are three sections involved in this banking model of BMMB corporate waqf. They are the fund accumulation, the management and the distribution of waqf fund. The fund accumulation is attained through individual or an organization where the fund is managed by Joint Management Committee (JPB) which showed a collaboration of Bank Muamalat Malaysia Berhad (BMMB) and Selangor Waqf Corporatization (PWS). Looking at BMMB specifically, this corporate entity has involved in the management of waqf fund by providing a banking service on the contribution of fund which the minimum contribution is RM10 by individuals and RM100 by institutions, and there is no

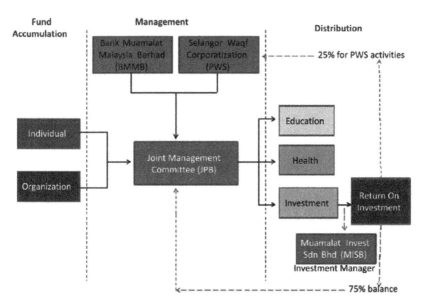

Fig. 28.2 Corporate Waqf Model Perbadanan Wakaf Selangor (PWS) and Bank Muamalat Malaysia Berhad (BMMB) (*Source* Ibrahim et al. 2016)

maximum amount for contribution by both. The fund will be managed and channelled by Join Management Committee (JPB) to three main sections, namely health, education and investment. These two sectors, healthcare and education for the needy irrespective of Muslim or non-Muslim healthcare and education, have been the major area of for waqf distribution. It is believed that waqf distribution to the public will eventually help to mitigate the cost of living and government spending (Jalil and Mohd Ramli 2014; Hanefah et al., n.d.).

For the investment, 25% of the return will then be distributed to the PWS, and 75% of them will be channelled back to JPB for redistribution in areas deemed appropriate by them (Jalil and Mohd Ramli 2014; Ibrahim et al. 2016). On the other hand, the waqf fund's goal is to accumulate a sum of RM50 million in three years' time, and BMMB itself has endowed RM1 million into the fund, and its staff has contributed RM74,040 at the launching ceremony of Wakaf Muamalat Selangor (Jalil and Mohd Ramli 2014).

Warees Investments Pte Ltd (Warees)

In Singapore, Warees Investments Pte Ltd (Warees) was created on 26th September 2001 and started its operations in January 2002. Warees is a wholly-owned subsidiary of Majlis Ugama Islam Singapura (MUIS) (Warees, n.d.). The governing bodies include the Board of Directors, Manager, and Operations Manager. The core business functions are real estate, project management, lease management, marketing and real estate investment. In the field of project management, Warees is in charge of all projects carried out by MUIS, including design, contract and implementation. In assets management, Warees also holds power over all MUIS properties (Haji Mohiddin 2015). By segregating this function, MUIS can focus on the regulatory roles and improving its corporate governance on Waqf (Abdul Karim 2010).

As part of Warees's portfolio, they are responsible for the management of Waqf and *Baitulmal* assets worth more than $250 million comprising religious, commercial, residential and educational buildings. Warees has successfully transformed a number of these low yielding assets into high income generating performers giving higher returns for the beneficiaries. Warees also holds some of MUIS assets directly for investment and development purposes (Md Saad et al. 2013). Warees also has effectively managed and constructed 27 mosques, also some 25 projects for commercial buildings and schools. It is also involved in mosque re-modification and maintenance, and the exchange of waqf lands that are considered useless for construction. One of Warees's significant projects was the issuance of SGD25 million worth of *musyarakah* bonds to purchase buildings in Beach Road in order to exchange 20 pieces of waqf land which were located in the insignificant (Haji Mohiddin 2015).

Warees play a role in any arrangement for the project given by MUIS, for example, the Bencoolen Waqf Project. Bencoolen Waqf Project is located near the city hall of Singapore (Bencoolen Street No. 59), and it was built by Syed Sharif Omar bin Ali Al-Junaied in 1845. For the purpose of raising fund for this development project, MUIS has given the approval to use the profit, and in this case, the trustees of the mosque contributed 51,900 SGD. MUIS also adopts the scheme of *Sukuk Musharakah* (Shinsuke 2016; Abdullah and Saiti 2016). Figure 28.3 illustrates the role of Warees in this development project.

Referring to the Fig. 28.3, it portrays that MUIS has issued sukuk to investors and collects 35 million SGD, while the trustees of the mosque provide funds. Through this *musharakah* framework in which MUIS and the trustees formed a joint venture, they managed to build new estate which consisted of 12 storey building, 107 service apartment units, three commercial office units and three commercial shops units (Shinsuke

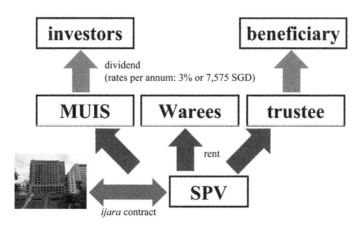

Fig. 28.3 Funding Scheme of the Bencoolen Street Waqf Project (*Source* Shinsuke 2016)

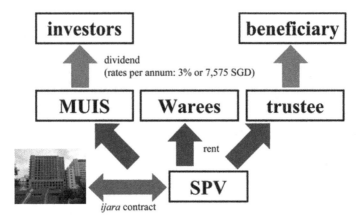

Fig. 28.4 Profit Distribution Scheme of the Bencoolen Waqf Project (*Source* Shinsuke 2016)

2016). Even with the several challenges due to contemporary financing option, this *musharakah sukuk* was 100% subscribed since MUIS carries a sovereign rating for its certificates issued (Md Saad et al. 2013). At this point, MUIS then improves the management efficiency and profitability of the waqf property. The joint venture leases apartments, offices and shops at the new building, based on an *ijarah* contract, and it receives rent from the lessees (Abdullah and Saiti 2016). While, Wareess is accountable to distribute the profit through the MUIS itself and the trustee, see Fig. 28.4 in order to understand this point.

This project has successfully improved the management, efficiency and profitability of this waqf property. It evident that the rent income in 2008 after the renewal reached 96,000 SGD, which was around 50-fold before the renewal; the expenditures in 2008 reached 146,090 SGD, which was around 20-fold. This development project is not only to enhance its charitable activities but also to sustain them based on a stable source of funding (Shinsuke 2016).

Discussion

Based on the experience of corporate waqf, it can be concluded that the corporate waqf institution has a great potential role in supporting some of SDGs. It can be discussed in these three following points:

28 HOW CORPORATE AWQAF CAN SUPPORT SDGS? 553

1. *Corporate waqf and its relation to the SDGs of No poverty, Good Health and Quality education.* The contemporary innovation of corporate waqf institution clearly reflects the objective of Shariah (*Maqasid al-Shariah*) on the creation of wealth. Moreover, the establishment of corporate waqf has successfully harnessed the potential of corporations to create wealth to combat the persistent poverty and marginalization among the community. This is in line with the objective of Shariah in the creation of wealth in Islam in which it emphasizes the rights of other people in the wealth, especially the poor and the needy. Thus, the Islamic concept of wealth in Islam is something that is not only benefits the individual itself but to others. Thus, corporate waqf is an effective mechanism for redistribution the wealth and to achieve inclusive economic development entirely. In fact, corporate waqf fulfils its Islamic Corporate Social Responsibility (ICSR).

2. The corporate waqf institution has provided a lot of benefit to the needy and the poor with a lot of the benefits. It is indicated in the distribution of corporate waqf proceed, and it covers the essential needs of the poor and the needy, particularly in the aspect of health and education. It is evident that the corporate waqf institutions have contributed immensely in the field of education, such as providing scholarship or training that will improve the quality of the community by enhancing their knowledge and skills. Evidently, health care and education for the needy have been the major area of for corporate waqf distribution regardless of Muslim or non-Muslim.

3. *Corporate waqf institution as a mean to promote peace, justice and strong institution.*

Sustainability cannot be achieved without the peace, justice and strong institution as the world are facing the ongoing crisis of corruptions due to the failure of the governance system, especially in Muslim developing countries. It is, therefore, highlights the importance of effective governance and the rule of law in an institution to combat this issue and ultimately contribute to peace and justice.

In response to this issue, it is the aim of the establishment of corporate waqf to address the current problem of underdevelopment of waqf properties as a result of weak governance of the waqf institution. Based on the experience of the joint venture programme between Islamic Religious Council and corporate waqf institution has resulted in the efficient and effective management of corporate waqf entity as they were able to get full flexibility in managing waqf professionally without the interruption of Islamic Religious Council. While the IRC focuses on their role to govern the activity of corporate entity must be in line with law and regulation of the country. As a result, the continuous benefit of waqf could be maintained despite the challenges they faced along the time of managing the waqf properties. They were able to work according to their expertise and professionalism in business, investment and the like.

Conclusion

This study explores the potential role of corporate waqf institutions in supporting SDGs. It mainly discusses the experience of corporate waqf institution in managing the waqf development in selected corporate waqf institution in Malaysia and Singapore. Waqf is known to have the potential to contribute to the economy and at the same time play a significant role in socio-economic development. This is in line with the main objective of SDGs to achieve the global goal of development in various aspect of the life of all human being in response to the global crisis of poverty, climate change, etc. Despite the potential role of waqf institution, the issue of inefficient management and poor governance that hampering waqf institution has led to its backwardness over a decade. This is resulting in the vast idle waqf properties have not been re-developed for the benefit of people. The initiative to establish waqf is one of the ways of resolving the managerial and legislative of the waqf institution. Corporate waqf refers to the creation, management and distribution of waqf by corporate entities collectively and independently. Generally, the experience of selected corporate waqf institutions in Malaysia indicated that large segment of vulnerable society regardless of Muslim and non-Muslim can enjoyed the benefit of corporate waqf proceed particularly in the aspect of education and health care. In view of SDGs, these two aspects are among essential goals that have been listed in the SDGs. Moreover, the creation of corporate waqf is also to tackle the issue of poverty whereby it has considered as an effective mechanism for redistribution of wealth. Lastly, this study recommends to expand the role of corporate waqf at the global level, and its establishment must be in line not only to the Shariah principles but also the SDGs. Since this study is confined to only selected corporate waqf institutions in Malaysia and Singapore, future studies can be undertaken by exploring the various model of corporate waqf in different

28 HOW CORPORATE AWQAF CAN SUPPORT SDGS? 555

countries so that an integrated and universal framework of corporate waqf can be formulated in line with SDGs. The framework must be easy to be practised and adopted, especially for developing countries.

REFERENCES

Abdul Karim, S. (2010). Contemporary Shari'a Compliance Structuring for the Development and Management of Waqf Assets in Singapore. *Kyoto Bulletin of Islamic Area Studies, 3*(2), 143–164. Available at: http://www.asafas.kyoto-u.ac.jp/kias/1st_period/contents/pdf/kb3_2/09shamsiah.pdf.

Abdul Latif, S., Nik Din, N. M., & Mustapha, Z. (2018). The Role of Good Waqf Governance in Achieving Sustainable Development. *Environment-Behaviour Proceedings Journal, 3*(7), 113–118. https://doi.org/10.21834/e-bpj.v3i7.1292.

Abdullah, A., & Saiti, B. (2016). A Re-examination of Musharakah Bonds and Waqf Development: The Case of Singapore. *Intellectual Discourse, 24,* 541–562.

Abdullah, M. (2018). Waqf, Sustainable Development Goals (SDGs) and Maqasid. *International Journal of Social Economics, 45*(1), 158–172. https://doi.org/10.1108/ijse-10-2016-0295.

Ahmad, M. (2017). Could a Waqf Company in Malaysia Expand Its Operation Through Initial Public Offering? In *Waqf Laws and Management* (pp. 214–229). Gombak: IIUM Press.

Al-Ghazali. (1973). *Al-Mustasfa min 'Ilm al-Usul.* Cairo: al-Maktabah al-Tijariyyah.

Ashur, M. A.-T. (2006). *Treatise on Maqasid al-Shari'ah.* (M. E.-T. El-Mesawi, Trans.). Herdon: International Institute of Islamic Thought.

Auda, J. (2010). *Maqasid al-Shariah as Philosophy of Islamic Law a System Approach.* Petaling Jaya: Islamic Book Trust.

Dusuki, A. W., & Bouheraoua, S. (2011). The Framework of Maqasid Al-Shariah and Its Implication for Islamic Finance. *ISRA Research Paper* (2), 1–49.

Haji Mohiddin, H. M. N. (2015). *Waqf Development in Malaysia and Singapore: A Comparative Study.* Durham University.

Hamid, Z., & Saleem, M. Y. (2017). Managing Corporate Waqf in Malaysia: Perspectives of Selected SEDCs And SIRCs. *Shariah Journal, 25*(1), 91–116.

Hanefah, P. D. H. M. M., et al. (2011). Financing the Development of Waqf Property: The Experience of Malaysia and Singapore. *The Journal of Mualamat and Islamic Finance, 8*(1), 89–104.

Ibrahim, S. S. B., et al. (2016). Analysis of Corporate Waqf Model in Malaysia: An Instrument Towards Muslim's Economic Development. *International Journal of Applied Business and Economic Research, 14*(5), 2931–2944.

Ihsan, H., Eliyanora, & Septriani, Y. (2016). Accountability Mechanisms for Awqaf Institutions: Lessons Learnt from the History. *Journal of King Abdulaziz University, Islamic Economics, 29*(1), 41–54. https://doi.org/10.4197/islec.29-1.3.

Ismail Abdel Mohsin, M. (2014). *Corporate Waqf: From Principle to Practice: A New Innovation for Islamic Finance*. Kuala Lumpur: Pearson Malaysia Sdn Bhd.

Jalil, A., & Mohd Ramli, A. (2014). Conceptualization of Corporate Waqf. In *Seminar Waqf Iqlimi 2014* (pp. 310–321). Available at: http://ddms.usim.edu.my:80/jspui/handle/123456789/9866.

Kahf, M. (2003). The Role of Waqf in Improving the Ummah Welfare. In *The International Seminar on "Waqf as a Private Legal Body"*.

Lasasna, A. (2013). *Maqasid Al-Shariah in Islamic Finance*. Kuala Lumpur: IBFIM.

Md Saad, N., Kassim, S., & Hamid, Z. (2013). Involvement of Corporate Entities in Waqaf Management: Experiences of Malaysia and Singapore. *Asian Economic Financial Review, 3*(6), 736–748.

Mohammad, M. T. S. (2018). Maqāṣid al-Sharī'ah and Waqf: Their Effect on Waqf Law and Economy. *Intellectual Discourse, 26*(Special Issue), 1066–1091. https://doi.org/10.1017/cbo9781107415324.004.

Mohd Ramli, A., & Jalil, A. (2013). Corporate Waqf Model and Its Distinctive Features: The Future of Islamic Philanthropy. In *World Universities Islamic Philanthropy Conference 2013*. Kuala Lumpur: Menara Bank Islam.

Omar, A. J., Wan Yusoff, W. Z., Mohamad, M., & Wan Zahari, W. A. M. (2018). Current Issue in Corporate Waqf in Malaysia. *Advanced Science Letter, 24*(5), 3045–3051. https://doi.org/10.1166/asl.2018.11315

Ramli, A., et al. (2018). Primary Drivers of Sustainable Performance : The Case of Corporate Waqf. *Global Journal Al-Thaqafah* (Special Issue), 207–218. https://doi.org/10.7187/gjatsi2018-14.

Sahih International. (n.d.). Retrieved from The Noble of Quran: https://quran.com/.

Shinsuke, N. (2016). Revitalization of Waqf in Singapore : Regional Path Dependency of the New Horizons In Islamic Economics. *Journal of Islamic Economic International, 9*(3), 4–18.

UNDP. (n.d.). *Sustainable Development Goals* [Online]. Available at: https://www.undp.org/content/undp/en/home/sustainable-development-goals.html. Accessed 1 May 2020.

WANCorp. (2018). *Annual Report Waqaf An-Nur Corporation Berhad.* Retrieved from http://www.wancorp.com.my/files/document/12/Waqaf%20Abridged%20Report.pdf.

Warees. (n.d.). *Warees Investments Pte Ltd.* Retrieved from https://www.warees.sg/.

Zahrah, A. (1971). *Muhadharat fi al-Waqf.* Dar Al-Fikr Al-'Arabi.

CHAPTER 29

Cash Awqaf: How It May Contribute to Sdgs?

Rusni Hassan, Jawwad Ali, and Fatimah Mohamad Noor

INTRODUCTION

Islam strongly encourages its followers to be involved in a viable eco-system and socio-economic practices for the well-being and welfare of the society, as for example: *Zakāt, Ṣadaqah*, etc. Remarkably, Islamic endowment (*Waqf*) is one of the Islamic paradigms under the funda-mental pillars to eliminate the deprivation of basic needs and removal or reduction of poverty from the society. This Islamic principle can be realized by establishment of right to education and health care, by giving control to resources which are tangible in nature, the facilities provided by them, and employment for the needy or poor. The charitable endowment (*Waqf*) as a practice of continual philanthropic deed (*Ṣadaqah Jāriyah*) is not mentioned in the explicit verses of Holy book of Qur'an. Though, some Qur'anic verses indicate the basic theory of this endowment. Allah (SWT) says in His Holy book: "you shall never attain righteousness unless

R. Hassan (✉) · J. Ali · F. Mohamad Noor
IIUM Institute of Islamic Banking and Finance, International of Islamic University of Malaysia (IIiBF/IIUM), Gombak, Malaysia
e-mail: hrusni@iium.edu.my

© The Author(s), under exclusive license to Springer Nature Switzerland AG 2021
M. M. Billah (eds.), *Islamic Wealth and the SDGs*,
https://doi.org/10.1007/978-3-030-65313-2_29

559

560   R. HASSAN ET AL.

you spend from what you love. Whatsoever you spend, Allah is fully aware of it" (Al-Qur'an, 3:92). In the same light, the messenger of Allah (PBUH) declares that *"when a man dies all his good deeds come to an end except three: Ongoing charity (Ṣadaqah Jāriyah), beneficial knowledge and a righteous son who prays for him"* (Al-Tirmidhê 1975, p. 652). The prophetic approach was passionately followed and supported by the Muslim society and regarded as a standard practice of Islamic ethos throughout the history (Ibn Qudāmah 1968a, pp. 3–4; Cizakca 1998; Kahf and Mohomed 2017). Previously, immovable assets such as land and building are considered as a familiar method of establishing a *Waqf* (Ahmed and Khan 1998; Cizakca 1998).

BACKGROUND OF WAQF AND MAQASID AL-SHARI'AH

Waqf and Maqasid al-Shari'ah

The term "*Waqf*" is derived from the word "*Waqafa*" which means to hold, to prevent, or to restrain. Technically, definitions of *Waqf* given by the jurists have varied according to their different perceptions. According to Ibn Qudamah and Shirazi, "*Waqf*" means "to hold up the root and spread its usufruct" (Ibn Qudāmah 1968a, p. 3; 1994b, p. 250; Al-Shirazi, n.d., p. 323). This definition is preferred due to its inclusiveness of main purpose of *Waqf* and harmonization with the common concept of *Waqf* that can be found in all four *Madhāhib*. Practically, *Maqāṣid al-Sharī'ah* is interpreted as the objectives, derived from the holy sources of 'Qur'an' and '*Sunnah*' for the consciousness of *Maṣāleh al-'Ibād* (public interest) (Mahmud and Shah 2010; Arshad et al. 2018, p. 160). Accordingly, *Maṣāleh al-'Ibād* conclusively encompass five main objectives of the *Sharī'ah* which are protection of *Dīn* (faith), *Nafs* (life), *Nasl* (progeny), '*Aql* (intellect), and *Māl* (wealth), also known as *kulliyyāt al-Khams* (the five basic principles) (Al-Shatibi 1997, p. 20; Ibn Ashur 2004, pp. 233–234). According to Al-Shatibi, the *Maṣāleh al-'Ibād* (public interest) is divided into three comprehensive categories: (1) *Ḍaruriyyāt* (necessities) which refers to the preservation of essential requirements of human. Thus, if these elements are threatened, it could lead to devastation of both individual and collective life. (2) *Ḥājiyyāt* (needs) denotes the complementary of *Ḍaruriyyāt*, which facilitates the necessity by providing ease and alleviation (*al-Taysīr*) and avoiding difficulty and hardship (*al-Ḥaraj*). However, the absence of these elements does not cause any disruption of human life. (3) *Tahsīniyyāt* (embellishments) signifies to the enrichment of value system and behaviours among the human beings. Though, the absence of these elements, neither result in disruption nor hardship to the human life (Al-Shatibi 1997, pp. 21–23; Ibn Ashur 2004, pp. 231–243).

Contribution of Waqf Towards Preservation of Kulliyat al-Khams

Hifz al-Din (Preservation of religion) involves its transmission and promotion in a better way and further involves protection of stated principles and its followers. This can be achieved by worshiping Allah (SWT), obeying His commands, performing religious practices and its obligatory duties, and establishing educational and academic seminaries (Al-Ghazali; Ibn Ashur, p. 303). Likewise, *Hifz al-Nafs* (Preservation of life) includes both protective steps and punitive actions. The former measure involves the basic needs of human being such as having food stuff, clothes, house for sustenance, prohibition of such activities which may jeopardize the life (Al-Ghazali; Ibn Ashur, p. 303). Similarly, *Hifz al-Aql* (Preservation of mind) protects individual mind that can be achieved with the help of retributive measures, such as prevention of wine and punishing those who are involved with this sinful act. Equally, *Hifz al-Nasl* (Preservation of posterity) preserves the human posterity for the maintenance and development of the eco-system. Hereby, Imam al-Ghazali counted the marriage among the elements which protects the human race and highlighted the prohibition of *Zina* (adultery) (Mohammad 2018, p. 72). Finally, *Hifz al-Mal* (Preservation of wealth) is a prerequisite for the achievement of *Maqasid al-Shariah* in totality, in all three levels. Importantly, Islamic law encourages people to seek wealth throughout the various legal means and however, forbids unlawful practice of acquiring wealth which belongs to others, and further prohibits its misuse and misappropriation (Al-Ghazali).

Significantly, *Waqf* institutions would be utilized for achieving the above-mentioned objectives. Historically, immense amount of *Waqf* properties was endowed for the establishment of mosque, *Madrasah* (religious school) and *Jamiat* (universities) for the performance of *Salah,* propagation of the Quran and various religious activities, which would be considered as *Hifz al-Din* and *Aql* as well. Importantly, according to Mohammad (2018), for the avoidance of evil from Islam, income of *Waqf* can be distributed among the non-believers as a *Taklif*. This Islamic act might lead to change their mentality towards Muslims which further take a lead to avoid the Islamophobic mindset to a certain level. Additionally, this religious institution was further engaged for the protection of life, posterity and wealth, throughout the Islamic history, by providing medicinal treatment and utilizing the Income of *Waqf* to support the poor and needy and to marry them. It should be taken into consideration, that moveable property (cash *Waqf*) can contribute towards achieving all these objectives of *Shariah* as immoveable property (general *Waqf*). Remarkably, these objectives are easily achievable throughout the cash *Waqf* compared to general *Waqf*, as it can be realized in the characteristics of cash *Waqf*.

Waqf and Its Relation to SDGs

As previously mentioned that Muslim scholars have recognized, that *Sharī'ah* preserves *kulliyyāt al-Khams* for public interests both in this world and the hereafter. And according to Shatibi and Ibn Ashur, the purpose of *Sharī'ah* is to maximize the advantage for human life and minimize or eliminate the evil from it (Al-Shatibi 1997, p. 8; Ibn Ashur 2004, p. 197). Remarkably, the philanthropic deed of *Waqf* could lead to the enrichment of benefit and avoidance of evil form the public interest, provided that all three levels of human interest are taken into consideration (Mohammad 2018, p. 1070). Noticeably, according to Ibn 'Ashur, *Waqf* (Islamic endowment) would fall under the category of *Ḥājiyyāt*, whose main purpose is to facilitate the ease and relief and eliminate the difficulty and hardship from the society. As he argued that *Waqf* is needed for the well-being of Muslim society and for the betterment and management of their issues in gentle manner, regardless of that its absence does not cause the destruction to the society, undeniably it impacts on the organized activities (Ibn Ashur 2004, p. 241).

Importantly, the framework of sustainable development goal (SDGs) is intently harmonious with the core spirit of *Sharī'ah* objectives. In thrust of developing a viable eco-system (e.g. healthy life, right to education, etc.) and socio-economic (sustainable consumption, social security, ecological development, etc.) growth, both SDGs and *Maqāsid al-Sharī'ah* reflect the parallel concepts of attaining same objective. Noticeably, the main purpose of both SDGs and *Maqāsid al-Sharī'ah* is to achieve the sustainable and comprehensive growth. The absence of these objectives results in dispossession of essential necessities, that may further result to imperil the dignity of human being, protection of which is the core objective of *Shariah*. In this vein, the approach of *Maqāṣid* requires the contemporary religious foundations (*Waqf*) to advance into a comprehensive institution that takes all matters of human sustenance on priority basis (Abdullah 2018, pp. 159–160). To achieve this approach, the contemporary pious foundation *(Waqf)* is required to be aligned with *Maqāṣid* approach, and hereby, these foundations would be headed for the safety of human life along with other objectives of *Sharī'ah*, as their primary objective. Remarkably, the approach of sustainable development goals (SDGs) could be important to the organizational partners of *Waqf* institution, for the adjustment of *Waqf*-based development policies, and this framework further provides a shared operational space for development among SDGs and the *Maqāṣid al-Sharī'ah* (Abdullah 2018, p. 160).

The Main Concept of Cash Waqf

Jurisprudential Boundary of Cash Waqf

As per Mohsin, "Cash *Waqf* can be defined as the confinement of an amount of money/cash from the founder and the dedication of its usufruct, according to the founder's condition (s), in perpetuity to the welfare of the society" (Mohsin 2009, p. 40). Importantly, this definition of cash *Waqf* harmonizes with the statement of Imam Zufar and al-Tusuli to enlighten the accurate description of cash *Waqf* (Ibn Nujaym, n.d., p. 219; Al-Tusuli 1998, p. 369). There has been disagreement of views among the Muslim jurists pertaining to the legitimacy of cash *Waqf*. This divergence of opinion among the jurist rests the issue of perpetual requirement (*Ta'bīd*) of Islamic endowment (*Waqf*) whether cash *Waqf* fulfils this basic nature of *Waqf* or not? In this context, cash endowment was legitimated during the era of Ottoman caliphate by the late *Ḥanafī Fuqahā*, realizing the view of Imām Muḥammad bin Ḥasan who based the legitimacy of *Waqf* on *'Urf* (custom). This view is also supported by late *Ḥanafī* jurists and particularly Imām Zufar who is with the opinion of, that anything which can be measured or weighed would be established as *Waqf* (Ibn 'Abidin 1992, pp. 363–364; Ibn Nujaym, n.d., p. 219). Importantly, this view of Imām Zufar played a significant role in legalizing the concept of cash *Waqf*. Contrary to this view, the concept of cash *Waqf* not approved by the vast majority of Shāf'aī and Ḥanbalī schools as it does not meet the basic nature of *Waqf,* i.e. perpetuity (Ibn Qudāmah 1968a, p. 35; Al-Haithami 1983, pp. 237–238; Al-Jumal, n.d., p. 578). However, in the recent years, contemporary *Fatāwā* issued in favour of legitimacy of cash *Waqf* by the renowned bodies such as international *Fiqh* Academy and Accounting and Auditing Organization for Islamic Financial Institutions (AAOIFI).

Arguably, cash endowment carries several advantages relative to other form of *Waqf* (movable *Waqf*), which can be achieved by the stakeholders of this endowment. Cash *Waqf* facilitates a great substitute for those, who only has movable assets, i.e. cash for the endowment. Additionally, charity through the cash endowment helps to produce more capital, which further can be utilized for the development of abandoned *Waqf* properties. Likewise, this form of *Waqf* is easy in nature to fulfil the day-to-day needs of the beneficiaries when compared to immovable *Waqf*. Also, this type of charitable deed could be a solution for the issue of liquidity which is faced by the manager of *Awqāf* (*Mutawallī*) for the development of *Waqf* assets (Al-Mayman 2009, pp. 29–30; Al-Thamali, n.d., pp. 21–24; Saifuddin et al. 2014).

Timeline of Cash Waqf

Historically, the concept of *Waqf* was established and developed in the era of Prophet (PBUH), and an immense amount of properties endowed by the companions and later in the era of *Khulafā al-Rashidīn*, however, a single example of cash *Waqf* could not be reported in these times (Al-Thamali, n.d., p. 16; Cizakca 1998; Aziz and 'Ali 2018). Remarkably, the *Fatāwā* of Imām Zuhri as reported by Imām Bukhari, and *Fatwā* of Imām Malik in this regard, can be considered as first reported cash *Waqf* (Ibn al-Ḥajar 1379, p. 405; Malik 1994, p. 343). Noticeably, with the establishment of Ottoman empire in fifteenth century, the concept of cash endowment was discussed and argued among the *Ḥanafī* jurists and later, this charitable deed evolved and flourished when Ottoman court legalized it by implementing the *Fatāwā* of Imām Muḥammad and Zufar (Al-Thamali, n.d., p. 6; Saifuddin et al. 2014). According to Cizakca, as a result of this approvement, the basic needs of the society, such as health care scheme and education system, were almost fulfilled throughout the use of endowment funds (Cizakca 1998).

Primary Restriction Validating Cash Endowment

There is consensus among the Muslim scholars that once any property is endowed as *Waqf*, it falls under three primary restrictions. Likewise, is the validity of cash *Waqf*, which is covered under these provisions, which includes:

- Perpetuity: this refers to the perpetuity of cash *Waqf* by ensuring the perpetual and ongoing support to the *Mawqūf 'Alih* (beneficiaries).
- Irrevocability: this includes that once the *Wāqif* (endower) declared the money as cash *Waqf*, he is not capable to revoke this declaration as it rests in the ownership of Allah (SWT).
- Inalienability: this means that once the cash *Waqf* is established, the corpus of this *Waqf* cannot be sold, gifted, inherited, etc. (Abdullah Nadwi and Kroessin 2013; Mohsin 2009, pp. 42–43).
- Importantly, from *Sharī'ah* perspective, there are some basic requirements for the endower of cash *Waqf* like other types of *Waqf*, which are as follows:

  - A *Waqf* will be valid only when established with an understanding mind, free from coercion, i.e. undue influence by others. Therefore, the *Wāqif* must be sane and mature and not suffering from idiocy. (Al-Haithami 1983, p. 236).
  - The *Mutawalli*/who is the caretaker of *Waqf* property would be explicitly stated that endower (*Wāqif*) of this deed himself/herself handles and manages it or he/she will appoint someone else to achieve this objective.
  - The *Mawqūf 'Alih* (beneficiaries) of *Waqf* are required to be registered by declaring the categories of *Waqf* and with the explanation of their particular shares of usufruct or revenue (Abdullah Nadwi and Kroessin 2013; Mohsin 2009).

Types of Cash Waqf Implementation Suggested by the Jurists

1. Mudārabah (profit and loss sharing)

In the implementation of mudārabah, the cash money is invested profitably. The surplus or profit of the share is divided between the investment expert and the rest shared by the eligible recipients. The cash is maintained in the form of shares. An example of profit and loss sharing using waqf property is mentioned by Imam al-Zuhri. An individual endowed 1000 gold dinars in the path of Allah by entrusting the sum to a trader to invest it in his business and declared that the profit accruing from the money invested would be given to charity. In the contemporary practice, this practice refers to the cash waqf investment. Fiqh Academy in its Resolution No. 140 (15/6) recommended the investment of cash waqf through both low-risk investment and high-risk investment while observing the following conditions (Resolution):

(i) Statement and scope of the investment should be Shari'ah compliant. Perpetuity of the waqf and its benefits must be ensured.

(ii) Observation of variation of investment scope in order to minimize risks or diversify business risks, taking guarantees, documentation of the contracts, conducting of feasibility study for the intended investment projects.

(iii) Selection of the safest modes of investment and keeping away from the high-risk investment modes.

(iv) Investment of waqf properties should be in accordance with the Shari'ah and modes suitable to those properties which serve and protect the waqf and beneficiary rights. Therefore, if the waqf properties are tangible assets, the investment should not lead to the termination of their ownership, and if they are in the form of cash, they can be invested in any Shari'ah compliant mode of investments, such as *Mudarabah, Murabahah, Musharakah, Istisna'*.

(v) There must be an annual disclosure on the investment activities and make such information available to the persons involved.

2. Al-Ibdah

The jurists also suggest a type of investment called *ibda'*. *Al-Ibda'* is a type of investments run by workers, investors, or businessman voluntarily without taking any wages from his efforts, this is done by using other people's capital in the investment, and if any profits are gained, the profits belong to the owner of the capital (Abd Rahman and Awang 2018).

3. *Interest-Free Loans*

Incurring a debt is understood as the act of giving the ownership of one's property to another person on the condition that the debtor will return it without any addition to the amount. If there is any addition involved in the debt, it is prohibited based on the legal concept: "Every loan with an addition is considered usury (*riba*)" (Abd Rahman and Awang 2018).

The Forms of Cash Waqf in Contemporary Practice

Generally, there are two forms of cash waqf that are commonly be practiced in waqf institutions (Ismail and Mohsin 2014). The forms are as follows:

1. *Direct Cash Waqf*

Direct cash waqf is an endowment created by the donors of waqf in cash to be channelled for the development of waqf property (Fig. 29.1).

2. *Indirect Cash Waqf*

Indirect cash waqf is an endowment made by the donors in cash form, but to be invested first and only the revenue generated to be channelled to the beneficiaries. Figure 29.2 portrays the common modus operandi of indirect cash waqf.

CASH WAQF AND ITS ROLES IN SUPPORTING SDGs

This study focuses primarily to uncover the potential role of cash waqf to attain two goals of SDGs. The rationale of selecting these two goals is due

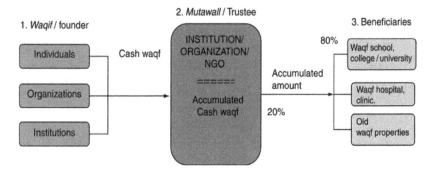

Fig. 29.1 Modus operandi of direct cash waqf (*Source* Ismail and Mohsin 2014)

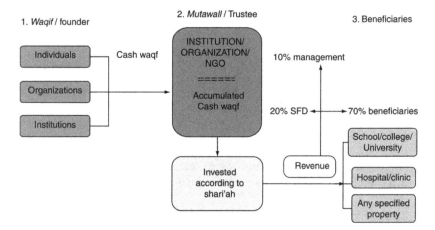

Fig. 29.2 Modus operandi of indirect cash waqf (*Source* Ismail Abdel Mohsin 2014)

to the prior study indicated that these two goals were the top priority of donors' motivation to contribute in cash waqf. This section will analyse several models and framework of cash waqf that possibly help to combat poverty and to improve the quality of education in the Muslim society as indicated in the SDGs.

Cash Waqf and Poverty Alleviation

It is believed that a cash waqf is an effective tool and strategy in combating poverty. This program, however, demands a large amount of fund while the government is not able to be a sole source of financing. In this situation, cash waqf can take place in this role. Usually, the waqf fund trustees will establish the fund by collecting cash waqf from the donors and invest the money in the real sector or any Shariah-compliant investment funds. The profit from the investment will be distributed to charitable means that benefits the society as a whole, including the poverty reduction programmes (Saiti et al. 2019). A study conducted by Ismail Abdel Mohsin (2013) discovers the role of cash waqf in different Muslim majority and minority countries. The study indicates that there are six types of cash waqf schemes that are being practiced in different countries, those waqf schemes are: waqf shares scheme, deposit cash waqf scheme, compulsory cash waqf scheme, corporate waqf scheme, deposit product waqf scheme, and co-operative waqf scheme. Based on the analysis from different types of cash waqf scheme, the author concludes that the cash waqf shows the potential of cash waqf as one of the financial institutions in providing different needs in the different societies without depending on government's budgets.

The researcher further comes up with the framework of Cash Waqf Financial Institution (CWFI). This framework reveals the potential cash waqf as an Islamic Micro-Finance Institution financing small business, as the beneficiaries, through *al-Qard al-Hassan* (Benevolent loan). It was supported by Robinson (2001) (as cited in Shahimi et al. 2013) emphasized the need for financial services both credit and savings for the economically active poor in the developing countries. An alternative financial service is highly demanded by this group of low income that could possibly assist improving their household and enterprise management, increase productivity, smooth income flows and consumption cost, enlarge and diversify their micro business and increase their income. Moreover, prominent factors that hinder micro enterprises from accessing external finance such as inadequate collateral; insufficient legal status; high transaction costs; insufficient information and documentation; lack of financial track record; nature and quality of business; rigidity of the financing procedure; and lack of awareness on financial facilities (Mohd Thas Thaker 2018).

570   R. HASSAN ET AL.

Generally, the modus operandi is started with the establishment of the cash waqf from the main founders, which can be individuals, organization, company, corporation, NGOs, or financial institution. Then, the CWFI in its role as the trustee can provide a list of beneficiaries and can call for more founders/contributors to donate/contribute cash waqf (either direct or indirect) for the selected beneficiary. The CWFI can then manage the accumulated cash waqf and channel it according to the type of the created cash waqf, either for direct or for indirect cash waqf. To ensure the perpetuity of the direct cash waqf, the accumulated funds of the cash waqf must be channelled directly to re-develop any old waqf property. In this case, exchange from liquid money to re-developing the real state can be made and which is acceptable in Shari'ah. This means that the funds can be channel directly to re-develop idle and unproductive old waqf buildings, such as waqf schools, waqf colleges, waqf universities, waqf hospitals, waqf clinics, waqf factories, and waqf agriculture lands.

In achieving so, all the old waqf properties can regain its role in providing the goods and services needed in each society besides employing the majority of people, for the indirect cash waqf. To ensure the perpetuity of the indirect cash waqf, the accumulated cash waqf must be invested, and only the revenue generated can be channelled to the beneficiaries. Hence, for the investment of the accumulated cash waqf, it can be invested in low-risk investment or high-risk investment as recommended by the contemporary Muslim scholars mentioned above. To ensure the perpetuity of the capital of liquid waqf, it is much recommended as an entail stage to invest only 50% and to keep 50% intact. Out of this 50%, which is meant for investment, it is also much recommended to invest 30% in low-risk investment and 20% in high-risk investment. Profit generated from the indirect cash waqf investment can be channelled to three parties in different proportions, for example 10% to go for the management team, 70% to be channelled to the beneficiaries (services needed), and 20% as a self-financing device (SFD) specifically to add up to the capital, i.e., to the 50% (to cater if any lose happened in the future). The framework of CWFI for investment, therefore, is divided into two categories: high-risk investment and low-risk investment as recommended by the Fiqh Academy. It has been illustrated in Figs. 29.3 and 29.4.

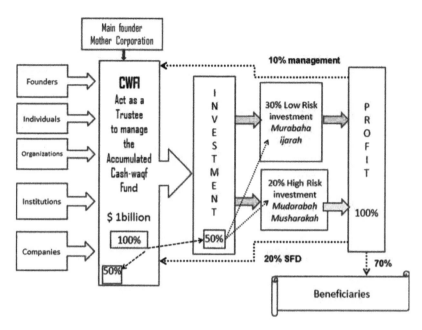

Fig. 29.3 CWFI framework for low-risk investment (*Source* Ismail Abdel Mohsin 2013)

Cash Waqf and Quality Education

Cash waqf has the potential to fulfil the goal of "Quality Education". In Islamic history, it was recorded the significant contribution of waqf in education during the period of Abbasiyah, Ayyubiah, Mamalik, and Uthmaniah, for example, the establishment of Waqf schools in many Islamic cities such as in Jerusalem, Damascus, Baghdad, Cairo, Balkan states, Morocco, Cordoba, Istanbul, and various part of the world including the Malay Archipelago (Bakar et al. 2019). While, the oldest University Waqf, Al-Azhar University of Egypt, was established in year 975AD and University of Al-Qurawwin, in Fez Morocco in the year 1200 AD. The waqf concept had been disseminated to Balkan states, and it is believed that Western universities in Europe adopted the same concept. At this time, waqf university has been establishing in many parts of the Muslim world. Such as there are more than 68 waqf universities in

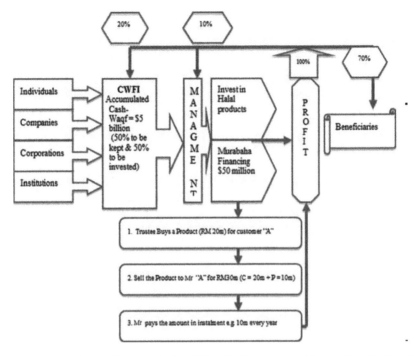

Fig. 29.4 CWFI framework for high-risk investment (*Source* Ismail Abdel Mohsin 2013)

Turkey, and 38 of them are located in the historic city of Istanbul (Bakar et al. 2019).

An example of university that using the cash waqf framework as a method of financing and development for university is the International Islamic University Malaysia (IIUM) (Saad et al. 2016). The International Islamic University Malaysia Endwoment Fund (IEF) was established on 15th March 1999 as a division of the IIUM. Structure-wise of the IEF is identical to Al-Azhar University Waqf and an endowment fund of eminent universities in the UK and USA. It is overseen by the executive board chaired by the honourable Rector while the deputy rector of student affairs is the deputy chairman along with six other members. The IEF is managed by the management team headed by a Director. The IEF has three units comprising of the Corporate Communication Unit, Investment and Business Development Unit and Zakat and Training Services

Unit (Saad et al. 2016). The main purpose of its establishment is to assist the poor and needy students in the University who are academically excellent but incapable of financing the fees and the cost of living. More specific objectives: to solicit and receive contributions in the form of movable and immovable properties, cash, shares, negotiable instruments, etc., from Malaysian and International donors for the purposes of education and research; to provide fund for scholarships and financial assistance to the needy students of IIUM; to fulfil specific wishes of a donor in so far as they relate to a particular objective within the parameters of IIUM; and to invest in investment avenues permitted by the Shariah for fund growth (IIUM Endowment Fund, n.d.).

IIUM Waqf Knowledge is a cash waqf model of IEF, also known as *Waqf 'Ilmi*. This program is initiated by the IEF itself, and according to it, the program strictly follows the principles of waqf. The projects long-term aim is to develop into a RM 1 billion trust fund. In this regard, 145 of IIUM staff joined this project during its launch. From the total source of collections, which was around RM 10 million in 2016, 5% of the sources (RM 509,951) were generated from the waqf knowledge project. This project shares a similar aim, which involves the broader source of funds for IEF, which are to be contributed among the needy, especially in IIUM. The concept used in IIUM Waqf Knowledge is the same concept as cash waqf. The annual report mentioned that the collections under this project are pooled and then invested in Shariah-compliant investments. Thus, it must be carefully managed and monitored to ensure the allocated investments return a profit to IEF. The yield is then used to assist the needy. The operational mechanism for IIUM Waqf Knowledge is reflected in (Firdaus et al. 2017). Figure 29.5 shows the model of cash Waqf of IEF.

Conclusion

It can be concluded that the framework of sustainable development goal (SDGs) is intently harmonious with the core spirit of Sharī'ah objectives of Waqf particularly in the aspect of the contribution Waqf towards Preservation of *Kulliyat al-Khams*, they are: preservation of religion, preservation of life, preservation of mind, preservation of posterity and preservation of wealth. All these aspects reflect the goals of SDGs. However, this study focuses on cash waqf and its potential roles in supporting the SDGs. Since the SDGs consists of 17 goals, encompass

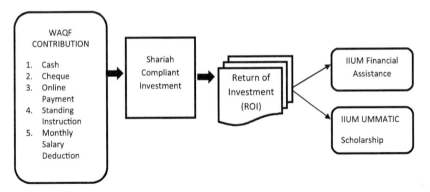

Fig. 29.5 Figure cash waqf investment model of IEF (*Source* Firdaus et al. 2017)

all the aspect of human life, this study, however, limited to the discussion of the two goals SDGs; no poverty and quality education. Several frameworks and model of cash waqf were analysed, particularly in these two aspects. In view of the potential role of cash wash in poverty alleviation, the researchers view that the framework of CWFI is a good initiative for the economically active poor or needy to get financial aid from this alternative financial institution. In the perspective of education, it is evident that cash waqf has contributed significantly to the advancement of quality education. Cash waqf has been used to provide scholarship and financial assistance for the poor and needy. In doing so, the cash waqf investment scheme has been used as a mechanism to grow the cash waqf fund, and the profits were distributed to educational ends. Future studies can be undertaken to uncover potential roles of cash waqf in another aspect of the SDGs.

References

AAOIFI, Qararat No: 60. Available online: https://iefpedia.com/arab/?p=41068. Retrieved on 12 June 2020.

Abd Rahman, A. A., & Awang, A. B. A. (2018). Exploring the Dynamism of the Waqf Institution in Islam: A Critical Analysis of Cash Waqf Implementation in Malaysia. *Intellectual Discourse, 26*(Special Issues), 1109–1128. https://doi.org/10.1017/cbo9781107415324.004.

Abdullah Nadwi, M., & Kroessin, M. (2013). Cash Waqf: Exploring Concepts, Jurisprudential Boundaries and Applicability to Contemporary Islamic Microfinance. *Islamic Relief Worldwide.*

Abdullah, M. (2018). Waqf, Sustainable Development Goals (SDGs) and Maqasid al-Shariah. *International Journal of Social Economics, 45*(1), 158–172.

Ahmed, H., & Khan, A. (1998). *Strategies to Develop Waqf Administration in India* (No. 50). The Islamic Research and Teaching Institute (IRTI).

Al-Haithamī, A. (1983). *Tohfah al-Mohtāj fi Sharḥ al-Minhāj* (n.p.) (Group of 'Ulama, Eds.) (Vol. 6, pp. 237–238). Misr: al-Maktaba al-Tijāriyyah.

Al-Jumal, S. A. (n.d.). *Futuḥāt al-Wahhāb bi Tawḍīḥ Sharḥ Manhāj al-Tullāb al-M'aruf bi Hāshiyah al-Jumal* (n.p.) (Vol. 3, p. 578). Bairut: Dar al-Fikr.

Al-Maymān, N. (2009). *Al-Nawāzil al-Waqfiyyah* (1st ed, pp. 29–30). Al-Mamalakah al-Saudiyyah: Dār Ibn al-Jawzi.

Al-Quran.

Al-Shātibi, I. (1997). *Al-Muwāfaqāt* (1st ed., Vol. 2, pp. 17–22). Al-Muhaqqiq: Abu 'Ubaiydah. Al-Nāshir: Dār Ibn 'Affān.

Al-Thamālī, U. (n.d.). Waqf al-Nuqood (Hukmuhu, Tārīkhuhu wa Aghrāzuhu, Ahmiyatuhu al-Mu'aāsrah, Istithmāruhu) (pp. 6–24). Jāmi'a Umm al-Qurā, Makkah al-Mukarramah.

Al-Shīrazī, A. I. I. (n.d). Al-Muhaddhab fī Fiqh al-Imām Al-Shāf'aī (n.p.). Bairut: Dār al-Kutub al-'Ilmiyyah (Vol. 2, p. 323).

Al-Tusuli, A. I. (1998). *Al-Bahjah Fi Sharḥ al-Tuḥfah* (1st ed., Vol. 2, p. 369) (M. 'Abdul Qādir Shaḥun, Ed.). Bairut: Dār Al-Kutub Al-'Ilmiyyah.

Al-Tirmidhī, A. M. (1975). Sunan al-Tirmidhī (2nd edn). Taḥqeeq wa T'aleeq: Aḥmad Muḥammad Shākir, etl, Miṣr: Shirkat Maktabah wa Matb'a Muṣtafā al-Yābi (Vol. 3, p. 652).

Arshad, R., Zain, N. M., Urus, S. T., & Chakir, A. (2018). Modelling Maqasid Waqf Performance Measures in Waqf Institutions. *Global Journal Al-Thaqafah, 8*(1), 157–170.

Aziz, A., & 'Ali, J. (2018). A Comparative Study of Waqf Institutions Governance in India and Malaysia. *Intellectual Discourse*, 1229–1246.

Bakar, R., et al. (2019). Corporate Waqf University : A Sustainability Model. *Journal of Emerging Economies and Islamic Research, 7*(1), 24–36.

Cizakca, M. (1998). Awqaf in History and Its Implications for Modern Islamic Economies. *Islamic Economic Studies, 6*(1), 43–70.

Firdaus, M., Rusli, M., & Abideen, A. (2017). A Waqf Concept Applied in Higher Education: An Exploratory Study on the Practice of the IIUM Endowment Fund. *Journal of Islamic Finance, 6*(2), 013–023.

Ibn 'Ābidīn, M. A. (1992). *Raddul Muḥtār 'Alā al-Durrul Mukhtār āshiya Ibn 'Ābidīn* (2nd ed., Vol. 4, pp. 363–364). Bairut: Dār al-Fikr.

Ibn al-Ḥajar, A. (1379). *Fatḥ al-Bārī Sharḥ Ṣaḥīḥ al-Bukhārī* (n.p) (Vol. 5, p. 405). Bairut: Dār al-Mʿarifa.

Ibn Ashur, M. (2004). *Maqasid al-Shariah al-Islamiyah* (Vol. 3, pp. 197–243) (M. al-Habib, Ed.). Qatar.

Ibn Nujaym. (n.d.). *Al-Baḥr Al-Rāiq Sharḥ Kanz Al-Daqāiq* (2nd ed., Vol. 5, p. 219). Cairo: Dār Al-Kitāb Al-Islāmi.

Ibn Qudāmah, A. M. D. (1968a). Al-Mughnī (n.p). Misr: Maktabah al-Qāhira (Vol. 6, pp. 3–4).

Ibn Qudāmah, A. M. D. (1994b). Al-Kāfī fi Fiqh al-Imām Aḥmad (1st edn). Beirut: Dār al-Kutub al-ʿIlmiyyah (Vol. 2, p. 250).

IIUM Endowment Fund. (n.d.). International Islamic University Malaysia. Available online: https://www.iium.edu.my/division/ief. Retrieved on 5 April 2020.

International Fiqh Academy of Jeddah, Fatwa on Cash Waqf. Available online: http://www.fiqhacademy.org.sa/qrarat/15-6htm. Retrieved on 12 June 2020.

Ismail Abdel Mohsin, M. (2013). Financing Through Cash-Waqf: A Revitalization to Finance Different Needs. *International Journal of Islamic and Middle Eastern Finance and Management, 6*(4), 304–321. https://doi.org/10.1108/imefm-08-2013-0094.

Ismail Abdel Mohsin, M. (2014). Corporate waqf from principle to practice a new innovation for islamic finance. Kuala Lumpur: Pearson Malaysia Sdn Bhd.

Kahf, M., & Mohomed, A. N. (2017). Cash Waqf: An Innovative Instrument of Personal Finance in Islamic Banking. *Journal of Islamic Economics, Banking, and Finance, 13*(3), 13–29.

Mahmud, M. W., & Shah, S. S. (2010). Optimization of Philanthropic Waqf: The Need for Maqasid-Based Legislative Strategies. *Shariah Law Reports, 2*, 45–59.

Mālik, B. A. (1994). *Al-Mudawwanah* (1st ed., Vol. 1, p. 343). Bairut: Dār al-Kutub al-ʿIlmiyyah.

Mohammad, M. T. S. H. (2018). Maqāṣid al-Sharīʾah and Waqf: Their Effect on Waqf Law and Economy. *Intellectual Discourse, 26*(2), 1065–1091.

Mohd Thas Thaker, M. A. B. (2018). A Qualitative Inquiry into Cash Waqf Model as a Source of Financing for Micro Enterprises. *ISRA International Journal of Islamic Finance, 10*(1), 19–35. https://doi.org/10.1108/ijif-07-2017-0013.

Mohsin, M. I. A. (2009). *Cash Waqf: A New Financial Product* (1st ed.). Petaling Jaya: Prentice Hall.

Saad, N., Kassim, S., & Hamid, Z. (2016). *Best practices of waqf: Experiences of Malaysia and Saudi Arabia, 2*(2), 57–74.

Saifuddin, F. B., Kadibi, S., Polat, R., Fidan, Y., & Kayadibi, O. (2014, June). The Role of Cash Waqf in Poverty Alleviation: Case of Malaysia. *International Journal of Business, Economics and Law, 4*(1). ISSN: 22891552.

Saiti, B., Salad, A. J., & Bulut, M. (2019). The Role of Cash Waqf in Poverty Reduction: A Multi-country Case Study (pp. 21–34). https://doi.org/10.1007/978-3-030-10907-3_3.

Shahimi, S., Mohd Marzuki, M. U., & Embong, Z. (2013). Potential of Cash Waqf for Poverty Alleviation in Malaysia: A System Dynamics Approach. *Jurnal Ekonomi Malaysia, 47*(2), 149–163.

PART V

How Sukuk Structure May Support SDGs?

CHAPTER 30

Analysis of *Sukuk* Al-*Waqf* Structure for Financing BOT-Based Development Programs

Mustafa Omar Mohammed, Mohamed Cherif El Amri, and Ramadhani Mashaka Shabani

Introduction

Sukuk, also known as the Islamic Bond, is a certificate of ownership of a tangible asset or use of a project, investment or service (AAOIFI 2010). The use of *Sukuk* funding began in the traditional Islamic era when the paper was used as a title document. *Sukuk* financing has a huge effect on the funding of social and economic activities as well as on the self-benefits of its organization. The growth of Islamic finance contributes to the development of new financial instruments. *Waqf* is one of the organizations that secure the benefits of this latest financing instruments by

---

M. O. Mohammed
Department of Economics, International Islamic University Malaysia [IIUM], Gombak, Malaysia

M. C. El Amri (✉) · R. M. Shabani
Department of Islamic Economics and Finance, Istanbul Sabahattin Zaim University, Istanbul, Turkey

© The Author(s), under exclusive license to Springer Nature Switzerland AG 2021
M. M. Billah (eds.), *Islamic Wealth and the SDGs*,
https://doi.org/10.1007/978-3-030-65313-2_30

581

incorporating *Waqf* assets into *Sukuk* financing. Currently, there is an increasing number of *Waqf* projects financed by *Sukuk*. For example, the ZamZam tower *Waqf* project in Mecca financed by *Sukuk* al-Intifa'a worth US$390 million (Kholid et al. 2008); the *Waqf* property development by the Majlis Ugama Islam Singapura (MUIS) financed using Musharakah *Sukuk* worth SGD 35 million (Nagaoka 2016); and the recent *Waqf*-linked *Sukuk* for social investment developed in Indonesia (Dea 2019).

The Islamic ethical wealth industry has been innovative and continues to develop various structures of *Waqf Sukuk*. The main structures prevalent in the market include the equity structure [Mudharabah and Musharakah] such as the Singapore MUIS Musharakah *Sukuk*, the Mecca Usufruct *Sukuk* or *Sukuk* al-Intifa'a, the Indonesian *Waqf*-linked *Sukuk* for social investment. Most of these *Waqf Sukuk* structures have adopted financing based on the principle of Build Operate Transfer (BOT), the focus of the present chapter. In this arrangement, *Waqf* institution moves the *Waqf* property to the financial institution in a limited number of years to build it, operate it to recover its cost plus profit and return the complete project back to the *Waqf* institution. The structure may include several parts and contracts, for example, it may be the *Waqf* institution that leases the property to the second party and the second party that issues *Sukuk* to finance the property. Initially, there were Shari'ah issues raised regarding *Waqf Sukuk* financing based on the principle of BOT. For example, the objective of *Waqf*'s property is to provide perpetual benefits to society and transferring or leasing such *Waqf*'s property leads to holding up the benefits from society. Nevertheless, Kahf (1999) argues that pledging or leasing of such property is permissible if the property and its usufruct or income return to the beneficiary after a certain period so that the beneficiary continues to receive such benefits perpetually.

Overview of *Waqf*

Waqf is an Arabic word that means a prohibition, containment, or retention. In Islam, *Waqf* refers to the activities of holding and saving certain property for the benefit of benevolence. The property shall not be disposed of or used for any purpose other than the intended purpose (Kahf 1992). *Waqf* is suitable for the development of a country in a variety of areas, such as religious, socioeconomic, and cultural development. Throughout Islamic history, *Waqf* programs have been successful in providing social goods such as education and health; public goods that include roads, bridges, utilities (water and sanitation); religious services that include building and maintenance of mosques and, graveyards; civil services in terms of helping the poor and the needy; creating employment in sectors such as agricultural and other industrial sectors (Sadeq 2002). *Waqf* projects expanded during the Ummayad and Abbasid eras to cover almost all social services beyond building of mosques, houses, and wells. Meanwhile during the Ottoman Caliphate, the entire health, education, and welfare budget was funded from *Waqf* (Çizakça 2000). Furthermore, the estimated population of 700,000, living in Istanbul were fed on daily basis by charitable complexes established under the *Waqf* system (Barkan and Ayyerdi 1970).

Waqf also played significant role in the development of Islamic cities. There were constructions and development of bakeries, grinders, shops, market places, religious, cultural and social institutions, libraries, hospitals, bath (*hamam*), roads, water and sanitation, among others. Prominent cities developed by *Waqf* were Fustat and Cairo in Egypt and Baghdad (Barkan and Ayverdi 1970) and other Islamic cities such as Istanbul, Bursa, and Edirne in Turkey were entirely financed from *Waqf* (Öztürk, 1995). Several land projects were also funded from *Waqf*. The economically productive land in the Ottoman Caliphate and later three-quarter of arable land in modern Turkey was controlled by *Waqf* institutions (Saduman and Aysun 2009). Beside land properties, Cash *Waqf* was also used for developing *Waqf* projects. According to (Çizakça 2000), healthcare, education, and welfare activities during the Ottoman Caliphate were funded from cash *Waqf*. To conclude on the role of *Waqf* toward the socioeconomic development of Muslim societies, Yediyildiz (1996) states:

Thanks to the *Waqfs* that flourished during the Ottoman Chaliphate, a person would have been born in a *Waqf* house, sleep in a *Waqf* cradle, eat and drink from *Waqf* properties, read *Waqf* books, taught in a *Waqf* school, received his salary from a *Waqf* administration, and when he dies, he is placed in a *Waqf* coffin and buried in a *Waqf* cemetery. In short, it was possible to meet all one's needs through goods and services mobilized by *Waqf* institution.

Overview of *Sukuk*

Sukuk in the plural "Sakk" means the certificate or document of the act. In financial terms, *Sukuk* is the security that is backed by the asset (Wijnbergen and Zaheer 2013)*Sukuk*, also known as the Islamic Bond, is a certificate of ownership of a tangible asset or use of a project, investment, or service (AAOIFI 2010). Based on the International Islamic Financial Market (IIFM) *Sukuk* Annual Report 2019, global *Sukuk* issuances during the year 2018 stood at USD 123.2 billion, which is a modest increase of 5.5% over 2017 primary market *Sukuk* issuances of USD 116.7 billion. The report also revealed that 90.44% of the USD 443.78 billion *Sukuk* outstanding globally are issued from few well-established markets namely Malaysia, Saudi Arabia, UAE, Indonesia, and Bahrain while other countries like Turkey, Pakistan, Qatar, Oman, and regions such as Africa in particular are likely to gradually increase their market share in the coming years.

The origin and significance of *Sukuk* are shown from the traditional Islamic era (700–1300AD) in which financial and commercial activities, such as trade, were carried out using paper as a means of recognition of the title (Karan et al. 2016). Those papers were issued following Surah Al-Baqarah (2:282) recommending the need to write down the contract. *Sukuk* financing has a significant impact on the financing of social and economic activities as well as on the self-benefits of its structure (Abdulkareem et al. 2019; Fathurahman and Fitriati 2013; Zolfaghari 2017).

The difference between the Islamic Bond and the conventional bond is that the *Sukuk* is the title of the asset and the conventional bond is the title of the debt to enable it to be traded on the secondary market. For *Sukuk* to be negotiable on the secondary market, interest on the actual asset should be borne more than liabilities or obligations. Some scholars suggest that the *Sukuk* asset structure can take up to 33% of the face value, while others propose that 51 and 70% of the underlying asset be tangible assets (Latham & Watkins 2014). *Sukuk* is issued by the originator and purchased by investors structured in different contacts that can be one or multiple contacts in compliance of Shari'ah which may include the sale and repurchase, lease, and partnership (Lewandowski et al. 2015). Although *Sukuk* has largely been issued by the Islamic Banking and finance industry, there are increasing issuance by Islamic social finance institutions, especially *Waqf*.

Before the evolution of *Waqf Sukuk*, there were five traditional models of financing of *Waqf* property. As explained by Kahf (1998), *Waqf* was financed by increasing the *Waqf* principle by adding new *Waqf*, Istibdal with higher usufructuary assets, borrowing on *Waqf* and repaying *Waqf* net revenue, al-Hukr and lease with dual payment. Permission to use the *Waqf* property to issue *Sukuk* should be based on the consensus of scholars on the intent. For example, if the *Waqf* institution issues Musharakah *Sukuk*, it is confusing, because if it is to be real Musharakah, it means that the title of the *Waqf* property will be in a partnership that is contrary to the nature of the *Waqf* (Mohammad Tahir Sabit 2005). The general rule of Shari'ah does not permit the property of *Waqf* to be sold, disposed, gifted, inherited, or used differently from what is decreed by the founder of the *Waqf* (Kahf 2016). However, upon the approval of the court, when it has determined that the *Waqf* property is not productive, it may be exchanged with a productive one in the process known as Istibdal (Laldin et al. 2013).

Waqf Sukuk is the integration of a contract based on *Sukuk* and *Waqf*. In this contract, *Waqf* institutions issue to investors commercial certificate of equal monetary value (Ramli 2014). The structure of *Waqf Sukuk* is not different from that of *Sukuk* for other investments, except for the objectives of their issuance. The objectives of the *Waqf Sukuk* are motivated by a desire for eternal life and the blessings of Allah to serve the public interest, while in the case of *Sukuk* for other investments, an investor intend to generate profits from the project (Umar and Aliyu 2019). From the Shari'ah perspective, the objectives of the *Waqf* are largely charitable rather than commercial. Whenever there is a profit, the profit is exempt from tax and should be channeled for the sake of public interest (Ismal et al. 2015). Below is a case of *Waqf Sukuk*.

Sukuk *Al-Musharakah: Majlis Ugama Islam Singapura (MUIS)*

The Majlis Ugama Islam Singapura (MUIS) is the institution in Singapore which is responsible for the religious affair of Muslim community such as the halal certification, managing zakah, *Waqf*, hajj, mosques, and madrasah. For *Waqf*, MUIS is responsible for the management of *Waqf* funds, distribution of Waqf income, upgrading of *Waqf* properties, and promoting the creation of new waqf. MUIS has come up with several innovative ways to develop *Waqf* assets and enhance their income in a Shari'ah-compliant manner. MUIS issued *Sukuk* al-Musharakah based in two tranches. The first portion was SDG25 million for the purchase of a building at 11 Beach Road and the second tranche was the raising of USD35 million for the development project at Bencoolen Street.

Musharakah Sukuk *Structure for 11 Beach Road*
This *Sukuk* was issued in 2001 on the basis of Musharakah or partnership between MUIS and the investor for the purchase and renovation of a 6-storey commercial property. The capitalization was made through SPV1 (Fusion Pte Ltd) which raised SGD 34 million. Out of this, SGD 9 million was funded from *Waqf* Fund obtained from the disposal of 43 *Waqf* properties that were unproductive. The fund was merged into the project. The remaining SGD25 million was funded by the investors. The profit-sharing ratio was 26.5% for the *Waqf* institution and 73.5% for the investors (Nagaoka 2016). Fusion Pte Ltd rented the property to SPV2 (Freshmill Pte Ltd) which is a subsidiary and fully owned by MUIS. Freshmill promised to manage the property and guarantee the rental income of SDG 1,190,000 p.a. paid semi-annually up to 2006 (Abdullah and Saiti 2016). This means that the *Sukuk* investors received SGD 875,000 and MUIS received SGD 315,000 per annum.

Musharakah Sukuk *Structure for Bencoolen Street*
The area in Bencoolen Street was very potential for commercial activities. MUIS decided to develop the land known as Lot 19 Town Division owned by the merchant named Shaikh Ali B Omar Aljunied. The project was 104 apartments, 6 storeys, and mosque. The estimated cost was SDG 39.7 million (Hasan 2014). Warees contributed SDG1,000 and *Waqf* Fund amounted to SGD 4,719,000 (comprising SGD 4,200,000 in property and SGD 519,000 in cash) both owned by MUIS and *Sukuk* Musharakah was issued by MUIS to raise SGD 35 million from *Sukuk* Investors (Abdullah and Saiti 2016). The profit-sharing ratio between MUIS and *Sukuk* investors was 11.88 and 88.12%, respectively. A leasing agreement followed between the Special Purpose Vehicle (SPV) and Ascott International Pte. Ltd with the agreement of 10 years. After the renovation of the land, the annual profit increased to $19,000 per year to gross income level of $5.3 million in 2006. The *Waqf* institution took possession of the commercial unit and mosque after completion. MUIS retained the income generated from the mosque and the commercial unit equivalent to 11.88%, and part of the apartment was vested to Warees.

Both financings used *Sukuk* al-Musharakah. This structure is based on the share of ownership of the asset. The Hanbali school define Musharakah as sharing the rights to collect benefits from or to deal in the properties of the partnership (Al-Zuhayli 2001). From this definition, it is obvious that the structure of the financing might be suitable but may not be suitable for BOT-based structure. This is because the BOT based contract gives the right to both parties on the property owned. Therefore, they will share the ownership of the property. Such arrangement contradicts the conditions of *Waqf* property which require the asset not to be owned, sold, transferred, or inherited (Kahf 2016). There are some arguments that the beneficiaries of *Waqf* property are entitled to receive continuous benefits from the property all the time when the property exists. Putting the property under the *Sukuk* financing will hold the benefit because during this time the beneficiaries will be cut off to receive any benefit. Hasan (2014) argued that during the development of *Waqf* property if the benefit will be put on hold then the *Waqf* institution should provide the means that the beneficiaries will continue receiving their benefits. Kahf (1999) argues that scholars consider the difference between the current *Waqf* institution and the Charitable Institution (Sadaqa). If *Waqf* pledges the income or usufruct of the asset for a specific time and after that, the asset, usufruct, and income return back to the owners then *Sukuk* al Musharakah will be suitable for financing *Waqf* property, though it may not be suitable for BOT-based financing.

Prior to a discussion on *Waqf Sukuk* for financing BOT-based *Waqf* programs or projects, it is desirable to facilitate the discussion by providing an overview of BOT. Build Operate Transfer (BOT) is the process of transferring ownership of the project from the government or project company to the private sector to return the project to the government or project company upon maturity or specified period (Markom et al. 2012). This is typical of most private sector investment in public infrastructure. The project is transferred to the private sector that builds, operates, and transfers it to the project company (Ozdoganm and Birgonul 2010). The advantage of BOT is that the project company reduces risk and does not incur liabilities in the balance sheet beyond the cash flow of the project (Salman et al. 2007). Islamic financing in BOT is a new type of financing based on the Shari'ah and used to fulfill the need for developing modern infrastructure (Markom et al. 2012). The contracts used to finance BOT are the same as those common in Muamalat, such as Mudarabah, Murabahah, BBA, Ijara, Musharakah, Intifa, Hybrid *Sukuk*

588   M. O. MOHAMMED ET AL.

(Hasan 2014; Lahsen 2018). Below is a case of Ijarah *Sukuk* used to finance BOT-based project.

Sukuk *Al-Ijarah Lebuhraya Kemuning-Shah Alam (LKSA)*

The Lebuhraya Kemuning–Shah Alam (LKSA), is 28.7 km (17.8 mi) highway in Malaysia which is also known as Bulatan Darul Ehsan Interchange. The construction began in 2007 and took 24 months to construct. It was completed in the middle of 2010. The expressway was opened to traffic on May 18, 2010. The financing was structured using *Sukuk Ijarah* based on BOT project which utilizes the Islamic financing principles to form the partnership between the originator and the investor until the completion and transfer of the project back to the originator. While operating on behalf of the originator, Projek Lintasan Shah Alam Sdn. Bhd. (PLSA) invited other investors, *Sukuk Ijarah* holders (the lessors) to participate in the construction and development of the Project (Markom et al. 2012). The project succeeded under the Ijarah *Sukuk* contract structure. The lessee pays rent and uses the part of proceeds to cover his cost.

Waqf has adopted the BOT framework for financing its projects through the use of *Sukuk* financing and benefits from risk, cost, and opportunity (*Revital. Waqf Socio-Economic Dev. Vol. I* 2019).

WAQF *SUKUK* STRUCTURE AND BOT-BASED PROJECTS

The development of Islamic finance fosters the development of new financing instruments. In the last two decade *Sukuk* has become an important financing instrument and is structured in different ways. *Sukuk* for financing BOT-based project has become among the viable models because it helps to reduce the risk and uncertainty of the developer. *Waqf* institutions are among those institutions which have adopted this model to finance what is called *Waqf Sukuk* for financing BOT-based projects. This is in addition to other non-BOT-based projects that are financed by *Waqf Sukuk* as discussed previously. Therefore, there are currently several projects financed BOT-based and non-BOT projects that are financed by *Waqf Sukuk*. Below are some selected cases.

Sukuk *Al-Intifa'a: ZamZam Tower*

Sukuk al-Intifa'a is a document of ownership of usufructs from leased property or asset over time (Rafay et al. 2017). *Sukuk* al-Intifa'a is not much different from the Ijarah *Sukuk*. It is an extension of Ijarah *Sukuk* based on time-sharing on segment ownership of leased property. In Saudia Arabia, this *Sukuk* was used instead of normal Ijarah *Sukuk* due to the reason that the law of Saudia Arabia does not allow foreigners to own real estate in the holy cities of Makkah and Madinah (Lahsasna et al. 2018). The *Sukuk* was issued to build the apartment and the high tower named ZamZam Tower on the land of King Abdul Aziz *Waqf* (KAAW) near to the Masjid Al-Haram in Makkah, Saudi Arabia.

The *Sukuk* was structured under the forward lease contract *(Ijarah Mawsufah fi dhimma)* (Hasan 2014). The *Waqf* land of KAAW was leased to Binladin Group under the concept of BOT. The Binladin Group was required to build the apartments shops and tower and receive payment from leasing. The Binladin Group then enter into another contract with Munshaat Real Estate Projects KSC from Kuwait. The Munshaat Real Estate Projects KSC required to construct such project and operate it and transfer back to Binladin Group after 28 years. To be able to finance this project, Munshaat Real Estate Projects KSC issued *Sukuk* al-Intifa'a with the value of US$390 million for 24 years. The *Sukuk* was time-sharing based and the usufruct was divided into weekly basis (Kholid et al. 2008). The *Sukuk* holder was given the right to sell, inherit, grant, and invest the *Sukuk* (Lahsasna et al. 2018).The *Sukuk* was structured as follows:

- KAAW leased the land to Binladin Group for 28 years
- Binladin Group subleased the land to Munshaat Real Estate Projects KSC
- Munshaat Real Estate Projects KSC issued *Sukuk* al-Intifa'a for 24 years valued at US$390 million
- The *Sukuk* holder bought the usufruct of the asset based on time-sharing and paid the forward lease rental which paid to Munshaat Real Estate Projects KSC to be used for the construction cost
- Munshaat Real Estate Projects KSC paid the lease of the land to KAAW.
- Binladin Group transferred the project to KAAW after 28 years.

The project of the seven towers with the highest tower of Royal Clock that stood 601 m above the ground was started in 2004 and completed in 2012. The project is helpful for the tourists and those who are visiting the holy cities of Makkah and Madinah. The financing shows success and there is no Shari'ah contradiction between the objectives of the *Waqf* institution, and the investors. The contract structured on *Sukuk* al-Intifa'a allows sharing of ownership of usufruct, there are no sales of the actual asset. Among conditions of *Waqf* property is the prohibition of selling (Markom et al. 2012). *Sukuk* al-Intifa'a becomes suitable for *Waqf* financing based on BOT, although another reason for the success of using this type of *Sukuk* is the fact that Saudia Arabia do not allow ownership of land to the foreigners (Hasan 2014).

CASH *WAQF* LINKED *SUKUK* STRUCTURE

In addition to *Sukuk* al-Intifa'a, which has suitable structure for financing *Waqf* BOT-based project, another *Sukuk* structure that recently evolved looks promising. The Cash *Waqf* linked *Sukuk*, which is developed in Indonesia, is a form of social investment. In this structure, endowments of money are collected by the *Waqf* Board as Nazhir and deposited to the bank after consultation from the Shari'ah advisory board (Dea 2019). The structure of *Waqf*-linked *Sukuk* is similar to project-based *Sukuk* which aimed at the real development of society. This *Sukuk* is utilized to enhance interaction between the real sectors and financial sectors (Ismal et al. 2015). The structure of this *Sukuk* is the idea of Indonesia government. It encourages economic growth reflected in GDP with emphasis on the real sector. The issuance of *Sukuk* is developed from the *Waqf* asset whether it is productive or non-productive. The asset can be used for commercial purpose, i.e., developing the asset or used as the underlying asset for originating *Sukuk*. The government uses the results of the issuance of the *Sukuk* to finance the state budget, including to finance the construction of public service such as infrastructure development on the *Waqf* land, educational institutions, and helping projects relating to the *Waqf* objective. The structure involves various parties including government sector, non-government sectors and investors. The following are the salient steps in the structure, which is also shown in Fig. 30.1.

- The National *Waqf* board (3) and Ministry of finance (2) are responsible for identifying the infrastructure that can be developed

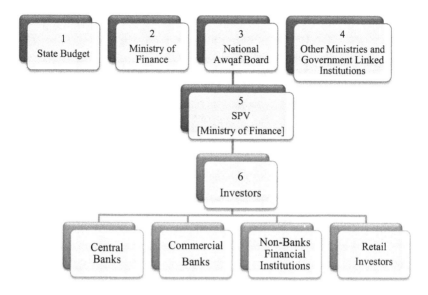

Fig. 30.1 Cash *Waqf* linked *Sukuk* structure (*Source* Authors' illustration)

using *Waqf* asset. In cooperation with the ministry of finance, other ministries (4) identify projects that are related to the *Waqf* asset that conform to their development targets.
- The Ministry of Finance establishes the SPV (5) which fulfills the Shari'ah-compliant requirement necessary for the issuance of the *Sukuk*.
- The investors (6) which comprise the central bank, commercial banks, non-bank financial institutions (NBFIs), and retail investors are attracted to invest in the Cash *Waqf Sukuk*.

This structure is proposed in Indonesia, to combine 3 sectors: Islamic capital market, National Awqaf board, and government sectors. Ismal et al. (2015) explained how the different contracting parties can benefit from the *Sukuk* structure shown in Fig. 30.1. Investors are expected to benefit from the returns generated by the projects the *Sukuk* is funding. Meanwhile the Cash *Waqf* linked *Sukuk* are deemed as liquid instruments, because of their sovereign class, for the banks, and the central bank may use the *Sukuk* as a monetary tool or retrench the assets through securitization process using the *Sukuk* inventory as the underlying assets. Furthermore, Islamic banks and non-bank financial institutions would use the acquired *Sukuk* for liquidity management purposes (e.g., as a secondary reserve requirement) in the inter-Islamic bank money market or with other financial institutions for the same liquidity reasons (Ismal et al. 2015).The structure seems interesting and sets direction for more innovations in *Waqf Sukuk*. The impact and benefits are diversified and the structure is incorporated into the development strategies of various ministries in the government. The investor base is also diversified.

Notwithstanding these merits of the structure, few pertinent questions arise to the extent of *Waqf* objectives that this structure has achieved. Secondly, what are the intentions or motives of the different contracting parties and how are they related to *Waqf*? For example as explained by Ismal et al. (2015) the central bank will use the *Sukuk* as policy instrument, and the commercial banks will use them for liquidity management. How then do these objectives relate to the objectives of *Waqf*? Thirdly, the inclusion of SPV in the *Sukuk* structure shows that the over-riding concern is investment. There is therefore a need for further research or at least explanation to respond to some of these queries. Otherwise it is a misnormer to call it *Waqf Sukuk* when the structure is still predominantly the conventional *Sukuk* structure. The main difference is that such *Sukuk* is used for the purpose of developing *Waqf* properties. In that case, any other Shari'ah compliant *Sukuk* can fulfill the requirement without the need of calling it *Waqf Sukuk*. Most of the current structure used for *Waqf* project are still the normal *Sukuk* and according to Chik (2012), there are six fundamentals of *Sukuk* structure.

- Funds raised must be used for Shari'ah-compliant (halal) activities.
- Fundraised may be used to finance needed tangible assets.
- Income received by *Sukuk* holders (investors) must be derived from the cash flows generated by the underlying.
- *Sukuk* holders have a right to the ownership of the underlying asset and its cash flows.
- Clear and transparent specification of rights and obligations of all parties to the transaction, the originator (customer) and *Sukuk* holders.
- No fixity in returns.

Conclusion

Waqf institutions have shown good track records in history in financing *Waqf* related projects. These projects covered various sectors related to religious, social and economic development of Muslim societies. The projects included mosques, graveyards, educational institutions, libraries, health care centers, hospitals, roads, parks, shops and animal and bird feeding places, among others. The modes of financing evolved over time with the needs of the society. In the past these modes included direct financing, leasing, and Istibdal. Most projects funded through *Waqf* showed successful completion without facing the problem of deficiency in fund. This was made possible due to generous contributions from the public who clearly understood that objectives of the *Waqf* institution are to serve public interests rather than make profits.

Today, the modes of financing *Waqf* projects include *Waqf Sukuk*. The various structures of *Waqf Sukuk* are used to fund several construction projects, infrastructures, and development projects. They are used in both the old and new projects. *Waqf Sukuk* structures vary in terms of contracts such as Mudarabah, Musharakah, Ijarah, and Intifa'a. They also vary in relation to BOT-based financing and non-BOT-based. A critical review of the literature shows that most of these *Waqf Sukuk* structures are basically the normal conventional *Sukuk* structures that are also used to finance other projects that are not related to *Waqf*. Yet some of them vary to the extent to which they achieve *Waqf* objectives. For example, the *Sukuk* al-Itifa'a used to fund the ZamZam tower is closer to the objectives of *Waqf* in terms of fulfilling the requirement of ownership. On the other hand, the structure of the Cash *Waqf* linked *Sukuk* introduced in Indonesia seem have larger socioeconomic benefits, which are in line with *Waqf* objectives, yet there are also over-riding commercial objectives which makes the intentions of the contracting parties ambiqious.

The Way Forward for New *Waqf Sukuk* Structure

Integrating the structure of *Sukuk* and the objective of *Waqf*, the existing structure which is also used to finance other projects seems to be successful in the objectives of *Waqf* institution. Based on the discussion above, it is obvious that not all *Sukuk* structures are suitable for *Waqf* financing. For example, the Mudarabah or Musharakah *Sukuk* used to finance *Waqf* projects have issues related to fulfilling the conditions of the ownership of the *Waqf* properties. Mudarabah *Sukuk* requires rab al-Maal and Mudarib to agree on sharing profit (Al-Zuhayli 2001). In contrast to such arrangement, the requirement of the *Waqf* property is to contribute social good for the welfare of the society and not for making a profit. Similarly, Musharakah *Sukuk* requires the contracting parties to contribute capital, have control over the capital and property under the partnership and share profit and loss (Saleem 2013). But the Ownership of *Waqf* property is limited to the Awqaf institution and can not be for sale, disposal, gift, inheritance or used differently as decreed by the founder of the *Waqf* (Kahf 2016). So this also makes the Musharakah *Sukuk* not ideal for financing *Waqf* projects.

Sukuk al-Intifa'a used to finance the ZamZam Tower project seems to be suitable in financing *Waqf* projects. The financing shows success and there is no Shari'ah contradiction between the objectives of the *Waqf* institution and the investors. The structure allows sharing of ownership of usufruct, there are no sales of the actual asset. Among conditions of *Waqf* property is the prohibition of selling (Markom et al. 2012). Meanwhile, as discussed earlier, the structure of the Cash *Waqf* linked *Sukuk* have larger socioeconomic benefits, which are in line with *Waqf* objectives, were it not for the over-riding commercial objectives the structure embodies.

What is the way forward? One interesting proposition that could drastically change the structure and align the intention of the investors to the objectives of *Waqf* is if they forego their profit portion in the project, and surrender it as charity for social good because *Waqf* is not a profit-making venture. As a start, it may be a good idea to integrate the structure of *Sukuk* al-Intifa'a with the structure of Cash *Waqf* linked *Sukuk*. The new *Sukuk* could still use the various government ministries in their structure. The originator and the investors will share the ownership of usufruct of the projects. There will not be the sharing of the actual asset. This will ensure the true objective of Awqaf properties to maintain the ownership of the actual asset. Therefore, the main components of the structure would consist of the originator, the SPV, the contracts and the investors, as follows:

- **Originator**: can comprise various government ministries and *Waqf* board who would identify the *Waqf* assets to be developed.
- **SPV**: can be determined and appointed from the ministries [preferably Ministry of Finance] or other efficient external body. The SPV would be responsible for issuing the *Sukuk* and mobilizing the funds

required for the project. Otherwise a trustee can be appointed for the task of managing the fund.

- **Contracts**: the underlying contracts will include Ijarah, al-Intifa'a which will enable the parties to share the usufruct of the project on a time basis, and Sadaqah for the investors to forego a portion of their profit for the sake of *Waqf*
- **Investors**: This will comprise mainly investors who fully understand the objectives of *Waqf*. The investors would use the usufruct or sublease of the asset, and surrender their profit as Sadaqah.

REFERENCES

AAOIFI. (2010). *Accounting and Auditing Organization for Islamic Financial Institutions.*

Abdulkareem, I. A., Sadad, M., & Mahmud, B. (2019). Infrastructure Project Financing Through Sukuk as an Alternative to Conventional Bond Financing. *Journal of Management and Operation Research, 1*(19), 1.

Abdullah, A., & Saiti, B. (2016). *A Re-Examination of Musharakah Bonds and Waqf Development: The Case of Singapore, 4878,* 541–562.

Al-Zuhayli, W. (2001). *Financial Transactions in Islamic Jurisprudence* (Vol. 1). Dar Al-Fikr, Damascus.

Barkan, Ö. L., & Ayverdi, E. H. (1970). *İstanbul Vakıfları Tahrir Defteri 953 Tarihli. Istanbul Fetih Cemiyeti Yayini,* Istanbul Enstitusu Dergisi. Retrieved from https://www.nadirkitap.com/istanbul-vakiflari-tahrir-defteri-953-1546-tarihli-barkan-omer-lutfi-ekrem-hakki-ayverdi-kitap18209747.html

Chik, M. N. (2012). *Sukuk:* (pp. 1–31). Central Bank of Sri Shariah Guidelines for Islamic BondsLanka: Centre for Banking Studies.

Çizakça, M. (2000). *A History of Philanthropic Foundations: The Islamic World from the Seventh Century to the Present.* Istanbul: Boğaziçi University Press.

Dea, M. N. (2019, November). Cash Waqf Linked Sukuk.

Fathurahman, H., & Fitriati, R. (2013). Comparative Analysis of Return on Sukuk and Conventional Bonds. *American Journal of Economics, 3*(3), 159–163. https://doi.org/10.5923/j.economics.20130303.05.

Hasan, S. M. (2014). Waqf Development Through Sukuk. *Global Islamic Economics Magazine,* 5. https://doi.org/10.1039/c5tc03776j.

Ismal, R., Muljawan, D., Chalid, M. R., Kashoogie, J., & Sastrosuwito, S. (2015). *Awqaf Linked Sukuk to Support the Economic Development.* Occasional Paper, 1–29.

Kahf, M. (n.d.). *Fiqhi Issues in the Revival of Awqaf.*

Kahf, M. (1992). *Waqf and Is Sociopolitical Aspects by Monzer Kahf.* Irti.

Kahf, M. (1998). *Financing Development of Awqaf Properties*. International Conference on Awqaf and Economic Development, Kuala Lumpur, 1–45.

Kahf, M. (1999, October). Towards the revival of awqaf: A few fiqhi issues to reconsider. In *Harvard forum on Islamic finance and Economics* (Vol. 1). New York, NY: Harvard University.

Kahf, M. (2016). Waqf: a Quick Overview, 2.

Karan, M. B., Arslan-ayaydin, Ö., & Dorsman, A. (2016). *Energy and Finance: Sustainability in the Energy Industry*. Cham: Springer.

Kholid, M., Sukmana, R., & Hassan, K. (2008). Waqf Through Sukuk Al-Intifa'a: A Proposed Generic Model. *Mbri.Ac.Ir*, 1–16.

Lahsasna, A., Ahmad, R., & Hassan, M. K. (2018). *Forward in Islamic Capital: Structure and Governing Rules*. London: Palgrave Macmillan.

Lahsen, O. (2018). *Sukuk-waqf: The Islamic Solution for Public Finance Deficits* (9). https://doi.org/10.13135/2421-2172/2413.

Laldin, A. M., Khir, M. F. A., Bouheraoua, S., Ansary, R., Ali, M. M., & Mustafa, M. M. (2013). *Islamic Legal Maxims and Their Application in Islamic Finance. First publication 2013* (First). International Shari'ah Research Academy For Islamic Finance (ISRA).

Latham & Watkins. (2014). *The Sukuk Handbook*.

Lewandowski, C. M., Johnson, H. T., Chatfield, M., Parker, R. H., Code, C., Sciences, M., et al. (2015). *Journal of Islamic Accounting and Business Research*. Financial Accounting Standards Board—FASB, *39*(Acc 6810), 154–157. https://doi.org/10.1017/CBO9781107415324.004.

Markom, R., Ali, E. R. A. E., & Hasan, A. (2012). The Current Practices of Islamic Build Operate Transfer (BOT) Financing Contracts: A Legal Analysis. *Pertanika Journal of Social Science and Humanities*, *20*(SPEC. ISS.), 73–85.

Mohammad Tahir Sabit, M. (2005). Innovative Modes of Financing the Development of Waqf Property. *National Wakaf Convention*, 1–29.

Nagaoka, S. (2016). Revitalization of Waqf in Singapore: Regional Path Dependency of the New Horizons in Islamic Economics. *Kyoto Bulletin of Islamic Area Studies*, *9*. Retrieved from www.muis.gov.sg.

Ozdoganm, I. D., & Birgonul, M. T. (2010). *A Decision Support Framework for Project Sponsors in the Planning Stage of Build-Operate-Transfer (BOT) Projects a Decision Support Framework for Project Sponsors in the Planning Stage of Build-Operate-Transfer (BOT) Projects*, 6193. https://doi.org/10.1080/014461900370708.

Öztürk, N. (1995). Türk Yenileşme Tarihi Çerçevesinde Vakıf Müessesesi. *Türkiye Diyanet Vakfı Yayınları*. Ankara.

Rafay, A., Sadiq, R., & Ajmal, M. (2017). Uniform Framework for Sukuk al-Ijarah—A Proposed Model for All Madhahib. *Journal of Islamic Accounting and Business Research*, *8*(4), 420–454. https://doi.org/10.1108/JIABR-09-2015-0042.

Ramli, H. (2014). Furas Tamwil Al-waqf Al-jaza'iri Bil-i'timad ala Sukuk Al-waqfiya. In *Product and Innovation by Financial Engineering Between Conventional Finance and Islamic Finance*.

Revitalization of Waqf for Socio-Economic Development, Volume I. (2019). *Revitalization of Waqf for Socio-Economic Development, Volume I*. Springer International Publishing. https://doi.org/10.1007/978-3-030-18445-2.

Sadeq, A. M. (2002). Waqf, Perpetual Charity and Poverty Alleviation. *International Journal of Social Economics, 29*(1/2), 135–151. https://doi.org/10.1108/03068290210413038.

Saduman, S., & Aysun, E. E. (2009). The Socio-Economic Role of Waqf System in the Muslim-Ottoman Cities' Formation and Evolution. *Trakia Journal of Sciences, 7*(2), 272–275. Retrieved from http://www.uni-sz.bg,

Saleem, M. Y. (2013). *Islamic Commercial Law*. Wiley, Singapore Pte. Ltd., 1 Fusionopolis Walk, #07–01, Solaris South Tower, Singapore 138628.

Salman, A. F. M., Skibniewski, M. J., Asce, M., & Basha, I. (2007, January). *BOT Viability Model for Large-Scale Infrastructure Projects*, 50–63.

Umar, A., & Aliyu, S. (2019). Sukuk: A Veritable Tool for Effective Waqf Fund Management in Nigeria. *Iqtishadia, 12*(1), 1. https://doi.org/10.21043/iqtishadia.v12i1.4618.

Wijnbergen, S., & Zaheer, S. (2013). Sukuk Defaults: On Distress Resolution in Islamic Finance. *SSRN Electronic Journal*. https://doi.org/10.2139/ssrn.2293938.

Yediyildiz, B. (1996). Place of the Waqf in Turkish Cultural System. In *Habitat II*. Istanbul. Retrieved from http://yunus.hacettepe.edu.tr/~yyildiz/placeofthewaqf.htm.

Zolfaghari, P. (2017). An Introduction to Islamic Securities (Sukuk), *2*, 1–42. https://doi.org/10.1109/68.841264.

CHAPTER 31

Sukuk and SDG-9 "Industry, Innovation and Infrastructure" in Sub-Saharan Africa: Achievements, Challenges and Opportunities

Abubakar Jamilu Baita and Hassan Hassan Suleiman

INTRODUCTION

The Sustainable Development Goals (SDGs) are the ambitious blueprint sustainable development agenda for the world set in 2015 and committed to by the United Nations General Assembly and 193 governments. The global development agenda—the successor of the Millennium Development Goals (Mdgs)—consists of 17 interrelated mutually supportive and inclusive goals as well as 169 underlying targets. The 2030 agenda envisage a better and more sustainable future for all by making the world's environments, economies, and societies a better place by the year 2030.

A. J. Baita (✉)
Department of Economics, Yusuf Maitama Sule University, Kano, Nigeria

H. H. Suleiman
Securities & Exchange Commission, Abuja, Nigeria

© The Author(s), under exclusive license to Springer Nature   599
Switzerland AG 2021
M. M. Billah (eds.), *Islamic Wealth and the SDGs*,
https://doi.org/10.1007/978-3-030-65313-2_31

A report by UNDOCO[1] and Dag Hammarskjold (2018, p. 3) shows that developing economies require $2.5 trillion annually to close the financing gap in order to attain SDGs. To increase the source of funds, the report called for innovative financing. Another report by SDG Centre for Africa (2019, p. 13) finds that Africa faces a funding gap of about 10–15% of GDP in financing "...*education, health, water, energy and road infrastructure.*" Its estimated annual deficit for financing SDGs is put between $500 billion and $1.2 trillion. Moreover, the region has not witnessed significant progress in innovative financial options for sourcing funds for development.

Sustainable Development Goal nine (SDG-9) is one of the 17 UN SDGs entitled "Industry, Innovation and Infrastructure." It aims to stimulate inclusive and sustainable industrialization, nurture innovation and build resilient infrastructure. Industry, innovation, and infrastructure are purported to promote welfare and output growth. SDG Centre for Africa (2019, p. 15) report that Africa performs poorly in realizing SDG-9.

Industry is central to efforts to promote sustainable output growth and enhancing the socio-economic well-being of countries. African Development Bank [AfDB] (2018, p. 64) believes that though inadequate "productive" infrastructure significantly hampers the pace of industrialization, the region must promote industrialization for sustainable and inclusive growth. World Bank (2020) report on SDGs reveals that manufacturing value added (MVA) as percent of GDP in 2017 was 10.25% in sub-Saharan Africa [SSA] compared to world average of 15.59%. This demonstrates the low level of industrial development in the SSA, thus requiring significant expenditures on industry to actualize SDG-9.

In the same vein, a strong innovation ecosystem is purported to be a key driver of output contribution. Innovation enhances economic productivity and investing in human capital will play a vital role in the next decade (World Economic Forum 2019). Xiong et al. (2020) finds that consistent growth rate of R&D activity is significantly linked to improved GDP growth and thus policy makers believe that innovation will drive consistent and sustainable economic growth in the future.

Infrastructure is particularly important to SDG-9. Quality infrastructure is pivotal in implementing SDGs as it supports economic growth.

---

[1] UN DOCO stands for United Nations Development Operations Coordination Office.

That is why World Bank Group (2017a) explains that adequate infrastructure is a leeway to economic development. To World Bank (2010, p. 1), infrastructure has contributed to over half of improved growth performance in Africa and it could potentially drive future growth in the region. However, Biancone and Radwan (2018) observe that countries across the globe continue to be challenged by deficits in infrastructure. Essentially, government has been the major financier of infrastructure. However, government's effort to finance the sector has been constrained by large deficits in budget and rising public debt (Ahmed et al. 2015, p. 28; COMCEC 2019, p. 1). In fact, reliance on public budgets to finance the infrastructure is no longer sustainable (Biancone and Radwan 2018).

In this connection, Africa faces inadequate infrastructure despite its enormous potentialities for realizing sustainable and all-inclusive growth. Though considerable success has been recorded in providing finance for infrastructure in the region, large-scale infrastructure development has not yet materialized (Global Infrastructure Hub 2018, p. 3). Africa requires infrastructure investment of US$184.03 billion in 2019 and US$190.1 billion in 2020. It has to close infrastructure deficits of US$47.07 and US$49.3 billion in 2019 and 2020, respectively (Global Infrastructure Hub 2020). In a different version, AfDB (2018, p. 64) estimates that Africa should make annual investment of $130–$170 billion in infrastructure to plug its funding gap of about $67.6–$107.5 billion.

In SSA alone, a minimum of $93.3 billion is required every year (nearly 15% of its GDP) to mitigate its infrastructure deficits. Capital expenditure amounting to $60.4 billion constitutes two-third of the total expenditure while operation and maintenance represents the remaining one-third. $40.8 billion, representing more than 40% of $93.3, is required to finance power sector only, while transport infrastructure accounts for one-fifth (World Bank 2010, p. 7). Additionally, SSA governments spend about 65% of their total spending on infrastructure (Gutnam et al. 2015, p. 3).

It is essential to note that public financing of infrastructure is not providing adequate support to the sector in Africa and other developing countries. Consequently, policy makers seek for alternative "innovative solutions" for financing the development of infrastructure (World Bank Group and PPIAF 2017, p. 8). There is also the need for finding alternative sources of finance to fund infrastructure using Islamic mode of financing such as sukuk (COMCEC 2019). This is in line with sustainability of development goals. Therefore, it is imperative to utilize alternative financing mechanisms that can be used to achieve the 2030 development agenda.

Islamic capital markets can generally serve as alternative options for financing development projects (Mohieldin 2018, p. 13). Sukuk financing, which continues to gain momentum particularly in some developing countries, can be utilized in financing infrastructure projects (Gelbard et al. 2014, p. 13). This financial instrument can effectively serve as an innovative financial technique for financing real sector development including industry and infrastructure. In this regard, Baita and Mustafa (2019, p. 153) view that sukuk bring a lot of economic advantages to issuer countries which include industrial and infrastructural development.

In this chapter, we provide an analysis on the role of sukuk as a means of financing SDG-9 "Industry, Innovation and Infrastructure" in SSA, and how the financial instrument could serve the purpose of achieving sustainable and all-inclusive development in the region. The analysis using recent data sets will focus on two main questions: (1) Are sukuk Instruments contributing toward achieving the SDG-9? (2) Are sub-Saharan African countries seizing the opportunity and aligning their financing strategy to this Islamic financing instrument? To the authors' knowledge, these questions have not been exhaustively studied in the context of SSA region.

The remainder of this chapter is organized as follows. Section "SDG-9 "Industry, Innovation and Infrastructure"" provides an overview of SDG-9 as well as the status of industry, innovation, and infrastructure in SSA. Section "Sukuk and SDG-9" reviews and sheds light on the link between Sukuk and SDG-9. The next section, Sect. "Achievements, Challenges and Opportunities" focuses on achievements, challenges, and opportunities, and the final section provides concluding remarks and recommendations.

SDG-9 "Industry, Innovation and Infrastructure"

An Overview

SDG 9 "Industry, Innovation and Infrastructure" is aimed at promoting inclusive and sustainable industrialization, fostering innovation, and building resilient infrastructure. It has eight targets while 13 indicators are used in measuring these targets (United Nations Industrial Development Organization [UNIDO] 2019).

There are five components of SDG-9. These include (i) developing quality, reliable, sustainable, and resilient infrastructure; (ii) promoting inclusive and sustainable industrialization; (iii) more access of small-scale industries and other enterprises to financial services; (iv) upgrading infrastructure, making industries sustainable, and increasing the adoption of clean and environmentally sound technologies; and (v) enhancing scientific research, upgrading the technological capabilities of industrial sectors, including more innovation by increasing public and private R&D spending among others (Schmidt-Traub 2015).

SDG-9 index is a composite index measuring the combined performance of industry, innovation, and infrastructure across the globe. It has 5 components. These include percentage of internet users, subscription for mobile broadband (per 100 persons), index of logistics performance, universities ranking of Times Higher Education (average score of top 3 universities), number of scientific and technical journal articles (per 1000 persons), and R&D spending as ratio of GDP. In the index, 0 stands for worst performance, while 100 represents best performance. In Fig. 31.1, a comparative analysis of SDG-9 is made across selected geographical regions.

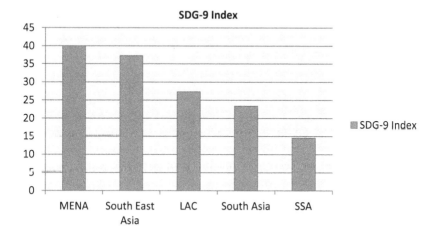

Fig. 31.1 Sustainable Development Goal 9 (SDG-9) Index in 2019 (*Source* Bertelsmann Stiftung and SDSN [2019])

Figure 31.1 presents SDG-9 index in selected geographical regions for the year 2019. All the regions perform below average with MENA region performing fairly well. This is followed by Southeast Asia and LAC which score 37.3 and 27.3, respectively. The low performers are South Asia and SSA scoring 23.4 and 14.5, respectively. SSA is the lowest performer with poorest SDG-9 score across the globe. This indicates the low level of industrialization, innovation, and infrastructure in the region which requires massive investments in the sectors. By implication, the traditional methods of financing, particularly in SSA, are not significantly effective in sustaining development. As such, innovative financing needs to be mainstreamed in the region's financial system to finance industrial and infrastructure development.

The Nature and Extent of Industry, Innovation and Infrastructure in SSA

This section is concerned with the nature of industry, innovation, and infrastructure in SSA. It is divided into three subsections based on the components of SDG-9. These include industry in SSA, innovation in SSA, and infrastructure in SSA.

Industry in SSA

UNIDO (2019) posits that industrial development is crucial to achieving SDG-9 goal. It annually publishes Competitive Industrial Performance (CIP) Index to compare industrial performance across the globe. In constructing CIP Index, UNIDO uses three indicators of SDG 9 which include (i) manufacturing value added (MVA) per capita and MVA as a ratio of GDP; (ii) carbon dioxide emissions per unit of value added; and (iii) percentage of medium- and high-tech industry value added in total value added.

CIP index takes the value of 1 for best performance in the rank. High value of the index represents low rank implying low industrial performance. Figure 31.2 presents CIP Index in 2019 to compare industrial performance across geographical regions.

Figure 31.2 shows the performance of selected geographical regions in CIP index between 2015 and 2017. As earlier stated, lower rank indicates better industrial performance. Europe is the best performer in industrial development ranking 42 in 2017 followed by North America with average rank of 53 in 2015 and 2017. Asia and Pacific, and Latin America

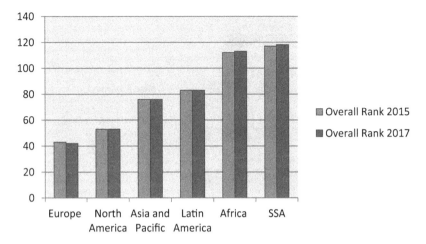

Fig. 31.2 Competitive Industrial Performance (CIP) Index (*Source* UNIDO [2019])

perform averagely with Asia and Pacific surpassing Latin America in 2015 and 2017. SSA is the worst performer with average rank of 117 and 118 in 2015 and 2017, respectively. In fact, SSA[2] successively performs below the average Africa's ranks in 2015 and 2017. On average, SSA lags behind its regional counterpart (North Africa) in industrial development, let alone other regions of the world.

Innovation in SSA
Innovation is vital for industrialization and sustainable development. This study uses Innovation Capability Index developed by World Economic Forum. Additionally, R&D is one of the major components of innovation index. R&D index consists of scientific publications, patents applications (per million population), ratio of R&D to GDP, and prominence of research institutions (see World Economic Forum 2019). Therefore, innovation can foster or hamper the attainment of development goals. Countries that vigorously pursue innovation enhancing policies are likely to attain sustained growth and development. Figure 31.3 compares the

---

[2] North Africa rank 72 in 2015 and 2017, respectively. This sub-region ranks higher than Asia & Pacific and Latin America in industrial performance.

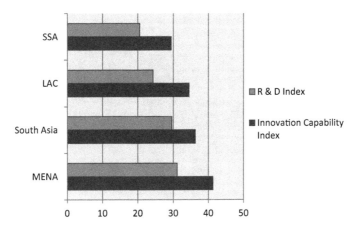

Fig. 31.3 Innovation index in 2019 (*Source* World Economic Forum [2019])

performance of some selected regions in innovation and R&D.

Figure 31.3 presents innovation and R&D indices for year 2019. In the sample geographical regions, MENA's performance is better compared to other regions. It scores about two-fifth in innovation index and about one-third in R&D. South Asia and LAC perform at relatively the same level with South Asia scoring slightly above LAC in both indices. SSA has the least score in innovation and R&D scoring 29.4 and 20.5, respectively. Though SSA has the lowest scores for innovation and R&D, other regions in the sample have low performance in both indices, signifying inadequate funding of innovation to achieve SDG-9.

Infrastructure in SSA

In developing economies, direct influence of infrastructure development on sustained increase in growth and productivity has been established. It is observed that low level of infrastructure retard growth in these economies leading to persistently high levels of poverty. In most cases, this part of the world does not have ample financial resources to finance infrastructure deficits (World Bank Group and PPIAF 2017, p. 9).

In SSA, there is serious need for financing infrastructure to foster development in the region (AfDB 2018; Baita and Mustafa 2019; Calderon et al. 2018; Gutnam et al. 2015). A report by World Bank Group and PPIAF (2017, p. 11) shows that economic infrastructure in SSA decreases

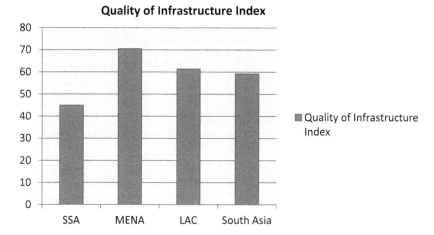

Fig. 31.4 Infrastructure index in 2019 (*Source* World Economic Forum [2019])

annual growth at national level by 2 percentage point and slashes productivity by nearly 40%. Figure 31.4 presents infrastructure quality index as reported by World Economic Forum (2019).

Figure 31.4 reveals that MENA, LAC, and South Asia perform above average in infrastructure index in 2019. The quality of infrastructure in MENA region is 70%, followed by LAC and South Asia which score about three-fifth. SSA[3] scores 45% which is closer to the average. Notwithstanding, it[4] has the lowest quality of infrastructure. This confirms the views and finding of AfDB (2018), Baita and Mustafa (2019), Calderon et al. (2018), and Gutnam et al. (2015). As such, the region requires innovative financing to fix the problem.

---

[3] It scores 22.91 in Africa Infrastructure Development Index (AIDI), developed by AfDB. Moreover, SSA has lower performance in AIDI compared to World Economic Forum's infrastructure index.

[4] SSA performs below average in both quality and quantity of infrastructure.

Sukuk and SDG-9

Accounting and Auditing Organization for Islamic Financial Institutions [AAOIFI] (2015, p. 468) in its Shariah standards (17) describes sukuk as *"...certificates of equal value representing undivided shares in ownership of tangible assets, usufruct and services or the assets of particular projects or special investment activity..."*. Similarly, sukuk are described as a certificate that entitles unbroken proportional ownership right in the underlying assets being financed through the issuance as opposed to a debt obligation (Iqbal and Mirakhor 2007).

Sukuk are classified into sovereign, quasi-sovereign, and corporate. Sovereign sukuk are issued by government or its agencies (such as ministries). Quasi-sovereign sukuk are issued by government corporations or bodies. They also include sukuk guaranteed by governments or its agency. Corporate sukuk are sukuk issued by corporate bodies such as public limited liability companies and other registered private corporations.

Sukuk can also be classified according to the currency used in its issuance. Domestic sukuk are sukuk issued in domestic or local currency such as naira in Nigeria, riyal in Saudi Arabia, or ringgit in Malaysia. International sukuk, on the other hand, are issued in foreign currencies such as dollar, pounds, and euro.

According to Economist Intelligence Unit [EIU] (2015), sukuk are sought-after instruments for financing African infrastructure gap. Islamic bonds, Sharia-compliant bonds, or sukuk, have been used in several countries to generate funds. Ahmed (2017) noted that its appeals are premised on its social and ethical ethos, asset-linked and risk-sharing features which makes it ideal for funding SDGs and other infrastructure projects. In the same vein, Ajanovic (2017) identified raising wholesale funding mostly from sukuk program as part of a comprehensive Islamic finance solution in supporting SDGs.

Mohieldin (2018, p. 15) observes that sukuk play an important role in financing development due to a number of factors. They are backed by assets and revenue from the underlying asset is linked to "investor's return" from sukuk. A large number of sukuk are issued to finance infrastructure. They facilitate sharing of risks in projects that are highly risky. In addition, there is flexibility of sukuk structures based on the various stages of a project. They promote public–private partnership and sukuk investors are largely available; i.e., there is high demand for sukuk.

Malikov (2017, p. 12) observed that "*Sukuk have been recognized as a viable financing method for infrastructure projects in developing nations.*" He added that risk sharing and socio-economic development are central to Islamic finance and sukuk issuances in infrastructure projects require both. Alshaleel (2019, p. 292) acknowledges that Islamic finance and instruments such as sukuk constitute innovative opportunity for a non-traditional financing which can play a substantial role in financing SDGs in developing economies. For him, "*sukuk represent an important tool for the financing of infrastructure, and other development projects.*" He added "*sukuk can play an effective role in partially financing large sustainable development projects in developing countries, where governments find difficulties in allocating sufficient resources*" (Alshaleel 2019, p. 293)

Al Amine (2016) also observed that Islamic finance, through its instruments like sukuk, constitutes a good fit for infrastructure and project finance helping to tap an additional source of funds. Similarly, Trepelkov (2017) observed that there a unanimous agreement on the imperative of mobilizing and utilizing additional financial resources from all available sources in order to achieve the 2030 sustainable development agenda. He notes that it is even more important in developing countries where funding challenges are prevalent for essential infrastructure. He further believes that Islamic bonds can help can generate the necessary financing for infrastructure investments needed. Despite these important features of Islamic finance, the full potential of its products has not yet been utilized. Therefore, a case should be made for the instruments where they are competitive and offer positive externalities in promoting sustainable development (Trepelkov 2017).

Biancone and Radwan (2018) observed that globally, there are a number of efforts to attract alternative financing toward large as well as long-term infrastructure projects. Such projects typically find it difficult to attract sufficient funding. The authors argued that Sharia-compliant financing represents a potential prospect for financing such public utility projects. They noted that different types of sukuk can be used to satisfy the short as well as long-term financing and refinancing needs. Lahsasna et al. (2018) acknowledge that sukuk will play a significant role in the future in building a more sustainable and eco-friendly economy.

As expressed by Ahmed (2017), sukuk have become a common means for generating financing for sovereign and corporate issues. For him, sukuk constitute single most significant instruments to raise finance through Islamic Capital Market (ICM) operations using Sharia-compliant regulation. He observed the absence of a separate and specialized regulatory framework for sukuk, and the instrument is subjected to the same regulations as conventional capital markets which may not be proper, and therefore recommended appropriate modification in order to treat sukuk with clear understanding.

ACHIEVEMENTS, CHALLENGES AND OPPORTUNITIES

Achievements

Several achievements have been made in sukuk issuances for accelerating development in a cross-section of countries. The study is concerned with sukuk issues by the sovereign and quasi-sovereign in SSA. There are eight SSA countries that have issued sovereign sukuk. These include Sudan, Gambia, Senegal, South Africa, Ivory Coast, Nigeria, Mali, and Togo. At least, this is a modest achievement. In this regard, this subsection will analyze and explain the role of sukuk in financing sustainable development. Facts will be presented and analyzed while a case study of infrastructure sukuk will be discussed focusing on Nigeria.

Sukuk as Instruments of Financing SDG-9

Sukuk serve as potential source of financing infrastructural projects based on success stories in some countries (Ahmed et al. 2015, p. 29). They provide various sources of funds to finance infrastructure (Ahmed 2017; COMCEC 2019; Gelbard et al. 2014). They are the second-largest aspect of global Islamic financial industry. Sovereign sukuk issues represent about three-fifth (60%) of the total sukuk issues while only 11.57% was used to finance infrastructure in 2018 (COMCEC 2019, p. 59).

In particular, huge infrastructure deficits in SSA can be financed by issuing sukuk which will be readily subscribed by investors in the Middle East, and Southeast Asia particularly Malaysia and Indonesia (Gelbard et al. 2014, p. 12). However, the region has not significantly utilized this financial instrument in achieving development (Bukhari 2015).

Islamic financial means of mobilizing resources for achieving SDG-9 exist (Ahmed 2017; Ahmed et al. 2015; Gundogdu 2018). Gundogdu (2018, p. 386) views that commercially priced loans, including issuance of investment sukuk, could be harnessed to provide infrastructure for sustainable development. By involving the private sector, the resource gap will be closed though this approach may seem costly in the short term. However, it is cost-efficient in the long term compared to financing infrastructure through public financing.

Abdurraheem and Naim (2018, p. 27) observe that SSA has mainly relied on public budget to finance infrastructure in the region. However, the region is financially and technically incapable of providing adequate infrastructure. The region requires large investment in infrastructure to close the infrastructure deficit. This, therefore, necessitates "...*the need to explore other sources of long-term funding to bridge the existing gap*" (Abdurraheem and Naim 2018, p. 28). The authors argue for increasing sukuk financing to reduce the infrastructure challenges in the region. In a related case, IISD (2018) reports that in 2018, HSBC's Islamic banking business in Malaysia issued an SDG sukuk to finance global initiatives in line with the bank's SDG Bond Framework. The effort represents the world's first sukuk issued by a financial institution solely centered on the SDGs. The financing instrument will support projects aligning with seven SDG goals including SDG-9 (industry, innovation, and infrastructure). Figure 31.5 presents distribution of outstanding global sukuk issuances

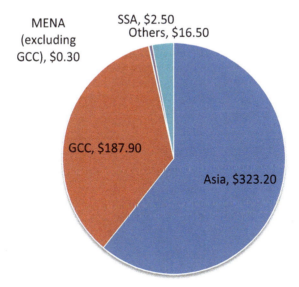

Fig. 31.5 Outstanding sukuk issues in 2018 (*Source* Islamic Financial Service Board [IFSB] [2019])

612 A. J. BAITA AND H. H. SULEIMAN

Table 31.1 Global sovereign sukuk issuances in sub-Saharan Africa (Jan. 2001–Dec. 2018)

Category	Number of issues	Amount US$ Millions	Percent
International	2	630	2.78
Domestic	366	21,048	97.22
Total	368	22,678	100

Source IIFM Sukuk Report (2019)

in 2019 including SSA.

Figure 31.5 shows the outstanding sukuk issues in 2018 across the globe. Asia accounts for about 60% of the outstanding sukuk in the year. However, SSA (Africa excluding North Africa) has outstanding sukuk of US$2.5 billion in 2018 representing 0.47% of the total. SSA records less than 1% of the outstanding sukuk.

From Table 31.1, the total sovereign sukuk issued by SSA countries amounted to $22.677 billion between January 2001 and December 2018. There are only 2 issues of international sovereign sukuk amounting to US$630 million which represents 2.78%. US$21.047 billion worth of domestic sukuk were issued during the period representing 97.22% of the total issuances in the region. The breakdown of global sovereign sukuk issues in the SSA region is presented in Table 31.2.

Table 31.2 presents global sovereign sukuk issued by SSA countries between January 2001 and December 2018. Gambia has the highest number of sovereign sukuk issues (321) followed by Sudan (36). In

Table 31.2 Global sovereign sukuk issuances by countries in SSA (Jan. 2001–Dec. 2018)

Countries	Number of issues	Amount US$ Millions	Percent
Gambia	321	383	1.69
Ivory Coast	2	460	2.03
Nigeria	4	714	3.15
Mali	1	285	1.26
Senegal	2	445	1.96
South Africa	1	500	2.20
Sudan	36	19,646	86.63
Togo	1	245	1.08
Total	368	22,678	100

Source IIFM Sukuk Report (2019)

terms of value, Sudan issued \$19.65 billion sovereign sukuk representing 86.63% in SSA. The amount of sovereign sukuk issued in the remaining countries represents about 13%. This shows the dominant role played by Sudan in sukuk issuance in SSA for over a decade.

Case Study of Sukuk Issuances in Nigeria
Investment in infrastructure is one of the major goals of Nigeria's Economic Recovery and Growth Plan [ERGP] (2017–2020). Sukuk financing is a positive driver to attainment of this goal (Debt Management Office [DMO] Press Release 2 2017). In line with ERGP, the Federal Government of Nigeria [FGN], on 14th September 2017, offers its 7-year debut sovereign ijarahsukuk worth N100 billion (equivalent to \$326.80), with 16.47% rate of return. FGN Roads Sukuk Company I PLC is the special purpose vehicle (SPV) (DMO 2017a). The sukuk bonds are over-subscribed by N5.878 billion. The funds generated from the SPV are to be used for constructing and rehabilitating 25 roads across the six geopolitical zones. Federal Ministry of Power, Works and Housing is the charged with the supervision of these public works (DMO Press Release 3 2017).

In December 6, 2018, FGN issues second N100 billion ijarah sukuk spanning for 7 years. The sukuk carry 15.743% rate of return (DMO 2018). The sovereign sukuk, oversubscribed by N32.2 billion, are earmarked for constructing and rehabilitating 28 projects across 6 geopolitical zones (*Vanguard* 2019). Similarly, the FGN, on 21st May 2020, issues its third N150 billion (equivalent to \$405 million) ijarah sukuk spanning for 7 years. The sukuk's annual rental rate is 11.2%. The subscription level stands at N669.124 billion, which represents 446%. This issuance is meant for construction and rehabilitation of 44 "*critical Road Projects*" across the 6 geopolitical zones in the country (DMO 2020).

Challenges

Several challenges have been identified that impede the growth of the global sukuk market and thereby inhibiting SDG-9 funding.

Legislative and Tax Framework
Legislative and tax framework constitutes a key challenge inhibiting the development of sukuk. The concept of trust and beneficial interest is alien

in civil law however recognized legislatively under common. Therefore, to ensure the commercial viability of a successful sukuk issuance where SSA countries adopt the civil law code, they need to integrate the recognition of trust and beneficial interest into its legal framework (Muhammad et al. 2018).

Tax liability such as stamp duty and capital gains tax positions sukuk at a disadvantage relative to conventional bonds given its asset-backed or asset-based nature. Therefore, modifications to tax legislation should be enacted to lessen the tax burden for sukuk issuers. A number of countries have started to integrate sukuk into their legal and tax codes (Muhammad et al. 2018). Adeola (2018) also identified the non-release of general tax guidelines clarifying tax neutrality of non-interest transactions by National tax body as one of the challenges of sukuk in Nigeria.

Lack of Uniform Interpretation in Structuring of Sukuk Across Jurisdictions
There is no uniform interpretation in structuring of sukuk across jurisdictions as a challenge facing sukuk. Each issue is characterized by bulky documentation and legal due diligence as each sukuk is unique though it may be structured under similar Islamic contract (Aliyu 2016; Bennet and Iqbal 2011). Shariah opinions among scholars vary around Shariah principles applicable to sukuk structuring and trading, such as bay' al-inah (sale and buy-back) and bay' al-dayn (sale of debt) (Muhammad et al. 2018).

Liquidity Management
Another challenge is the use of sukuk in liquidity management and product range (Alvi 2019). Aliyu (2016) identified liquidity management issue as inhibitive of global sukuk growth. He observed that the exclusion on interest bearing investment, financial transactions and treatment of money as a medium of exchange not as a commodity, results in inadequate tradable instruments and quality assets leading to sub-optimal deployment of excess liquidity. This leads to slow face of development of liquidity management instruments and reliance on balance sheet assets for liquidity management. Adeola (2018) lamented the failure of the Nigerian Central Bank to Issue sukuk-backed treasury bills to create liquidity instruments for non-interest banks as challenging for Sukuk development. Bennet and Iqbal (2011) also noted the lack of liquidity in the market due to low activity in the secondary market, as well as the limited opportunity for portfolio selection/diversification as inhibitive of sukuk.

Skills, Technical Capacities Gap and Limited Islamic Finance and Shariah Experts

There is a clear dearth of identified skills and technical capacities and Shariah experts in government, financial institutions, central banks, and regulatory bodies (EIU 2015). The capacity gap observed is felt in the long time lags in deploying instruments.

Opportunities

According to Malikov (2017, p. 10), "*Numerous emerging and frontier economies are paving the way for the enlargement of the sukuk market through appropriate regulations.*" Looking at the most recent estimates, global outstanding sukuk stood at $443.78 billion as at 2017, with global sukuk issuances up 5.5% at $123.2 billion in 2018 (IIFM 2018). Islamic finance is still at a bourgeoning stage of development in SSA. There is a positive outlook for non-interest compliant financing (Aliyu 2016; Biancone and Radwan 2018).

Market analyst project a positive outlook for sukuk and opportunities for utilizing sukuk instruments for SDGs are encouraging. There is high investor appetite fueled by the opportunity it presents for diversification (Gelbard et al. 2014). In addition, the forecasted rise in Muslim population in SSA will contribute a rise in demand for Shariah-compliant products and services (EIU 2015). There are also other expected demands from non-Muslim populations given that interest in shariah-compliant instruments is not limited to majority or even large Muslim populations. Non-Muslims who identify economic potential in halal sectors and sukuk are among its chief consumers (ibid.).

According to EIU (2015), sukuk can serve as another prospective driver for financing SSA infrastructure deficit. Poor roads, railways, and ports infrastructure are insufficient and power need urgent financing. In any case, as noted in the report, infrastructure projects are perfect for sukuk due to their long timelines to completion, large values, and link to the real economy in the form of the asset.

The sukuk market is a potent conduit for the growing pool of Shari'ah compliant capital to be employed for financing sustainable and equitable economic development (Zulkhibri 2015). The 2018 HSBC's pioneering "SDG sukuk" is a model for SSA countries to follow on how sukuk can be employed as an innovative financing for achieving sustainable development goals.

Africa is a destination where Islamic finance can and ought to thrive (Dey and Jin 2018). According to IIFM 2018 annual sukuk report, 90.44% of the $443.78 billion sukuk outstanding globally come from few well-established Asian and Middle East markets. It projects that the African region will gradually increase their market share in the coming years. Bearing in mind investors' appetite, the number of issuances in the pipeline, as well as the positive growth pattern, growth in sovereign issuers, as well stable quasi-sovereign, corporate, and financial institution issuances are all indicative to a bright outlook (IIFM 2018).

CONCLUSION AND RECOMMENDATIONS

This chapter investigates the potential role of sukuk in promoting and achieving Sustainable Development Goal-9 (SDG-9), with particular focus on sub-Saharan African countries. Our aim is to shed light on the role sukuk can play in promoting industrial development, fostering innovation, filing the infrastructure gap, and accelerating growth and progress toward the SDGs with a focus on SDG-9. The study sets out the imperative of sukuk in achieving the United Nations Sustainable Development Goals (SDGs) and makes a case for why sub-Saharan African countries should embrace sukuk as part of their financing strategy. Achieving the goals of SDG-9 will require rallying the needed scale of sukuk financing, and enacting strong policies and incentives to facilitate its growth and addressing its challenges in SSA countries.

Sukuk instruments contribute toward achieving the SDG-9 albeit below par. Out 46 SSA countries, only eight (8) have issued sukuk. At the same time, few SSA countries have so far aligned their financing strategy to this Islamic bond instrument.

The following recommendations are therefore proffered:

- Governments of SSA countries should set up new sukuk integrated legal framework and trust laws, to establish a strong governance framework for sukuk issuances where absent.
- Strengthen and standardize the regulatory framework and support product innovation, and provide some legislative accommodation by amending tax legislation to lessen the tax burden for sukuk issuers.
- Standard & Poor's as cited in EIU (2015) suggested countries may not require unique legislation for issuing sukuk as in the case of Senegal's which used existing financial legislation, not a

new regulatory framework, although other experts favor unique legislation.

- SSA countries should promote more sovereign sukuk issuances to facilitate liquidity management by central banks.
- There is need to improve skills, technical capacity, and availability of Islamic finance and Shariah experts in governments and financial institutions of SSA countries.

REFERENCES

AAOIFI. (2015). *Shariah Standards*. Manama, Bahrain: Author.

Abdurraheem, A., & Naim, A. M. (2018). Sub-Sahara Africa's Infrastructure Funding Gap: Potentials from Sukuk Financing. *Indiana-Pacific Journal of Accounting and Finance, 2*(4), 26–34.

Adeola, H. (2018). *Non-Interest Capital Market Sub-Committee Update at Q3 2018: Capital Market Committee Meeting*. Retrieved from http://www.sec.gov.ng/cmc/2018/11/19/cmc-2018-presentations-and-reports/.

Africa Development Bank. (2018). *African Economic Outlook 2018*. Abidjan, Ivory Coast: Author.

Africa Development Bank. (2020). *Africa Infrastructure Development Index (AIDI), 2019*. Abidjan, Ivory Coast: Author.

Ahmed, H. (2017). *Contribution of Islamic Finance to the 2030 Agenda for Sustainable Development* (with special reference to infrastructure finance). Retrieved from https://www.un.org/esa/ffd//////high-level-conference-on-ffd-and-2030-agenda/wp-content/uploads/sites/4/2017/11/Islamic-Finance_Ahmed.pdf.

Ahmed, H., Mohieldin, M., Verbeek, J., & Abdoulmagd, F. (2015). *On the Sustainable Development Goals and the Role of Islamic Finance* (Policy Research Working Paper, 7266).

Ajanovic, N. (2017). *Islamic Finance and SDGs*. A Paper Presented at the Senior Partnership Specialist High-Level Conference on Financing for Development and the Means of Implementation of the 2030 Agenda for Sustainable Development, November 19, 2017, Doha, Qatar. Retrieved from: https://www.un.org/esa/ffd/high-level-conference-on-ffd-and-2030-agenda/wp-content/uploads/sites/4/2017/11/Islamic-Finance_Ayanovic.pdf.

Al Amine, M. (2016). Islamic Finance in Africa: Current Penetration. In *Islamic Finance and Africa's Economic Resurgence*. Palgrave Studies in Islamic Banking, Finance, and Economics. Cham: Palgrave Macmillan.

Aliyu, S. U. R. (2016). *Challenges to the Development of Sukuk*. A Paper Presented at the 3-Day Workshop on Viability of Non-interest Bond (Sukuk)

618   A. J. BAITA AND H. H. SULEIMAN

in the Era of Dwindling Economy, organised by the Nigerian Capital Market Institute (NCMI), Abuja-Nigeria held on 30 August–1 September, 2016. Retrieved from https://www.academia.edu/37544179/Challenges_to_the_Development_of_Sukuk.

Alshaleel, M. (2019). Islamic Finance, Sustainable Development and Developing Countries: Linkages and Potential. In O. Osuji, F. Ngwu, & D. Jamali (Eds.), *Corporate Social Responsibility in Developing and Emerging Markets: Institutions, Actors and Sustainable Development* (pp. 281–305). Cambridge: Cambridge University Press. https://doi.org/10.1017/978110 8579360.016.

Alvi, I. A. (2019). *Developments in the Global Sukuk Market*. IIFM Awareness Seminar on Islamic Finance organised by Bank Indonesia-Jakarta held on 12 November.

Baita, A. J., & Mustafa, D. (2019). Appraisal of Economic Benefits of Sukuk in Financing Budget Deficits in Nigeria. *Journal of King Abdulaziz University: Islamic Economic, 32*(1), 145–158.

Bennet, M., & Iqbal, Z. (2011). The Role of Sukuk in Meeting Global Development Challenges. In S. Jaffer (Ed.), *Global Growth, Opportunities and Challenges in the Sukuk Market* (pp. 68–74). EuroMoney.

Bertelsmann Stiftung & Sustainable Development Solutions Network [SDSN]. (2019). *Sustainable Development Report 2019*. New York: Author.

Biancone, P. P., & Radwan, M. (2018). Sharia-Compliant Financing for Public Utility Infrastructure. *Utilities Policy*. Retrieved from https://doi.org/10.1016/j.jup.2018.03.006.

Bukhari, I. (2015). *Financing Solutions for SDGs: Examining the Role of PPP and Islamic Finance*. Jeddah: Islamic Development Bank.

Calderon, C., Cantu, C., & Chuhan-Pole, P. (2018). *Infrastructure development in Sub-Saharan Africa: A Scorecard* (Policy Research Working Paper, 8425). Washington: World Bank Group.

COMCEC. (2019). *Infrastructure Financing Through Islamic Finance in the Islamic Countries*. Ankara, Turkey: Author.

DMO. (2017a). *Sovereign Sukuk Offer for Subscription*. Abuja, Nigeria: Author.

DMO. (2017b). *FGN Prospectus Execution Version*. Abuja, Nigeria: Author.

DMO Press Release 2. (2017, September 11). *Financing Infrastructure*. Abuja, Nigeria: DMO.

DMO Press Release 3. (2017, September 26). *FGN Debut Sukuk Offer Oversubscribed*. Abuja, Nigeria: DMO.

DMO. (2018). *Sovereign Sukuk Offer for Subscription*. Abuja, Nigeria: Author.

DMO. (2020, June 12). *Investors Scramble for Third Sovereign Sukuk*. Abuja, Nigeria: Author.

Dey, D., & Jin, X. (2018). *Islamic Finance in Africa: Opportunities and Challenges*. Retrieved from https://www.whitecase.com/publications/insight/islamic-finance-africa-opportunities-and-challenges.

Economist Intelligence Unit [EIU]. (2015). *Mapping Africa's Islamic Economy*. Dubai, UAE: Author.

Gelbard, E., Hussain, M., Maino, R. Mu, Y., &Yehoue, E. B. (2014). *Islamic Finance in Sub-Saharan Africa: Status and Prospects* (IMF Working Paper, 149).

Global Infrastructure Hub. (2018). *InfraCompass: Set Your Infrastructure Policies in the Right Direction in the Compact with Africa Countries*.

Global Infrastructure Hub. (2020). *Global Infrastructure Outlook Data for Africa*. Retrieved from outlook.gihub.org/region/Africa.

Gundogdu, A. S. (2018). An Inquiry into Islamic Finance from the Perspective of Sustainable Development Goals. *European Journal of Sustainable Development, 7*(4), 381–390. https://doi.org/10.14207/ejsd.2018.v7n4p381.

Gutnam, J., Sy, A., & Chattopadhyay, S. (2015). *Financing African Infrastructure: Can the World Deliver?* Washington: Brookings Institution.

IFSB. (2019). *Islamic Financial Services Industry Stability Report 2019*. Kuala Lumpur, Malaysia: Author.

IIFM. (2018). *Sukuk Report* (7th ed.). Manama, Bahrain: Author.

IIFM. (2019). *Sukuk Report* (8th ed.). Manama, Bahrain: Author.

IISD. (2018). *HSBC Malaysia Issues Islamic Bond to Support SDGs*. Retrieved from http://sdg.iisd.org/news/hsbc-malaysia-issues-islamic-bond-to-support-sdgs/.

Iqbal, Z., & Mirakhor, A. (2007). *Introduction to Islamic Finance: Theory and Practice*. Hoboken, NJ: Wiley.

Lahsasna, A., Hassan, K. M., & Ahmad, R. (2018). *Forward lease Sukuk in Islamic Capital Markets*. Cham, Switzerland: Palgrave Macmillan. https://doi.org/10.1007/978-3-319-94262-9.

Malikov, A. (2017). How Do Sovereign Sukuk Impact on the Economic Growth of Developing Countries? An Analysis of the Infrastructure Sector, In V. Etendić, F. Hadžić, & H. Izhar (Eds.), *Critical Issues and Challenges in Islamic Economics and Finance Development*. Cham: Palgrave Macmillan.

Mohieldin, M. (2018). *Islamic Capital Markets and the SDGs*. Jeddah and Washington: Islamic Development Bank and World Bank Group.

Muhammad, M., Ramli, R., Sairally, S., Kasri, N. S., & Zaki, I. A. M. (2018). *The Role of Sukuk in Islamic Capital Markets*. Retrieved from:http://ebook.comcec.org/Kutuphane/Icerik/Yayinlar/Analitik_Calismalar/Mali_Isbirligi/Toplanti10/files/assets/common/downloads/publication.pdf.

Schmidt-Traub, G. (2015). *Supplemental Material to: Investment Needs to Achieve the Sustainable Development Goals*. New York: SDSN.

SDG Centre for Africa. (2019). *Africa 2030: Sustainable Development Goals Three-Year Reality Check*. Kigali, Rwanda: Author.

Trepelkov, A. (2017, November 18–19). *Opening Remarks*. Presented at the High-Level Conference on Financing for Development and the Means of Implementation of the 2030 Agenda for Sustainable Development, Doha, Qatar. Retrieved from https://www.un.org/esa/ffd/high-level-conference-on-ffd-and-2030-agenda/wp-content/uploads/sites/4/2017/11/MOI-plenary-session_Trepelkov.pdf.

UN DOCO & Dag Hammarskjold. (2018). *Unlocking SDG Financing: Findings from Early Adopters*. Retrieved from http://daghammarskjold.se/wp-content/uploads/2018/06/UNDG-CountryStudy-Kenya.pdf.

UNIDO. (2019). *Industrial development report 2020: Industrializing in the digital era*. Vienna: Author.

Vanguard Newspaper. (2019, January 11). Finance Minister Hands over N100b Sukuk Proceeds to Works Minister. Retrieved from https://www.vanguardngr.com/2019/01/finance-minister-hands-over-n100b-sukuk-proceeds-to-works-minister/.

World Bank Group. (2017a). *Africa's Pulse*. 15. Washington: World Bank Group.

World Bank. (2010). *Africa's Infrastructure: A Time for Transformation*. Washington: Author.

World Bank. (2020). *WDI: Sustainable development goals (SDGs)*. Washington: Author. Retrieved from https://datatopics.worldbank.org/sdgs/ (Accessed on 20/05/2020).

World Bank Group. and PPIAF. (2017). *Mobilising Islamic Finance for Infrastructure Public-Private Partnerships*. Washington, DC: World Bank Group and Public Private Infrastructure Advisory Fund.

World Economic Forum. (2019). *Global Competitiveness Report*. Geneva, Switzerland: Author.

Xiong, A., Xia, S., Ye, Z., Cao, D., Jing, Y., & Li, H. (2020). Can Innovation Really Bring Growth? The Role of Social Filter in China. *Structural Change and Economic Dynamics*. https://doi.org/10.1016/j.strueco.2020.01.003.

Zulkhibri, M. (2015). A Synthesis of Theoretical and Empirical Research on Sukuk. *Borsa Istanbul Review*. https://doi.org/10.1016/j.bir.2015.10.001.

CHAPTER 32

How Green *Sukuk* Structure Contributes to SDGs?

Mohamed Cherif El Amri, Mustafa Omar Mohammed, and Mohamed Hamoud Abdi

INTRODUCTION

Sukuk is the Islamic alternative for bond securities. It serves the purpose of raising funds for the *sukuk* issuer. The rapid growth and the worldwide acceptance of the Islamic finance allowed the expeditious development of the *sukuk*, which in its structure or practice possess an interesting component that set it apart from its conventional counterpart. This component is the underlying asset for the investment (Safari 2012; Usmani 2008). According to the International Islamic Financial Market (IIFM) 2019 report, the global *sukuk* issuance grew from 20 billion to 138 billion, in the period between 2001 and 2013 before drastically declining to 67,82

M. C. El Amri (✉) · M. H. Abdi
Department of Islamic Economics and Finance, Istanbul Sabahattin Zaim University, Istanbul, Turkey

M. O. Mohammed
Department of Economics, International Islamic University Malaysia [IIUM], Gombak, Malaysia

© The Author(s), under exclusive license to Springer Nature Switzerland AG 2021
M. M. Billah (eds.), *Islamic Wealth and the SDGs*,
https://doi.org/10.1007/978-3-030-65313-2_32

621

billion in 2015. Based on the report, after 2016 it started increasing with a score of total global issuance of *sukuk* of 123,15 billion USD in 2018 (International Islamic Financial Market 2019).

Sukuk has been issued to carter for various kinds of projects both in the public and private sectors. The present chapter focuses on Green *sukuk*, issued for climate and environment-related projects such as those related to preventing pollution, providing efficient energy, sustaining agriculture, fishery and forestry, providing clean water and transportation, and protecting the aquatic ecosystem. All these objectives for the issuance of Green *sukuk* are in line with the Shari'ah that strongly opposes any form of environmental degradation and instead promotes sustainable environment free from pollution and the mismanagement of the ecosystem. Muslim scholars have provided several Shari'ah guidelines, norms, and moral values to limit human greed in utilizing earthly resources. They advocate moderation in the use of these resources. Such moderation creates a balance between the individual and societal goals and rights. Green *sukuk* is also seen as one of the means for achieving the sustainable development goals or SDGs. There are already substantial evidences from Muslim governments like Indonesia, Malaysia, and many others, who are embracing SDGs in their financing modes, including *sukuk*, for the greater purpose of economic growth and social welfare (Mat Rahim and Mohamad 2018; Usmani 2008). Green *sukuk* issuance for SDGs-related projects includes the solar power plants, clean technology investments, and climate adaptation projects (Dorsman et al. 2016; Islamic Development Bank 2019).

Green *Sukuk* and the Projects They Fund

The dynamism of project financing and the well-established financial systems have helped communities grow and prosper, which in turn have enhanced their social development in many aspects. Finance methods vary in their uses, for example syndication, SPVs, public leasing, structured financing, and many more in accordance with the specificity of the projects they fund. From an Islamic perspective, the project financed must be of great relevance to the interest of the society as a whole and obviously does not in conflict with the Shari'ah requirements. The Shari'ah compliance must also extend to the financing methods as well, free from interest and risk shifting, which are the features of the conventional financing methods (Moghul and Safar-Aly 2014).

As already established, Islamic finance promotes social welfare through various forms of financing that are based on equity and fairness, preservation of ethical values, and ensuring financial inclusion. The Islamic finance industry continues, in addition to the already existing Shari'ah compliant products and services, to develop new products and instruments, including *sukuk*, which is perceived as the Islamic alternative for the conventional bonds. *Sukuk* entered the financing world with their unique features and continue to attract the attention of the Islamic as well as the non-Islamic markets. *Sukuk*, which was first introduced in the late 1980s, are financial assets issued to investors entitling them a risk-shared profits and are free from elements deemed unlawful in the Shari'ah such as interest and speculation. The participants in the *sukuk* market now comprise largely the growing Muslim populations especially the middle east, north Africa and Asia, making them the second fast growing market of Islamic finance (Dorsman et al. 2016). According to (Bahari et al. 2016; IIFM 2017), the global *sukuk* issuance was US$138 billion in 2013 and US$100 billion in 2014. Meanwhile based on the report from (Thomson Reuters 2014), the global *sukuk* issuance is estimated to reach US$250 by 2020. This figure is slightly higher based on Dorsman et al. (2016), which was estimated at US$116.4 billion in 2014 of global *sukuk* issuance with a market value of US$300 billion in the same year resulting in an increase of 11.4% compared to 2013. Despite all these variations in the estimate, the figures show significant growth rate in the *sukuk* market. There was only a huge decline in 2015 of nearly US$68 billion of global *sukuk* issuance, but at the end of 2018 the global *sukuk* issuance picked up and recorded a figure of US$123.2 billion (International Islamic Financial Market 2019). The *sukuk* structure has many layers, which may be complicated and challenging to understand. This at the initial phase of *sukuk* issuance compelled many investors to opt for the simple debt-based conventional bond structure rather than issuing *sukuk*. Nevertheless, Dorsman et al. (2016) stipulate, the US and the Eurozone crisis and the credit crunch forced many more to shift to *sukuk* market. Also due to the low volatility of *sukuk* and the risk-sharing aspect, make *sukuk* more prosperous in comparison with the conventional bond (Thomson Reuters 2014).

Sukuk and conventional bonds have some similarities, but in theory they structurally vary significantly. Regarding similarities, *sukuk* and bonds are issued to raise funds for generally large projects, where these are often for long periods of time and with lower risks (relatively). They are also, due to the substantial amount of capital involved, issued by large entities and governments, and exclude individual contribution (if not as investors) most of the time. On the other hand, they are different in operations, legal and regulatory frameworks, where conventional bonds consist of funds lent to the bond issuer and at the maturity paid back with interest, whereas in the *sukuk*, in addition to the absence of interest, a tangible asset is at the center of the operation and the investors get returns from the funds generated by the asset. Also, the projects funded through *sukuk* must be Shari'ah compliant, though there is no such restriction for the conventional bond. Moreover, beyond the yield to maturity differences, in *sukuk* the risk is shared and the returns are not predetermined or fixed as in conventional bonds, whereby the risk is borne by the bond issuer which makes the investors entitled to predetermined and fixed returns (Safari 2012; Usmani 2008).

Sukuk has different types of structures, such as Ijarah *sukuk*, Istisna *sukuk*, Musharakah *sukuk*, Murabahah *sukuk*, Mudharabah *sukuk*, Salam *sukuk*, and Wakalah *sukuk*. These structures combined with other Islamic finance instruments are determined in accordance with the nature of the project in hand (Bahari et al. 2016; Moghul and Safar-Aly 2014; Mat Rahim and Mohamad 2018).

While *sukuk* in general are used to fund wide range of products, Green *sukuk* are specifically directed to funding environmentally friendly projects. The term 'green' refers to the *sukuk* focus on environmentally sustainable initiatives and renewable energy projects. The global environmental concern and the urgency for response to such concern have motivated people to come up with different solutions, which include Socially Responsible Investments, Circular Economy, the Green *sukuk*, the Green Bonds, among others. The motivation for Green *sukuk* is driven not only by global concern but by the Shari'ah regards for the environment as well. Green *sukuk* is similar in form and substance to the general *sukuk* structures, which grant investors the ownership of the underlying asset used to raise funds for the green projects—a feature that sets Green *sukuk* apart from its conventional counterpart—the Green bond (Dorsman et al. 2016). The generic structure for Green *sukuk* is shown in Fig. 32.1.

The use of an underlying asset and the proceeds derived from it are evident that this kind of structure contributes to the real economy, hence ensuring prosperity and sustainability of the economy. The projects funded by Green *sukuk* are Shari'ah compliant and environmentally

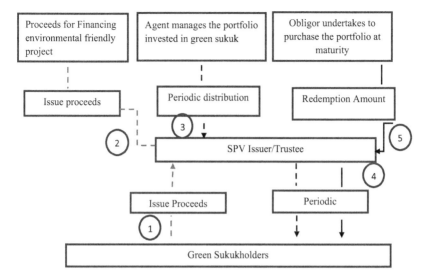

Fig. 32.1 Generic structure for Green *sukuk* (*Source* Adapted from [Mat Rahim and Mohamad 2018])

conscious projects aimed at preserving the natural resources and assuring the next generations of their fair share. Green *sukuk*-funded projects include the solar power plants, clean technology investments, clean energy, climate adaptation and low-carbon projects, financing construction light rails, and electric vehicles. Below are examples of selected projects funded by Green *sukuk*.

The 'One solar watt per person,' a 50 MW photovoltaic solar project, illustrates a great example for projects invested or funded by Green *sukuk*. This project was mandated by two Australian lighting/solar companies; 'Mitabu Australia and Solar Guys International' for Indonesia but initiated and issued by Malaysia. The US$550 million multi-phases project was funded US$150 million in the first phase in late 2012 (Dorsman et al. 2016). Solar projects are known for their advantages, whether the light and smooth installation process or the quick revenue streams just after several months and this project was designed to provide clean and renewable solar power (Reve 2013).

Tadau energy solar photovoltaic and Bakun Hydroelectric are other Green *sukuk*-funded projects, issued, respectively, by China and Malaysia.

Tadau issued in 2017, a 10-year project of RM 250 million [Malaysian Ringgit] to set up a 50 MW solar photovoltaic for a small region called Kudat in the district of Sabah. Bakun hydroelectric on the other hand was 2400 MW hydroelectric plant with 30 years of period project managed by Sarawak Energy Berhad owned by Sarawak state, for the purpose of building a 205-meter high wall with an estimated cost of US$1.6 billion. The electricity charges were planned to be 6.25 cents per kilowatt with an increase (annually) of 1.5% (Mat Rahim and Mohamad 2018).

The Green Building *sukuk* project by PNB Merdeka Ventures Sdn. Bhd is 15 years project to build 83 story building in Malaysia. The project was issued by Permodalan Nasional Bhd., a government-linked company, with a cost of RM 2 billion.

The Green Building *sukuk* project has several benefits from the building, the issuer, investors, and the society at large. For example, the building adopts a feature of low-carbon emission, the issuer and the investors earn good reputation from the eyes of the society, and the society develops social conscience toward the environment. Owing to the Green *sukuk* requirements, the issuer is obliged to disclose the use of the proceeds to the investors along with an annual report comprising the amount disbursed and the use of the funds. Moreover, the building must manifest sustainability features that affirm low waste and carbon emission, low consumption of water and energy...(Kamil et al. 2019).

The Orasis *sukuk* were other Green *sukuk*-funded project. The *sukuk* were 10 years, French issued Green *sukuk* project in 2012 by solar energy specialized and real estate investment company, Legendre Patrimoine and Anouar Hassoune Conseil, an Islamic Finance consultancy firm (Dorsman et al. 2016). The *sukuk* were the second to ever be issued in France after the Shari'ah compliant catering SME project of €500,000 in the same year. This project also enabled individual contributions or investments alongside institutions with a single overseas share cost of €5425 and a cost of €5890 in France. Depending on the shares acquired, the investor becomes entitled to ownership of solar farm shared ownership (Alam et al. 2016). Figure 32.2 shows the structure of the Orasis Green *sukuk* funded project

Despite the robustness of the Orasis Green *sukuk* structure in Fig. 32.2, the project failed 2 years after the issuance. This is due to numerous factors that included crisis couple years prior to the project, liquidity crunch, and decrease of redemption value. Nevertheless, this Green *sukuk* displayed unprecedented features, the first of their kind that

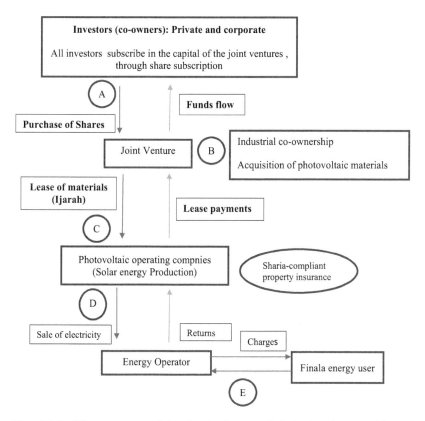

Fig. 32.2 The structure of the Orasis Green *sukuk* Project (*Source* Adapted from Dorsman et al. [2016])

paved the way for many other green *sukuk* projects (Dorsman et al. 2016). Green *sukuk* has enormous capacity to finance housing, clean transportation, sanitation, and water projects, among many others. This is despite the fact that it is a new concept and constitute less than 0.25% of the bond market (Dorsman et al. 2016).

628 M. C. E. AMRI ET AL.

GREEN *SUKUK* AND SDGs

This section comprises two interconnected subsections, sustainable development goals (SDGs) and the contributions of Green *sukuk* structure to SDGs.

Sustainable Development Goals

Sustainable development in the wider meaning refers to finding ways of improving the present without affecting negatively the future (Kates et al. 2005). There is yet the universally accepted definition with the underlying meaning that progress and advancement should not be at the expense of the future generations, the familiar slogan, 'leave no one behind.' The sustainable development goals set by the UN, came in the aftermath of the climate and global crisis, which also coincided with the failure of the Millennium Development Goals (MDGs) (Sachs 2012), proposed in the Rio + 20 summit in June 2012. This international framework of SDGs involves civil society, governments, international Institutions, academics, private sector... basically all people (United Nations 2015), and the main topics (where almost 300 issues were evoked) evolved mostly around; 'Oceans, sustainable development as an answer for economic and financial crisis, Water, Forest, Sustainable development for poverty, food nutrition security, innovation and cities, unemployment, decent work and migration, sustainable energy for all, consumption and production patterns...(United Nations General Assembly 2015) After 3 years, following the 2015 Addis Ababa summit (United Nations General Assembly 2015), 17 goals (and 169 targets) were proposed.'

These goals are 'No poverty, zero hunger, good health and wellbeing, quality education, gender equality, clean water and sanitation, affordable and clean energy, decent work and economic growth, life below water, climate action, responsible consumption and production, industry, innovation and infrastructure, life on land, reduced inequalities, peace, justice and strong institutions, sustainable cities and communities and finally partnership, to stimulate action for the next 15 years.' These 17 goals are often broadly categorized into 6 (sometimes 5) general goals, which are people, dignity, prosperity, planet, justice (or peace), and partnership. To achieve these 17 goals, immense data collection would take place beforehand, to determine on the equitability and fairness in the implementation process, taking into consideration the different communities within a country as well as between countries. This implies that if one community in a country failed to attain those goals, the whole country is deemed a failure. The structures of the SDGs are extremely interconnected and require interdepartments (between countries also), efficient relations, cross sectoral activities/information and policy coherence, whereby in results, the development indicators of the country is regarded as more accurate with SDGs, in comparison with MDGs (Sachs 2012). Furthermore, the MDGs had only 8 goals (and 21 indicators) and were designed to address only developing countries-related issues. Whereas sustainable development goals address global issues and require collective work to obtain sustainability in social, economic, and environmental dimension. These are fundamentally the main differences that set the SDGs apart from the MDGs (United Nations 2015; Sachs 2012).

Green sukuk *Structure and Its Contributions to SDGs*

The Green *sukuk* as discussed earlier is an environmentally friendly Shari'ah compliant *sukuk*. Their features embody moral, ethical, social, and economic dimensions, in addition to the values of inclusive participation, risk sharing, and ownership of assets (asset backed/based). They are also free from interest, uncertainty, and speculation. Some of the objectives embodied in the structure of Green *sukuk* have commonality with the sustainable development goals. This facilitates for Green *sukuk* to become a great contributor to the SDGs (Ebrahim 2019). Hence, as Shiller (2012) mentions in his Finance and the Good Society' book 'The better aligned a society's financial institutions [including the instruments] are with its goals and ideals, the stronger and more successful the society will be.' Some of the shared objectives between Green *sukuk* and SDGs include risk-sharing, focus on equity, absence of speculation, and presence of tangible physical assets.

The risk sharing aspect in the Green *sukuk* (especially in asset-backed) structure is useful toward attaining the SDGs in the sense that the issuer does not bear the liabilities and losses all alone, rather they are shared with other involved parties (Ebrahim 2019; Wilson 2008). This aspect corresponds to the SDG 8, 'Decent work and economic growth,' and also SDGs 10 and 17 related to 'Partnership' and 'Reduced Inequalities,' respectively (United Nations 2015). Needless to say, risk transfer is one the features of the conventional finance, which evidently is one of the root problems to unfair income and wealth disparities.

Another aspect of the Green *sukuk* structure that shares commonality with SDGs is the focus on 'equity,' which has relevance to SDGs 9 and 11, 'Industry, Innovation and Infrastructure and Sustainable Cities and Communities.' Green *sukuk* and, in fact, all *sukuk* structures have the key feature of the 'underlying asset,' that could notably be a piece of land, building, and other movable assets (Dorsman et al. 2016; Ebrahim 2019; Wilson 2008). The underlying asset makes the financing instrument more attractive and an integral part of the real economy, rather than a simple debt-based commercial paper. The assets are generally attained through Murabaha and Ijarah, but often at times through Musharakah, Mudharabah, Salam, Wakalah, and Istisna as well (Bahari et al. 2016; Wilson 2008; Mat Rahim and Mohamad 2018).

In the case of the Murabahah Green *sukuk* project, an Islamic Financial Institution or any other company or sovereign body (willing to issue GS) issues a Murabahah *sukuk* to investors. The originator appoints an SPV as a purchase agent for the Murabahah Green *sukuk* holders, which will provide the amount required for the project—100USD million (cash) for instance. The purchase agent now buys the commodity (a land, solar panels, etc.) on behalf of the GS holders, on spot from the seller. Straightaway the originator signs a purchase agreement from the investors with regard to the commodity, with an amount higher than the purchase price (i.e., will paid 120USD million) on installment basis [This is Tawarruq/Inah sale, a contentious structure]. The Green *sukuk* issuer generates funds through the asset (land, building, solar panels, etc.) and is able to repay the GS holders gradually (Mat Rahim and Mohamad 2018; Wilson 2008). This is a very simple Murabahah Green *sukuk* structure as an example, although in practice, the process is longer and involves many other parties (trustee, rating agency, arranger, brokers, etc.). The Green Building *sukuk* project by PNB Merdeka Ventures Sdn. Bhd mentioned earlier in Table 32.1 (Kamil et al. 2019) is a typical example of a Murabahah Green *sukuk* issuance to finance a green project.

The Ijarah Green *sukuk* project is a bit different from the Murabahah GS, where in the case of Ijarah, the ownership of the asset is not transferred immediately, rather gradually (Dorsman et al. 2016; Wilson 2008). A case of GS based on Ijarah structure is the Bakun Hydroelectric which supplied electricity to the Sarawak state. The project was managed by the Sarawak Energy Berhad company. The company (Sarawak Energy

32 HOW GREEN *SUKUK* STRUCTURE CONTRIBUTE TO SDGS? 631

Table 32.1 PNB Merdeka Ventures Sdn Bhd *sukuk* Highlight

Issuer	PNB Merdeka Ventures Sdn Bhd
Issue Size	RM2 Billion
Issuance date	December 2017
Purpose	The proceeds shall be utilized to partly finance the Merdeka PNB118 tower
Tenor	15 years
Profit rates	Fixed profit rate to be agreed between the issuer and the lead manager(s) prior to each issuance of the Merdeka ASEAN Green SRI *sukuk*
Payment	Semi-annual basis
Currency	Malaysian ringgit
Lead arranger	MIDF Amanah Investment Bank Bhd
Governing law	Malaysian law
Solicitor	Zul Rafique & Partners
Rating	Unrated
Sharia advisor	MIDF Shari Committee
Structure	Murabahah Tawarruq arrangement and Wakalah

Source Kamil et al. (2019)

Berhad) first issued an ijarah Green *sukuk* to the investors and through an agreement is appointed as agent to purchase the asset. After the transaction, the GS holders own the solar panels and through an Ijarah contract (rent, plus an added markup which signifies the profit), leased them to Sarawak Energy Berhad. The company benefited from the usufruct of the solar panel and generated funds to repay the investors and gradually becomes the full owner of the panels. This Ijarah GS is asset-backed Ijarah contract. Other Ijarah *sukuk* are asset-based Ijarah contract, where the company uses superficial asset, which it does not own, to raise funds to finance a green project. Table 32.2 shows the major differences between asset-based and asset-backed contracts.

From Table 32.2, in the case of ownership for asset based *sukuk*, the beneficial ownership is transferred rather than full ownership, also the risk of default is more significant compared to the asset-backed Ijarah. This risk in case of a default is tied to the credit profile of the issuer, given that the investors have no recourse to the asset. Moreover, asset-based *sukuk* structure includes the feature of the 'buy back the asset,' which is considered by some scholars as non-Shari'ah compliant, as it resembles bay' al Inah. For this reason, the asset-backed Ijarah, according to the

632   M. C. E. AMRI ET AL.

Table 32.2 Asset-based and Asset-backed *sukuk* compared

Criteria	Asset-based sukuk	Asset-backed sukuk
Ownership	Provides beneficial ownership rights to the usufruct of certain physical underlying assets, and relies on the obligor's credit quality to ensure that the *sukuk* performs	Ownership rights extend to the actual underlying assets such as physical real estate or rights/usufruct from particular intangible but valuable assets
Recourse to Asset/investor	The recourse of the investor is to the creditworthiness of the ultimate obligor	Recourse of the investor is to the underlying asset and the *sukuk* investors bear any losses in case of impairment of the *sukuk*
Rating	Corporate rating methodology is used for asset-based transaction of *sukuk* whenever a corporate obligor is the key driver affecting credit risk of *sukuk*	Asset-backed rating methodology will be used for the asset-backed *sukuk* transaction, which involves securitization. Here, credit risk is determined solely by the performance or the underlying asset

Source Adapted from Muhamed and Radzi (2011)

majority of scholars, is much preferred since the actual reason behind the issuance is to acquire the asset (Muhamed and Radzi 2011; Wilson 2008). The Musharakah *sukuk* is less frequently used in Green *sukuk* but at the same time constitutes a very sophisticated and innovative feature for financing green projects. Nevertheless, the Musharakah GS would not involve the same Shari'ah issues as the Ijarah asset based, unless its structure is also asset based. Otherwise, in such structure the risk would be shared and the transaction would involve a tangible and fund generating asset which would encourage the green project financing as it is profitable, and at the same time preserving the environment (Wilson 2008).

Besides the risk sharing and equity focus, there are other unique features of the Green *sukuk* structure, which contribute to SDGs. These features are the absence of speculation and the presence of tangible physical assets. Green *sukuk*, and indeed other *sukuk* structures as well, should not be used for speculation. They are securities for investment of long-term periods to fund climate change mitigation and adjustment projects. The investors comprise socially conscious individuals rather than quick income or revenue chasers (Dorsman et al. 2016). Furthermore, the presence of a tangible asset makes the Green *sukuk* market much more stable and resilient to recessions and crises compared to debt markets (Ahmad and Radzi 2011). Green *sukuk* includes securement of future income cash flows, socially driven projects that minimize economic impact on the environment. These unique features of GS harness their objectives to the shared interest and mission of the sustainable development goals.

Identifying and Analyzing the Issues

In spite of the great structure of the Green *sukuk*, at least in theory, and the immense innovation and services they offer, there are numerous issues that cannot be overlooked and need to be addressed. In the same vein, the SDGs also are not exempted as they too have some criticism despite the ambitious and global agenda they promote. Both GS and SDGs share a great deal of principles and goals, yet they have their fair share of drawbacks. As for the sustainable development goals, one of their shortcomings is that they are legally non-binding goals, making them vulnerable of dismissal and setbacks. In addition to the non-binding issue, lack of awareness in some places creates hardships against the accomplishment of the SDGs (United Nations General Assembly 2015; Sachs 2012). Moreover, according to (Carant 2017) SDGs address problems without deeply examining the real causes, hence the proposed goals appear to a lot of people, as well-structured facade to calm critics and allow the prevailing world order to persist. Ignoring the underlying causes, for example inequalities borne by the current financial system, in addition to the global decision making being exclusive, thus shows lack of presenting serious reforms embedded in the goals, and pictures the SDGs as unrealistic as its predecessor, the MDGs. Another concern related to SDGs is the data collection. Millions of people are involved in reaching out to achieve 17 goals, 169 targets, and 230 indicators altogether. Unfortunately, again, the data focus on the problems and their interconnection and not exactly the cause (United Nations 2015).

With regard to GS, the issues include the structure, Shari'ah compliance, transparency, pricing model, and reputational risk. The structure of the Green *sukuk* is no different from the structure of the regular *sukuk*, which makes the so-called 'Green *sukuk* structure' a misnomer. The structure remains the same. The only difference is the kind and nature of projects Green *sukuk* funds, which are environmentally friendly projects.

Furthermore, the Green *sukuk* issuance is profit oriented and the social orientation is not embedded in the structure.

According to (Bahari et al. 2016; Dorsman et al. 2016; Usmani 2008), the most revealing issue with *sukuk* in general [including Green *sukuk*] is Shari'ah compliance. One of the critical issues, as already mentioned, is the 'sell-buyback' feature, which also represents the key feature of the controversial 'sale of Inah.' It poses a serious Shari'ah issue to the extent that most Islamic scholars consider any Inah-based structure as impermissible. The controversy of the sale of Inah also includes a moral dimension, where the real intention of the transaction is not to acquire asset or commodity, rather it is to engage in loan transaction disguised as deferred sale with 'profit'—the surplus above the loan. Some scholars argue that the sale of Inah (as well as Tawarruq) is innovative back doors to interest, and therefore immoral and impermissible. Accordingly, the Ijarah asset based and Musharakah *sukuk* that are structured using the sell-buyback feature could actually lose their potentials. Another Shari'ah issue (Bahari et al. 2016; Usmani 2008) is the fixed cash flows (other than ijarah and Murabahah) and the guaranteed revenue. These Shari'ah issues, as (Dorsman et al. 2016; Usmani 2008) argue, result from a poor regulations and incompetent Shari'ah advisory.

Moreover, according to Wahida Ahmad and Rafisah Mat Radzi (2011), these issues originate from a conventional banking and finance rules, regulations and setting, upon which Islamic finance operates. Apart from the Shari'ah issues, the Green *sukuk* market according to Bahari et al. (2016) lacks transparency, while Dorsman et al. (2016) reproach it (GS as a derivative to *sukuk*) of using unfavorable *sukuk* pricing models. Naturally, this leads to mistrust of investors and the decrease of Green *sukuk* demands in comparison with the Green bonds. Furthermore, the structure of the Green *sukuk* (*sukuk* in general as well) suffers from reputational risk. The structures remain inconsistent, and their flexibility which varies with the conventional finance structures lead to the mistrust of the vast majority of people and project a negative image of what was supposed to be a well-intended financing product.

Conclusion and The Way Forward

Green *sukuk* ideally has a lot of advantages. They are directed toward environmentally friendly investments. Their structure is based on tangible physical assets [rather than debt-based commercial papers], which have direct link to the real economy. GS promotes risk sharing as opposed to risk transfer. Such arrangements make them, obviously attractive tradable capital market product. The risk sharing aspect addresses the problem of income and wealth disparity in the society in addition to the environmental concern. Furthermore, the risk sharing aspect of Green *sukuk* promotes financial inclusion. The features of GS relate to SDGs as follows: 13th goal: climate action, 11th goal: sustainable cities and communities, 8th goal: decent work and economic growth, 17th goal: partnership for the goals, 15th goal: life on land, 10th goal; reduced inequalities,9th goal; Industry, Innovation and Infrastructure and 7th goal; affordable and clean energy.

Despite their merits, both GS and SDGs have some drawbacks. The GS offers plausible investing answers, but if not improved and gone through strict Shari'ah regulations, it will die out because of strong competitive advantages of its counterpart, the Green Bonds. As for the sustainable development goals, the framework must promote serious reforms, to assure the participation and the involvement of everyone, otherwise, yet again, it will just represent an ambitious attitude of the United Nations. Improvements could include examining underlying causes of the challenges, and managing data, among others.

Therefore, the Green *sukuk* embodies the Islamic Finance moral philosophy of elevating the standard living and the creation of prosperous and harmonious environment for societies. Sustainable development goals also upheld the responsibility of strong commitment to eradicate inequalities, poverty, and hunger around the world. The novelty of this chapter, therefore, lies in charting a new direction of GS–SDGs relationship.

References

Ahmad, W., & Radzi, R. M. (2011). Sustainability of Sukuk and Conventional Bond during Financial Crisis : Malaysia's Capital Market. *Global Economy and Finance Journal, 4*(2), 33–45.

Alam, N., Duygun, M., & Ariss, R. T. (2016). Green Sukuk: An Innovation in Islamic Capital Markets. In A. Dorsman, Ö. Arslan-Ayaydin, & M. B. Karan (Eds.), *Energy and Finance* (pp. 167–185). Cham: Springer.

Bahari, N. F., Ahmad, N. W., Shahar, W. S. S., & Othman, N. (2016). A Review on the Potential Growth of Sukuk, Issues and Its Challenges. *International Conference on Economics and Banking, 2016*(2), 395–403.

Carant, J. B. (2017). Unheard Voices: A Critical Discourse Analysis of the Millennium Development Goals' Evolution into the Sustainable Development Goals

Development Goals. *Third World Quarterly, 6597*, 1–26. https://doi.org/10.1080/01436597.2016.1166944.

Dorsman, A. B., Arslan-Ayaydin, Ö., & Karan, M. B. (2016). *Energy and Finance: Sustainability in the Energy Industry* (pp. 1–203). https://doi.org/10.1007/978-3-319-32268-1.

Ebrahim, M. (2019, October). *Islamic Finance for Green Sustainable Projects.* https://doi.org/10.6084/m9.figshare.10068596.

IIFM. (2017, July). A Comprehensive Study of the International Sukuk Market IIFM Sukuk Report 6th Edition.

International Islamic Financial Market. (2019, July). Iifm Sukuk Report 2019, 202.

Islamic Development Bank. (2019). *Sustainable Finance Framework.*

Kamil, W. A. R., Bakhor, S. A. S. M., De Luna-Martinez, J., Zhang, W., & Aziz, A. H. A. (2019). *Islamic Green Finance: Development, Ecosystem and Prospects.*

Kates, R. W., Parris, T. M., & Leiserowitz, A. A. (2005). What Is Sustainable Development? Goals, Indicators, Values, and Practice. *Environment, 47*(3), 8–21. https://doi.org/10.1080/00139157.2005.10524444.

Mat Rahim, S. R., & Mohamad, Z. Z. (2018). Green Sukuk for Financing Renewable Energy Projects. *Turkish Journal of Islamic Economics, 5*(2), 129–144. https://doi.org/10.26414/m031.

Moghul, U. F., & Safar-Aly, S. H. K. (2014). Green Sukuk: The Introduction of Islam's Environmental Ethics to Contemporary Islamic Finance. *Georgetown International Environmental Law Review, 27*(1). https://doi.org/10.1093/ww/9780199540884.013.u15278.

Muhamed, N. A., & Radzi, R. M. (2011, July). Implication of Sukuk Structuring: The Comparison on the Structure of Asset Based and Asset Backed. *2nd International Conference on Business and Economic Research (2nd ICBER 2011) Proceeding*, 2444–2460.

Reve. (2013). *Sukuk to Fund an Indonesian Solar Power Project.*

Sachs, J. D. (2012). From Millennium Development Goals to Sustainable Development Goals. *The Lancet, 379*(9832), 2206–2211. https://doi.org/10.1016/S0140-6736(12)60685-0.

Safari, M. (2012). Are Sukuk Securities the Same as Conventional Bonds? *SSRN Electronic Journal*, 1–31. https://doi.org/10.2139/ssrn.1783551.

Shiller, R. J. (2012). *Finance and the Good Society.* Princeton, NJ: Princeton University Press.

Thomson Reuters. (2014). *Thomson Reuters Sukuk Perceptions & Forecast 2015 Beyond Traditional Markets.*

United Nations. (2015). *Transforming Our World: The 2030 Agenda for Sustainable Development.* New York: United Nations.

United Nations General Assembly. (2015). *Addis Ababa Action Agenda of the Third International Conference on Financing for Development*. Addis Ababa: United Nations.

Usmani, M. (2008). *Sukuk and Their Contemporary Applications* (pp. 1–15). South Africa: Mujlisul Ulama of South Africa.

Wilson, R. (2008). Innovation in the Structuring of Islamic Sukuk Securities. *Humanomics, 24*(3), 170–181. https://doi.org/10.1108/082886608 10899340.

Index

A

Achievement, 4, 5, 10, 90, 92, 101, 102, 147, 173, 186, 203, 221, 222, 234, 245, 249, 326, 353, 417, 480, 487, 542–545, 553, 554, 561, 602, 610

Asset, 35, 37, 39, 40, 43, 44, 46, 47, 58, 72, 74–76, 108, 117, 119, 126, 144, 150, 157, 176, 178–182, 185, 186, 188, 190, 198–200, 222–227, 229, 233, 234, 281, 285, 287, 305, 306, 330, 335, 345, 347, 348, 365, 368, 369, 375, 379, 397–399, 426, 428, 471, 472, 485–488, 490–495, 497, 502, 503, 516, 522, 525, 532, 535, 543, 545–547, 550, 560, 564, 566, 581, 582, 584, 585, 587, 589–592, 594, 595, 608, 614, 615, 621, 623, 624, 629–634

B

Baitul Maal wat Tamwil (BMT), 107, 115, 176–186, 188–194
Banking, 107, 108, 115, 117, 118, 126, 161, 168, 173, 176, 188, 198, 275, 291, 293–295, 300, 380, 442, 444, 462, 466, 503, 504, 516, 517, 519, 532, 549, 584, 611, 634
Bookkeeping, 232, 235
Build Operate and Transfer (BOT), 513, 518, 582, 587–590, 593
Business zakat, 221–223, 228, 230–235

C

Cash waqf, 39, 45–47, 109–115, 118, 119, 121, 176, 178–191, 194, 248, 296, 306–308, 311, 313–315, 317, 319, 323, 462–464, 485, 487, 488, 493, 495, 496, 503, 516, 518, 524, 540, 562–574, 583, 590, 591, 593, 594

© The Editor(s) (if applicable) and The Author(s), under exclusive license to Springer Nature Switzerland AG 2021
M. M. Billah (eds.), *Islamic Wealth and the SDGs*,
https://Doi.org/10.1007/978-3-030-65313-2

639

640 INDEX

Charity, 13, 16, 31, 33, 35–37, 40–42, 45, 46, 62, 80, 105, 106, 166–168, 170, 242–245, 251, 286, 287, 290, 293, 297, 332, 347, 348, 366, 393, 423, 424, 426, 430, 431, 440, 456–461, 470–472, 478, 485–488, 491, 493–495, 522, 525, 541, 544, 547, 548, 564, 566, 594

City, 4, 19, 130, 132–140, 142, 144, 145, 149–151, 204, 222, 309, 354, 376, 380, 432, 442, 478, 480, 495, 551, 572

Commercial, 41, 105–109, 115–118, 120–123, 126, 138, 143, 144, 175–178, 181, 185–188, 191–194, 223, 264, 277, 280, 306–309, 311, 313, 319, 323, 369, 399, 424, 425, 434, 466, 504, 511, 540, 550, 551, 584–586, 590–594, 614, 630, 634

Compatibility, 5, 7, 9, 10, 24, 25, 96, 98, 101

Contributions, 5, 36, 45, 48, 64, 90, 93, 102, 107, 108, 144, 159, 188, 223, 245, 248, 281, 289, 297, 350, 351, 377, 380, 383, 393, 394, 416, 428, 477, 486, 487, 493, 514, 525, 533, 546, 548–550, 571, 573, 593, 600, 624, 626, 628

Corporate, 46, 116, 157, 199, 200, 248, 285, 295, 297, 369, 395, 396, 412, 425, 444, 448, 526, 529, 530, 532–535, 540, 542, 543, 545–547, 549, 550, 552–555, 569, 572, 608, 609, 616, 632

Corporate Zakat, 424, 425

Corporatization, 369, 395–397, 413, 416, 417

COVID-19, 117, 184, 186, 325, 395, 408, 409, 414–416, 439, 525, 527, 530, 532, 535

Crowdfunding, 194, 334, 441, 444–448

D

Development, 539, 540, 542, 545–547, 550–554

Divine principles, 3–5, 8, 18, 22, 24, 25, 88–90, 94–96, 98–102, 342

Divine status, 466

E

Economic wellbeing, 356

Education, 9, 14, 49, 58, 60, 62–66, 75, 80, 91, 115, 122, 123, 155, 156, 170, 171, 191, 202, 203, 206, 208, 209, 211, 246, 249, 309, 313, 315, 316, 326, 332, 334, 345, 346, 349, 351, 352, 354, 356, 360, 367, 377, 380, 381, 383, 384, 389, 397, 401, 402, 409, 410, 421, 427, 429, 432–435, 440, 445, 448, 462–464, 466, 473, 477, 486, 487, 489, 490, 493, 494, 502–506, 511, 512, 515, 518, 519, 522–525, 532, 534, 539, 544, 548, 550, 553, 554, 559, 562, 564, 568, 571, 573, 574, 583

Egypt, 352, 376, 459, 460, 464, 480, 571, 583

Ending poverty, 71, 155, 170, 234

Ethical finance, 168, 169, 200, 201, 214, 275

Ethical wealth management, 55, 66, 258

Ethics, 7, 17, 71, 75, 197, 199, 201, 245, 275–277, 286, 328, 360, 361, 370, 446

F

Finance, 40, 47, 90, 105–110, 114–116, 120, 121, 123–126, 145, 156, 157, 168, 173, 175–177, 179, 180, 184, 190, 191, 193, 200, 202, 214, 232, 246, 275, 276, 285, 287, 290, 296, 307–311, 316, 319, 330, 342, 348, 353, 362, 377, 379, 380, 382, 383, 422, 427, 445, 448, 462, 464, 473, 493, 496, 503, 504, 516, 517, 540, 569, 582, 584, 588–590, 592–594, 601, 604, 606, 608–611, 622, 626, 627, 629–631, 634

Financing, 31, 40, 46–49, 81, 106, 107, 110, 114, 115, 117–123, 125, 126, 142, 144–147, 151, 177–179, 187–191, 194, 198, 263, 264, 275, 280–283, 285, 287–290, 295, 297, 299, 307, 316, 332, 333, 342, 348, 380, 383, 394, 427, 439, 462, 466, 482, 485, 486, 488, 493, 495, 496, 512–515, 517, 524, 525, 531, 546, 552, 569, 572, 573, 581, 582, 584, 585, 587, 588, 590, 593, 594, 600–602, 604, 606–611, 613, 615, 616, 622, 623, 625, 630, 632, 634

Foundation, 5, 6, 11, 25, 79, 88, 95, 113, 146, 184, 186, 201, 202, 204–214, 289, 308, 313–318, 341, 429, 432, 433, 441, 463, 464, 466, 470, 502, 522, 526, 532, 533, 563

G

Global, 3, 5, 6, 9, 10, 12, 69, 70, 78, 90, 95, 99, 102, 118, 119, 125, 129, 136, 139, 155–157, 173, 198–200, 220, 251–253, 262, 274, 277–279, 288, 291, 322, 325–327, 334, 342, 349, 360, 377, 381, 383, 384, 402, 442, 448, 470, 481, 491, 529, 530, 554, 584, 599, 610–615, 621–624, 628, 629, 633

Goals, 10, 12, 48, 49, 53–56, 59–63, 69, 71, 78, 81, 82, 88, 90, 101, 102, 106, 120, 124, 125, 155, 156, 168, 191, 192, 194, 199–201, 246, 249, 251, 268, 274, 276, 320, 326, 348, 350, 351, 355, 361, 364, 382–390, 399, 400, 406, 410, 413, 416, 425, 428, 433, 440, 474, 481, 485–487, 489, 491, 492, 504, 518, 539, 550, 554, 568, 599, 601, 605, 613, 616, 622, 628, 629, 633, 635

Good health, 11, 13, 48, 54–57, 61, 62, 64, 91, 121, 192, 211, 320, 322, 330, 342, 381, 384, 385, 387, 400, 409, 422, 504, 505, 527, 528, 553, 628

Green finance, 124

Green Sukuk, 124, 622, 624–635

H

Health, 5, 9, 49, 58, 60, 61, 64–66, 155, 156, 184, 191, 203, 206–208, 211, 287, 290, 306–309, 311–314, 317–323, 325–327, 330–333, 335–339, 341, 342, 348, 360, 380, 381, 383, 384, 400–402, 409, 410, 421, 427, 429, 435, 440, 448, 462, 463, 466, 480, 486, 487, 489, 490,

492–494, 502, 505, 506, 518,
526–530, 532–535, 539, 550,
553, 583
Healthcare, 75, 98, 115, 122, 123,
207, 306–314, 316–318, 320,
322, 323, 327, 352, 397, 430,
432, 435, 473, 503, 504, 511,
512, 515, 523–530, 532–535,
547, 548, 550, 553, 554, 559,
564, 583, 593

I

Implication, 6, 25, 32, 33, 36, 37,
74, 79, 82, 250, 327, 340, 342,
416, 428, 604
India, 4, 58, 106, 264, 290, 441,
459, 466, 467, 514, 516
Indonesia, 58, 61, 62, 64–66, 106,
107, 176, 186, 245, 262–265,
270, 305, 308, 309, 311–314,
322, 323, 368, 376, 377, 380,
381, 402, 425, 429, 441, 445,
525, 582, 584, 590, 591, 593,
610, 622, 625
Inequality, 5, 6, 11, 18, 48, 49,
54, 56, 57, 60–62, 65, 70, 71,
75, 78, 81, 82, 91, 121, 123,
124, 155, 157, 193, 200, 258,
260, 270, 274, 320, 326, 348,
359–361, 365–370, 377, 378,
381–387, 398–400, 402, 409,
422, 423, 425, 427, 428, 435,
439, 486, 487, 489, 524, 539,
628, 629, 633, 635
Institutions, 5, 12, 22, 23, 30, 33,
34, 36, 39, 40, 42, 48–50,
54–56, 58, 77, 78, 80, 87, 88,
90, 92–94, 101, 102, 106–109,
111–114, 116, 117, 125, 134,
141, 142, 145, 189, 197, 200,
202, 220, 242–248, 251–253,
259, 262, 285, 287, 289, 297,

311, 312, 320, 322, 323, 326,
334, 341, 342, 346, 350–356,
382–385, 387, 393, 394, 400,
401, 403, 404, 409, 412, 416,
422, 423, 427, 428, 433–435,
440–442, 444, 447, 448, 464,
466, 473, 477, 479–482, 485,
487–491, 493–495, 497, 502–
504, 506, 507, 512–514, 516,
517, 519, 523–526, 530–535,
539, 540, 542, 546, 547, 549,
552–554, 561, 564, 567, 569,
583–585, 588, 590, 592, 593,
605, 608, 615, 617, 626, 628,
629
Integration, 62, 109, 175, 177, 202,
221, 291, 321, 339, 433, 585
Investment, 37, 40, 46, 47, 61,
73, 77, 79, 82, 99, 106, 110,
113, 117–119, 135–137, 142,
144, 146, 147, 149, 150,
168, 177–179, 189, 190, 198,
200, 201, 214, 225, 248, 250,
275, 279, 296, 330, 332, 333,
379–382, 387, 397, 398, 422,
426, 462, 473, 481, 485–495,
497, 503–506, 508, 511–519,
524, 531–534, 544, 545, 547,
550, 554, 566, 567, 569,
570, 572–574, 581, 582, 584,
585, 587, 590, 592, 601, 604,
609–611, 613, 614, 621, 622,
624–626, 632, 634
Investment waqf funds, 486, 487,
489–493, 495–497
Islam, 3–5, 7, 8, 10, 12, 13, 15,
17–25, 30–33, 38, 53–55, 59,
63, 65, 66, 87–90, 94, 95,
100, 102, 105, 123, 157–159,
162–164, 166, 167, 169, 170,
197, 199–201, 220, 224, 234,
242, 243, 245, 257–262, 270,

INDEX **643**

273, 274, 276, 277, 279, 287, 299, 328–330, 333, 334, 342, 347, 350, 352, 361, 364–366, 375, 378, 379, 386–388, 394, 396, 400, 423–428, 434, 439, 440, 447, 458, 459, 461, 469, 470, 477–479, 481, 482, 486, 502, 518, 526–528, 542, 543, 553, 559, 561, 582

Islamic, 539, 541, 546–548, 553, 554

Islamic accounting, 233

Islamic Ethical Wealth (IEW), 29, 30, 32, 34, 36–42, 45, 48–50, 54, 137, 142–148, 151, 245–253, 263, 264, 274–277, 285–288, 326–328, 330, 332, 333, 341, 342, 361, 370, 582

Islamic finance, 7, 93, 106, 157, 162, 168, 174, 193, 198–201, 214, 275, 280, 291, 332, 352, 423, 445, 466, 581, 588, 608, 609, 615–617, 621, 623, 624, 634, 635

Islamic social finance (ISF), 54, 61, 64, 106, 107, 115, 116, 118, 120–126, 175–177, 185, 186, 191, 194, 199, 203, 258, 263, 264, 270, 275, 285, 286, 288, 383, 390, 423, 584

Islamic wealth management, 55, 64, 245, 249, 250, 258, 263, 276, 362, 363, 365–367

K

Kano State, 220–223, 227–229, 232–235, 355, 356

L

Lesson, 137, 250

M

Malaysia, 31, 106, 107, 144, 228, 262, 368, 380, 381, 394–396, 398, 404, 405, 412–414, 425, 428, 429, 444, 446, 448, 464–467, 485, 487, 489, 522–527, 529–535, 540, 546, 547, 554, 584, 588, 608, 610, 611, 622, 625, 626

Maqasid al-Shari'ah/Maqasid shariah/Maqasis al-Shari'ah, 96, 100, 322, 365, 370, 471, 473–476, 481, 541, 553

Mega-cities, 132–138, 140, 142–144, 147–151

Microfinance, 46, 47, 62, 106, 107, 109, 181, 184–187, 193, 248, 250, 448, 486, 490, 493, 496, 512, 569

Mission, 17, 106, 189, 210, 211, 342, 528, 535, 633

Muslim, 4, 7, 10, 13, 17, 25, 31, 35, 58, 88, 94, 96, 99, 101, 102, 108, 111, 112, 139–141, 170, 171, 176, 180, 186, 187, 193, 197–199, 201, 220, 221, 223, 234, 243, 246–249, 261, 287, 293, 306, 309, 322, 323, 328, 334, 338, 339, 346, 347, 350–352, 363–366, 376–380, 383, 394, 399, 400, 424, 427, 435, 440, 441, 444, 446–448, 453, 459, 462, 466, 471–474, 479, 480, 482, 485, 502, 514, 516, 517, 519, 523, 525, 527, 528, 539, 540, 543, 547, 550, 553, 554, 560, 562, 563, 565, 568–571, 583, 585, 593, 615, 622, 623

644 INDEX

N

Nigeria, 106, 220–223, 225, 226, 234, 235, 345, 442, 466, 467, 608, 610, 612–614

O

Oman, 107, 488, 495, 584
Organization of the Islamic Cooperation (OIC), 65, 129, 130, 132–135, 137, 138, 143, 150, 173, 342, 394, 466, 488, 495

P

Pakistan, 58, 106, 202–213, 264, 282, 285, 368, 422, 426, 428–430, 432–435, 584
Poverty, 5, 7, 9–13, 30, 32, 41, 48, 49, 53–58, 60–64, 70, 78, 80, 98, 106, 107, 110, 121, 122, 145, 156, 164, 169, 170, 177, 178, 182, 187, 191, 192, 199, 200, 211, 219–222, 227, 228, 232, 234, 235, 242–251, 262, 274, 278, 282, 289, 320, 326, 327, 332, 348, 349, 360, 369, 370, 377, 379–381, 383–386, 389, 397–403, 407, 409, 421–423, 425–428, 434, 435, 440, 441, 462, 470, 475, 486, 487, 489, 490, 492–494, 512, 523, 553, 554, 559, 568, 569, 574, 606, 628, 635
Poverty alleviation, 58, 60, 62, 74, 82, 232, 234, 245, 246, 248–250, 252, 345, 368, 377, 379, 380, 387, 423, 424, 427, 432, 493, 502, 512, 574
Program, 48, 57, 59–66, 70, 81, 110–117, 119, 121–123, 126, 135, 178–180, 182, 184, 185, 187, 190, 191, 193, 204,

205, 209–211, 232, 252, 253, 262–268, 270, 288, 289, 308, 311, 313–316, 322, 338, 350, 356, 383, 395, 397, 399, 402, 404, 406–410, 412–414, 416, 428, 432, 433, 493, 502, 512, 517, 519, 532, 547, 553, 569, 573, 582, 587

Q

Qard Hasan, 80, 503
Quality education, 5, 11, 14, 49, 54, 56, 57, 60, 62, 63, 65, 70, 82, 121, 122, 192, 320, 345, 346, 348, 349, 351–356, 377, 382, 383, 385, 387, 400–403, 409, 422, 433, 507, 510, 553, 571, 574, 628

R

Recordkeeping, 222, 225–227, 229, 230, 233–235
Risk, 60, 77, 81, 117, 119, 134, 156, 157, 161–163, 168, 176, 190, 198–201, 205, 260, 264, 280, 282, 289, 299, 329–332, 342, 428, 445, 446, 462, 492, 496, 503, 566, 570, 571, 587, 588, 608, 609, 622–624, 629, 631–635

S

Saudi Arabia, 144, 376, 428, 440, 442, 485, 487, 488, 496, 497, 584, 589, 608
Shari'ah, 25, 30, 37, 96, 108, 158–160, 168, 169, 173, 174, 198–200, 214, 215, 221, 224, 329, 381, 384, 423–425, 428, 469, 471, 474–476, 478, 503, 504, 515, 516, 519, 566, 570,

582, 592, 615, 622–624, 626, 629, 631–635

Shari'ah objectives, 173, 481, 482

Social, 539, 541

Social welfare, 350, 367, 368, 379, 409, 421, 460–462, 465–467, 470, 481, 504, 523, 542, 622, 623

Socio economic development, 203, 204, 208, 233, 246, 253, 377, 427, 583, 609

Strategies, 92, 93, 133, 149, 155, 203, 225, 245, 246, 248, 250, 275, 280, 285, 288, 290, 380, 425, 427, 428, 485, 487, 489, 491–494, 497, 540, 569, 592, 602, 616

Structure, 33, 37, 72, 94, 95, 99, 101, 108, 110, 112–114, 116, 117, 138–142, 144, 149, 150, 168, 283, 297, 307, 308, 310, 312, 315–319, 333, 337, 349, 370, 395, 396, 404, 533, 535, 572, 582, 584, 587, 588, 590–594, 621, 623, 624, 626, 628–634

Sub-Saharan Africa (SSA), 106, 134, 220, 277, 600–602, 604–607, 610–617

Sukuk, 283, 285, 488, 503, 513, 515, 518, 546, 551, 552, 581, 582, 584–594, 601, 602, 608–617, 621–624, 626, 629–634

Support, 22, 24, 25, 30, 32, 49, 56, 59–64, 107, 117, 134, 145, 147, 148, 151, 157, 160, 188, 192–194, 204, 205, 208, 213, 214, 233, 244–248, 250–253, 258, 267, 275, 280, 287, 290, 291, 300, 315, 316, 351–353, 380, 382, 398, 401, 402, 413, 423, 427, 429, 431, 434, 463, 467, 473, 480, 481, 493,

502–504, 511–514, 518, 523, 525, 532, 533, 535, 542, 552, 554, 562, 565, 601, 611, 616

Sustainability, 5, 9, 17, 21, 32, 36, 37, 73, 78, 82, 89, 92, 93, 95, 101, 106, 120, 132, 133, 136–138, 142, 144, 146–151, 176, 177, 182, 204, 221, 252, 261, 262, 268, 274, 278, 285, 293, 295, 296, 309, 326, 349, 382, 394, 399, 400, 442, 485–487, 492, 497, 517, 540, 553, 601, 624, 626, 629

Sustainable development, 3, 5, 9–12, 22, 25, 78, 87–89, 91–96, 98, 99, 101, 125, 133, 137, 148–150, 155, 199–202, 214, 249, 274, 326, 346, 348, 349, 351, 353, 355, 486, 489, 495, 508, 599, 605, 609, 610, 628

Sustainable development goal nine (SDG-9), 600, 602–604, 606, 610, 611, 616

Sustainable development goals (SDGs), 4–6, 9–11, 22, 24, 25, 48, 49, 53–66, 69–72, 74, 78–83, 87–90, 92–94, 96, 98–102, 120, 121, 123–125, 136, 137, 142, 147, 148, 151, 155, 156, 169, 173, 174, 192–194, 202–204, 206, 245, 246, 248–254, 260, 262–265, 267, 270, 274, 277, 320, 321, 326, 327, 342, 348, 350, 351, 360, 377, 381, 383, 384, 386, 389, 395, 397, 400–404, 406–413, 416, 417, 422, 424, 425, 427, 429, 434, 440, 441, 446–448, 485–487, 489–493, 496, 497, 504, 506, 508, 511, 513, 514, 518, 522, 539, 546, 552–555, 562, 563, 567, 568, 573, 574, 586, 599,

600, 608, 609, 611, 615, 616, 622, 628–630, 632, 633, 635

T

Technicalities, 14, 115, 178, 180, 182, 184, 185, 187, 191, 615

Threat, 17, 19, 126, 249, 331, 445

U

United Arab Emirates (UAE), 290, 440, 442, 584

Urban, 129, 132–151, 207, 213, 268, 368, 435

W

Waqf funds, 47, 248, 267, 320, 322, 352, 353, 466, 471, 485–491, 493–497, 523, 533, 534, 549, 550, 569, 585, 586

Wealth, 542, 544, 553, 554

Wealth purification, 55, 59, 64, 66, 363, 365

Welfare, 8, 23, 32, 33, 36, 49, 63, 99, 106, 156, 157, 164, 168, 169, 175–177, 203, 204, 211, 213, 244, 287, 296, 367, 370, 398, 423, 426, 429, 434, 435, 440, 441, 469, 471, 473–475, 485, 487, 542, 545, 559, 563, 583, 594, 600

Wellbeing, 5, 8, 11, 13, 62, 120–122, 125, 192, 313, 320, 325–327, 330–333, 335, 336, 339–342, 381, 474, 524, 541, 544, 545, 628

Worldview, 30–32, 34–38, 40–42, 45–50, 158, 248, 259

World Zakat Forum, 440, 441, 447, 448

Y

Youth Empowerment, 352, 356

Z

Zakat Fund Mechanism, 441, 448

Zakat impact, 395, 402–404, 406, 408–413, 416, 417

Zakat institutions (ZIs), 109–111, 113–118, 178–181, 184–189, 233, 234, 307, 310–312, 318, 394, 402, 406, 408, 426, 441, 445, 446

Zakat program, 58, 59, 64–66, 116, 182, 187, 246, 377, 398, 399

Zero hunger, 11, 13, 48, 54, 56, 57, 60–62, 64, 70, 71, 74, 91, 121, 122, 192, 258, 263–265, 267, 268, 270, 274, 275, 277, 279, 280, 286, 288, 290, 294, 296, 297, 300, 320, 381, 385, 387, 400, 409, 422, 504, 505, 507, 509, 628